54.00 R

D0913112

ALFA BOOK CO.
1ST. FLOOR. No 12.
9, BATTERY ROAD,
TEL: 915635.

MARINE
DIESEL ENGINES

MARINE DIESEL ENGINES

C. C. POUNDER

LONDON
NEWNES-BUTTERWORTHS

THE BUTTERWORTH GROUP

ENGLAND
Butterworth & Co (Publishers) Ltd
London: 88 Kingsway, WC2B 6AB

AUSTRALIA
Butterworth & Co (Australia) Ltd
Sydney: 586 Pacific Highway, Chatswood, NSW 2067
Melbourne: 343 Little Collins Street, 3000
Brisbane: 240 Queen Street, 4000

CANADA
Butterworth & Co (Canada) Ltd
Toronto: 14 Curity Avenue, 374

NEW ZEALAND
Butterworth & Co (New Zealand) Ltd
Wellington: 26-28 Waring Taylor Street, 1

SOUTH AFRICA
Butterworth & Co (South Africa) (Pty) Ltd
Durban: 152-154 Gale Street

First published by
George Newnes Ltd, 1952
    second impression 1954
    third impression 1955
Second edition 1960
    second impression 1963
Third edition 1964
    second impression 1965
Fourth edition 1968

Fifth edition published by
Newnes-Butterworths, an imprint
of the Butterworth Group, 1972

© Butterworth & Co. (Publishers) Ltd, 1972

ISBN 0 408 00077 5

Filmset by V. Siviter Smith & Co. Ltd, Birmingham

Printed in England by Fletcher & Son Ltd, Norwich

Preface

It is fully twenty years since the publishers persuaded me to undertake the compilation of this book. During these two decades it has passed through the printing press no fewer than ten times, either as new editions or as repeat impressions.

At this point it is, perhaps, apposite to repeat what was written in the preface to the first edition.

'When the invitation to write this book was first received from the publishers, I suggested that there were two courses open to them: one was to offer the authorship to an engineer having wide, if second-hand, knowledge of all representative engine types; the other was to invite one man to write the main part of the book from direct experience and to describe those engines on which he was said to be an authority, and then to incorporate for other engine types, descriptions by their respective exponents. The publishers decided upon the second of these alternatives and requested my acceptance of authorship; and so the book came to be written.

This book must be unique amongst marine-engineering tomes; it is international in its authorship and in its scope, and it can reasonably be expected to be international in its appeal.

My day-to-day work brings me into frequent contact with the operating engineer, often in his shipboard environment; and, as a result, many questions arise in discussion. Some of these matters are profound, but, mercifully, many of them are simple. Be that as it may, the consequence is that there is probably not a paragraph anywhere in those parts of the book for which I am responsible which has not been influenced, both in matter and in scope, by questions thus raised. This will explain why many of the deeper and more profound problems—which it might have been expected that a designer would, with relish, seize upon and proceed to expound in detail—are touched upon but lightly, while simpler things are treated at considerable length.

The book is restricted in scope to propulsion machinery. The engine types described are, in all instances, those in service.'

In recent years there have been a number of significant trends both at home and abroad. The resultant effects have included the merging of firms, changes in proprietorship and policies, discontinuance of some types of engine with concentration upon other types and so on. The change of emphasis has not always been founded upon matters of technical superiority or even technical parity, but rather upon the dominance of specific commercial interests which have pulled in such directions as seemed politic and profitable.

By reason of the need for controlling costs, the book remains approximately the same size as before. Accordingly, to make room for new items, certain chapters which formed part of earlier editions and dealt with their respective matters at great length have been shortened.

In accordance with my terms of reference, the SI system has been used. Those many engineers to whom the code is new will, I hope, receive a measure of guidance from the last chapter of the book.

Belfast, N.I.   C. C. POUNDER

Acknowledgements

The thanks of the publishers are due to all those firms who have facilitated the references to machinery and equipment which appear in the text of this book. These include: Allmanna Svenska Elektriska A/B; American Bureau of Shipping; Paul Bergsøe & Søn; Board of Trade; British Internal Combustion Engine Research Institute Ltd.; British Ship Research Association; Brown Boveri & Co. Ltd.; David Brown Gear Industries Ltd.; Burmeister & Wain A/S; Crossley Brothers, Ltd.; Doxford & Sunderland, Marine Engine Division; *Engineering*; Fiat, Divisione Mare; Fluidrive Engineering Co. Ltd.; Götaverken A/B; Graviner Manufacturing Co. Ltd.; Institute of Marine Engineers; Institution of Mechanical Engineers; Lloyds Register of Shipping; Lohmann and Stolterfoht A.G.; Maschinenfabrik Augsburg-Nürnberg A.G.; Ministry of Transport & Civil Aviation; Modern Wheel Drive Ltd.; North East Coast Institution of Engineers & Shipbuilders; Power Plant Co. Ltd.; Pyropress Engineering Co. Ltd.; Ruston & Hornsby, Ltd.; Alexander Stephen & Sons, Ltd.; Stork-Werkspoor Diesel; Sulzer Bros. (London) Ltd.; F. Tacke KG; *The Engineer*; *The Motor Ship*; The Scandinavian Metal Corporation Ltd.; The Stephenson Society (King's College, Newcastle-upon-Tyne); Weser A.G.

Contents

Contributors

I. M. Bull
Design Manager, D. Napier & Son Ltd.

J. F. Butler
*Engine Works Technical Director,
Doxford & Sunderland Ltd.*

D. Castle
Engineering Manager, Crossley-Premier Engines Ltd.

Niels Gram
Metallurgist, Paul Bergsøe & Søn, Copenhagen

Søren Hansen
Engineering Consultant, Burmeister & Wain A/S.

Ir. A. Hootsen
*Promotion and Marketing Research, Stork-Werkspoor
Diesel, Amsterdam*

E. T. Kennaugh
Manager, Diesel Division, Sulzer Bros. (London) Ltd.

P. Pfeifer,
British Brown Boveri Ltd.

Ing. Walter Ragazzini,
Vice-Director, Marine Division, Fiat, Turin

Dr. Ing. F. Schmidt
Consultant Engineer, formerly M.A.N. Werk, Augsburg

H. Watson, B.SC., PH.D.
Engineering Manager, Ruston Paxman Diesels Ltd.

Ir. J. H. Wesselo
Engineering Director, Stork-Werkspoor Diesel, Amsterdam

Ing. Åke Westlin
Engineer, Diesel Engine Department, Götawerken, Göteborg

Chapter 1

Elementary Theory

By the term diesel engine is to be understood—for present purposes —any reciprocating engine in the cylinders of which an introduced charge of air is compressed sufficiently to ensure the spontaneous ignition and combustion of an atomised stream of fuel oil injected into the said charge of compressed air.

Theoretical Heat Cycle

The thermodynamic cycle most apposite to present-day airless injection practice is probably the so-called dual or mixed cycle, diagrammatically illustrated in Figure 1.1.

Starting from point C, the air is compressed adiabatically to a point D. Fuel injection begins at D, and heat is added to the cycle partly at constant volume—as shown by vertical line DP—and partly at constant pressure—as shown by horizontal line PE. At a point E, expansion begins; this proceeds adiabatically to point F, when the heat is rejected to exhaust at constant volume, as shown by vertical line FC.

The ideal efficiency of this cycle—of the hypothetical indicator diagram—is about 55–60 per cent; that is, about 45–40 per cent of the heat supplied is lost at the exhaust.

For a four-stroke cycle, the exhaust and suction strokes are shown by horizontal line at C, which has no effect upon the cycle.

Figure 1.2 may be deemed to approximate to a perfect, attainable diagram.

Thermal Efficiency

The irrecoverable heat loss inherent in the theoretical cycle is

1

substantial, as mentioned above, and there is nothing that the marine engineer can do to improve it. That is the first loss.

An actual indicator diagram must fall short of the perfect diagram visualised in Figure 1.1, because of thermal and other losses at the cylinder. That is the second loss.

By the time the power has been transmitted from the cylinder through the engine to the aft end of the crankshaft, there is a further loss by friction in the engine mechanism. That is the third loss.

The activities of the marine engineer must necessarily be confined to obtaining a good working indicator diagram, to ensuring an efficient, smooth-running engine and to achieving a low fuel consumption for the power developed. The thermal efficiency is the overall yardstick of performance.

Thermal efficiency (absolute)

$$= \frac{\text{heat converted into useful work}}{\text{total heat supplied}} \tag{1.1}$$

This may be expressed in two ways:

a indicated thermal efficiency; *b* brake thermal efficiency.

The equations, expressed in metric technical units, are:

a indicated thermal efficiency

$$= \frac{\text{one horse-power hour}}{g \times K \times E} = \frac{270\,000}{g \times K \times E} = \frac{632 \cdot 6}{g \times K} \tag{1.2}$$

b brake thermal efficiency

$$= \frac{\text{one horse-power hour}}{G \times K \times E} = \frac{270\,000}{G \times K \times E} = \frac{632 \cdot 6}{G \times K} \tag{1.3}$$

where g = wt. of fuel burned, in kg/ihp h (metric);
$\quad\quad G$ = wt. of fuel burned, in kg/bhp h (metric);
$\quad\quad K$ = calorific value of fuel burned, in kcal/kg;
$\quad\quad\quad$ one metric horse-power = 75 kg/metres per sec;
$\quad\quad\quad$ one horse-power hour (metric) = 60 × 60 × 75
$\quad\quad\quad$ = 270 000 kg/metres;

$\quad\quad E$ = 426·8 kg metres = one metric heat unit (kcal/kg);

$$\frac{270\,000}{426 \cdot 8} = 632 \cdot 6 = \text{one horse-power hour (metric) in kcal/kg.}$$

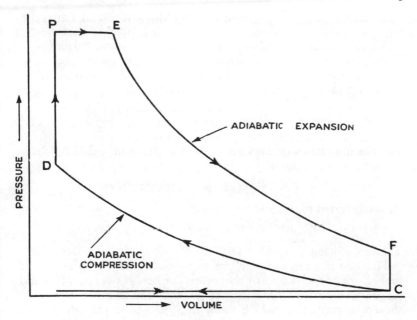

Figure 1.1 Theoretical heat cycle

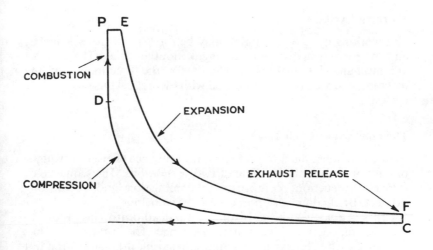

Figure 1.2 Perfect indicator diagram

As an exercise in expressing thermal efficiency in SI units, the following example is given.

A single-acting two-stroke trunk engine, 6 cylinders, 250 mm bore (area 0·0493 m²), 300 mm stroke, 450 rev/min (7·5 revs per sec), 13 bar bmep, consumes 170 kg of fuel per hour, calorific value 46 MJ/kg. Determine the brake thermal efficiency.

$$\text{Thermal efficiency} = \frac{\text{heat converted into work}}{\text{total heat supplied}}$$

Total heat supplied per second $= 170 \times 46\text{MJ}/3600 = 2\cdot17 \times 10^6 \text{J}$
By definition:

$$\text{bar} = 10^5 \text{N/m}^2 \text{ where N} = \text{newtons}; \text{ N} = \text{J/m}$$

Heat converted into work per second

$$= 6 \times 13 \times 10^5 \text{J/m}^3 \times 0\cdot0493\text{m}^2 \times 0\cdot300\text{m} \times 7\cdot5 = 8\cdot65 \times 10^5 \text{J}$$

Thermal efficiency $= 8\cdot65 \times 10^5 \text{J}/2\cdot17 \times 10^6 \text{J} = 0\cdot399$

The calorific value K may be expressed either in terms of the higher—or gross—value, or the lower—or net—value; equally valid reasons can be given for either usage. In citing efficiency figures, it should be made clear which value of K is used in the calculation. Otherwise the gross value is normally assumed.

The above formulae are for the absolute thermal efficiency, as distinct from the relative thermal efficiency, which is the ratio of the actual to the hypothetical diagram.

Working Cycles

The working cycle of an engine may be four-stroke or two-stroke; and the engine may be single-acting or double-acting. These cycles are mechanical sequences of events for the functioning of the machine, and are not to be confused with theoretical thermodynamic cycles.

The Four-stroke Cycle Engine

Figure 1.3 shows, diagrammatically, the sequence of events throughout a typical four-stroke cycle of two revolutions. The sequence of strokes is: suction; compression; combustion and expansion; exhaust. Brief comment upon each is given below.

SUCTION STROKE. With the piston at top dead-centre, just about to descend, the suction valve is already opened. The exhaust valve has not yet closed. The partial vacuum created by the out-flowing hot gases assists the inflow of fresh air through the suction valve and the cleansing of the cylinder of residual gases. As the piston descends, the suction valve remains open until about 25–30° beyond bottom dead-centre. Thereby more air flows into the cylinder than if the suction valve were to close on bottom dead-centre.

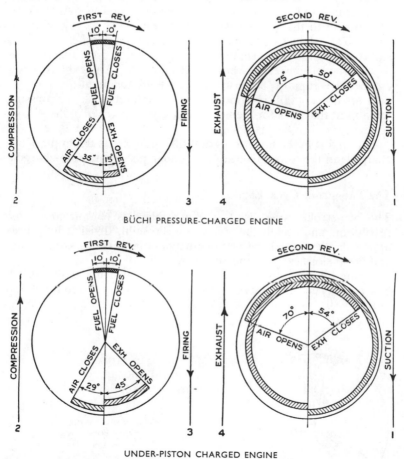

BÜCHI PRESSURE-CHARGED ENGINE

UNDER-PISTON CHARGED ENGINE

Figure 1.3 Four-stroke cycle, sequence of events

COMPRESSION STROKE. On the piston up-stroke the charge of air is compressed to about 35 kgf/cm². The temperature rises, but the compression is only roughly adiabatic, as heat is lost to cylinder walls and cover. The final compression temperature may be about 550°C. The clearance volume may be approximately 9 per cent of the working stroke volume.

EXPANSION STROKE. Near the end of the piston up-stroke, at about 10° before top dead-centre, the fuel valve opens. The injected fuel burns immediately. Combustion does not cease with fuel-valve closure, but continues for some distance as the piston descends. Expansion is only approximately adiabatic, as it is accompanied by loss of heat to the cylinder walls. With mip about 8·5 kgf/cm² the pressure at exhaust valve opening may be about 3 kgf/cm².

EXHAUST STROKE. The exhaust valve opens about 50–20° before the descending piston reaches bottom dead-centre. The exhaust gases escape very rapidly, because of their high temperature, and the pressure quickly falls to atmospheric, or thereabouts. The pressure remains at that level for the upward or exhaust stroke of the piston. A new cycle then begins *da capo*.

The engine in the upper diagram of Figure 1.3 is Büchi pressure-charged; in the lower diagram it is under-piston pressure-charged.

The Two-stroke Cycle Engine

The two-stroke cycle, as its name implies, is completed in one revolution, and usually the revolution is roughly divisible into three approximately equal periods, namely: compression; combustion and expansion; exhaust and scavenge.

Figure 1.4 shows the sequence of events diagrammatically. As will be seen, only insignificant fractions of the expansion and compression

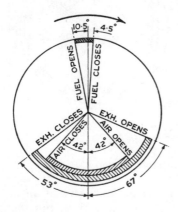

Figure 1.4 Two-stroke cycle, sequence of events

strokes are lost, because the exhaust and scavenge periods occur and are completed as the piston is approaching and leaving bottom dead-centre.

Indicated Horse-power

$$\text{ihp} = \frac{N \times p \times l \times a \times n}{4500}$$

where ihp = indicated horse-power of engine (metric horse-power);
 N = number of cylinders on engine;
 p = mean indicated pressure (mip) in cylinders, kgf/cm^2;
 l = engine stroke, in metres;
 a = cross-sectional area of one cylinder, in cm^2;
 n = number of *working* strokes per min;
 4500 = kg metres per min = metric horse-power. (1.4)

Cylinder Constants

As the engineer on board ship is interested in only one engine size and type, at any one time, much arithmetical labour can be eliminated, in routine use of the *plan* formula, by an evaluation of the constant quantities.

That is, in general terms, and in metric units:

$$\text{ihp} = \text{mip} \times R \times C \text{ (per cylinder)} \qquad (1.5)$$

where   mip = mean indicated pressure, in kgf/cm^2;
 R = rev/min;
 C = cylinder constant.

and $\text{ihp} = \text{mip} \times R \times K$ (per engine)   (1.6)
where $K = C \times$ number of cylinders.

The derivation of 5 is simple.

$$\text{ihp} = \frac{p \times l \times a \times n}{4500} \text{ per cylinder.}$$

For a single-acting four-stroke engine, $n = \dfrac{R}{2}$,

$$\therefore \quad \frac{p \times l \times a \times n}{4500} = p \times R \times \left(\frac{l \times a}{9000}\right),$$

where $\dfrac{l \times a}{9000}$ = cylinder constant.

For a single-acting two-stroke engine, $n = R$,

$$\therefore \quad \frac{p \times l \times a \times n}{4500} = p \times R \times \left(\frac{l \times a}{4500}\right),$$

where $\dfrac{l \times a}{4500}$ = cylinder constant. And so on.

Examples of Cylinder Constants

650 mm bore, 1400 mm stroke, S.A. 4C:

$C = 0.5162$ (one cylinder)
$K = 4.1296$ (eight cylinders)

740 mm bore, 1500 mm stroke, S.A. 4C:

$C = 0.7168$ (one cylinder)
$K = 4.3008$ (six-cylinder engine)

750 mm bore, 2000 mm total stroke, S.A. 2C:

$C = 1.9635$ (one cylinder)
$K = 13.7445$ (seven-cylinder engine).

The cylinder constants for some engine types may be rather difficult to determine, e.g., double-acting two-stroke engines with exhaust piston valves of diameter less than the cylinder bore and with piston-rod in the lower cylinder. It is advisable, in such instances, to obtain the cylinder constants from the builders. Cylinder constants receive further attention in the chapter which deals with conversion factors.

Mechanical Efficiency

Mechanical efficiency $\eta = \dfrac{\text{output at crankshaft}}{\text{input at cylinders}} = \dfrac{\text{bhp}}{\text{ihp}}$

or $\quad\quad\quad\quad\quad\quad\quad \text{bhp} = \text{ihp} \times \eta$ (1.7)

The brake horse-power (bhp) is normally determined by brake-dynamometer on the builder's test-bed. In the ship there may be a torsionmeter, arranged abaft the thrust block. The shaft horse-power (shp) at the torsionmeter is less than the bhp of the dynamo-meter, by the frictional horse-power lost at the thrust block.

Analysis of many test-bed results shows that the difference between ihp and bhp for an engine remains fairly constant through-out a wide range of loading. If the full-load efficiency, therefore, is known, the efficiency can be calculated for fractional loads.

Cylinder Mean Pressures

The mean indicated pressure (mip)

$$= \dfrac{\left(\begin{array}{c}\text{work done in cylinder}\\ \text{on working stroke}\end{array}\right)}{\text{swept volume}} = \dfrac{4\text{mip} \times a \times l}{a \times b}$$ (1.8)

The mip, in practice, is obtained by measuring the area of the indicator diagram, usually in square centimetres, and dividing it by the length of the diagram, in centimetres. The quotient of this process is the mean height of the diagram in centimetres. The scale of the indicator spring is usually, but not always, 1 mm of height = 1 kgf/cm² of mean indicated pressure.

For small engines, especially those which are not fitted with indicator gear, the term brake mean effective pressure (bmep) is used. This is determined from the bhp, the stroke-volume of the cylinders and the number of strokes. That is, equation (1.4) may be used, but for bhp and bmep instead of ihp and mip. The bmep is the product of the mip and the engine mechanical efficiency. There is a growing tendency to use bmep instead of mip, even for large engines. The author dislikes this usage, and prefers the simple and direct mip to the artificial bmep.

Piston Mean Speed

$$\text{Piston mean speed (metres/sec)} = \frac{l \times R}{30} \qquad (1.9)$$

where
$$l = \text{stroke in metres};$$
$$R = \text{rev/min}.$$

Fuel Consumption per 24 Hours

In metric units:

$$W = \frac{w \times \text{shp} \times 24}{1\,000\,000} \qquad (1.10)$$

$$w = \frac{1\,000\,000 \times W}{24 \times \text{shp}} \qquad (1.11)$$

where
$$W = \text{total fuel consumed per day, metric tons};$$
$$w = \text{fuel consumption rate, g/shp h (metric)}.$$
One metric ton $= 10^6$ grams

In SI units:
$$W = \frac{w \times kW \times 24}{1000}$$

$$w = \frac{1000\,W}{kW \times 24}$$

where
$$w = \text{fuel consumption rate, kg/kW h};$$
$$W = \text{total fuel consumed per day, tonnes}.$$
One tonne $= 1000$ kg

A Note on Systems of Dimensions

After due consideration the author has retained, for the purposes of this chapter, the familiar MKS system—i.e. that based on the metre, the kilogramme and the second.

Although the change to the Système International d'Unites—for which the symbol SI is now used in all languages—has been planned to be completed in the United Kingdom by the end of 1975, there is no doubt that the normal metric system will be used by many men in their individual capacities in marine engineering circles for some time to come, at least until all experiential and comparative records of performance data, voyage results and so on, have been established in terms of SI units.

The effect of applying the SI code to the metric equations quoted in this chapter will be to substitute the bar for the kilogramme force per square centimetre (one bar = 1·0197 kgf/cm^2) and the kilowatt for the horse-power (one British horse-power = 0·7457 kW; one metric horse-power = 0·7355 kW).

In Chapter 18, 'Conversion Factors', the SI system receives detailed attention.

Chapter 2

Rating of Engines

It is of the greatest importance for the shipowner that his engines should not be too highly rated. An attractive initial price will never compensate him for the recurrent vexatious delays and heavy replacement costs which are the inevitable concomitants of an over-rated engine. Nothing has harmed the reputation of the diesel engine so much as over-rating, and the worst offences have concerned auxiliary engines. It is all wrong for an important ship to be at the mercy of two or three undersized, over-rated auxiliary engines. Fully adequate auxiliary power should always be insisted upon; and auxiliary engine sizes should be based upon nothing less than a continuous night and day rating.

Maximum Rating

The practical limit of output in a diesel engine may be said to have been reached when one or more of the following factors operate:

1. The maximum percentage of fuel possible is being burned effectively in the cylinder volume available. (For the fuel to burn most effectively, the combustion must be perfect and completed at the earliest possible moment during the working stroke.)

2. The stresses in the component parts of the engine generally, for the mechanical and thermal conditions prevailing, have attained the highest safe level for continuous working.

3. The piston speed and revolutions per minute cannot safely be increased.

For a given cylinder volume, it is possible for one design of engine effectively to burn considerably more fuel than another design. This may be brought about by more effective scavenging, by a more

11

suitable combustion space and by a more satisfactory method of fuel injection. Similarly, the endurance limit of the materials of cylinders, pistons and other parts may be much higher for one engine than for another; this may be achieved by the adoption of more suitable materials, by better detail designing as regards shapes, thicknesses, etc., more satisfactory cooling and so on.

The piston speed is limited by the acceleration stresses in the materials, the speed of combustion and the scavenging efficiency, i.e., the ability of the cylinder to become completely rid of its exhaust gases. Cylinder-liner wear may possibly be considered, in certain circumstances. Within limits, so far as combustion is concerned, it is possible sometimes to increase the speed of an engine if the mean pressure is reduced—which may be of importance for auxiliary engines.

For each type of engine, therefore, there is a top limit beyond which the engine should not be run continuously. This limit is the maximum rating for that engine type. It is not easy to determine this maximum rating; in fact, it can only satisfactorily be established for each size and type of engine by exhaustive tests.

It is not prudent for a superintendent engineer, when considering new tonnage, to settle upon what appears to be a moderate rating for an engine without having available all relevant comparative data.

If a cylinder is overloaded by attempting to burn too much fuel, combustion may continue to the end of the working stroke and perhaps also until after exhaust has begun. Besides suffering an efficiency loss, the engine will become overheated, and piston seizures, or cracking of engine parts, may result; or, at least, sticking piston-rings will be experienced, also dirty and sticking fuel valves, with consequent heavier upkeep costs.

Acceptance Ratings

It is a common procedure for owners to insert in their contracts some such phrase as: 'The engines are to be capable of maintaining the designed sea speed of the vessel, fully loaded, when developing not more than 80 per cent [or some other percentage] of their rated bhp.' This type of clause leaves the full-rated power undefined, and therefore does not necessarily ensure a moderate rating.

An alternative practice is to agree upon the mean pressures and revolutions which the engines can carry continuously; to determine from them the somewhat lower figures to be used on trials; then, by prescribing a sufficient margin between trial-trip power and service power, a moderate rating in service is assured. On trials the engines should not be run one revolution more than is essential to fulfil the contract trial speed. This procedure has much to recommend it, being something which is proper to all high-class machinery until it is run-in.

The acceptance of a ship and its machinery must necessarily be based on a sea trial; a builder cannot be expected to accept a contract based on service speed—where there are many variable factors, all out of his control. In his own interest the owner should so arrange the requirements of the sea trials that the most economical results are assured in service.

Some General Comments on Rating

In considering the rating of diesel machinery a sharp distinction must be drawn between genuine over-rating and some purely local fault, such as may occur at one time or another with almost any engine part, a fault which may be fully explicable by a retrogression in design, unsatisfactory material, bad fuel oil, a local lubrication problem and so on. The over-rating of an engine must also not be confused with some propeller difficulty, which may simply mean that the propeller is not the most suitable one for the particular conditions of power, revolutions and speed of ship.

Definite scales of rating are laid down by some superintendent engineers for different types of engine, these being based upon observation and analysis over a long time, showing that beyond certain revolutions, piston speed, power per cylinder, mean pressure, exhaust temperature, etc., maintenance costs begin to rise quickly. This is an excellent notion if founded on sound experiential knowledge; the difficulty then is to deal with engines of newer types.

Exhaust Temperatures

The exhaust temperature can prove to be a limiting factor for the maximum output of an engine.

An exhaust-temperature graph—a diagram in which mean indicated pressures are plotted as abscissae and exhaust temperatures as ordinates—will generally indicate when the economical combustion limit, and sometimes when the safe working limit, of an engine has been attained. The economical limit is reached shortly after the exhaust temperature begins to curve upwards from what was, previously, almost a straight line. Very often the safe continuous working-load limit is also reached at the same time, as the designer naturally strives to make all the parts of an engine equally suitable for withstanding the respective thermal and mechanical stresses to which they are subjected.

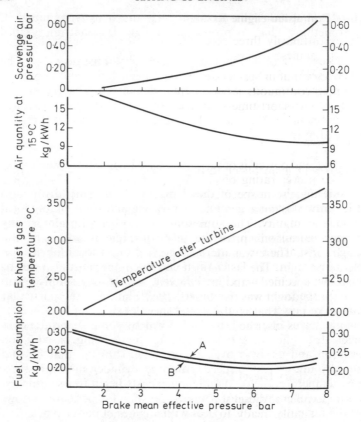

Figure 2.1 Performance curves

Exhaust temperature cannot be taken as proportionate to mean indicated pressure, when comparing different engine types.

Figure 2.1 shows guidance performance curves for single-acting, two-stroke, eccentric-type engines. Curves 'A' and 'B' are respectively for boiler oil and diesel oil, at 43 and 45 MJ/kg gross calorific value.

Sometimes it is said that power is limited by exhaust temperature. What is really meant is that torque is so limited. Exhaust temperature is a function of torque and not of power. The exhaust temperature is influenced by the lead and dimensions of the exhaust piping. The more easily the exhaust gases can flow away, the lower their temperature, and *vice versa*.

Levels of Propulsion-engine Rating

There are ordinarily three sets of requirements to be fulfilled for propelling engines:

normal continuous sea-service rating;
maximum continuous service rating;
trial trip—i.e. short time—rating.

Legend Power

The term 'legend power' is occasionally used to denote the maximum continuous power rating of an engine; that is, the power output corresponding to some specified value of piston speed, mean pressure and so on. But it is not a very satisfactory expression, if only because of possible ambiguity. The term probably had its origin in an old Admiralty expression—probably now in desuetude—namely, the legend draught. There was the light draught, the load draught and the legend draught. The last-named was the draught corresponding to a definite, specified—and intermediate—condition. Appropriate to the legend draught was the legend speed, and thus, by declension, the legend power. That is, the word 'legend' is used in the sense of something that is inscribed; it is not a synonym for something that is mythical.

Rating of Auxiliary Diesel Engines

The total number of diesel sets should be such that a stand-by unit is always available, ready to come into operation at a moment's notice. Thus, if the engines are of such a size that one can carry the sea-load, then three sets should be provided; i.e. two sets will normally share the load, so that, if one fails, the other will immediately take over the full load; the third set will be available for overhaul at sea. Similarly, if the relation between sea-load and engine output is such that two sets are needed for the load, then four sets should be installed, i.e. three will run at reduced power normally and, if one set fails, the other two will take the full load; the fourth set will be available for overhauling purposes.

The maximum continuous electrical load at sea, for which the engine-builder must provide, is the total connected load, multiplied by a diversity factor, the latter being deduced from voyage results of comparable ships. Sometimes, in the builders' analysis, the total connected load is split up and each section is multiplied by its own diversity factor. Thus the auxiliaries which continuously carry a full load at sea, e.g. the refrigerator, the main circulating pumps, the forced-lubrication pumps and so on, are grouped together, and the total motor brake horse-power obtained. This figure is multiplied by 0·9, because the motors supplied by reputable makers always have power in hand. The remainder of the sea connected load, excluding stand-by units, is then grouped and the aggregate power is multiplied by a lower factor; this may be of the order of, say, 0·45. The mixed diversity factor thus obtained may vary from, say, 0·60 to 0·75.

By way of example: one 14 000 shp twin-screw vessel showed, when homeward bound, a maximum sea load of 1600 A, a minimum of 1300 and an average of 1400. In this particular ship there were four 330 kW generating sets. In another vessel, having four 250 kW sets, the average amperage on the outward voyage was 1350 with 1700 on the homeward run. The maximum was 2000.

In yet another comparable twin-screw vessel, which had four 350 kW auxiliary diesel generators, the maximum sea load was 650 kW, the average 550 kW and the minimum, at night, 460 kW. In this vessel the maximum engine-room load was 200 kW, with an average of 140–150 kW. In passenger-carrying vessels the two extreme conditions are the load at midnight, which is a minimum, and the load when manoeuvring into port, which is a maximum.

Chapter 3

Engine Performance

The work of a marine engineer comprises, and is confined to, the successful operation of machinery which has already been designed and built into a ship. Accordingly, neither the designing of propellers, nor the determination of hull forms, nor the powering of ships lies within his province. All these things are decided by other people. But, as the function of a marine engine is the effective propelling of a ship, it is necessary that the operating engineer should have a working knowledge of at least the simpler parameters and the more frequently used methods of comparison, whereby the overall performance of ship and engines can be equitably adjudged.

In this chapter brief consideration is given to such matters as the propeller law, propeller slip, performance coefficients, fuel constants, propulsive coefficients, power build-up and so on.

The instruments normally provided by the engine builder for the assessment of power are few in number and simple of manipulation. They comprise: engine indicators, tachometer, revolution counter, pyrometers and possibly a torsionmeter. Sometimes there is a thrust meter, but this is an instrument of direct value only to the naval architect, for whose benefit it is fitted.

Cylinder Mean Pressures

The term bmep (brake mean effective pressure), although very useful for industrial and auxiliary engines which are not provided with cylinder indicating gear, has no meaning for marine propelling engines. On shipboard, where only indicated mean pressures can be measured, it is an artificial and superfluous term, despite its growing use. Indicated mean pressures do not involve any assumptions; brake mean pressures involve the assumption of mechanical

17

efficiency. In assessing engine performance, the greater the number of assumptions to be made, the wider can be the influence of the personal equation towards optimistic and sometimes unreal results —which is always a matter for deprecation.

Horse-power and Swept Volume

A ready yardstick of comparison, which is regarded as useful by some superintendents, is the relationship between horse-power and swept volume. An average figure, for two-stroke pressure charged engines under description, is 14·5–15 bhp/m³ min, a rating in which inherent reserve power is implicit.

Levels of Engine Rating

As maintenance costs are a function of the wear and tear experienced by a marine diesel engine, and as wear and tear is a function of rating, it is advisable—in the author's opinion—for three levels of rating to be assigned to an engine:

   (i)   normal continuous sea service rating;
   (ii) maximum continuous service rating;
   (iii) trial trip rating.

The values for bhp, mip and rev/min are, of course, capable of mutual variation within reasonable limits, the horse-power developed per cylinder being the product of the mean pressure, the revolutions per minute and the cylinder constant. The stated, and recommended, power and speed ratings are obtainable from the engine builder.

Propeller Slip

The slip of the propeller is almost invariably entered on the voyage log sheets, as being a useful pointer to overall results. It is true that the term 'slip' may never be used by naval architects, nor may the word ever be heard in the precincts of Tank establishments; and it may also be correct to state that the amount of apparent slip is no index to propulsive effectiveness in a new design, because a sound design may well have a relatively high slip. Nevertheless, the variation in propeller slip from day to day can be symptomatic of changes in the relationship of propulsive power and ship speed, and the entity, therefore, is a useful parameter.

The effect of ocean currents on ship speed 'over the ground' is sometimes appreciable. Thus, a following current in fine weather, may be as much as 2 per cent and 2·5 per cent; an adverse current, with heavy weather ahead, may have an effect of more than twice these amounts.

The Propeller Law

When a designer is powering a ship he is at liberty to make the engine mean pressure and the engine revolutions what he will, within the practicable and experiential limits of the engine design. It is only after a decision has been made and the engine has been coupled to a propeller that the propeller law operates in its effect upon horse-power, mean pressure and revolutions.

$$\text{shp varies as } V^3 \qquad\qquad (2.1)$$
$$\text{shp varies as } R^3 \qquad\qquad (2.2)$$
$$T \text{ varies as } R^2 \qquad\qquad (2.3)$$
$$P \text{ varies as } R^2 \qquad\qquad (2.4)$$

where $\text{shp} =$ aggregate shaft horse-power of engines, metric or British;

$V =$ speed of ship in knots;
$R =$ revolutions per minute of engines;
$T =$ torque, in kg metres or lb ft $= Pr$;
$P =$ brake mean pressure, kgf/cm^2 or lbf/in^2;
$r =$ radius of crank, metres or feet.

Propeller slip assumed to be constant.
That is:

$$\text{shp} = KV^3 \qquad\qquad (2.5)$$

where $K =$ constant, determinable from shp and V for a set of conditions.

But R is proportional to V, for constant slip,

$$\therefore \qquad \text{shp} = K_1 R^3 \qquad\qquad (2.6)$$

where $K_1 =$ constant, determinable from shp and R for a set of conditions.

But $$\text{shp} = \frac{P \times A \times c \times r \times 2\pi \times R}{33\,000}\text{(British)} = K_1 R^3,$$

where $A =$ aggregate area of pistons, cm^2 or in^2;
$c = 0.5$ for two-stroke, 0.25 for four-stroke engines.

or $$T = PAcr = \frac{33\,000}{2\pi \times R} \times K_1 R^3 = K_2 R^2 \text{ (British)}$$

or $$T = PAcr = \frac{4500}{2\pi \times R} \times K_1 R^3 = K_2 R^2 \text{ (metric)}$$

i.e. $$T = K_2 R^2 \qquad (2.7)$$

where $K_2 = $ constant, determinable from T and R for a set of conditions.

$$PAcr = T \text{ or } P = \frac{T}{Acr} = \frac{K_2}{Acr} \times R^2$$

i.e. $$P = K_3 R^2 \qquad (2.8)$$

where $K_3 = $ constant, determinable from P and R for a set of conditions.

The propeller law index is not always 3, nor is it always constant over the full range of speeds for a ship. Approaching top speed, it may exceed 3; for short, high-speed vessels—such as cross-channel ships—it may approach 4. But 3 is satisfactory for all ordinary calculations. The index for R, when related to the mean pressure P, is 'one down' from the index for V.

On the builders' test-bed, when the engine is coupled to a brake dynamometer, the propeller law is followed, to obtain data which will be useful at the ship.

The Fuel Coefficient

For measuring machinery performance, the most easily applied yardstick is the fuel coefficient:

$$C = \frac{D^{\frac{2}{3}} \times V^3}{F}$$

where
$C = $ fuel coefficient;
$D = $ displacement of ship in tons;
$V = $ speed in knots;
$F = $ fuel burned per 24 hours, in tons

Strictly, this method of comparison is applicable only if: the ships are similar; they are run at approximately corresponding speeds; they are running under the same company's flag, i.e. under the same conditions; the routes are the same; the quality of fuel is the same.

The displacement in relation to draught is obtained from a scale provided by the builders.

As a guide, the undermentioned values of the coefficient are quoted. They are averages from many logs and many ships.

Cargo vessels, 70 000–95 000;
Tankers, 70 000–95 000;
Cargo liners, 80 000–100 000;
Large passenger vessels, 90 000–110 000.

The Admiralty Constant

$$C = \frac{D^{\frac{2}{3}} \times V^3}{shp}$$

where $C =$ Admiralty constant, dependent upon ship form, hull
finish and other factors. Typical values, using trial-trip
powers, are: tanker 500–530; cargo ship 450; cargo
liner 400; passenger vessel 350; cross-channel ship
250–280.

If C is known for a ship the approximate shp can be computed for
given conditions of speed and displacement.

Apparent Propeller Slip

Apparent slip, per cent $= \left(\dfrac{P \times R - 101 \cdot 33 \times V}{P \times R} \right) \times 100$

where $P =$ propeller pitch in ft;
$R =$ rev/min;
$V =$ speed of ship in knots;
$101 \cdot 33 =$ one knot, in ft/min.

The real propeller slip is the slip relative to the wake stream, which
is something very different. The engineer is normally interested in
the apparent slip.

Acceptance of Ship and Machinery

There are so many variables which affect machinery performance
at sea that the only practicable basis for a contract is acceptance
on sea trials, where everything is under the builders' control. This
means that the margin between trial-trip powering and sea-service
requirements of speed and loading must ensure that the machinery
has ample capacity.

In this connection one of the factors is the propeller surface. A
propeller which provides the most efficient smooth-water performance on acceptance trials is not necessarily the best propeller for
sea service. In recent years there has been a tendency to reduce
propeller surface. The result is that under strong head winds and

heavy weather the propeller is unable to provide the necessary thrust, and slip increases rapidly.

Normal propeller performance is fairly insensitive to surface, and accordingly many propellers have had their surface increased as much as 30 per cent, with decided benefit to average speed on passage. It is important that a propelling engine should be able to provide heavy torque when required, which implies an ample number of cylinders combined with ability to carry high mean pressure. When a propeller reaches its limit of thrust under head winds increase of revolutions can be unavailing.

On the tank-test result sheets the following particulars are given:

Quasi-propulsive coefficient (Q)

$$Q = \frac{\text{Model resistance} \times \text{Speed}}{2\pi \times \text{Torque} \times \text{rev/min}} = \frac{\text{Work got out per min}}{\text{Work put in per min}}$$

Total shaft horse-power at propeller (EHP)

$$\text{EHP} = \frac{ehp + p}{Q}$$

where ehp = effective horse-power for naked model, as determined by tank experiments;

   p = increase for appendages and air resistance = 10–12 per cent of the naked model EHP; this is for smooth-water conditions.

The shaft horse-power at the propeller needed for smooth sea trials, say in the Firth of Clyde, is about 10 per cent more than in tank tests. The additional power, compared with sea trials, which is necessary for South Atlantic service is 11–12 per cent, with 20–25 per cent for the North Atlantic. The size of ship enters into these allowances; a small ship needs greater margins. By way of example: 15 per cent margin over trial conditions equals 26·5 per cent over tank tests.

The torsionmeter shp, just abaft the thrust block, exceeds the EHP by the power lost in friction at stern tube and plummer blocks. This is usually reckoned to be 5 or 6 per cent. Torsionmeter error is usually said to be ±0·5 per cent, but the author has known it to be several per cent—sometimes as high as 6, 8 and possibly 10 per cent. The error becomes apparent when a well-understood ship form shows a propulsive power several per cent unexpectedly good and at the same time the propelling engine—the performance of which is also fully understood—shows a fuel consumption unexpectedly bad and to the same extent.

The brake horse-power (bhp) exceeds the torsionmeter shp by the frictional power lost at the thrust block. On board ship the bhp

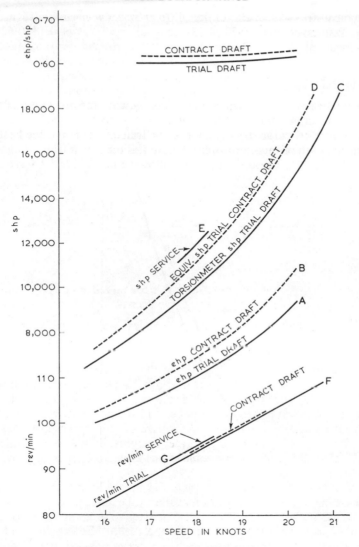

Figure 3.1 Propulsion data

can be determined only by multiplying the ascertained ihp by the mechanical efficiency stated by the builder.

To summarise: the required bhp for a propelling engine = (EHP + sea-service margin) + hp lost at stern tube and plummer blocks + hp lost at thrust block.

Typical values of Q are: tanker 0·67–0·72; slow cargo boat 0·72–0·75; fast cargo liner 0·70–0·73; cross-channel vessel 0·58–0·62; passenger ship 0·65–0·70.

Power Build-up

Figures 3.1 and 3.2 are typical diagrams showing the powering data for a twin-screw ship.

In Figure 3.1 curve A is the EHP at the trial draught; B is the EHP corrected to the contract draught. Curve C is the shp at trial draught

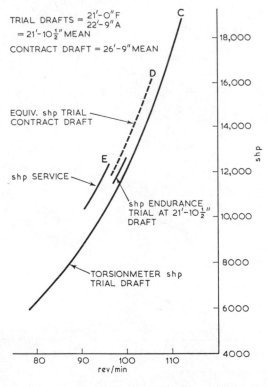

Figure 3.2 Propulsion data

on the Firth of Clyde; D is the shp corrected to the contract draught. E is the power-service curve, from voyage results. Curve F shows the relation between speed of ship and revolutions of engines on trial; G is the service result. The full power rating of the propelling engines is 18 000 bhp, the continuous service rating 15 000 bhp.

In Figure 3.1 curves *A* to *D* show shp as ordinates and speed of ship as abscissae; curve *F* shows engine revolutions as ordinates and speed of ship as abscissae. In Figure 3.2 powers are shown as ordinates, revolutions as abscissae.

Figure 3.3 shows the relationship between revolutions, powers and brake mean pressures for the conditions summarised in Figures 3.1 and 3.2. A fair line drawn through the observed points for the

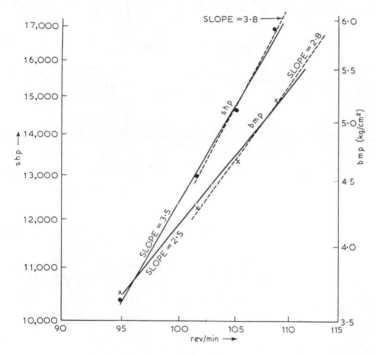

Figure 3.3 Engine trials; power, revolutions and mean pressure

whole range shows the shp approximately to increase as the cube of the revolutions and the bmep as the square. For the range 95–109 rev/min, the index increases to 3·5 for the power and 2·5 for the bmep. Between 120 and 109 rev/min a more closely drawn curve shows the index to rise to 3·8 and the bmep to 2·8. In Figure 3.3 ordinates and abscissae are plotted to a logarithmic base, thus reducing the power/revolution and the pressure/revolution curves to straight lines, for simplicity of construction and computation.

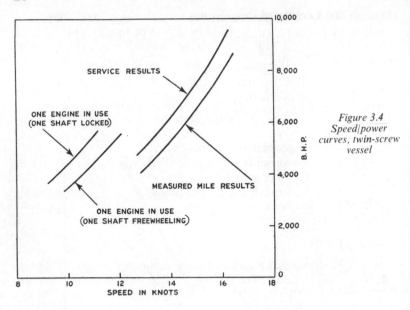

Figure 3.4
Speed/power
curves, twin-screw
vessel

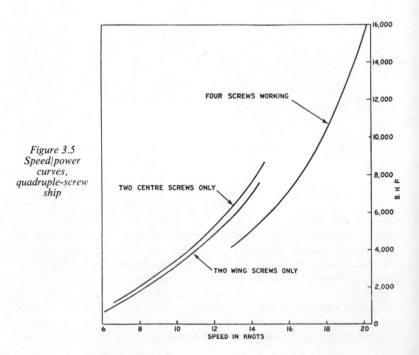

Figure 3.5
Speed/power
curves,
quadruple-screw
ship

Trailing and Locking of Propellers

In Fig. 3.4 there are shown the normal speed/power curves for a twin-screw motor vessel on the measured mile and in service.

The effect upon the speed and power of the ship when one of the propellers is trailed, by 'free-wheeling', is indicated in the diagram. The effect of one of the propellers being locked is also shown.

Figure 3.5 shows the speed/power curves for a four-screw motor ship:

    (a) when all propellers are working;

    (b) when the vessel is being propelled only by the two centre screws, the two outer screws being locked; and

    (c) when the ship is being propelled only by the two wing screws, the two inner screws being locked.

Astern Running

Figure 3.6 summarises a series of tests made on the trials of a twin-screw passenger vessel, 716 ft long, 83 ft 6 in. beam, trial draught 21 ft forward, 26 ft aft, 26 000 tons displacement.

As plotted in Figure 3.6, tests I to VI show distances and times,

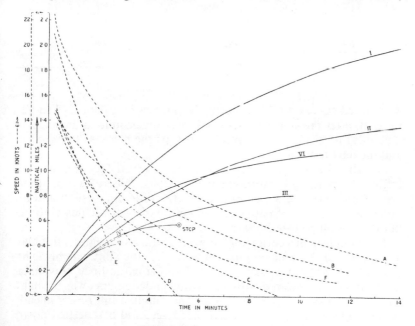

Figure 3.6 Ship stopping trials

the speed of approach in each test being as stated at column 2 in Table 3.1. The dotted curves show reductions of speed and times.

Table 3.1 SHIP STOPPING TRIALS

1	2	3	4		5	6
	Ahead speed of approach		*Propellers stopped (min)*			*Distance travelled*
Test No.	*knots (rev/min)*	*Propellers*	*P.*	*S.*	*Ship stopped (min)*	*(nautical miles)*
I	23·0 (119)	Trailing; unlocked	16·4	14·9	—	2·0
II	14·5 (75)	Trailing; unlocked	12·5	12·1	17·0	1·4
III	13·5 (75)	Trailing; locked	1·5	1·5	13·0	0·8
IV	15·0 (75)	Ahead running checked; no additional astern power	1·3	1·3	5·2	0·5
V	14·8 (75)	Engine stopped; astern as quickly as possible	0·7	0·8	3·1	0·4
VI	22·4 (116)	Trailing; locked	1·5	1·6	15·0	1·1

The dotted curves *A* to *F* respectively correspond to curves I to VI. In test I, after the ship had travelled, over the ground, a distance of 2 nautical miles (1 nautical mile = 6080 ft) the test was terminated and the next test begun.

In Table 3.2 a typical assortment of observed facts relating to engine stopping and astern running is given. Where two or three sets of readings are stated, these are for different vessels and/or different engine sizes. Space does not permit of extended description, but the overall picture is clear.

Trials made with a cargo liner, powered with a six-cylinder double-acting two-stroke cycle engine, showed that the ship was brought to rest from 20 knots in 65 seconds. Another cargo liner, travelling at 16 knots and powered with an eight-cylinder engine, was brought to a stop in a similar period. The engine, running full power ahead, was brought to 80 rev/min astern in 32 sec, and had settled down steadily at full astern revolutions in 50 sec.

Table 3.2 ENGINE REVERSING AND SHIP STOPPING

Ship	Engine type	Ahead (rev/min)	Time for engine stopping (sec)	Engine moving astern (sec)	Astern running Rev/min	sec	Ship stopped min	sec
Large passenger	D.A. 2C. (twin)	65	—	30	—	—	4	2
Small fast passenger	S.A. 2C. tr. (twin)	217	53	63·5	160	72·5	2	15
		195	35	45	160	60	1	54
		220	45	59	170	81	2	5
Passenger	Diesel-electric (twin)	92	110	—	80	225	5	0
Cargo	S.A. 2C. (twin)	112	127·5	136	100	141	—	
Cargo	D.A. 2C. (single)	90	24	26	90	115	2	26
		88	12	14	82	35	3	25
		116	35	40	95	50	—	
Cargo	S.A. 2C. (single)	95	31	33	75	45	—	
		110	12	21	110	53	3	21
		115	10	55	110	110	4	6

Effect of Hull Fouling

The deterioration in the performance of new ships, as a result of fouling of the hull by marine growths, can sometimes be startling, especially if the trade route lies across tropical waters.

Thus, under exactly comparable conditions of trim, draught, weather and speed, an increase in voyage fuel consumption of 25 per cent can result from a ship not being drydocked at the normal time, but being allowed to continue for an additional voyage. Expressed in different terms, a ship travelling at 17 knots with clean hull can be reduced by fouling to 14·3 knots. In older less-efficient, hulls a deterioration of 8–10 per cent would be expected.

Some Recapitulative Comments

The shipbuilder necessarily thinks of ship speed in terms of trial performance in fair weather; but to the shipowner ship speed is inevitably related to scheduled performance on a particular trade route. A number of factors are involved in relating trial results to working schedules. Considerations of money and time result in sea trials being almost invariably run with deadweight limited to fuel, fresh water and ballast. Because of the difference between load draught and trial draught, the hull resistance may be 25–30 per cent greater for the same speed. This has a consequential effect upon the relation between engine torque and power, and in the reaction upon propeller efficiency. Adverse weather, marine growths and machinery deterioration necessitate further power allowance, if the service speed is to be maintained.

At this point it is instructive to compare the behaviour of diesel engines with that of steam turbines. As already mentioned, propeller torque, in relation to engine revolutions, increases with draught, adverse weather and hull fouling. The steam turbine responds automatically, with high torque, to meet the stalling effect of the additional resistance. The cycle of heat temperatures is constant at all points of the installation for any given speed. Once the machinery is set, there is no necessary fluctuation of temperature. The torque that can prudently be exerted by the diesel engine is controlled by the heat stresses; power is therefore reduced when circumstances are adverse. The reduction in power is taken further in the diesel engine than it is in the turbine. Higher marginal provision of cylinder capacity is therefore necessary to ensure the scheduled speed. Moreover, the diesel engine has no reserve which corresponds to the operation of the turbine by-pass valves. These valves permit a substantial margin of power being available over the normal designed power, at only a small increase in specific fuel consumption and a small additional cost.

On trials, new diesel machinery, with no wear, is run at ratings higher than that prudent for long distances and steady running. Neither power of machinery nor speed of vessel can be defined without reference to other factors, as mentioned earlier. The maximum power that can be developed tends to diminish as the draught increases, and the speed is consequently reduced; adverse weather and fouling of bottom have similar and additional effect. There is thus the double diminishment, in that the factors which result in increased resistance and against which more power is needed to maintain the ship's speed, in themselves reduce the maximum power that can be developed.

Diesel machinery is subjected to heavy fluctuations of temperature and stress in each revolution. The result is not infrequently failure of parts by fatigue. Inevitably there are wear and tear, calling in time for correction or renewal. Judgment is required in deciding the length of life before renewing these expensive wearing parts. As a result, diesel machinery can never be maintained continuously at maximum efficiency. A balance has to be accepted between frequency of renewal and efficient service. The outstanding effect of the necessary inefficiency is reduction in the maximum power which may prudently be used. Imprudently, it is possible in all conditions to develop higher power at corresponding risk. Mean wear and tear may result in a reduction of 10–15 per cent in maximum power. Alternatively, a loss of prudent maximum speed up to 1 knot may be experienced.

A further allowance must be made for the difference between speed maintained in fair weather and the mean for a voyage from departure to arrival. The deduction may be of the order of one half-knot.

In this chapter metric and British dimensions have been retained, being those in which the technical records were made. The only changes required by an application of the SI code would be in relation to powers, i.e. kilowatts instead of horse-powers and the international nautical mile instead of the British nautical mile. One international nautical mile is 1·8520 km; one U.K. nautical mile is 1·8532 km. In this chapter it is the underlying principles and systems that are of value to the marine engineer in his assessment of ship performance.

Chapter 4

Pressure-charging

In an engine which draws its combustion air direct from the atmosphere the density of the induced air charge is approximately the same as the ambient air density. As this air density determines the maximum weight of fuel that can effectively be burned per working stroke in the cylinder, it also determines the maximum power that can be developed by the engine. If, therefore, the charge-air density is increased by the interposition of a suitable compressor between the ambient air and the cylinder, it follows that the weight of air per working stroke is increased and thereby a greater weight of fuel can be burned in the same cylinder, with proportionate augmentation of power. This is a self-acting process, which does not require an external governor.

The power for driving the compressor has an important influence on the operating efficiency of the engine. For example, it is relatively uneconomical to drive the compressor direct from the engine by chain or other mechanism because some of the additional power is absorbed thereby and there is thus an increase in specific fuel consumption for the extra power obtained. But if the compressor is driven by the heat energy in the engine exhaust gases—about 35 per cent of the total heat energy in the fuel is discharged to the exhaust gases—then an increase in power is obtainable which is about proportional to the increase in the charge-air density. This is the essential principle of exhaust turbo-charging.

The turboblower comprises a gas turbine, driven by the engine exhaust gases, direct-coupled to a compressor, i.e. a blower, which draws air from the ambient atmosphere and discharges to the air inlet manifold on the engine. The power generated in the turbine must equal that required by the compressor. The advantages of pressure-charging by means of an exhaust turboblower system are:

32

(i) a substantial increase in power output for any stated engine size and piston speed, alternatively, a substantial reduction in engine dimensions and weight for any stated horse-power;

(ii) an appreciable reduction in the specific fuel consumption rate at all engine loads;

(iii) a reduction in initial cost;

(iv) increased reliability and reduced maintenance costs, resulting from less-exacting conditions at cylinders.

In pressure-induction engines the components which sustain the increased piston loads and reactions may or may not be heavier than those in non-P.I. engines. This is a problem for resolution by a careful analysis of the working stresses in the respective components.

FOUR-STROKE ENGINES

Exhaust turbocharged, single-acting, four-stroke cycle marine engines are in successful operation which deliver as much as 200 per cent more power than atmospheric induction engines of the same speed and dimensions. Almost all marine four-stroke engines at present in service operate on the pulse system.

In matching the turboblower to the engine, a free-air quantity in excess of the swept volume is required to allow for the increased density of the charge-air, and to provide air for through-scavenging. For example, an engine with a full load bmep of 150 lb/in² (10·4 bar) would need about 100 per cent excess of free air, about 60 per cent of which is retained in the cylinders, the remaining 40 per cent being used for scavenging.

To ensure adequate scavenge/cooling, a valve overlap of approximately 140° is normal. In a typical valve timing arrangement the air inlet valve opens at 80° before top dead-centre and closes at 40° after bottom dead-centre. The exhaust valve opens at 50° before bottom dead-centre and closes at 60° after top dead-centre.

To obtain the air needed for a bmep of 150 lb/in² (10·4 bar)—compared with a bmep of about 80 lb/in² (5·5 bar) for atmospheric induction—a boost pressure of approximately 7·5 lb/in² (0·5 bar) is required, corresponding to a compressor pressure-ratio of 1·5:1 for a medium-speed direct-injection engine.

Optimum values of power output and specific fuel consumption can be achieved only by effective utilisation of the high-energy engine exhaust pulses. The engine exhaust system should be so designed that it is impossible for gases from one cylinder to contaminate the charge-air in another cylinder, either by blowing back through the exhaust valve or by interfering with the discharge of gases from the cylinder. During the period of overlap the exhaust pressure must be less than the air-charging pressure. This ensures effective scavenging of the cylinder for elimination of all residual exhaust gas, and for cooling purposes. It has been found, in practice, that if the period between discharge of successive cylinders into a common manifold is less than about 240°, then interference will take place between the scavenging of one cylinder and the exhaust of the next. This means that engines with more than three cylinders must either be fitted with more than one turboblower, or the turboblower must have multi-inlet casings which have separate passages right up to the turbine nozzles. Either method can lead to inefficient turbine operation, which will be discussed in more detail later.

The exhaust manifold system should, in general, be as small as possible in terms of both pipe length and pipe bore. The shorter the pipe length, the less likelihood there is of pulse reflections occurring during the scavenge period, particularly in high-speed engines. The smaller the pipe bore, the greater the preservation of exhaust-pulse energy, although it has been shown that a minimum bore may be reached beyond which the increase in frictional losses of the high-velocity exhaust gas more than offsets the increased pulse energy. As a first approximation, the ratio of pipe area to maximum exhaust valve or port area should be about unity. Sharp bends or sudden changes in pipe cross-sectional area should be avoided wherever possible.

TWO-STROKE ENGINES

In comparison with four-stroke engines, the application of pressure-charging to two-stroke cycle marine engines is relatively difficult because, until a certain level of speed and power is reached, the turboblower is not self-supporting. That is, at low engine revolutions there is insufficient energy in the exhaust gases to drive the turbo-blower at the speed required for the necessary air-mass flow. In addition, the small piston movement during the through-scavenge period does nothing to assist the flow of air, as in the four-stroke engine. Accordingly, starting is made very difficult and off-load running may be very inefficient, or even impossible, unless the scavenging is assisted by, for example, having a scavenge pump in series with the turboblower.

Two-stroke engine turbocharging is achieved by two distinct methods, respectively termed the constant-pressure and the pulse system.

For constant-pressure operation, all cylinders exhaust into a common receiver which tends to dampen-out the pulses and to

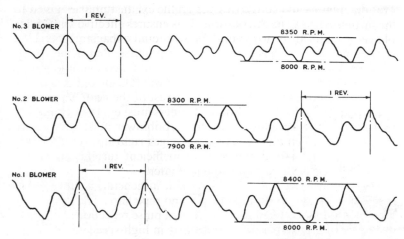

Fig. 4.1 Cyclic variations in turboblower revolutions

maintain an almost constant pressure. The advantage of this system lies in the ease with which normally aspirated engines may be adapted for pressure-charging, because a complicated multi-pipe exhaust arrangement is not needed, and also little change in port timing is required. It also leads to much higher turbine efficiencies, a matter which will be later discussed in greater detail. An additional advantage is that the lack of restriction, within reasonable limits, on exhaust-pipe length permits greater flexibility in positioning the the turboblower relative to the engine. The main disadvantage of the constant-pressure system is the poor performance obtained at part-load conditions. In addition, owing to the relatively large exhaust manifold, the system is insensitive to changes in engine operating conditions; and the resultant delay in turboblower acceleration, or deceleration, results in poor combustion during transition periods.

For operation under the pulse system, the comments made for the four-stroke engine under this system generally apply. The acceptable minimum firing-order separation for cylinders exhausting into a common manifold is about 120°. The sudden drop in manifold pressure, which follows each successive exhaust-pulse, results in a greater pressure differential across the cylinder during the scavenge period than is obtained with the constant-pressure system. This is a factor which makes for better scavenging.

Figure 4.1 shows the variation in rotational speed of a turboblower during each working cycle of the engine, i.e. one revolution.

This diagram clearly illustrates the reality of the impulses given to the turbine wheel. The fluctuation in speed is about 5 per cent. Each blower is coupled to two cylinders, with crank spacing 135°, 225°.

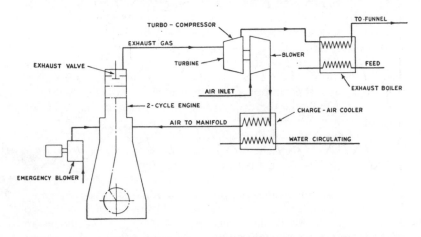

Figure 4.2 Exhaust turbocharging system

It is usually desirable to fit charge-air coolers to turbo-charged two-stroke engines. The coolers are located between the turbo-blowers and the cylinders, as shown in the diagrammatic arrangement of Figure 4.2.

CHARGE-AIR COOLING

As already mentioned, the increased power output obtained by pressure-charging is the result of an increased weight of air trapped in the cylinder, enabling a greater weight of fuel to be burned. The increase in air density is fractionally offset by the increase of air temperature consequent upon adiabatic compression in the turbo-blower, the amount of which is dependent on compressor efficiency. This reduction of air density due to increased temperature implies a loss of potential power for a stated amount of pressure-charging. For example, at a charge-air pressure of, say, 5 lb/in² (0·35 bar) the temperature rise is of the order of 33°C—equivalent to a 10 per cent reduction in charge-air density. As the amount of pressure-charging is increased the effect of turboblower temperature rise becomes more pronounced. Thus, for a charge-air pressure of 10 lb/in² (0·7 bar) the temperature rise is approximately 60°C, which is equivalent to a reduction of 17 per cent in the charge-air density.

By the use of charge-air coolers this potential loss can be mostly recovered. In four-stroke engines, with a moderate amount of pressure-charging, the cooling of the charge-air is not worthwhile; but in two-stroke engines it is an advantage to fit charge-air coolers.

Charge-air cooling has a double effect upon engine performance. By increasing the charge-air density, it thereby increases the weight of air flowing into the cylinders; and by lowering the charge-air temperature it reduces the exhaust temperature and the engine thermal loading. The increased power is obtained without loss of fuel economy. It is important that charge-air coolers should be designed for low pressure-drop on the air side; otherwise, to obtain the required air pressure, the turboblower speed must be increased. The favoured type of charge-air cooler is the water-cooled design. To ensure satisfactory effectiveness and a minimum pressure-drop on the charge-air side and on the cooling-water side, the coolers are designed for air speeds of the order of 35 ft/sec (11 m/sec) and water speeds in the cooling tubes of approximately 2·5 ft/sec (0·75 m/sec).

Charge-air cooler effectiveness is defined as the ratio of charge-air temperature drop to available temperature drop between charge-air inlet temperature and cooling-water inlet temperature. This ratio is approximately 0·8.

IMPORTANCE OF ADEQUATE SCAVENGING

It is essential that each cylinder should be adequately scavenged before a fresh charge of air is compressed; otherwise this fresh air charge is contaminated by residual exhaust gases from the previous cycle. Further, the cycle temperature is unnecessarily high if the air-charge is heated by mixing with residual gases and by contact with hot cylinders and pistons.

In the exhaust turbocharged engine the necessary scavenging is obtained by providing a satisfactory pressure-difference between the air manifold and the exhaust manifold. The air-flow through the cylinder during the overlap period has a valuable cooling effect; it helps to increase the volumetric efficiency and also to ensure a low cycle temperature. Also, the relatively cooler exhaust allows a higher engine output to be obtained before the exhaust temperature imposes a limitation on the satisfactory operation of the turbine blades.

The 140° overlap in four-stroke engines has already been mentioned. In two-stroke engines the exhaust/scavenge overlap is necessarily limited by design characteristics. Thus, in Figure 4.3 a comparison of the exhaust and scavenge events for poppet-valve engines and opposed-piston engines is given. In the poppet-valve engine the camshaft lost-motion coupling enables the exhaust pre-

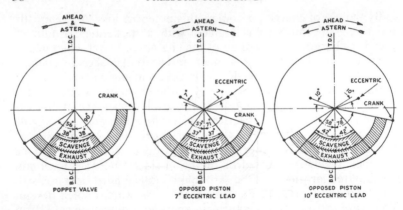

Figure 4.3 Single-acting two-stroke engine timing

opening angle to be 52°, ahead and astern. In the opposed-piston engine, with eccentric advance angle of 7°, the exhaust pre-opening angle is only 34° ahead and 20° astern; and with eccentric advance angle of 10°, the exhaust pre-opening angle is 36° ahead and 16° astern. Against this, however, the rate of port opening in opposed-piston engines is quicker than that in poppet-valve engines.

The essential difficulty in a reversible opposed-piston engine is the obtaining of a sufficiently large pre-exhaust area for astern running. In principle, the normal timing of non-pressure-charged engines has been retained, without any complication—such as reversing devices for the exhaust piston movement or valves in the exhaust line. A turbine area is chosen, so small that the scavenging air pressure is higher than the pressure needed at the beginning of compression, to compensate for that part of the scavenging which takes place as in non-turbocharged opposed-piston engines, namely, in the period between scavenge-port and exhaust-port closure.

In the four-stroke engine the substantial increase in power per cylinder, obtainable by turbocharging, is achieved without increase of cylinder temperature. In the two-stroke engine, with augmented cylinder loading, the increase of thermal loading—if any—is without significance. At the present time the exhaust gas temperature limit at the turbine inlet branch is of the order of 1200°F (650°C).

Engineers are sometimes puzzled by the fact that the engine exhaust gas raises the blower air to a pressure-level greater than the mean pressure of the exhaust gas itself. The explanation is to be found in the utilisation of the kinetic energy of the exhaust gas leaving the cylinder, and the energy of the heat-drop as the gas passes through the turbine. In Figure 4.4 the blower pressure gradient

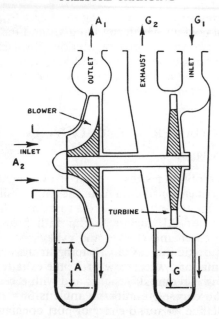

Figure 4.4 Scavenge gradient

A exceeds the turbine pressure gradient G by the amount of the scavenge gradient. The design of the engine exhaust-pipe system can have an important influence on the performance of the turbo-blowers. The overall adiabatic efficiency of a turboblower is about 60 per cent.

Examination of turbo-charged engine test results shows, both for four-stroke and two-stroke engines, that there is an increase in temperature of the exhaust gas between the cylinder exhaust branch and the turbine inlet branch, the rise sometimes being as much as 200°F (93°C). The explanation of this apparent anomaly is that the kinetic energy of the hot gas leaving the cylinder is converted, in part, into additional heat energy as it adiabatically compresses the column of gas ahead of it until, at the turbine inlet, the temperature exceeds that at the cylinder branch. At the turbine some of the heat energy is transformed into horse-power, lowering the gas temperature somewhat, the gas continuing to flow to a boiler.

This explanation might not, perhaps, always be the whole truth. The temperature recorded by the thermometer at the cylinder is a time-average figure, and some experts maintain that there is a cooling effect from the exhaust-pipe water-jacket. Moreover, during the exhaust/scavenging stroke the last thing to emerge from the exhaust ports is a slug of cold air which can hang around the thermometer stem for about two-thirds of a revolution, thus influencing the reading towards a lower temperature. Whatever effect these other factors might have, adiabatic compression can be accepted as the chief reason for the temperature difference.

NAPIER TURBOBLOWERS

Capacity of Turboblower

To determine turboblower sizes for four-stroke engines the maker requires the undermentioned data from the engine builder: size and number of cylinders; rev/min; firing order; maximum firing pressure; non-P.I. output; non-P.I. fuel rate; bhp with pressure-charging; type of combustion chamber; inlet and exhaust valve particulars; compression ratio; timing; exhaust piping arrangement; exhaust temperature limitation; water-flow rate and inlet temperature, if charge-air cooling is required.

For two-stroke engines, additional information is required as follows, viz.: method of turbo-charging, i.e. constant-pressure or pulse system; full technical details of engine-driven scavenge blower, if used; air consumption and air manifold pressure, under non-P.I. conditions.

From the engine swept-volume and the appropriate excess-air factor, the free air capacity for the turboblower is calculated. With this information, and knowing the blower pressure-ratio, the maker can determine the basic turboblower size, and also decide upon the correct compressor diffuser and the turbine area necessary.

De-rating of Turboblowers

Diesel engines may be required to operate under atmospheric conditions far removed from standard operating conditions. In marine engines the change is usually confined to one of temperature or humidity, although pressure changes have to be considered for altitude operation on lakes. Because of this change of ambient conditions, it is often necessary to de-rate the engine to suit them. Failure to do this can result in excessive engine thermal loading, together with increased exhaust manifold temperatures, causing possible overspeeding of the turboblower. The de-rating of diesel engines is covered by British Standard 649:1958.

Reduction of the ambient pressure lowers the density and hence the weight of the charge-air in nearly direct proportion. A proportionate reduction in fuel must therefore be made in order to maintain the correct fuel/air ratio. This results, in turn, in a reduction of engine output. The reduction in output is somewhat less than the reduction in charge-density, due to the slightly lower flow losses in engine and turboblower.

The effects of an increase in ambient temperature are more complex. For a given turboblower rotational speed, the inlet manifold temperature (for non charge-air cooled engines) is very nearly proportional to the ambient temperature. The manifold pressure will also decrease, but this decrease is a non-linear function of the ambient temperature change. Thus, the overall effect is again a decrease in charge-density and output. If the engine is fitted with a charge-air cooler a de-rating factor must be applied to take account of any increase in cooling water temperature.

A further factor is introduced to allow for variations in humidity, the effect of this being to decrease the weight of air in unit volume of free air.

In practice, where an engine is operated permanently at non-standard ambient conditions, the engine is not always de-rated in this manner. For example, a non charge-air cooled engine with a specified standard sea-level rating may be required to run permanently on a lake at high altitude. Such an engine could be fitted with a smaller turbine build and a charge-air cooler, thus restoring the engine inlet manifold pressure and temperature to their values for sea-level operation. Thereby the sea-level power output would be fully restored.

Matching of Turboblower and Engine

The correct matching of a turboblower to an engine is extremely important. After a certain size of turboblower has been correctly matched with a certain type and size of diesel engine, individual matching of other engines of the same type and size should not be necessary, unless a change in engine rating or in engine design is made. With correct matching, the engine operating point should be close to optimum efficiency, as shown by the blower characteristic curve, *see* Figure 4.5. In this diagram the ordinates indicate pressure-ratio; the abscissae show blower capacity.

During the initial shop trials of a new size of engine, with the turboblower recommended by the maker, test data are recorded and analysed. If the turboblower is correctly matched to the engine, there is no more to be done. Should the matching be incorrect, however, the turboblower will supply charge-air at either too low or too high a pressure, or surging may occur at the blower. Mis-matching can usually be corrected by a change of turbine capacity and/or blower diffuser. This change can often be made in place, at the engine builders' works.

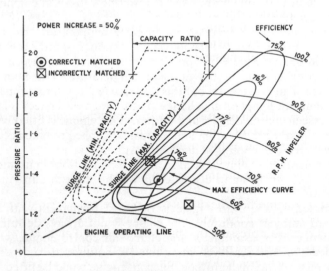

Figure 4.5 Turboblower characteristics

Compressors can be designed which maintain a high efficiency at a constant pressure-ratio over a wide range of air mass-flows by providing alternative forms of diffuser for any one design of impeller. This range can be further extended by the use of different impeller designs, each with its own set of diffusers, within a given frame size of turboblower. By this means, each frame size can provide a mass-flow capacity range having a maximum to minimum ratio of about 3:1. Advantage is taken of this fact to reduce the number of basic turboblower sizes required to cover the total range of diesel engine powers. So that some overlap of capacity is provided from one frame size to another, each size is increased in capacity from the next smaller size by a factor of about 1·6:1.

Too low and air-mass flow at a given speed, or pressure ratio, will cause the blower to surge. Surge-pressure fluctuations are accompanied by a loss in pressure-ratio and efficiency at a given speed, and must therefore be avoided when matching a turboblower to an engine. Too high a mass-flow causes the blower to choke; this also results in a loss of pressure-ratio and efficiency at a given speed.

In addition to matching the blower to the engine, it is also necessary to match the turbine to the blower. This is achieved by designing the rotor blades and nozzle assembly in such a way that the blade height can be incrementally adjusted within a given turboblower size.

These days, increasing use is being made of computers for evaluating engine performance and predicting the correct match of turboblower. In addition, the computer can be used to optimise many of the engine design features such as manifold size, valve timing, ignition timing, etc.; hence, the computer offers the prospect of reducing the cost of engine development.

Surge

In the determination of satisfactory running conditions the problem of surge is important. There is shown a line in Figure 4.5 which, from its designation, is the surging limit.

What happens is that the blower impeller, as it rotates, accelerates the air-flow through the impeller, and the air leaves the blower with a velocity which is convertible into pressure at the diffuser. If, for one reason or another, the rate of air-flow decreases, then its velocity at the blower discharge will also decrease; there will thus come a time when the air pressure that has been generated in the blower will fall below the delivery pressure. That is, there will be a sudden breakdown of air delivery, followed immediately by a backward wave of air through the blower which will continue until the delivery resistance has decreased sufficiently for air discharge to be resumed. This periodical break-down of air delivery is called 'surging'.

In the lower speed ranges surging is manifested variously as humming, snorting and howling. If its incidence is limited to spells of short duration it may be harmless and bearable. In the higher speed ranges, however, prolonged surging may cause damage to the blower, in addition to being most annoying to the senses. Close attention to the surging limit is always necessary in the designing and arranging of blowers.

If one of the cylinders of a two-stroke engine should stop firing— perhaps by reason of fuel injection failure—when the engine is running above, say, 40 or 50 per cent of full load, it is possible that the turboblower affected may begin to surge. This will be recognisable as a repeated changing in the pitch of the blower noise. In these circumstances the engine revolutions should be reduced until the surging stops and firing is resumed in all cylinders.

Characteristics of the Turboblower

COMPRESSOR. From considerations of cost, size, strength and flexibility, the centrifugal compressor has been universally adopted for use in turboblowers. This compressor consists essentially of a radial-vaned impeller with a central 'eye'. The suction air, flowing through the inlet passages of the compressor to the eye of the rotating impeller, is forced outwards to the tip of the impeller by centrifugal force. This displacement of air creates a continuous suction at the entry, thus inducing more air to flow into the eye. As it passes through the impeller, work is done on the air by increasing its momentum, and it finally leaves the impeller at high velocity and with high kinetic energy. The work done on the air during its passage through the impeller is a function of the impeller diameter and its rotational speed. On leaving the impeller, the air enters a number of stationary diverging passages which convert the kinetic energy of the air into pressure energy. This process of conversion is known as diffusion, and hence this part of the compressor is termed the diffuser. As some compression takes place in the impeller, the air leaves the impeller with a higher static pressure than at entry. In fact, the static pressure-rise in the compressor takes place about equally in the impeller and in the diffuser. When it leaves the diffuser section the air enters a spiral volute which acts as a collector, conveying the gas at constant velocity and pressure to the exit flange.

TURBINE. For the size of turboblower fitted to medium and large marine engines, the turbine is almost always of the axial type. With this turbine, the exhaust gas enters through a row of fixed-nozzle-guide vanes. These guide vanes consist of a number of converging channels where the gas is turned from the axial direction and ex-panded to a high velocity so that it leaves with considerable tangential momentum. The gas then enters a single row of rotating blades, which further expand it and absorb most of the tangential momentum so that it leaves approximately axially.

In the constant-pressure system, the turbine operates under nearly constant conditions throughout each complete engine cycle. It can thus be made to operate at, or near, its design conditions, with high efficiency results.

For pulse operation, the turbine speed varies by a few per cent during each engine cycle, but the gas velocity can vary between sonic velocity and zero. This results in velocity triangles in the turbine which can vary considerably from the design triangles. The effect can be high blading incidences and outlet whirl velocities, with high pressure-losses and low efficiencies. In addition, with partial admission to the turbine, certain cylinder groupings can result in periods when the rotor blades are receiving gas from one sector or certain sectors of the nozzle ring only. Thus, while work is performed on a part of the wheel, windage losses are incurred in the remaining sector(s). There are also losses due to the blades entering and leaving the sectors of gas-flow. These three sources of loss can result in turbine efficiencies considerably lower than those in constant-pressure turbines. Care must therefore be taken to avoid cylinder groupings which may result in long periods of no-flow to the turbine.

In general and except at very high pressure-ratios the pulse system, despite partial admission and low turbine efficiencies, is superior to the constant-pressure system with high turbine efficiency.

As there is no mechanical connection between the turboblower and the engine, the former adapts itself to variations in engine load. It therefore needs no form of regulator either for speed or for load. The speed of the turboblower depends upon the available maximum flow of exhaust gas, upon its pressure, its temperature and upon the design characteristics of turbine and blower.

Construction of Turboblower

As there is not space to describe more than one type of turboblower, one of large size has been chosen, see Figure 4.6.

The rated air flows of the blower are given below.

Pressure ratio	Free air delivery
1·5:1	5 500–18 000 ft^3/min (160–520 m^3/min)
2·0:1	8 700–22 000 ft^3/min (250–630 m^3/min)
2 5:1	11 000–26 000 ft^3/min (310–740 m^3/min)

The turbine is designed for an inlet temperature of 650 C.

The main structure of the blower consists of four major casings which can be bolted together in various positions relative to each other to fit in with different arrangements of engine ducting.

The turbine inlet and outlet casings are of high-grade cast iron, arranged with water cooling jackets. Various types of turbine inlet casing are available to suit different arrangements of cylinders under pulse conditions. There is also an alternative single-entry type of casing specially designed for constant-pressure conditions.

The compressor inlet and outlet casings are of aluminium. The inlet casing is designed for low aerodynamic losses with near ideal conditions, while preventing noise from coming back through the compressor inlet. The casing is lined with sound absorbent material. An air filter of the separate panel type is fitted.

The rotor comprises two half-shafts spigoted and bolted to the turbine disc. The blades are laced and fitted in the disc with fir-tree roots, secured by special lockwashers.

The compressor impeller comprises two aluminium forgings, an inducer and a main impeller section. Four sizes of impellers are

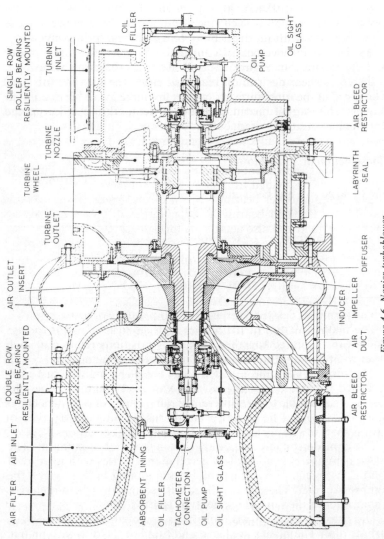

SINGLE ROW ROLLER BEARING RESILIENTLY MOUNTED

TURBINE INLET

OIL FILLER

OIL PUMP

OIL SIGHT GLASS

AIR BLEED RESTRICTOR

TURBINE NOZZLE

TURBINE WHEEL

LABYRINTH SEAL

TURBINE OUTLET

DIFFUSER

AIR OUTLET INSERT

INDUCER

IMPELLER

AIR DUCT

DOUBLE ROW BALL BEARING RESILIENTLY MOUNTED

AIR INLET

AIR BLEED RESTRICTOR

AIR FILTER

ABSORBENT LINING

OIL FILLER

TACHOMETER CONNECTION

OIL PUMP

OIL SIGHT GLASS

Figure 4.6 Napier turboblower

available, together with a range of diffusers which allow wide variations in capacity. This range of compressor/diffuser sizes is matched by a range of turbine rotor/nozzle sizes. Compressor diffusers and turbine nozzles may be increased in size by machining, to facilitate initial matching with an engine.

The overall design is such that the complete rotor assembly can be withdrawn, without disturbing the air and gas flow connections to the casings. Sleeve bearings, or ball and roller bearings, may be fitted as desired. In Figure 4.6, ball and roller bearings are shown.

The plain bearings run on hardened steel sleeves, and both fixed and rotating bearing surfaces may be extracted and replaced. The white metal journal bearings have been reduced in size, compared with former designs, to reduce frictional losses, but the load-carrying capacity has been adequately maintained. The thrust bearing is separated from the compressor journal bearing and is so arranged that end-float adjustment can be made before assembly on the shaft. Lubrication is provided from an external source.

The ball and roller bearing version of the design has a two-row angular contact ball bearing at the compressor end which carries the journal load and also acts as the thrust bearing. A roller bearing is fitted at the turbine end; both bearings being carried in resilient mountings to provide damping. Each bearing is lubricated by a separate gear-type oil pump driven by the rotor shaft and contained in its own oil sump.

The turboblowers are made in seven basic sizes, covering a range of air capacities suitable for pressure-charging four-stroke and two-stroke engines of 200 to 10 000 bhp. For engines of greater power, more than one turboblower is used. All of the larger sizes and some of the smaller ones can be supplied with resiliently mounted ball and roller bearings or, alternatively, sleeve bearings. All ball and roller bearing types are fitted with self-contained oil lubrication systems which function satisfactorily when the turboblowers are level or permanently tilted at up to 15° to the horizontal, or momentarily tilted at 22·5° as in a heavy sea-way. The turbine inlet casings are made with two, three or four entry branches, as may be desired.

Charge-air Cooler

The water-circulated air coolers in general use with the type of exhaust-driven turboblower described in this chapter are built-up of standard cooling elements, each element being approximately 4 in. (100 mm) square and of a length to suit the required application. There are twenty-three aluminium-brass water tubes in each element; these are $\frac{7}{16}$ in. (11 mm) outside dia., 20 gauge thick, and are threaded through a large number of thin square copper finplates, pitched at approximately 0·1 in. (2·5 mm). The tubes are secured in naval brass tubeplates.

The cooling-element block determines that the header tank must have basic dimensions which are multiples of 4 in. (say 100 mm). Using more than three blocks in series results in a disproportionate cooling-air pressure-drop for only a small gain in effectiveness. The frontal area, and hence the charge-air speed through the cooler, is adjusted by increasing the number of elements in parallel. The cooler side plates are made of ribbed aluminium-alloy castings.

Small coolers are usually, but not necessarily, arranged with a single-pass for the circulating water. For large coolers, to reduce the quantity of cooling water required, a double-flow is arranged. The coolers should be circulated by the coldest water in the engine circuit.

The coolers are installed as close to the turboblower as possible. There is a diverging air duct before the cooler and a converging duct between it and the air manifold; these ducts reduce the air speed through the cooler, minimising air-pressure losses and increasing the cooler effectiveness.

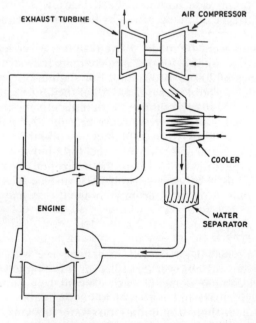

Figure 4.7 Arrangement of water separator

Water Separators

As the air passes through the charge-air cooler, its temperature may be reduced until it is below the saturation temperature. Heavy condensation of water vapour may then follow, this water being carried into the engine.

For a ship whose trade route lies across hot, humid zones, water separation is essential; for other services it is desirable. A water separator can be mounted at any convenient point between the charge air-cooler and the engine air-inlet manifold. Figure 4.7 shows, diagrammatically, the position of the water separator in a turbocharged engine arrangement.

NOISE

When a noise problem arises in a turbocharging system it is manifestly necessary to locate the place of origin of the noise—the focal point, as it were—before effective remedial measures can be applied. The three most common sources of noise are:

(i) the blower suction inlet;
(ii) the air and gas pipes, passages and ducts;
(iii) the turboblower proper.

The noise may originate in one place or in more than one place. It will usually be necessary to carry out a survey with a probe microphone and a sound analyser to determine both the place of origin and the spectral distribution of the offending noise. Generally it will be found that the noise from the compressor will be a discrete frequency of the number of compressor vanes multiplied by the revolutions per minute (i.e., compressor-vane passage frequency) added to the air noise. The latter will not have particular frequencies included unless sharp edges, etc., are present in the system.

Usually it is the suction noise which is noticed first. When strong emphasis is laid on silent running the suction silencer may have to be enlarged and perhaps removed some distance from the blower. In general, it may be stated that the ultimate result will probably be determined by the amount of sound-proofing material which is used.

If the noise originates in the ducts and pipes a careful examination must be made for sharp edges, protuberances and irregularities—against which the gases can impinge—and for large, thin, unsupported, metal plate surfaces which might respond to airborne vibrations, such as guides in exhaust ducts. Such metal plates should be stiffened, replaced by thicker plates or deadened with a suitable vibration damping compound. Radiation from the compressor casing or delivery duct may be dealt with by cladding with a material such as 'Sound Barrier Mat'—consisting of a sandwich of alternate layers of dense limp damping material and either felt or plastic foam—or a lead loaded polyvinylchloride sheet applied over felt or plastic foam. These porous materials must be made impervious to oil, etc., by coating with a sealing compound. Pipe passages, suction chambers and similar places may be lined with soft material, or with perforated non-conducting material; but the sound-insulating material must be securely and permanently fastened.

It is sometimes found that discrete frequencies exist which are linked to the compressor vane passage frequency, or, as also sometimes occurs, excitation of the compressor impeller vibration modes by interference from the diffuser vanes (number of diffuser vanes multiplied by the revolutions per minute). In this case, an increase in the impeller/diffuser gap produces a marked improvement. An alternative method is to change the number of diffuser vanes, thus altering the rotational speeds at which particular vibration modes are excited.

The amount of noise which will be air-borne to engine spaces and ship spaces, and the amount which will be structure-borne, is a matter for analysis. In some passenger vessels and cargo liners the engine casings are sound insulated, as well as heat insulated.

I.M.B.

BROWN BOVERI TURBOBLOWERS

The development of Brown Boveri exhaust-gas turbochargers dates back to 1924. The current VTR range of turbochargers is, therefore, the outcome of many years of research, development and experience. The present range of units was conceived in 1943. Through all the intervening years the basic design principles have been adhered to, thus confirming the inherent soundness of the design. Since their inception, the external dimensions of the nine sizes of VTR 'Standard Type' turbochargers have remained the same, despite the fact that the internal parts have had to follow the requirements imposed by engine developments.

With this design one turbocharger can be assembled in a number of different ways. Thus, an optimum match can be made between the turbocharger and a given engine, whether two-stroke or four-stroke, with different ratings and having different numbers of cylinders, with variations in cylinder arrangement, firing order, turbocharging and scavenging systems, also when burning different fuels and when designed for different engine applications.

Basic Design

The basic design of the turbocharger is shown in Figure 4.8. It comprises a single-stage gas turbine driving a blower. The exhaust gases from the diesel engine enter the turbine through the water-cooled gas inlet casing, expand in the nozzle ring, and drive the rotor of the turbine. This, in turn, drives the compressor. The exhaust gases leave the turbine through the water-cooled gas outlet casing and then flow to a waste-heat boiler and/or the atmosphere.

The combustion air required for the diesel engine enters the centrifugal blower through a suction branch or a filter-silencer. The air is compressed in the inducer and the impeller, whence it flows through the diffuser out to the blower casing and so to the engine. A partition wall separates the blower from the turbine. Through the duct, marked X in Figure 4.8, air flows from the blower to the labyrinth gland on the turbine side. This prevents the exhaust gases from entering the bearing space through the duct marked Z.

The bearings at each end of the rotor are elastically supported on spring mountings. The turbine wheel and shaft are made in one piece. In the following notes the component parts are described in detail.
BLOWER. The blower wheel is of the radial type. As shown in Figure 4.8, it is open, i.e. it consists of a single hub disc manufactured from a light-alloy forging. At the outer end of this disc are the grooves for the labyrinth glands. A slight flow of air through these glands into the exhaust casing cools the turbine shaft. The labyrinth glands are fixed in such a position that the thrust on the shaft remains within admissible limits.

At the inlet to the blower impeller is located what is known as the inducer. Its purpose is to lead the air into the impeller proper without shock.

For each size of turbocharger a number of different inducers and impellers can be supplied, according to the pressure ratio and the flow capacity desired. The air leaves the impeller at a high velocity and, consequently, with a high kinetic energy. It is the duty of the diffuser, which is made from light metal, to slow-down the air and convert its kinetic energy into pressure. The dimensions and the shape of the diffuser are adapted to suit the particular kind of impeller, and also the operating conditions. Diffusers may be supplied with or without vanes. The main feature of vaneless diffusers is that they have a wider characteristic but a lower maximum efficiency than diffusers with vanes.

In the blower casing there is a special duct arranged for cleaning the impeller and the diffuser by pouring in a specified amount of water.

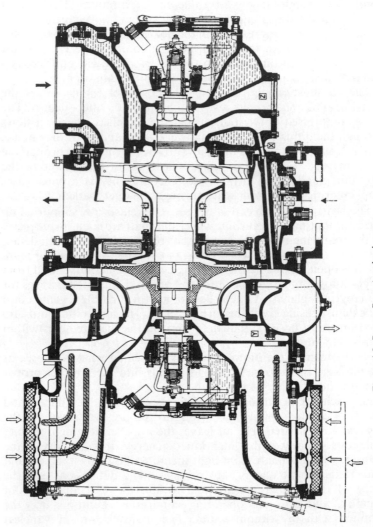

Figure 4.8 Brown Boveri turbocharger

On the reverse side of the impeller there is a partition with thermal insulation, which separates the air casing from the gas casing. If, for any reason, the rotor has to be removed from the casing, there is no need to take the impeller or the turbine wheel off the shaft, as the partition is drawn out with the shaft.

The air is fed to the blower either from the atmosphere through a pipe leading into the suction branch, or it is drawn-in from the engine room through a silencer-filter. This filter is very useful, because the air in the engine room always contains a certain amount of oil vapour, soot and dust. Without the filter the compressor would rapidly become clogged, with the result that the charging-air pressure would drop and less air would be delivered to the engine. The filtering medium is copper mesh, enclosed in separate segments. The segments can be detached from the turbocharger and the copper removed for cleaning, this being a simple operation. The filter inevitably collects dirt as time passes, and the pressure-drop across the filter increases. A U-tube pressure gauge indicates this pressure-drop and, when it has reached the permitted limit, the filter can be taken off and cleaned.

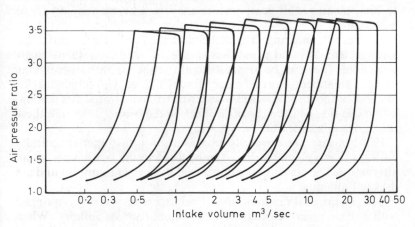

Figure 4.9 Operating ranges of Brown-Boveri turbochargers

Figure 4.9 indicates the capacity range of the various sizes of VTR turbochargers. As will be observed, the ranges of the individual sizes overlap appreciably. This means that there is a suitable turbo-charger available for every operating requirement.

TURBINE. As already stated, this is a single-stage axial-flow design. The gas inlet and outlet casings are of high-grade grey cast iron. They are double-walled, on account of the need for water cooling. The casings are protected, by the cooling, against thermal deformation, while the bearing at the turbine end is protected against the high temperature of the exhaust gas. On the water side, anti-corrosion wear plates are fitted to the core-hole covers; and baffles are incorporated in the water inlet openings, also serving to prevent corrosion. Depending upon the number and arrangement of the cylinders and the firing order of the engine, the gas inlet casing may have one, two, three or four inlet openings.

The nozzles which admit the gas to the turbine blading are of high-grade heat-resistant sheet steel. They are cast-in between an inner and an outer ring of cast iron, thus ensuring that the entire assembly is very rigid and strong.

In the turbine wheel, grooves are cut for the fir-tree roots by means of which the blades are attached. To prevent harmful vibration, a circumferential damping wire is run through the blades, which can be individually replaced. The length of the blades and the nozzle area can be adapted individually to suit operational requirements.

The maximum admissible gas inlet temperature to the turbocharger may lie between 600° and 650°C, depending upon the particular design. When special metals are used for nozzle rings and turbine blading, this temperature may be increased by 50°C, or even more.

BEARINGS. The bearings are situated at the ends of the shaft. This arrangement has the great advantage of rendering them easily accessible. They can be inspected without the turbocharger having to be dismantled. Furthermore, forces caused by unbalance for instance of the turbine wheel—resulting from deposited dirt flaking-off on one side—have very little effect on the bearings because these forces occur between the two bearings.

Ball bearings are normally used, but, if a customer specifically requests them, plain bearings can be fitted to the larger sizes, as an alternative. The bearings are contained in spring mountings and are thus self-aligning.

The operational features of turbochargers respectively equipped with ball or plain bearings can be summarised as follows. When fitted with ball bearings, the turbochargers need no additional lubrication system. Because of the small amount of friction, the surface of the bearing space is sufficient for cooling purposes. Each bearing is provided with a lubricating pump mounted on its respective end of the shaft. There are no external oil pipes. The small amount of bearing friction simplifies the starting-up of the diesel engine and enables some types of engine to maintain a lower dead-slow speed. By reason of their simplicity, ball bearings are ideal for ships selected for automation which, incidentally, is being applied to an ever-increasing extent. The bearings can be run for at least 8000 hours before they have to be changed. It is quite a simple matter to remove a worn ball bearing and replace it with a reconditioned unit. With VTR turbochargers, 'brinelling' of ball races has never been experienced.

Plain, or sleeve, bearings require an external lubricating arrangement comprising pipes, pumps, oil-tank and cooling system. It is important to ensure that the flow of oil is never interrupted, also that the oil is clean when it enters the bearings. As the oil film in the bearings is extremely thin, an oil filter is necessary, being arranged with a mesh or a gauge smaller than would correspond to the thickness of the film at its thinnest point. If the oil film contains foreign bodies that are larger than the film thickness, the bearings will wear and thus will need renewal from time to time.

Because the rotor of the turbocharger is relatively light, only a slight amount of unbalance is sufficient to produce radial forces which exceed the static load on the bearings due to the weight of the rotor. The result of this is a bearing load that circulates in the radial direction. For this reason the plain bearings are designed as multiple-wedge bearings. Ball bearings withstand this form of load with ease.

Operating Performance

Figure 4.10 shows a typical pressure-volume curve of a turbocharger, the operating characteristics of a two-stroke diesel engine fitted solely with turbochargers being indicated. This means that there are no additional blowers which might operate in series with, or parallel to, the turbochargers. A further assumption is that the engine load varies in accordance with the propeller law.

As will be seen, the operating curve runs almost parallel to the surge line. Every value of the engine output corresponds to a point on the curve, and this point, in turn, corresponds to a particular turbocharger speed which is obtained automatically. There is consequently no need for any system of speed control for the turbocharger.

By comparing the relationship between the charge-air pressure, the speed of the turbocharger and the engine output, it is possible to draw conclusions regarding possible irregularities. If, for instance, at a definite turbocharger speed the charge-air pressure is lower than normal—the admission pressure and temperature, also the engine power, being otherwise unchanged—the conclusion may be drawn that the compressor is contaminated. By spraying a certain amount of water into the compressor the deposit can be removed, provided it has not already become too hard. A special duct is provided for the injection of this water into the type VTR turbochargers. Encrus-

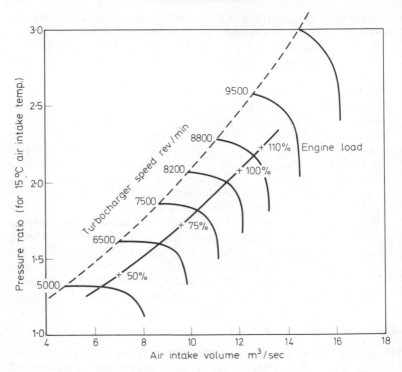

Figure 4.10 Typical pressure-volume curve

tations on the turbine blading can be removed by a similar method.

The operating curve and the behaviour of the turbocharger may vary, depending upon whether the constant-pressure system or the pulse system of turbocharging is employed and depending also upon how volumetric compressors and turbochargers are connected together. By reason of the many different combinations which are possible, no attempt is here made to discuss specific examples of abnormal operation and their consequences. By observing changes in behaviour it is usually possible to deduce causes and to prescribe the measures necessary to rectify the difficulties.

In conclusion, it may be worthwhile mentioning the following matters regarding the reliability of the VTR turbochargers. Sometimes users are a little apprehensive of employing turbochargers, as they are fast-running machines, the peripheral speed of the blading of a turbocharger fitted to a modern two-stroke diesel engine being about 350 metres per second. But it has been many times demonstrated that the maintenance costs of such a turbocharger are indeed low, being in fact much lower than those for the additional cylinders that would be required to develop the same total output on a non-supercharged basis.

The suction noise of the impeller is reduced by the silencer. A cover-plate, as shown in Figure 4.8, absorbs the radiated solid-borne noise which would otherwise escape from the central part of the silencer. With increasing levels of pressure-charging and higher speeds of turboblowers, the importance of noise reduction becomes more and more evident.

An objection that is frequently raised against the application of turbocharging in general is the suction noise that can be created at the impeller. This matter has received special attention in the designing of the Brown-Boveri turboblowers.

P.P.

Chapter 5

Götaverken Engines

More than 800 Götaverken engines are at present in service, about 450 of them being of the older non-turbocharged types, mostly built during the decades 1940 and 1950.

The introduction of turbocharging in the midfifties initially necessitated only a few, slight modifications to the non-turbocharged engine designs. Apart from the addition of turboblowers, air-coolers and air receivers, the crankshaft scantlings had to be increased, which also involved minor alterations to the bedplates.

The first part of the following description deals with the moderately turbocharged types, but it is also applicable to the earlier normally-aspirated engines. The later part of the description refers to the most recent high-pressure, turbocharged engines. These engines entered the market in 1964 and have been built in three sizes with cylinder bores 850, 750 and 630 mm respectively.

MODERATELY TURBOCHARGED ENGINE TYPES

Figure 5.1 shows the cross-section of a turbocharged engine having a cylinder bore of 760 mm and a piston stroke of 1500 mm. The normal revolutions per minute are 120.

This type belongs to an engine series having bores, strokes and outputs in accordance with Table 5.1. The illustration shows an engine with fabricated frame and bedplate, but the engines were also built as cast-iron designs.

The large-bore engine, 850/1700 VGA-U, with cast-iron A-frames and welded bedplate, is in most respects built-up in accordance with the same main features, as can be concluded from Figures 5.1 and 5.2. This type is however dimensioned for higher mean pressures, see Table 5.1.

58

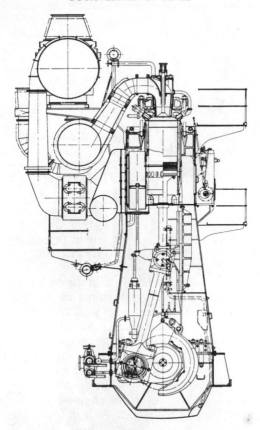

Figure 5.1 Turbocharged engine 760 mm bore, 1500 mm stroke

Table 5.1 TURBOCHARGED GÖTAVERKEN ENGINES

Bore	Stroke	Speed	Max. continuous cylinder output	MIP
mm	mm	Rev/min	kW	bar
520	900	185	440	9·0
630	1300	135	700	9·0
680	1500	130	885	9·0
760	1300	125	935	9·0
760	1500	120	1030	9·0
850	1700	119	1765	10·5

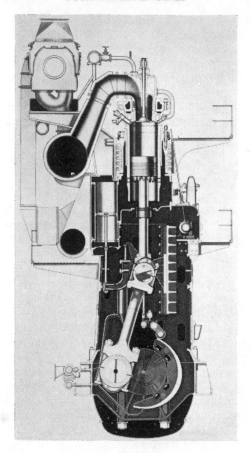

Figure 5.2 Large-bore engine, 850/1700 VGA-U

Bedplate and Frames

The bedplate of the welded engine is of steel, divided into a suitable number of sections and assembled with fitted bolts. Each section consists of two rigid longitudinal girders, with transverse cross-members of I-section welded between them. The cross-members, or cross-girders, are fitted with cast-steel saddles, which carry the main bearings, and with heavy bolt connections which transmit the forces from the entablatures directly to the bedplate. The cross-girders are annealed before being welded to the longitudinal girders.

The after part of the bedplate carries thrust bearing of Michell type, with self-adjusting cast-iron pads thrust lined with white metal. A sheet-steel oil tray is welded to the underside of the bedplate.

For the cast-iron engine the bedplate is cast in three or more parts, depending on the number of cylinders, and these parts are joined together by strong bolts. The main bearings are seated in the transverse girders of the bedplate, and on each side of the bearings there are holes for the tie-bolts.

The welded bedplate for the 850/1700 engine is arranged in two parts. The transverse cross-girders are mainly of steel castings which are welded to the longitudinal girders. The oil trough is in two pieces, divided horizontally. The upper part is welded to the bedplate and the lower piece is bolted to the upper part.

The main bearing shells for the above-mentioned engines are white-metal-lined steel castings, with shims for bearing clearance adjustment. The normal clearance for the bearings is about 0·4 to 0·5 mm, where 0·5 mm refers to a new bearing, and 0·4 mm to a run-in bearing.

The entablatures for the welded engine are of steel plate and form closed units, one for each cylinder. A heavy steel casting forms the top of each welded entablature. The castings are provided with heavy fitted bolts which connect all the entablatures, thus forming a very strong longitudinal girder. Furthermore, they are fitted with long studs to hold down the cylinder covers. The upper parts of the entablatures together form a common and continuous scavenging-air receiver, extending down to the top of the crankcase, from which it is completely isolated by means of a diaphragm plate carrying piston-rod stuffing boxes having scraper and sealing rings.

The A-columns of the cast engines and type 850/1700 are horizontally connected by tie-bars and crankcase door landing strips. Cast-iron scavenging-air receivers are arranged on the columns and form vertical distance-pieces between the columns and the cast-iron cylinder frames. The scavenging-air receivers are linked together through large openings and form a scavenging-air manifold which is common to the whole engine.

Through the bedplate, columns, scavenging-air receivers and cylinder frames, vertical tie-bolts are fitted for transmitting the combustion loads from the cylinder covers to the bedplate. The cylinder frames are box-shaped and interconnected by bolts, hence a solid girder construction is obtained in the longitudinal direction of the engine.

The guide-plates are constructed of cast iron, being secured to the entablature by means of fitted bolts. They are provided with shims for the adjustment of guide clearances. Figure 5.1 shows a single-screw engine, looking forward.

Turning Gear

The turning gear is driven by a three-phase, squirrel-cage motor. The transmission system consists of a steel worm and a bronze worm-wheel located in a robust cast-iron housing. The upper part of the housing forms a tray for the worm gear oil. The oil level can be checked with a graduated dipstick. The worm, which is horizontal, is supported in bushings and axial ball bearings; the wormwheel is fitted on a vertical steel shaft. The main worm, located at the lower end of this shaft, engages the main turning wheel, which is mounted on the thrust shaft. The upper bearing of the vertical shaft is lubricated by a syphon lubricator and the lower bearing from a grease cup.

The turning gear is brought into position by means of a bar and, when the turning engine is engaged, the fastening bolts must be tightened, otherwise the gear may be damaged.

Crankshaft

The crankshaft is of the semi-built type and is made in two parts. The thrust shaft is separate. The crankpin and the pair of webs comprising each crank-throw are formed from a single open-hearth steel casting. This casting is shrunk on to the main journal-pieces, which are of forged steel. The generous fillets provided between the crankpin and the crank-webs to obviate dangerous stress concentrations are contained entirely within the webs so as not to reduce the effective bearing length. Each crankpin and journal-piece is bored to reduce weight, the holes being used for lubrication purposes. Each crank-web is fitted with a cast-steel cam holder, to which cam segments for actuating the exhaust valve are bolted.

Connecting Rod and Bottom-end Bearing

The connecting rod is an open-hearth steel forging, drilled throughout to reduce weight and to provide passage for lubricating oil from the crankshaft to the crosshead and guide bearings. The top-end of the connecting rod is flanged to seat the crosshead bearing and the bottom-end is arranged for attachment to the bottom-end bearing.

The bottom-end bearing is designed with top and bottom halves of cast steel, white-metal lined and provided with shims for adjusting the clearance. The complete bearing is secured to the bottom-end of the connecting rod by two large drilled bolts of heat-treated steel.

The normal clearance of the bottom-end bearing is the same as that of the main bearings. When measuring the clearance the working piston of the cylinder concerned must be in either top dead-centre or bottom dead-centre position.

Crosshead

The crosshead proper is of cast steel, incorporating a white-metal-faced guide shoe. It is drilled for the passage of lubricating oil to the guide-plate. A cast-steel bracket, with one or two arms, is bolted to the crosshead and carries the scavenging-pump piston rods. The crosshead pin, which is of special steel, carefully ground and polished, is drilled throughout its length to provide passages for the cooling oil to and from the piston. The crosshead pin is provided with four studs and nuts which secure it to the crosshead, and which also secure the bottom flange of the piston rod to the crosshead. A cast-steel arm is fitted to one end of the crosshead pin and carries the piston cooling telescope pipe. This arm is provided with a cast oil-passage which connects the telescope pipe to the drilled hole in the piston rod, and through which cooling oil flows to the piston. The cooling oil discharge is led through a steel outlet bend carried on the other end of the crosshead pin. This bend is connected to the centrally placed outlet pipe in the piston rod.

Crosshead Bearing

The crosshead bearing consists of one bottom-half and two top-halves of cast steel, white-metal-lined. The bottom-half bearing extends for the full length of the crosshead pin, ensuring the largest possible bearing surface. The complete bearing is secured to the top-end of the connecting rod by four heat-treated steel bolts.

The working conditions at the crosshead bearing in any type of single-acting two-stroke engine are extremely unfavourable, due to the very limited oscillating movement of the bearing and the lack of pressure-change. Between about 75° before top dead-centre and top dead-centre the magnitude of the gas force on the crosshead bearing is reduced by the inertia force, but the resulting force is, nevertheless, always in the same direction.

Resulting from the introduction of heavy fuel oils with the harmful and dangerous components of the residue, and the application of supercharging with its higher peak pressures and scavenging-air pressures, the adverse circumstances are even more accentuated. Accordingly, the crosshead bearings must be kept carefully under observation and, by regular examination and survey, be maintained in the best possible condition. The intervals between inspection are suitably chosen in such a way that each crosshead bearing is examined at least twice a year or after a maximum of 2000 hours of service.

In this connection it is of importance that the edge profiles of the lubrication grooves should be correct, so that no sharp edges appear in the transition area between lubrication groove and bearing surface, thereby preventing the lubrication oil from reaching the bearing surface. For this purpose there is provided a special tool for checking each lubrication groove, using blue marking paint.

White-metal Lining

The bearing metal must everywhere be solidly attached to the bearing shell, and if any loose pieces are discovered, the bearing must generally be replaced.

When checking the crosshead bearing the pin must be carefully examined for adherent bearing metal or scratches. If necessary, the pin must be carefully freed from metal and scratches by polishing them away, using first a fine enamel cloth and then finishing with a polishing cloth until a completely shining surface is obtained. If the scratches are deep, then the pin must be restored in the workshop.

When assembling the crosshead bearing it must be ensured that the crosshead pin and lower bearing half are in parallel. After mounting, the clearance must be checked and adjusted by shims. A normal clearance for the crosshead bearing is calculated to be about 0·3 to 0·4 mm, measured when the piston is at its bottom or its top dead-centre position.

Working Piston and Piston Rod

Many types of working piston have been used during past years. The latest type—and the only type used for the large-bore engine—is made of chrome-molybdenum steel, forged in one piece. It has six compression rings and, to keep the ring wear in the piston-ring grooves on a low level, these are usually provided with caulked and welded wear rings of cast iron. At the lower part of the piston there are two lead-bronze wear rings, see Figure 5.18.

It is of the utmost importance for the operational safety of the engine that the piston rings should work satisfactorily. Piston inspections must therefore be made at regular intervals and so frequently that the piston rings will have no time to stick. Piston overhauls are, as a rule, carried out after about 4000 operating hours, which means once or twice a year. The vertical clearance between the rings and the ring grooves must be 0·15 to 0·25 mm. Wear edges, if any, in the liñer as well as sharp edges at the scavenging ports must be eliminated.

Effective cooling is achieved by the use of oil, which is forced against the crown through a labyrinth insert. Sealing against oil between piston and piston-rod flange is ensured with a rubber ring.

The piston rod is manufactured from forged open-hearth steel.

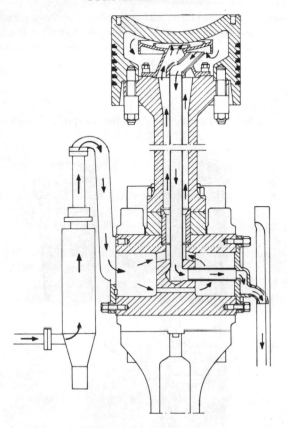

Figure 5.3 Piston cooling oil flow

The rod is drilled throughout its length and a steel pipe, centrally placed in this drilled passage, carries the cooling oil discharge from the piston. The top and bottom ends of the piston rod are flanged. The top flange has a ground surface and is bolted to the piston; the bottom flange, which is square, is bolted to the crosshead.

Telescopic Pipes

The fixed part of the telescopic tube for the piston cooling inlet consists of a large steel pipe mounted on one corner of the crankcase and connected to the cooling-oil system. The upper part of this pipe is provided with a spherically mounted stuffing box, fitting around the moving pipe. A slotted discharge pipe of steel is mounted on the opposite side of the crankcase and collects the cooling oil discharge from a bend fitted to the cross-head. The slotted pipe is connected to a device on the manoeuvring side of the engine, through which the return oil-flow from the piston can be observed.

Cylinder Liner

The cylinder liners are made of vanadium–titanium cast iron, *see* Figure 5.4.

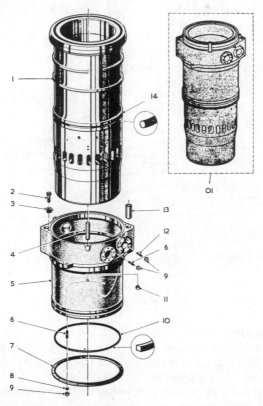

Figure 5.4 Cylinder liner and jacket, 850/1700 engine

The top of the liner is provided with a flange having ground faces. The flange is clamped between the cylinder cover and the cooling-water jacket. The jacket encircles the liner, the top part forming a collar with ground faces clamped between the cylinder liner and the entablature—for type 850/1700 between cylinder liner and cylinder frame. The jacket, which is of cast iron, is provided with the necessary water connections. It is also provided with a stuffing box at the bottom end, which permits the axial expansion of the cylinder liner. Cylinder liner and jacket can be withdrawn together, as they comprise a complete unit.

The liner of a cast engine is located in the cylinder block in such a way that a closed chamber is formed, through which the cooling water passes. The upper part of the cylinder liner is provided with a flange which rests on a ring on the cylinder block. The cooling water is discharged through this ring. Liner, ring and block are ground together, to obtain a good fit. The top of the liner is provided with a recess into which the cylinder cover is ground. The lower part of the liner is, for all engine types, provided with scavenging ports equally spaced around its periphery. The shape of the ports is such that the air is given a swirl during scavenging.

Cylinder Head

For all engine types the cylinder cover is in two parts, comprising a cast-iron water-cooled lower half and a cast steel uncooled upper half. (The 520/900 engine is an exception, having a one-piece cover of cast iron.) The lower half is the cylinder cover proper, which seals against the combustion chamber and contains all the valves. The exhaust valve is located centrally in the cylinder cover, the other valves, i.e. fuel injection, starting and safety valves, are mounted on the periphery. The two parts of the cylinder cover are bolted together, to form one unit, by four heavy studs which also serve as holding-down bolts for the exhaust valve.

The exhaust-valve housing is made of cast iron and is water-cooled. The lower end of the housing is provided with a replaceable valve seat of cast iron. The valve spindle is spherically mounted in the cast-steel yoke.

Exhaust-gas System

Each exhaust valve is operated by the cam segments mounted on the crank-webs, the movement being transmitted by rollers, levers and pull-rods to the yoke into which the valve stem is fitted. The valve is closed by heavy encased helical springs fitted between the yoke and the cylinder cover.

The exhaust-gas receiver is connected to the inlet of the exhaust turbine. To permit the operation of the engine when a turbocharger is out of service, there is a by-pass between the receiver and the exhaust pipe after the turbine. Under normal operation of the engine the by-pass is closed by a spectacle-flange or a mushroom valve.

In old-type engines, where under-piston scavenging is used, the cylinder liner is fitted with an external air sleeve operated by the exhaust-valve pull-rods. This sleeve covers the scavenging ports in the cylinder liner during the compression stroke of the piston, which is also the suction stroke at the underside of the piston. The opening of the exhaust valve coincides with the uncovering of the ports when scavenging takes place.

Chain Transmission System

The camshaft is driven from the crankshaft by a roller chain, the entire transmission gear being mounted in a separate entablature situated between the two groups of cylinders, *see* Figure 5.5.

There are four cast-steel sprockets in the transmission system.

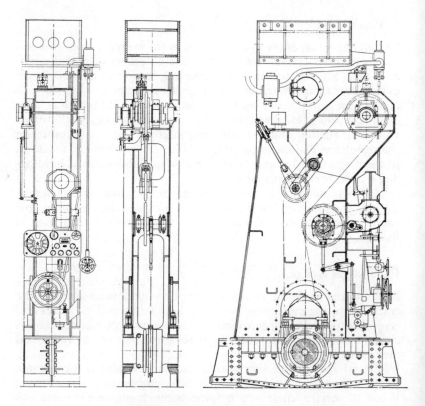

Figure 5.5 Manoeuvring system, 760/1500 VGS-U engine

One, a split-sprocket, is keyed to the coupling flange of the forward half of the crankshaft. The second, a sprocket for the camshaft, is mounted on the driving sleeve of the shaft by fitted bolts. The third sprocket is located on the shaft which operates the governor, fuel-oil delivery pump, starting-air distributor and tachometer. The fourth sprocket is the driving-chain tensioner and is arranged on a cast-steel hinged yoke. Adjustment to tension is made by means of a screw, connected to the yoke, and a spring which is located outside the entablature at the back of the engine.

Camshaft

The camshaft, which is arranged along the front of the engine, is fitted with symmetrical cams which are adjustable within limits, to enable, *inter alia*, the fuel-injection pump timing to be altered to suit the fuel being used.

The camshaft is driven by a dog-clutch having a clearance between the dogs equal to the reversing angle of the camshaft. This arrangement permits the same cams to be used both for ahead and for astern running. There is also an air-operated lock which moves longitudinally on the camshaft and locks the camshaft and driving sleeve during the normal running of the engine.

Fuel-injection Pump

The fuel-injection pump for each cylinder is mounted over the camshaft. The lift of each cam is transmitted to its respective pump plunger by a roller and a spherically mounted pushrod. A typical fuel pump is shown in Figure 5.6.

Each fuel pump barrel has a special hardened-steel liner which is a press fit. Into this liner the plunger is lapped. The fuel-pump plunger is of special steel and has two helical grooves which communicate with an axial hole in the plunger opening into the pressure chamber of the barrel. The fuel oil is fed to the upper side of the plunger, which, when it nears the lower turning point, uncovers the inlet pipe for the oil from the supply pump. During the fuel-injection pump stroke the oil is pressed through the fuel pipes to the fuel-injection valves.

The supply pump is generously dimensioned, so that a large oil excess is obtained. This excess, if diesel quality fuel is used, is employed for cooling the fuel-injection valves. If the installation uses heavy fuel oil, the excess is led back to the suction side of the supply pump.

The amount of oil delivered by each injection pump is regulated by rotating the plunger within the barrel, so as to make the point of cut-off later or earlier in the stroke. There are no delivery valves, but a cylinder having a spring-loaded piston is fitted at the inlet port to act as a shock absorber at the end of delivery, that is, when high-pressure fuel is being returned to the pump inlet port.

The injection-pump plunger can be rotated by a longitudinal regulating shaft on which a lever and a rod are mounted for each pump. The regulating shaft is connected to the manoeuvring wheel, by levers and pull-rods. The emergency governor can operate the regulating shaft in such a way that the plungers are rotated towards the stop position as soon as the engine shows a tendency to race.

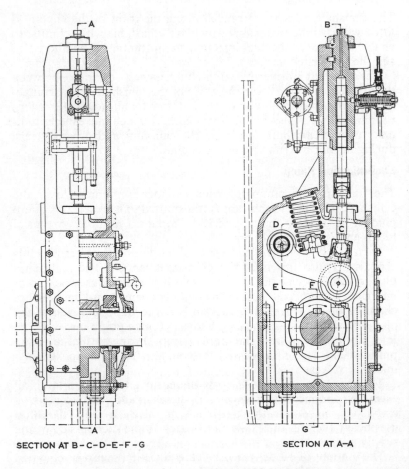

SECTION AT B-C-D-E-F-G   SECTION AT A-A

Figure 5.6 Fuel pump, 760/1500 VGS-U engine

Fuel-pump Operation

The beginning of fuel injection is determined by the moment when the plunger has completely covered the inlet hole for fuel oil. This can be delayed if there is, for instance, a clearance in the spherical coupling of the pushrod. The delay means that, at a given plunger angular position, too small a fuel quantity is injected into the cylinder before the piston reaches top dead-centre. The total oil quantity injected during the stroke remains unchanged. This means that after-burning increases, giving a lower maximum pressure, high exhaust-gas temperature and increased fuel consumption.

If the maximum pressure must be increased, the plunger advance can be increased, i.e. the distance which the plunger has moved from its bottom position in the pump to the position it has reached when the working piston is on top centre.

If it is desired to increase the plunger advance, this is done by moving the cam in the same direction as its rotation for 'Ahead'. The cam consists of two components bolted together. The cylindrical cam component cannot be turned on the shaft because its position is fixed by a key; but the curved half-cam can be turned on the shaft in either direction by loosening the bolts on one side of the shaft and tightening them on the other side.

Higher maximum pressure can also be obtained by lowering the pump barrel. This is done by altering the shims on the upper side of the pump barrel for a welded engine, or at the flange coupling in the pushrod for a cast engine. The maximum lowering of the barrel is determined by the position of the plunger in relation to the inlet hole for the fuel oil. The upper edge of the sealing surface of the plunger must in its lowest position be not more than 3 mm (or 2 mm for 520/900 VGS) from the lower edge of the inlet hole.

Fuel-injection Valve

The fuel-injection valve is designed for operation both on diesel quality oil and on heavy fuel oil, *see* Figure 5.7.

The valve housing is provided with a central bore for fuel injection, and also with bores for pumping-through, for cooling and for de-aeration. The de-aeration is accomplished by opening the air relief screw. The atomiser and the lower side of the valve housing are thoroughly ground, to ensure an oil-tight joint when the bottom nut holding the atomiser against the housing is tightened. The valve needle is carefully ground into the atomiser. The valve seat is conical, with an angle of 62° on the needle and 60° on the seat, whereby a narrow contact is obtained at the end of the seat, thus improving the sealing and the functioning of the valve.

To obtain the correct position of the atomiser in the combustion chamber, the housing is provided with a location pin corresponding to the holes in the atomiser so that it cannot be wrongly mounted. The valve position in the cylinder cover is also locked by location pins. The fuel-injection valve is held against the cover by two bolts; on the larger engine types it is provided with a yoke to obviate obliquity of the fuel-injection valve housing, when fastening it.

The opening pressure of the valves is determined by a screw which adjusts the spring load transmitted to the valve needle through a thrust spindle. The lifting height of the valve needle is adjusted by varying the height of the thrust washer.

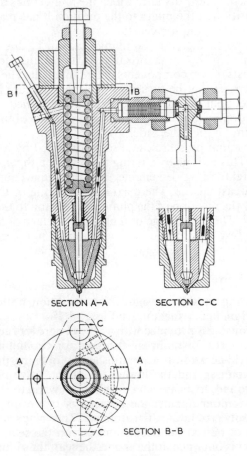

Figure 5.7 Fuel-injection valve

The cooling-oil connections are located on the sides of the valve-housing flange. The cooling liquid is led to one side of the atomiser and then circulated around the space between the surface of the atomiser and the bottom nut. It then leaves by the other side of the atomiser and so proceeds to the outlet connection. *See* section through C–C, Figure 5.7.

Fuel-valve Inspection

When inspecting the fuel-injection valves great care and cleanliness must be observed.

In the atomiser the needle must bear only on the extreme end part of the seat. The valve needle must move easily in the atomiser. With cleaned surfaces the needle must automatically glide out from the atomiser, if it is turned downwards from the horizontal position.

It must be checked that the spring discs are easy to move and fit to the adjusting screw and thrust spindle respectively. Otherwise the contact surfaces must be ground together. It is most important that the end surfaces of each spring are carefully ground, forming a right angle with the longitudinal centre-line of the spring, so that the latter will not tend to lie obliquely and thus chafe against the housing. The lower end surface of the thrust spindle is slightly spherical, to ensure a central contact with the valve needle.

After assembly, the opening pressure must be adjusted to 216 bar (147 bar for 520/900). Before assembly the lifting height is checked, which must be about 1·0 to 1·3 mm. If the lift exceeds 1·5 mm, the thrust washer must be replaced. The cooling chamber of the fuel-injection valve must be pressure-tested. It must be confirmed that the rubber ring between the valve housing and the bottom nut is tight. The pressure, which must not exceed about 10 bar, must therefore be maintained for a while.

When an engine is running on diesel oil, so called, the fuel-injection valves are cooled by the excess oil from the fuel-oil supply pump. When heavy fuel oil is being used, the fuel-injection valves are cooled by a special cooling system, entirely separated from the injection system. Diesel oil is normally used as the cooling medium, but if a more efficient coolant is needed, it is possible to use water with a suitable additive, *see* Figure 5.8.

The cooling system consists of two electrically driven circulation pumps, one cooler and one expansion tank. When stopped for other than short periods, also during manoeuvres, or when slow-running on very thick fuel oil, the cooling system can be used for heating the fuel-injection valves. When that happens, the tubes of the cooler are circulated by steam instead of by sea-water.

74

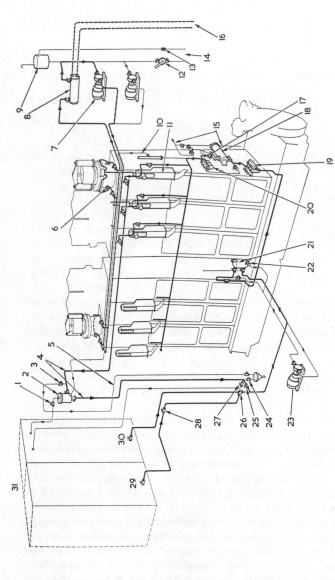

Figure 5.8 Heavy fuel operation and fuel-valve cooling

1. Air relief
2. Float valve
3. Reserve
4. Return line
5. Tell-tale line
6. Fuel-injection valve
7. Circulation pumps
8. Cooler
9. Expansion tank
10. Air relief
11. Fuel-injection pump
12. Hand pump
13. Sight glass
14. Filling of cooling system
15. Steam
16. Cooling water
17. Thermostat
18. Heater
19. Auto-Klean filter
20. Fine filter
21. Direct driven supply pump
22. Cleaning valve
23. Electrically driven supply pump
24. Test cock
25. Return valve
26. Change-over valve diesel heavy fuel oil
27. Drain valve
28. Non-return valve
29. Diesel oil
30. Heavy fuel oil

Fuel-oil System

Heavy oil is stored in steam-heated bunker tanks and is pumped by means of the transfer pump to the steam-heated heavy oil settling tanks. The fuel oil is then fed through heaters, and usually through two separators in series, to the steam-heated heavy oil daily service tank.

Between the daily service tank and the fuel-injection pumps on the main engine there are both a double-acting piston pump—placed on the chain entablature—and an electrically driven pump. These pumps, which are provided with relief valves, are so generously dimensioned that they provide a large excess of oil, which is circulated through the fuel system of the main engine. The pumps, of which the electrically driven one is a stand-by to be used for pumping-through, draw from the daily service tank and discharge through an Auto-Klean filter with several inserts to the oil heater, which is steam-heated and provided with thermostatic regulation. From the heater the oil is pumped through a fine filter to the fuel-injection pumps, from where the excess oil is led through a connecting pipe and a float valve to the suction side of the supply pump.

Manoeuvring and Reversing System

The engine is controlled by means of a single handwheel, from the movement of which starting, reversing and speed regulation are effected. This wheel is mounted on a control shaft and is situated at the front of the intermediate entablature at floor-plate level (*see* Figure 5.9).

The handwheel is provided with a pointer which moves around a graduated backplate. The graduations are duplicated on each side of the STOP position and indicate AHEAD and ASTERN. The graduations correspond to the rotary movement of the fuel-pump plunger, by means of which speed regulation is obtained. An eccentric mounted on the control shaft transmits the movement of the control wheel to the fuel-pump plungers by a system of links and rods.

The whole of the control system, including the starting-air slide, starting-air distributor, starting-air valves and the lock on the camshaft, are operated by compressed air. This air is controlled by mechanically operated valves, actuated by cams mounted on the control shaft. When starting in either ahead or astern direction, the control wheel is turned to the starting position indicated on the backplate, and air is admitted immediately to the starting slide, which, in turn, admits air to the operating side of the starting-air valves. The air distributor, in its turn, opens the air valve for the

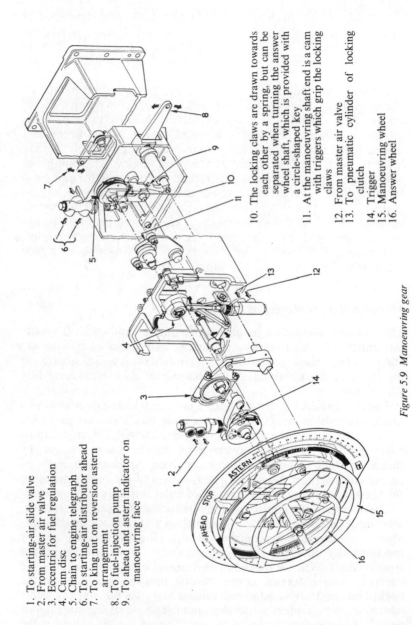

1. To starting-air slide valve
2. From master air valve
3. Eccentric for fuel regulation
4. Cam disc
5. Chain to engine telegraph
6. To starting-air distributor ahead
7. To king nut on reversion astern
   arrangement
8. To fuel-injection pump
9. To ahead and astern indicator on
   manoeuvring face

10. The locking claws are drawn towards
    each other by a spring, but can be
    separated when turning the answer
    wheel shaft, which is provided with
    a circle-shaped key
11. At the manoeuvring shaft end is a cam
    with triggers which grip the locking
    claws
12. From master air valve
13. To pneumatic cylinder of locking
    clutch
14. Trigger
15. Manoeuvring wheel
16. Answer wheel

Figure 5.9 Manoeuvring gear

cylinder, which is in the starting position. When the engine begins to rotate, the handwheel is turned to the running position and the starting air is automatically cut off.

Figure 5.10 illustrates the reversing gear for the 760/1500 VGS-U engine type. When reversing the engine, the camshaft with its corresponding cams does not move while the crankshaft turns 100°. During reversing, the rollers for the fuel-injection pumps remain all the time on the cams. Assume that the engine camshaft is ready for running AHEAD and the engine is to be started ASTERN. The master air valve is opened. The air passes through the piping R_1 to the change-over valve Z_1, and through R_2 to the pneumatic cylinder of the starting-air slide-valve and presses the slide against its seat. At the same time the chamber E, under the piston, is filled with air. The air passes farther through R_5 to the change-over valve Z_2.

The manoeuvring wheel is turned over to start ASTERN, whereby the following events happen:

(a) The switch lever S prevents the manoeuvring wheel from turning over to FUEL OIL, before the reversing of the camshaft and its fuel cams to ASTERN has been made.

(b) The change-over valve Z_1 is lifted by the trigger Q, and the pneumatic cylinder of the starting-air slide-valve is de-aerated through the pipe R_2.

(c) The starting-air slide-valve lifts, and through the pipe R_3 all starting valves are supplied with air. The air passes simultaneously through the pipe R_4, the change-over valve Z_3, and the pipe R_8 to the starting-air distributor.

(d) The air passes farther from the change-over valve Z_2 through the pipe R_6 to the pneumatic cylinder, the piston of which is pressed down, and the locking clutch is brought over to a neutral position in relation to the hub N.

(e) The starting-air distributor rotates with the same speed as the crankshaft. The slide in the starting-air distributor now distributes the air through R_9 to the pneumatic cylinder of the respective starting valve, and, due to this over-pressure, the starting valve opens and supplies starting air to the working cylinder. The engine begins to rotate and all starting valves open one by one, when their working pistons reach their starting positions.

(f) The sprocket wheel K is, through the driving chain, connected to the crankshaft and follows it. The worm M has been threaded-out and has made the sector V free, whereby the change-over valve Z_2 de-aerates the pneumatic cylinder through the pipe R_6. The locking clutch again takes its original position.

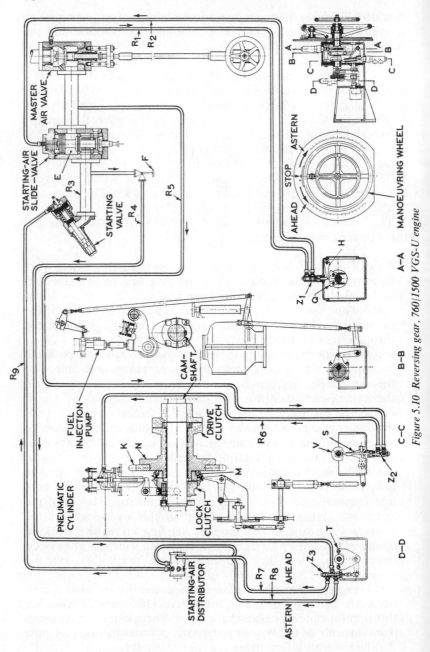

Figure 5.10 Reversing gear, 760/1500 VGS-U engine

(g) When the manoeuvring wheel is turned over to FUEL OIL the change-over valve Z_1 opens again for the air to the starting-air slide-valve, whereby this cuts off the air supply to the starting valves.

The engine telegraph receiver is placed at the instrument board in front of the chain entablature and can be either electrically or mechanically operated. In front, on the manoeuvring wheel, there is a smaller 'reply' wheel, which is connected to the receiver by a chain. With the reply wheel, any manoeuvring order received is repeated. If the order received is correctly repeated by the reply wheel, a locking arrangement in the manoeuvring box prevents the manoeuvring wheel from turning in the wrong direction. A correctly repeated order can consequently never be wrongly executed.

Governor Operation

The governor is mounted on the entablature and is driven from the intermediate gear of the chain transmission by a small chain and bevel gearing. For the 520/900 engine the governor is driven by bevel gear from the camshaft.

The governor for the cast engines consists of two spring-loaded weights and a servo-motor supplying the regulating force by means of oil pressure. The governor transmits its motion by an oil-regulating slide to the regulating piston of the servo-motor which, by a system of links and rods, controls the shaft regulating the fuel-injection pumps. The oil for the regulating piston of the servo-motor is taken from the engine lubricating-oil system. The maximum speed of the engine can be changed during operation by regulating an external spring arrangement, thus giving a small adjustment of the speed upwards or downwards.

For the welded engine and for type 850/1700 the regulating movement from the governor to the fuel-injection pumps is transferred directly from the governor weights, without the aid of a servo-motor system, see Figure 5.11. In order to allow an increase or decrease of the maximum speed while the engine is running, the governor has an external spring.

The governor serves to prevent racing, coming into operation only when the engine has exceeded the predetermined speed.

During recent years the governor types described above have tended to be superseded for application to new engines. A hydraulic speed governor of the Woodward design is more sensitive and better adapted for application to remote-control systems.

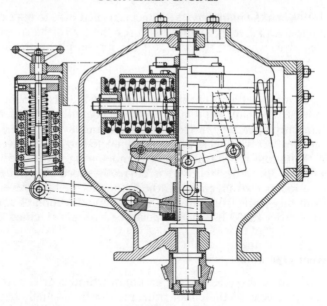

Figure 5.11 Governor

Indicator Gear

An indicator valve is provided in each cylinder cover, with a suitable connection for the indicator. Reciprocating motion for the indicator drum is provided by an eccentric mounted on the camshaft, which operates a spring-loaded pushrod to which the indicator cord can be attached.

Cylinder Lubrication

Cylinder lubrication is effected by means of mechanical lubricators provided with sight-feed glasses, each lubricator being operated by a pushrod from the indicator cam. There is a non-return valve for each point of lubrication on the cylinder, and the valves are assembled on the entablature of the cylinder concerned. The quantity of oil delivered to each lubrication point can be regulated by means of screws in the lubricator.

A feed rate of 0·00055–0·00060 kg/kWh is recommended as a reasonable guidance but this can, of course, be departed from if the liner and piston ring conditions require a higher rate or, and this is often the case, allow a lower feed rate.

Lubricating and Cooling Oil System

Lubricating oil for the engine and for piston cooling is stored in two double-bottom tanks, usually situated under the engine and connected to the engine sump by drain pipes and shut-off valves. Electrically driven lubricating oil pumps, of the screw-type, draw oil from these double-bottom tanks and discharge through filters and coolers to the engine. Each pump is fitted with a spring-loaded discharge valve, by means of which the discharge pressure can be regulated within wide limits. It also acts as a safety valve.

The main inlet for the cooling oil and the circulating lubrication oil to the engine is divided into two pipes, namely, a cooling-oil pipe, from which the inlet pipes to the piston cooling are branched, and a lubrication oil pipe, from which the lubrication oil is led to main bearings, bottom-end bearings, thrust bearings and so on.

For adjustment of the oil quantities in both pipes there is a control valve at their branching point which must be adjusted to give equal distribution of oil between both systems. The valve lid has a hole in it so that the lubrication oil cannot be shut off completely. The pressure of the cooling oil is adjusted by the control valve, so that a maximum oil quantity is led to the piston cooling. A tell-tale device on the manoeuvring side of each entablature indicates that cooling oil is passing through the piston. It must be systematically checked that lubrication oil reaches the control tap on the highest point of the circulating lubrication-oil system, on top of the chain entablature.

A pressure of 2·0 to 2·4 bar before the engine, for lubrication and cooling oil, is considered normal; the minimum pressure is 1·5 bar. The cooling-oil outlet temperature must normally be 45 to 50°C, with a maximum of 55°C.

Turboblower Lubrication

Turboblower units with plain bearings are gravity-lubricated from a separate system. A main tank is provided, into which the oil drains from the bearings. Pumps deliver oil from this tank through automatic non-return valves, multi-element Auto-Klean filters and heat exchangers, to a branch pipe which is connected to both a gravity tank and to the turboblower bearings. The oil pressure at the bearings is determined by the level in the gravity tank, which, in turn, is controlled by an overflow pipe connected to the main tank. This overflow pipe is fitted with a sight-glass for checking the flow of oil, ensuring that the gravity tank is full. The gravity tank also acts as an emergency reservoir in the event of the pump's ceasing to operate. The bearings are then supplied with lubricating oil for a limited period, determined by the capacity of the gravity tank. During the running-down time the standby pump must be started-up, or the unit stopped.

To prevent impurities out of the piping from entering the bearings with the oil, a multi-element Auto-Klean filter is fitted before each of the two bearings of the unit; moreover, the oil-flow can be inspected through a sight-glass arranged at each bearing housing, in the drain pipe to the main tank.

Cooling-water System

The main engine receives its cooling water from two or several sets, one of which functions as standby. Further there is usually a special system for the auxiliary engines. Each set consists of two pumps, one for sea-water and one for fresh water, these being coupled to the same electric motor on a common base-plate.

The cooler works in accordance with the counter-flow principle. Its design is usually the same as for the lubrication-oil cooler, except that it is not provided with air-relief arrangements.

The main engine is cooled with fresh water, to which are added suitable small quantities of chemicals to prevent corrosion. The fresh-water pump draws from the outlet piping of the engine and discharges through the cooler back to the engine. An expansion tank is placed in the engine-room casing.

The sea-water is fed through one of the valves in the bottom of the ship, or through the high suction valve on the side of the ship, and discharged through the oil cooler and the fresh-water cooler and then overboard. If necessary, the sea-water can bypass the cooler, and it is also possible to cool the engine directly with sea-water.

The fresh cooling water is supplied to the engine from a main line along the engine. For each cylinder there is a branch pipe with a closing valve, and the cooling water is supplied to the upper part of the cooling jacket (for cast engine to the lower part of the cylinder frame) and thereafter through the lower cylinder cover and the exhaust-valve housing, through the outlet, to a common collecting pipe for all cylinders.

Turbocharging and Scavenging

Götaverken engines are turbocharged on the constant-pressure system, with the blowers acting in series with the reciprocating scavenging-air pumps at each cylinder. The constant-pressure principle gives an effective protection against turbine damage caused by pieces of piston ring and other solid particles. The pieces are trapped in the exhaust-gas receiver. The ashes in the fuel oil are built-up in the exhaust pipe after the cylinders and in the exhaust-gas receiver. No danger is involved. The turbine blades remain clean and uninjured and the turbine efficiency is retained intact.

The reciprocating scavenging-air pumps result in a slight increase in fuel consumption, because of the reduced mechanical efficiency. The fuel consumption in service is maintained at the same value as during the delivery trials, owing to the above-mentioned factors. In addition, the mechanical air pumps ensure reliable starting and provide ample scavenging air for manoeuvring and slow-running. It is not necessary to use excessive air–fuel ratios at high engine load, as the normal ratio is sufficient even at considerably reduced outputs. This can be deduced from Figure 5.21.

The turboblower unit is made up of a single-stage centrifugal compressor and a single-stage axial-flow turbine, both mounted on the same shaft. The speed of the rotor depends solely on the engine load and the scavenging resistance. Thus, the turbocharged engine is controlled in the same manner as the non-turbocharged engine.

The rotor shaft and the turbine disc are made of steel, and the turbine blades of a heat-resisting alloy. The compressor impeller is shaped as an open radial wheel and is made of forged aluminium alloy. The rotor is supported at both ends by plain bearings lubricated from an external system. The turboblowers, except for one larger type, have also, on request, been supplied with ball and roller bearings lubricated from an internal oil system.

The compressor housing is an aluminium-alloy casting and consists of a guide-vane diffuser directly after the impeller, and a spiral diffuser discharging into the air-outlet pipe. The turbine casing, which is water-cooled, is divided into an inlet and an outlet section. The inlet section contains the nozzle ring of the turbine, with blades of heat-resisting steel.

The unit is cooled by fresh water, the piping being connected in parallel to the engine-cylinder cooling circuit.

From the compressor outlet of the turboblower unit the compressed air passes through a welded pipe to an intermediate air-cooler, cooled by sea-water. The cooling-water tubes, of bronze, have copper fins soldered on to them to provide a large cooling surface. The complete cooler insert is submerged in a metal bath for soldering, a procedure which ensures good heat conductivity between fins and tubes. Inspection covers are fitted so that the cooler can be inspected from both inlet and outlet ends. For easy cleaning of the tube-stacks, these are made as casettes, which can be taken out without dismantling the air side.

After the coolers the air enters the outer scavenging-air receiver, which is connected to the double-acting reciprocating pumps by means of non-return valves. This type of valve is also directed towards the engine room and remains closed as long as the pressure in the receiver is the same as, or higher than, that in the engine room. When the turboblower unit is disengaged, the reciprocating scavenging pumps draw in air at atmospheric pressure, both through the non-return valves and through the turbocharger unit at rest.

HIGHLY TURBOCHARGED ENGINE TYPES

The application of high-pressure turbocharging to Götaverken's slow-running marine diesel engines was started by the introduction of the large-bore type 850/1700 VGA-U, which was among the types described in the previous section.

An increase in mean pressure means an increase in output per unit of cylinder volume. The earlier engines permitted such an increase of pressure level to a certain extent, but beyond this limit it was not possible to go further without an essential revision of the design. Thus a development programme for entirely new engine types, suitable for high mip values, was decided upon.

The three basic sizes of the new Götaverken engine are designated 630/1400 VGS-U, 750/1600 VGS-U and 850/1700 VGS-U.

When designing these new engines Götaverken strictly adhered to most of the main features of the older types. The uniflow-scavenged, two-stroke, single-acting crosshead engine types have, through the years, proved to be reliable in service, economical in running and requiring low maintenance costs. These comments also apply to the turbocharging system adopted, which is based on the constant-pressure principle with scavenging-air pumps arranged in series with the turboblower. It therefore seemed sound and natural to adhere to these principles in the latest designs.

Table 5.2 HIGHLY TURBOCHARGED GÖTAVERKEN ENGINES

Bore	Stroke	Speed	Cylinder output	MIP
(mm)	(mm)	(Rev/min)	(kW)	(bar)
630	1400	135/139	955/1030	11·1–11·6
750	1600	120/124	1400/1510	11·2–11·8
850	1700	115/119	1765/1950	11·0–11·5

The two speed and power values for each engine size have reference to continuous service output and maximum continuous output respectively.

Retained Design Features

It can be seen from the cross-sections of the 850/1700 VGS-U engine type given in Figure 5.12(a) and (b) that many of the components are very similar to the corresponding parts of the previous engine types. This means that the earlier descriptions are to a great extent also applicable to the latest engines dealt with in this part, as exemplified by the connecting rod and bottom end bearing; crosshead and crosshead bearing; white metal lining; working piston and piston rod; cylinder lubrication; cylinder head; telescopic pipes; fuel oil system including injection pump, valve and valve inspection; turning gear; indicator gear; lubricating and cooling oil system; cooling water system; also turbocharging and scavenging.

The following description is therefore limited to departures in design from the older engines, not only new design solutions but also added details and maintenance routines.

Frame Structure

The engines are designed with welded framework. The box-type entablatures without through-going staybolts have been retained, giving a minimum of machined surfaces. The cylinder units can be assembled before being placed on the bedplate, and complete cylinder units can be transported from the engine shops to the ship. All welds which are stressed by gas pressure, e.g. the welds between the cast-steel top and the plates of the entablature, are continuous full-strength butt welds with complete fusion. All horizontal tee connections are designed to ensure complete penetration.

An open cofferdam is arranged between the scavenging-air belt and the crankcase. This arrangement gives an efficient sealing, which is most valuable, bearing in mind the high scavenging-air pressure. Moreover, the risk of a crankcase explosion caused by fire in the scavenging-air belt is practically eliminated. There is ample room for two piston-rod boxes, as shown in Figure 5.13, and it is possible, therefore, to inspect the functioning of the scraper boxes. To facilitate the dismounting of the boxes they are assembled in one common cast-iron housing which is bolted to the lower intermediate plate only. In the upper intermediate plate there is a sliding fit with sealing ring. The housing can thus be lowered into the crankcase towards the crosshead; or it can follow the piston and piston rod when these are lifted for overhaul.

Bedplate

The customary design of bedplate is, on the whole, retained. Figure

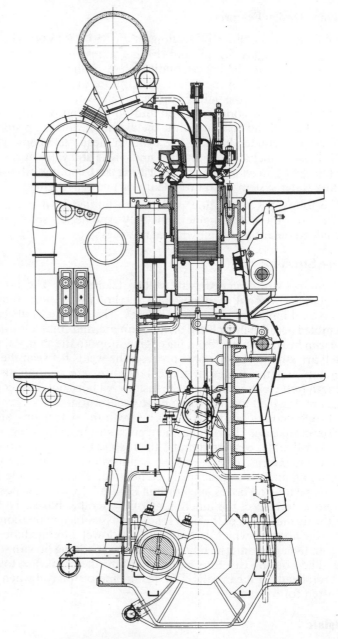

Figure 5.12(a) 850/1700 VGS-U engine. Transverse section

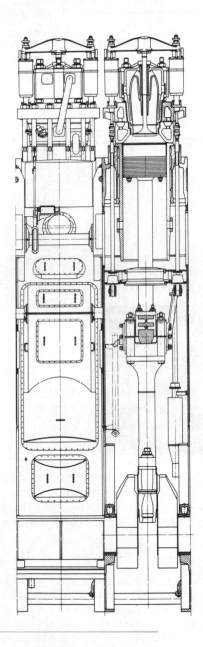

Figure 5.12(b) 850/1700 VGS-U engine. Longitudinal section

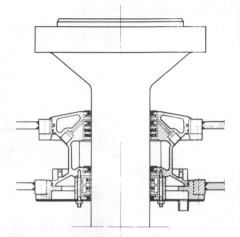

Figure 5.13 Piston rod boxes

5.14 shows one of the cross-girders. The aft end of the bedplate together with the thrust-bearing housing form an integral unit. Stiff

Fig. 5.14 Bedplate cross-girder

plates transmit the forces from the thrust shaft directly to the engine foundation. The thrust bearing is separated from the crankcase by a complete transverse partition, thus reducing the risk of a crankcase explosion in the event of a thrust-bearing failure by overheating.

Crankshaft

The crankshaft is semi-built, in accordance with the normal practice for Götaverken engines. To make the distance between cylinder centres as small as possible, and thus to reduce the overall engine length, specially large crankshaft diameters are used. The specific pressures for the main bearings and for the bottom-end bearings are about the same as for the previous, turbocharged engine types.

Exhaust-valve Mechanism

The large crankshaft diameters, the balance weights and the demand for a good accessibility to the main bearings made it impossible to retain the cams on the crankshaft. Accordingly, a separate camshaft for the operation of the exhaust valves has been introduced, *see* Figure 5.15. The exhaust-valve gear has been arranged in the upper

Figure 5.15 Exhaust valve operating

part of the crankcase. The bearing housings for the camshaft are mounted on brackets on the crosshead guides. By means of a roller, a Y-shaped lever and two pull-rods, the motion is transmitted to the yoke into which the valve stem is fitted. From six or eight springs on each cylinder the required spring force is obtained.

The exhaust gas valve is dimensioned and designed to ensure the least possible flow-resistance during the exhaust and scavenging periods. The valve stem and the disc are an integral part. The yoke arrangement on the top of the engine provides easy handling for the engine top details when maintenance work is required to be carried out, and this feature has therefore been retained intact.

Camshaft Drive

The chain transmission for the two camshafts of the 630 mm and 750 mm bore engines includes one $3\frac{1}{2}$ in duplex chain, while the 850 mm bore engines has two $4\frac{1}{2}$ in simplex chains for the same purpose. These last-mentioned chains are matched, which means that they have been chosen in such a way after manufacture that they are as nearly identical as possible as regards tolerances, *see* Figure 5.16.

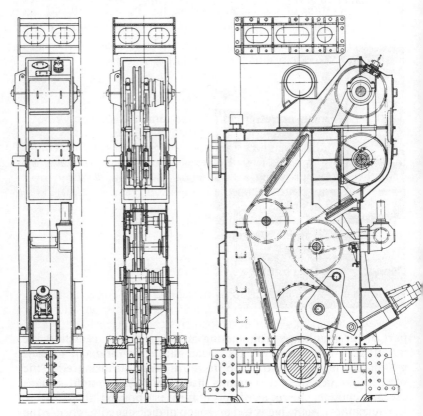

Figure 5.16 Camshaft chain transmission, 850/1700 VGS-U engine

The chain tension, being effected by means of a chain adjuster with two heavy springs, should under normal service conditions be inspected at 500 hour intervals. The condition of the chains and the chain wheels must also be carefully inspected at regular intervals, say at approximately 1000 hours for the first 6 months. Thereafter, inspection at 3000–4000 hourly intervals is recommended.

To prevent transverse chain vibrations in the 850/1700 engine, steel guide bars provided with a vulcanised rubber layer are used. These dampers can be adjusted in relation to the chains by means of shims. A normal clearance along the whole rubber lists of 0·5–1·5 mm should always be aimed at. When this clearance has increased to 5 mm, by reason of rubber wear, the damper must immediately be readjusted.

A smaller $1\frac{1}{2}$ in simplex chain drive, obtaining its motion from the lower intermediate shaft, drives the governor, the starting air distributor, and the tachometer generator. The whole chain transmission assembly is lubricated from a number of splash pipes which are connected to the ordinary oil circulation system.

Cylinder Liners

The cylinder liners are essentially of the same design as previously described; see Figure 5.4. For the 850/1700 VGS-U-type, however, a modification has been necessary, due to the increased turbocharging rate. This liner has a wall of even thickness all over and the cooling jacket is provided with a helical, inside guide rib giving a higher and more clearly defined cooling water velocity. In this way the temperatures on the inner wall of the liner have been decreased to values well below those of the earlier large-bore engines, despite the increased mean pressure level.

Cooling Water De-aeration

Gas or air quantities circulating in the cooling water can considerably reduce the cooling action, for which reason a de-aeration system for the water circuit has been developed. As can be seen from Figure 5.17, the cooling water from the top of the engine is led to a cyclone vessel, in which the air or gas contents are thoroughly separated from the water. The main pipe from this vessel to the suction side of the main cooling water pumps has a restriction flange, so that there is enough pressure-difference to give a positive stream from the top of the de-aerating vessel to the top of the fresh water expansion tank.

Furthermore, there are smaller de-aerating pipes from the turbocharger cooling pipe and from the ends of the main engine outlet. From the bottom of the expansion tank an equalising pipe is led to the suction side of the cooling water pumps and, with this arrangement, if there is any gas or air in the cooling water it is efficiently separated and brought to the vent pipe.

Piston Cooling System

Oil cooling of the pistons has been retained, see Figures 5.18 and 5.19.

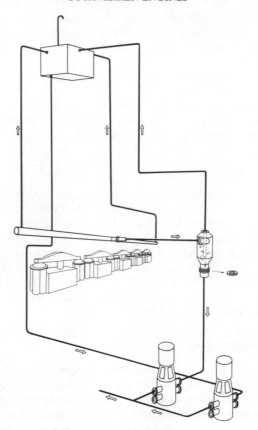

Figure 5.17 Air relief arrangement

If an owner desires completely to separate the cooling oil from the lubricating oil this can be done by means of an extra telescopic pipe for the cooling-oil outlet from the piston. A long pipe in the bottom of the crankcase collects the cooling oil from all the pistons and leads it to a separate bottom tank. A separate pump and cooler are necessary for this system.

Exhaust Manifold Arrangement

The exhaust-gas manifold has been moved to a position above the turbochargers, which are placed on the top platform. This arrangement reduces the maximum width of the engine and also provides a

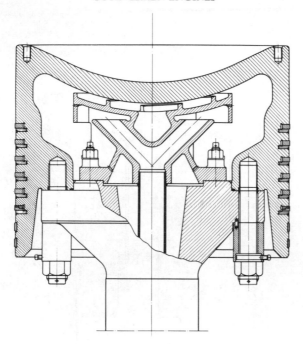

Figure 5.18 Piston 850 mm bore

large free area at one single level around the engine top, for convenient handling of engine parts when maintenance work is being carried out.

Turbocharging Installation

The by-pass arrangement for the exhaust gases, previously described in this chapter when dealing with the older engine types, was adopted from the very first turbocharged installation in 1955. Not knowing at that time what degree of reliability could be expected from the turbocharger, the Götaverken engine was judged to have a specifically good point in being able to operate non-turbocharged, in event of a turbocharger breakdown.

Several years of experience in this field, however, proved that this kind of breakdown was so extremely rare that it was justifiable to dispense with the by-pass valve when designing the new range of engines. For an intermediate period, a by-pass pipe was adopted. This pipe was normally blind-flanged; but it was opened when

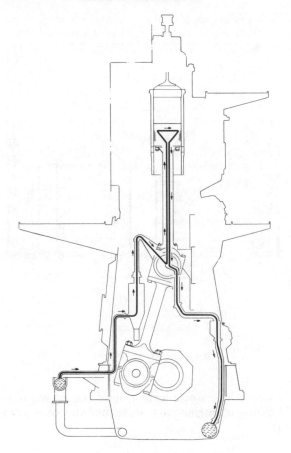

Figure 5.19 Piston cooling oil charge and discharge

operating the engine without the turbocharger, thus reducing the
pressure-loss in the exhaust system and making higher outputs
possible without exceeding the maximum permissible exhaust
temperature.

Special tests showed, in due course, that the same result was
reached by simply blocking the damaged turbine and allowing the
gases to pass through the unit. The whole by-pass idea was thereafter discarded and the routine in event of a breakdown now follows
one or other of the following alternatives:

(a) All turbocharger rotors of the engine are locked and two or
three inspection covers on the scavenging air receiver are opened,

i.e. at least one on each of the fore and aft receiver halves. The engine is thereafter operated non-turbocharged, the air being drawn through the above-named openings and through the blower compressors. About 40–45 per cent of the normal engine output can be utilised in this way. It should be mentioned that this procedure is followed when circumstances allow of only a minimum of time being spent on the change-over or when the ship is close to a port where more thorough steps can be taken.

(b) The rotors of the damaged turbochargers are locked and the remaining turbochargers are allowed to be free-running. Two or three inspection covers on the air receiver are opened, as described above.

(c) The rotors of the damaged turbochargers are locked, whereafter the respective turbine inlets and compressor outlets are blind-flanged. The remaining turbochargers continue in operation. These steps are obviously more circumstantial but ensure in return a smaller reduction of the engine output than do the steps with methods (a) and (b).

The scheme to be followed must depend on the number of turbochargers installed on the engine and on the number of damaged turbochargers. Table 5.3 indicates the possibilities and also shows the approximate maximum engine output for the respective alternatives.

Table 5.3

Number of turbochargers out of order	Number of turbochargers installed				
	1	2	3	4	5
1	a (40–45%)	c (45–50%)	c (70–75%)	c (80–85%)	c (90–95%)
2	—	a (40–45%)	b (40–45%)	c (45–50%)	c (65–70%)
3	—	—	a (40–45%)	b (40–45%)	b (40–45%)
4	—	—	—	a (40–45%)	b (40–45%)
5	—	—	—	—	a (40–45%)

Since 1966, washing equipment on both the compressor and turbine sides of the blowers has been standard for these engines. Deposits in the turbochargers of some engines and the demand for prolonged service periods between overhauls were the incentives for introducing this equipment.

The compressor is washed at full speed by injecting 1–3 litres of pure water by means of compressed air. The quantity used depends on the turbocharger size. The impact of the individual droplets removes the deposit mechanically. The turbine side is also washed with pure water, obtained from the cooling water outlet of the turbocharger through a nozzle in the turbine inlet. The washing is carried out at reduced speed for 8–10 minutes, and the water flow can be up to 30–50 litres per minute for the larger turbocharger types. These procedures are usually repeated 2–3 times every month.

Air Cooler Cleaning

Each air cooler comprises two tube stacks, these being so dimensioned that at full engine load the air side pressure-drop through the cooler is less than 120 mm water gauge as long as the tubes are in clean condition. This pressure-drop increases gradually due to air impurities adhering to the tube surfaces. Simultaneously the cooling efficiency deteriorates. Thus, the coolers must be maintained in a condition of maximum cleanliness, particularly on the air side. The condition of the compressor filter silencer is also important.

As a general recommendation the cooler elements should be cleaned at least twice a year. For this purpose the engines are provided with lifting-bars over all cooler elements, to enable the engine staff to dismount, clean and replace them easily. A washing tank for the cooler elements is included in the standard equipment. Three alternative cleaning fluids are recommended, namely trichlorethylene, varnolene and white spirit.

In order to simplify further the air-side tube cleaning a new washing arrangement has been developed, thus making it possible to carry out the operation *in situ*. A cleaning insert is mounted in the scavenging air receiver, above the corresponding cooler, *see* Figure 5.20. Each insert has eight atomisers which distribute the cleaning liquid, or hot water, over the entire cooler. The procedure cannot be carried out while running the engine.

Engine Performance

The Götaverken engine is subjected to thorough shop tests. The initial running-in routine includes two idle running periods of short duration, with bearing and camshaft chain inspections interposed. The engine is thereafter operated at 25 per cent load for twelve hours, after which a component inspection and a short 'adjustment trial' at half-load take place.

The engine is run in accordance with two propeller curves, corresponding respectively to 80 per cent and 100 per cent of the normal engine output. All performance data of interest are measured at 5 load points on the 100 per cent-curve and at 3 load points on the 80 per cent-curve. The diagrams in Figure 5.21, based on diesel oil

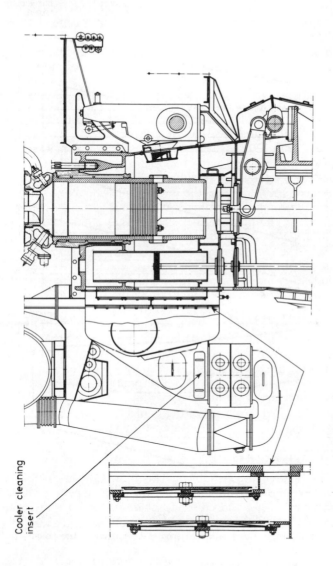

Cooler cleaning insert

Figure 5.20 Air cooler cleaning arrangement

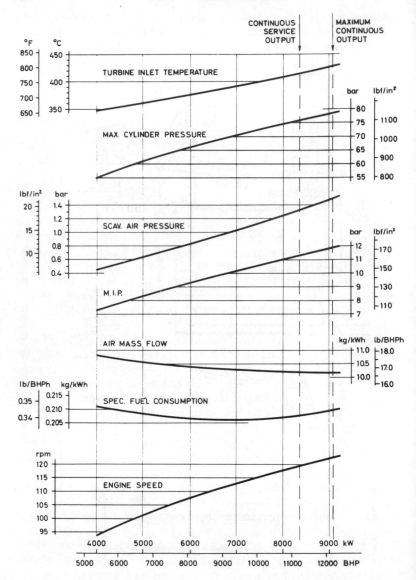

Figure 5.21 Results from testbed trials, 750/1600 VGS-6U

trials with a six-cylinder production unit of the 750/1600 engine type, have reference to the 100 per cent load-curve. This means an engine output of 8400 kW at the normal service speed of 120 rev/min. In

addition to the values given in the diagram, the following data
referring to the load mentioned may be of interest;
  Exhaust temperature, after the cylinders (in the outlet
  bends),   355°C
  Exhaust temperature, after the turbine   310°C
  Scavenging air temperature, after the cooler   45°C
  Mechanical efficiency   88·5 per cent
  Figure 5.22 shows a six-cylinder 630/1400 engine type on the
test bed.

Telegraphic Reports

The instrumentation for the main engine on board ship mainly
corresponds to that used during shop trials, and diagram sheets are
supplied to the chief engineer together with instructions, thus
enabling him to judge the various instrument readings. After the
delivery of a ship, the guarantee engineer and subsequently the chief
engineer, send periodical reports to the builders by telegram, using
a specially developed code system for supplying the maximum
amount of information with a minimum number of words. When
they reach the manufacturer the reports are dealt with in the way
described below.

The values are plotted into the diagrams from the shop trials. If
pressures and temperatures coincide with the load condition of the
engine, the report will simply be filed. But if any value or values are
obviously abnormal or if the report has been accompanied by a
question, a complete computer calculation is made not only based
upon this particular report but upon all those filed earlier. Such an
analysis provides a quick response regarding the location of any
disturbance. The result is reported to the ship and the system therefore functions as a service to the owner.

Experience gained from engine reports has shown the necessity
for keeping instruments in good order, so that readings made and
reported will show the existing conditions correctly. If a telegraphic
report contains incorrect values these can often be discovered when
the values are treated in the computer. But as the programme treats
the whole process, and as each series of measuring data satisfies a
determined state of balance between compressor, engine and turbine,
an incorrect primary value will often show an unreasonable result.

Inspection and Maintenance

A clear tendency has been apparent in recent years towards reducing
the size of ship's crews and to arrange machinery maintenance in

Figure 5.22 Six-cylinder 630/1400 engine on testbed

accordance with a fixed plan which partly apportions work to the crew and partly to organisations ashore. Relating this reduction in crew numbers to the increased size of engines and components, it has become of vital importance to develop suitable tools and engine room equipment for easing the burdens of maintenance.

Götaverken has met this requirement by developing a wide range of hydraulic tools for various purposes. Thus the hydraulic tightening of cylinder cover bolts and exhaust valve housing bolts gives not only an easier, faster and safer result than the earlier routine with sledge hammers, but the tightening accuracy is considerably improved.

The same principle is used also for the various bolt connections of the crank mechanism, including such smaller nuts as those located at the piston rod foot and at the crosshead bearing. The idea is to avoid the use of hammers, which often leave unpleasant marks on piston rod surfaces. The oil pressure is delivered by pumps of hand-operated or electrically driven types.

Table 5.4 indicates numbers of men and hours required for overhaul routines.

MANOEUVRING SYSTEM

A pneumatic remote control system has been developed which, from the very beginning, was intended as a complete system for remote control and automation, directly actuating the fuel injection and starting-air devices of the engine. This completeness makes it possible to install the system in older ships, which can be done even while the ship is in operation, the final connecting to the engine being carried out during the first convenient stay in harbour.

Nowadays the engine-room manoeuvring device is mostly placed in a console at some distance from the engine. If the movements of this device are transmitted mechanically to the engine there will always be a play involved, which depends on the distance and on the number of joints in the linkage. The pneumatic remote-control system is free from this disadvantage, and it is therefore very suitable for engine-room control, no matter whether or not the engine is simultaneously equipped with bridge control. If the owner does not want to install a bridge-control console at the beginning, but the need of this equipment should arise later in service, the addition is very easy to apply, assuming that the described remote-control system (Figure 5.23(a)) has been originally applied. The system is therefore standard equipment for the new highly turbocharged Götaverken main engines.

The manoeuvring system in Figure 5.23(a) is pneumatic. The impulse air is taken from the starting-air receivers through air filters, oil-mist lubricating devices and pressure regulators, reducing the air pressure to 8 bar. The components of the system are of standard

Table 5.4 SOME TYPICAL NUMBERS OF MEN AND HOURS REQUIRED FOR DIFFERENT OVERHAUL ROUTINES

Routine description	Men needed	Hours	Routine description	Men needed	Hours
Draw, clean and re-ring a piston, replace and box up, including adjusting jobs	5	8	Replacement of a fuel injection pump	2	2
Overhaul of piston, inspection of cooling space etc.	2	8	Dismounting of scavenging air valves, inspection, cleaning and mounting	2	8
Cylinder liner replacement (with piston kept in place)	4	5	Stripping and inspection of bottom end bearing and pin. Box up	2	4
Disconnect and replace a complete exhaust valve, including normal grinding of the corresponding contact surface in the cylinder head	3	3	Stripping and inspection of main bearing and pin. Box-up	2	5
Overhaul of exchanged exhaust valve, cleaning and normal grinding	2	5	Inspection of crosshead bearing and pin	2	3
Exchange of starting air valve	1	1	Overhaul of one turbocharger unit	2	10
Exchange of fuel injection valve	1	$\frac{1}{2}$	Inspection and cleaning of a scavenging air cooler, water and air side	2	10
Cleaning up of the scavenging air belt	1	8	Opening up and inspection of a thrust bearing, including cam and segments	2	6

type and widely available. They require a minimum amount of maintenance and are easy to overhaul.

When the remote console is connected the cylinder *SC* turns the regulating shaft of the fuel pumps to STOP position. The shaft is then locked in this position by cylinder *SPC*. The two cylinders *SC* and

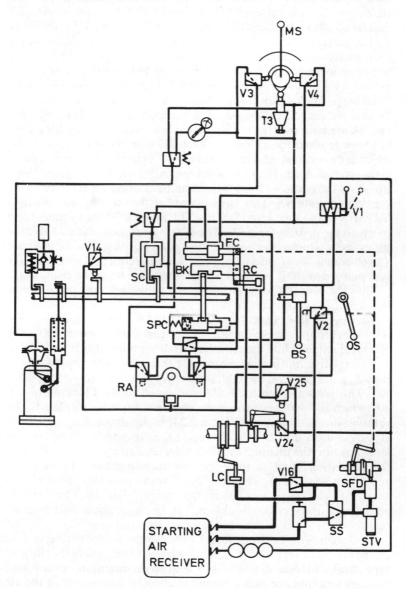

Figure 5.23(a) Pneumatic remote control system

SPC are actuated by impulse air from *V1*. When remotely operating the engine, the control lever *MS* is moved directly to a position which corresponds to the intended engine speed. The valve *V3* (AHEAD) or *V4* (ASTERN) is then opened, thus transmitting the impulse air to the switch-over cylinder *FC* of the starting-air distributor *SFD*. If the engine is to be reversed, the camshaft of the distributor is axially moved by *FC*, and this motion also brings the piston *BK* into a blocking position. Thus the regulating shaft is locked in STOP position by two pistons, *SPC* and *BK*. The components *SC*, *SPC*, *FC*, *RC* and *BK* are built into the manoeuvring box. After the switching-over has been finished the air passes through *FC* to the stop-cylinder *SC* which is disengaged, and to the valve *V14*, being held open by a lever in the STOP position. The valve *V16* (opened by an air signal from *V14*), transmits the control air, 25 bar, from the starting-air receiver to the starting-air slide *SS*. This slide opens for the starting air, which is led partly to the starting-air valves *STV* in the working cylinders and partly to the distributor *SFD*. The distributor opens the air valve for the cylinder which is in convenient starting position. The air cylinder *LC* (through *V16*) disengages the locking clutch connecting the fuel-pump camshaft to the chain transmission from the crankshaft.

Thus the camshaft can remain at rest while the crankshaft rotates through the reversing angle.

The engine now begins to rotate, started by the air from the slide *SS*. The driving sleeve of the upper camshaft rotates 100°, the reversing angle, while the camshaft itself remains at rest.

This relative motion by means of a threaded sleeve opens one of the valves *V25* or *V24*, through which the air then passes to the piston *RC*. This piston is mechanically connected to the blocking piston *BK*, which is disengaged when the reversing angle is completed. The rotation direction sensor (Figure 5.24) is simultaneously in action. If the rotation direction of the engine corresponds to the control lever position the piston *SPC* is also declutched by air from *RA* and the regulation shaft is then free for fuel injection. Turning the regulating shaft from STOP position means that the valve *V14* is switched over, relieving *V16* and the starting slide *SS*. The starting-air delivery to the engine is closed, but the engine now continues on fuel.

The functioning of the different valves in the manoeuvring system can be visually checked on a mimic diagram board during the starting procedure. This board, which is located on the engine-room console, includes a number of lights being actuated by pressostats in the air pipes, and also a manometer giving the air pressure at the governor actuator.

The regulating shaft of the fuel pumps is actuated by the speed governor when the engine is remotely operated. The control lever *MS* guides the pressure regulator *T3*, which in turn gives signal air to the actuator of the speed governor. This actuator contains a spring-loaded diaphragm, the movement of which is transmitted by rods and levers to the speed control shaft of the governor. The signal air pressure is by means of *T3* adjusted between 4 bar (corresponding to the lowest engine speed) and 1 bar (highest engine speed).

The governor includes an oil pump delivering the necessary oil at the required pressure to the power piston of the governor. The force is transmitted to the regulating shaft by levers, rods and a spring coupling. A separate booster pump, driven by impulse air, ensures the oil pressure during the start of the engine.

Bridge Control

The bridge manoeuvring system in Figure 5.23(b) includes the basic system just described, which can easily be seen by comparing the Figure 5.23(a) and (b). In Figure 5.23(b) there are, however, shown a number of supervision and alarm systems, which are necessary for the safety of the machinery.

The bridge staff demand the engine operation by means of a push button on the bridge console. The engaging of the remote-control system is then executed by the engine-room staff by pushing the telegraph lever over FULL AHEAD to the BRIDGE CONTROL position. After that, the engine is operated by means of the control lever *MS* at the bridge console. Control lamps at both consoles indicate which of them is connected at the time. The engine-room staff can, at any moment, take over the control of the engine, for instance in event of machinery emergency.

In a system equipped for bridge control, the engine room control function is directly connected to the telegraph receiver in such a way that when answering the telegraph order the manoeuvre is simultaneously carried out. Thus, if the order is correctly answered, it is also correctly carried out.

If, however, for some technical reason the engine speed has to be limited, this can be done by means of the pressure regulator *T6*. After this an order of, for instance, FULL AHEAD from the bridge can be correctly answered but the engine speed is increased only to the speed limit (or above that value at a pace decided by the engine staff).

Regarding the position of the two valves *V3* and *V4*, alternatives are given in Figure 5.23(a) and (b). In the first figure they are directly actuated by the control lever *MS*, and this arrangement is used when the distance between the control console and the manoeuvring box is less than about 60 m.

BRIDGE CONSOLE

ENGINE ROOM CONSOLE

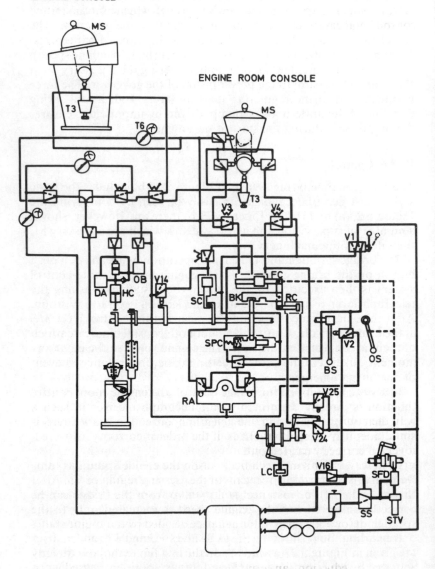

Figure 5.23(b) Complete bridge-control system

At longer distances, e.g. when an amidship navigating bridge is combined with an aft engine installation, the alternative in Figure 5.23(b) has to be used. The two valves *V3* and *V4* are located in a valve cabinet and they are actuated by the control lever on the bridge console by means of two electric circuits.

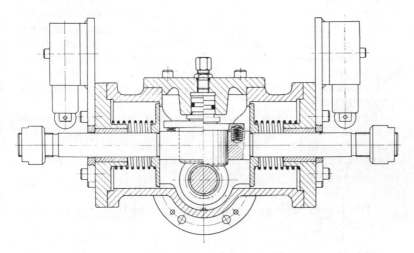

Figure 5.24 Rotation direction sensor

As mentioned previously, the safety of the machinery requires a number of supervision and alarm systems, when the engine is bridge controlled and the engine room staff are thus not constantly checking the well-being of the machinery. These systems include pneumatic, electric and also hydraulic components, some of the valves being brought together in special cabinets.

If the lubricating-oil pressure of the engine falls below a fixed limit, a switch-over valve cuts-off the signal air from *T3* to the governor and connects the actuator to a reducing valve in the impulse air system. This valve gives a fixed air pressure to the actuator, and the engine speed is thus reduced to the corresponding rev/min. A further reduction in lubricating-oil pressure to a lower, fixed value closes the electric circuit through *V30*, thus engaging the stop cylinder *SC*, which turns the regulating shaft of the fuel pumps to STOP position. Both the bridge console and the engine-room console have indicating lights for these procedures. The described systems for speed reduction and engine stopping can be immediately eliminated with a push button on the bridge console, if necessary for the safety of the ship.

When the engine is remotely started, the control lever can be brought directly to the required operational position. If this position corresponds to an engine load exceeding a certain fuel supply, the engine immediately accelerates to the speed given by this fixed-pump setting. The remaining acceleration, however, is directed by a 'load timing device'. At each start the oil in the container *OB* is pressed by impulse air (from *V14*) through a non-return valve to one side of the piston in cylinder *HC*. The piston rod is then pressed against an arm on the fuel regulating shaft, thus limiting the turning of this shaft. During the subsequent engine acceleration the oil in the cylinder *HC* is slowly pressed through the timing device *DA* back to the container *OB*, thus slowly increasing the turning angle of the regulating shaft.

The load increase period can in this way be set between 4 and 60 minutes. The timing device can be by-passed in emergencies by means of a push-button in the bridge console.

Among other functional disorders being automatically revealed the following can be mentioned:

Too low impulse air pressure—giving rise to alarm and speed reduction;

Too low starting-air pressure—giving rise to alarm and start blocking, which can, however, be immediately done away with in event of ship manoeuvring emergency;

Overload or overspeed—giving rise to alarm and engine stop respectively;

Wrong direction of rotation—giving alarm and stop;

Start failing—giving alarm.

A large number of further connections are available for optional input signals, for which alarm, speed reduction or engine stop is needed.

Emergency Control

For the unlikely event of a control system breakdown, a simple mechanical emergency device is placed on the engine. This comprises two levers, one for the switching-over of the starting-air distributor and another for starting and fuel regulation. The cylinder *SPC* is always in neutral position during hand-control, while *BK* works in the way previously described. The actuator of the speed governor is relieved, and consequently the governor endeavours to turn the fuel-regulating shaft to the maximum-speed position.

During local hand operation, the control lever MS at the bridge console is used as the engine telegraph and the given order is confirmed by means of a reply lever at the emergency control stand. After the lever OS has been brought to the required position, AHEAD or ASTERN, the control lever BS is moved to the left, thus actuating the impulse valve $V2$ for the starting-air supply. The lever is held in this position until a suitable engine speed is reached. The lever is then moved forward, which turns the fuel-regulating shaft to injection position. The valve $V2$ is simultaneously disengaged.

A.W.

Chapter 6

M.A.N. Engines

The main marine diesel engines built by M.A.N. are mostly single-acting two-stroke engines of crosshead design. Double-acting engines, which were formerly built by M.A.N. in considerable numbers, have gradually been superseded by supercharged single-acting crosshead engines. During the same period the medium-speed two-stroke trunk engines have been replaced by supercharged four-stroke engines.

These engines with cylinder diameters of up to 520 mm were mostly used as propulsion units for smaller vessels and as auxiliaries; but their range of output has been extended more and more by supercharging. During the last few years two special types, highly supercharged to 16–18 kgf/cm² (15·7–17·7 bar), with piston speeds of 7·8–8·0 m/s have been designed.

These medium-speed four-stroke engines have an output of 500 and 1000 hp (370 and 750 kW) per cylinder respectively at 400–430 rev/min. The engines are built both as in-line and as V engines. In the complete range extending from 6-cylinder in-line engines up to V engines having 18 cylinders, an output per unit is available of 3000 to 18 000 hp (2240 to 13 500 kW) suitable for all kinds of marine service, especially for vessels requiring low weight and low headroom for the propulsion plant. A twin-engine geared plant develops a shaft output up to 35 000 hp (26 000 kW), equalling the power of a 9-cylinder large-bore engine and approaching the maximum power possible for a normal propeller. With the development of suitable gear boxes, geared plant are feasible with three and four engines having an aggregate output up to 70 000 hp (52 000 kW), which may be required in the near future.

A description of these new four-stroke engines is given in the second part of the present chapter.

110

SINGLE-ACTING TWO-STROKE CROSSHEAD ENGINES

The development of this engine type has shown great progress since about 1950, leading to seven cylinder-sizes being standardised according to Table 6.1.

All of these engines are supercharged. Ratings without supercharging have been omitted, but they can be calculated on the basis of mep of 5·15 to 5·25 kgf/cm² (5·05 to 5·15 bar). The figures in the code of the types show respectively the cylinder diameter and the stroke in cm.

Until now the Type KZ70/120 has been the most commonly used engine for marine purposes. Within the last eighteen years M.A.N. and their licensees have built more than 800 engines of this type and size.

The steady demand of shipowners for high outputs without increase in bulk and weight, and for long running periods without inspections, overhauls or repairs resulted in certain alterations to the KZ-design and finally prompted the development of a new series of large marine diesel engines, termed KSZ, the dimensions of which are given in Table 6.1. The largest type, KSZ 105/180, was developed and tested in 1966/68, and three engines are now in service with twelve under construction.

The most important improvements incorporated in the KSZ-design are mentioned in the following description of the KZ-series.

Construction

The engines have the following constructional features. The engine foundation is a strong welded bedplate; the columns straddle the main bearings and carry—with a welded entablature in the middle—the cylinders, which are bolted together to form one block. The bedplate, columns, entablature and cylinders are connected by means of steel tie-rods, which relieve them of stresses caused by the firing pressures. Easy access to the crankcase is an important feature of the engines.

The crankcase is enclosed by easily removable covers. The cylinder liners are arranged in the cylinder block with adequate seals against cooling water, scavenging air and exhaust gas. The cylinder covers are bolted down to the liners through strong studs, which are anchored in the cylinder block.

Scavenging System

M.A.N. two-stroke engines are scavenged according to the loop-scavenging system. The exhaust ports are located above the scavenging ports on the same side of the liner, occupying approximately

Table 6.1 POWERS AND SPEEDS OF M.A.N. MARINE ENGINES, SINGLE-ACTING, TWO-STROKE CROSSHEAD TYPE

No.	Type	No. of cylinders	Rev/min	Output turbocharged (hp)	Output turbocharged (kW)	Max. cont. output hp/cyl.	Max. cont. output kW/cyl.	Max. m.e.p. kgf/cm²	Max. m.e.p. bar	Max. piston speed m/s
1	KZ57/80 F	5–12	187–225	3 750–10 800	2 800– 8 000	900	670	8·8	8·6	6·0
2	KZ60/105 E	5– 9	130–165	3 935– 9 000	2 900– 6 700	1 000	750	9·2	9·0	5·8
3	KZ70/120 E	5–10	130–150	6 500–14 000	4 900–10 500	1 400	1 050	9·75	9·6	6·0
4	KZ78/140	6– 8	100–130	4 700–13 200	3 500– 9 900	1 650	1 240	8·55	8·4	6·0
5	KZ78/155 F	5–10	105–122	8 170–19 000	6 000–14 000	1 900	1 400	9·45	9·3	6·3
6	KZ86/160 F	6–12	105–122	12 900–30 000	9 600–23 000	2 500	1 850	9·9	9·7	6·5
7	KZ93/170 E	6–12	100–115	14 300–33 000	10 600–24 000	2 750	2 000	9·3	9·1	6·5
8	KSZ70/125	6–10	130–140	8 910–16 000	6 600–11 900	1 600	1 190	10·7	10·5	5·8
9	KSZ78/155	6–10	110–122	11 370–21 000	8 500–15 600	2 100	1 560	10·45	10·3	6·3
10	KSZ90/160	6–10	105–122	14 940–29 000	11 000–22 000	2 900	2 200	10·5	10·3	6·5
11	KSZ105/180	6–12	90–106	20 400–48 000	15 200–36 000	4 000	3 000	10·9	10·7	6·4

Types 4 and 7 are now omitted.

Nos. 8–11: new types KSZ recently under development, with delivery as from 1970.

Nos. 3, 5, 6: production is gradually being discontinued as these engines will be replaced by Nos. 8, 9, 10 in the near future.

one-half of its circumference. The scavenging air is admitted through the scavenge ports, whence it passes across the piston crown and ascends along the opposite wall to the cylinder cover, where its flow is reversed. The air then descends along the wall in which the ports are located, expelling the exhaust gas into the exhaust pipe. The piston closes the scavenging ports and then, on its further upward travel, also closes the exhaust ports compressing the charge of pure air in the cylinder.

Engines built immediately after the war were equipped with rotary slide valves in the exhaust sockets, which close the exhaust ports as soon as the scavenging process is terminated. The weight of the air charge in the cylinder is thus increased, as no air can escape through the exhaust ports during the upward travel while the piston is closing the exhaust ports, i.e. the compression is already beginning with the closing of the scavenging ports and at a pressure which is close to the charging pressure. With supercharged engines the gain of air-weight is decreasing as the difference between scavenging and exhaust back pressure with relation to the charging pressure is decreasing more and more. Furthermore, for the three-cylinder groups having a crank-displacement of 120°, a strong pressure-wave in the exhaust line, emanating from the neighbouring cylinder, has almost the same effect as the rotary slide valve. So it was decided to abandon the exhaust slide-valve in all supercharged engines of recent design.

The earlier, non-supercharged, engines used the undersides of the main pistons as scavenging pumps together with a relatively small additional pump. With the introduction of supercharging, this small pump was soon abandoned but, in most units, piston undersides are still used as additional pumps, the number depending on the system and the degree of supercharging.

Figure 6.1 illustrates a two-stroke engine, of type and size KZ 57/80, which is supercharged according to the pulse series parallel system.

SUPERCHARGING

(a) Exhaust Arrangement

The principle of exhaust turbocharging is widely known and need not be described here. In the course of their development M.A.N. engines have been supplied with various systems of exhaust turbo-charging. The systems differ in the lead of the exhaust and charging-air pipe systems.

There are two possibilities on the exhaust side; the constant-pressure system and the impulse system. In the *constant-pressure*

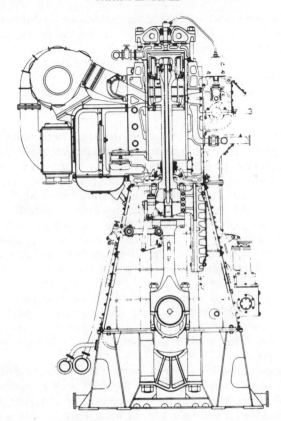

Figure 6.1   Two-stroke engine type KZ 57/80 supercharged on pulse series parallel system

system the exhaust gas is led to the turbine through an amply dimensioned manifold under a constant mean pressure, *see* Figure 6.2. In the *impulse system* the exhaust gas is led to the turbine through individual pipes of a small diameter, thus exploiting the kinetic energy of the exhaust gas, *see* Figures 6.1 and 6.3.

(b) Charging-air Arrangement

The charging-air side affords three possibilities, namely, the series system, the parallel system and, a combination of these, the series–parallel system. In the *series system*, Figure 6.4(a), the charging air supplied by the blowers is compressed further by the attached piston pumps. That is, with the M.A.N. engines the undersides of the main cylinders and a small additional pump, as mentioned before, are

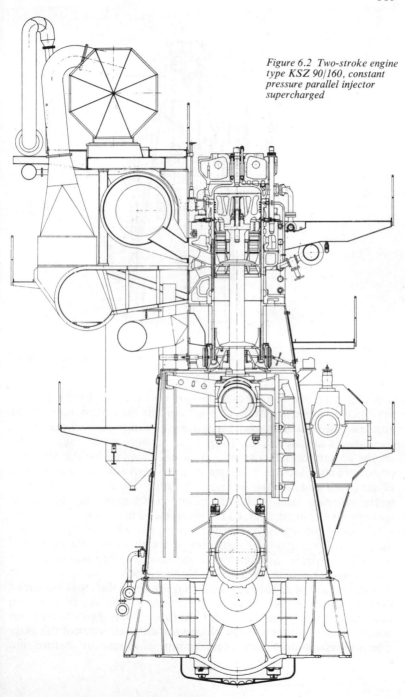

Figure 6.2 Two-stroke engine type KSZ 90/160, constant pressure parallel injector supercharged

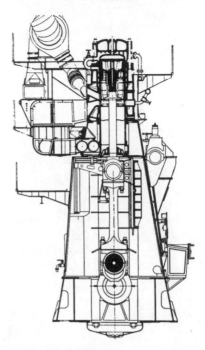

Figure 6.3   Two-stroke engine, KZ 93/170 type, supercharged according to pulse parallel system

used. The undersides of the cylinders are not sufficient, by themselves, for efficient supercharging. This system has the advantage that, in any case, the attached pump takes over the compression work which the blowers cannot deliver. Even if the blowers are failing, or if the engine is running DEAD SLOW, air is still supplied by the attached pumps. (This system is not used any more.) In the *parallel system* (Figures 6.3 and 6.4(b)) the blowers supply the charging air direct to the cylinders, part of the piston undersides supplying additional scavenging air, in parallel, to the blowers. With regard to the accessories and piping, this system is the simplest when compared with the others. But it requires turbochargers with a high efficiency and, sometimes, special auxiliaries to secure a reliable service in the whole service range down to DEAD SLOW.

A combination of the two systems is possible, thus making use of the advantages of both systems. This *series-parallel system* is shown in Figure 6.4(c) and in Figure 6.1. In this version the exhaust gases are led into a common manifold on the constant-pressure system. The blowers supply the charging air, through an intercooler,

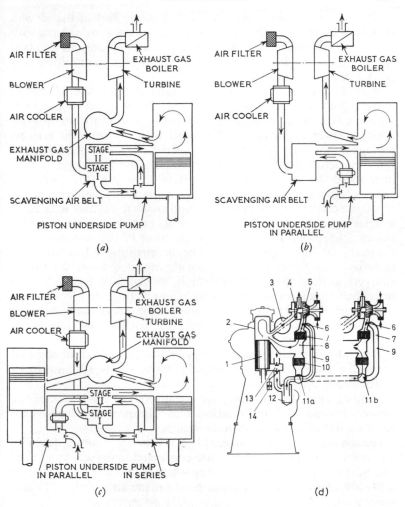

Figure 6.4 Pressure-charging systems

into the first stage of the charging-air belt. Approximately one-third of the piston undersides supply, in parallel, charging air from the atmosphere straight into the second stage of the charging-air belt. The remaining piston undersides draw the air supplied by the blowers from the first stage and supply it to the second stage of the charging-air belt; i.e. they operate in series. The partition wall between the 1st stage and the end stage of the scavenge air belt is provided with non-return valves which are closed until the pressure in the 1st stage exceeds that of the 2nd stage. Part of the air will then flow direct into the 2nd stage through by-pass valves, with the piston undersides connected in series serving only as a means for transporting the additional air without accomplishing any further compression work.

With the increase in the degree of supercharging the advantage of the pulse system, i.e. the higher turbine output, becomes increasingly smaller. The latest development therefore tends to the constant-pressure system, which is much simpler with regard to the exhaust piping and the arrangement of the turbochargers. To overcome the poor efficiency during starting and manoeuvring, M.A.N. have introduced the so-called injector system (Figure 6.4(d)), whereby some of the piston-undersides, which normally deliver the air through a cooler to the scavenging main are changed over to injector nozzles arranged in the delivery pipes of the blowers. The two-way valves operate automatically as a function of the scavenging air pressure, i.e. the engine load. The accelerating effect, and the quantity of compressed air passing the nozzles, assist the turbochargers, as their operating level can be moved away from the surge line. Thus enough air is available for manoeuvring and for part-load conditions. For full load, too, the operating point of the blower can be moved into the range of optimum efficiency, resulting in an improved air-delivery rate.

Depending on this effect, it is possible to shut-off all or some of the piston undersides by opening the delivery valves by means of hydraulically operated pistons.

In some units, the auxiliary air is delivered to the blades of the blowers instead of to the nozzles. This 'compressor-drive system' has a similar effect as the injector system.

In each system the air delivered by the blowers is cooled down by air-coolers of ample size, which are connected to the sea-water line. The heat transferred to the cooling water is about 65–90 kcal/bhp (364–504 kJ/kW). The resistance head for the air is about 125 mm water gauge.

The air delivered by the parallel bottom-sides is also cooled. As this air may have a light content of oil-mist, a vortex-type cleaner is located before the coolers. Such a cleaner is built for easy cleaning without the necessity of removing components.

(c) M.A.N. Turbochargers

Based on scientific research and on the successful results of many tests, M.A.N. developed turbochargers of their own design for all sizes of M.A.N. engines.

The engine builder as well as his client benefits if the turbochargers are designed and built in the workshops of the engine builder. Matching of the turbochargers for each engine type and for each system of supercharging is much easier; moreover, the responsibility for the blowers and the engine is undivided, which is very convenient for the customers.

The main features of the design are shown in Figure 6.5. There are plain bearings between the impeller and the turbine-wheel. Both

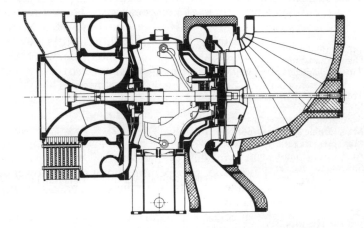

Figure 6.5 Turbocharger for two-stroke engines

wheels are of the overhung type, resulting in reduced length and in reduced rotating masses. A further advantage is that the nozzle-ring at the turbine-side and the diffuser at the blower-side can be changed very quickly, to meet differing specifications inside the standard types.

Lubrication is effected from the main engine oil-circuit or, on request, by an independent oil system. The bearing casings are water cooled. Turbine-disc and rotor shaft are in one piece. The turbine blades are welded to the turbine-disc.

For the larger types the exhaust gases are led axially through the turbine, i.e. from the inside to the outside, thus compensating for axial thrust and reducing the load on the axial bearing. Furthermore the bearings can be inspected and dismantled through openings in the casing without having to remove the rotor. Only the bearing casings are water cooled. The casings for exhaust gas inlet and outlet are not cooled but insulated. Thus the loss of heat and the danger of corrosion are avoided. Owing to the favourable curves of optimum efficiency, four fundamental types are sufficient for supercharging the whole range of two-stroke engines, from 2000 to 15 400 hp (1500 to 11 500 kW) per turbocharger. For the largest turbocharger the turbine output is about 3600 hp (2700 kW), its weight being about 5 tonne.

Table 6.2 gives the principal characteristics of a medium-size turbocharger, preferably for four-stroke engines, and of the largest type for two-stroke engines, representing a unit with an output of 3600 hp (2700 kW).

Table 6.2

	Middle size turbocharger type N 34	Largest turbocharger Z 1298
Length (max.) mm.	1 250	3 900
Height (max.) mm.	832	1 980
Outside diameter (max.) mm.	963/710 for the intake damper	1 800
Total weight, (kg)	550	5 400
Max. intake volume, m³/s (with pressure ratio = 2)	2·0	25·5
Max. turbine speed, rev/min	21 500	8 200
Max. pressure ratio	3·05	3·2
Admissible exhaust temp.	620°C	500°C
Suitable for max. engine output of (per set)	1 900 hp (1 400 kW)	15 400 hp (11 500 kW)

(d) Test Results

Figures 6.6(a) and 6.6(b) provide some test-results on the behaviour of two M.A.N. two-stroke engines, both supercharged according to the system: constant-pressure–parallel injector, *see* Figure 6.4(d).

Figure 6.6(a) shows the curves for the 6-cylinder engine of the Type K6Z 78/155F, based on the speed and load according to the propeller law. The rated output is attained with 122 rev/min and a mep of 9·45 kgf/cm² (9·27 bar).

Three bottom-sides are working in parallel; for slow speed they are switched over to two injector nozzles.

Figure 6.6(b) shows the test results of an 8-cylinder engine, Type KSZ 105/180, with the rated output of 32 000 hp, $\eta = 106$ rev/min, mep $= 10·9$ kgf/cm² (10·7 bar). As the capacity of the water brake did not allow higher load, the overload-tests were limited to 10 per cent, e.g. 35 200 hp (26 400 kW) with about 110 rev. According to the results of the experimental engine a maximum output of over 40 000 hp (30 000 kW) would be possible.

The diagram shows also the range where the four bottom-sides are switched over from injector to parallel operation.

In the following pages the characteristic features of the different

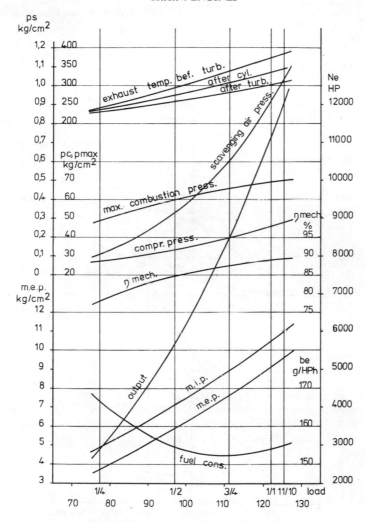

Figure 6.6(a) Test results of K6Z 78/155 engine

engine types are given. The many common features have been
described earlier in the chapter.

PARTICULARS OF DESIGN

The crankshaft is of the semi-built type, i.e. each throw is either
individually forged or made from cast steel, the journals being

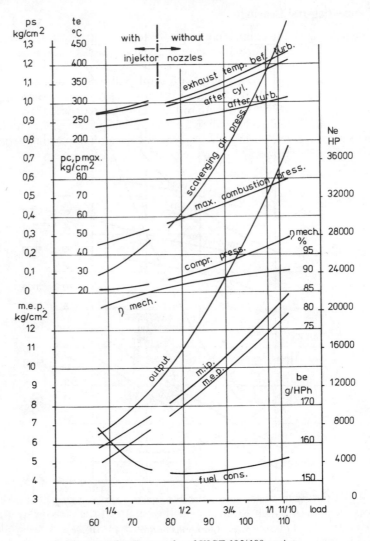

Figure 6.6(b) Test results of K8SZ 105/180 engine

shrink-fitted. The crankshaft of the KZ57/80 engine is forged in one piece. Unless a separate thrust bearing is mounted, the aft journal carries a flange which transmits the thrust to the thrust bearing mounted direct on the engine.

Connecting-rod Bearings

The top-end of the connecting rod is forked and carries two bearings for the crosshead. Particular care is given to the lubrication of the crosshead bearings because no pressure reversal occurs in two-stroke engines. A special lubricating oil pump is attached to the crosshead, or to the upper part of the connecting rod. The angular movement between connecting rod and crosshead drives, through a linkage, the two plungers which force the oil into the bearings under high pressure, i.e. during the lower half of the piston-stroke, when the load is a minimum, *see* Figure 6.7.

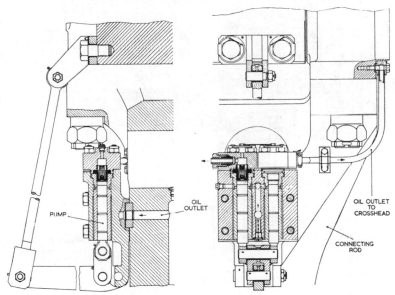

Figure 6.7 Crosshead oil pump

The crosshead bearings of the KSZ-types consist of a shell, the bottom part of which extends over the length of the crosshead, the two upper parts being arranged on each side of the crosshead body (*see* Figure 6.8). The advantages are:

The shell is lined with a thin layer of white metal which has a higher fatigue limit than a thicker one; Maintenance is easier, because only the shell has to be replaced; The bottom-side of the shell has an increased bearing surface. As the throttling distance from the oil supply to the bearing ends is much longer, the oil cushion effect is improved, i.e. the thickness of the oil-film is increased, especially in the middle with the highest bearing load.

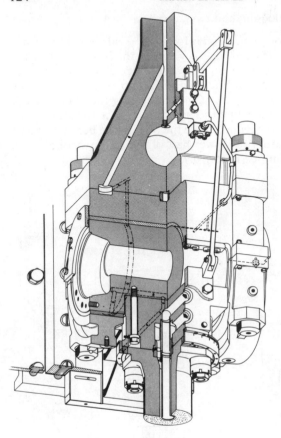

Figure 6.8 New crosshead design, KSZ type

Furthermore the pressure pump is modified, so that each plunger has its own drive and also its separate circuit, leading into separate grooves on both sides. Thus a higher degree of reliability is attained, because if one pump fails the lubrication of the whole bearing is ensured. The bottom-end bearings are also provided with thin bearing shells. In the main bearing the dovetailed grooves, formerly used, which were sometimes the cause of fatigue cracks in the white metal lining, have been omitted.

Pistons

The piston, Figure 6.9, consists of the piston crown, made of cast steel with molybdenum content, and the cast-iron piston-skirt. For cylinder diameters 700 mm, and over, a special cast-iron guide ring is inserted between the crown and the skirt. Both cast-iron parts are equipped with slide-rings of lead bronze. The piston crown has five or six piston rings of standard design, the ring-grooves being flame-hardened to reduce the wear to a minimum.

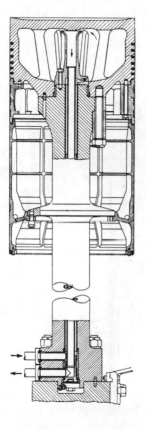

Figure 6.9 Piston and piston rod

All two-stroke engines now have water-cooled pistons. Telescopic pipes are arranged inside the crankcase in a recess of the columns. Tightened by special glands they plunge into large dashpots, thus avoiding 'water-hammer' in the piston-cooling system. A small compressor attached to the engine, or arranged separately, continuously maintains an air cushion in the air vessels. The telescopic pipes are fastened to a bracket bolted to the crosshead. The cooling arrangement and the path of the water through the rifle-bored piston rod to the piston and back to the outlet is shown in Figures 6.9 and

6.10. The piston-cooling pressure is $2\cdot5$–$3\cdot5$ kgf/cm^2 ($2\cdot4$–$3\cdot4$ bar), depending on the size, speed and loading of the engine.

Up to 1965, the smaller types KZ57/80 and KZ60/105 had oil-cooled pistons. Link pipes led the oil to the crosshead from where it passed to the rifle-bored piston-rod and the piston crown. For the KSZ-types the higher mep made it essential to reduce the temperatures as well as the mechanical and thermal stresses in the piston crown. The conflicting requirements were reconciled after careful research work led to the following techniques, *see* Figure 6.11.

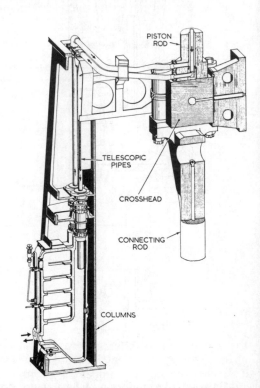

Figure 6.10 Piston cooling arrangement

The wall thickness of the piston crown has been reduced and to compensate for its reduced strength a double row of supporting ribs is arranged. These are made as long as possible so that they can follow the thermal expansion of the piston without undue stresses. The improved cooling effect is manifested by the low temperatures of the piston crown and especially of the ring grooves. Figure 6.11 shows the piston crown of the experimental engine KSZ102/180, the temperatures being measured at full load.

Because of higher cooling water and lubricating oil pressure, droplets of oil or water might pass the opening in the column where the bracket for the telescopic pipes moves up and down. The openings are closed now during the whole stroke by a sliding shield made of ferrocell. The complete separation of the gland-space made it possible to simplify these glands. The cuffs formerly used are replaced by simple rings made of special plastics, water lubrication ensuring a long operational life. In addition, it was possible to alter their arrangement so that the glands can now be overhauled and replaced without removing the telescopic pipes.

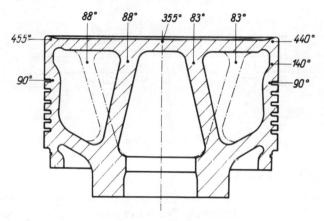

Figure 6.11 Piston crown of experimental engine, KSZ 102/180

Piston Rod Gland

Figure 6.12 shows the piston rod scraper box, which separates the underpiston space from the crankcase. The scraper box has three distinct functions. The upper part, with one scraper ring, prevents sludge and dirty oil from passing into the crankcase. Leakage is drained away outside, through the pipe indicated.

Two gas-tight rings seal against the scavenge-air pressure in the underside space.

The next four scraper rings prevent crankcase oil from passing upwards with the movement of the piston rod. These rings are drained to the crankcase through the holes marked. The scraper rings are double-edged and made in three or four segments, tightened inwards by garter springs.

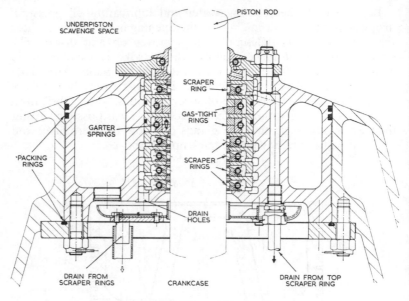

Figure 6.12 Piston rod scraper box

Cylinder Liners and Covers

The cylinder liners, with the exhaust and scavenging ports, are
arranged in the cylinder block. The water space is sealed by means of
a stuffing-box, with a leakage groove underneath. In event of leakage
the water is visibly discharged through the groove. The liners are
made of a special alloyed cast iron, the wearing properties of which
have been proved over many years.

Figure 6.13 shows a cylinder liner and jacket in section.

In the middle of the cylinder, at the manoeuvring side, an inspection hole is provided through which the pistons can be inspected
when the engine is shut down. The inspection hole allows cleaning
of the exhaust ports when the piston is at bottom dead-centre, by a
special tool which is combined with a kind of soot-blower.

For smaller types the liner is one-piece, inserted from the top of
the cylinder block. The larger types have mostly two-part liners, the
lower part being inserted from the bottom-side of the cylinder block
and fastened to it by a flange. A one-piece liner design is used, sometimes, also for the larger engine types. Both designs have their
advantages as regards manufacturing and servicing of the engine.

When going over to high-supercharge for their two-stroke engines,
M.A.N. introduced an effective cooling of the 'lands' between the

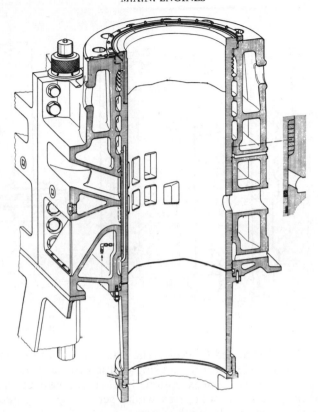

Figure 6.13 Cylinder liner and jacket

exhaust ports, *see* Figure 6.13. For this purpose, special cooling-water pipes are cast into these 'lands' by a method which was developed after extended trials. The cooling of the liner flange has also been improved, *see* Figure 6.14. In the latest design a deep groove is cut into the flange and a two-part steel ring is shrunk into the groove. Cooling water passes at high velocity through the annular space. The design also includes a cast-steel backing ring arranged between the liner flange and the upper edge of the cylinder block. This ring is fitted to the liner in such a manner that the thermal expansion of its upper part causes a shrink-fit, thus reducing the tangential stresses in the liner itself.

The cylinder covers consist of two parts. The lower part, made of cast steel, carries the openings for the fuel valve, arranged vertically in the centre, and those for the starting- and relief-valve and the

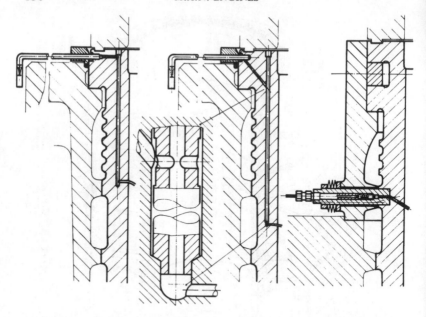

Figure 6.14 Development of upper part of cylinder and of cylinder lubrication

indicator cock, arranged laterally. The thin-walled bottom ensures effective heat transfer without causing undue thermal stresses. The upper part of the cover is an exceptionally stiff casting which supports the bottom-part by circular ribs which serve also as guides for positive circulation of the cooling water.

FUEL-INJECTION SYSTEM

Fuel-pump Design

Since 1956 all single-acting two-stroke engines have had fuel pumps with helical control edges, as shown in Figure 6.15.

In this design the quantity of fuel injected is regulated by turning the pump plunger. Two helical grooves arranged opposite each other are provided in the top of the plunger, one of which passes the suction hole during the upward travel—thus regulating the quantity of fuel injected—the other one serving for pressure compensation. The grooves are connected with the delivery space through drilled passages in the plunger.

Because of the heavy fuel service, the suction space 5 has, in its upper part, the special connection shown at 6 for continual venting and rinsing of the pumps.

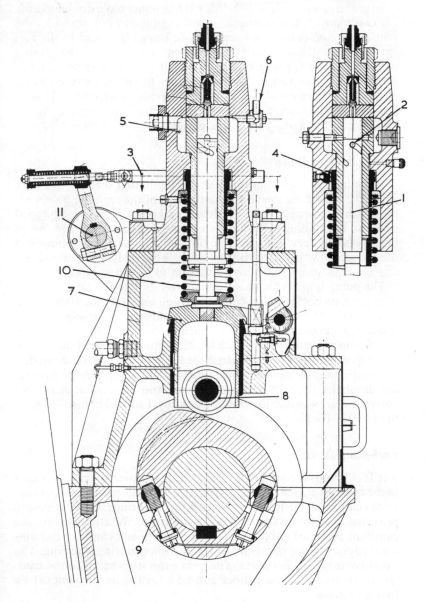

Figure 6.15 Fuel-injection pump

In the largest type, KSZ105/180, each cylinder has a double-pump, i.e. two plungers are arranged in one casing and are driven by the reinforced cam-drive. Two separate delivery pipes lead to the fuel valve. The control-racks are displaced in such a manner that during part-load only one plunger delivers fuel, the second one being out of action. The main purpose of the design is to ensure exact metering of the fuel during part-load. For this purpose the second fuel-line is provided with a non-return valve near the fuel valve separating the two injection-systems during this period.

Setting the Fuel Pump

The quantity of fuel is set through the regulating shaft 11, the rack 3 and the regulating sleeve 4. The top end of the regulating sleeve is located in the casing proper. The lower part of the plunger is equipped with two lugs sliding in the axial slots of the regulating sleeve. When the regulating sleeve is turned the position of the control groove 2 in the plunger 1 with regard to the suction hole is changed, allowing a stepless regulation from zero admission to full admission.

The pump is in correct position with relation to the cam when the plunger in its bottom dead-centre position uncovers the 10-mm-dia. suction-hole by only 8 mm. The zero admission is already attained when the regulating rack is put on mark 2, and this should be observed when connecting the pumps with the regulating shaft, see Figure 6.16.

Ignition control is not required for these pumps, as for the earlier spill-valve pumps, because the beginning of the injection is advancing automatically with increased speed and admission. A further correction is possible, in special cases, by a helical control-edge of the plunger itself.

Fuel-pump Drive

The fuel pumps are actuated by the camshaft over rollers 8, located in the cylindrical guide 7. The upward travel of the plunger is operated by the cam, and the downward travel by the spring 10. Two cams are provided, one for AHEAD and one for ASTERN. When reversing, the camshaft is shifted axially, and as the rollers and cams have chamfered edges, it is not necessary to lift the rollers during reversing. The cams are made in two parts. The cam support is keyed to the camshaft, whereas the cam proper can be adjusted on the support by two set-screws 9.

Basic adjustment of the pumps as regards injection point is determined by the position of the cam and is measured by the lift of the plunger when the main piston is in its top dead-centre position.

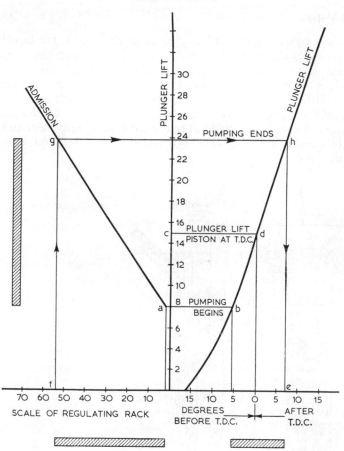

Figure 6.16 Fuel-pump delivery

For the smaller type KZ57/80, shown in Figure 6.1, the camshaft is arranged near the upper edge of the cylinder block and extends over the length of the engine. Each pump is located in front of its cylinder. The camshaft drive is through a roller chain from the crankshaft.

With the larger types, the fuel pumps are mounted in two casings arranged at about mid-level of the engine. Each casing has a short camshaft, and their common drive is through a gear train from a flange wheel of the crankshaft.

Fuel Valves

As will be seen in Figure 6.17, the valves are designed as needle valves, consisting of the needle 1 with the guide 2 into which the needle is lapped, easily movable, but giving a seal against high pressure. The nozzle 3, with the 0·4–0·9 mm orifices, is fitted against the needle guide with a polished even face. The needle lift is limited by the intermediate plate 4 through which an extension of the needle projects. All parts are made of hardened high-quality steel and are rigidly connected to the valve body and sealed against high pressure by the nut 6.

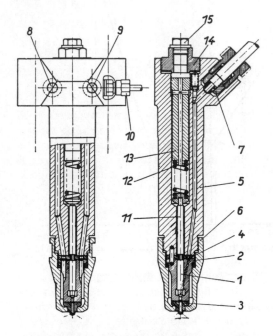

Figure 6.17 Fuel valves

The valve is set to a blow-off pressure of 220–250 kgf/cm² (215–245 bar), by adjusting the spring 12 by means of the thrust bolt 13. The fuel is admitted through the delivery pipe 7. Fuel leaking along the needle is led through the passage in the thrust bolt 13 into the leakage fuel-discharge pipe 10.

The holes 8 and 9 represent the admission and discharge connections for the nozzle coolant. In most of the cases water is used as the coolant. The holes lead the coolant through the guide down to and around the nozzle itself. For heavy fuel operation, intensive cooling is of great importance to avoid carbonisation of the nozzle tips and clogging of the nozzle holes. Fresh water cooling is, therefore, specified for heavy fuel service, and it is recommended to install an independent circuit with pumps, tank and cooler. An anti-corrosive oil should be added to the water. At least 0·90 kg/kWh should pass through the nozzles; the temperature difference should be not more than 3–4°C; and the maximum temperature not higher than 45°C.

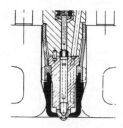

Figure 6.18 Fuel valve needle guide

In the KSZ-engines the fuel valve has been improved with particular regard to the needle guide, Figure 6.18. Needle guide and nozzle are now a single piece, both parts being welded together by electron-beam. Thus the seat can be arranged in the nozzle itself, and fuel quantity trapped between seat and nozzle-bores, which is sometimes liable to coking, is much smaller than before.

Governor with Servomotor

The standard governor, Figure 6.19, used for many years, acts as overspeed governor, i.e. it enters into action only when the service speed is exceeded by 5–10 per cent, which may happen in a heavy sea or by a failure of the shafting. The governor is horizontally positioned before the fuel-pump drive and driven through an inter-mediate wheel, gear-wheel 1, and a flexible coupling 3. The levers of the fly-weights engage with a cross key 4 on the governor spindle 5. The spring-loaded sleeve 6 acts on the governor spindle through a ball bearing. The sleeve 6 moves a bell crank by means of the bolt 7 protruding laterally. The slide valve of the servomotor 9 is controlled by the bell crank. The tension of the springs in the governor sleeve can be altered from the outside by means of a hand-wheel, thus setting the speed at which the governor will enter into action.

All rotating parts are provided with ball bearings. The governor is lubricated through the spray pipe 10 protruding into the governor spindle. The small buffer-spring 11 is provided to dampen governor action during sudden load-changes. Adjustment by means of the

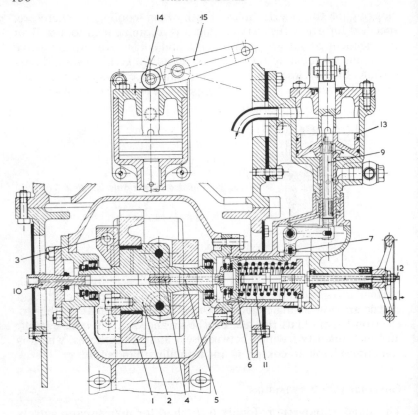

Figure 6.19 Governor and servomotor

threaded spindle 12 is determined by the measure *a*, which is entered
under the adjusting data annexed to the operating manual. It must
not be altered without ensuring that the governor will attain the
zero-admission point. The force of the fly-weights is not sufficient
to shift the regulating rods. The governor is therefore connected to
an oil-pressure controlled servomotor, operating as described below.

The power piston 13, of the servomotor, moves towards zero
admission under oil pressure. Movement towards full admission is
under the force of the spring inserted into the regulation linkage, *see*
Figure 6.22. Between the control-edges of the slide-valve 9 and those
of the power piston 13 the oil-flow is controlled in such a manner
that the piston must follow exactly the movement of the slide valve,
i.e. the governor spindle. This movement is transmitted to the
regulation shaft of the fuel pumps by the roller 14 and the lever 15.

The oil-pressure for the servomotor should be 3·0–3·5 kgf/cm² (2·9–3·4 bar); the connection is to be branched-off from the delivery pipe of the lubricating oil pump before the filter and the cooler. A special filter is provided directly before the servomotor.

Because of the higher requirements and the introduction of remote control, M.A.N. now use Woodward governors for all higher-output engines. This special design has many advantages, namely:

(1) by reason of the higher speed—about 800 rev/min— the governor is highly sensitive and responds instantly;

(2) the servomotor is built-in;

(3) the main characteristics, such as speed and speed-drop, can be easily adjusted;

(4) it permits admission control, as well as speed control, over a wide range;

(5) with supercharged engines it may be provided with an admission limit, depending on the supercharging pressure, thus avoiding overloading in event of insufficient scavenging air.

The Woodward governor is arranged vertically at the same place as where the safety governor used to be installed. It is driven from the camshaft-drive with a gear-ratio of nearly 8:1. For the largest engines, where its servomotor is not sufficient, the output-lever is connected to a special servomotor, arranged in a control-unit, where the admission controls and all automatic shut-off devices are assembled. To ensure high output-torque and quick action a high oil pressure of about 18 kgf/cm² (17·6 bar) is delivered to the servomotor by two separate gear-pumps, one pump being a stand-by.

Starting Valves and Pilot Valves

Part of the starting air is branched off and led through pilot valves to the starting valves, which are opened by this control air, *see* Figure 6.20. The valve cone 6 of the starting valve opens towards the inside of the cylinder, i.e. the starting valve remains closed until the pressure inside the cylinder is overcome by the pressure of the control air. The piston 2 is seated loosely on the extended spindle 1. The control air is admitted to the piston 2. The valve is kept closed by the spring 3.

The pilot valves 4 are located by the side of the fuel pumps and actuated by 'negative' cams 5. When starting air is admitted to the engine through the main starting valve the control slide valve—the roller of which faces the negative side of the cam—is opened. The control air is led to the control piston and opens the starting valve

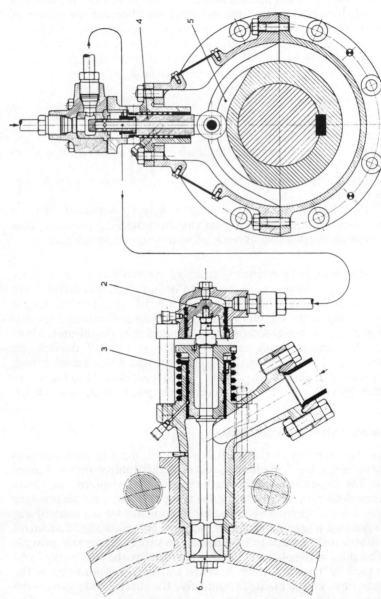

Figure 6.20 Starting valve and pilot valve

of the appropriate cylinder. The crankshaft turns, roller and piston of the pilot valve are pushed upward by the cam, the control air is cut off, the connecting pipe leading from the pilot valve to the starting valve is vented and the starting valve in the cylinder is closed.

Relief Valves

The relief valves, Figure 6.21, open when the pressure in the cylinder exceeds the maximum admissible limit. They are set to a blow-off pressure of up to 10 kgf/cm² (9·8 bar) above the highest admissible firing pressure. The valve spindle is pressed to its seat by the spring.

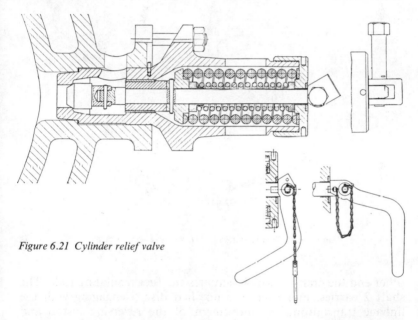

Figure 6.21 Cylinder relief valve

The valve spindle is guided in such a way that the escaping exhaust gas flows out sideways without touching the valve spring. The figure also shows a device for opening the valve by hand. This is necessary when repair work is being done in the crankcase, to ensure the safety of men, and when the cylinders must be blown-out by starting air after a long shutdown. For remote control, this device can be replaced by small pistons operated by compressed air.

MANOEUVRING AND REVERSING GEAR

Up to the introduction of remote control almost all two-stroke engines were equipped with a standard-type manoeuvring gear having a handwheel controlling reversing, starting and fuel regulation, *see* Figure 6.22. The hand-wheel 1 is attached to a camshaft 2 which controls three valves I, II and III. The shaft 2 carries on the

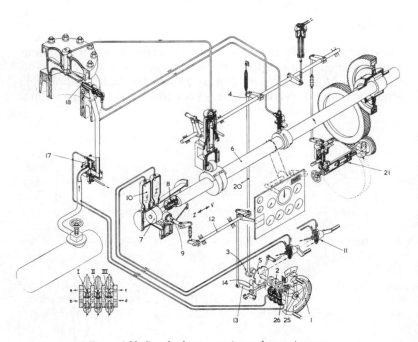

Figure 6.22 Standard manoeuvring and reversing gear

other end the crank 3, which actuates the fuel-regulating rods. The shaft 2 carries, moreover, the notched disc 5 engaging with the linkage transmitting the movement of the reversing piston and blocking the hand-wheel. The individual manoeuvres are described in the following paragraphs.

Reversing

Reversing is performed by simply shifting the camshaft 6, which carries AHEAD and ASTERN fuel and starting-cams, in axial direction. The fuel-pump rollers need not be lifted for this purpose. The camshaft is shifted by means of the piston 7, which is connected with the camshaft through the dog 8. The piston is actuated by oil pressure. To retain the piston in one of its end positions it is provided with the lever 9, which, by means of a spring, locks the piston in one of the two end positions. The pressure oil actuating the reversing cylinder is stored in the two vessels 10, to which starting air is admitted alternately. This process is controlled by the valve I.

Only one control valve being available for reversing, a change-over cock 11 is required to determine the sense of rotation, i.e. depending on the position of the cock, starting air is admitted either to the AHEAD or to the ASTERN vessel. The lever of the change-over cock has two positions, AHEAD and ASTERN, which are marked accordingly. The space on the one side of the reversing piston is vented while air is admitted to the space on the other side, and *vice versa*, through the change-over cock. In order to be able to reverse the engine without compressed air the shaft of lever 9 has a toothed segment engaging with a gear-wheel, which can be operated by hand.

If the engine is started in the same direction as it ran prior to shutting down, the change-over cock must not be actuated. Although the control valve I is opened when the hand-wheel 1 is turned, the camshaft is not shifted.

An interlocking device prevents starting air from being admitted to the cylinders before the reversing process is terminated, which might happen when the hand-wheel is turned too quickly beyond the reversing range. The interlocking device consists of a linkage transmitting the movement of the reversing piston to the hand-wheel, which is blocked until the reversing process is terminated. Linked to the lever 9 is a lever shaft 12 which also actuates the pointer which indicates the position of the reversing gear and the interlocking lever 13 carrying the stop 14.

Starting

After the termination of the reversing process, and when the hand-wheel is released, the wheel is turned further, to starting. The control valve III is opened and simultaneously the valve II closed. The space above the main starting valve 17 is vented so that it can open and the starting air be admitted to the starting valves 18 in the cylinder covers and the starting-air pilot valves.

It is important that the valves II and III are not actuated when the hand-wheel is turned towards STOP. The two cams have a loose fit on the shaft 2 connected only by a pin. At the end of the starting range the dog 26 forces the cam-support to move in axial direction out of the range of the pin. Thus the cams return into the stop-position under the effect of the auxiliary starting lever 25. Only when the hand-wheel and the camshaft return to stop-position are the cams coupled with the shaft again.

Fuel Regulation

During the second half of the starting period the fuel-regulating rods 20 are actuated by the crank 3 on the end of the shaft 2, through lever 4 so that fuel is admitted to the cylinders simultaneously with the starting air. When turning the hand-wheel further, air is admitted to the control line of the main starting valve, thus closing the valve.

The governor 21 enters into action only when the speed limit to which the governor is set is exceeded by 10 per cent. Usually there is a clearance between the roller and the contact piece of the power piston so that the fuel regulation linkage is free in the whole range of admission.

REMOTE CONTROL AND AUTOMATION

In course of the general automation of large marine diesel engines, the operation of the main machinery by remote control has been introduced more and more. In its most simple form this can be achieved by providing a separate manoeuvring stand beside, or in front of, the engine. Mostly, this stand is widened to become a large desk or console, comprising all the instruments needed for manoeuvring and servicing the main and auxiliary engines, together with all measuring instruments.

In these first equipments the standard manoeuvring hand-wheel, with the valves I to III (Figure 6.22), was installed into this desk, the pneumatic control of starting and reversing being led by pipes to the engine. With a short distance between the desk and the main engine there is no difficulty in designing a mechanical transmission to the fuel-regulating shaft, also the blocking device for the reversing gear and, if necessary, for the adjustment gear of the governor.

The further development of automation requires remote control from any place of the engine room or a special control room and, in many instances, from the bridge. Further progress has been full automation, with the intention of relieving the engineers, and especially the men on the bridge, from paying any attention to levers, instruments, etc. Therefore a special kind of engine telegraph receives the orders and sets off a sequence of individual operations which are run-off according to a programme.

With such installations the handwheel is turned according to the orders of the telegraph by an electropneumatic or an electro-hydraulic gear, some further controls or blocking devices being operated pneumatically or electrically. In most cases a manoeuvring stand at the engine is retained, to permit direct operation of the engine in event of emergency.

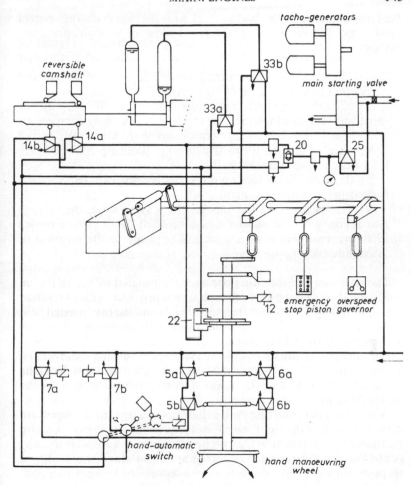

Figure 6.23 Schematic manoeuvring system, with function units of remote control

Because many different systems of remote control and the development of complete automation schemes are normally in the hands of the shipyard or specialised firms, the engine builder must aim at a manoeuvring gear which is most simple and which can be connected to any scheme without the need for extensive alterations. M.A.N. have designed such a universal manoeuvring system for their large marine diesel engines. As the schematic drawing (Figure 6.23) shows, the fundamental elements of the M.A.N. manoeuvring gear are retained, namely, the hand-wheel with the camshaft, the control valves and the reversing gear. The following modifications are embodied:

(1) The hand-wheel is turned anti-clockwise for AHEAD and clockwise for ASTERN. *The change-over cock is omitted.*

(2) All other elements are controlled by small two-way, or three-way, valves which are—or can be—operated by compressed air. These valves are so interconnected that, when turning the hand-wheel, the operations Reversing, Blocking and Starting follow each other automatically.

(3) Resulting from this method, the scheme can also be used for pneumatic remote control.

(4) The whole system is blocked by a valve when the turning gear is engaged. The hand-wheel is blocked by an electric device 12 to prevent turning in a direction opposite to the position of the engine telegraph.

The reversing and starting processes are initiated by the valves 5a, 6a, 5b, 6b. For safety purposes each way is provided with two valves arranged in series. Between the valve-heads and the cams, small bell-cranks are fitted which operate the valves only in one direction. Air is then led to the valves 33a or 33b respectively for the reversing piston, and also to the valves 14a or 14b respectively for the reversing control. As soon as the reversing gear is in its end position, blocking valve 22 is released and the main starting valve is opened by the valves 20 and 25.

After the main starting valve has opened the next important operation is to stop the flow of starting air at the right moment. Normally the starting air is shut off by a tachometer and an electrically controlled air valve, when the engine has attained about 20–30 rev/min. Furthermore, there is a time-controlled valve which ends the starting process after some seconds, i.e. if the engine fails to start. After some time the device repeats the starting automatically, then also a third time. After that no further starting is initiated, but an alarm is given to the control room and to the bridge.

In the present remote control system the hand-wheel is disengaged during remote automatic control and turned into position 'automatic'. With a small lever the system is changed over to 'automatic' whereby the valves 5 and 6 (Figure 6.23) are cut out and their function replaced by two electrically operated solenoid-valves 7a and 7b. Simultaneously the handwheel is blocked in its 'automatic' position indicated by a signal-light. When the telegraph (e.g. on the bridge) has excited the valve for the direction required, all the following sequences for reversing, starting, and the necessary control-devices are controlled by a series of pneumatic switching valves. The starting procedure is controlled in the same manner as described before. Admission or speed, respectively, are prescribed by the telegraph and transferred to the so-called actuator which is arranged within the fuel admission unit.

Normally, admission is regulated over the speed prescribed; in the upper speed range, it is possible also to switch over the pure admission control. Then the Woodward-governor preserves only a certain speed limit. The first method is preferable for low engine speeds or when the ship is operated in a high sea, because, with fixed admission the influence of sea, propeller and blowers may cause inadmissible speed drift. For normal service fixed admission has some advantages. The regulating gear does not have to compensate for smaller influences (e.g. of the swell) and, should one cylinder fail, the other cylinders are not overloaded because the speed drop shows that there is a fault condition. The complete system incorporates some additional pneumatic controls or blocking devices which cannot be specified here.

About the further elements for the automation of a large diesel plant the following remarks are relevant:

(a) Before starting, it is necessary to control all preparations. A special check shows if the pumps for lubrication, cooling and fuel are running, and the valves are in the correct position; also if the starting air vessels are filled. If anything is not in order the starting is blocked and an alarm is given, indicating the place of failure.

(b) Naturally these controls also operate during service, with the effect that in the event of failure of a pump the standby pump is automatically put into service. In some cases the engine load is reduced, or the engine is stopped.

(c) When switching over from one control-stand to another, special blocking and indicating devices must ensure that no control-stand can interfere with the other, also that switching-over is possible within the shortest time and without faults.

(d) As reduction of the personnel and the increasing of relia-bility is the main purpose of automation, the complete control of the main and auxiliary engines, the electric plant and part of the ship's services is to be placed in one room. The supervision of 100–250 instruments and of many alarms would mean a heavy burden; therefore automatic supervisory systems are a great help. These logging plants print all measured values at predetermined time intervals, indicating the date and the hour. If limit values—

which are set in advance—are exceeded, an alarm is given immediately and the item concerned is printed in red.

Because experience has shown that it is hardly possible to check the long tapes with all measuring results later, data-logging is mostly limited to printing out the point and duration of an alarm.

A similar automatic writer is provided to take down all orders coming from the bridge, also the order confirmations. Thus a complete log-book for the ship and the machinery is recorded for the whole voyage, giving a valuable means of control for the staff and the owners' superintendent.

The most difficult manoeuvre to be performed by the remote control gear is the so-called *crash stop*. Owing to the high kinetic energy of large ships in loaded condition, the ship's speed decreases but slowly. Accordingly, the drift tends to turn the propeller in the ahead direction. A high torque results, offering strong resistance to starting the engine in the astern direction.

When the telegraph is put to *full astern* reversing and starting of the engine are controlled by a tachometer which delays the programme until the engine is slowed-down to about 35 rev/min. During trials the successive steps must be programmed to agree with the type of engine and ship. Moreover, a special alarm signal should be given to the watch-keeper in the engine or control room, so that he can take over should the need arise.

HEAVY FUEL EQUIPMENT

Almost all marine diesel engines are provided with special equipment for the use of heavy fuel, which is conditioned and led to the engine at a certain temperature. Apart from a slight increase in the clearance of the fuel-pump plunger and injection-valve needle, the diesel oil injection elements can be used for heavy oil without change.

Heavy-fuel equipment has now become standard and its particulars are described in the earlier edition of this book. The most important development necessary during the last years was to adapt the fuel system to full automation, i.e. to unattended operation. Consequently pressure, temperature and viscosity of the fuel must be controlled automatically by a suitable monitoring system. In the same manner cleaning plant such as separators, heaters and filters are automated. By the permanent control of the whole fuel system much better conditions are ensured for using heavy fuel during manoeuvring. Following some further improvements and preliminary tests, all M.A.N. two-stroke engines can now be started and manoeuvred on heavy fuel if required.

CYLINDER LUBRICATION

With the introduction of heavy fuel for use in internal-combustion engines, special attention had to be paid to cylinder lubrication. Extensive investigations during the pre-war decade revealed that corrosion caused by the acids which were produced in the combustion process was of greater consequence than the wear of liners, piston rings and ring grooves due to abrasion. The new knowledge led to the development of special alloys for liners and piston rings which were able to withstand the corrosive effect of acids and, even more important, to the development of lubricating oils capable of counteracting acidic deposits by a very high neutralising effect. The two new products—but in particular the latter—brought down the liner and piston-ring wear to values which formerly could be expected only when using a good-grade diesel oil. Today it should not be forgotten that correct cylinder lubrication does not merely serve the purpose of providing an oil film between the liner and the piston ring, but it is also responsible for the neutralising of harmful acids which tend to condense on the cylinder walls. Consequently, the quantity of cylinder oil required does not depend solely upon the surface to be lubricated per second but also upon the quantity of fuel burned in the cylinder and, moreover, upon its sulphur content. In other words, the total consumption of cylinder lubricating oil must be increased approximately in proportion to the bhp developed per hour, because the larger quantity of fuel consumed implies a larger amount of sulphur to be neutralised.

Even distribution of the lubricating oil over the cylinder walls is also of importance. M.A.N. have therefore increased the number of feeding points to 8 for each cylinder of 700 mm and 780 mm bore, and to 10 or 12 for the larger cylinder diameters. For the large-stroke engines 2 or 4 additional feed points are arranged underneath the ports. The oil is led to the liners through connections fitted into the liner flange, whence it flows downwards through axially drilled holes in the liner wall to the feeding points. Care has been taken to place the feeding holes closer to the cooled outside of the liner, *see* Figure 6.13.

A design somewhat more effective, introduced for the KSZ-types, is shown at Figure 6.14. There is only a short distance between the non-return valves and the oil outlet, thus the danger of blow-back or formation of air bubbles or overheating is reduced considerably and the exactness of lubrication ensured.

The mean indicated pressure of highly supercharged two-stroke engines running under the varying requirements of sea service can range from 2 up to 12 kgf/cm² (say 1·95–11·77 bar). With the common constant-rate adjustment of the lubricators, the supplied oil quantity is only proportional to the speed of the engine, whereas the mip increases with the square of the speed, *see* Figure 6.24. To

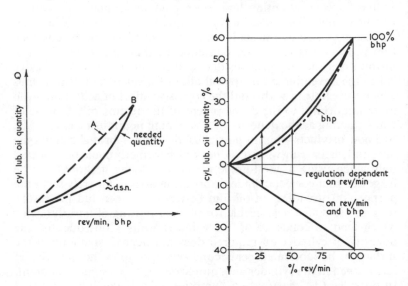

Figure 6.24 Regulation of cylinder lubrication

avoid excessive lubrication of the cylinders at reduced load, M.A.N. developed a variable adjustment of the lubricators, controlled by the fuel admission control. This gear is outlined in Figure 6.25. The crank of the lubricator is driven by the indicator linkage, through the rod and lever. These two parts are connected by the sleeve shown, which is shifted on the extension of the lever by means of the linkage illustrated. The angular movement of the lubricator crank is thus adjusted according to the load approximately following the curve in Figure 6.24. In the near future this regulating mechanism will be incorporated into the lubricator. The lubricating oil consumption for cylinders only, is roughly 0·8 g/kWh.

ENGINE OPERATION

Irregularities

After extended shut-down the engine must be checked and turned by means of the turning gear, all indicator cocks and relief valves in the cylinders being kept open and the hand-wheel on the manoeuvring stand being set to STOP.

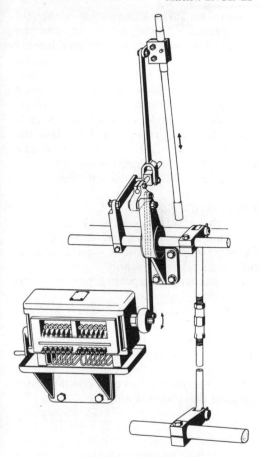

*Figure 6.25 Regulation gear
for lubrication*

All valves in the cylinders must be checked for easy movability and proper operation. This applies also to the fuel pumps, the manoeuvring gear and the reversing gear. Moreover, a thorough check of the roller clearances and of the setting of the fuel regulation and bearing clearances is required.

The systems for lubricating oil, cooling water, fuel and starting air must be inspected and deficiencies, if any, immediately eliminated. Then the pressure tests should be carried out. When all is clear and ready the turning gear must be cut out. The crankshaft is then turned by means of starting air, at first with the relief valves open so as to blow-out the cylinders. After closing the relief valves the engine is ready for starting.

Indicator diagrams must be taken to check the setting of the fuel regulation. The compression pressure, the firing pressure and the mean indicated pressure should be the same for all cylinders. It must be borne in mind that, with supercharged engines, compression and maximum firing pressures depend on the supercharging pressure. The relation between these pressures, the load and the engine speed must be known, so as to determine if a failure is due to a defect in the supercharging arrangement or in the cylinders, e.g. a leaky valve, a broken piston ring or a fault in the injection system. If the last, the indicator diagram mostly shows too small an area, or the exhaust temperatures are too high, or perhaps the exhaust is smoky.

At first the fuel valves should be checked for the following:

(1) Jamming of needles in needle guide.

(2) Poor atomisation, which is mostly due to leaky valve seats. This can be checked with the test device for fuel valves. Regrinding these seats requires the utmost care and skill; it should be done by a specialist, if possible, and preferably ashore.

(3) Incorrect valve adjustment: the opening pressure and needle-lift should be checked on the test stand.

(4) If the nozzle tips show tubular carbon residues and the orifices are partly clogged the causes may be insufficient cooling or very bad heavy fuel. The results obtained in operation before the trouble arose will give some hints regarding the measures to be taken. If the fuel valves are in order and the trouble has not been eliminated the fuel pump setting and the fuel cam position must be checked. See the section on fuel pump testing.

Running temperatures

A good way to assess the load on the individual cylinders is to make a comparison of the exhaust temperatures. This method is, however, not always authoritative without the aid of the diagrams.

The temperatures of the cooling water and lubricating oil, possibly also the piston cooling oil, should be regularly checked during operation. Because of the use of heavy fuel with high sulphur content, high cooling water temperatures are recommended, and fresh water cooling is absolutely necessary. The discharge temperature of the cylinder and piston cooling water should be about 55–65°C. To ensure the necessary water velocity in the cooling spaces, the quantity of water must be kept as high as possible. The difference between inlet and outlet temperatures should not exceed 7–9°C at full load. It is wrong to regulate the water quantity to maintain the same difference when the engine load is reduced.

During manoeuvring and when running slow in narrow waters the sea-water flow through the air coolers should be throttled or shut-off, so as to avoid excessive condensation in the scavenge air spaces. For the same reason, in hot and humid climates, the air must not be cooled down to a temperature below 40–42°C.

Lubrication and Cooling

If oil is used as coolant for the pistons, the quantity flowing through the pistons is more important than the temperature. The temperature difference between inlet and outlet should not exceed 8–10°C. As the cooling circuit is generally combined with the circuit for lubrication, and as the oil temperature should not exceed 45°C when entering the bearings, the outlet temperature of the piston cooling is specified to be about 52–55°C.

The oil filters require special care to make sure, always, that there is clean oil in the engine. Repeated separation is recommended.

For the operational safety and economy of the engines, the use of suitable lubricating oils for cylinder lubrication is of greatest importance. Unsuitable lubricants will result in burnt piston rings, pitting on the cylinder liners and a disproportionately high wear of these parts. This problem is most important to heavy fuel operation, and it has therefore received attention in the section dealing with cylinder lubrication.

After each overhaul, and within certain periods, the lubricators must be checked so as to ensure that the delivery at each feed pump is in order and that the number of droplets is as specified. Further on, from time to time, an exact control of the oil consumption is necessary. This is done by weighing the refilled quantity.

It may here be mentioned that the highly alkaline lubricating oils are mostly unsuitable for running-in new engines, or for new liners and piston rings. For this purpose it has been proved to be of advantage to use a straight oil of good quality. The running-in period should extend over 80–100 service hours. Diesel oil or a better quality of heavy fuel should be used during this period.

Scavenge Fires

The valves of the cylinder undersides as well as the by-pass valves between the 1st and 2nd stage in the scavenge air system—if the engine is turbo-charged according to the series-parallel system—should be checked regularly at intervals. Cylinder indicator diagrams should be taken when tracing a deficiency which may originate in the scavenge air system, e.g. when the scavenging air pressure drops.

Considerable deposits of dirty oil, sludge or coke in the piston underside space, the scavenging air space in the cylinders and in the scavenging line, can be the cause of fires. All drain-pipes of these spaces should be watched carefully and opened as soon as they seem to be blocked. At every convenient opportunity the spaces should be checked and if necessary cleaned, especially when heavy fuel of bad quality is used. In spite of these precautions a fire may occur in the scavenging air space of a cylinder, ignited by sparks blown through the gap between piston and liner. Therefore some plants are now provided with special pipes directing carbon dioxide to the scavenging spaces.

In event of difficulty during operation the engine should, if possible, be immediately shut down and not restarted until the cause of the difficulty has been traced and eliminated.

Starting and Stopping

Irregularities encountered during starting may originate in the various valves controlling the starting air and in those leading the starting air to the cylinders. If the engine reaches the requisite speed by means of compressed air without ignition occurring the cause originates in the fuel system. The fuel pipes are either insufficiently primed or the fuel contains water or air. Fuel with a high-ignition lag may cause difficulty when the engine is started cold. The engine should then be heated by means of hot water, which is usually tapped-off the cooling circuit of the auxiliary engines.

Should the engine stop without apparent reason, the following possible causes should be investigated, viz.: the fuel tank is empty; the filter is clogged; the fuel contains water or air; or the governor has cut off the fuel admission. If the speed of the engine drops without the admission setting being changed the fuel pumps are drawing in air, parts of the pumps are leaky, suction valves are jamming or plungers are sticking. It is also possible that either a piston or a bearing is beginning to seize. If this should be so, the engine must immediately be shut down. The speed of the engine may also drop due to a decrease in the scavenging air pressure, causing poor scavenging and thus poor combustion. This may be due either to leaky scavenging-pump valves or broken valve discs. It may also happen that one or several cylinders fail to fire. This may be due to a failure of the injection pump or other injection elements. A nozzle may be broken, which is indicated by a heavily smoking exhaust.

The engine may operate irregularly or knock for the following reasons: fuel needle valves are defective; the nozzle or the needle guide is cracked; improper setting of a fuel-injection pump or its cam, whereby the injection is either advanced or retarded; unsuitable fuel is used; the fuel-injection pumps require resetting; a piston or a bearing may run hot—when the engine must be shut down immediately; the regulating rods may be out of order so that too large a quantity of fuel is being injected into the cylinder; or, the air vessel of the telescopic pipes for the piston cooling requires more air.

Smoky exhaust indicates that the injection elements are out of order. Mostly it is likely to be fouled or leaky nozzles. It may also be that the engine is overloaded or the load is not being evenly distributed to all cylinders. Bad exhaust may also be due to the use of unsuitable fuel or to the fact that the injection elements and the regulating rods are not set for this particular fuel. Dropping scavenging air pressure may also be the cause of poor combustion.

Turbochargers

With turbocharged engines, a damaged or fouled turbocharger or also intercooler may exert an influence on the combustion because the quantity of air is reduced thereby. If there are undersides working in parallel, special attention should be given to the examination and cleaning of the respective coolers. The degree of contamination of the coolers should be checked constantly by determining the resistance with the help of the pressure gauges. Special tools and devices permit careful cleaning, which in most cases is possible also without removal from the engine. If one of the turbo-sets fails the engine will, no matter which system is used for supercharging the engine, continue operating at about 45 per cent of its full-load performance.

With nine- or twelve-cylinder engines, supercharged on the pulse system and equipped with three or four turbochargers, the output may be about 55 per cent if one blower fails. For some installations with special requirements, electrically driven emergency blowers are provided. In any case, all measures necessary in event of turbocharger failure are described in detail in the operating manual.

A defective turbo-set should be shut down by means of the blocking device. It is, however, not to be recommended that the engine should be run with a blocked rotor for several days; this may cause damage to the rotor and the bearings. If possible, the rotor should be removed and the openings in the blower closed.

ENGINE OVERHAUL

The designers of M.A.N. diesel engines, by their endeavours, have successfully increased their reliability and reduced the maintenance work to a minimum. For this reason, completely new operating manuals, giving an extremely detailed description of the engines, with many drawings and sketches and clear instructions for supervision and maintenance, are provided by the engine builders for the use of customers. Furthermore, intensive reliability studies are continually being made to collect statistical data for determining optimum schedules for maintenance and for indicating working times as well as the personnel and material required for the different tasks. This maintenance programme is now included in the operating manual and ensures maintenance-free periods for the propulsion plant. It enables the shipping company to plan ahead with regard to ship and machinery maintenance. To support world-wide shipping, M.A.N. have set-up service stations in major ports all over the world, where marine engineers can find assistance and obtain essential spare parts. A list of these service stations—about 36 in number—is given in the operating manual together with addresses and further notes, especially mentioning if M.A.N. experts and spare parts are available. It should be mentioned that the M.A.N. works in Augsburg and the special service station in Hamburg, have available a staff of experienced service engineers who are prepared to fly to any part of the world, if shipowners require assistance in overcoming serious difficulties. The cooperation with M.A.N. licensees in Germany, the Netherlands, Belgium, Sweden, Great Britain, Jugoslavia and Japan is expanding steadily so that they are all in a position to service M.A.N. engines. Every care is taken to ensure that important spare parts manufactured in the works of the licensees fit any M.A.N. engine.

An extract from the instructions for the most important inspections is given in the following section:

The main bearings and the connecting-rod bearings should be checked at definite intervals, these usually being specified by the classification societies. The bearing clearance is $0.5-0.6/1000$ of the bearing diameter, and this may increase by about 50 per cent after several years of service. Considerable wear within a shorter period indicates faulty lubrication or a very bad condition of the lubricating oil. The clearance can be set by removing shims from the gaps between the bearing shells. Defective bearing shells can be turned out of the bedplate by means of a special device, without having to lift the crankshaft.

When checking the position and the alignment of the crankshaft the undermentioned two measurements are important:

(a) The measurement of the position of the crankshaft journal against the bedplate by the so-called Lloyd's V depth gauge. On comparing the results with the original figures recorded in the operating manual, the wear-down of the bearing will be deducible. When carrying out this check it must be ensured that the journal is pressing against the bearing.

(b) The measurement of the crank deflection of each throw in four positions, which controls the alignment of the shaft. The deformation of the ship and also the temperature of the engine during measurement have a very significant influence upon the results. It is recommended therefore that the deflections should be checked during the first running period when the vessel is respectively laden and under ballast, as well as when the engine is cold and when it is warm. The original deflections are recorded in the operating manual.

As a rule the pistons are taken out after 4500–6500 operating hours. Depending on their state, they are dismantled and cleaned and the piston rings are renewed if necessary. If the piston-rod stuffing box is carefully handled and thoroughly greased it requires overhaul only when the piston is removed. On this occasion the gap clearance of the sealing rings and scraper rings must be reset to the original value and worn-out parts replaced.

The withdrawing of the cylinder liners, in general, depends on their wear. This may amount to approximately 0·05 of the diameter The cylinder liners are dismantled with the help of a special device which works hydraulically in the larger crosshead engines, *see* Figure 6.26.

When carrying out overhaul work it must be thoroughly checked that all bolts are properly retightened. The bolts for the piston rods, connecting rods, tie-rods and all other important bolts must be given a proper pre-stress. Special instructions are laid down for each engine regarding the elongation of the bolts and the method of measuring the same. Hydraulic devices are used for tightening the tie-rods. With the larger engines, such devices are used also for tightening the cylinder cover, crosshead and connecting-rod bolts.

SUPERCHARGED FOUR-STROKE TRUNK ENGINES

Of the various sizes and types of four-stroke engine built by M.A.N. for all applications, only the two largest types, GV40/60 and GV52/74, are described here, because they are to be found in ships belonging to almost all the seafaring nations of the world. The range of output and the speed of the engines are listed in Table 6.3. The figures in the type-code are to be read as in Table 6.1, i.e. as cylinder bore and piston stroke. Both types are of similar design, with the characteristic features described below, *see* Figure 6.27.

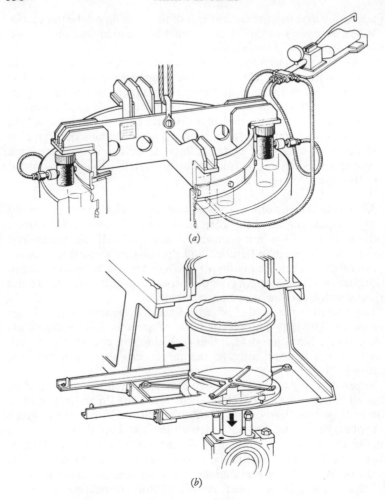

Figure 6.26 Cylinder-liner dismantling gear
(a) For upper liner   (b) For bottom liner

Construction

A single-piece cast-iron bedplate is used. The bedplate of the earlier
models was fabricated, and it incorporated a cast-steel girder placed
in the middle of the bedplate to support the bearings. The underside
of the bedplate is closed by the oil trough.

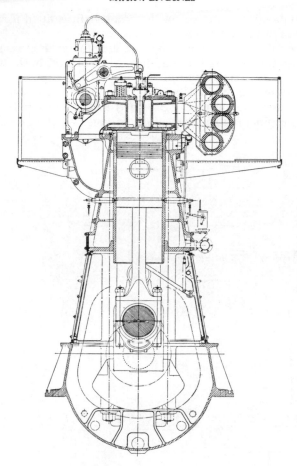

Figure 6.27 Four-stroke trunk-piston engine

The engine frame consists of short columns of cast iron, which carry the cylinder blocks. Three or four cylinders are combined into one casting with integrally cast air-intake pipe. The tie-rods are arranged in the usual manner.

The cylinder liners are made of a special alloy cast iron.

The crankshafts are solid forgings, made in a single-piece for engines up to eight cylinders, and in two pieces, coupled by fitted bolts, for nine- and ten-cylinder engines. Instead of a built-in thrust bearing, external thrust blocks are usually provided. The M.A.N.

vibration damper, mounted on the crankshaft, is fitted if required on account of torsional vibrations.

The die-forged steel connecting rods are of circular cross-section. The piston pin bearing is a lead-bronze-lined steel bush, which is pressed into the connecting rod.

The pistons are made of special light metal alloy castings. An integrally cast cooling coil is provided in the upper part of each piston of engines with higher supercharging, *see* Figure 6.28. The

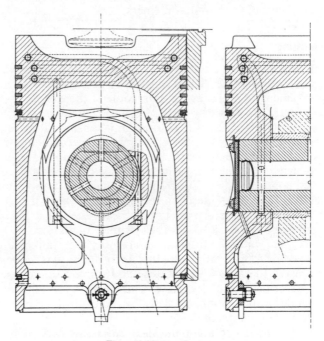

Figure 6.28 Trunk piston

cooling oil is branched-off from the oil supply to the upper bearing. The latest design, specially for heavy fuel operation, has a cast-in ring insert for the first ring. The number of piston rings is reduced to four.

The camshaft is arranged at cylinder-head level. It is driven from the crankshaft through a sturdy roller-chain having a double tension adjuster. The coupling between the camshaft and the sprocket wheel is so designed that the tension of the chain does not affect the axial shifting of the camshaft nor the force necessary to accomplish it.

The fuel injection system is similar to that of the two-stroke engine, and the same can be said of the method of reversing. Starting and reversing, and also adjustment of fuel admission, is by means of a single hand-wheel, the operation of which is almost the same as that in Figure 6.22. A safety governor, with servomotor, is driven by a gear train from the crankshaft.

The pump for the lubricating oil system may be attached to the engine, but electrically driven pumps are often used. Special lubricators are provided for cylinder lubrication, supplying an accurately metered amount of fresh oil to the liners.

Supercharging

As mentioned previously, almost all engines are now turbocharged. Owing to a considerable increase in turbocharger efficiency and to the arrangement of charging-air intercoolers, the degree of super charging could be raised 1·75–2·2, resulting in a mep of 10·3–12·5 kgf/cm² (10·1–12·25 bar) without any substantial increase in mechanical or thermal loads. Exhaust turbochargers arc now mostly of M.A.N. design. Turbochargers of marine engines are usually arranged on the coupling side, on one level with the exhaust manifold.

The fuel consumption of supercharged engines is approximately 210 g/kWh at full load, if diesel oil with a caloritic value of 42 MJ/kg is used. The engines can also operate on heavy fuel oil, if the necessary equipment is provided. If fuels with a high viscosity, high sulphur content and carbon residues are used the crankcase oil is liable to become spoiled rather quickly. Accordingly, it is economical to select heavy fuel oils with viscosity and sulphur content within suitably prescribed limits. It is always advisable to obtain from the engine-builder a fuel specification which indicates the range of the several important characteristics.

It is quite possible that in the near future M.A.N. will cease production of these two types, as smaller engines with higher speeds and much higher mep are economically superior, even if a gearbox is necessary to obtain a suitable propeller speed.

During the past fifteen years M.A.N. have developed highly supercharged four-stroke engines. Mean effective pressures of 16–20 kgf/cm² have been attained. A small crosshead engine, with a bore of 450 mm and a stroke of 660 mm, was built for marine service. The cylinder output of that engine was about 470 hp (350 kW) (mep = 16 kgf/cm² (15·7 bar), speed = 250 rev/min). In the following years numbers of six-cylinder engines were installed in German and Japanese merchant vessels. After some time this engine proved to be too small for the ever-increasing requirements of shipping.

M.A.N. MEDIUM SPEED FOUR-STROKE V-ENGINES

Arising from the experiences described in the last paragraph, M.A.N. decided to develop an engine having a far higher speed, adapted for geared drive or for installations requiring reduced weight and a very low head room. After extensive trials, the VV40/54 engine was built and installed in medium-sized passenger boats and ferries. The chief features of the design are shown in Figure 6.29.

The main technical data are given in Table 6.4 (upper part).

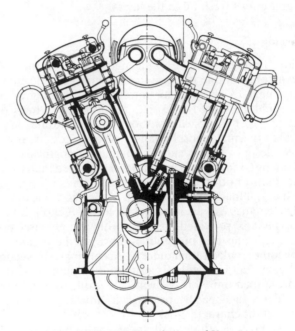

Figure 6.29 M.A.N. medium speed V-engine

The engines are mostly built as V-engines, the banks of cylinders being arranged at an angle of 45°. In-line engines with 6 to 9 cylinders are also in the current programme, the output per cylinder being the same as in the V-engines. The success of the VV40/54-type (within 6 years more than 280 engines have been delivered or ordered, totalling nearly 2·0 m. hp) and the ever increasing demand for higher outputs prompted the development of a similar type of larger dimensions. Owing to the experience gained with the first type and by using scientific research and computers, design construction and testing of the new type required only some 18 months. The main

Table 6.3 POWER AND SPEEDS OF M.A.N. FOUR-STROKE TRUNK-PISTON MARINE ENGINES

Type	Swept vol. per cyl. (litres)	No. of cylinders	Rev/min	Mep (kgf/cm²)	Mep (bar)	Bhp	kW	Kg/bhp	Kg/kW
GV40/60	75·4	6–10	225–310	9·0* 12·5†	8·83 12·25	1020–2350 1420–3250	760–1750 1060–2420	30–22 25–19	40 –29·5 33·5–25·5
GV52/74	157	6–10	200–250	10·3†	10·09	2160–4500	1610–3360	36–26	48 –35

*Standard supercharging without intercoolers (air-coolers).
†With intercoolers for charge-air.

technical data of the new VV52/55-type are shown in the lower part of Table 6.4. As the leading design features are almost the same for both types, the section of Figure 6.29 applies and the following description of the VV52/55-type holds good for the smaller type in almost every respect.

The progress in the latest design is illustrated by the specific-weight figures. With the same speed and with only slightly increased mep (+ 4 per cent) the power/weight ratio has been reduced by approximately 22 per cent. This fact is remarkable as M.A.N. adhered to cast-iron construction for the framework, i.e. the combined crankcase, bedplate and oil trough and also for the cylinder block.

The transverse girders of the crankcase are open so that the crankshaft and the main bearings may be installed from the top. These openings are closed off by cast-steel transverse members bolted to the crankcase by strong vertical and horizontal bolts. The cylinder block is fastened to this extremely stiff box-section by tie rods. The crankshaft is solid forged from high tensile steel and meets the requirements of the various classification societies. By adoption of the well-proved articulated connecting rod design (Figure 6.30), it is possible to arrange the respective cylinders of both banks in the

Figure 6.30 Articulated connecting rods

Table 6.4 MAXIMUM CONTINUOUS OUTPUT OF V ENGINES

Type*	Swept vol. per cyl. litres	Rev/min	Mep kgf/cm²	Mep bar	Output hp	Output kW	Weight tonnes	Weight kg/hp	Weight kg/kW
V5V40/54	67·9	360–430	17·2	16·9	4 850– 5 600	3 600– 4 200	73	13·1	17·6
V6V40/54					5 850– 6 700	4 400– 5 000	84	12·5	16·8
V7V40/54					6 850– 7 800	5 100– 5 800	97	12·5	16·8
V8V40/54					7 800– 8 900	5 800– 6 700	108	12·2	16·4
V9V40/54					8 800–10 000	6 500– 7 500	119	11·9	16·0
V5V52/55	116·8	360–430	17·9	17·6	8 100–10 000	6 000– 7 500	106	10·6	14·2
V6V52/55					9 720–12 000	7 200– 9 000	121	10·0	13·4
V7V52/55					11 340–14 000	8 400–10 500	138	9·8	13·1
V8V52/55					12 960–16 000	9 600–12 000	153	9·5	12·8
V9V52/55					14 580–18 000	10 900–13 500	168	9·3	12·5

*The figures in the code show the cylinder diameter and stroke in cm, respectively.

same plane. Thus the whole design of the engine is simplified and the overall-length is reduced by approximately 12–13 per cent compared with engines with offset cylinders. A further advantage may be mentioned, that the pistons can be withdrawn without removing the crank bearing and that a lower dismantling height for the pistons is attained.

The pistons consist of two parts. The aluminium piston skirt, with the piston pin bearing and the piston crown of alloy steel which is cooled by oil branched off from the oil supply to the upper connecting-rod bearing. The thin walls of the steel-crown ensure effective cooling and, in consequence, there is very little change in piston crown clearance; there is also low temperature at the ring grooves which are flame-hardened. Thus low wear and good partial-load service are attained, particularly with heavy fuel operation.

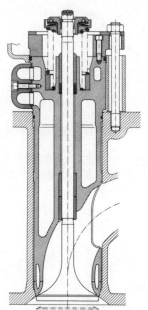

Figure 6.31 Exhaust valve with water-cooled seat ring

Separate cylinder lubrication is provided, permitting the feeding of small quantities of fresh oil, suitable for the fuel grade used, to the exact point at which the oil is required. The oil is fed to the cylinder liners from below and, consequently, it is not exposed to the danger of carbonisation or the separation of additives.

The inlet and exhaust valves are installed in cages so that they can be removed without lifting the cylinder head. Intensive cooling of the exhaust valve seats (Figure 6.31) lowers the temperature of the valve-cones to a point where, in heavy fuel operation, dangerous vanadium and sodium deposits are reduced to a minimum. Moreover, a special device to rotate the valve-cones during operation is provided. Fuel ignition is effected by cam-operated pumps similar to those of the two-stroke engines. For special plants, where high flexibility is required, e.g. for high-speed ships which have to operate in narrow waters at $\frac{1}{4}-\frac{1}{5}$ of the normal speed, or for dual-fuel engines

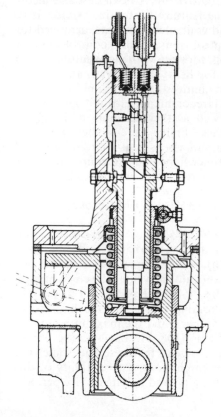

Figure 6.32 Tandem fuel pumps

the pumps have two plungers of different diameters arranged in tandem (Figure 6.32). The camshafts, arranged on the outer side of the cylinder blocks, are driven by a four-wheel gear train from the crankshaft.

With regard to periodically or permanently unattended engine rooms, special care has been taken to avoid pollution of the main oil circuit by leakage of the fuel-valves or fuel pipes. For each bank of cylinders a high-pressure M.A.N. turbocharger delivers the combustion air. These turbochargers are mostly arranged on the coupling-side, together with the air-coolers. Both medium-speed engines are normally direct-reversible except in those instances where manoeuvring is taken over by controllable-pitch propellers. The standard reversing system of four-stroke engines is used, i.e. double cams and shifting of the camshaft by a hydraulically operated piston.

The manoeuvring gear is of standard M.A.N. design and incorporates all necessary interlocking features for marine service. It is, together with the measuring and control instruments, arranged for full automation with remote control from a central control room or from the bridge. The engine itself, together with the injection system and the fuel lines, is arranged for heavy fuel service. In order to ensure long periods between oil changes and long running periods for pistons and exhaust valves, it is recommended to limit the sulphur-content and coke residue, as well as the vanadium and sodium content of the fuel. Usually these limits are complied with if a residual fuel is blended to a maximum viscosity of 1500 sec Redwood No. 1. Because of the weight, dimensions and stiff framework, it is possible to arrange these engines on resilient mountings, a fact which is very important for passenger-ships and ferries. Such a plant with 4 engines R9V40/54, 18 000 hp (13 500 kW) has proved to be a remarkable success.

The test-results (Figure 6.33, V9V52/55) show a fuel consumption rate at full load, i.e. mep $= 17 \cdot 9$ kgf/cm^2 (17·6 bar), $\eta = 417$ rev/min, of about 150 g/Hph (200 g/kWh), which also applies to heavy fuel service when allowing for the lower calorific value. The consumption of lubricating oil has proved to be $1 \cdot 0 – 1 \cdot 2$ g/Hph ($1 \cdot 34 – 1 \cdot 61$ g/kWh) for long service periods. Outstanding values are the high boost pressure, about $1 \cdot 6$ kgf/cm^2 ($1 \cdot 57$ bar), and the maximum ignition pressure of about $110 – 120$ kgf/cm^2 ($108 – 118$ bar). As the framework and the running gear are designed for these and somewhat higher pressures after careful research work, the reliability of this engine is not impaired and has been proved in long service periods.

Maintenance Problems

As with the new two-stroke engines, every effort was made to facilitate maintenance and accessibility. Thus, the work necessary for loosening and tightening of all important bolts has been reduced by the new heating-up method. Electric heater rods are inserted into bores in the bolts, and within a few minutes the bolts are heated to

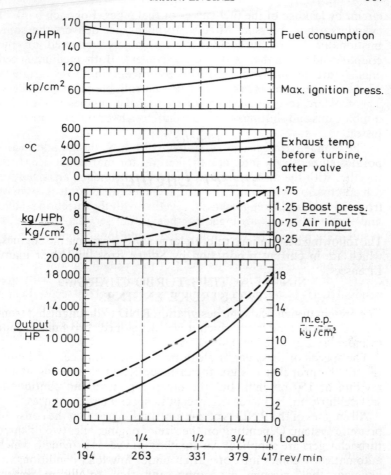

Figure 6.33 Test results of V9 V52/55 engine; rated output 17500 hp (13000 kW) at 417 rev/min

250–280°C, so that the thermal expansion corresponds to the prescribed preloading. Special valve grinders have been developed for maintenance of the valve seats. Furthermore, special tools and devices are available for all standard dismantling work.

F.S.

Chapter 7

Sulzer Engines

The following descriptions refer to large slow-speed marine engines, which are in current production by Sulzer Bros. and their many Licensees.

SINGLE-ACTING TURBO-CHARGED TWO-STROKE ENGINES

The present design bears the designation RND to distinguish it from the RD engine type from which it was developed. It is built in four cylinder sizes as listed in Tables 7.1 to 7.4.

The speeds of these engines can be varied, within certain limits, to suit the propeller design, for instance RND 68 running at 137 rev/min or 150 rev/min, but the bmep for maximum continuous service must not be increased, except in special circumstances.

All engines of the RND type are pressure-charged on the constant pressure system. Depending on the size of engine, one, two or three turbochargers are supplied. An auxiliary blower is provided, which automatically comes into operation under low-load conditions, to augment the scavenge air supply and thus to ensure perfect combustion.

Figure 7.1 shows a cross-section and Figure 7.2 a longitudinal section through the engine, these sections being representative of all engines in the RND series, *see also* Figure 7.3.

The design incorporates several of the basic features which have always been characteristic of large Sulzer engines, e.g. cross-scavenging and a cylinder cover with centrally placed fuel valve, but without mechanically operated inlet and exhaust valves.

Bedplates, Frames and Tie-rods

The bedplates and A-frames are fabricated from steel plates. Longi-

168

Table 7.1 SULZER TYPE RND 68, 680 MM BORE, 1250 MM STROKE

Type	5RND68	6RND68	7RND68	8RND68	9RND68	10RND68
Cylinders	5	6	7	8	9	10
Max. continuous output, bhp (metric)	7 500	9 000	10 500	12 000	13 500	15 000
kW	5 520	6 620	7 720	8 830	9 930	11 030
Corresponding rev/min	137	137	137	137	137	137
Bmep, kgf/cm²	10·9	10·9	10·9	10·9	10·9	10·9
Bmep, bar	10·7	10·7	10·7	10·7	10·7	10·7

Table 7.2 SULZER RND 76. 760 MM BORE, 1 550 MM STROKE

Type	5RND76	6RND76	7RND76	8RND76	9RND76	10RND76
Cylinders	5	6	7	8	9	10
Max. continuous output bhp (metric)	10 000	12 000	14 000	16 000	18 000	20 000
kW	7 350	8 830	10 290	11 770	13 240	14 710
Corresponding rev/min	122	122	122	122	122	122
Bmep, kgf/cm²	10·5	10·5	10·5	10·5	10·5	10·5
Bmep, bar	10·3	10·3	10·3	10·3	10·3	10·3

tudinal and transverse members of the bedplate are respectively shown in Figures 7.4 and 7.5.

The transverse bearing saddle supports are solid steel forgings or castings, and are stress-relieved before final welding into the complete bedplate. At the bottom of each crank-pit a strainer is fitted to exclude dirt from the oil system.

The bedplate carries the main bearings, each of which consists of two identical white-metal-lined bearing shells, a bearing keep and shims. To reduce to a minimum the bending moment on the transverse members of the bedplate, set-up by the pull of the tie-rods and

Table 7.3 SULZER RND 90, 900 MM BORE, 1550 MM STROKE

Type	6RND90	7RND90	8RND90	9RND90	10RND90	11RND90	12RND90
Cylinders	6	7	8	9	10	11	12
Max. continuous output bhp (metric)	17 400	20 300	23 200	26 100	29 000	31 900	34 800
kW	12 800	14 930	17 060	19 200	21 330	23 460	25 600
Corresponding rev/min	122	122	122	122	122	122	122
Bmep, kgf/cm^2	10·85	10·85	10·85	10·85	10·85	10·85	10·85
Bmep, bar	10·63	10·63	10·63	10·63	10·63	10·63	10·63

Table 7.4 SULZER RND 105. 1050 MM BORE. 1800 MM STROKE

Type	8RND105	9RND105	10RND105	11RND105	12RND105
Cylinders	8	9	10	11	12
Max. continuous output bhp (metric)	32 000	36 000	40 000	44 000	48 000
kW	23 540	26 480	29 420	32 360	35 300
Corresponding rev/min	108	108	108	108	108
Bmep, kgf/cm^2	10·7	10·7	10·7	10·7	10·7
Bmep, bar	10·5	10·5	10·5	10·5	10·5

the downward load on the crankshaft, the main bearing keeps are held down by jack-bolts, allowing closely-pitched centres for the tie-rods, *see* Figure 7.6.

Figure 7.7 shows the method of dismantling the bearing shells. The crankshaft is raised a maximum amount 'S' so as to avoid scoring the back of the bottom half-shell and the bearing housing while turning-out the bearing. Care should be taken to place the beam 941.41, in the plane of the tie-bolts and the jacks at centres 'A'.

The frames are symmetrical and carry oil-cooled crosshead guides lubricated from the crosshead slippers. The individual frames are held together on both sides of the engine by longitudinal stiffening plates, which are bolted-on. Large rectangular doors allow access to the crankcase from both sides of the engine, and those on the fuel pump side are fitted with inspection hole covers. The doors on the exhaust side carry crankcase relay valves, fitted with protective caps.

The cylinder block A-frames and bedplate are held together by long tie-bolts which transmit the combustion forces from the tops of the cylinders down to the bedplate cross-members. Figure 7.8 shows the hydraulic device for tightening the tie-bolts.

The tie-bolts are tightened in two stages, with the main bearing jack bolts slackened off. The increase in dimension X, i.e. the stretch of each tie-bolt, is checked against the engine builders' records. After the tie-bolts have been stressed, the main bearing jack bolts are tightened in a similar manner.

Cylinder Jackets, Liners and Piston-rod Glands

The cylinder jackets are cast separately, but are bolted together to

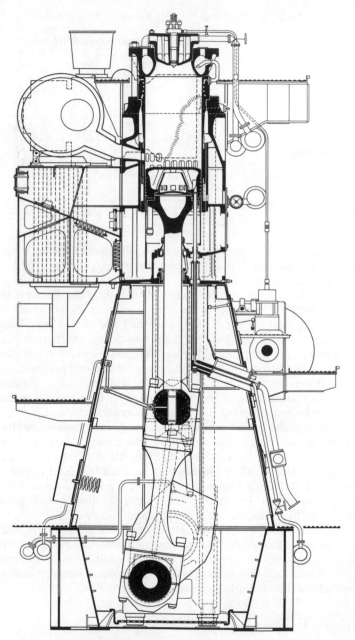

Figure 7.1 Type RND engine, transverse section

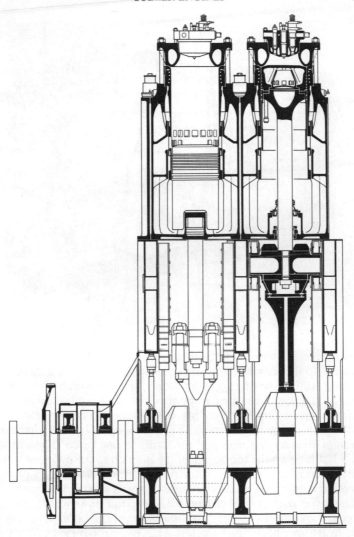

Figure 7.2 Type RND engine, longitudinal section

form a rigid block. The assembly of the bedplate, frames and cylinder block, held together by the tie-rods, forms an extremely rigid structure which remains completely free from deformation under the most severe service conditions.

Each cylinder jacket is provided with an opening on the fuel pump side, to facilitate access to the piston rod gland, piston cooling

Figure 7.3 Eight-cylinder type RND engine, 760 mm bore

telescopic pipe, top packing rings and piston skirt. Above it the
openings to the scavenge spaces are located, as well as the inspection
opening leading to the cylinder bore through which the exhaust
ports on the opposite side can be checked. This construction forms
a diaphragm, completely sealing the cylinder from the crankcase.

The cylinder liners, as shown in Figure 7.9, are of special vanadium-
titanium alloyed cast iron and are made in one piece. The cylinder
cover holds down the top flange of the liner on to the cylinder jacket.
The top flange of each liner is constructed in such a way as to provide
intensive cooling by means of water passages drilled tangentially.

The lower part of the liner is free to expand downwards, and the
scavenge and exhausts ports are sealed from the cooling spaces by
heat-resisting rubber rings. Each seal has two rubber rings. An empty
inspection groove is machined between each pair of rings and
connected to the outside of the engine by a hole in the cylinder jacket.
If a ring adjacent to the water space, or gas side, should leak it can
be detected easily. The bridges between the exhaust ports are drilled
to form cooling water passages. The cooling of the exhaust ports
prevents deformation of the liner and greatly lessens the formation
of carbon deposits in the ports.

The running surface of the liner is lubricated by eight evenly spaced quills fitted with non-return valves, feeding into grooves cut into the liner wall.

The lubricating quills are extended through the cooling water space and are protected from the cooling water by special pipes, 215.05, Figure 7.10. Any leakages of combustion gas or water pass to the outside between the lubricating connection and the protection pipe. The lubricating quill can be removed for inspection without draining the jackets.

The glands for the piston rods are situated in the central bores of the bottom floors of the cylinder jackets and separate the main cylinders from the crankcase, as shown in Figure 7.11. The gland is divided into a top and bottom group between which is a neutral chamber open to the atmosphere. The top group serves as a seal

Figure 7.4 Longitudinal member of bedplate

against scavenge air and scrapes off dirt. The bottom group prevents crankcase oil leaking out. The oil scraped by the lower packing rings is led back into the crankcase. All packings can be inspected and replaced without removing the piston.

Cylinder Cover and Valves

The cylinder cover is in two pieces and is fresh water cooled. The outer cover is of cast steel, of symmetrical shape, and is held down on to the cylinder liner flange by long studs screwed into the cylinder jacket. The centre-piece is of special spheroidal graphite cast iron

Figure 7.5 Transverse member of bedplate

and carries the fuel valve in the centre, also the starting air valve, the relief valve and the indicator cock. It is held down on to a soft iron joint ring at the bottom of the central bore in the outer cover, by studs held in the latter. A copper joint ring is fitted between the outer cover and the top of the cylinder-liner flange. All valves are in separate housings and can be dismantled as complete units.

The fuel valve, Figure 7.12, consists of a spring-loaded needle valve cooled by fresh water from a separate closed system. The fuel valve is held in place by studs fitted with special spring washers. The main components are the nozzle holder, the nozzle and the retaining nut.

The needle, which has been lapped into the nozzle, is held on the conical seat immediately above the spray holes by a guided push-rod and spring. The pressure of the fuel at which the needle lifts from its seat is set to about 270 kgf/cm² (265 bar), by adjusting the thickness of the spacing ring under the top collar of the spring tensioner to a tolerance of ±5 kgf/cm² (4·9 bar). The cooling-water passages are shown in the section on the right of Figure 7.12. They allow the cooling water to be brought relatively close to the tip of the nozzle, thus giving the effective cooling necessary to prevent formation of carbon trumpets around the spray holes when burning heavy fuels. The nozzle is fitted with a shrunk-on cooling jacket of heat resisting stainless steel and is provided with a locating pin. This pin ensures the correct lining-up of the fuel and water passages, when the nozzle retaining nut is tightened.

The spring must always be completely relieved of stress before tightening or slackening the nozzle retaining nut. If this is not done the pin will be sheared and the faces of the nozzle holder and nozzle will be badly damaged.

Fuel valves are tested with a device which comprises a hand-pump and a pressure gauge having range of 150–1200 kgf/cm² (147–1176 bar) (which also covers the checking of fuel-pump relief valves). The opening pressure can be set and, if the valve and nozzle are in good order, slow pumping will produce a mist from the fuel jets in which there should be no large drops and no drips at the end of the pump stroke.

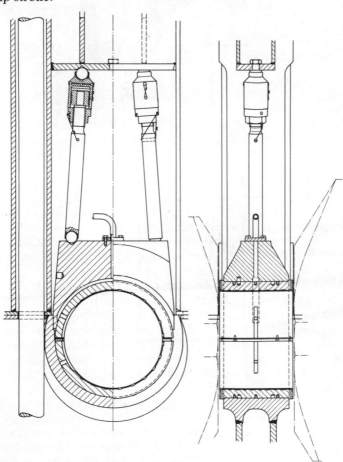

Figure 7.6 Jackbolts on main bearing keeps

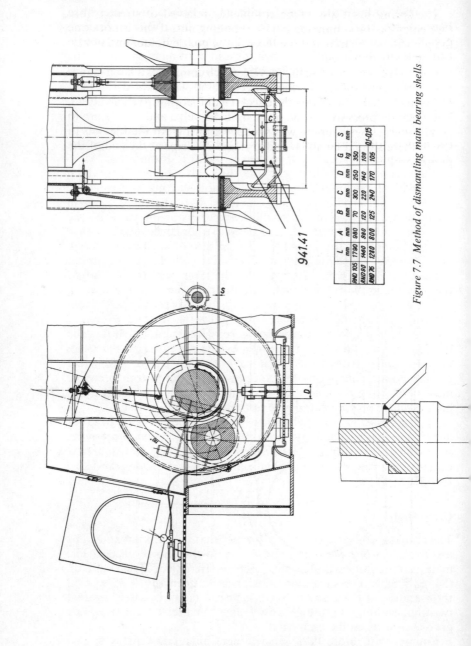

941.41

	L mm	A mm	B mm	C mm	D mm	G kg	S mm
PN0 105	1790	980	70	300	250	350	0.1–0.15
RN0 90	1460	980	120	220	140	108	
PN0 76	1280	800	125	240	170	105	

Figure 7.7 Method of dismantling main bearing shells

Nozzles with needles must be changed if only a few holes have been eroded oval, or have worn to a diameter more than 10 per cent greater than the original size. Enlarged nozzles holes, or bad atomisation of the fuel, will cause overheating and burning of the top of the piston head, also high cylinder and piston ring wear. The needle lift should be checked, if the nozzle and needle have been reseated, because excessive lift will cause hammering of the seat and premature failure of the fuel valve.

A mixture of white lead and oil should be put on the threads of the nozzle holder and smeared lightly on the narrow collar on the nozzle, to prevent sticking when the valve is next dismantled.

Each cylinder is provided with a starting valve, Figure 7.13, which is controlled pneumatically by one of the starting control slide valves, arranged radially as shown to the right of the figure. Control air from the slide valve enters and leaves the starting valve by the two small-bore pipes. It opens and closes the valve rapidly with a damping action at the end of the closing motion, to obviate shock on the valve seats. Starting air enters the valve at a maximum pressure of 30 kgf/cm² (29·4 bar) by the large-bore pipes. Should the pressure in the cylinder be substantially higher than the starting air pressure the valve will not open, thus preventing hot gases from entering the starting air manifold and allowing starting with very low air pressures. When the engine is being reversed, i.e. during the braking phase, the stepped piston prevents the rapid pressure-rise in the cylinder from forcing the valve to shut before its correct closing point. This allows air compressed by the piston to escape into the starting air manifold, through flame traps which prevent high cylinder pressures and give optimum braking action.

Each cylinder is provided with a relief valve which is set to lift at a pressure higher than the normal maximum cylinder pressure. Adjustment of the lifting pressure is ensured by altering the thickness of a spacing ring under the gland nut which compresses the valve spring.

Crankshaft

The crankshaft is of the semi-built type; that is, crankpin and webs are forged in one piece and shrunk on to the journal pieces. The material is open-hearth steel with a tensile strength of 55–65 kgf/cm² (54–63·5 bar). The shrinking allowance of, normally, 1·75 to 1·82 thousandths of the diameter gives a liberal factor of safety against twisting, without the use of dowel pins. Neither oil passages nor grooves are cut in the crankshaft.

Engines with more than six cylinders have crankshafts in two

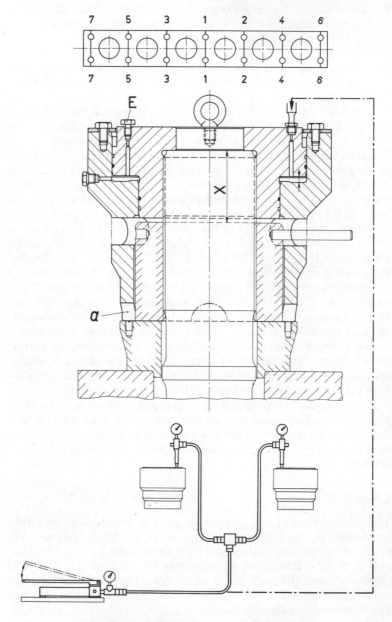

Figure 7.8 Hydraulic device for tightening tie-bolts

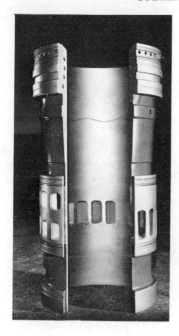

Figure 7.9 Cylinder liner

sections, joined by flanges with fitted bolts. The crankshafts for engines with six cylinders and fewer are in one piece. The aft end of the crankshaft is coupled by flanges and fitted bolts to a thrust shaft of similar material. The forward end of the crankshaft is provided with a flange to take a vibration damper, if this should be necessary.

The alignment of the crankshaft should be checked from time to time, and always when main bearings are being replaced, or if the ship's bottom should have suffered damage in way of the engine room. The distances between the crankwebs are measured at top and bottom dead-centres with a special crankshaft alignment gauge. The difference between the two measurements gives the amount of crankshaft deformation. The measurements are taken opposite the crankpin at a radius from the crankshaft centre-line equal to the crankshaft journal radius. The crankshaft deformation at each crank-throw should not exceed the following measurements:

Engine type	RND68	RND76	RND90	RND105
Good figure, mm	0·12	0·15	0·15	0·18
Maximum, mm	0·25	0·31	0·31	0·36

The crankshaft must rest on the bottom bearing shells while the measurements are being taken. This is for normal conditions; but,

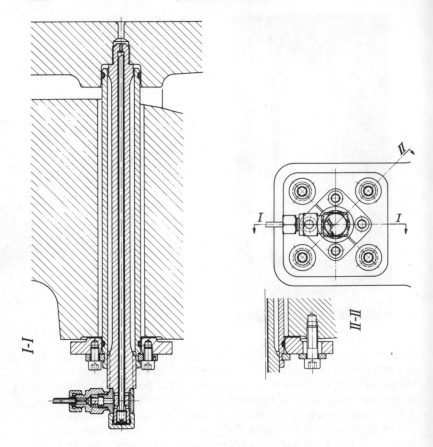

Figure 7.10 Lubrication quill

if there has been distortion of the seatings, then pressure must be
used to force the shaft down on to the bearing shells.

Thrust Bearings

The thrust bearing is of the single-collar type designed on the
Michell principle. The collar is solid forged with the thrust shaft,
and bears respectively on either the AHEAD or the ASTERN ring of
white-metalled bearing segments. The shaft is supported on two
journal bearings which are lubricated from the engine system. The
collar runs in an oil bath, which is continuously being replenished
from the engine system.

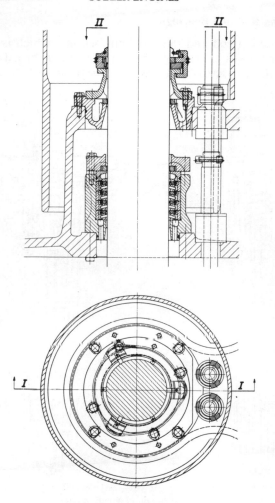

Figure 7.11 Piston rod gland

The thrust collar should have an axial clearance of 0·5 mm, on either side, which is adjustable by altering the shims behind the rings on which the bearing pads pivot. The collar should be so located that the crank-throw next to the thrust bearing is displaced about 1·0–1·5 mm towards the bearing. This allows for expansion of the crankshaft when running with optimum clearances between all crank-webs and main bearings.

Connecting Rod and Bearings

The connecting rod and the crankpin bearing, which is in halves, are of forged steel. The top of the rod forms a broad flange for carrying the two crosshead cast steel bearings which are also in

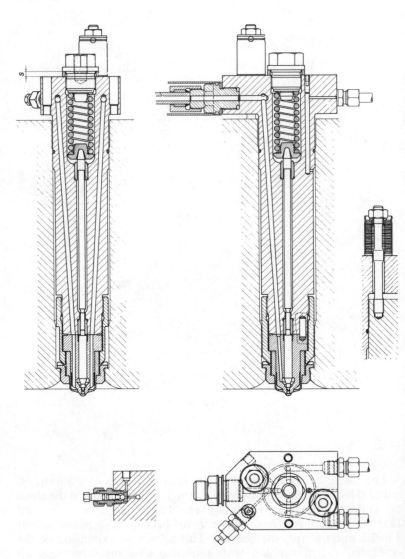

Figure 7.12 Fuel valve

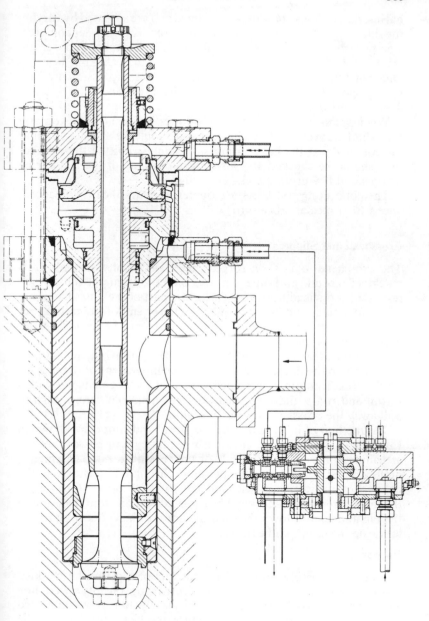

Figure 7.13 Starting valve

halves. All bearings are white-metal lined and are adjusted by varying the shims between the top and bottom halves. The cylinder compression pressure can be adjusted by altering the thickness of the single shim between the connecting-rod foot and the crankpin bearing. One mm difference in shim thickness alters the compression pressure 0.5 kgf/cm² $(0.49$ bar) for RND 105, RND 90 and RND 76 and 0.59 kgf/cm² $(0.58$ bar) for RND 68.

When shims are changed, the clearance between the piston and the cylinder cover must be checked and should be at least 5 mm in the cold state. If thicker compression shims are fitted the cylinder liner should be checked and any ridge at the top of the piston ring travel should be ground away carefully

The connecting-rod bolts are tightened hydraulically in accordance with a special procedure.

Crosshead and Slippers

The crosshead pin is of forged steel, electrically melted. It is machined, ground and super-finished on the journal portions, which rest in the crosshead bearings. The centre part of the pin is flattened-off on four sides and bored to take the lower end of the piston rod. Both ends of the pin are turned down, to form smaller journals to make the crosshead slippers.

The slippers are of cast steel and are lined with white metal in the bores and on the flat sliding surfaces. The movement of the slippers on the crosshead pin is restricted so that, if the engine is run with a piston and rod withdrawn, then the crosshead pin cannot turn to pull away the crosshead lubricating pipes.

The method of lubricating the crosshead and slippers is shown in Figure 7.14. Oil from the medium-pressure system passes through articulated pipes 339 to the side of the crosshead pin 337 which is hollow bored. Oil led into the pin flows through oil passages to the connecting-rod top-end bearings and to the slippers. Grooves in the lower halves of the top-end bearings collect oil from the bores in the pin and lead it down through the bore of the connecting rod to lubricate the crankpin bearings.

Pistons

The piston assembly, Figure 7.15, consists of a piston head, skirt, piston rod with nut, and pipes for conveying the piston cooling water. The head is of cast steel, with a relatively thin crown supported by internal ribs. The thin walls reduce the heat stresses, and the outside of the piston remains relatively cool. This precludes the danger of corrosion by vanadium, which is present in most heavy

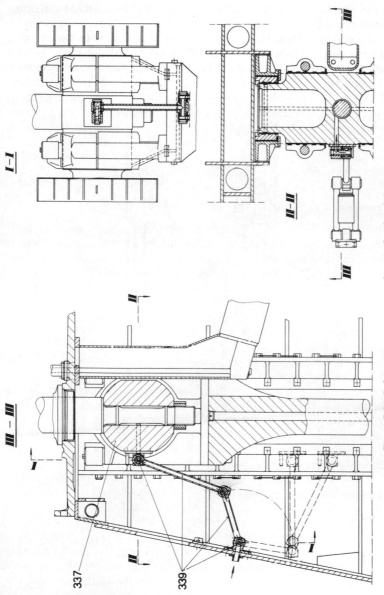

Figure 7.14 Lubrication arrangement for crosshead and slippers

fuels. The five piston-ring grooves are chrome-plated on their lower landing faces, to reduce the rate of groove wear.

Piston rings should be handled with care and only fitted by making use of the special tools provided.

The piston skirt is of cast iron and is provided with two bronze wearing rings, which are hammered into dovetailed grooves before they are machined slightly proud of the skirt. The bronze rings assist

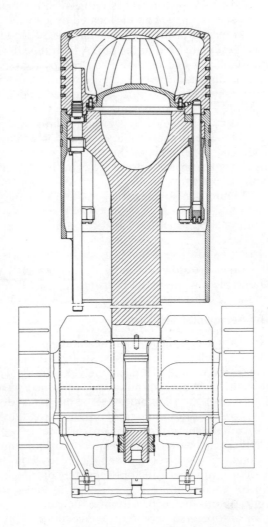

Figure 7.15 Piston assembly

in the running-in of the liners and pistons; they are not replaced when they have worn down flush with the skirt surface.

The piston rod is of forged steel, with a wide flange at the top. Long studs, screwed and locked into the piston head, pass through a flange on the piston skirt and the flange on the piston rod. Nuts, with tubular extensions, clamp the whole piston assembly together and allow considerable elasticity in the bolting arrangement.

The lower end of the piston rod is reduced in diameter to pass through the crosshead pin, where it is located by a dowel. The crosshead pin is held by the piston-rod nut, having a serrated circumference, locked by a plate fixed to the pin. A hydraulic device is used for stretching the lower end of the piston rod by a predetermined amount, thus allowing the nut to be tightened with a small tommy-bar.

The piston cooling running pipes are located and fixed in the piston-rod flange. This arrangement simplifies correct alignment, which is checked by a gauge or by sighting against the piston rod with the piston in the vertical position, using a source of light behind the piston rod. The upper ends of the running pipes, which are of chrome-plated bronze, project into recesses in the piston head and are sealed with rubber rings.

The glands, Figure 7.16, are designed so that they can be checked without dismantling the working piston. The glands consist of inlet and outlet components, which are identical, and a top and bottom scraper group.

The top scraper group seals against the scavenge air pressure. The bottom scraper group, which seals against water from below, consists of a one-piece white-metal bearing.

Camshaft with Servomotor and Drive

The camshaft is situated at the level of the middle platform. Engines with four to six cylinders have the drive at the aft end and others have the drive in the middle of the engine. The drive, Figure 7.17, consists of four straight-toothed spur gears. The wheel on the crankshaft is in halves, but the remainder are of one-piece design. The intermediate wheel bearings and spray nozzle D for the gear teeth are lubricated from the engine low-pressure oil system.

The camshaft is fitted with cams driving the fuel injection pumps. These are arranged in groups so that the fuel pipes from the pumps to the fuel-injection valves are all approximately of the same length. A single cam for each cylinder is used for both ahead and astern running and, to obtain the correct timing, the camshaft is put into position by an oil-operated servomotor incorporated in the camshaft gearwheel. Each cam is in halves and is mounted on a sleeve

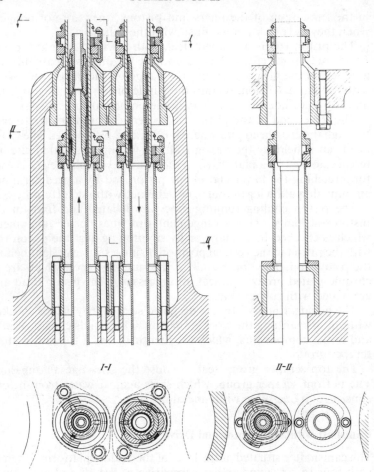

Figure 7.16 Piston cooling glands

keyed to the camshaft. Radial serrations on one end of the cam, and on the collar formed on the sleeve, secure the cam when the cam nut is tightened. The camshaft is supported in white-metalled bearings split vertically, so that it can be removed outwards without dismantling the fuel pumps.

The vertical drive, Figure 7.18, is taken from the reversing servomotor shaft, between its coupling to the camshaft and camshaft drive 411, through a pair of helical gears. The lower shaft of the drive is coupled to a gearbox at its upper end. The gearbox drives the engine governor 511, the transmitter for a remote tachometer,

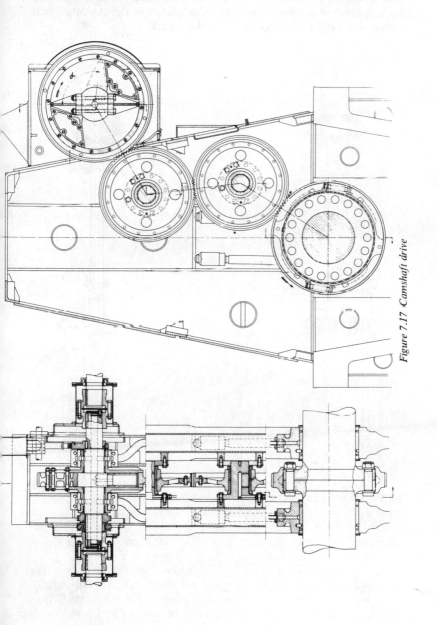

Figure 7.17 Camshaft drive

and a second governor for controlling starting air to the engine if remote control is fitted. The upper shaft leads to the starting-control valves 431 near the top of the cylinder block.

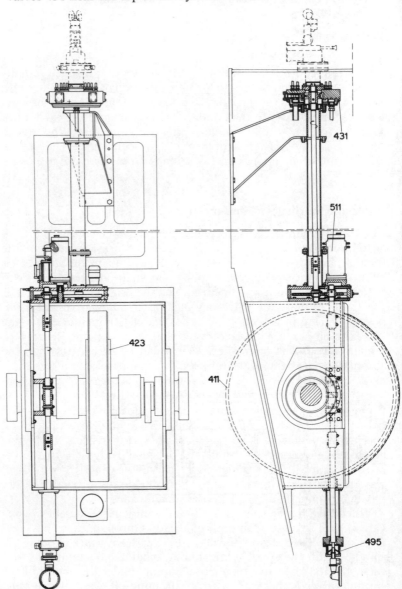

Figure 7.18 Vertical drive to starting control valves

On engines which have the control stand near the camshaft drive, the vertical drive is extended downwards to drive the tachometer 495, which usually incorporates the stroke counter.

Starting-control Valves

The starting valves of the cylinders are controlled pneumatically by the starting-control valves, Figure 7.19, which are arranged radially and driven by a cam pinned to the upper portion of the vertical shaft. When the engine is reversed the vertical drive, together with the cam, is turned in relation to the crankshaft by the camshaft servomotor 423, Figure 7.18, so that similar timing is obtained for either ahead or astern running. The starting-air valves open, theoretically, with air pressure in the upper control air lines, from 4° before top dead-centre to 104° after top dead-centre, both $\pm 2\frac{1}{2}°$ crank angle.

Automatic Starting Air Shut-off Valve

The valve, Figure 7.20, is normally fitted near the control stand so as to be easily accessible from the middle platform; and the spindle for the handwheel is extended for operation from the floor. It is connected in the starting air supply to the engine and remains closed automatically in normal operation of the engine, although it is preferable to close the valve manually after manoeuvres are completed. During overhauling of the engine it is imperative that the valve should be closed manually and that the venting needle valve E remains open. The handwheel 437.34 can be turned to open the automatic starting air shut-off valve for manoeuvring, if the automatic action is out of order, but normally it is turned to the 'Automatic' central position and locked by the handle 437.46.

On pulling the engine starting lever, pilot air enters the space below the piston which actuates the valve 436.51. The valve rises, venting the underside of valve 436.10 and its inner space A. Starting air from the reservoir surrounds the outside of valve 436.10 and the pressure acting on the annular area B causes the valve to open downward to its stop C. Starting air then lifts the non-return valve before passing through flame traps to the starting valves.

When the starting lever is released the pilot air is vented, causing valve 436.51 to close. Compressed air flows through to two passages D into the space A and through the clearance space around the spindle to fill the space under the automatic starting air shut-off valve 436.10. The valve then closes rapidly under the action of the spring. Valves E and K are used for draining-off water, which must be done after every manoeuvring period.

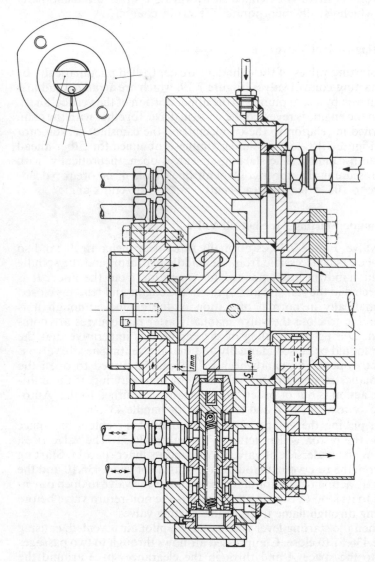

Figure 7.19 Starting control valves

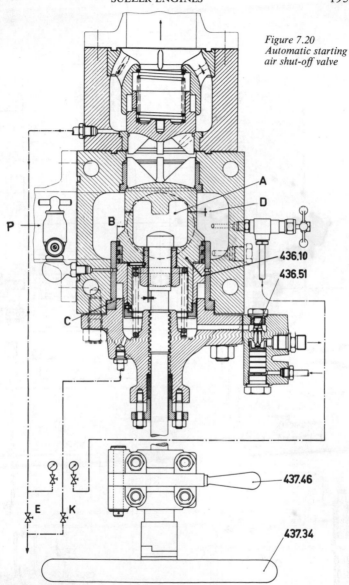

Figure 7.20
Automatic starting air shut-off valve

The function of the automatic starting air shut-off valve may be checked, even when the engine is running, by setting the spindle with hand-wheel to the 'Automatic' position and opening the needle valve *K*. This causes the automatic valve to open. When *K* is shut, pressure builds-up under the valve, causing it to close.

196

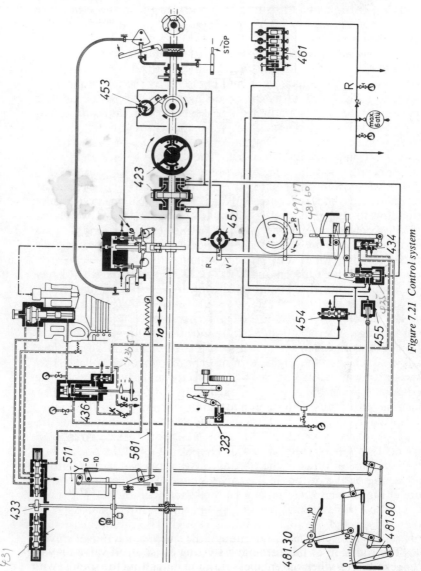

Figure 7.21 Control system

Starting-control System

The control media are lubricating oil from the medium-pressure system at 6 kgf/cm² (5·9 bar), maximum, and starting air at 30 kgf/cm² (29·4 bar), maximum.

The engine is started by the lever 481.60 (Figure 7.21) on the control stand, with the fuel lever 481.30 set no higher than position 3.5. The direction of running is set by the telegraph reply lever 491.17, which turns the reversing valve 451 to the desired position. The corresponding oil passages to the camshaft servo-motor 423 are put under pressure. When the servomotor has reached approximately the end of its travel, pressure oil is admitted to the starting lever blocking device 435. The starting lever is then freed for movement. At the same time pressure oil moves a second valve 454 upwards, admitting oil to the cylinder 455 and the movement of its piston frees the fuel control linkages to take-up a position corresponding to that indicated by the load indicator 481.80, which, in turn, is determined by the position of the fuel lever 481.30. This assumes that the pressures of the lubricating oil supply, bearing oil, jacket cooling water and piston cooling water are all above the minima for which the oil and water-pressure safety device 461 has been set. If not, valve 454 moves downwards, venting cylinder 455, which brings the fuel linkages to zero position.

The starting lever 481.60 is held in its normal position by a spring. On pulling the lever to the 'Starting' position, pilot air valve 434 is raised. Pilot air taken from the reservoir passes through the blocking valve attached to the engine turning gear 323, through valve 434 to the starting air control valves 431 and to the actuating valve 436.51 (Figure 7.20) of the automatic starting air shut-off valve 436. The last-named is caused to open and admit starting air to the engine manifold, feeding the starting valves and also feeding the starting air control valves. Pilot air reaching the latter forces them with their rollers on to the starting cam 433. Depending upon the position of the cam, one or other of the starting valves is opened by the control air acting on the piston on the valve spindle. Thus the engine turns under the action of the starting air, fires, and then the starting lever is released to its normal position by the spring fitted. Valve 434 is then closed and the pilot air line is vented. The rapid collapse of pressure on the pilot air connection of the starting air control valves 431 allows their springs to move the valves and rollers away from the cam 433. Thus the starting air valves are no longer actuated.

The collapse of pressure in the pilot air line causes the automatic starting shut-off valve to close. The pressure in the manifold is gradually relieved through small leakage points in the starting valves and can be vented through a needle valve E before the engine overhauls; *see* Figure 7.21.

Reversing

A reversing manoeuvre from ahead to astern running is normally carried out as described below, *see* Figure 7.21.

The operation is started by moving the telegraph reply lever 491.17 from AHEAD to STOP, the fuel lever 481.30 being brought back to about position 3.5 so as to avoid excessive fuel injection on restarting the engine. As long as the telegraph reply lever is at STOP, the starting lever 481.60 is held in the resting position by the mechanical blocking device 435. By the movement of the telegraph reply lever to STOP, the camplate 492 is turned and the reversing valve 451 is brought to the stop position, which relieves the oil pressure from the valve to the reversing servomotor 423. This drop in pressure causes the slide valve 454 to move downwards under the action of its spring, and this relieves the pressure on the piston of the fuel cut-out servomotor 455, which cuts-off fuel injection.

The oil pressure under the piston of the hydraulic starting lever blocking device 435 is relieved by the slide valve 454 and thus the starting lever is held by both interlocks. When the engine speed has dropped sufficiently, the telegraph reply lever is set to ASTERN, bringing reversing servomotor 423 into the ASTERN position. Control oil is then pressurised to valve 454 and the hydraulic starting lever blocking device 435 frees the starting lever, 481.60. The mechanical starting lever blocking device 435 has already released the lock on the starting lever when the telegraph reply lever 491.17 was moved from STOP to a running position.

By pulling the starting lever into the starting position all the control operations described previously under the heading Starting-control system, are set in motion. The engine now turns astern, and as the running direction corresponds with the telegraph reply lever, the running direction safety interlock 453 releases the fuel supply.

A shortened reversing manoeuvre may be employed by bringing the telegraph reply lever straight from AHEAD to ASTERN without waiting in the stop position for the engine to slow down. As soon as the reversing servomotor has completed the change-over, the starting lever 481.60 is released by the hydraulic starting-lever blocking device 435 and can be operated immediately. The engine, turning ahead, is quickly stopped and immediately started astern. The running direction interlock 453 releases the fuel supply automatically as soon as the engine begins to turn astern.

In an emergency manoeuvre, the fuel lever may be set somewhat higher than usual, say position 5 instead of 3·5. This type of manoeuvre naturally makes more demands on the engine than the normal procedure and should be resorted to only in emergencies, such as danger of a collision.

Running Direction Safety Interlock

The interlock, Figure 7.22, is situated at the forward end of the fuel pumps. Its function is to withhold the fuel supply while the engine is manoeuvring, as long as the running direction of the engine does not coincide with that to which the telegraph reply lever 491.72, Figure 7.21, is set.

Oil- and Water-pressure Safety Device

The engine is safeguarded by an automatic cut-out, Figure 7.23, against seizure, overheating, etc., which may occur by the loss of lubricating oil pressure or the failure of the cooling water supplies. The cut-out is set by altering the spring pressures with the screws 461.13 so that, with the pressures in Table 7.5, piston 461.06 rises

Table 7.5 OIL AND WATER PRESSURES FOR SAFETY DEVICE

	Normal pressure kgf/cm²	bar	Cut-out operates at kgf/cm²	bar
Piston cooling water	3·5–4·5	3·43–4·41	2·5	2·45
Cylinder cooling water	3·0–4·5	2·94–4·41	2·0–2·5	1·96–2·45
Bearing oil	1·5–2·5	1·47–2·45	1·0–1·2	0·98–1·18

and allows the pressure in the control oil line A to drop, by connecting space B with the relief chamber C. The drop in pressure of the control oil through control valve 454 causes the cut-out servomotor 455 to move into the stop position, thus stopping the supply of fuel from pumps to injectors.

The crosshead oil supply is safeguarded by the spring in the cut-out servomotor 455 at about 1·8 kgf/cm² (1·76 bar). The upper face of each piston is sealed by a diaphragm 461.33, which can be checked for leakage at the orifices K.

In emergency, the cock 461.60 can be closed by holding it against a spring 461.19, thus making the automatic cut-out inoperative and enabling the engine to continue running, preferably at much reduced speed, if the pressure of any one of the oil or water supplies is low.

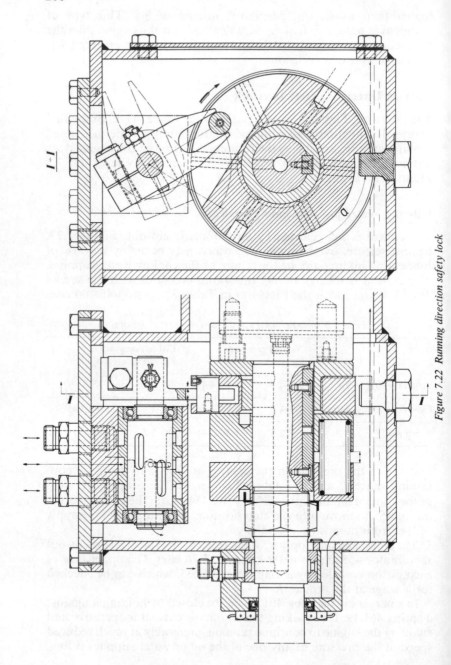

Figure 7.22 Running direction safety lock

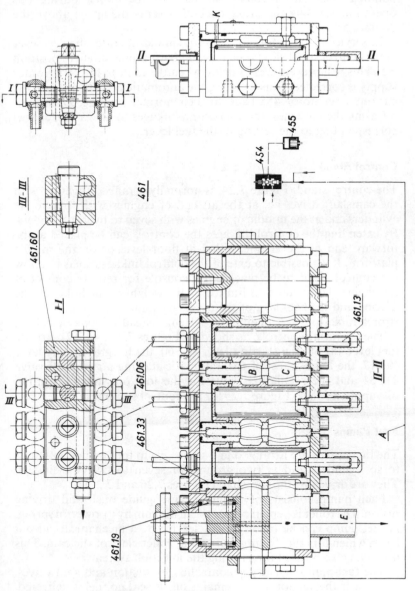

Figure 7.23 Oil and water-pressure safety device

It can be closed also for the renewal of a diaphragm. The corresponding cock on the block 461.60 must be closed during this operation. Closing the latter cock also vents the space above the diaphragm.

In service if the automatic cut-out should operate, the fuel lever at the control stand should be brought back immediately to position 3.5. This will prevent heavy firing when the fault in the oil or water supply is corrected, thus bringing the automatic cut-out 461 and the cut-out servomotor 455 back to their normal running conditions, releasing the governor and fuel-pump linkages to give a fuel charge corresponding to the setting of the fuel lever.

Control Stand

The control stand, Figure 7.24, is normally arranged together with the camshaft drive, i.e. at the aft end of engines with four to six cylinders and at the middle of engines with seven to twelve cylinders. By extending the control linkages the controls can be placed at the forward end of the engine, either at floor level or on the middle platform. It is possible to extend the control linkages so as to allow the control stand to be placed in a console for remote control of the engine. The distance is limited by the weight of the linkages, the friction and the backlash of the necessary joints, pivots, etc., and it is preferable to use a pneumatic system instead of rods or cables.

The operating controls, as shown in Figures 7.24 and 7.21, are the fuel lever 481.30, the starting lever 481.60, the telegraph reply lever 491.17, the hand-wheel of the automatic starting air shut-off valve 437.34 and the regulating valve for the low pressure lubricating oil supply. See also Figure 7.25 for the control station.

Fuel Pumps

The fuel pumps are arranged in a single group for engines with four to six cylinders and in two groups for seven to twelve cylinders. They are driven by the camshaft (Figures 7.26 and 7.27).

Each pump consists of a plunger and guide bush and driving piston. The roller is kept in contact with the cam by a powerful spring. A fuel pump can be taken out of service by a mechanical cut-out lever, which lifts the driving piston and roller clear of the cam. This lever can also be used for priming the injection system.

The fuel-pump delivery is controlled by suction and spill valves. As long as the suction valve remains off its seat no fuel is delivered. When the fuel-pump plunger is raised, the suction valve is lowered on to its seat. As soon as the suction valve closes, fuel is delivered.

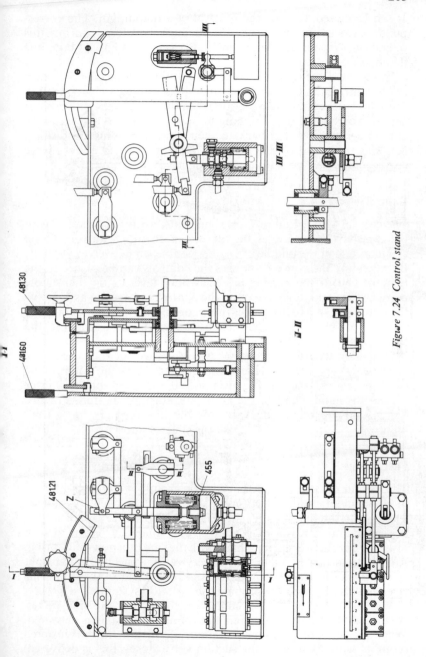

Figure 7.24 Control stand

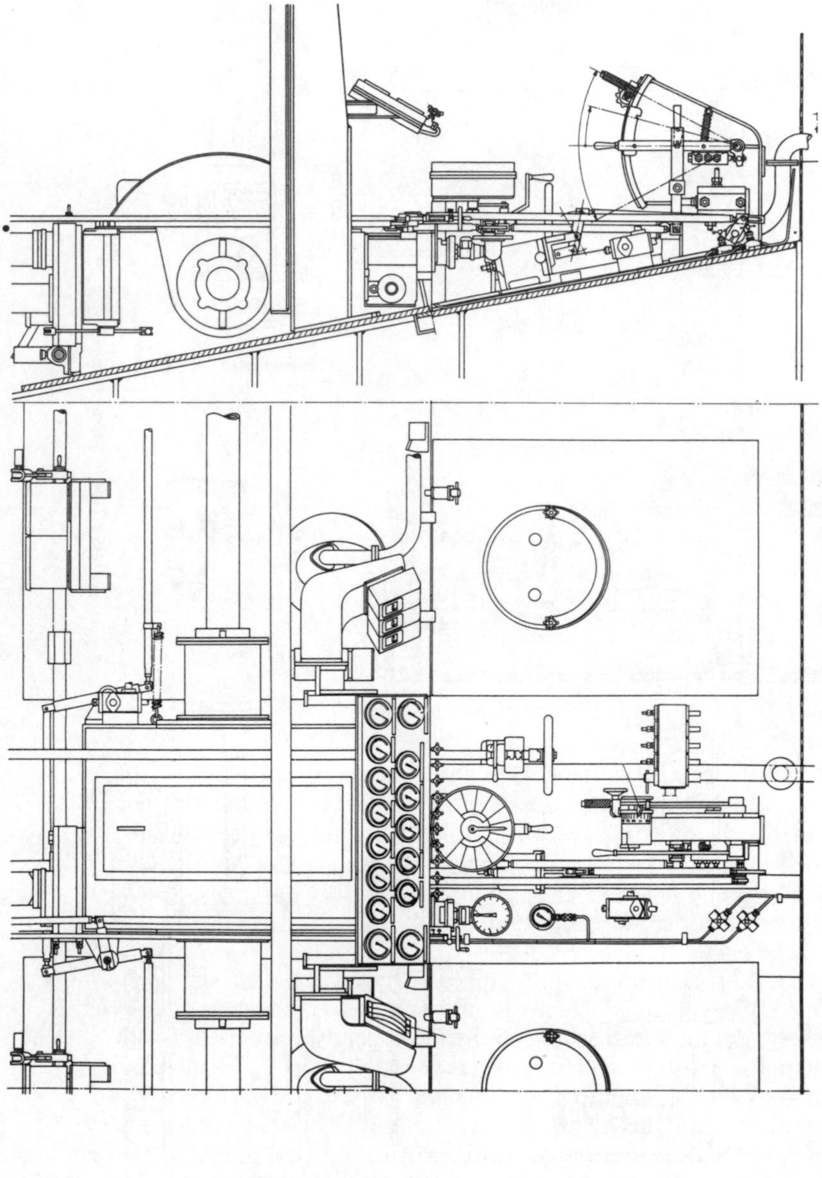

Figure 7.25 Control station

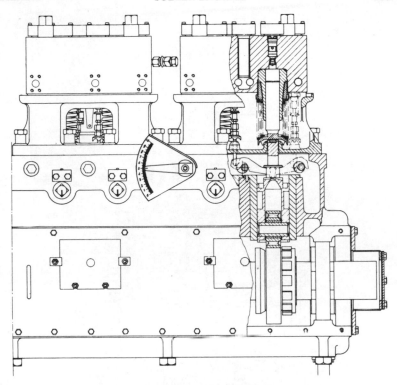

Figure 7.26 Fuel pump, longitudinal section

Normally the start of delivery is constant and the effective stroke is controlled by adjusting the spill valve. Retarding the spill valve increases the effective delivery stroke, while advancing reduces the effective stroke. These adjustments must be made when the engine is stopped and never when running. Ignition pressures are equalised only by turning the cams and not by altering the length of the pushrods.

The fuel charge for individual cylinders can be temporarily reduced, for instance when running-in an essential spare part such as a cylinder liner, piston, etc., by fitting a spacer between the pushrod and the regulating rod. This raises the suction valve by 2·4 mm. When adjusting the fuel-pump control valves no spacers should be fitted.

The effective fuel charge can be read-off on the load indicator which has a scale graduated from 0 to 10. The load indicator serves as a guide for adjusting the fuel pumps, and for this reason its linkages

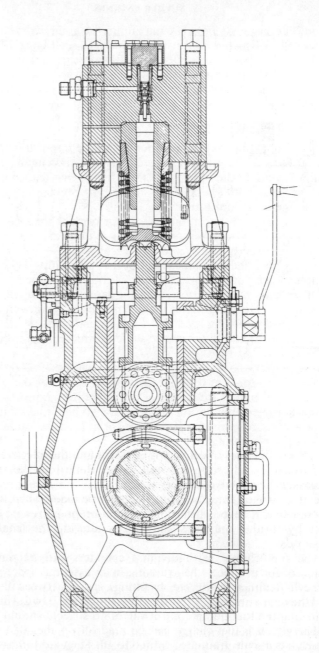

Figure 7.27 Fuel pump cross section

should never be altered. The maximum fuel charge is set by a stop piece 481.21 which is set during engine tests, *see* Figure 7.24.

The pump bodies are safeguarded against excessive pressure by relief valves which are fitted on the backs of the fuel-pump blocks and connected to the delivery passage above the plunger.

Adjusting the Fuel Pumps

Correct adjustment of the fuel pumps is very important and should be carried out carefully in accordance with the engine instruction book. Whenever the engine-control system is overhauled the following cut-outs should be checked in order to prevent any possibility of the engine 'running away'.

1. Check the 0 positions. The 0 positions of the load indicator, fuel lever, cut-out servomotor and Woodward governor must coincide exactly, *see* Figure 7.21.

2. Check the manual cut-out of the fuel pumps. When the fuel pumps are cut-out by hand the clearance between the driving rollers and the raised portion of the cam must be at least 0·5 mm.

3. Check cutting-out of the fuel pumps by the governor. When the speed adjusting lever and the terminal shaft of the governor are at position 0 the eccentric shafts of the fuel pumps must also be at 0

4. Check the fuel pump valve strokes at position 0. When the load indicator is at 0, either the suction valves or the spill valves of all fuel pumps must be in a raised position constantly during the complete revolution of the cam. When the suction valve closes the spill valve must be lifted for at least the value indicated in the valve setting tables.

5. Check the minimum position of load indicator at commencement of discharge. No fuel pump must deliver fuel when the load indicator is lower than position 1, because this margin is absolutely essential for safety. The effective strokes must *not* be increased by reducing the idle regulating range between position 0 and 1·0, otherwise it may not be possible safely to stop the engine.

6. Testing the safety cut-out device. When the safety governor has been tripped by hand, the suction valves of the fuel pumps must be lifted by at least 6 mm when the rollers of the driving pistons are on the cam crowns. This must be checked.

Important. When tripping the cut-out shaft by hand for testing purposes, the motion of the latter should be slowed down with the aid of a spanner until it rests against the stop. In order to avoid damage to the dial gauges during this test, the latter should be removed from the suction valves.

Preparation for adjusting the Fuel Pumps

1. Adjust the fuel cams according to instructions.

2. Close the fuel pipes leading to and away from the pumps. Remove the screw plugs from the fuel pump blocks and allow the fuel to drain away from the pumps.

3. Dismantle the fuel delivery pipe sections, which are situated immediately above the pumps.

4. Set the telegraph lever and the running direction safety interlock to the running direction, for which the fuel pumps are to be adjusted. Open-up the oil pressure so as to move the reversing servomotor to the correct position.

5. Tie-up the hand grip of the automatic cut-out device with a piece of wire against the spring force, so that the cut-out servomotor releases the fuel charge. (*Note:* Remove wire after completing adjustments).

6. The terminal shaft *see* 511, Figure 7.21, of the Woodward governor, namely the shaft of the power booster, should be set at least to the position necessary for adjusting, so that a fuel charge is released.

7. Set the speed adjusting lever so that the load indicator is exactly at adjusting position (see the valve setting tables for adjusting position).

8. Dismantle the connecting nipples, spring cap, spring, delivery valve and valve cover, pressure nipples, springs, and suction and spill valves. Test and adjust the pump, make the cut-out tests and assemble the parts again, before starting the work on the next pump.

9. The suction and spill valves, which are to be adjusted and/or checked, should at the same time be cleaned and inspected for free motion of the valve in the valve guide. The valve and valve seat are to be refitted without the spring.

10. Test the spacers of the dial gauge holders and the dial gauges for free motion, and screw the dial gauge holders in place.

11. If the adjusting work has to be carried out, as an exception, without oil pressure, the wing of the reversing servomotor rests against the stop for the running direction for which the adjustment is done. This is carried out with the aid of a tool, which is fitted to the free end of the camshaft. Furthermore, pin Z must be removed from the cut-out servomotor, in the case of no oil pressure being available (*see* Figure 7.24), so as to permit the load

indicator to move to adjusting position. After completion of the adjusting work, pin Z must be immediately refitted and secured.

12. In order to avoid errors due to play in the camshaft drive when adjusting the fuel pumps, the engine should always be barred over in the direction of rotation for which adjustment is carried out, before the angle is read-off from the flywheel scale.

When adjusting the fuel pump control system, no spacers for fuel charge reduction must be fitted.

Readjusting the fuel pumps:

Fuel pumps with spill valve control; constant commencement of delivery

Working principle: Constant commencement of delivery, controlled by suction valves. Variable termination of delivery, controlled by spill valves.

Check data for a given load indicator position (see valve setting tables for special instructions).

Idle stroke up to commencement of delivery in mm.

Effective delivery stroke in mm.

Effective commencement of delivery in degrees before top dead-centre.

When adjusting the fuel pump control system, no spacers for fuel charge reduction must be fitted.

(a) *Preparations for adjustment;*
(b) *Load indicator to adjusting position (see valve setting tables);*
(c) *Adjusting the effective delivery stroke.*

1. Bar the engine over until the roller is on the apex of the cam. Fit the dial gauge above the closed suction valve and set the dial to 0·00 mm.

2. Bar the engine over until the driving roller runs again on the base circle of the cam, fit the dial gauge above the plunger and set the dial to 0·00 mm. After this fit the dial gauge above the spill valve and set the dial to 0·00 mm.

3. Bar the engine over in the running direction for which the fuel pumps are to be adjusted, until the dial gauge above the plunger indicates the end of the idle Stroke S1, i.e the point where the delivery stroke commences.

4. Adjust the pushrod of the suction valve so that the dial gauge above the suction valve indicates 0·02 mm. When taking the reading, the tensioning nut of the pushrod must already be tightened.

Suction valve closes = effective commencement of delivery

5. Read the crank angle for commencement of delivery in degrees before top dead-centre off from the graduated flywheel.

6. Bar the engine over in the same running direction until the dial gauge above the plunger indicates the end of the effective delivery stroke.

7. Adjust the pushrod of the spill valve so that the dial gauge above the spill valve indicates 0·02 mm.

Spill valve opens = effective termination of delivery

8. Read the crank angle for termination of delivery in degrees after top dead-centre off from the graduated flywheel scale and note it down.

9. Uniform effective delivery strokes of the individual fuel pumps bring about equal cylinder outputs. The maximum admissible difference between the largest and smallest delivery stroke is 0·2 mm. The admissible deviation of effective delivery strokes from the values in the valve-setting tables is $\pm 0·1$ mm.

10. When lengthening the pushrods of the suction valves, a larger idle stroke will be the result. When lengthening the pushrods of the spill valves, the effective delivery stroke is reduced.

11. After timing the valves, the adjustment of the push rods should be marked with $L = \ldots$ mm. Enter the idle strokes and the effective delivery strokes in the valve-setting tables. The effective commencement and termination of delivery can be entered in the valve-setting tables only after the fuel cams have been adjusted and the ignition pressures equalised.

(d) *Carry out cut-out test*

On this occasion the safety cut-out device must be tested also.

Governor

All RND type engines are fitted with Woodward governors. The governor is of flyweight type, with an adjustable spring. Regulating movements of the flyweights are transmitted to the fuel pump regulating rods by means of a built-in servomotor. The oil pressure necessary for operating this governor is generated by a gear-type oil pump built into the governor.

Fuel Regulation

Referring to Figure 7.26: the effective fuel charge is shown by the load indicator. It may coincide with or be smaller than the position of the fuel lever 481.30 in Figure 7.24 but can never be greater. The fuel pump regulating linkage is constantly forced by the spring in the direction of increased fuel charge, i.e. towards position 10.

The cut-out servomotor 455, Figure 7.24, is connected to the fuel regulating linkage through a slotted links and pin Z. The slot allows a full range of fuel charge as long as the cut-out servomotor is not operated by the running direction interlock 453, Figure 7.21, by the oil and water pressure safety device 461. If the cut-out servomotor 455, Figures 7.21 and 7.24, is operated by one of the above devices then link S moves, causing the end of the slot to engage the pin Z, thus pulling the fuel-regulating linkage and the load indicator to zero fuel-charge position.

The Woodward governor 511, Figure 7.21, is coupled to a slotted rod attached to the fuel-regulating linkage 581 by a lever on the terminal shaft. Thus the governor can only reduce the fuel charge when the clearance Y is zero and can never increase the fuel charge beyond that set by the fuel lever, *see* Figure 7.21.

Fuel System Fittings

Figure 7.28 shows the fuel system. The engine is supplied with fuel

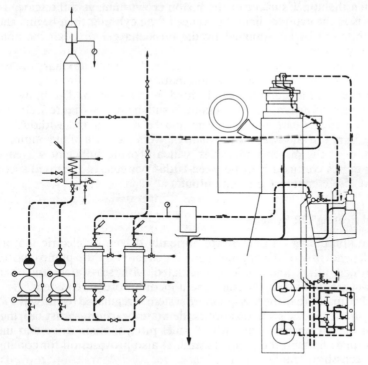

Figure 7.28 Fuel system

by a fuel-oil booster pump, electrically driven, capable of increasing fuel pressure to a maximum of 10 kgf/cm^2 (9·8 bar), and circulating a fuel quantity several times more than that burned by the engine.

The fuel filter contains several filter elements which can be switched over, during running, for cleaning. It is designed for steam heating and each individual filter chamber is fitted with a safety valve.

Scavenge System and Turbochargers

In Figure 7.29 the scavenge air flow is shown by white arrows and the exhaust gas flow by black arrows.

Air drawn in by the turbocharger is compressed and flows through a cooler (1) into a manifold (2) running the full length of the engine. That part of the manifold to the cylinder block side of the vertical non-return valves is subdivided for each cylinder.

The upward motion of the piston draws the scavenge air through the non-return valves 3 into the piston underspace C. There it is compressed and delivered into the space d. The compression ends when the upper surface of the piston crown uncovers the scavenge parts in the cylinder liner. Scavenge of the cylinder then begins and is followed by air supplied by the turbocharger through the non-return valves.

For operation at part loads, an electrically driven auxiliary blower 4 is provided. The blower is automatically brought into operation by means of a pressure switch fitted in the space a. The blower is switched-off when the air pressure is sufficient, *see* Figure 7.30.

The engine can, however, run and be manoeuvred without the auxiliary fan and without the main blowers, because of the pumping action of the piston undersides, which provide sufficient scavenge air to run continually at between 60–64 per cent of the rated speed and 25 per cent of the rated output.

Lubricating Oil Systems

The lubricating oil pumps are normally driven by electric motors independently of the engine. The oil delivered by the pumps passes through filters and coolers, circulated with sea-water, and then branches into a low-pressure and a medium-pressure system.

The pressure in the low-pressure system is regulated by the valve R, Figure 7.21. The system supplies the main bearings, thrust bearing, camshaft, camshaft drive wheels, fuel pumps, chain drive and the rotating shafts in the control stand. It also provides oil for cooling the crosshead guides.

The medium-pressure system lubricates the crossheads, lower

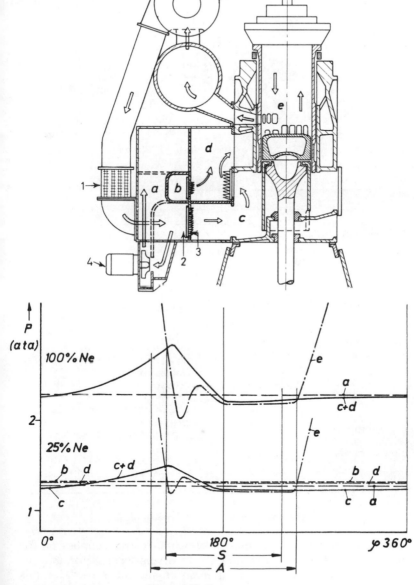

Figure 7.29 Scavenge system

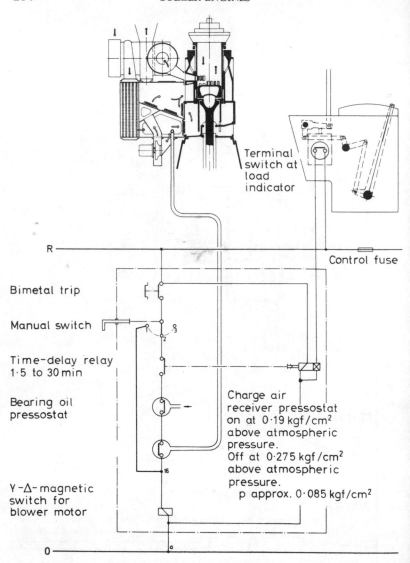

Terminal
switch at
load
indicator

R

Control fuse

Bimetal trip

Manual switch

Time-delay relay
1·5 to 30 min

Bearing oil
pressostat

Charge air
receiver pressostat
on at 0·19 kgf/cm²
above atmospheric
pressure.
Off at 0·275 kgf/cm²
above atmospheric
pressure.
p approx. 0·085 kgf/cm²

Y–Δ–magnetic
switch for
blower motor

0

Figure 7.30 Arrangement of auxiliary blower

connecting-rod bearings, and the slippers. It also supplies oil for
the control-oil system, including the reversing servomotor, and for
the turbocharger lubrication, if main engine oil is used for this
purpose.

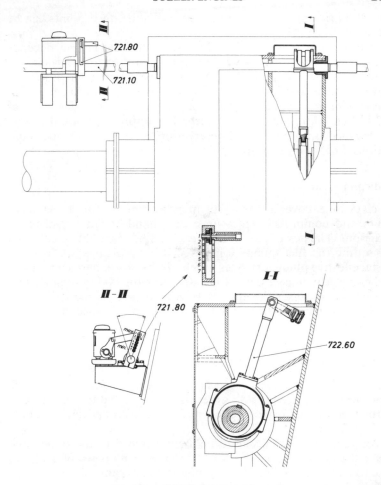

Figure 7.31 Lubricator drive

The cylinder lubrication is independent of the rest of the lubricating system, and usually the engine is provided with lubricators
of the Ivo type located at middle platform level, *see* Figure 7.31.
They are driven from an oscillating shaft 721.10, which is connected
to a crank on the aft end of the camshaft by a connection rod 722.60.
The oscillating shaft is fitted with drive levers 721.80, one for each
lubricator, which can be adjusted by hand while the engine is
running. Seven different drive positions are possible, from position
1 giving maximum oil feed from the lubricator, to position 7, where
the oil feed is a minimum. Normally, all the levers are set the same

for all lubricators on an engine. The individual feed points can be adjusted in the lubricator itself.

The amount of cylinder oil necessary for the engine depends mainly upon the type of oil used, the quality of the fuel and the loading of the engine. For most of the special cylinder lubricants now available, and for a range of outputs from 80 to 100 per cent of the maximum continuous rating of the engine, an oil feed rate of 0·3–0·6 gm/bhp/hr is recommended. The optimum amount can be determined only by careful observation of piston and liner conditions, liner and piston-ring wear, etc.

Indicator Gear

Each cylinder cover is fitted with an indicator cock for taking maximum and compression pressures, also hand-drawn out-of-phase diagrams. The power output from each cylinder should be balanced by setting the fuel pumps for correct timing of injection and for equal effective plunger strokes which makes power cards and hence indicator gear unnecessary. Indicator gear for taking diagrams by mechanical means is therefore only fitted on special request.

No adjustment to the fuel pumps, in order to balance the engines, should be made whilst running.

Cooling Systems

(a) *Cylinder Jacket and Turbocharger Cooling.* A closed circuit with a header tank is used. Fresh water, suitably treated to prevent scale formation and corrosion, is circulated by an electrically driven pump and cooled in a heat exchanger.

Air vent cocks are fitted at the highest points of the system and these should be connected by continually rising pipes of generous size to a common rising pipe leading to the expansion tank.

(b) *Fuel-valve Cooling.* A separate closed fresh-water cooling system is used for cooling the fuel valves. It has an electrically driven pump, a heat exchanger, heater and an overhead expansion tank. The fuel-valve casings are connected in parallel with shut-off valves in each inlet and outlet line, which enables each fuel valve to be dismantled without draining the whole system. An inspection cock is fitted to each outlet line from the fuel valves. The surface of the water in the expansion tank should be examined regularly, and, if traces of fuel are then seen by observing the water bled-off from the inspection cocks, the faulty fuel valve can be located quickly.

(c) *Piston Cooling.* An independent open fresh water cooling system is used for piston cooling. An electrically-driven pump draws the fresh water from a collecting tank and supplies it through a heat exchanger, to a manifold extending along the engine under the first platform. The pistons are circulated in parallel and the outlet from each is taken to a flow indicator, before joining-up in a manifold leading to the collecting tank.

Leakage water from the top scraper groups runs into a neutral chamber which is accessible from the outside.

(d) *Sea-water System*. The heat exchangers necessary for cooling the engine are circulated with sea-water by an electrically-driven pump. The pump draws from the sea connections, through a filter, and delivers to the air coolers, lubricating oil cooler, and piston water cooler, all connected in parallel. All the sea-water from these coolers passes through the cylinder jackets and turbocharger cooler, before going overboard through a spring-loaded valve. Immediately before the spring-loaded valve, a three-way automatic, temperature-controlled valve is fitted. This valve passes some of the warm sea-water back to the pump suction so that the temperature of the sea-water circulating the coolers is kept more or less constant, whatever may be the actual sea temperature or the load on the engine. This arrangement makes much easier the task of the automatic temperature control of fresh water and oil circuits to the engine.

SERVICE AND MAINTENANCE

Starting after overhauls or long periods out of commission

The engine should never be started-up without first subjecting it to a thorough inspection.

1. Check the levels in all tanks. Replenish if necessary.

2. Check all shut-off valves in the cooling and lubricating systems of the engine for correct position.

3. Start-up all cooling water and lubricating oil pumps. Put the systems under service pressure. Repair any leaks immediately.

4. Open the vent cocks on the cooling water outlets of the main cylinders so as to allow the air to escape from the cooling spaces of the latter. The cooling water spaces of the turbines and charge-air coolers are to be vented also. Poorly vented cooling spaces may give rise to the formation of steam, corrosion, local over-heating or other shortcomings.

5. Make sure that no tools, devices, or cleaning cloths are left in the engine after overhauls, which might later impede the motion of the running gear or obstruct any ducts or pipes. Check the control linkage for free motion.

6. Open the indicator cocks on the cylinder covers and turn the engine over for a few revolutions with the aid of the turning gear, so as to ensure that the running gear is in perfect order and that no water, oil or fuel has collected in the main cylinders.

7. Check the low- and medium-pressure oil systems. Start-up the turning gear and turn the engine over until oil emerges from all running gear bearings. Check the sight glasses of the turbo-charger lubricating oil system. Check the cooling water outlets of the piston cooling system at the inspection (outlet) funnels.

8. Fill-up the cylinder lubricating pipes by giving the cylinder lubricators 50 to 60 turns by hand. Should the lubricating pipes have been dismantled or blown-through for checking, they must be filled-up again to the point where they enter the cylinder. Check the sight feed indicators of the cylinder lubricators.

9. While the engine is being turned-over with the aid of the turning gear, the cylinder lubricators should be turned-over by hand some 50 times, or so. Check that all cranks can be turned without applying more than normal force.

10. If the engine is to be started-up on high viscosity fuel the latter must be preheated, *see* Figure 7.28. In this event the cooling water for the fuel injection nozzles must be preheated also.

11. Check the pressure in the starting air system and refill the starting-air bottles if necessary. Drain air pipes and bottles of water, as well as the shut-off valve and the non-return valve for starting air.

12. Check the engine room telegraph for proper functioning.

13. Oil or grease all those parts which must be lubricated by hand.

14. Check the reversing servomotor by moving the telegraph lever several times from AHEAD to ASTERN and vice versa. At the same time check the blocking system of the starting and fuel lever.

15. Check the running direction safety interlock, both for ahead and astern. Bring the speed adjusting lever to position 10. The Woodward governor and cut-out servomotor must both be at position 10, otherwise they will not release fuel. Set telegraph lever to AHEAD. If the engine is turned over ahead, the load indicator must automatically move to maximum fuel charge, while it must move to position 0 if the engine is turned in the reverse direction. The same test is to be repeated with the telegraph lever at ASTERN. The load indicator must then move to maximum fuel charge if the engine is turned-over in reverse direction, and vice versa.

16. Check the automatic cut-out device. Set the fuel lever to maximum fuel charge. The Woodward governor and cut-out

servomotor must both be at position 10 in order to release the fuel charge. Both the telegraph lever and the running direction safety interlock must be set to the same running direction, i.e. either both to AHEAD or ASTERN. Turn the three-way cocks on the supply pipes to position 'drain' one after the other and check that the load indicator moves to position 0.

17. Check the regulating linkage. Set the telegraph lever and the running direction safety interlock to the same running direction, either AHEAD or ASTERN. When the speed adjusting lever is now moved from position 0 to position 10, the load indicator must follow this movement without any delay.

18. Drain condensation from the charge-air receiver and the air coolers. As the charge-air receiver is subdivided into individual chambers by longitudinal and transverse partitions, care must be taken that each chamber is drained.

19. Disengage the turning gear and secure the lever.

20. Close the indicator cocks on the cylinder covers again.

21. Prime the fuel pumps, fuel pressure pipes and fuel injection valves.

22. Open the shut-off valve on the starting-air-bottle. Set the automatic starting-air stop valve to position AUTOMATIC. Close the vent cock on the starting-air distribution pipe. A small quantity of oil should be filled into the opening in the top flange of the starting valves, which is closed by a screw plug. This opening should be checked for the presence of oil, particularly after extended periods during which no engine manoeuvres have been made.

23. Adjust the pressures for water, oil and fuel, and check them on the instrument panel, *see* Table 7.6.

24. Move the speed adjusting lever to a position corresponding to at least maximum manoeuvring speed.

25. Report readiness of the engine to the bridge.

Each time, before the engine is started-up, unless it has been stopped only for a short interval during a manoeuvring period, the engine should be turned-over by means of the turning gear, and with the indicator cocks open, for one full revolution to make sure that nothing impedes the motion of the running gear.

Priming the Fuel System

To ensure that the engine will fire immediately, the fuel pumps, fuel pipes, and fuel valves of all cylinders must be primed in accordance with instructions.

Table 7.6 PRESSURES AND TEMPERATURES AT CONTINUOUS-SERVICE-OUTPUT

Measuring point		Pressures kgf/cm² (bar) see note [1] Min.	Max.	Temperatures °C Min.	Max.	Diff see [2]
Jacket cooling water	Inlet	*RND* 90, 105 3·5 (3·43)	4·5 (4·4)	50	60	
		RND 68, 76 3·0 (2·94)	4·0 (3·92)			
	Outlet			60	75	15 [3]
Cooling water for turbines (connected in series after cylinder cooling)	Inlet			60	75	10
	Outlet				85	
Fuel-valve cooling water	Inlet	2·5 (2·45)	4·0 (3·92)	70		
	Outlet				90	
Piston cooling water	Inlet	3·5 (3·43)	4·5 (4·4)	40	50	15 [3]
	Outlet				65	
Charge-air cooling water	Inlet		2·0 1·96)	25	33	
	Outlet				44	

(a) *Priming with booster pump*

   1. Start-up fuel booster pump.

   2. Open the vent cock on the fuel filter to allow the air to escape from the fuel supply pipe. Close vent cock again.

   3. Open the priming plugs on the fuel valves. Raise the fuel pressure, by adjusting the pressure retaining valve, until fuel emerges from the drain openings at the priming plugs. Keep the priming plugs open until fuel flows into the drain funnel without any accompanying air or gas bubbles.

   4. Close the priming plugs again and tighten the locknuts. Readjust the pressure retaining valves to service pressure.

(b) *Priming with hand lever*

   1. Start-up oil pump to obtain control-oil pressure in the cut-out servomotor.

Table 7.6 PRESSURES AND TEMPERATURES AT CONTINUOUS-SERVICE-OUTPUT *(cont.)*

		Pressures kgf/cm² (bar) *see note* [1]		*Temperatures* °C		
Measuring point		Min.	Max.	Min.	Max.	*Diff see* [2]
OIL Engine bearing oil	Inlet	1·5 (1·47)	2·5 (2·45)	35	45	
Turbocharger bearing oil		see instruction for turbochargers				
Crosshead lubricating oil	Inlet	3·0 (2·94)	4·0 (3·92)	35	45	
FUEL Fuel after filter	Inlet	3–6 (2·94– 5·88) normal (4·9)	6·5[4] (6·37) 5			
CHARGE AIR Air filter before turbocharger	Admissible pressure drop	150–200 mm (water gauge)				
Charge air in receiver	Outlet from cooler			35 normal 40–45	60	
Charge-air cooler	Admissible pressure drop	200–300 mm (water gauge)				
EXHAUST Exhaust	Inlet to turbine				500	
	Pressure after turbine	max. 300 mm (water gauge)				

[1] Pressures refer to a height of the pressure-gauge about 2 m above crankshaft centre, i.e. as with manoeuvring stand at bottom platform.
[2] Approximate temperature rise under service output.
[3] For RN 105 . 12°.
[4] During priming, temporarily higher.

2. Bring both telegraph lever and running direction interlock to the same running position, to allow the cut-out servomotor to release the fuel supply.

3. Set fuel lever to maximum charge; load indicator must assume the corresponding position.

4. With about one-half of the fuel pumps, the actuating rollers run on the base circles of the fuel cams. For the time being only these pumps can be primed.

5. Open the priming plug on the fuel valve of the cylinder to be primed.

6. Operate the cut-out lever of the fuel pump to be primed until fuel flows out of the priming pipe into the drain funnel without bubbles.

7. Close the priming plug and operate the cut-out lever to test whether or not priming has been carried out correctly. A strong resistance is a sign of correct priming.

8. Repeat this operation with all cylinders, barring the engine over at the same time.

9. Disengage the turning gear and secure the lever.

Starting the Engine

The engine must not be started without first ensuring that the adjustment of the fuel pumps, the Woodward governor, and the entire regulating linkage is in order. Check the shut-off valves.

All tools used for the adjustment of the control system must be removed. Check the regulating linkage for free and easy motion before starting the engine.

1. Check that the starting-air supply to the engine is opened, the turning gear is disengaged and secured, the automatic starting-air stop valve is at position AUTOMATIC and the speed adjusting lever is positioned so that a charge sufficient for starting is released (normally not beyond 3·5).

2. Repeat the starting order by means of the engine room telegraph. Thereby the mechanical blocking device of the starting lever is released and the slide valve of the reversing servomotor is brought to the desired position for either AHEAD or ASTERN. The oil pressure then moves the reversing servomotor to the corresponding position. As soon as the servomotor has reached its correct end position, the hydraulic blocking device releases the starting lever.

3. Pull the starting lever to position STARTING and release it again as soon as the cylinders fire correctly. The starting lever is pulled back to its resting position by the return spring and the starting control elements are vented of air.

4. The engine is now running on fuel. Adjust the manoeuvring speed by means of the speed adjusting lever.

5. As soon as the engine is turning over correctly, check the pressure on the pressure gauges and adjust the pressures to the proper values, if necessary. Check the turbocharger speed.

6. Make a tour of inspection all over and all around the engine.

7. Observe temperatures, see Table 7.6, listen carefully for unwanted running sounds.

After service speed has been ordered:

8. Close the automatic starting air stop valve by hand. Open the vent cock on the starting air distribution pipe.

9. Raise the engine speed slowly, particularly if the engine has been cold, until the service speed is reached. The load indicator position for full load must not be exceeded, *see* trial reports.

10. Adjust the temperatures.

Table 7.7 shows the recommended temperatures to which fuel oils must be heated. During the normal full-speed running the temperature of the fuel oil leaving the preheater must be kept at least 10°C above the minimum temperature given in the table below. This allows for cooling between the preheater and the injection nozzles, with the steam heating of the pipes and filter shut-down.

Table 7.7 HEAVY FUEL VISCOSITIES AND TEMPERATURES

Viscosity (sec)		Temperature
Redwood No. 1 at 100°C	Saybolt universal	°C
200	226	65– 75
300	340	75– 85
400	455	82– 92
500	570	85– 95
600	683	90–100
800	910	95–105
1 000	1 137	100–110
1 200	1 365	103–113
1 500	1 705	107–117
2 000	2 275	113–123
3 000	3 410	120–130
4 000	4 550	124–134
5 000	5 690	127–137
6 000	6 826	131–141

Manoeuvring can be carried out when running on heavy fuel oil, but extra vigilance is needed to ensure that the necessary preheat temperature is maintained.

Before overhauling the engine, it is best to run for about half-an-hour on heated diesel oil. The temperature should at first be the same as that of the heavy fuel oil, and then gradually reduced.

Sudden changes in the temperature of the fuel should be avoided at all times. In particular a sudden temperature drop may cause operating troubles, such as sticking of fuel-pump plungers.

Checks during Normal Operations

The inspections and precautions which contribute towards the avoidance of difficulties must be carried out constantly under normal operation. The most important checks are as stated below.

1. Regular checks of pressure and temperatures on pressure gauges and thermometers. The prescribed limits must be adhered to. When comparing temperatures the thermometer readings should not be relied on exclusively but, whenever possible, the pipes in question should be felt by hand.

2. The temperature differences between the inlets and outlets should be as small as possible, i.e. the throughput should be as large as possible. For this reason the cooling systems must not be throttled down. The shut-off valves of the cooling-water inlets and outlets must be fully open during operation. They serve only to cut-off individual cylinders from the cooling-water circuit during overhauls. The outlet temperatures are adjusted by regulating the oil or cooling-water by-passes of the installation.

3. If the cooling-water pressure is too low the individual outlets must not be touched either but, instead, a throttling disc should be fitted at the end of the cooling-water manifold.

4. Check all shut-off valves of the cooling and lubricating system for correct positioning. The oil and water-pressure safety device trips only if there is insufficient pressure in the main distribution pipe.

5. If abnormally high or low temperatures are encountered at an outlet, the temperature must be brought up or down to the prescribed value only by steps. Abrupt temperature changes cause severe thermal stresses, which may give rise to trouble.

6. Special attention is to be paid to the correct charge-air temperature after air coolers. Basically, the charge-air temperature should be kept as low as possible because high charge-air temperatures result in a poor air charge for the cylinder in question, causing increased fuel consumption and high exhaust temperatures. In hot and moist climates, however, water may condense in the charge-air receiver if the charge-air temperature after air cooler drops to below the point of condensation. To avoid the formation of rust inside the charge-air receiver, the charge-air must be cooled down only to a value which is safely above the dew point.

7. Check the pressure-drop of the charge-air through the air filters of the turbochargers and the air coolers. Too great a resistance causes insufficient air supply to the engine.

8. The fuel must be kept at a temperature which ensures a viscosity figure which is safely below the prescribed limits, before it is delivered to the engine.

9. The values read off from the instruments, compared with the values given in the trial reports under consideration of engine speed, are a reliable yardstick for the behaviour of the engine during operation. The most essential instrument readings are: position of the load indicator, speed of turbochargers, scavenging-air pressure, and exhaust temperature after turbochargers. A valuable criterion is also the daily fuel consumption referred to the lowest calorific value.

10. It is particularly important to check the exhaust temperature after the turbine, which is indicated by the remote thermometers in the control stand. The maximum admissible temperature must not be exceeded. The exhaust temperatures read off from the instruments during operation should be compared with the values given in the trial reports. If major deviations are noted with individual cylinders, the cause is to be investigated.

11. Check combustion by observing the exhaust gas colour.

12. Adjust the correct feed rate for cylinder lubricating oil and calculate the consumption. The optimum consumption under different load conditions is a matter of experience acquired during extended periods of operation.

13. The cylinder lubricators must be checked and filled-up at regular intervals. If cold, viscous oil is used for refilling, the lubricators should be filled gradually.

14. The temperature of the running gear should be checked by feeling the crankcase doors by hand. Bearings which have been replaced, or rescraped, must be given special attention for some time after being put into service. The prescribed precautions for observing crankcase explosions must be observed.

15. Regular listening to the noise of the engine may reveal irregularities.

16. The fuel should be carefully cleaned before being used. Water and sludge should be regularly drained away from the service tank and fuel filter.

17. Open the drain cocks on the air-coolers and charge-air receiver at regular intervals, for a check. Should any water be present it must be drained-off. Make sure whether or not it is sea-water (from a leaking cooler) or fresh water (water of condensation): air temperature after cooler must be increased.

18. Drain the spaces below the piston undersides. During each watch the drain cocks should be opened, one after the other, and kept open for a short while.

19. The vent cocks on the topmost points of the cooling water spaces (cylinder covers, turbochargers, air coolers, etc.) must always be kept open so as to permit air to escape along with the water.

20. Check the pressure-drop through the air filters of engine and turbochargers. Clean them if necessary.

21. Check the level of liquids in all water and oil tanks as well as in all drain tanks. Investigate any abnormal findings.

22. Check the cylinder, piston and fuel valve cooling water for dirt. If any contamination is found the cause must be investigated and rectified.

23. Check, and if necessary clean, the filter tank for the piston cooling water. Excessive fouling points to poor working condition of the glands.

24. Check the piston cooling glands for abnormal leakages.

25. Hand-drawn indicator diagrams should be taken from time to time.

26. Centrifuge the lubricating oil. Test samples should be taken at regular intervals and analysed by a reliable laboratory.

Instructions Concerning Overload Operation

The engine can be run at the overload conditions for a limited period. Overload operation is restricted to 110 per cent of the full load output, which in accordance with the propeller law means a speed of 103·23 per cent and a mean effective pressure of 106·56 per cent. The following instructions should be remembered:

1. During normal operation with the fuel pump control system correctly adjusted the overload position of the load indicator is only admissible under exceptional circumstances and for no longer than one hour or so. The load indicator position and the exhaust temperature after the turbines serve as a yardstick for the degree of overloading of the engine.

2. When the vessel is proceeding against strong head winds or heavy seas, or when the hull is heavily fouled, the speed of the vessel drops and consequently the revolutions of the engine also fall. The speed drop must not be compensated by simply setting the speed adjusting lever to a higher position as this would amount to overloading the engine, even though the engine speed would not exceed the value for normal operation.

3. The maximum admissible overload position of the load indicator is laid down in the trial reports of the engine and must not be exceeded. The same restriction also applies to the maximum

exhaust temperature after the turbines which, in no circumstances, should exceed the prescribed maximum admissible values.

4. The limiting stop for the maximum fuel charge, 481.21 on Figure 7.24, fitted to the speed adjusting lever by the engine maker, which is fixed after acceptance of the engine and secured against displacement, must not be wilfully moved or dismantled.

5. When running at overload, the delivery rate of all cylinder lubricators must be increased by moving the adjusting levers of the lubricators towards MAXIMUM position.

6. The outlet temperatures for water and oil must not exceed the prescribed maximum values.

7. The regular tours of supervision and inspection must be carried out frequently when operating the engine at overload, and the instrument readings for pressures and temperatures must be taken at shorter intervals.

Instructions Concerning Manoeuvring

1. Keep the automatic starting air stop valve open in position AUTOMATIC. Check the starting air pressure (maximum 30 kgf/cm^2; 29·4 bar). During manoeuvring the starting air compressors are to be kept in operation so as to maintain the starting air pressure as high as possible.

2. Set the repeating lever of the engine room telegraph either to AHEAD or ASTERN, whereby the reversing manoeuvres are initiated.

3. The reversing servomotor moves the fuel and starting cams into the new position for the desired running direction.

4. The speed adjusting lever is pulled back, but only as far as the position necessary for restarting the engine.

5. After the reversing functions are completed, the blocking device releases the starting lever.

6. The engine, which in most instances will still be turned over in the old running direction by the propeller, is stopped by the starting air and started-up in the new running direction.

7. The running direction safety interlock and the cut-out servomotor automatically release the fuel supply, as soon as the engine turns over correctly in the desired running direction.

8. When the cylinders fire the starting lever is released, where-upon it returns automatically to its resting position.

9. Adjust the manoeuvring speed by means of the speed adjusting lever.

10. All the instruments of the engine must be continuously checked, especially pressure gauges and thermometers.

11. During manoeuvres the cooling water supply to the air coolers must be reduced or cut-off completely, to avoid condensation of water inside the charge receiver and the resultant danger of corrosion.

12. If the engine has not been switched over to diesel fuel prior to manoeuvring, i.e. if the manoeuvres are carried out on fuel of high viscosity, the fuel must be constantly kept at a sufficiently high temperature. Keep fuel valve cooling water at normal temperature.

13. The engine should be stopped, as a rule, with the repeating lever of the engine room telegraph. If this lever is set to STOP position, the fuel is automatically cut-off by the reversing control valve and the cut-out servomotor. If no further manoeuvres are ordered, i.e. if the engine is put out of operation for some time, the first lever should be set to position 0.

Running at Minimum Speed

The engine speed which is just sufficient to permit all cylinders to fire regularly is referred to as minimum speed. With the engine being warm this speed is about $\frac{1}{6}$ of the rated speed. The following instructions should be remembered for minimum speed operation:

1. When running at minimum speed, the water and oil temperatures should be kept at the normal values.

2. At extremely low speeds, the engine is no longer respectively regulated by the governor and the speed. Accordingly the fuel charge is adjusted manually with the aid of the speed adjusting lever (fine control).

3. At low loads, the cylinder lubricating oil feed rate should be reduced correspondingly by moving the adjusting levers of the cylinder lubricators towards MINIMUM position.

4. The cooling water supply to the air coolers should be cut-off completely, to avoid condensation of water inside the charge-air receivers, leading to the formation of rust.

Operation in Heavy Seas

In heavy seas it is desirable to reduce the engine speed correspondingly and to remember the following points:

1. The governor establishes the new equilibrium without lag as soon as the propeller emerges, thus keeping the resulting speed fluctuations at a minimum.

2. When the propeller is again immersed, the governor increases the fuel charge to the value allowed by the torque limit fitted in the governor.

Instructions for Putting the Engine out of Operation for an Extended Period of Time

After the engine has been stopped, the following measures have to be taken if the engine is to be put out of operation for an extended period of time:

1. Set the telegraph lever to position STOP and the speed adjusting lever to 0.

2. Close the automatic starting air stop valve by means of the hand wheel. The shut-off on the starting air containers must be closed also.

3. The starting air pipes before and after the automatic starting air stop valve should be vented by opening the appropriate valves at the control stand. Make sure that there is no longer any pressure left in the starting air pipes by checking the manometers.

4. The water and oil pumps should be kept running for at least 20 minutes after the engine has been stopped, so as to bring all cooled engine parts to an even temperature as far as possible. Thereby the engine is not to be cooled down, but the inlet temperature of the cooling water maintained unchanged.

5. Engage the turning gear and keep it engaged as long as work is being performed on the engine. While the cooling system is still in operation, the engine should be turned over by means of the turning gear, with the indicator valves open. At the same time the cylinder lubricators should be operated, unless the cylinders had been amply lubricated prior to stopping.

6. Leave the turning gear engaged, so that the engine cannot be turned over by the propeller.

7. Open the crankcase doors and check all running gear parts for overheating, by feeling them with the hand. Observe the prescribed safety precautions.

8. Close the shut-off valves on the fuel tank.

9. Open the drain valves on the exhaust manifold pipe and exhaust chamber.

10. Keep the cooling water at about normal temperature, by utilising either a heating system or the heat of the cooling systems of the auxiliary engines.

11. The engine should be turned over at intervals by means of the turning gear, with the indicator cocks open, and the oil pump

running. In moist climates the engine should be turned over daily.

12. Any damages, leakages or other shortcomings noticed during the preceding spell of operation, or during inspection, must be put right without delay.

13. Carry out any due overhauls. Take notice of all prescribed safety precautions.

14. If the engine is to remain idle for several weeks, or if the ship is taken out of commission, the engine must be cleaned and all bright parts greased.

The cylinder liners and pistons should likewise be thoroughly oiled, which is best done by ample lubrication prior to stopping. After the engine has been stopped it should be turned over with the turning gear, while at the same time the cylinder lubricators are operated. This is also recommended as a protective measure against corrosion, if the engine is put out of service for only a day or two.

15. If the auxiliary engines and boilers are also put out of operation and there is danger of frost, all cooling systems must be carefully drained.

If the engine is stopped, e.g. for loading or unloading the ship in port, the pumps for cylinder and piston cooling water, lubricating oil, etc., must be kept in operation for at least another twenty minutes to equalise the engine temperature. To maintain operational readiness and to eliminate the formation of water of condensation and corrosion, the temperatures of the cooling media must not fall too low. The crankshaft should be turned over for a few revolutions with the turning gear, while at the same time the hand cranks of the cylinder oilers are to be given some 40 turns.

Instructions concerning operation with the Propeller Uncoupled

After major overhauls, the engine should be run-in with the propeller coupled-up at 60 per cent of the full load speed as a minimum. The usual checks of the running gear can be carried out best this way. If, however, the ship's berth does not permit this standing pull test with the vessel made fast to shore, the engine can be run with the propeller uncoupled. Experience has shown, however, that this carries the risk of the engine running away unless the following safety precautions are observed:

1. After completion of the overhaul, make sure that the fuel regulation and fuel pump control systems are correctly adjusted and functioning properly.

2. Before starting-up the engine, the prescribed fuel pump cut-out check must be carried out. No pump should deliver fuel with the load indicator at position 1.3 or below.

3. The engine must in no circumstances be started-up if the governor is disconnected from the regulating linkage, blocked, defective or not adjusted according to instructions.

4. Before starting the engine make sure that the regulating linkage can be moved to position 0 of the load indicator by both the governor and the fuel lever.

5. The regulating linkage must be checked for free and easy motion also. It must be possible to move the linkage by hand without difficulty and the load indicator must follow the movements of the speed adjusting lever instantly, that is, without lag.

6. When the engine is started, at least one man is to be stationed at each fuel pump group ready to cut it out by hand.

7. When running the engine with the propeller uncoupled, an engineer must always be at the control stand ready for immediate action. The engine speed must be watched carefully.

8. During the running-in period, attention should be paid to any unusual noises and vibrations. These are to be eliminated, if possible, by selecting the appropriate speed.

Instructions concerning the Cutting-out of Individual Cylinders

1. Should a cylinder sustain damage, the engine must be stopped immediately and the defect put right. If this is not possible, the fuel pump of the defective cylinder must be cut-out at once by means of the cut-out lever.

2. If the damage to the cylinder in question is of a nature making any further operation of the running gear impossible, the latter is to be immobilised in the following manner: support the piston, together with the crosshead, by means of special device; dismantle the connecting rod.

3. If the piston, or cylinder, only has been damaged while the connecting-rod bearings and crosshead are still in operating condition, only the piston and piston rod are to be removed. In addition to this, the following measures are to be taken: seal-off the cylinder bore, and piston rod gland bore, with special device; dismantle the standpipe of the piston cooling system and seal-off the bore with plug; seal-off the crosshead bore with special device.

4. In any event the following preventive measures must be taken: reduce the lubrication of the cylinder in question to a minimum; dismantle and block-off the control air pipe to the starting valve; distmantle and block-off the starting air pipe to the cylinder cover.

5. With a cylinder cut-out, the normal service speed of the engine can no longer be maintained. To avoid thermal overloading of the engine, the full load position of the load indicator or the full load exhaust temperature must on no account be exceeded. Also, the colour of the exhaust gases is to be constantly checked. Should the exhaust temperature rise to an excessive value the engine speed must be reduced correspondingly.

6. With individual cylinders cut-out the turbochargers are forced to operate outside their normal speed range. The delivery rate of the chargers decreases, so that they may start surging, a fact which manifests itself in the form of a loud howling noise and pronounced fluctuations of the scavenging pressure. If this occurs at brief intervals, or is continuous, the engine cannot be run at this speed on account of lack of air, and the speed must be reduced until the surging ceases.

7. With individual cylinders cut-out, the engine may be stopped in a position still working within the starting range. In this event the engine should be started briefly in the opposite running direction, to bring the crankshaft to a more reasonable position. The possibility of poor response of the engine during manoeuvres must be taken into account.

8. Whenever parts of the running gear of individual cylinders are removed, or immobilised by supporting them, the mechanical equilibrium of the engine is disturbed and considerable vibration may be set-up within certain speed ranges. If exceptionally severe vibration is encountered, the engine speed must be reduced further. In instances such as this, extended voyages should be avoided, if possible.

Instructions concerning Operation with Defective Turbocharger

If turbochargers are damaged to an extent which makes normal operation impossible, special measures are to be taken. These will depend upon the time available and the number of turbochargers involved.

If the necessary alterations cannot be made right away, operation with the defective turbocharger should be continued, but only for a short time and at strongly reduced engine speed, so as to obviate considerable further damage.

If the defective turbocharger cannot be repaired on the spot and there is no spare turbocharger, or if there is not enough time for replacement or repair, then the engine must be started-up again only after the alterations described in Table 7.8 have been carried out, see Figure 7.32.

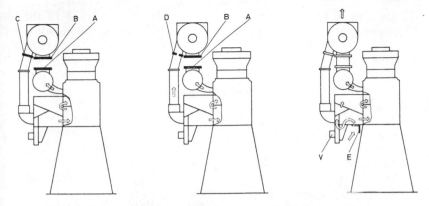

Figure 7.32 Turbocharger emergency conditions

The upper limits of Table 7.8 are for guidance and may have to be further reduced, depending on the condition of the engine.

The position of the load indicator, the blackening of the exhaust and the exhaust temperature after the turbine must be constantly checked. To avoid overloading of the engine, the values measured during normal service must in no circumstances be exceeded

Operation with Defective Air-cooler

If the tubes of an air-cooler should leak, cooling water will enter the charge-air cooler. The latter is equipped with drain pipes for leak water and condensed water, so that the engine room staff are able to see a defect in good time. As the charge-air is, as a rule, cooled with sea-water, cooler leakages may cause serious corrosion in the lower part of the charge-air receiver. For this reason, the cocks of the drain pipes should be opened from time to time. If no charge-air blows through while the engine is running, the drain is clogged and needs cleaning.

On detecting a cooler defect the following remedial measures should be taken:

(a) As soon as operation permits, dismantle the defective cooler and replace it with a spare unit.

(b) Put the defective air cooler out of operation and drain it.

(c) Disconnect the individual supply and drain pipes leading to and from the defective air cooler C. The air cooler is drained by opening the screw plugs A. Leak water can be drained away from the charge-air receivers by opening the cocks of the drain pipes.

Table 7.8 BLOWER DEFECTS, COUNTER MEASURES AND ATTAINABLE REVOLUTIONS, LOAD AND MEP—RN ENGINES

No. of Blowers		Counter measures	Refer to emergency case	Upper limit in %			Supervise
Total	Defect			Rev/min	Power	Mep	
3	1	1. Remove expansion piece between exhaust manifold and turbocharger gas inlet. Fit blank flanges A and **B**. 2. Fit blank flange C to blower air outlet. 3. Shut-down turbocharger lubrication and water cooling systems.	034-20 1	81	53	65·5	Scavenge pressure; Blower rev/min; Firing pressure.
2	1	1. Remove expansion piece between exhaust manifold and turbocharger gas inlet. Fit blank flanges A and **B**. 2. To the blower air outlet fit flange D. This flange to have hole of diameter given in *Table 034-20* 3. Reduce bearing lubrication and water cooling according to extent and type of damage. Lubricating oil pressure to be reduced in relation to reduction in sealing air pressure, so that no oil leaks to gas side.	034-20 2				
1	1	1. Block the rotor of damaged blower. 2. Shut-off turboblower bearing lubrication. 3. Open all covers E on air receiver. 4. Switch-on auxiliary blower if not fitted with automatic start.	034-20 3	63	25	39·5	Exhaust temp. before turbine smoke***
2	2						
3	2 or 3						

*The power obtainable from the engine in these emergency cases is also dependent on the general condition of the engine.
**None of these values may exceed the values obtained at normal service power.
***Heavy black smoke is to be avoided; the visible exhaust must remain translucent.

During this kind of emergency operation the charge-air temperature and also the exhaust temperature will rise. For this reason the engine should be loaded only to a degree at which the normal full-load exhaust temperature after the turbine is not exceeded. The exhaust temperature must be carefully observed. Should the exhaust temperature rise too high, the engine speed must be reduced accordingly.

Safety Measures to be taken before Overhauls

Before any overhaul work is started, particularly on the running gear, the following safety precautions must be taken:

1. Close the automatic starting air stop valve and the shut-off valves on the starting air bottles.
2. Vent all starting air pipes before and after the automatic starting air stop valve. Check pressure gauges. Leave the vent cocks open.
3. Leave all indicator cocks open as long as the overhaul work is being carried out.
4. Engage the turning gear and secure the lever.
5. If the engine has to be stopped on account of running gear components, or bearings running hot, the engine should be allowed to cool-off for at least 10 minutes before opening the crankcase doors.
6. If carbon dioxide had been used in the crankcase, the latter should be thoroughly vented before any man is allowed to work inside it.

OPERATING TROUBLES

Breakdowns can be normally avoided by conscientiously observing the service instructions. But if serious trouble should arise in spite of this, the cause must be traced systematically and not by making random searches. The following notes will assist in tracing the cause of trouble:

Engine does not fire when the Starting Lever is pulled

Possible causes for this are:

1. The turning gear is engaged. Its blocking valve prevents pilot air flowing to the pilot valve on the control stand.
2. The shut-off valves on the starting air containers and/or pipes are closed.

3. The automatic starting air stop valve does not work on account of having been closed by hand, either being jammed or its internal outlet ducts being obstructed.

4. The actuating valve for the automatic starting air stop valve is jammed or opens only partially.

5. The non-return valve in the starting air pipe is stuck and does not open.

6. Starting air pressure is too low, the engine only oscillating. Flame baffle is obstructed.

7. The starting air control slide valves are either stuck or the control air is not able to force them down on to the starting cam. Vent opening may be obstructed.

8. The starting valves do not open.

9. A working piston or any other running gear component prevents starting of the engine by reason of being seized or defective.

10. One or more starting control air pipes, or control oil pipes, are incorrectly connected or obstructed.

11. If the blocking device of the starting lever has been un-coupled by hand, the engine can only be started if the reversing servomotor is close to its end position.

The engine oscillates when being started or does not gain speed

Possible causes for this are:

1. Individual cylinders receive only an insufficient amount of starting air, or none at all.

2. The starting air pressure is too low in general and cannot overcome the compression counter-pressure. This happens more frequently with engines having only a few cylinders.

3. One or more starting air control slide valves are stuck.

4. One or more starting valves are stuck or defective.

5. Obstructed starting air pipes (flame baffles).

The Engine turns over on Compressed air but Receives no Fuel Charge

(a) *Load indicator does not indicate a charge.*

1. Oil or water pressure is too low (automatic cut-out device).

2. Fuel lever is at position 0.

3. Regulating linkage is jammed or blocked.

4. Return springs are loose or defective: regulating linkage does not move to a position releasing a fuel charge.

5. Governor is defective: it does not release a fuel charge.

6. Starting lever blocking device is jammed and does not release control oil supply to the cut-out servomotor.

7. The cut-out servomotor, or its control valve, is jammed in cut-out position.

8. The running direction safety interlock is uncoupled (defective).

9. The rotary slide valve of the running direction safety interlock is seized in an end position.

10. The automatic cut-out device is defective.

11. The three-way cocks of the automatic cut-out device are closed.

12. Control oil pipes are incorrectly connected.

13. Control oil pipes are obstructed or defective due to leaking.

(b) *Load indicator indicates a charge but cylinders do not receive fuel.*

1. Fuel supply is interrupted or obstructed.

2. The fuel pump plungers had been raised by hand and are still lifted.

3. The fuel pump control system is incorrectly adjusted (suction valves remain open).

4. The safety governor is in tripped position.

5. The priming plugs on the fuel valves are open.

6. Leaking fuel delivery pipes or fuel pumps.

Cylinders do not Fire

Possible causes for the cylinders not firing are:

1. The shut-off valves on the fuel supply pipes, or before the fuel filters, are closed.

2. Insufficient fuel supply pressure.

3. Fuel is either unsuitable or contains water.

4. The fuel pump chambers, or delivery pipes, have been only insufficiently primed, or not at all, and contain air or fuel vapour.

5. Compression pressure is too low.

6. The quantity of injected fuel is insufficient. The speed adjusting lever should be moved to a somewhat higher position.

7. The regulating linkage or one or more eccentric shafts are stuck. The load indicator should be checked.

8. The Woodward governor sticks in an extremely low position and releases only an insufficient fuel charge, or none at all.

9. One of the control elements is stuck; the cut-out servomotor does not release a fuel charge.

10. The fuel pump plungers are either raised or seized.

11. The fuel pump valves are either leaking or stuck.

12. The safety governor has tripped and fuel pump suction valves remain constantly open.

13. The fuel valve nozzles are either obstructed or defective, or their needles are stuck.

14. The priming plugs of the fuel valves are open or leaking.

15. Oil and/or water pressure is too low. The automatic cut-out device does not release fuel supply.

Individual Cylinders do not Fire correctly

Possible causes for individual cylinders not firing correctly are:

1. The fuel pump drive of the cylinder in question is still raised or the fuel pump plunger is stuck.

2. The fuel pump or fuel delivery pipe of the cylinder in question has not at all, or only insufficiently, been primed and still contains air or water.

3. The suction and/or delivery valve of the fuel pump is leaking or stuck.

4. The relief valve of the fuel pump of the cylinder in question is leaking.

5. The fuel delivery pump is leaking.

6. The priming plug of the fuel valve is still open or leaking.

7. The fuel valve nozzle is obstructed or leaking. The nozzle needle is seized.

8. The compression pressure is too low for firing.

Heavy Ignitions occur when the Engine is Started

Possible causes for heavy ignitions are:

1. Fuel had inadvertently entered the cylinders when priming the fuel injection system.

2. The injected fuel quantity is too large for starting. The speed adjusting lever should be set to a lower position (about position 3·5).

3. The fuel cams or fuel pumps are incorrectly adjusted. Compare adjustment with the values given in the valve setting tables.

4. One or more fuel cams have been turned relative to the cam shaft. Check whether or not the cam nuts are correctly tightened and if the cam locking device teeth engage properly.

5. If the reversing servomotor on the camshaft has stuck before reaching its proper end position and the blocking device of starting and fuel lever had been released by hand. Fuel is injected into the cylinders too early. Caution when unblocking by hand.

Poor Combustion, Discoloured Exhaust

Possible causes for poor combustion with discoloured exhaust are:

1. The engine is overloaded. The load indicator and the exhaust temperatures should be checked.
2. An excessive quantity of fuel is injected into individual cylinders. These cylinders are therefore overloaded.
3. The charge-air pressure is too low, resulting in a lack of air. This may be due to fouled blowers or fouled protective gratings.
4. The scavenging and/or exhaust valves are fouled.
5. Loss of air through defective scavenging air valves.
6. Insufficient compression pressure.
7. The fuel pumps, or fuel cams, are incorrectly adjusted.
8. The fuel is either unsuitable or insufficiently preheated.
9. The fuel valve nozzles are either obstructed, encrusted with coke, or atomise the fuel only poorly on account of formation of 'trumpets'.
10. The fuel valve nozzles are either defective or leaking.
11. The nozzle holes are enlarged by erosion in the course of operation, or their outlet edges are no longer sharp.

Engine cannot be Reversed or can be Started only in one Running Direction

1. There is only an insufficient control oil pressure or none at all.
2. If the engine cannot be reversed when stopping the vessel, this may also be due to an inadequate torque on account of insufficient starting air pressure or a defective starting air control slide valve or starting valve.
3. The reversing servomotor is either stuck in an end position or shortly before an end position, thus not releasing control oil to the blocking device of the starting lever. Unblocking the starting lever by hand will be a remedy only if the incorrect reversing angle is not excessive. Caution when unblocking by hand.
4. The running direction safety interlock, or its control slide valve, is stuck in an end position so that the engine may be started in the opposite running direction; however, the cut-out

servomotor does not receive control oil pressure, thus not releasing a fuel charge for the opposite running direction.

5. Control oil pipes, or ducts of the reversing servomotor, are obstructed or heavily leaking, so that the oil pressure is too low to move the turning arm.

6. The reversing valve has become loose and has been turned relative to the lever (incorrect assembly).

7. If this shortcoming is encountered already during the first reversing manoeuvre, this may be caused by incorrect positioning of a blocking duct, so that control oil passage to the blocking device of the starting lever does not open.

Engine Starts in the Wrong Running Direction when being Reversed

1. The cam disc of the engine room telegraph has been fitted facing in the wrong direction. Check the markings.

2. The reversing valve, or the rotary slide valve, of the running direction safety interlock has been incorrectly fitted. Check the markings on housing and valve.

3. The control oil pipes of the reversing servomotor are incorrectly connected. This may happen at initial erection.

4. Incorrect assembly of the reversing servomotor. Check the markings on the bearing sides.

5. The running direction safety interlock is out of action if the cut-out servomotor is stuck.

Scavenging Air Pressure in the Charge-air Receiver drops with the Load Indicator remaining in the same position

Possible causes for this are:

1. Turbocharger is either fouled or defective.
2. Loss of exhaust gases before turbine.
3. Increasing exhaust gas back-pressure after turbine.
4. Intake filters of turbocharger or air cooler are fouled. Protective grating before turbocharger is fouled.
5. Air losses on account of leakages (leaking stuffing boxes).

Exhaust Temperature in Manifold Pipe rises with Load Indicator remaining in the same position

Possible causes for this are:

1. The engine is thermally overloaded.

2. Ports in working cylinders are fouled.

3. The engine does not receive enough air because of defective or fouled turbocharger or air cooler. Protective grating before turbocharger may be fouled.

4. There is a fire in a scavenging air space.

Exhaust Temperature after an Individual Cylinder drops with Load Indicator remaining in the same position

Possible causes for this are:

1. If the compression and ignition pressures of the cylinder in question did not change along with the exhaust temperature, the exhaust thermometer of this cylinder is probably defective and should be checked or replaced.

2. If the compression and ignition pressures of the cylinder in question dropped along with the exhaust temperature, the following causes may be to blame, provided that neither the indicator bore nor the indicator valve are obstructed:

(a) Defective piston rings. Piston rings are either sticking or leaking. Piston ring gaps are right above each other.

(b) The cylinder in question fires irregularly or not at all, or does not receive enough fuel.

(c)' The fuel injection system is either leaking or defective (there are leaking fuel pump valves or fuel injection valves).

Engine Speed falls with Load Indicator remaining in the same position

Possible causes are:

1. A component of the running gear is running hot. Stop the engine immediately.

2. The hydrodynamic resistance of the ship's hull is increasing.

3. The propeller is absorbing greater power.

4. The propeller shaft friction in stern tube is excessive.

5. A fuel pump or fuel pipe is defective.

6. The priming plug on a fuel injection valve is either loose or leaking.

7. The holes of a fuel valve nozzle are obstructed.

8. Defective scavenging air valves.

9. Defective or fouled turbocharger or air cooler (inadequate air supply). Protective grating before turbocharger may be fouled.

12. Fouled scavenge or exhaust ports.

13. Poor combustion.

Irregular Running: Intermittent Cutting-out

Possible causes:

1. All or individual cylinders fire irregularly or intermittently.
2. Fuel circulating pump out of service or defective.
3. Fuel transfer pressure before fuel pumps is too low.
4. Fuel temperature before fuel pumps is either too high or too low.
5. Fuel pipes have been poorly ventilated.
6. Fuel contains water.
7. Leakages or defects in the fuel injection system.
8. Hot running gear component causes severely alternating friction.
9. Woodward governor does not function properly, or it sticks.
10. Pressure surges in the charge-air receiver (turbocharger 'pumping').
11. Temporary tripping of the automatic cut-out device by reason of the cut-out pressure being reached.

Engine stops spontaneously

Possible causes of engine stopping are:

1. The automatic cut-out device had tripped by reason of inadequate oil and/or water pressure.
2. The oil pressure acting on the cut-out servomotor 455, on its control slide valve 454, or on the blocking valve for the starting lever 435 is too low, so that the springs of these units cut-out the fuel supply. The numbers refer to Figure 7.21.
3. Control oil pipes are either obstructed or defective (leakages).
4. The Woodward governor is either defective or blocked.
5. Fuel tanks are empty, or their shut-off valves are closed or obstructed. Filters are fouled or clogged.
6. The fuel contains water, or the fuel pumps draw-in air.
7. The telegraph lever was inadvertently moved to STOP.
8. The running direction safety interlock 453 has been uncoupled because of the sliding ring running hot or the stop pin having come loose, thus interrupting the supply of control oil to the cut-out servomotor.
9. A working piston, or another part of the running gear, has seized or is blocked due to a defect. Caution when opening the crankcase.
10. The propeller is obstructed or the propeller shaft has seized.

11. Air supply to the turbochargers is blocked (fouled filters). The protective gratings before the turbocharger are fouled.
12. The safety governor has tripped.

Individual piston Knocks at Top Dead Centre

Possible causes are:

1. Early fuel injection. The adjustment of the fuel pump and fuel cam should be checked.
2. The cylinder in question is overloaded. The effective delivery stroke of the corresponding fuel pump should be checked.
3. The needle of the fuel valve nozzle in question sticks.
4. The fuel used is unsuitable.
5. The cylinder is fouled.
6. The top piston ring strikes against the ridge worn at the top of the cylinder bore.
7. Excessive clearance between piston and cylinder.
8. Excessive bearing play of the running gear.
9. Bolts of the running gear have loosened.
10. The working piston is riding too high and strikes against the cylinder cover at top dead-centre.

Piston running hot

If a cylinder knocks increasingly at the end of each piston stroke, with the engine speed decreasing and the outlet temperature of the cylinder cooling water rising, then the piston has run hot and is seizing.

Remedial measures:

1. Cut-out the fuel pump of the cylinder immediately. Lubricate the cylinder additionally by hand.
2. If possible, stop the engine and allow the cylinder and piston to cool down.
3. Remember safety instructions concerning the prevention of fires in the buffer space underneath the piston undersides.
4. Check and dismantle the defective piston.
5. If piston and liner are only slightly damaged, the scored areas should be cleanly smoothed with carborundum stone and emery cloth.
6. If piston and liner have sustained serious damage, then spares are to be fitted.
7. Check the cylinder lubrication before re-erecting the piston.

8. Check piston clearances.

9. If the voyage has to be continued and the repair of piston and liner postponed owing to shortage of time, then the piston must be taken out together with the piston rod and the cylinder and the gland sealed off.

Running Gear Bearings become hot

Possible causes are:

1. Inadequate lubricating oil pressure. The pressure gauges should be checked and replaced if necessary.

2. The oil level has fallen too low in the tank and the pump is drawing-in air.

3. Bearing clearances are too small.

4. Lubricating orifices, or grooves of the bearing, are obstructed or clogged.

5. An oil pipe or pipe connection is defective. Closed shut-off valves.

6. There is water in the lubricating oil. Rusty pins.

7. There is air in the lubricating oil.

8. There are metal particles, or sand, in the lubricating oil system. New piping should be carefully cleaned.

9. The bearing or journal pin is damaged mechanically.

10. Excessive bearing wear.

11. The bearing has been deformed, resulting from inexpert tightening of the bolts.

Remedial measures

1. Increase the lubricating oil pressure as far as possible.

2. Should the temperature keep rising in spite of this measure, the engine should be stopped immediately and allowed to cool down.

3. Note the safety precautions concerning the prevention of crankcase fires or explosion.

4. Check and dismantle the hot bearing.

5. If the damage is only slight, the bearing and journal should be repaired.

6. If the damage is severe, a spare bearing and journal should be fitted. Recondition if possible.

7. If the dismantling and reconditioning of the bearing and journal have to be postponed due to lack of time, and the voyage has to be continued, the speed of the engine must be substantially reduced and the fuel supply to the cylinder in question cut-off.

Difficulty with the Oil System

(a) *Insufficient oil pressure.*

Possible causes are:

1. Defective oil pump.
2. Inadequate delivery rate of the oil pump. The prescribed delivery rate should be adhered to.
3. The by-pass in the installation is opened too far.
4. The oil regulating valve is not opened far enough.
5. Excessive bearing clearances.
6. Defective oil supply pipes.
7. Defective crosshead lubricating system.
8. The oil level in the tank has fallen too low. The oil pump is drawing-in air.

(b) *Oil supply is interrupted.*

Possible causes are:

1. Oil passages or grooves are obstructed.
2. Defective oil supply pipes.
3. There is air in the oil supply pipes.

Difficulty with the Cylinder Lubricating System

Possible causes are:

1. The non-return valve for the lubricating stud is defective.
2. The cylinder oiler or its drive are defective.
3. Lubricating oil pipes or pipe connections are defective.
4. Lubricating oil pipes, or cylinder lubricating studs, are defective.
5. The cylinder lubricators need replenishing.
6. There is air in the piping.

Difficulty with the Cooling Water System of the Engine

If the cooling water temperature or pressure rises, falls, or fluctuates continually in spite of correctly set regulation, the cause of this shortcoming should be traced and rectified.

Fluctuating Pressure of the Cylinder Cooling Water

Possible causes are:

1. There are accumulations of air in the cooling chambers, or pipes, by reason of inadequate venting during replenishing and operation.

2. The static pressure head of the cylinder cooling water system has fallen due to the expansion vessel running empty, or because the vent cocks of the cooling water outlets on the cylinder covers are closed.

3. Gas is entering the cooling water as the result of a defect.

4. Cooling water pipes are clogged; regulating valves are defective or almost closed.

Rising Outlet Temperature of the Cooling Water with Individual Cylinders

Possible causes are:

1. The cylinder in question is overloaded.

2. The working piston in the cylinder is running hot or has seized.

3. The cooling chambers have been insufficiently vented. Check this.

4. The shut-off valves on the cylinder have been closed inadvertently or are defective.

5. Cooling water pipes or ducts are obstructed.

6. Gas is entering the cooling water due to a defect.

Rising Cooling Water Temperatures with all Cylinders

Possible causes are:

1. Overloading of the complete engine. The load indicator and the exhaust temperature after the turbines should be checked.

2. The cooling chambers and pipes have been inadequately vented. This is to be checked.

3. Shut-off valves have been inadvertently closed or throttled too far.

4. Cooling water pipe or manifold pipe obstructed.

5. Recooler is fouled or defective.

6. Defective cooling water pump (inadequate delivery rate).

Difficulties with the Fuel System of the Engine

(a) *Preheater, filter, and fuel pipes remain cold:* A state which applies particularly to operation on heavy fuel oil.

Possible causes:

1. No steam pressure.
2. Steam pipes obstructed.
3. Failure of the steam pressure-reducing valve.
4. Condensate accumulating in the heating pipes.
5. Water accumulating in the steam trap.
6. Inadequate venting of the heating pipes.

(b) *Fuel does not circulate and unheated portions remain cold:* A state which applies particularly to operation on heavy fuel oil.

1. Fuel circulating pump is defective, or out of service.
2. Fuel tank is empty.
3. Fuel cannot be pumped because of inadequate heating.
4. Shut-off valves or change-over cocks, before or after the fuel circulating pump, are either closed or else set wrong way.
5. Fuel pumps inadequately vented.
6. Fuel pipes clogged by congealed fuel. When the fuel delivery pipes are obstructed, the engine should be barred over with the turning gear for several revolutions, with maximum fuel charge and the priming plugs open.
7. Individual fuel pipes inadequately heated or not heated.

TURBOCHARGER RUNNING DEFECTS

Charging-air pressure too low or too high

Charging-air pressure falls if:

(a) Air filters are blocked or there is too great an air pressure-drop in the suction air duct.

(b) Air loss in the air ducting, caused by a damaged gasket.

(c) Loss of exhaust gas in the ducting between diesel engine and exhaust gas inlet housing.

(d) Too high an exhaust gas back-pressure after the turbine; foreign body in the exhaust pipe after the turbine.

(e) Excessive dirt deposit on the turbine, impeller, spiral insert with diffuser and air cooler.

(f) Damaged labyrinth rings on the blower side of the gas inlet housing.

Charging-air pressure increases if:

(g) There is incorrect combustion.

(h) Drop in the mechanical efficiency of the diesel engine (piston seizure).

Vibrations

Vibrations are caused by:

(a) Broken turbine blades. In this event, rotor to be removed and forwarded to the manufacturers.

(b) Defective or badly worn bearings leading to rubbing of the rotor on the guide ring or on the labyrinth ring. Bearing to be changed according to the maker's instructions.

(c) Badly out-of-balance turbine wheel, caused by breakage of a blade.

Abnormal noise can be caused by the rubbing of the impeller wheel on the guide ring, or by the turbine blades fouling the diffuser on the turbine side.

MAINTENANCE SCHEDULE FOR RND ENGINES

The time intervals should correspond to the operational conditions; this may necessitate a change of the intervals stated in this schedule.

I Before and after each Starting Manoeuvre

Thrust bearing; crankshaft bearing. Check oil circulation and temperature after each overhaul.

Chamber below piston undersides. Drain away water; during each watch open one drain-cock after the other for a short time.

Fuel injection valves. Prime after extended period out of service.

Starting valves. Check temperature of starting air pipe after valve, by feeling. Lubricate during manoeuvres.

Top and bottom connecting-rod bearings; crosshead slippers. Check oil circulation and temperatures after each overhaul.

Automatic starting air-stop valve and non-return valve. Drain after each manoeuvring period.

Oil and water pressure safety device. Check functions after leaving port.

Woodward governor. Check oil level.

Charge-air receiver. Drain.

Charge-air coolers. Check vents at regular intervals.

II Every 150 hours running

Piston cooling-glands. With new engine, check glands and reciprocating tubes after the first 1000 hours.

Regulating linkage. Oil.

Turbochargers. See special service instructions for turbochargers.

Charge-air coolers. Clean as soon as admissible pressure-drop is exceeded.

Chamber below piston undersides. During each watch open one drain cock after the other for a short time.

III Every 1500 hours running

Piston cooling-glands. Check glands and reciprocating tubes after the first 1000 hours.

Camshaft drive. Check gear-wheels and nozzle.

Woodward governor. Drain oil every six months; rinse housing with gas oil and replenish with new oil.

Regulating linkage. Grease.

Turbochargers. See special service instructions for turbochargers.

Charge-air coolers. Clean as soon as admissible pressure-drop is exceeded.

Piston-rod glands. With new engine, check one gland after 1000 hours of operation.

Fuel-injection valve. Clean and check. Readjust injection pressure if necessary.

Starting valves. Retighten valve spindle after 200–300 starting manoeuvres.

Crankcase. With new engine, retighten all screwed connections after the first 500 to 1000 hours.

Crankshaft bearing. With new engine, retighten the thrust bolts after the first 500–1000 hours.

IV Every 3000 hours running

Thrust bearing. Check axial play.

Crankshaft bearing. Check clearance and readjust if necessary. Dismantle bearings according to regulation of classification societies at least every 15 000 to 20 000 hours of operation.

Tie rods. Check the prestressing of all tie bolts after approximately one year of operation.

Cylinder liners. Clean the scavenge and exhaust ports if necessary.

Cylinder lubricating studs. Check for satisfactory seal against water and proper functioning of cylinder lubricating system during each piston overhaul.

Chamber below piston undersides. Clean if necessary.

Fuel injection valves. Check holes for wear.

Crankshaft. Check crank spread.

Top and bottom connecting-rod bearings. During each second piston overhaul dismantle the corresponding bearings. Check play and readjust if necessary.

Piston cooling-glands. Clean and check. Replace rings if necessary.

Woodward governor. Drain oil every six months. Rinse housing with gas oil and replenish with new oil.

Charge-air coolers. Clean as soon as admissible pressure-drop is exceeded.

V Every 6000–8000 hours running

Crankcase. Clean; retighten all screwed connections.

Crankshaft bearings. Check clearance and readjust if necessary. Dismantle bearings according to regulation of classification societies, at least every 15 000–20 000 hours of operation.

Tie-rods. Check the prestressing of all the bolts after approximately one year of operation.

Cylinder liners. Remove ridge from top of cylinder liner and check internal diameter.

Cylinder lubricating studs. Check for satisfactory seal against water and proper functioning of cylinder lubricating system during each piston overhaul.

Piston-rod glands. Clean and check. Readjust the lateral play of sealing and scraper elements, and replace them if necessary.

Cylinder covers. Check copper sealing rings.

Starting valves. Clean and check at least once a year. Grind-in if necessary.

Z TYPE ENGINES

The Sulzer Z and ZV engines are turbocharged trunk-piston engines of light, compact design and are suitable for a wide range of applications. Both two-stroke and four-stroke versions are available in two configurations, i.e. in-line and V form. The engine has a bore of 400 mm and a stroke of 480 mm and covers an output range of 2500 to 9600 bhp (say 1900 to 7200 kW). *See* Figures 7.33 and 7.34, illustrating an in-line engine and Figure 7.35 a V engine.

Several new design features have been incorporated which will permit substantial increases of the specific output in the course of further development. The new design features are: 1. Rotating piston eliminating risk of piston and piston ring seizure; 2. Effective bore cooling in the top part of the cylinder liner; 3. Cylinder head with a double-bottom plate, the lower one being relatively thin to permit low thermal stresses.

The crankcase is of welded construction. Together with the

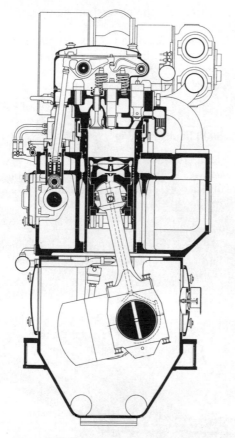

Figure 7.33 Z40/48 cross-section in-line engine

cylinder block it forms a stiff and compact structure.

The cylinder liners are of special cast iron with the top ends reinforced. They are watercooled, with cooling bores in the top part for reducing the temperatures on the running surface. The cylinder cover is likewise watercooled and consists of special cast iron. It has four exhaust valves and a centrally arranged fuel valve, *see* Figure 7.36.

The fuel valve is watercooled, including its nozzle as far as the tip, in order to preclude residues when running on heavy fuel oil. The fuel pumps are of the double-chamber type, with slanting control edges. Each cylinder has its own fuel pump, which can be cut out individually.

Figure 7.34 6Z40/48 in-line engine

The exhaust valves are made from special steel, and their seats are given a special treatment to withstand corrosive attack by heavy oil residues. The camshafts are arranged along the side and carry the cams actuating the exhaust valves and fuel pumps. The cams are shrunk-on hydraulically, with neither keys nor grooves, so that they can be removed or repositioned at any time with a simple device.

The piston is cooled with lubricating oil and turns on its own axis. The rotary motion is caused by the swing of the connecting rod, acting through a toothed rim and two pawls; the force is absorbed by a circular spring which transmits the thrust evenly to the piston. The rotating piston results in less and more uniform wear on cylinder

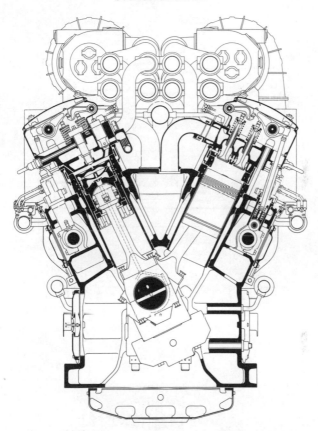

Figure 7.35 ZVB cross-section V engine

liners and piston rings and therefore better running conditions. It demands a spherical bearing instead of a gudgeon pin, *see* Figure 7.37.

The connecting rod is drilled to enable lubricating oil to be supplied to the top-end bearings and cooling oil to the piston crown. The big end is bolted-on separately; shims to adjust compression can be fitted between the big-end and the shank, *see* Figure 7.38.

The main bearings and big-end bearings are of the familiar trimetal type. The bearing cap thrust bolts and big-end bolts can be tightened hydraulically with a simple device.

The crankshaft is forged in one piece from special steel, and machined all over. It is drilled to convey the lubricating and cooling oil, which enters at the main bearings and passes into the piston crown from the top-end connecting-rod bearing. At the front end

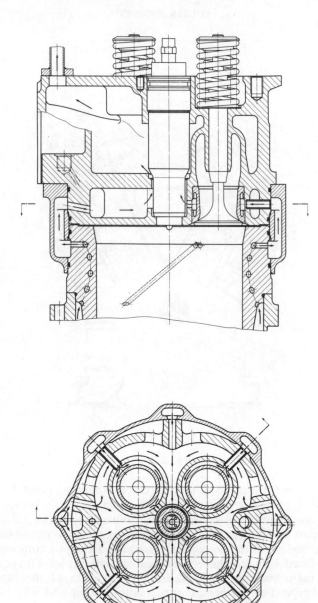

Figure 7.36 Z engines. Cylinder cover cooling system

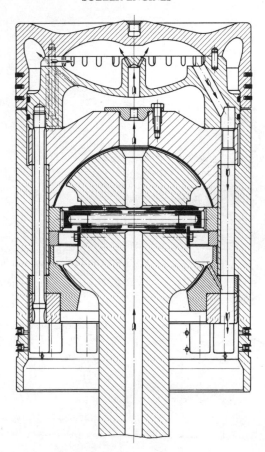

Figure 7.37 Z40 rotating piston

of the shaft a vibration damper may be mounted, and auxiliary
drives can also be arranged, for cooling water and bilge pumps, etc.
At the rear end of the crankshaft is a flywheel with barring rim. For
normal duties the last main bearing is designed as a thrust bearing.
For direct screw propulsion a separate thrust bearing can be built on.

Lubrication of the complete engine is provided by a separately
driven oil pump. Cylinder lubrication is effected by special lubricators, controlled according to the engine load.

Engine control takes place from a manoeuvring stand, with
starting and fuel lever and a speed and safety governor. A running
direction safety interlock prevents incorrect manoeuvres, and

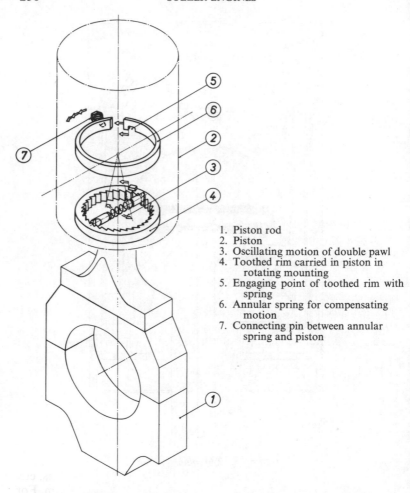

1. Piston rod
2. Piston
3. Oscillating motion of double pawl
4. Toothed rim carried in piston in
   rotating mounting
5. Engaging point of toothed rim with
   spring
6. Annular spring for compensating
   motion
7. Connecting pin between annular
   spring and piston

Figure 7.38 Drive principle of rotating piston

further safeguards prevent operation without cooling water or
lubricating oil. Starting and reversing are accomplished with dual-
controlled starting valves, which rule out all incorrect manoeuvres
and ensure speedy reversing.

Turbocharging is applied on the pulse system, with a number of
cylinders connected to one charger. Various turbocharger makes
can be used. The combustion air delivered by the chargers is cooled
again in an intercooler, and led into a common receiver for pressure
equalisation. From here it enters the cylinders through the scavenge

ports in the bottom of the liners.

Remote control is quite feasible, as the necessary connections are already available on the manoeuvring stand.

SULZER REMOTE CONTROL

The remote control system developed by Sulzer, is based on pneumatic elements with a relatively simple electronic control incorporated for fine speed adjustment. This brings the engine speed over a pre-set period to the required service speed.

The system provides automatic control of the main engine from the wheel house and manual control from the control room in the engine room. The manual controls may be retained on the engine if required. *See* Figure 7.39 for schematic layout.

The pneumatic system is most reliable and positive; and the electronic system is simple, robust and easily maintained. The electronic system contains only three insert type packs; one is a power pack containing transformer and rectifier to give 24 V dc and 115 and 200 V ac; the second is a programme unit for various fine speed adjustments; and the third is an electronic control for the electric step motor. Even if all electronics should fail, bridge control with the pneumatic system is possible.

Crash manoeuvres, if absolutely necessary, can still be performed even with complete power failure, as the electronic programming controls are in parallel with the pneumatic system, i.e. they are additional to the pneumatic system and not in series.

Basically three different remote control arrangements are in general use, (*a*) from engine control room to engine; (*b*) from bridge to engine; the remote control is purely pneumatic up to 30 metres and electro-pneumatic beyond this distance; (*c*) from bridge and from engine control room to engine. Controls from the bridge are the same as for arrangement (*b*); and those from the engine room as for arrangement (*a*).

Method of Control

When the officer on the bridge moves a selector switch on the bridge console to BRIDGE CONTROL, a special 12th section (BRIDGE CONTROL) on the control room telegraph lights up and an alarm sounds on the telegraph until acknowledged. Moving the telegraph lever to acknowledge this actuates a pneumatic switch which transfers control to the bridge, whereupon the telegraph is automatically disconnected and free for control of the engine.

Movement of the telegraph lever thereafter gives the correct

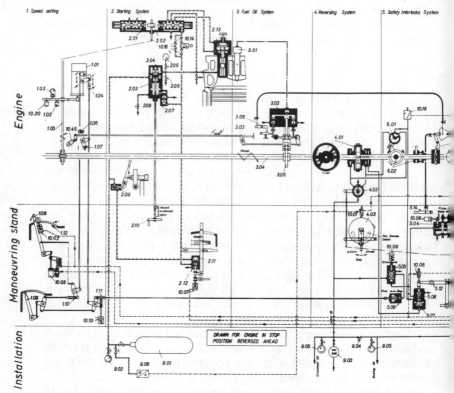

Figure 7.39 Schematic layout of RND control system with the adoption of Sulzer engines

1.01 Woodward governor UG 40 TL
1.03 Tachometer
1.04 Fuel linkage
1.05 Governor and starting distributor
1.06 Minimum fuel limit screw
1.07 Maximum fuel limit screw
1.08 Speed setting screw
1.09 Load indicator
1.10 Feedback linkage
1.11 Stop linkage
1.12 Speed setting maximum limit
2.01, 2.02 Starting air distributor
2.03 Starting air master valve
2.04 Check valve
2.06, 2.08 Drain cock
2.07 Control valve
2.09 Interlock valve on turning gear
2.10 Starting air master handwheel
2.11 Starting lever
2.12 Starting air pilot valve
2.13 Starting valve
3.01 Fuel valve
3.02 Fuel pump
3.03 Fuel rack control spring

3.04 Camshaft
3.05 Fuel pump cam
3.06 Overspeed safety cut out system
4.01 Reversing servomotor
4.02 Reversing valve
4.03 Reversing lever
5.01 Direction safeguard valve
5.02 Friction coupling
5.03 Safety cut out device
5.05 Shutdown hydraulic pilot valve
5.06 Shutdown servomotor
5.07 Starting lever reversing interlock
    servomotor
5.08 Fuel interlock cylinder
5.09 Starting lever interlock
5.10, 5.11 Interlock cam
5.12 Starting lever hydraulic interlock
5.13 Overspeed trip
5.14 Manual operation of overspeed
    trip
6.01 Telegraphic receiver
6.02 Speed setting lever
6.03 Starting lever
6.04 Main shut off handle

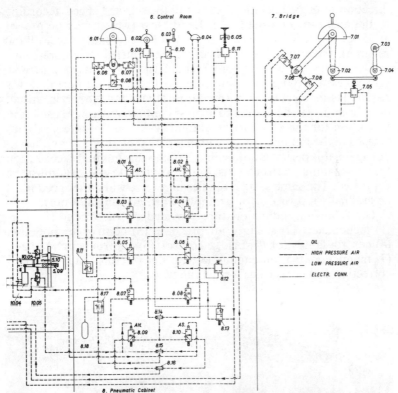

Figure 7.39 (contd.) Pneumatic remote control from the bridge and from a control room

6.05 Maximum bridge speed control	9.02, 9.05 Pressure gauge
6.06 Changeover bridge/control room pilot air valve	9.03 Main lubricating oil pump
6.07 Ahead selecting pilot air valve	9.04 Pressure reducing valve
6.08 Astern selecting pilot air valve	9.06 Remote control pressure reducing and air cleaning station
6.09 Valve on speed setting lever	10.01 Pilot air valve on telegraph
6.10 Pilot air valve on starting lever	10.02 Handgrip lifting cylinder
6.11 Control valve on maximum speed	10.03 Speed setting servomotor
7.01 Telegraph transmitter	10.04 Reversing servomotor
7.02 Speed setting cam	10.05 Direction interlock control valves
7.03 Programming motor	10.06 Reversing interlock control pilot air valves
7.04 Speed setting cam for fine speed	
7.05 Control valve	10.07 Starting cylinder
7.06 Control cam for ahead/astern	10.08 Safety cut-out device
7.07, 7.08, Pilot air valve for ahead/astern	10.09 Emergency stop cylinder
	10.10 Slow-down cylinder
8.01–8.10 Pneumatic relay air valves	10.14 Starting cut-out solenoid
8.11 Flow control valve	10.15 By-pass cocks
8.12 Starting speed control valve	10.16 Direction interlock switch
8.13 Solenoid valve	10.17 Direction of rotation transmitter
8.14–8.16 Double check valves	10.20 Rev/min transmitter for remote indication
8.17 Flow control valve	
8.18 Timing volume	10.45 Fuel rack indicator transmitter
9.01 Starting air tank	

direction of engine rotation, start and the selected speed according to the quadrant indicated: e.g. Dead Slow (which may be pre-set at 35 rev/min); Slow (50 rev/min); Half (65 rev/min); and Full (80 rev/min). These speeds can, of course, be adjusted to requirements.

There are also two buttons marked FINE SETTING UP and FINE SETTING DOWN. When the ship is manoeuvred out of port and it is required to increase the ship speed from FULL AHEAD to service speed, the officer on watch has only to depress the AUTOMATIC ACCELERATION UP button for the speed to be automatically and progressively increased to the nominal speed within a period of about 30 minutes—but again, this period is adjustable. To stop this gradual acceleration the programme button AUTOMATIC ACCELERATION OFF must be depressed. The same system applies in reverse when the speed must be gradually returned—for example, when arriving at a port.

The following indications are provided on the bridge console: (1) tachometer, (2) starting air pressure, (3) control air pressure, (4) control lamps for (5) bridge control, (6) control room control, (7) manual control on engine, (8) transfer of command, (9) speed correction and (10) critical speed range.

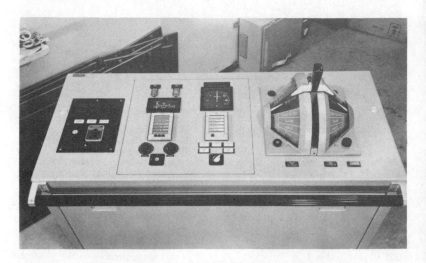

Figure 7.40 Panel for bridge console

Also fitted in the wheelhouse console are an emergency stop button and control lamp and an emergency run button and control lamp; there are also alarms for engine overload, engine tripped, engine fails to start, starting air pressure too low, control air pressure too low and electric power failure. Push buttons are provided for STOP HORN, STOP FLASH and for the test circuit. As the conventional telegraph is also used for the engine control, the STANDBY and FINISHED WITH ENGINES orders are performed by using separate buttons.

See Figure 7.40 for bridge console panel.

Control from the Control Room

A complete rack is delivered to be fitted in a shipyard-built general control desk. Controls in the control room are operable when the telegraph handle on the engine is set on the special position REMOTE CONTROL. In this position, air at 7 kgf/cm² (6·85 bar) is applied to the remote control system and in particular, to the various servomotors fitted on the engine. With this movement the engine control is automatically transmitted to the control room and vice versa. On pulling the lever out of the section REMOTE CONTROL, commands are immediately transferred to the mechanical stand without any further action being necessary.

In the control room, handling of the engine is practically identical to using the manual controls on the engine. Reversing of the engine is automatically performed with the telegraph when acknowledging the bridge order. Speed is regulated by the separate control lever with fine setting and starting air is applied also on pulling a separate lever.

Method of Operating

The following have been attached to the control gear on the engine and on the manoeuvring stand to enable the system to be remotely controlled, *see* Figures 7.39 and 7.41.

Pilot air valve 10.01 on the manoeuvring stand on the engine. This is actuated when the reversing lever is set on a special 12th section, REMOTE CONTROL.

Speed setting servomotor 10.03. This is an actuator which moves the speed-setting lever on the engine from zero to full position when a linear 0·7 to 4·2 kgf/cm² (0·68 to 4·12 bar) modulated air signal is applied to it.

Reversing cylinder 10.04. This servomotor unit is a three-position cylinder which is connected to the reversing valve 4.02 on the engine through the starting lever interlock system. Of special design, this cylinder is locked in the middle position, when air is applied on both sides, which corresponds on the engine to the STOP position. When that on the other side is vented, the cylinder moves—thus moving the reversing valve 4.02 on the engine to the ahead or astern position.

Pilot air valves 10.05. These two valves are mounted on the engine to check if the reversing gear actuated by the three-position cylinder 10.04 has moved into the correct position.

Pilot air valve 10.06. This air valve, also is mounted on the engine and is actuated by the hydraulic servomotor 5.07. This servomotor is energised when reversal of the main engine has taken place.

Starting servomotors 10.07 actuate directly the starting pilot valve normally operated by the starting lever in the control room without moving this lever.

Handgrip lifting cylinder 10.02. This lifts the handgrip of the speed control lever in the control room when air is applied to the control system.

Figure 7.41 Panel for engine room control

When bridge control is required the deck officer has to move a special selector on the bridge console to the position BRIDGE CONTROL. The 12th position, BRIDGE CONTROL, lights up and the telegraph alarm bell sounds until the engineer in the control room has acknowledged the order by putting the telegraph lever on this special section. Pilot air valve 6.06 is then actuated and control air at 7 kgf/cm² (6·85 bar) is led from the main control room shut-off valve 6.04 placed in the main control desk to changeover valves 8.03, 8.04 and 8.05 in the pneumatic cabinet; this system is then ready to be manoeuvred from the wheelhouse.

Manoeuvring from the Wheelhouse

Control from the bridge is effected by the main telegraph transmitter 7.01. The pilot air valves 7.07 and 7.08 on the bridge as well as control air valve 7.05 are actuated by cams 7.06 and 7.02. These cams are moved by sprocket wheels and chains by the telegraph. In reality, the two cams 7.02 and 7.06 are mounted on the same shaft but in the accompanying diagram they are shown separately for easier comprehension.

The control air valve 7.05 is indirectly actuated by cam 7.02 through a link which can be actuated by the cam 7.04 on the other side and moved by a small electric step motor. This motor is controlled by two buttons and takes care of the fine setting of the speed between the different orders of the telegraph. By moving the telegraph from one position to the other, the motor 7.03 automatically returns to the neutral position, thus avoiding an eventual speed correction to be carried over to the next step.

Manoeuvring from the bridge is effected as follows. When the telegraph is moved to, say, DEAD SLOW AHEAD, the pilot air valve 7.08 is actuated, thus sending an air signal to relay air valve 8.02 via 8.04 and setting the three-position cylinder 10.04 in the ahead position. The engine will now set hydraulically the control gear into the corresponding direction which takes approximately one second if it has already been AHEAD beforehand, or approximately five to six seconds if the previous manoeuvre was ASTERN.

When the reversing gear has moved on to its end position, the servomotor 5.07 is energised thus actuating the pilot air valve 10.06 and leading an air signal via the pilot air valve to interlock relay valve 8.09. This signal is also led through double check valve 8.15 to relay air valves 8.07 and 8.08 and thence to the starting air cylinder 10.07.

Simultaneously, this air signal is led to relay air valve 8.06. This valve changes over the air signal from control air valve 7.05 on the bridge to a fixed value given by reducing valve 8.12. During starting, therefore, the speed setting lever will always move to a previously set fixed position.

The starting cylinder having been actuated, the engine begins to turn on compressed air. At firing speed, an electric signal is given through a tachogenerator to a solenoid valve 8.13 which, energised, sends an air signal to relay air valve 8.08, thus cutting off the starting air sequence.

At the same time, relay air valve 8.06 is released and the air signal from the bridge, corresponding to the DEAD SLOW position, is led to the servomotor 10.03 on the engine.

Failure-to-start Sequence

Should the engine fail to start, e.g. the engine speed falls below the firing speed, the solenoid valve 8.13 is de-energised and a starting air signal is again led to starting servomotor 10.07. The starting sequence is definitely stopped when the relay air valve 8.07 closes after approximately six to seven seconds and the lamp ENGINE STALLED will light up on the bridge console. The delayed closing time of this valve is made by using control valve 8.17 and timing volume 8.18.

A timed cutting-out system has been preferred to a counting relay, as by lower starting air pressure only two instead of three starts are performed during the six seconds of time, thus preventing unnecessary waste of air.

Bridge Facilities

When putting the telegraph lever to one of the four orders ahead or astern, to which a fixed speed corresponds each time, this speed may be changed in a limited range over or under the fixed point by depressing the two 'fine setting' buttons 'up' or 'down'. Each time one of these two buttons is pressed an annunciator lamp engraved SPEED CORRECTION lights up. The SPEED CORRECTION lamp is automatically put off when moving the telegraph from one order to the other; for example, when moving from DEAD SLOW to SLOW ahead. In fact, in any changing of telegraph position the little electric motor 7.03 is brought automatically to its neutral position, cancelling any speed correction.

However, when the telegraph is in the FULL AHEAD position, which corresponds to the full manoeuvring speed ahead (approximately 70 per cent of service speed) if the button AUTOMATIC ACCELERATION UP is pressed, the engine speed is automatically increased from full manoeuvring speed to the service speed in an adjustable time some 30 minutes during which time this button light blinks constantly until the engine has reached its maximum speed.

The same sequence is possible from full navigation speed when the control button AUTOMATIC ACCELERATION DOWN is pressed. If required, arrangements can be made to pass through the engine barred speed range automatically.

E.T.K.

Chapter 8

Fiat Engines

Fiat production of four- and two-stroke diesel engines extends over a wide range, namely, between 150 kW at 1500 rev/min and 35 400 kW at 106 rev/min: it is thus capable of complying with the most widely differing fields of application, including marine propulsion of many ship classes, stationary power plant, marine generating sets, industrial engine installations of different types, and so on.

For the propulsion of merchant ships, Fiat has developed two-stroke low-speed diesel engines and four-stroke medium-speed engines. Although in recent years there has been a remarkable tendency to adopt multi-engined geared sets for the propulsion of medium and even large ships, Fiat is of the opinion that, until such installations have had exhaustive experience in practical service, especially in regard to the use of heavy fuels, it is prudent to cultivate, in parallel, the fields of traditional large-bore units and the new medium-speed engines.

The current range of direct-driven two-stroke cycle, single-acting supercharged, crosshead-type marine engines, as built by Fiat and their licensees, is indicated in Table 8.1. The powers extend from 3400 to 36 000 kW (4600 to 48 000 bhp) approximately. The designating symbol for each engine size is the cylinder bore in millimetres followed by the letter S for supercharged engines.

Apart from a few variations of detail due to size and to the period of design, all these engines show the same constructional features and the same basic operating characteristics.

It should be noted that the type 600S engines have a comparatively higher rotating speed by reason of the smaller stroke/bore ratio. This has been adopted to limit as much as possible the vertical overall dimensions the engine being mostly intended for propelling ferries and vessels characterised by very low engine rooms.

To better explain the features of the Fiat two-stroke engines, it is advisable to refer specifically to the two most recent types, i.e. those of 1060 mm and 780 mm bore respectively.

Table 8.1 TWO-STROKE FIAT ENGINES

Class	No. of cylinders	Bore mm	Stroke mm	Stroke/ bore	rev/min	mep bar (kgf/cm²)	Output kW/cyl (hp, metric)
B600 S	5, 6, 7, 8, 9, 10, 12	600	800	1·33	220	8·16 (8·32)	676 (920)
B680 S	5, 6, 7, 8, 9, 10, 12	680	1 200	1·77	155	8·82 (8·99)	992 (1 350)
780	5, 6, 7, 8, 9, 10	780	1 600	2·05	126	9·18 (9·35)	1 470 (2 000)
A900 S	6, 7, 8, 9, 10	900	1 600	1·78	125	10·07 (10·26)	2 130 (2 900)
1060 S	5, 6, 7, 8, 9, 10, 11, 12	1 060	1 900	1·79	106	9·94 (10·13)	2 940 (4 000)

The largest 1060S engine, corresponding to a maximum continuous rating of 4000 hp/cyl (3000 kW) at 106 rev/min, has been developed to fulfil, with a limited number of cylinders, the propulsion needs of mammoth tankers. The 780S engine is to be considered the latest evolved form of the 750 type which for over 20 years, was the strong point of Fiat production for the propulsion of the largest merchant ships of that time. Against the 1500 hp/cyl (1120 kW) at 135 rev/min of the latest version of the 750 type engine, stands the 2000 hp/cyl (1470 kW) at 126 rev/min of the slightly larger bore 780S engine.

Besides obtaining a remarkable reduction of longitudinal dimensions, for the same installed power the new 780 type engine allows a saving of 1–2 cylinders and consequently a reduction of length between 10 and 20 per cent, this engine has a higher stroke/bore ratio (2·05 against 1·76) than the 750S engine, so that it was possible to meet the demand of some ship designers to have slower rotating speeds (126 rev/min) to obtain higher propeller efficiencies.

GENERAL CHARACTERISTICS

Apart from the difference in size, and also some detail variants mainly connected with the different stroke/bore ratio, the 1060S and 780S engines are of closely similar design following, in outline, the traditional one of Fiat two-stroke engines, *see* Figures 8.1, 8.2, 8.3, 8.4.

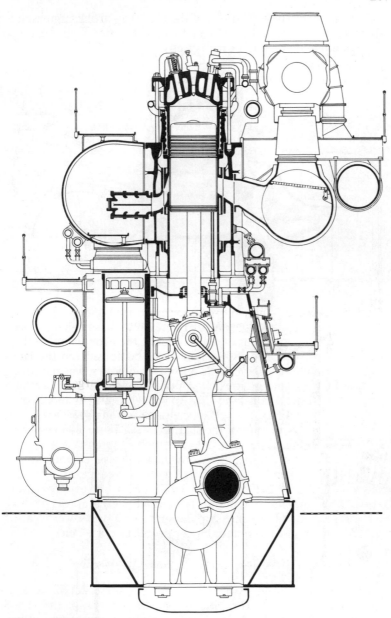

Figure 8.1 Cross-section of engine, 1060 mm bore, 1900 mm stroke

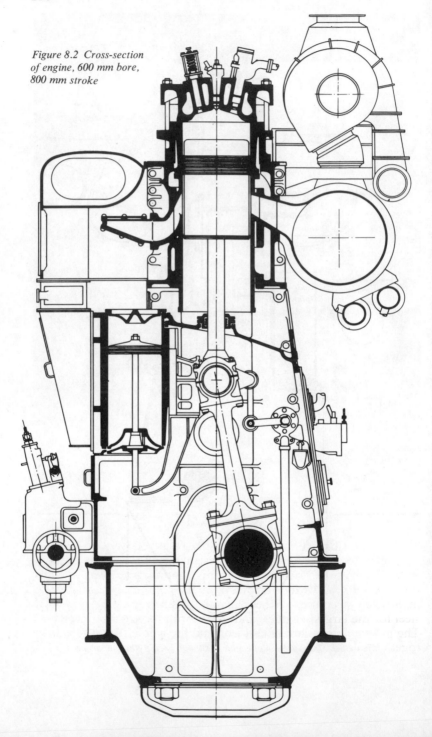

Figure 8.2 Cross-section of engine, 600 mm bore, 800 mm stroke

Figure 8.3 Six-cylinder A900S engine

The main characteristics are summarised as follows:

There is the utmost simplicity of design, together with the rational distribution of the various components, to make as easy as possible the access to the various engine parts for maintenance work. The main fixed structure, i.e. bedplate and main frames, is of welded steel for the largest engines, and of cast-iron for the smallest types. The main cylinders are of cast iron and the whole structure is held together by steel tie-rods.

Figure 8.4 Ten-cylinder 600 S engine

The cross-scavenging is simply controlled by the movement of the piston, which covers and uncovers the air intake and the gas exhaust ports located in the lower part of the cylinder liner. There are non-return valves, consisting of movable blades housed in suitable cages, which are fitted upstream of the scavenge ports. There are no driven valves along the exhaust gas passages.

Supercharging is accomplished by turbochargers operating on the constant-pressure system. This system, adopted by Fiat since the first application of supercharging to its engines, is now generally recognised as the only way to achieve the ever-higher performances demanded by the market. The second stage of the supercharging system is represented by reciprocating air pumps arranged aside each cylinder and driven through a rigid arm by the crosshead shoe. Unlike other engine designs, this avoids using as a scavenging pump the lower part of the cylinder and results, instead, in being completely open to the atmosphere, easily to be inspected and cleaned of the sludge which, especially when operating on poor quality fuels, drains from the cylinder liner and collects on the upper crankcase wall. Any risk of fire in the scavenging belt, and therefore the adoption of corresponding alarm systems, otherwise required when the plant is destined for periodically unattended operation, are thus avoided.

The solution with independent air pumps ensures the availability of a sufficient amount of scavenge air, even when running at low speed, for avoiding any auxiliary electrically-operated blower as required by engines supercharged on the constant pressure system and utilising the main piston bottom as a scavenge pump. The double-stage supercharging system has also the advantage of allowing operation of the engine as a naturally-aspirated type, in case of failure of the first-stage turbochargers, by using the second-stage reciprocating pumps. Under these conditions the available output is yet sufficient to ensure a ship speed of about 80 per cent of the normal.

THE CONSTRUCTION OF THE ENGINE TYPES

Bedplate and Frames

For the largest engines, types 1060S, 900S and 780S, the bedplates and frames are normally built as a welded steel structure, with the inclusion of cast steel elements. The cast-iron construction is needed for reasons of lightness, the welded structure, with interchangeability of corresponding parts, can be considered.
changeability of corresponding parts, can be considred.

The bedplate consists of sections that are strongly bolted together. Figure 8.5 shows the bedplate of a ten-cylinder engine. The aftermost section is connected to the thrust-block section, Figure 8.6, thus providing great rigidity and ensuring complete and easy alignment. The thrust block is lubricated with oil directly drawn from the general lubricating system.

The transverse girders of the bedplate contain the main bearing housings. These are all machined together for obtaining perfect crankshaft alignment. The A frames are mounted on the bedplate, Figure 8.7, and support the cylinders. The A frames, on one side of the engine, are connected to each other by the crosshead guides and, on the other, by simple strut elements. The openings between the frames, on the back and front of the engine, are closed by large access doors. In Figure 8.8 a ten-cylinder 900S size engine is being assembled. The arrangement of the frames and cylinders is clearly seen, together with the vertical steel columns or tie-bolts which brace together the whole structure of bedplate, frames and cylinders, thus obviating tensile stresses.

The crankcase top, at each cylinder, is closed by a diaphragm which incorporates an oil-scraping device for effectively sealing the crankcase against lubricating oil pollution by unconsumed fuel residues from the cylinder and also for preventing lubricating oil from escaping from the crankcase. Figure 8.9 shows the diaphragm.

Figure 8.5 Ten-cylinder 900S engine bedplate and crankshaft

Cylinder

The cylinder (Figure 8.10) comprises a cast-iron body in which the liner, slightly forced, is located. The cylinder carries the scavenge air and exhaust gas passages and is the external wall of the cooling water jacket. The cylinder head is tied to the top of the body by means of stud bolts, as shown in Figure 8.11. The head, or cover, carries a single fuel valve, located in the centre, an air-starting valve, a safety valve and a gas inspection cock. A thin-walled strong-backed design has been adopted for the cylinder liner. Cooling is obtained with forced water circulation through suitably shaped ducts obtained by means of helical-shaped ribs between the inner cast iron liner and the outer high-tensile steel reinforcement. The liners can expand freely downwards. The lower part of each liner is open to the

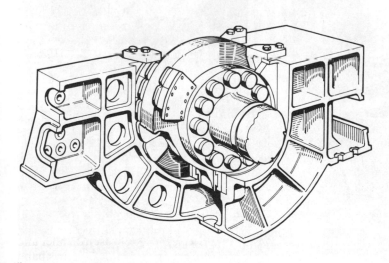

Figure 8.6 Thrust bearing and connection to bedplate

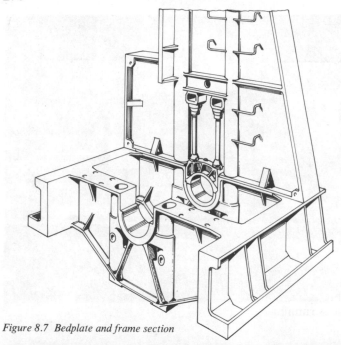

Figure 8.7 Bedplate and frame section

Figure 8.8 Ten-cylinder 900 mm stroke engine being assembled

Figure 8.9 Diaphragm between crankcase top and cylinder liner

atmosphere, thus permitting inspection to take place even when the engine is running.

Lubrication System

The internal surfaces of the cylinder liners are lubricated with special oil by open circuit. Through groups of adjustable delivery pumps the oil is admitted all around the liners, through a series of quills. The pumps are mechanically driven through a hydraulic servomotor, operated by the general lubrication system oil. The delivery can be adjusted either for all pumps or for any one of them, and can be checked by the position of a ball through a glass tube.

The general lubrication is accomplished with closed-circuit oil.

Cylinder Cooling System

Cylinder jacket and cylinder head cooling chambers are circulated by fresh water in closed-circuit, which in its turn is cooled through a suitable heat exchanger. A separate fresh water circuit is provided for the fuel valve cooling.

The piston cooling is accomplished according to the following respective arrangements.

For the largest engines, the water is sent through a separate fresh water circuit, being discharged from the piston crown through a couple of pipes which follow the piston motion and pass through

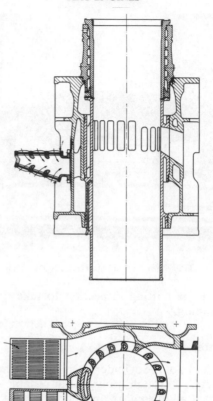

Figure 8.10 Main cylinder

special stuffing boxes into two feeding and collecting chambers located in the upper part of the crank chamber.

For the smallest types, the piston is cooled by means of oil carried and discharged from the piston crown through a system of oscillating pipes and suitable holes inside the crosshead connecting rod.

Fuel oil System

Fuels of the poorest quality can be used on Fiat two-stroke diesel engines as shown in Table 8.2. According to the viscosity grade of

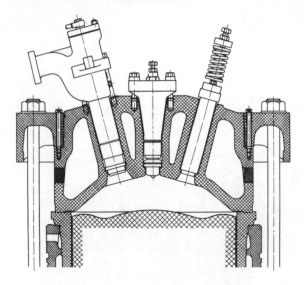

Figure 8.11 Cylinder head

the respective fuels, suitable cleaning and heating process are to be adopted.

Crankshaft

The crankshaft is of the semi-built type; that is, it is formed by C-shaped sections, which are the cranks, connected by shrinking with the sections that form the journals. An exception to this form of construction is represented by the crankshafts of the engine size 600 which, being of short stroke-bore ratio, are fully forged.

The aft end of the crankshaft is coupled to the thrust-block shaft. The thrust is of the oscillating shoes type and receives its lubricating oil from the general forced-lubrication system of the engine.

Piston

The main piston is the engine component which transmits the thrust of the hot gases to the engine mechanism and to the crankshaft. Because it is subjected to severe mechanical and thermal stresses, it is one of the parts to which, in recent years, builders and researchers have paid the greatest attention.

The major problems to be faced in the design of a piston essentially concern the following points:

Table 8.2 FUEL OIL SPECIFICATIONS

	No. 4		No. 5				No. 6	
A.S.T.M. designation	No. 4		No. 5				No. 6	
B.S. 2 designation			E				G–H	
Usual marine denominations	Marine diesel 100		Intermediate fuel oils				Intermediate–bunker C	
	Marine diesel 100		Light marine fuel oil		Medium marine fuel oil		Marine fuel oil	
Italian designation		Fluidissimo		Fluido		Semifluido		Denso
Specific gravity at 15°C		0·89–0·92		0·89–0·94		0·92–0·95		>0·94
Engler Viscosity at 15°C max.	17	12·5	(5)	[4·5]		11 [15]	(>7)	84 [45]
Engler Viscosity at 50°C max.	(3)	2·4	1·58	1·55	(7)	2·2		5·2 [3·6]
Engler Viscosity at 100°C max.	1·4				1·7			
Pour point (°C) max.		−7						
Flash point (°C) min.	(65)	54	(65)	54	(65)	54	(65)	66
Gross calorific value (Kcal/kg) min.	(10 300)	10 300	(10 200)	10 200	(10 100)	10000	(10 000)	9 900
Mineral acidity and alkalinity		nil		nil		nil		nil
Water and sediment % max.	(0·5)	0·5	(1)	1	(2)	1	(2)	2
Sulphur % max.	(2·5)	2		2·5		3·5		5 [4]
Ash % max.	(0·03)	0·1	(0·1)	0·1		0·1		0·15 [0·12]
Conradson residue % max.	(4)	5		6		10		15 [12]
Hard asphalt % max.		2·5		4		6		10 [8]
Distilled at 350°C % min.	(30)							
Cetane No. min.								

(a) The external temperature of the crown, which must not exceed a given limit if it is not to give rise to oxidation of the metal and excessive reduction of its mechanical properties;

(b) thermal stresses induced by the non-uniform temperature field, which must comply with the resistance of the material;

(c) mechanical stresses due to the gas thrust, which must comply with the fatigue strength of the material;

(d) corrosive action of the hot gases on the piston head, due to their temperatures and chemical composition;

(e) wear of the piston ring grooves, which must be as low as possible to ensure correct behaviour of the piston rings.

The solutions adopted by the Fiat Company are illustrated in Figure 8.12.

Piston and Connecting Rods

The piston rod passes through the crankcase sealing gland and is attached at its lower end to the crosshead block. The block is a

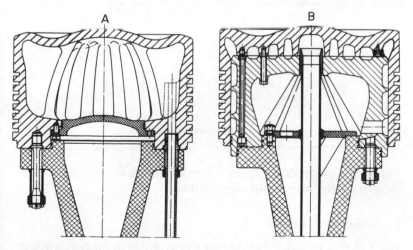

Figure 8.12 Water-cooled piston (A) and oil-cooled piston (B)

solid-forged parallelpiped with two projecting pins of ample diameter in the fore-and-aft plane, on which the connecting rod top-end bearings oscillate (Figure 8.13).

At the back of each crosshead is secured the guide shoe which reciprocates on a guide surface fixed to the A frames. The bottom

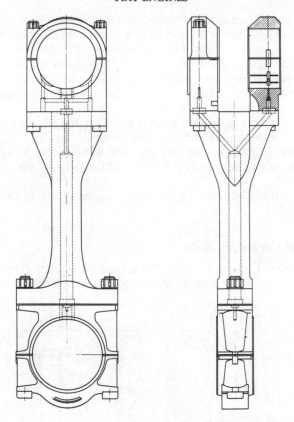

Figure 8.13 Connecting rod

face of the guide shoe carries a bracket which constitutes an arm for driving the scavenge-pump piston.

Fuel-injection System

The Fiat type of fuel-injection pump provides both for regulation of the injection timing and for controlling the fuel supply to the cylinders per cycle. Adjustment of the fuel delivery is obtained by the opening of a discharge valve about the end of the useful stroke of the fuel-pump plunger. Figure 8.14 shows a fuel pump in section.

The fuel-injection valve, Figure 8.15, which is of the multi-hole type, has only one function, namely, the admission of finely atomised fuel into the cylinder.

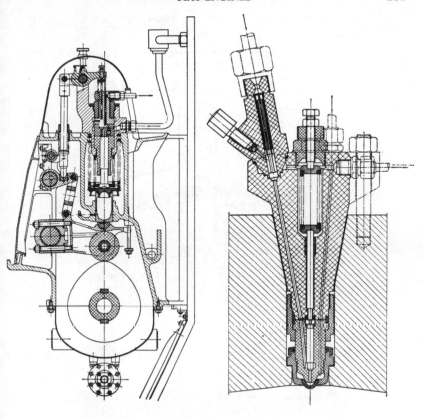

Figure 8.14 Fuel-injection pump   Figure 8.15 Fuel valve

SUPERCHARGING ARRANGEMENT

The supercharging system of Fiat engines is shown in Figure 8.16
which also includes, as an example, the values of pressure and temperature at various points for the 1060S engine functioning at a
normal output of 2940 kW/cyl at 106 rev/min and with ambient
temperature of 30°C.

The exhaust turboblower is shown at the top right-hand corner,
where 1 is the centrifugal air blower, or compressor, and 8 the
exhaust gas turbine. Atmospheric air enters the blower and is
circulated to the first stage of compression. A set of sea-water
circulated inter-coolers is interposed in the path of the air at 2, in
order to remove the heat introduced with the compression process.
From the inter-cooler 2 the air enters a manifold, then proceeds to

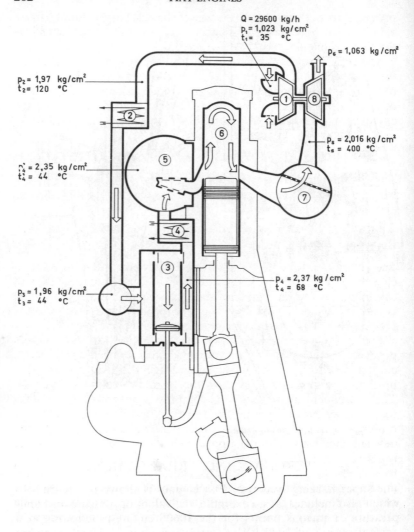

Figure 8.16 Supercharging system

the reciprocating air pumps at 3, wherein the air pressure is further augmented. The heat of compression is dissipated by passing the air through the second set of inter-coolers at 4. From these inter-coolers the air flows into the second scavenge air manifold 5, which is of large capacity; thence into the engine cylinders at 6. The exhaust gas from the cylinders flows into the exhaust manifold 7, and proceeds to the exhaust turbine 8, to be discharged finally to an exhaust heat boiler and/or silencer, and so to the atmosphere via the ship's funnel.

The constant-pressure system has also the advantage of allowing the most appropriate number of turboblowers to be chosen, thus obtaining the best operating conditions independently of the number of cylinders. The turboblowers can also be placed away from the engine as may be required by special circumstances and conditions.

MANOEUVRING AND REVERSING GEAR

The engines are started by compressed air at 30 kgf/cm² (29·4 bar). This air is delivered to the cylinders at the required instant, that is, about 5 degrees after top dead-centre.

Reversing

The engines are directly reversible, i.e. they can rotate in either a clockwise or an anti-clockwise direction. This is accomplished with ease, by changing the timing of the shafts which control the timing system components—namely, the starting air distributor and the fuel pumps relative to the engine crankshaft, see Figure 8.17.

By bringing the manoeuvring lever from the AHEAD RUNNING position to the ASTERN RUNNING position, or vice versa, some compressed air is sent to the starting distributor, which then takes up the position corresponding to the desired direction of running. The consequent introduction of compressed air into the cylinders forces the engine to assume the desired new direction of rotation; however, if this reversal has not been really effected, an automatic device excludes the fuel injection, which begins again only when the injection pump shaft reaches the angular positions corresponding to the new direction of rotation. The angular positioning of the injection pump shaft takes place automatically by means of a sector-coupling between the shaft itself and the engine crankshaft, which allows an angular displacement corresponding to the reversal angle.

Manoeuvring

The engine controls consist of one manoeuvring lever for starting, reversing and stopping, and one handwheel for fuel regulation, i.e. for controlling the engine output.

Orders from the manoeuvring lever are transmitted to the various actuating devices on the engine through totally pneumatic systems.

The connection between the fuel handwheel and the regulation

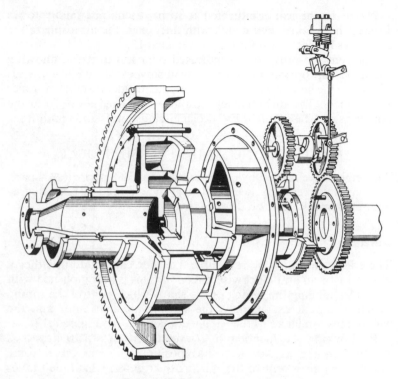

Figure 8.17 Engine reversing gear

shaft on the injection pumps is, however, accomplished by means of a mechanical transmission. Figure 8.18 shows a schematic arrangement.

The manoeuvring lever is shown at *A* and the fuel control handwheel at *B*. The pneumatic valves are located in the manoeuvring console 19.

The ahead starting line is shown at 17 and the astern line at 18. The starting air distributors and their positions are at 2 and the starting air valves on the cylinder heads at 1. The main shut-off air valve is indicated at 5; 3 and 4 are safety valves for ensuring the correct sequence of the operations and to preclude starting with the turning gear in place.

One of the compressed air bottles, carrying 30 atmospheres pressure, is shown at 7, and is also connected through a suitable reducing valve to the bottle 12 at reduced pressure for feeding the various manoeuvring systems.

The reversing gear is indicated at 8, with its oil pilot valve at 14. The fuel pumps are shown at 9, with their cut-off servomotor at 10, the valves for fuel cut-off during reversal at 13.

The overspeed governor is indicated at 11 and controls the valve 15, placed on the line of the fuel cut-off servomotor 10.

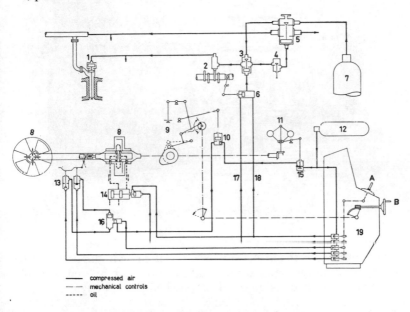

——— compressed air
— — mechanical controls
- - - - - oil

Figure 8.18 Engine manoeuvring system; schematic view

In Figure 8.19 is shown a standard manoeuvring console suitable for placing anywhere in the neighbourhood of the engine, particularly in a control, separate from the machinery space.

OPERATION AND MAINTENANCE

Starting of the engine must be preceded by the starting of the independent oil and water pumps. The load on the engine must be increased gradually, to avoid thermal unbalance. When running in service, the engineer's duty is simply to check the normal operation of the unit.

Performance Data

In Figure 8.20 the test graphs of a 1060 mm bore engine are shown. Graph 1 is the specific fuel consumption; 2 is the air pressure after

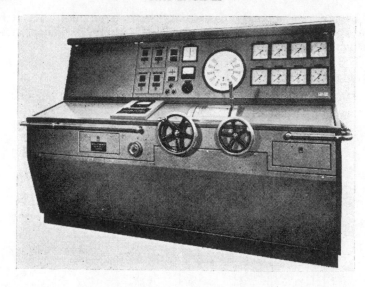

Figure 8.19 Independent manoeuvring console

the turboblower; 3 is the scavenging pressure; 4 is the turbine inlet temperature; 5 is the firing pressure; 6 is the maximum combustion pressure. If more extended information is needed, reference should be made to the makers' manual supplied with every engine.

Pressures

Cylinder gas pressure at beginning of ignition
$$= 55-60 \text{ kgf/cm}^2 \ (54-58 \cdot 8 \text{ bar})$$
Cylinder gas pressure at maximum combustion
$$= 65-70 \text{ kgf/cm}^2 \ (63 \cdot 7-68 \cdot 6 \text{ bar})$$
Oil pressure at engine inlet for general lubrication, also piston cooling
$$= 2 \cdot 0-3 \cdot 5 \text{ kgf/cm}^2 \ (1 \cdot 96-3 \cdot 43 \text{ bar})$$
Fresh water cooling, at engine inlet
$$= 1 \cdot 0-2 \cdot 5 \text{ kgf/cm}^2 \ (0 \cdot 98-2 \cdot 45 \text{ bar})$$

Temperatures

Piston cooling oil temperature at outlet = 45–60°C.
Fresh water cooling at engine outlet   = 50–65°C.

Maintenance Inspection

The maintenance inspections of the various engine components must

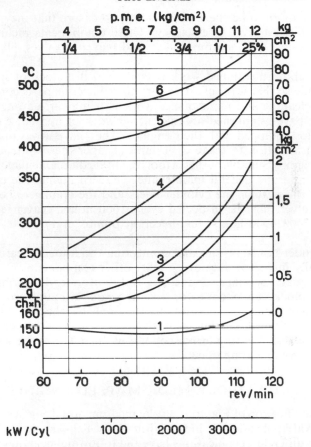

Figure 8.20 Performance data

be accomplished at regular intervals of time, according to a pre-established programme. The examinations can be subdivided into: routine checks which are made after every voyage, minor maintenance inspections which are made either when calling at intermediate ports or during the voyage, and medium and general maintenance.

Checks made after the arrival of the ship in port are carried out for ascertaining that everything is in order, and for making decisions on eventual maintenance inspections in addition to the scheduled ones. They consist of internal examination of the crankcase to check the condition of the crankgear components and to make inspection of the pistons through the exhaust ports.

Minor maintenance matters concern those engine components

which require to be checked frequently to ensure that they remain at the highest level of efficiency. These components include fuel pumps and valves, starting, safety and scavenge valves, filters and coolers.

The above-mentioned work is facilitated if a stock of spares is available so that it is only necessary to replace the parts concerned while cleaning and maintenance work is being carried out at sea.

Fiat have established an efficient network of assistance centres for ships equipped with their engines. They have always paid the utmost attention to make easier and cheaper the maintenance of their engines. Suitable outfits of tools facilitate the maintenance work.

Medium and general maintenance concern mainly the cylinder heads, the pistons, the cylinder liners and the crankgear bearings. Fuel valves must be inspected every 1000 hours, scavenge valves every 3000–4000 hours, fuel-injection pumps every 10 000–12 000 hours.

Cylinder heads, pistons and connecting-rod top-end bearings are generally inspected once every year; other components, e.g. guide shoes, main bearings, connecting-rod bottom-end bearings and thrust block can operate for several years without need of any particular inspection, except as required by the Classification Societies. The cylinder liners must be replaced when the wear limits are exceeded. Under normal conditions their life is not less than four to five operating years.

FOUR-STROKE MEDIUM-SPEED ENGINES

The classification of Fiat four-stroke medium-speed engines, mainly for naval application, is indicated in Table 8.3. The symbols used for the different classifications have the following meanings:

1. The number corresponds to the cylinder bore in millimetres;
2. The letters SS which follow the number indicate that the engines are of the turbocharged version with air inter cooling. The same classes of engines can, if required, be built also in the aspirated version, or turbocharged without inter cooling.

The output range extends from about 1100 to 17 600 kW. They can easily be used in multiple units, thus forming installations having a very high output.

General Characteristics

The engines can be built in the 'in-line' version up to ten cylinders and, in the 'V' type, for a higher number of cylinders; all follow an analogous design, even if dimensional differences have raised the need for some variations for constructional and functional reasons, *see* Figures 8.21 and 8.22.

Table 8.3 FOUR-STROKE FIAT ENGINES

Class	Cylinders		Bore mm	Stroke mm	rev/min	Mep bar (kgf/cm²)	Output kW/cyl (metric hp)
	Arrangement	*Number*					
C 420 SS	In line	6, 7, 8, 9, 10	420	500	450	14·16 (14·44)	368 (500)
	'V'	12, 14, 16, 18, 20					
550 SS	In line	6, 7, 8, 9, 10	550	590	430	17·55 (17·9)	882 (1 200)
	'V'	12, 14, 16, 18, 20					

Cast iron is the material chosen for the main structure of all engines. This is because cast iron allows better proportioning for the structure dimensions relative to the internal stresses.

As the following descriptions will show, the engines have been designed to obtain; maximum reliability, also when operating on high loads; easy access to all parts, thus allowing prompt and inexpensive maintenance; operation with heavy fuels.

Bearing structure

The engine bearing function is accomplished by a cast-iron structure, consisting of bedplate and frame, kept in compression by steel tie-rods extending throughout the structure. In this way, the gas action inside the combustion chamber does not stress the cast-iron structure which, therefore, can operate under the most favourable conditions. This arrangement allows the designer conveniently to limit the weight and yet maintain a particularly sturdy structure.

The lower part of the structure, i.e. the bedplate, sustains the crankshaft while the upper part, i.e. the frame is provided with seats and holding elements for the cylinder liners, camshaft and cylinder heads (Figures 8.23 and 8.24).

Main Cylinder

The fluids concerned with the thermodynamic cycle, i.e. air, fuel,

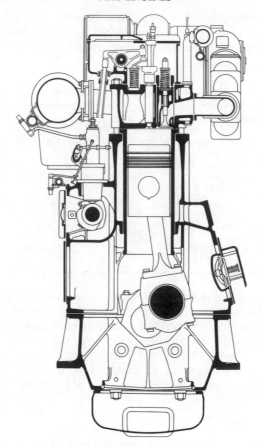

Figure 8.21 C420SS engine (line version)—transverse section

oil and exhaust gases, operate within a space limited by the cylinder liner, the piston and the cylinder head. These components, directly exposed to the action of gases at high temperature and pressure, are required to possess particular resistance and cooling characteristics, which fundamentally affect the nature of the components themselves.

The cylinder liner is of special grey cast-iron which, in addition to possessing good wear resistance, is characterised by high mechanical strength. Cooling of the cylinder liner is accomplished by water circulating in a jacket between the frame and the liner.

The cast-iron cylinder head, Figure 8.25, located on the top of the combustion chamber, is provided with passages for the air inlet and the gas exhaust as well as for the fuel valve. Air inlet to the

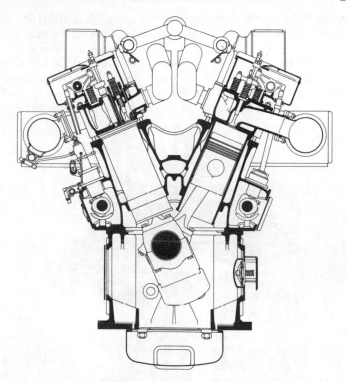

Figure 8.22 C420SS engine (V-version)—transverse section

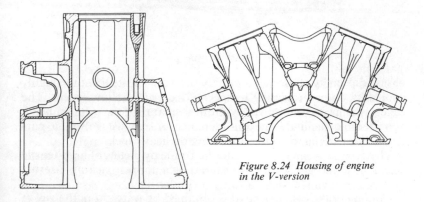

Figure 8.24 Housing of engine in the V-version

Figure 8.23 Housing of engine in the line version

cylinder at the proper time and for the required duration is controlled by two intake valves, operating in parallel, fitted at the inlet passage end. Analogously, the combustion gases are exhausted at the proper time by the opening of two exhaust valves tilted at the beginning of the relative passage; hence, through suitable pipes, the gases are conveyed to the turboblower. Each exhaust valve is contained in a cage, Figure 8.26, the parts of which, in contact with the exhaust

Figure 8.25 Cylinder head

gases, especially those adjacent to the valve seat, are thoroughly cooled by water circulating in special ducts and hollow spaces. The cages, which can be removed without dismantling the cylinder head, considerably facilitate the maintenance of exhaust valves, a particularly useful factor when operating on heavy fuel.

The cylinder head is secured to the frame by means of high-tensile steel studs; and gas sealing is ensured by a copper packing inserted between the cylinder head and the cylinder liner.

Cooling of the cylinder head is obtained by water from the jacket between frame and cylinder liner; this water enters the cylinder head at four different points and is conveyed so as to ensure uniform cooling of the head itself.

Crank Mechanism

The thrust caused by the gas pressure is taken by the piston, which is an aluminium-silicon alloy to minimise the weight, and which reduces the magnitude of the inertia forces. To maintain the temperature in the upper portion of the piston within limits which will

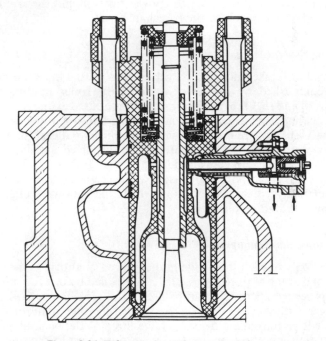

Figure 8.26 Exhaust-valve with water-cooled cage

ensure good preservation the piston is cooled with oil circulating in a proper coil incorporated in the piston itself. Moreover the groove for the first sealing ring is arranged in a special nickel cast-iron element, for improving wear resistance at the groove.

The gas thrust is transmitted from the piston to the crankshaft through the connecting rod. The latter, of high-tensile steel, is designed to take, at the upper end, the gudgeon pin which oscillates in a bronze bush. The lower end is provided with a bottom-end bearing which encircles the crankshaft. The bottom-end bush comprises a three-metal bearing consisting of a thin steel shell on which a copper-lead, i.e. leaded bronze, layer and a thin lead-tin electrolytic film are successively applied.

In the V-type engines, the connecting rods for the two cylinder rows are mounted side-by-side on the same crankpin. A hole drilled longitudinally in the connecting rod conveys the oil to the small-end bush for lubrication, and to the piston for cooling.

The crankshaft, which is a one-piece steel forging, is supported in the bearing structure by three-metal journal bearings analogous to the connecting rod ones. At the power take-off end the crankshaft carries the gear wheel for the camshaft drive.

Timing System

Control of intake and exhaust valves, and of fuel injection pumps, is accomplished by means of a camshaft, roller holding slides, pushrods and rocker arms. The camshaft is housed at one engine side, with bearing caps which allow lateral dismounting of the camshaft.

The V-engines are provided with one camshaft at each side. In the reversible engines, the camshaft can be displaced axially to bring the ahead and astern cams under the relative follower.

The cams corresponding to each follower are inter-connected by proper intermediate sections, on which the follower rollers slide during camshaft displacement.

Fuel-injection Equipment

Fuel supply to each fuel valve in the desired quantity, at the proper time and at the required pressure, is controlled by one fuel-injection pump per cylinder. The pumps are of the type characterised by a plunger with helical grooves for adjusting the quantity of fuel injected; an automatic delivery valve fitted at the beginning of the pipe conveying the pressure fuel from the pump to the fuel valve, controls suitably the residual pressure between the pumping strokes to avoid secondary fuel injection phenomena.

Fuel atomising is accomplished by the fuel valve, which is of automatic valve type, arranged in the centre of the cylinder head. The fuel valve is cooled by fresh water circulating around the needle guide.

Supercharging

Supercharging air is delivered under pressure to the air manifold by the turboblowers which are operated by the exhaust gases. Air flowing from the turboblower to the manifold passes through a cooler in which its temperature is reduced.

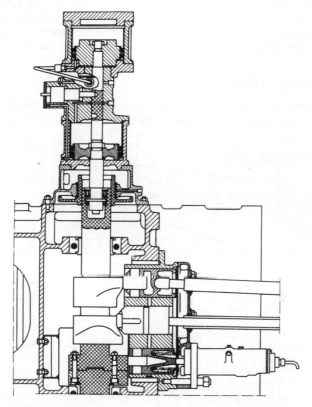

Figure 8.27 Camshaft displacement control for reversing engines

Lubrication

Pressure lubricating oil is sent into the main manifold, from which it is conveyed to the crankshaft journal bearings and, through holes drilled in the crankshaft, to the connecting rod bottom-end bearings, the small-end bushes and the pistons. A suitable piping system conveys the oil from the main manifold to all the remaining parts to be lubricated.

Reversing Device

The reversal of the engine is accomplished by the axial translation of the camshaft, on which a double series of cams are arranged. Figure 8.27 illustrates the system. The servomotor consists of two double-acting cylinders which are actuated by the air compressed at 30kgf/cm², (29·4 bar). The ahead and astern running cams are connected to each other through inclined surfaces, or ramps, on which the tappet roller must slide during the reversal phase.

Performance Data

The performance curves, Figure 8.28, relate to the C420SS engine equipped with six cylinders, on the basis of the mean effective pressure.

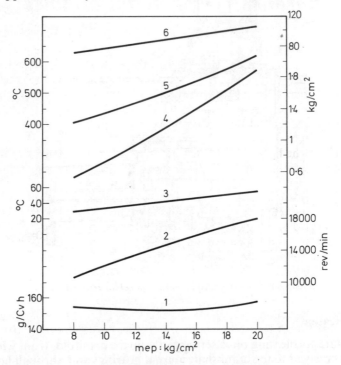

Figure 8.28 Main operating data

The curves refer to a constant speed of 450 rev/min. Curve 1 represents the fuel specific consumption; curve 2, the turboblower speed; curve 3, the supercharging air temperature; curve 4, the supercharging air pressure; curve 5, the gas temperature at the turbine inlet; curve 6, the maximum combustion pressure.

W.R.

Chapter 9

Burmeister and Wain Engines

The current marine engines of Burmeister and Wain design are high-pressure, turbocharged, longitudinally scavenged, single-acting two-stroke crosshead types, with centrally arranged exhaust valves.

The engines are built with fabricated steel bedplates and frames or, alternatively, as cast-iron designs, according to the requirements of the purchaser. Both designs have long vertical steel tie-bolts, which extend for the height of the engines. The thrust block may be incorporated in the engine or it may be separate. The turbochargers are normally of Burmeister and Wain design and make.

This well-established design has led to types showing even further advances, the engines being designated the K–GF series. These engines are described later in the chapter, at page 338 *et seq.*

Hitherto it has been customary to state the engine powers as points on one and the same propeller curve.

When the ship owner and the ship builder have to decide on the characteristics of the propeller for a given ship, however, such a single line is of little help in obtaining optimum conditions, because the propeller characteristics will change as a function of changing hull resistance—brought about by differences in draught, marine growths on the hull, sea and wind conditions, and so on.

Burmeister and Wain, therefore, recently decided to change this practice by stating the power range and the rev/min range that, with safety, are available for the different mean effective pressure levels.

This new method is illustrated in Figure 9.1, which gives the power ranges and the power field in logarithmic scales. In this diagram the continuous service power range is that corresponding to a mean effective pressure of $9 \cdot 6 \, \text{kp/cm}^2$. The maximum continuous power range is that on the $10 \cdot 2 \, \text{kp/cm}^2$ line, being the conditions upon which the engine design is based. The overload power range

297

is that corresponding to 10·9 kp/cm².

In Table 9.1 the power/speed ranges are classified for the three current engine sizes of the K-EF type. Table 9.2 shows the engine weights and overall dimensions.

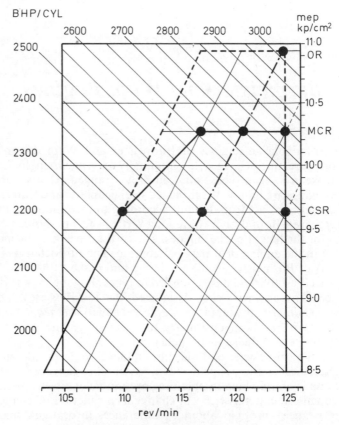

Figure 9.1 Power and revolution ranges; engine K84EF
CSR.   Continuous service rating
MCR.   Maximum continuous rating
OR.   Overload rating

CROSSHEAD TYPE ENGINES

General Construction

Figure 9.2 shows a transverse section through a typical engine. The bedplate is bolted to the seating, which forms part of the

Table 9.1 POWER DATA K–EF ENGINE TYPE

Engine type cylinder dia/stroke	Continuous service power			Max. continuous power	Overload power
	mep 9·40 bar 9·6 kp/cm²			mep 10·10 bar 10·3 kp/cm²	mep 10·70 bar 10·9 kp/cm²
mm	Units	Range	Nominal	Range	Range
K62EF 620/1 400	rev/min kW shp	141– 160 930–1 060 1 270–1 440	150 990 1 350	150– 160 1 060–1 130 1 440–1 540	150– 160 1 130–1 210 1 540–1 640
K74EF 740/1 600	rev/min kW shp	122– 139 1 310–1 500 1 780–2 040	130 1 400 1 900	130– 139 1 490–1 590 2 030–2 160	130– 139 1 590–1 700 2 160–2 310
K84EF 840/1 800	rev/min kW shp	110– 125 1 730–1 970 2 350–2 680	117 1 840 2 500	117– 125 1 960–2 090 2 660–2 840	117– 125 2 090–2 230 2 840–3 030

Table 9.2 ENGINE WEIGHTS AND SIZES

	Approximate dimensions							
	Approximate weight coefficient		Length coefficient				Heights	
							H₂	
Type	Cast	Welded	L	W	H₁		Norm.	Min.
K62EF	35	32	1 140	32	7 600		9 330	9 000
K74EF	55	51	1 360	51	8 730		10 750	10 400
K84EF	78	72	1 540	83	10 000		12 050	11 500

Weights in Mg = t = weight coefficient × (n + 1·8)
n = number of cylinders, for engines with semi-built crankshafts.
Overall length of engine, mm = L × (n + 2·6).
Length of engine over frames, mm = L × (n + 1·2).
H_1 = height from centre-line of crankshaft to top of engine, mm.
H_2 = height from centre-line of crankshaft to crane hook, mm.
W = width of base, mm.

double-bottom of the ship. The crankshaft main bearings are arranged in the bedplate cross-girders. The thrust block, located at the aft end of the engine, may be integral with, or separate from, the bedplate.

The main structure of the engine, which may be built in cast-iron or in fabricated steel, comprises the A-frames, which are bolted to the upper face of the bedplate, and the scavenging air box which is

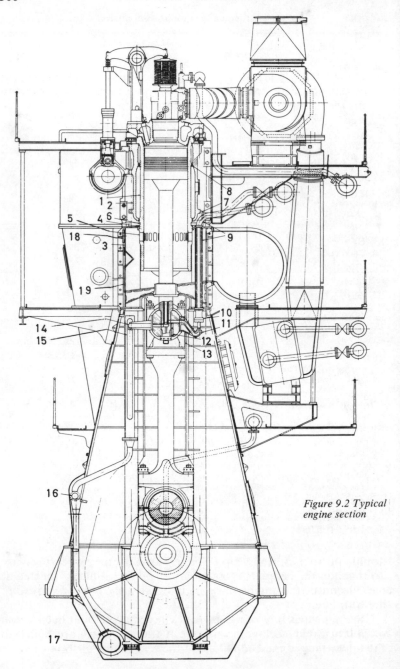

Figure 9.2 Typical engine section

supported by the A-frames. Each cylinder unit includes a heavy cast-iron frame fitted on top of the scavenging air box. The cylinder frame is provided at its top and bottom faces with large circular openings into which the cylinder liner is inserted. All the cylinder frames are strongly bolted together to form solid blocks.

The cylinders are divided into two groups. Between these two groups the chain-drive for the valve motion and the fuel pumps is arranged.

The scavenging air manifold extends the full length of the engine, and into it is discharged the air from the turboblowers. At each cylinder large air inlet orifices are provided. The crankcase top is isolated from the scavenging box bottom by a double diaphragm construction. An effective stuffing and scraper box is arranged for each piston rod where it passes through the double diaphragm.

A characteristic of the engine type is the system of vertical through-bolts, extending from the top of the cylinder frames down through the scavenging air boxes, A-frames and bedplate. The through-bolt nuts are tightened against the upper faces of the cylinder frames by hydraulic jacks. The bottom nuts bear upon the bottom faces of the bedplate transverse girders.

The engines are normally started and manoeuvred from a remote control room by means of pneumatic or electric signals with feed-back from the engine. On the engine proper is, therefore, installed only an emergency manoeuvring stand placed abreast of the chain-drive casing on the intermediate platform.

Cylinder Assembly

Figure 9.3 shows an assembled cylinder unit. The cylinder liner 1, which is made of pearlitic cast iron, is suspended in the heavy cast-iron cylinder frame 2, which is located on the top of the scavenging air box 3. The arrangement enables the cylinder liner freely to expand and contract with changes of temperature. Centring of the cylinder liner in the circular openings of the cylinder frame is obtained by means of a guide surface on the liner which fits into the opening. The liners extend well downwards into the scavenging air box 3. Airtightness is ensured by rubber rings 4, which are arranged at the top of the scavenging air box in grooves turned in the liners.

Scavenge air ports are provided in the cylinder liner as indicated at 5. They are arranged at such a height that they are uncovered by the upper edge of the piston when this is in its bottom position.

There are eight lubricating oil holes in each cylinder liner placed at the free circumference of the liner at 6 and as shown on Fig. 9.4 at (a). The quills are connected by oil grooves, as shown at (b).

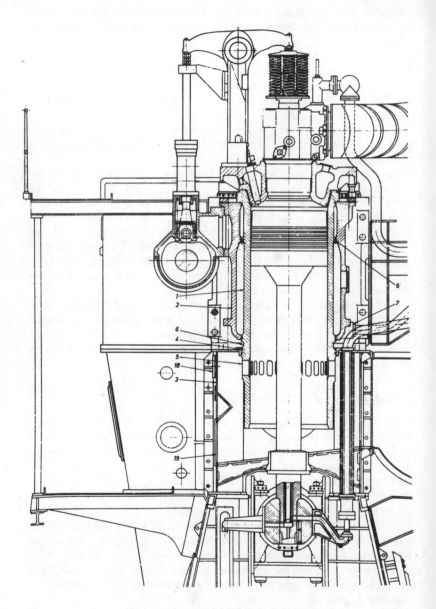

Figure 9.3 An assembled cylinder unit

Check valves, Figure 9.4 at (c), are screwed into the liner, and extensions into the check valve housing, to place the unions for pipes conveniently.

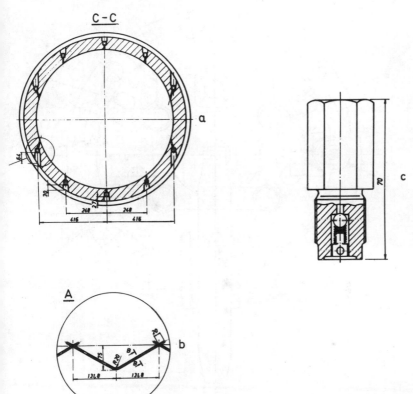

Figure 9.4 *Lubricating oil holes*

Cylinder Cover

The cylinder cover is made of special heat-resisting steel. The cover rests with one surface against the liner and guided on to it by a turned edge. In a machined groove on the conical part of the cover is placed a tightening ring which is carefully adjusted in the conical bearing surface.

The cylinder cover is assembled on the liner and cylinder frame by means of heavy, closely arranged studs on the cylinder frame. Figure 9.5 shows how the valves are arranged on the cylinder cover.

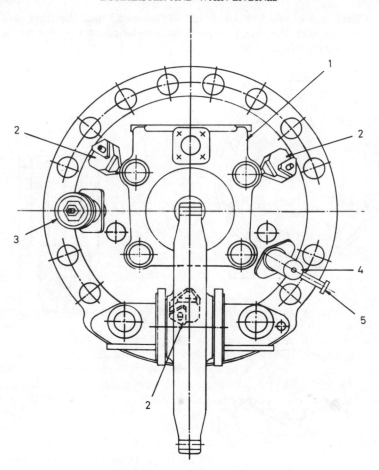

Figure 9.5 Valves on cylinder cover

There is one central exhaust valve 1; and, depending upon the engine size, two or three fuel valves 2; a starting air valve 3; and a safety valve 4. Also, there is an indicator cock 5. The valves are placed in bushes inserted in the cylinder cover as shown on Figure 9.6. The bushes have a press fit at the bottom end and tightening rings 2 and 4 at the upper end.

The fuel valve is tightened against the bottom seat of the bush 1, and the starting valve against the top of bush 3. The bushes for starting air valve and safety valve have heat shields inserted.

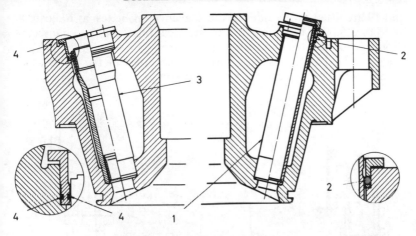

Figure 9.6 Valve bushes in cylinder cover

Cylinder Cooling

Referring to Figure 9.3, the cylinder-liner cooling space is formed by the walls of the cylinder frames which surround the liner some distance above the scavenge ports. The cooling water is led to the cooling space through the bottom inlet 7, placed eccentrically to the cylinder centreline. Water tightness at the bottom of the cylinder frame is ensured by two silicone rubber rings. At 8, at about $\frac{3}{4}$ height, is arranged a ring that closes tight against water jacket and liner, and in which are drilled a number of 10 mm dia. holes that direct the water at a small angle with the cylinder axis and tangentially giving effective cooling to the upper part of the liner.

From the cylinder frame the water passes to the cylinder cover by two external pipes, each in two pieces, Figure 9.7. They are joined by a tightening arrangement, with a silicone rubber ring. Thus the cylinder cover may be lifted without having to dismantle these connections. From the cover the water flows through similar connections to the exhaust valve, and from there to the outlet manifold.

Cylinder Inspection

For the periodical inspection of the cooling surfaces and spaces, the cylinder frames are provided with cleaning doors on front and rear sides and the cylinder covers with screw plugs and cleaning doors. For the inspection of the scavenge air chamber, removable doors 18 and 19 are fitted to the sides of the scavenge air boxes, as indicated in Figure 9.3. It is essential that the cleanliness of the chambers should be under strict and frequent control. The state of the piston rings can be partly observed through the holes of the inspection covers and from the scavenging air receiver.

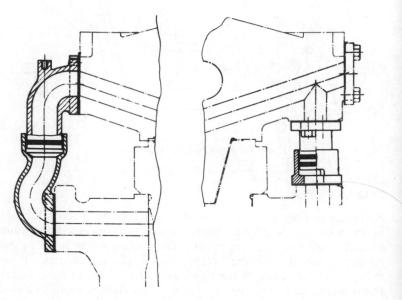

Figure 9.7 Cooling water connections

Pistons and Piston Rods

Figure 9.8 illustrates the piston and piston-rod assembly.

The piston consists of three parts. The piston crown 1 is a heat-resisting molybdenum steel casting or forging, machined all over. There are six piston rings, located in grooves with caulked-in cast-iron wear rings, or as an alternative with chrome-plated lands. The two upper piston rings are narrow rings with diagonal cuts; and the next three rings are wider and have S-seals. The lowermost ring is an oil distributor ring. All the rings are slightly chamfered on their top and bottom edges, to preserve the oil film during the running-in period.

A cast steel cylinder 8 supports the crown at about three-quarters of the outside diameter and transmits the gas forces to the piston rod, to which it is secured by screws 10. The piston crown is clamped

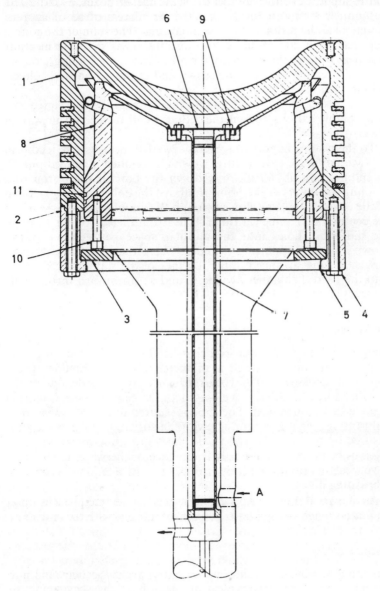

Figure 9.8 Arrangement of piston rod and crosshead

to the support cylinder by means of the cast-iron guide skirt 2 and an annular spring of the Belleville type. This method of support has enabled the piston crown, and particularly the outer cylindrical wall that is not now required to transmit the gas forces, to be made relatively thin. By this means, and by the efficient oil cooling arrangement, the temperatures at the crown and at the piston ring belt are kept moderate.

Each piston rod is bored longitudinally from the top flange to a point about half-way down the reduced end of the rod in way of the crosshead.

To the piston support ring there is welded, near its top, a conical wall with a flange at its centre, to which is bolted a flanged pipe 7, extending centrally all the way down the bore in the piston rod. Cooling coil enters at the point A, above the collar at the lower end of the central pipe, and flows through the annular space upward to the central oil chamber in the piston. From there it passes through the tangential holes into the annular space between the piston crown and the supporting cylinder. From there, it flows through tangential slots arranged in the top face of the supporting cylinder into the central chamber at pipe 6, and so downward through the central pipe in the piston rod.

Crosshead

Figure 9.9 shows the piston-rod crosshead assembly. The lower end of the piston rod is reduced in diameter to form a shoulder at the top of the crosshead. The rod is attached at the underside of the crosshead by a nut that is well-secured. On each crosshead journal a guide shoe is arranged. The shoe is secured to the crosshead by a tight-fitting spigot and four screws. The correct angular position is ensured by two dowels. The guide shoes are white-metal lined, oil grooves being cut horizontally in the face of the white-metal, with a vertical distribution groove to ensure an adequate supply of lubricating oil.

As shown at Figure 9.3, the crosshead shoes reciprocate upon accurately machined guide strips that are integral with the A-frames.

Piston Cooling

Referring to Figure 9.2, cooling oil enters from the manifold into the telescopic pipes 9 arranged at the top of the scavenging air receiver. There are two concentric, vertical stationary pipes which intersect the scavenging air receiver. The annular space between the pipes forms a cofferdam, if the inner one should become leaky. At the lower end there is a stuffing box, consisting of a floating white-metal lined bush. Each telescopic pipe is secured to the crosshead by a bracket 11, to which it is flanged. The vertical holes 12, and the corresponding horizontal holes in the crosshead, convey lubricating oil to the crosshead bearings, to the guide shoes 13, and

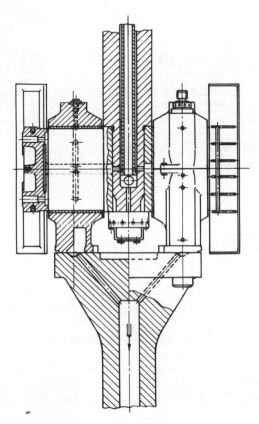

Figure 9.9 Piston rod top-end arrangements

through a longitudinal hole in the connecting rod to the connecting-rod big-end bearing. The cooling oil from the piston leaves by the bracket 14, which moves up and down in the slotted pipe 15, and finally it reaches the outlet pipe 17 in the oil pan. As it passes the sight glass window 16, the flow of oil may be checked and the temperature noted by a thermometer.

Piston-Rod Stuffing Box

The piston-rod stuffing box, which is introduced at the bottom of the scavenging air reservoir, comprises two elements respectively fitted with air sealing rings and oil scraper rings, *see* Figure 9.10. Each sealing ring consists of two internal rings of lead bronze contained in an outer ring of cast iron. The rings are in four sections,

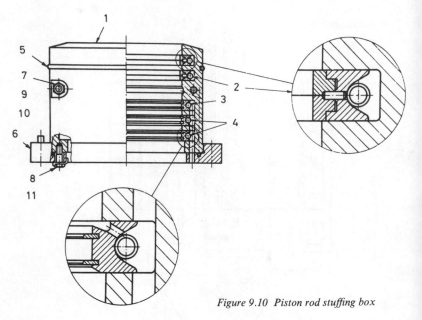

Figure 9.10 Piston rod stuffing box

staggered in relation to each other and maintained in that position by dowels. They are held together and against the piston rod by a garter spring 2. The three oil scraper rings at 3 and 4 are each in three pieces, held together by the garter spring 4. The scraping edges are formed on two replaceable insert rings that slide into the ring bodies.

The upper scraper ring has no drain from above, but the two lower rings have, on their upper faces, a groove with drain holes that drain the oil into the chambers around the rings. From here the oil from the three stuffing-box grooves flows through ducts into the crankcase. The oil from the two sealing rings is drained away through ducts which terminate in a connection leading to a cock for each stuffing box, arranged on the manoeuvring platform.

By observing the outlet from the cocks it is possible to check the condition of the sealing and scraping rings. Leakage of air shows that the sealing rings are out of order; and an excessive oil discharge means that the scraper rings are in need of examination. The stuffing box is held to the crankcase diaphragm plate by flange 11.

Connecting-Rod Top-End and Bottom-End Bearings

Connecting-rod top-end and bottom-end bearings are respectively illustrated at Figures 9.9 and 9.11. They are made of cast steel in two parts, bolted together by two bolts for each bearing. The nuts

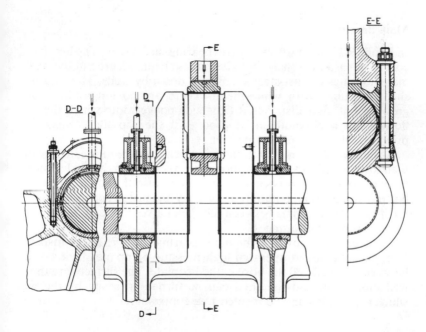

Figure 9.11 Bottom end and main bearings

are locked by Penn-type rings. The bearing halves are maintained in correct relation to each other and to the connecting rod by fitted bolts placed adjacent to the big bolts.

The feet of the crosshead bearings are so dimensioned that the angular deflection of the centre-line of the bearings under load is equal to the combined deflections of crosshead and connecting-rod flange. The centre-lines thus remain parallel at all times and the load remains evenly distributed. The crosshead bearings are provided with precision-type, steel-backed, white-metal shells with a thin layer of soft running-in alloy. The bearings are arranged to have longitudinal oil grooves spaced to ensure wetting of the entire sliding surface.

The big-end bearings are lined with white-metal, run directly into the castings. They have no longitudinal oil grooves but oil pockets are provided at the sides and there is a circumferential oil distribution canal at mid-bearing which does not extend through the upper half, but about one-third of the circumference. For adjustment of bearing clearances, arising from wear, shims of assorted thicknesses are inserted between the upper and lower bearing bushes.

Main Bearings

In Figure 9.11 the crankshaft main bearings are shown. The bearings consist of cast-steel shells in halves, these being secured in the bedplate housings by cast-steel keeps held down by studs. The bearing shells are lined with white-metal. There are no longitudinal oil grooves, but oil is distributed from side pockets into which the oil flows from a circumferential groove in the top shell, which is provided with a supply connection.

As indicated in Figure 9.2, the main bearings are lubricated from their own manifold. As mentioned in the section headed Piston Cooling, the crosshead bearings and shoes, also the connecting-rod bottom-end bearing, obtain their oil from the piston cooling system. Each bearing has shims between the shell halves to facilitate adjustment of running clearances.

To facilitate removal of the main-bearing lower shell for inspection, oil from a hand-operated high-pressure pump may be injected between the shell and the bore in the bedplate. The surfaces are thus well lubricated, and the shell can be turned-up easily by the jig which is provided and connected to a crankweb.

Crankshaft

Crankshafts are of two kinds, namely, fully-built and semi-built, depending upon the torsional vibration characteristics of the engine. Figure 9.11 shows a semi-built crankthrow.

The crankwebs of fully-built shafts and the crankthrows of semi-built shafts are steel castings. They are cast with large, heavy, casting heads for reducing casting imperfections to a minimum. The castings are carefully heat-treated and, after rough machining, they are thoroughly inspected by magnetic-particle and by ultrasonic tests.

The crankshaft journal pieces are made of forged, mild steel. They are hollow-bored only where it is desirable to do this, because of balancing or torsional frequencies. Webs and journal pieces are shrunk together with an adequate shrinking allowance for strength, and in accordance with classification society requirements.

Thrust Block

The thrust block is normally incorporated in the bedplate, at the aft-end; but it may be a separate unit, if so desired. The thrust block is of the single-collar pivoted pad type, *see* Figure 9.12.

The thrust shaft is, at its forward end, bolted to the crankshaft by a large diameter flange of which the part extending beyond the diameter of the crankshaft flange serves as the thrust collar. The pivoted pads 7 and 8 are guided in recesses in the retainer segments 6. These transmit the thrust to faces in the housing that are machined accurately normal to the crankshaft centre-line. The housing is integral with the aft part of the bedplate, with which it forms a rigid structure that transmits the thrust to the ship's foundation.

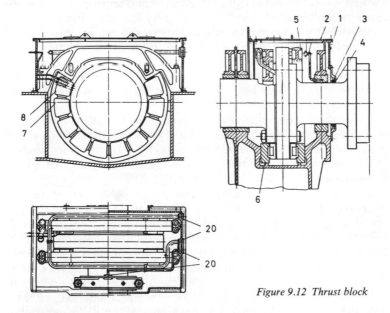

Figure 9.12 Thrust block

The housing also carries the aft main bearing and a smaller bearing aft of the thrust bearing proper. The thrust pads are lined with white-metal. The pads and the retainer segments are prevented from turning by the crossbars 5. The thrust bearing is lubricated from the engine forced-lubrication system, the oil pipe being at 20.

To prevent the escape of lubricating oil from the bearing, the end covers 1 and 3 are provided with a scraper ring 4, from which the leakage oil is led through a pipe to the oil pan of the engine. The lubricating oil from the pads drains through holes in the lower part of the bearing to the oil pan. The location of the drain holes ensures a correct level of oil in the thrust bearing.

For temperature control, one or two thermometers are inserted in the thrustpads, according to the control or alarm system being used in the ship.

Camshaft Chain Drive

The camshaft which actuates the exhaust poppet valves and the fuel-injection pumps, is driven from the crankshaft by a transmission system which comprises two matched roller chains of identical size. This chain drive is shown in Figure 9.13.

The main chains 1 run over an idler wheel 2 and a tightening wheel 3 which is located on the tightening arm 4 and tensioned against the chain by the threaded spindle 5 loaded by spring 6. The chains are prevented from generating transverse vibrations by two sets of rubber-clad guide bars 7 securely fixed to longitudinal bars.

The chains are lubricated by the injection of a jet of oil between the chain wheels and the chain rollers just before the rollers are about to engage the wheel. Thereby an oil cushion is formed to dampen the impact.

Two auxiliary chain-drives are taken from the idler wheel shaft. One drives the central lubricator for the rocker arms, the cylinder lubricators, the tachometer generator and the starting air distributor, and is marked 8 in Figure 9.13. The other, marked 9, drives the engine governor.

The tightening of the chains has to be controlled at regular intervals. This referring to Figure 9.14, is done as follows. Nuts 1 are loosened and turned away from the thrust plate 2 for the spring 3, until the length of the spring becomes equal to that stated in the engine builder's instruction book. Thereupon nuts 4 are loosened and turned away from the supporting beam. To take the slack out of the chain, the engine is turned in the direction that makes the tightening wheel strands of the chains the slack side. At the same time the upper of the nuts 1 is manipulated until the prescribed spring-length is obtained, making sure that nuts 4 do not touch the beam. When the length of the spring is correct, the lower nut 4 is turned lightly against the beam, and keeping it in that position, the upper nut is tightened against it and then secured. The upper nut 1 is next turned, until the flange 2 rests lightly on the distance piece 5.

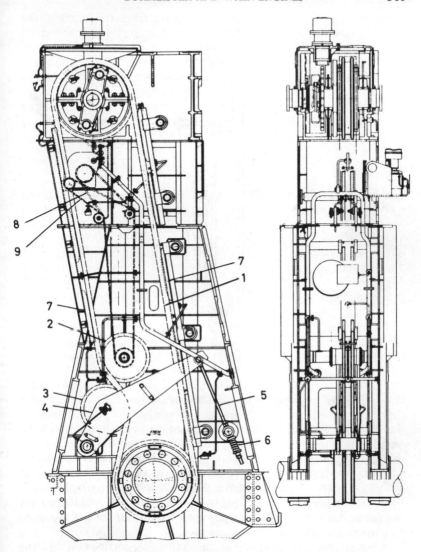

Figure 9.13 Camshaft chain drive

It is then tightened further according to instruction book and then secured.

In the course of time, as the camshaft chains increase in length, the retightening of the chains will gradually cause the camshaft to be displaced in its angular relation to the crankshaft and, as a result,

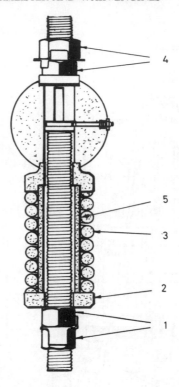

Figure 9.14 Chain drive adjustment

the leads of the fuel pumps and exhaust valves will also suffer an angular displacement. If these displacements exceed the limits given in the engine builder's instruction book they must be corrected. This may be done jointly for each half of the engine at the camshaft couplings nearest the chain-drive. These couplings may be loosened by hydraulic pressure, according to the SKF method, and thereupon the shafts aided by the proper jigs are turned into correct position. The hydraulic pressure is then released.

When changing links in one of the chains, the corresponding links in the other chain must also be changed. Similarly, if one complete chain is changed the other chain must also be changed.

Exhaust Valve

Figure 9.15 shows an exhaust valve in section.

The valve housing 1 is made of cast-iron and is water cooled.

317

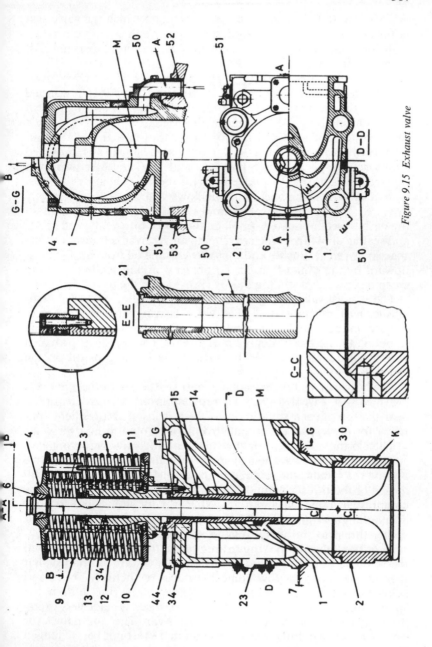

Figure 9.15 Exhaust valve

The valve seat 2 is made from steel tubing, on which the valve seat is formed in a welded-on hard surfacing cobalt chromium alloy, with high resistance to chemical attack and high temperatures. It is secured in place by screws 30.

The exhaust valve is arranged at the centre of the cylinder cover, as indicated at 1 in Figure 9.5. The valve in Figure 9.15 is secured tight on the ground seat K by four studs. To cope with the heat expansion of the valve housing without causing excessive forces, the studs are undercut and the forces are transmitted from the nut over elastic cast-iron liners 21. Each valve housing is provided with a spindle guide in two parts, 12 and 14. The lower part 14 is pressed into a hole in the valve housing and bears against the faces with a collar. The upper and the lower guides are respectively provided with wearing bushes 13 and 15, made of brass. To maintain the bushes well lubricated, small quantities of oil are injected at 34; and sealing air 44 from the scavenging air receiver is blown into the space between the bushes and thus prevents the oil from being blown upward by the exhaust gases. To prevent oil and sealing air from escaping upwards a stuffing box 3 is provided at the top of the guide.

The exhaust valve and spindle comprise a forging of special high-tensile, heat resistant steel. The valve bearing surface is conical, is hard surfaced and is ground to match the seat of the housing to obtain the necessary degree of tightness. The spindle is provided with a shrunk-on guard M to obviate the burning of oil on the spindle and guide.

The bearing face for the rocking lever on the top of the spindle is provided with a welded-on, wear-resistant layer. A groove is turned near the top of each spindle, into which is inserted a resilient split ring 7 for preventing the spindle from falling out during overhaul.

The closing movement of the valve and the valve actuating gear is brought about by six helical springs 9 that are placed on a circle around the spindle and secured to the discs 4 and 10 by recesses. By means of the threaded pin 11 and a special nut the spring may be compressed, removed and replaced in a very short time without dismantling anything else. The upper disc 4 transmits the upward spring thrust to the valve spindle through the split conical lock-rings 6. The halves of the rings 6 are pressed by the spring thrust into the recess in the valve spindle. The ring halves are so shaped that they rest with two narrow conical surfaces respectively above and below the waist of the spindle recess. The fit of the rings both in the spindle recess and in the conical faces of the disc 4 is made very exact. 'Play' at the bearing faces would cause wear. The ring halves for each valve are carefully mated together and must not be exchanged for rings from another valve.

Exhaust Valve Cooling

The water supply to the cooling spaces of the exhaust valve housing (Figure 9.15) enters at A and C on the short pipe bends 50 and 51, having risen from the cooling spaces of the cylinder cover. The bends 50 and 51 fit into holes bored in the upper sides of the cylinder cover, tightness being obtained by means of the rubber rings 52 and 53.

The cooling water is discharged through the opening B, whence the water passes through pipe bends to the common discharge line. The bends are provided with thermometers and de-aeration cocks. A cleaning door 23 is provided on the cooling spaces of the exhaust valve housing. The exhaust pipe from each exhaust valve is taken to the main exhaust system, from which the exhaust turbochargers are supplied.

Exhaust Valve and Fuel Pump Actuating Gear

Referring to Figure 9.16, the housing marked 1 that is bolted to the frame in Figure 9.3 near the top of the cylinder, carries the camshaft in an underslung bearing with white-metalled precision steel shells.

The camshaft is in pieces of one cylinder-distance length flanged together, and carries the fuel cam on the left of the diagram and the exhaust cam on the right. Cams and flanges are secured to the shaft by the SKF hydraulic method. The correct angular position for the flanges and exhaust cam is given by marks, and for the fuel cam by a scale to facilitate any possible readjustment. Such adjustments are particularly easy to make by the hydraulic method. The cams are hardened and ground. The roller guides move in vertical cylindrical bores in the housing. The roller guides are made of cast steel. They are secured from turning by keys, and they have oil distributing grooves. The hardened and ground rollers run in SKF needle bearings, the pins of which are secured to the roller guides by expansion bushes and location screws.

The springs for the fuel pump motion 7 and 8, Figure 9.16, rest against the heavy top flange 3, that is bolted to the housing and to which the fuel pump in turn is bolted. The pushrod for the exhaust valve motion passes through an oil scraper ring assembly 13 bolted to the housing. To the extreme left of Figure 9.16 is a pneumatic cylinder that is used for lifting the fuel pump motion away from the cam in the event of the particular cylinder having to be put out of action.

The entire motion receives oil from a separate lubricating system and the oil is drained from the underslung cover. Scraper rings at the ends of the housing obviate oil leakage.

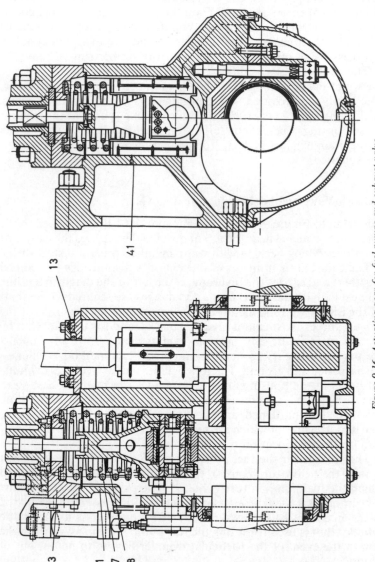

Figure 9.16 Actuating gear for fuel pumps and exhaust valve

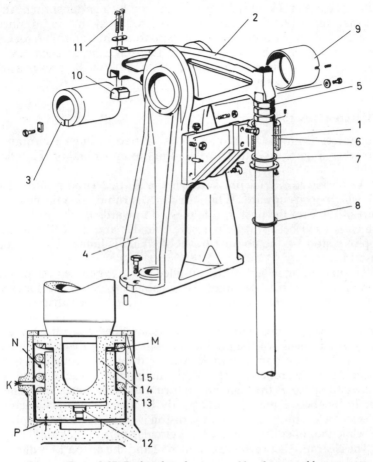

Figure 9.17 Push-rod, rocker arm and bracket assembly

Figure 9.17 shows an isometric view of the pushrod, rocker arm and bracket assembly. The motion of the roller guide is transmitted through the pushrod 1 to the rocker arm 2, the fulcrum of which is at the pin 3 located in bracket 4 and that is bolted on to the cylinder cover. On each pushrod there is a welded-on top piece having an internal thread for the thrust screw 5, by which the movement of the pushrod is transmitted to the rocking lever.

There is a side bracket 6 fitted with a bush for guiding the pushrod, on the fulcrum bracket. At the lower end of this bush there is a tightening ring 7 to keep the oil in the bush, and 8 is a Z-shaped rubber ring that is kept tight against the rod by a garter spring. Any oil that might possibly drain down the rod is at the ring drained into the hollow pushrod and from there to the housing. The rocker arm has a bronze bushing 9 at the fulcrum, and at each end a hardened thrust-piece 10 fits closely into slots in the rocker arm, being secured by screws 11.

Clearance Absorber

The forces from the pushrod are transmitted through a clearance absorber, Figure 9.17, that is placed in the upper end of the roller guide.

At the bottom of each pressure cylinder is fitted a non-return valve 12, which opens upward. When the roller is running on the circular part of the cam the push-rod is pressed upwards by the spring 13, which is fixed between the pressure cylinder and the collar at the top of piston 14, the upward travel of which is limited by the stop disc 15.

The maximum height of the oil-filled space P between the piston and the cylinder has been made large enough to permit the longitudinal expansion which results from the heating of the valve spindles when the engine is being run-up to maximum load. The spaces N and P are kept filled with oil, which is supplied from the forced-lubrication system of the engine through a pipe to which is fitted a filter. The oil is admitted at K, whence it passes through ducts to space M in the roller guide. When the engine is running the oil passes to space P through non-return valve 12, which is opened partly by the oil pressure and partly by the momentary suction effect which is produced when the piston is lifted upwards by spring 13 while the roller is running on the circular part of the cam.

The clearance between the cylinder 12 and the piston 13 is dimensioned such that the forces on the pushrod during one valve movement squeeze a predetermined small amount of oil from space P into space N resulting in a small downward movement of the piston. When the roller is running on the base circle of the cam where there are no forces on the pushrod, oil may again be admitted to space P through the checkvalve by the force from the spring that lifts the piston and the pushrod to contact with the rocker arm. During a transition period following a change in load on the engine, the exhaust temperatures and the length of the valve spindle and thereby the position of the lower face of the pushrod also change, but the piston is immediately brought in the no-clearance position either by squeezing out of more oil than is being sucked in or by sucking in more oil than has been squeezed out.

As a result, the pressure cylinder will always enclose exactly the quantity of oil needed to make the exhaust valve just close tightly against its seat. The arrangement thus ensures an automatic equalising of clearances when the temperature changes from cold engine to hot engine, and vice versa.

Lubrication

The rocking-lever contact faces which abut the valve spindles and the pushrods, as well as the rocking-lever bushes, are lubricated from a central lubrication system which automatically distributes the required oil quantities to the different points of lubrication. The oil supply to the roller guides is led through the pipe connection on Figure 9.16.

The needle bearings of the rollers are not in direct connection with the oil system, but are lubricated through the ducts with oil from the surfaces of the roller guides. The camshaft bearings are served by oil pipes connected to the housing and through bores to the bearing.

Valve Gear Adjustments

To ensure tight closing at the seats of the exhaust-valve spindles it is necessary that the valve actuating gear should be correctly adjusted by ensuring correct clearance between moving parts. The engine is turned so that the valve guide roller is placed on the base circle of the exhaust cam. Then the locknut of the thrust screw 5 (Figure 9.17) is loosened and the thrust screw is turned until a clearance of 0·3–0·5 mm is obtained between the pushrod and the rocker arm. During the adjustment the rocker arm is pressed lightly against the exhaust valve spindle. Thereafter, the locknut is tightened and the clearance checked.

Running Noises

If heavy noise should occur at a valve when the engine is running, this may be due to a clearance having developed between the end of the pushrod and the piston 14, Figure 9.17. The reason for this will be that the automatic clearance control has become defective and thus does not function correctly. The difficulty can be provisionally overcome by lengthening the pushrod while the engine is running. This is done by slackening the locknut of the thrust screw and then adjusting the thrust screw, so that the automatic clearance control is put out of action. To obviate the burning of the exhaust-valve spindles, it must be ensured that, at full load, there is still clearance.

Fuel Injection Pumps

There is one fuel pump for each cylinder. Figure 9.18 (a) and (b) shows a pump in section. Each fuel pump consists of a housing of cast steel 1, secured to the housing of the actuating gear, Figure 9.16.

A heavy flange 3 is fastened by studs 18 to the top of the fuel pump housing. The cylindrical part of the tubular flange projects down into the housing and is provided with an external thread that matches

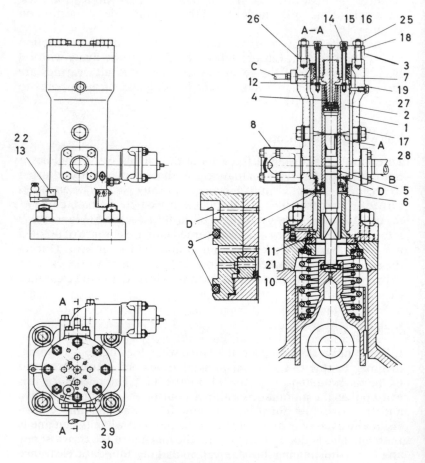

Figure 9.18(a) Fuel pump

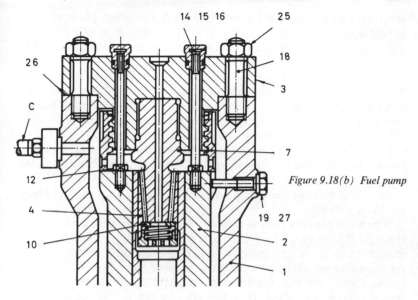

Figure 9.18(b) Fuel pump

the internal thread of the adjustment ring 7. On the upper part of the adjustment ring are cut external gear teeth that match with a pinion that is solid with its shaft which fits into bores in the top flange.

The pump barrel 2 is of forged steel and is guided at the top by a valve piece 4 that is screwed into the top flange and extends down into the bore of the barrel with a close fit of adequate length to give sufficient tightness for the injection oil when the pump is working. Below, the barrel is guided in the housing 1 and there are two synthetic rubber rings 9 for tightening.

When the pump is in operation, the barrel is fastened to the adjustment ring and to the top flange by studs 14 which extend through the top flange. The barrel has a shrunk-in liner of nitrided steel, into which the plunger 5 is accurately ground. The plunger terminates in a foot which is fixed in the roller guide by a bayonet at the top of the neck of the roller guide.

Above the foot there is a guide block whose plane surfaces slide in grooves in the regulating guide 6 to which a regulating arm 13 is bolted through a slit in the housing. A graduated scale 22 shows the angular position of the fuel pump plunger. The regulating guide rests against the flange 11. There is also a spigot for guiding the actuating gear housing to the pump housing.

At its top, the plunger has two helical edges as boundary between the plunger surface and an undercut relief space. The relief space is connected to the pressure chamber by a bore in the plunger. The helical edges terminate the injection when they pass the two diametrically opposed radial holes A in the fuel pump barrel.

The injection oil passes through the central hole in the valve piece and through the top flange to which the injection pipe is fastened. The valve piece has furthermore a number of longitudinal suction holes extending from the neck of the valve piece above the barrel down to the valve seat, where they are closed by a spring-loaded valve ring 10. The fuel pump works as indicated below.

Fuel oil under booster pump pressure enters at B into the annular space between housing and barrel. At the top of the housing there is a pipe connection C by which an amount of the heated fuel oil is recirculated to keep the pump equally warm at all times, including stand-by periods.

When the plunger moves downward, oil enters the barrel partly through the suction valve and partly through the radial holes A, except when the latter are covered by the plunger. In its bottom position, the top of the plunger is below the upper edges of the radial holes A, and, on the upward movement of the plunger, injection pressure builds-up when the holes are covered by the plunger top-edge. The timing of the beginning of injection may be altered by lifting or lowering the barrel, by loosening the top nuts of studs 18 and turning the distance ring 7 by the pinion, which also has a graduated scale.

The termination of injection, and thus the quantity of fuel injected, is changed by turning the plunger, whereby the helical edge opens earlier or later for the spill holes A. There is a hole D which connects a groove in the barrel with the annular space and thus there is only booster pressure below the groove. High pressure leakage is thereby returned to the inlet.

A tightening ring 10, of synthetic rubber, is placed between the tightening rings and the oil that is leaking through. This is drained away to a spill oil tank, from where it is pumped back to the system at intervals. A shock absorber 8, that has a spring-loaded floating piston, reduces the inertia pressure variations in the suction pipe.

Fuel Valves

Each cylinder is provided with two or three fuel valves of the type illustrated in Figure 9.19.

The atomiser elements 2 and 20, the spindle 21, and the spindle guide 3 are assembled at the lower end of the valve body 1 and held in place by nut 4. Tightness at junction of nut 4 and body 1 is obtained by a rubber ring 16. The valve is seated on an internal ledge or lip in the liner in the cylinder cover, see Figure 9.6.

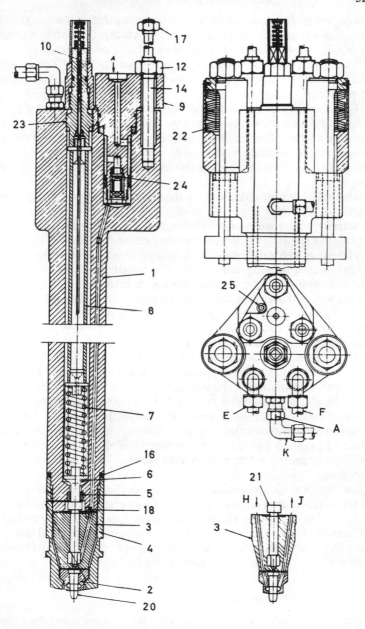

Figure 9.19 Fuel valve

The heavy flange of body 1 is held on to the cylinder cover by means of long studs, the nuts of which clamp the flange through Belleville springs 22. The relative positions of the atomiser, the spindle guide and the valve body are determined by dowel pins. The position of the valve in the cylinder cover is located by shoulders on the studs.

To obtain optimum oil-tightness, the spindle 21 and the guide 3 are ground very carefully together. Also, absolute oil-tightness is achieved by the plane-grinding of the jointing surfaces between the valve housing and the spindle guide, and between the spindle guide and the atomiser, as well as at the valve spindle seat in the spindle guide.

The valve spindle is loaded by the spring 7, the load being transmitted to the spindle by the lower spindle guide 6. The spring is compressed by means of the thrust spindle 8 and the thrust screw 23, the tightening of which determines the opening pressure of the valve.

The lift of the valve spindle is limited by the spindle head. This strikes against the stop disc 5 when the spindle is in its top position. The lift should not be allowed to become too great, because the spring would thereby be subjected to increased stresses. By placing a finger on the tip of the test pin 10 in the thrust screw 23, the knocking of the valve can be felt, this being a ready method of detecting whether or not the valve is functioning.

The fuel oil inlet connection A is on top of the filter body that is clamped to the valve by studs. When the oil has passed the fine slots in the filter it passes through the spring-loaded check valve 24, the dual purpose of which is, in event of a hanging fuel valve spindle, partly to prevent gas being blown back into the injection system when the engine is running and partly to prevent oil being pumped into the cylinder when the engine is standing and the booster pump is running. A vent screw 25 is also placed in the filter body.

The fuel valves are cooled by diesel oil. The oil is stored in the diesel oil tank, from which it is drawn by an electrically driven pump and circulated through all the fuel valves. The oil is admitted at E and returned to the tank at F. It flows through longitudinal bores in the valve body and enters and leaves the spindle guide at H and J respectively. K is a drain connection for leakage oil.

Fittings for High-pressure Fuel Pipes

Figure 9.20 shows the connection between the high-pressure pipes and the fuel pump and fuel valves respectively.

To prevent fuel oil from being squirted over the engine should a pipe 1 crack, it is surrounded by a flexible hose 2 in which building-up of pressure is prevented by the provision of adequate drains. The pipe has a ball-shaped abutment at its lower end that tightens against a conical recess in the fuel pump or valve, 3, and a thread to which the thrust piece 4 is fitted. The thrust piece, at its top end, fits tightly to the pipe and has a ball-shaped abutment that is in

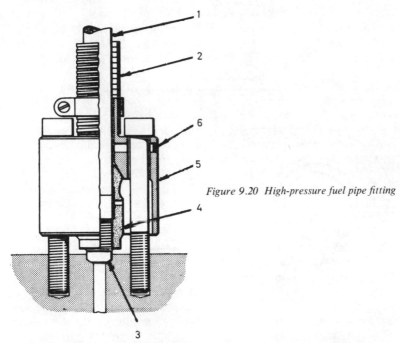

Figure 9.20 High-pressure fuel pipe fitting

contact with the cone on the flange 5 and presses it down. At the same time the pipe with which it makes a firm but not too hard contact is pressed down, thereby relieving the threat of any bending moment from possible pipe vibrations. Any possible leakage from the pipe is drained away either by holes down through the bolt holes or through a special drain pipe in the flange 6 to the drain tank.

Cylinder Lubrication

Each cylinder has its separate lubricator, *see* Figures 9.21 and 9.22.

The lubricator consists of a reservoir, 1, in which are arranged a number of small pumps, each pump supplying oil to its designated point of lubrication. The pump plungers 38, which are driven from the small camshaft 22, draw oil from the reservoir through the lower

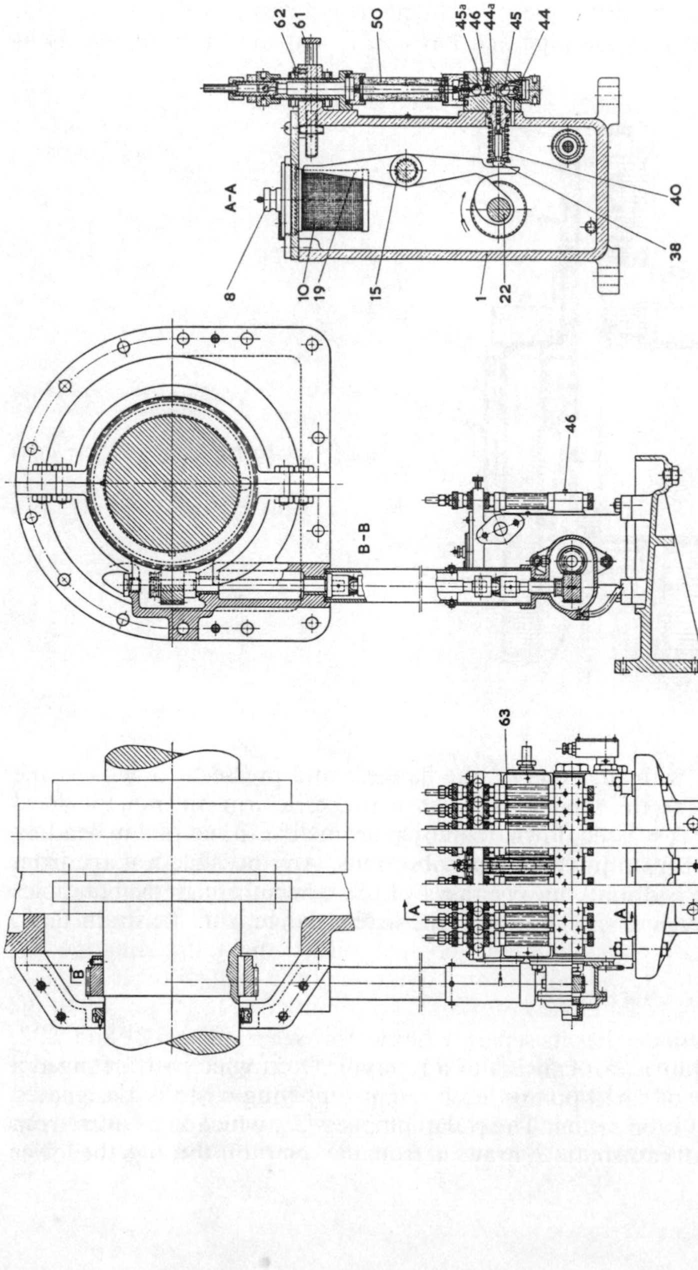

Figure 9.21 Cylinder lubrication

set of valves 44 and 45 and deliver it through the upper set of valves 44a and 45a, up the transparent plastic tube 50, to the assigned lubricating points.

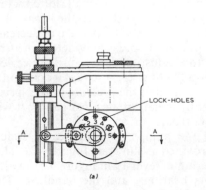

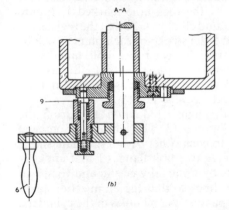

Figure 9.22 Lubricator detail

Each synthetic tube contains a steel ball. The internal hole in the tube is tapered, increasing in bore towards the top. In accordance with the amount and viscosity of the oil that ascends through the tube, the ball will rise to a proportionate height. This is a ready means of controlling the flow of oil to the lubricating points. Contacts may also be arranged in one of the control tubes, to close an alarm circuit when the ball is bottoming due to lack of oil in the lubricator.

The capacity of the unit oil pump is determined by the stroke of its plunger, which may be varied to suit immediate requirements. The stroke of each individual pump may be altered or, alternatively, all the plungers on one lubricator may be adjusted together. The latter course is adopted when it is desired for a period, say, during the manoeuvring of the engine, to feed more lubricating oil to the cylinder.

To alter the stroke of an individual pump, the small slotted screw 62 above the adjustment screw 61 is loosened; then the screw 61 is turned to the right or to the left, respectively, to increase or decrease the stroke. The stroke of the plunger is preferably determined by measuring the movement of the adjusting screw during service, exerting a slight pressure on the adjusting screw so that it constantly touches the lever 19 without overcoming the pressure of the spring 40. The movement is measured by means of a caliper gauge; it will always be equal to the plunger stroke.

To alter the strokes of all the pumps on a lubricator simultaneously, a special device is provided as shown in Figure 9.22. This comprises the shaft 15, the fulcrum of lever 19 in Figure 9.21, which is eccentrically mounted in its bearings, and the handle 6. The position of the handle during normal running should be such that the registering pin, 9.22(b), is in the lock-hole marked 1, Figure 9.22(a). If the handle is shifted round clockwise so that the registering pin 9 is in the lock-hole marked 5 the stroke of each plunger will be increased by 6 mm, being 1·5 mm for each lock-hole movement. Besides permitting the simultaneous adjustment of all plunger-strokes, the special regulating device can also be used for ventilating and priming the cylinder lubricating oil system.

The lubricators are driven through a reduction gear from the auxiliary chains marked 8 in Figure 9.13. The lubricators on each side of the chain are connected to each other by intermediate shafts marked 8 in Figure 9.23 that have two bolt flanges 1 that are connected to the lubricator flanges by an axially elastic and torsional stiff disc 2. The lubricators are times so that the oil injection takes place while the piston rings are passing the oil holes in the cylinders, during the upward travel of the piston. The lubricators may also be provided with a float that keeps a constant oil level from a filling pipe.

Manoeuvring

The engines are, as a rule, remotely controlled from an enclosed control room or from the bridge, but manual manoeuvring is also possible as an emergency, if the speed governor or the signal transmission system should fail.

Figure 9.24 shows the control console that contains all instruments for monitoring the engine during starting, reversing and running. There are three manoeuvring handles and, to the extreme left on

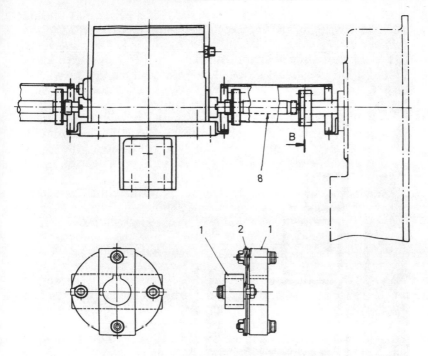

Figure 9.23 Lubricator drive

the table, alarm panels for temperatures and pressures of lubricating and cooling fluids, etc.

By means of the short handle to the left, the manoeuvring control may be switched to Bridge, Engine room or Emergency. The centre handle is the manoeuvring, i.e. start and speed control, handle; and the handle to the right is the telegraph reply handle which, at the same time, adjusts the engine for ahead or astern running.

During normal running, i.e. Bridge control or Engine room control, the engine revolutions are controlled by a hydraulic governor which has a hydraulic amplifier.

The transmission of signals from the console to the engine is pneumatic; starting and reversing are with on-off switches; and rev/min governing is by adjusting the level of a control pressure that in turn adjusts the governor. This pressure is determined by the position of the manoeuvring handle, which adjusts the spring in a pressure regulator.

When the manoeuvring handle is put into the start position, a stop cylinder keeps the fuel pumps in the no-fuel position against a

334

Figure 9.24 Remote control console

spring in a connecting rod between governor and fuel adjustment shaft. By moving the handle into the running section the pressure in the cylinder is released, whereupon the spring and the governor bring the fuel pumps into the position that ensures the desired rev/min.

The signals from the bridge control are electrically transmitted to the pneumatic system on the engine, by electro-magnetic positioning of the on-off valves and by a servomotor to the pneumatic fine-regulating valve that adjusts the pressure level for the rev/min control.

A tachometer generator, driven by the engine, transmits to the bridge control cabinet a voltage that is proportional to the engine rev/min. There it is used to ensure that, by bridge manoeuvring, the rev/min levels are suitable for beginning the reversing procedure, for going on to fuel at starting, and for actuating the overspeed relay. There are also timing units for slow turning of the engine before starting, if the engine has been standing still for a prolonged period, and for effecting a somewhat delayed stepwise running-up to full power after prolonged periods of no-running.

The previously mentioned stop cylinder is also used by: emergency stopping of the engine from the bridge; overspeed; too low lubricating oil pressures and too high coolant temperatures.

The bridge manoeuvring system being fully automatic, the navigator need not concern himself about the engine. He has only to move his telegraph handle to any new-desired running position, when his orders will be carried out in correct sequence and with correct timing. The system also reacts automatically, by slowing-down or stopping the engine, in event of emergencies or grave abnormal behaviour.

Starting Air System

The starting air system (Figure 9.25) consists of the stop valve A, master valve B, starting air distributors C and starting air valves D. The system is shown in the stand-by position.

The bushing 1, which has an external thread, is in its upper position, whereby the valve spindle 2 is free to move. The master valve spindles are in their lower position, in which the chambers 3 and 4 are connected, and the centre collar on the stop valve is closing upon its seat.

In the position for starting, (Figure 9.26(a)), the cylinder 5 is pressurised and lifts the master valve spindle, whereby the pressure in chamber 4 is released and spindle 2 lifts and admits air to C and D,

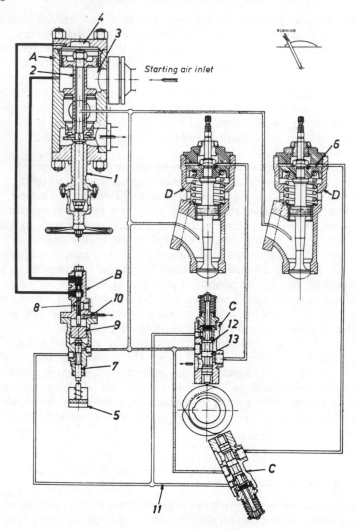

Figure 9.25 Starting air system

the spindle of the former being pressed down on to the cams. When the spindles are at the smaller diameter region of the cams, air is admitted to space C in the starting air valve, which opens and admits air to the engine cylinder.

In Figure 9.26(b) the air pressure is relieved from cylinder 5, the spindle 7 closes the de-aeration pipes 11, although the spindle 8

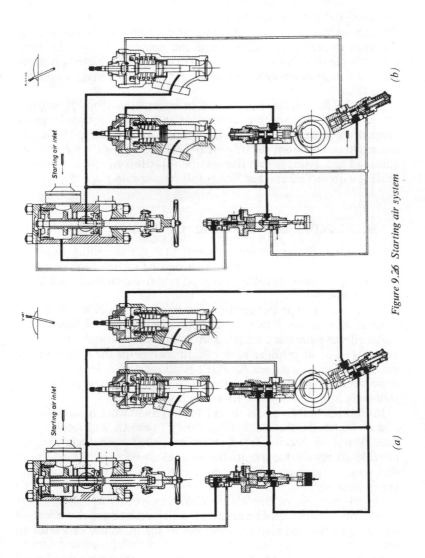

Figure 9.26 Starting air system

Starting air inlet

Starting air inlet

(a)

(b)

remains in the open position, due to the delayed action caused by the large diameter piston 9, which has to draw air through the small hole 10.

In the starting air distributor the collars 12 and 13 are of equal diameter and the spindles that are on the small diameter region of the cams remain open and starting air continues to be admitted to the corresponding cylinders, until the spindles are on the large diameter region of the cams from where they go to their top position; they do not go down again, even if the stop valve remains open for some time.

With this system there continues to be a torque from the starting air on the engine, to help to overcome an opposite torque from the propeller during stopping of the engine at reversing, i.e. in the transition period from starting air to fuel oil, without any fuel being admitted to a cylinder that has an open starting air valve. A section dealing with service and test bed results is given on page 353 *et seq.*

HIGH POWERED ENGINES OF ADVANCED TYPE

In due course, the engine series described in the preceding pages will be superseded by a two-stroke cycle marine engine type which, in a number of ways, breaks with traditional Burmeister and Wain diesel engine design.

The builders' type designation for the engine is K90GF. In this symbol, K indicates a two-stroke crosshead engine; G signifies the mean effective pressure range; and F implies a marine engine. The numeral 90 is the cylinder bore in centimetres for the first engine of the series. Other sizes are K67GF, K80GF, and K98GF. In order to appreciate the approach of the builders to these new engines, the following introductory remarks may be helpful.

In addition to their research and development work in laboratories and on test beds, the continuous flow of records and information that B and W receive from ships propelled with their engines, provide an invaluable aid to the final evaluation of the ability of their engines to cope with the many varied service conditions that are encountered.

In the analysis of service records received from ships, there necessarily enters consideration of hull conditions, the effect of marine growths and also to some extent the influence of wind and sea.

To evaluate these variables B and W have, through a number of years, used power-field diagrams in which by simply plotting the mip or mep against rev/min one not only obtains the shaft horse-power corresponding to a certain point but also valuable information on the hull conditions. The experience thus obtained has made the firm feel that they would better serve shipowners and shipyards to decide on propeller characteristics by introducing the concepts power-range and power-field, instead of giving results for a certain power-propeller curve only.

Power-field Diagram

In the future Burmeister and Wain will state the data for their engines on special data sheets that include a power-field diagram. Also they will include diagrams for the particular engine which will provide an easy means for shipowners to keep track of marine growths and dockings.

Table 9.3 POWER DATA K–GF TYPE

Engine type cylinder dia/stroke		Continuous service power mep 10·8 bar 11·0 kp/cm²		Max. continuous power mep 11·60 bar 11·8 kp/cm²	Overload power mep 11·60 bar 12·5 kp/cm²
mm	Units	Range	Nominal	Range	Range
K67GF 670/1 400	rev/min	131– 150	140	140– 150	140– 150
	kW	1 160 1 330	1 240	1 330–1 420	1 420–1 520
	shp	1 600–1 820	1 700	1 810–1 940	1 930–2 070
K80GF 800/1 600	rev/min	114– 131	122	122– 131	122– 131
	kW	1 650–1 900	1 760	1 880–2 020	2 010–2 160
	shp	2 250–2 580	2 400	2 560–2 750	2 740–2 930
K90GF 900/1 800	rev/min	103– 118	110	110– 118	110– 118
	kW	2 130–2 440	2 270	2 420–2 600	2 590–2 770
	shp	2 910–3 330	3 100	3 300–3 540	3 530–3 780
K98GF 980/2 000	rev/min	94– 107	100	100– 107	100– 107
	kW	2 550–2 900	2 710	2 890–3 100	3 100–3 300
	shp	3 470–3 960	3 700	3 940–4 200	4 200–4 500

Figure 9.27 is a power-field diagram for a K90GF engine.

All the scales on the diagram are logarithmic and, accordingly, all exponential relationships are shown as straight lines having different slopes. The abcissae are revolutions per minute and the ordinates are mean indicated pressures and mean effective pressures.

The lines sloping downwards from the right are constant brake horse-power lines; those sloping upwards from the right are propeller

Table 9.4 ENGINE WEIGHTS AND SIZES

	Approximate weight coefficient		Approximate dimensions				
			Length coefficient			Heights	
							H_2
Type	Cast	Welded	L	W	H_1	Norm.	Min.
K67GF	—	38	1 140	36	7 100	8 500	8 000
K80GF	—	62	1 360	59	8 600	10 300	9 600
K90GF	—	85	1 540	85	9 500	11 500	10 750
K98GF	—	125	1 900	130	11 000	13 000	11 850

Weights in Mg = t = weight coefficient × (n + 1·6)
n = number of cylinders, for engines with semi-built crankshafts.
Overall length of engine, mm = L × (n + 2·6).
Length of engine over frames, mm = L × (n + x·2).
H_1 = height from centre-line of crankshaft to top of engine, mm
H_2 = height from centre line of crankshaft to crane hook, mm
W = width of base, mm.

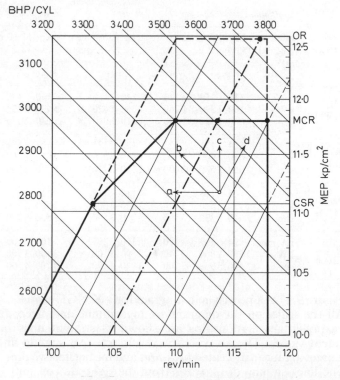

Figure 9.27 Power and revolution ranges, engine K90GF

lines, for constant hull and weather conditions. The slope of the propeller lines shows bhp proportional to rev/min³ and mep proportional to rev/min². Depending upon type and speed of ship, the exponent may be higher in the upper speed range.

Consider, as an example, a trial trip point 0. The movement of a service point in direction 'a' (constant mep), indicates an increase in hull resistance which, in turn, causes a decrease in rev/min and power. Movement in direction 'b' (constant power), indicates simultaneous increases in rev/min, mep and hull resistance.

A movement in direction 'c' (constant rev/min) indicates simultaneous increases in mep, bhp and hull resistance. Movement in direction 'd' (constant hull resistance) indicates a simultaneous increase in mep and rev/min, resulting in an increase in power.

The distance between the propeller lines through any two operating points thus gives an indication of the change that has occurred in the hull resistance and may be referred to constant rev/min or constant mep. The different power-ranges and fields are defined as follows:

C.S.R. (Continuous service-power range) is on the 9·6 kp/cm² mep line and shows the powers that are recommended for average service conditions, with about 6 per cent margin for increase in mep when desirable. The C.S.R. field is below the 9·6 kp/cm² line, within the heavy border lines.

M.C.R. (Maximum continuous-power range) is on the 10·3 kg/cm² line and shows the powers for which the engine is designed and approved. The M.C.R. field is between the 9·6 and 10·3 kp/cm² mep lines, within the heavy full border lines.

O.R. (Overload-power range) is on the 10·9 kp/cm² mep line. The O.R. field is between the heavy dotted lines and the heavy full lines.

Table 9.3 shows the power/speed data for the K-GF engine series. In Table 9.4 the corresponding weights and dimensions are indicated.

The preferred form of engine crankshaft has hitherto been the fully-built, where torsional and axial vibration conditions have permitted, because of the advantage with regard to production. The necessity for a shrinkage length at the crankpin, of the same dimensions as for the main bearing, requires a larger cylinder distance than is necessary for cylinder cover, liner, and other moving parts of the engine. Accordingly, a semi-built crankshaft is necessarily favoured in the new engine series, to obtain optimum crankshaft design with reference to minimum engine length linked to optimum supercharging arrangement for efficiency and economy.

ENGINE CONSTRUCTIONAL DETAILS

Bedplate

As seen in Figure 9.28, the standard bedplate is of the high type and of fabricated design. The centre-piece that carries the main bearing is provided with bosses for the staybolts, and is cast steel. The bedplate as normally constructed is in two parts, flanged together at the chain-drive.

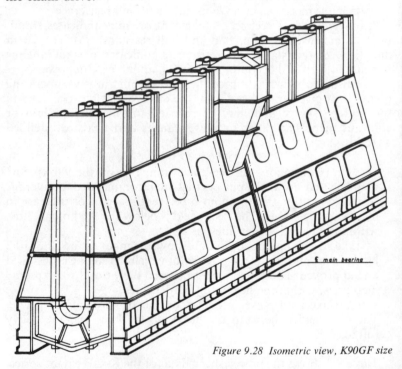

Figure 9.28 Isometric view, K90GF size

The lengths of the bedplate holding-down bolts have been increased, compared with previous practice; also the total elasticity has been further increased by adding cast iron space pieces. By this means the safety margin against bolts working loose has been increased to such an extent that spherical washers can now be omitted.

The standard thrust bearing is of the built-in, short type, and separated from the crankcase by a partition wall.

The turning gear is of the type with cylindrical teeth on the turning wheel to mesh with a drive movable in the longitudinal direction of the engine.

Frame

As shown in Figures 9.28 and 9.29 the frame section consists of three units: a frame box of a height corresponding to the length of the crosshead guides, bolted together in the longitudinal direction in the chain drive section only, and two longitudinal girders, also bolted together in this section.

This design gives rigid units of a size designed for easy handling and mounting, both on test bed and in the ship. The rigid design with few joints further ensures oil tightness, and the hinged crankcase doors located in the longitudinal girders on the manoeuvring side make the crankcase, as well as the crosshead sections, easily accessible for inspection, overhaul and replacement work.

The crosshead guides, consisting of heavy I-sections, are attached at top and bottom in the frame boxes. The lower attachment is flexible in longitudinal direction of the crosshead guides which are thus not influenced by deformations of the frame arising from gas forces.

Cylinder

The cooling jacket/scavenging air box section consists of cast one-cylinder sections connected in the vertical plane by fitted bolts.

This section is attached to the frame section and the bedplate by means of stay bolts and the horizontal joints are secured against relative movements by fitted bolts.

The cylinder liner is provided with a water cooled flange low down, which means a low temperature level in the most heavily loaded area, a feature essential to the reliability of the engine. The cast iron liner and the flange are, due to their low position, protected by the piston against direct temperature influence from combustion, which means that the heat stress is kept at a moderate level.

Crankshaft

The crankshaft is semi-built for all cylinder combinations. For six- to ten-cylinder engines, the crank throw is made of cast steel, whereas for 11 and 12 cylinders, it is forged.

Balancing of the engine is undertaken by varying the crank pin bores. Bolted-on counter weights are entirely eliminated.

Lubrication of the crank bearing is from the crosshead through the connecting rod and consequently significant stress raisers like transverse bores in the crankshaft have been eliminated.

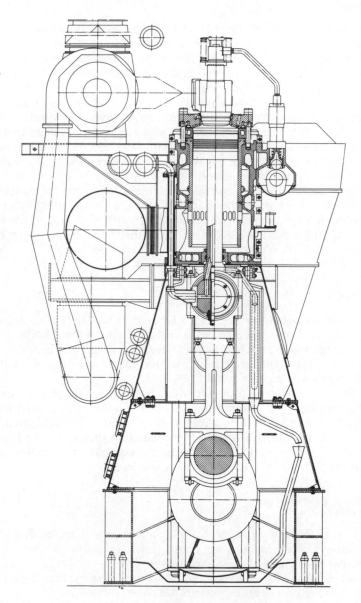

Figure 9.29 Engine section K90GF size

Crosshead

The crosshead is short and rigid and the bearings are so constructed that the bearing pressure between journal and bearing is distributed evenly over the entire length of the bearing. The bearing pressure is smaller than in previous engine types, and the peripheral speed is higher, which improves the working conditions of the bearings. The construction is such that, in event of surface damage, say by dirt particles, the pin can be turned 180° and continue operation.

Interchangeable bearing shells of steel with 1 mm white metal babbitting are fitted to the crosshead bearings. The bearings are finish-bored precision items. The main reason for choosing bearing shells is that improved binding between the white metal and the steel shells is obtained, as well as improved structure of the white metal, owing to faster cooling after casting. Also, loose bearing shells are easily replaced. The bearing shell halves are identical and so the upper bearing shell can replace the lower while a worn or damaged lower shell may be used temporarily as upper shell.

Figure 9.30 shows the crosshead arrangement.

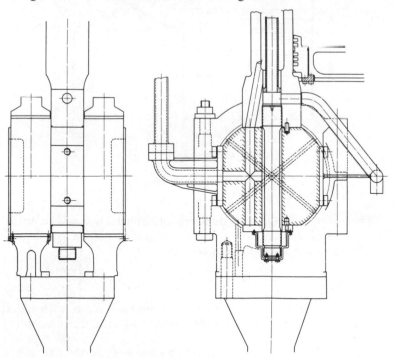

Figure 9.30 Crosshead arrangement

Piston

The design of the piston follows established principles as used in recent engine types, *see* Figure 9.31. The piston top is supported by a ring with a diameter of about three-quarters of the cylinder diameter and fixed to the piston rod top through a cast-iron skirt and a heavy Belleville-spring.

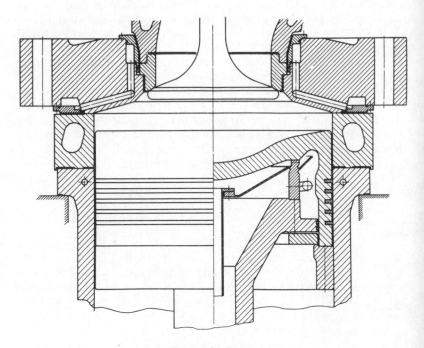

Figure 9.31 Piston

The comparatively small thickness of material behind the piston rings gives, in conjunction with effective oil cooling, a satisfactory low temperature level in the piston ring zone.

Cylinder Cover

The cylinder cover is in two parts, a solid steel plate, with radial cooling water bores, to which a forged steel ring with bevelled cooling water bores is bolted.

The fact that the radial cooling bores are close to the gas side of the cover causes the drop in temperature to be mainly concentrated on a small area between the gas side of the channels. No tensile stresses of consequence, resulting from the heat stresses, will arise in the cover. Due to the tightening of the studs for the cover, and to the gas pressure, compressive stresses are induced in the lower part of the cover and tensile stresses in the upper part. The cooling bores will thus be located only in a compression-stressed area and the risk of cracks, arising from the notch effect of the borings, will be insignificant. Because of the temperature distribution, with the almost constant temperature over the cooling bores, it will be possible to decide on the height of the cover by considering only the varying stresses from gas forces and other relevant elements of design, without this having any noticeable influence on the heat stresses. For dismantling, the cover is one unit.

The advantages of a cover of this design are:

1. short and light valves;
2. low temperature level;
3. low tensile stresses;
4. small varying stresses;
5. simple mounting of valves;
6. easy dismantling.

Exhaust Valves and Gear

In principle the exhaust valve is made like those in the most recent Burmeister and Wain engines. The valve bottom piece and valve spindle are made of steel with stellite welded on to the seats. This design has operated in service for 12 000–15 000 hours without grinding, so that an average of at least 8000 operating hours without grinding can be expected.

The engine is arranged for hydraulic operation of the exhaust valve. The system consists of a piston pump which is driven through the roller guide by a cam disc on the camshaft. The pressure oil is led through a pipe to a working cylinder placed on top of the exhaust valve housing. The maximum oil pressure in the system is below 200 kN/m^2 and, in the design, special attention has been paid to reliability and simple maintenance. Besides saving space and weight, the system has a number of other advantages over the conventional arrangements. For instance, the exhaust valve is not subjected to guide forces. This, in conjunction with effective insulation to prevent hot gases passing along the exhaust valve spindle, considerably improves the working conditions of the spindle guide bushes.

For the exhaust valve and hydraulic valve gear see Figure 9.32, which is self-explanatory.

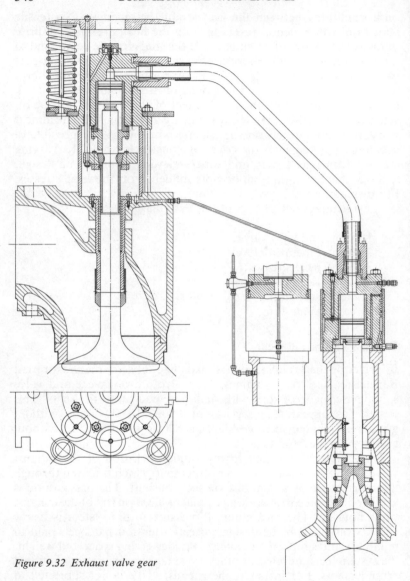

Figure 9.32 Exhaust valve gear

Fuel Pump

In principle, the fuel pump is of the latest, very successful design, as shown in Figure 9.33.

The fuel pump housing is of cast steel and the fuel pump barrel is placed centrally, guided below by the housing and above by a central guide protruding from the housing cover. For adjusting the firing pressure the position of the barrel may be altered by changing the number of shims between the top flange and the barrel.

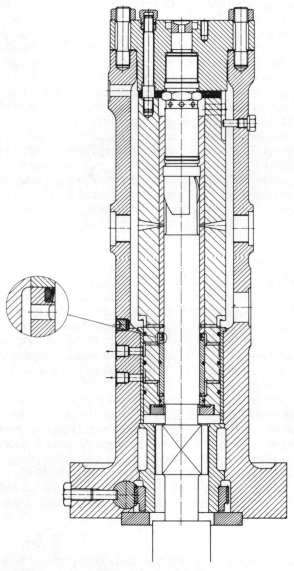

Figure 9.33 Fuel pump

Fuel oil enters the lower part of the housing, passes the annular space between housing and barrel, and enters the barrel through drillings in the central guide piece, which, at its lower face, forms the seat for an annular, spring-loaded, suction valve. The high pressure fuel passes through the central boring in the suction valve to the high pressure pipe, the distributor, and the fuel valves. Neither in the fuel pump nor in the fuel valve do these high pressure borings cross each other, which means that the traditional stress raiser that has most often caused cracking has been obviated.

With this pump design, a uniform heating of piston and liner has been attained, which has reduced considerably the risk of the plunger sticking, and the operation figures have been as expected. Only minor modifications have been made, after some time in service, mainly to reduce oil leakage down to the camshaft housing and to avoid oil spray from the cut-outs for the regulating lever. The pump piston is turned by a toothed rack built into the baseplate, which eliminates completely the traditional recess in the pump housing. The pump plunger can be lifted and retained in or released from the top position by an automatic pneumatic gear, even with the engine running.

Camshaft and Drive

The camshaft is divided into sections, one for each cylinder, enclosed and suspended in roller guide housings with replaceable, ready-bored bearing shells. The individual shaft parts are hollow ground, and cams and couplings are floated-on by means of the SKF oil-injection pressure method. The design of the camshaft chain drive is in accordance with the latest successful practice, with the chain tightener placed low on the frame section and with inclined chains and outside guideways.

The vertical joint of the frame sections is positioned at the chain drive front so that the intermediate wheel, the chain tightener, and the guideways belong to the aftermost part and need no dismantling where transport conditions and crane capacity make it necessary to separate the frame sections. The starting air distributor, the governor, the cylinder lubricators and the overspeed unit are driven from the chain drive intermediate shaft, through chains on either end of this shaft to gears on either side of the upper chain wheel frame.

Fuel Valves

The cylinder cover is provided with three fuel valves of a new type.
The high pressure fuel is led through a central bore in the valve via

the spindle to the atomiser. The non-return valve is built into the spindle in conjunction with an automatic vent slide. This positioning of the non-return valve results in a short distance between the fuel valve mitre seat and the non-return valve, diminishing vibration in the oil column and ensuring increased life for the non-return valve.

The vent slide has been so designed that a moderate circulation through the fuel valve is maintained so that the matching parts reach a temperature close to the working temperature and the risk of sticking is reduced. This arrangement further renders manual venting of the fuel injection system superfluous. Improved contact between the valve and the cylinder cover, ensuring good heat transmission, together with the improved cooling of the new design of cylinder cover, makes it possible to dispense with separate cooling of the fuel valve.

Manoeuvring and Reversing

The engines have a pneumatic manoeuvring system consisting of three units: the separate manoeuvring stand, component box and regulation unit.

The main variation from the earlier manoeuvring system is in reversing; this is carried out hydraulically.

In the reversing gear the chain wheel floats in relation to the camshaft which is driven through a self-locking crank gear. Whereas until recently the reversing has been done by the camshaft in relation to the chain wheel and by braking on a camshaft brake disc; in the new engines instead of braking, the reversing crank pins are turned by means of built-on hydraulic motors. Figure 9.34 shows the reversing gear arrangement.

Turbocharging

Scavenging and charging air are delivered by exhaust-gas driven blowers, arranged in accordance with the B and W turbocharging system, with exhaust pipes of relative small volume connecting the exhaust valve outlet and the turbine gas inlet. the turbochargers have been arranged with a view to providing good access for overhaul and cleaning, and are equipped with slide bearings.

Engines connected to controllable pitch propellers, or engines for specially slow running with fixed pitch propellers, are provided with auxiliary blowers.

The air coolers and the pipe connections are constructed for minimum pressure drop. The air coolers are of the established type, divided, however, into sections arranged for quick replacement with

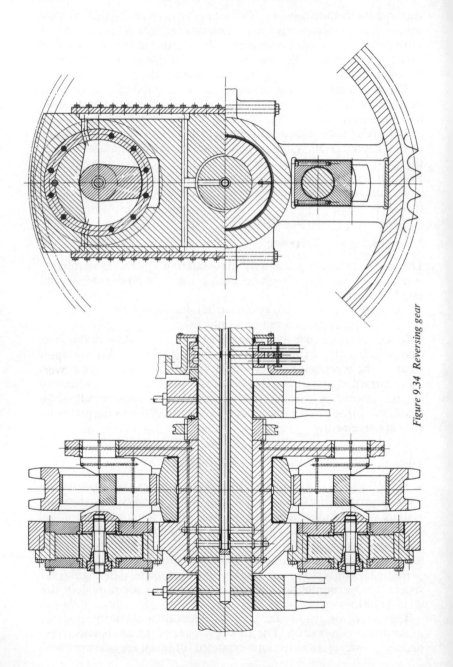

Figure 9.34 Reversing gear

spare cooling elements. This ensures sufficient time for cleaning the dismounted element as well as a decrease in off-hire time.

Service Results

The new piston design has contributed to low temperatures in the piston ring zone, giving low piston ring as well as low cylinder wear rates.

On the majority of pistons dismantled after the test running, distinct wear marks were found on the outer half of the contact faces between support and piston top, due to bending of the piston crown, caused by the temperature gradient.

In order to examine the development of wear, pistons were dismantled after 10 500 hours service. Measurement on the piston crown showed wear, at the outer half, of about 0·01–0·02 mm, while there was still no wear at the inner half. It has not been possible to obtain any clear measurement on the supporting ring, but the wear pattern had the same extent as on the piston top.

The wear observed does not appear to be of importance to the function of the piston, and the wear of the contact faces is a running-in phenomenon that will gradually disappear when the two contact faces have adjusted to each other and the load is distributed over a larger part of the face.

Crosshead bearings, crank bearings and main bearings have worked without any problems. The chain drive with guide bars has operated trouble-free.

On eight-cylinder engines, the torque variations in the camshaft are larger than on other cylinder combinations, and with a chain incorrectly tightened, transverse vibrations of a free chain strand are excited which creates a considerable increase in load on the chain drive. By fitting guide bars on this free strand, extra security is obtained.

The new type of fuel pump has worked well. Due to the uniform heating of piston and liner there is no risk of the piston seizing, e.g. when changing from diesel oil to heavy oil. The sealing rings for the plungers at the bottom of the fuel pump barrel have sometimes leaked. A new sealing ring has been tested with good results and has been introduced as standard.

The fuel valves with mitre seats have given satisfactory results.

Bearings in rocker arms on some plants have shown a tendency to heat. By increasing the oil rate for lubrication of these bearings and also introducing cooling of the hollow shafting, satisfactory results have been obtained. Roller bearings instead of plain bearings have been tested with favourable results. On some engines a spring guide is built on the exhaust valve springs to obtain the necessary natural frequency of the complete valve gear with reasonably low varying stresses in the springs.

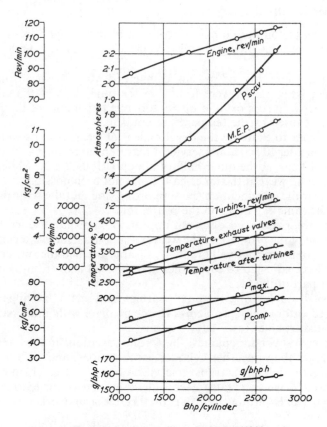

Figure 9.35 Test results for eight-cylinder 840/1800 engine

Good results have been obtained with an arrangement consisting of six springs with a shorter total height than the original arrangement. The springs, replacing the original springs and guide, are arranged in a circle around the valve stem. Because of the smaller wire dimensions, the material for these springs is easier to procure in a good quality and higher varying stresses as normal for smaller engine types are allowable. It means that the same high natural frequency as for the original spring arrangement is obtained. In this design also, a broken spring is easily removed.

Typical Test Results

In Figure 9.35 typical test results are given for an eight-cylinder, 840 mm bore, 1800 mm stroke engine of the class KEF.

KEF is the symbol designation of the direct-coupled engine design which forms the greater part of the descriptive matter in the present chapter, that is, from pages 297 to 338.

The set of tests shown in the diagram was very comprehensive, including compression; maximum, minimum and scavenge pressures; fuel consumptions; temperatures; revolutions; and so on, for both engine and turbochargers.

S.H.

Chapter 10

Doxford Engines

The Doxford engine is a vertical opposed-piston two-stroke engine, each cylinder having two pistons which move in opposite directions from a central combustion chamber. The lower piston uncovers a row of scavenging ports in the cylinder liner at the bottom of its stroke, and the upper piston uncovers a row of exhaust ports at the upper end of its stroke. On present-day engines, scavenging air is supplied by exhaust turbochargers driven by the exhaust gases from the engine cylinders, a centrifugal blower supplying the air at 0·70 to 0·825 bar gauge pressure. Each cylinder has a three-throw crankshaft, the centre crank being approximately opposite the two side cranks. On turbocharged engines, the exhaust cranks are given a lead of 9° on the P-type engines, and 8/10° on the J-type. The lower piston drives the centre crankpin by a single connecting-rod connected to a crosshead, while the upper piston is connected to a transverse beam which has two side-rods connected to crossheads, which are, in turn, connected to the two side crankpins by connecting-rods. To secure primary balance of the reciprocating masses, the stroke of the lower piston is greater than the stroke of the upper piston. The original Doxford engines were built in normal aspirated form; but now all engines are turbocharged, and to provide larger powers the J-type engine has been introduced. The P-range of engines was built in only one cylinder size to give 1660 bhp (1250 kW) per cylinder so that the six-cylinder engine gave 10 000 bhp (7500 kW) *see* Table 10.1. The J-range of engines is being built in three cylinder sizes, powers from 5500 to 22 500 bhp (say 4000 to 17 000 kW). For typical sections of the J engine *see* Figure 10.1.

Figure 10.2 shows a diagrammatic arrangement of one cylinder, from which it will be appreciated that the weight of the upper piston, with the transverse beam, two side-rods, crossheads and connecting-

Table 10.1 RANGE OF P-TYPE ENGINES

No. of cylinders	bhp	kW	Length mm	Height mm	Width mm	Weight tonne
4	6 640	5 000	10 600	9 500	3 710	250
5	8 300	6 200	12 600	9 500	3 710	325
6	10 000	7 500	13 900	9 500	3 710	380

rods, is heavier than the lower piston with one crosshead and connecting-rod.

Phases of the Cycle

Figure 10.2 shows the cycle phases which take place every revolution.

1. Engine on bottom centre, with scavenge and exhaust ports fully open, allowing scavenging air to flow through the cylinder.
2. Scavenge ports closed.
3. Exhaust ports closed, from which point the compression commences as the pistons move together.
4. Pistons approaching top dead-centre, at which point combustion takes place, fuel being injected at full load from approximately 14° before to 20° after T.D.C., whereas for slow running, fuel is injected from approximately 5° before to 5° after T.D.C.
5. The pistons have moved apart on the power stroke, and the exhaust ports are just commencing to release the products of combustion to the exhaust pipe.
6. The scavenge ports are just starting to open, to permit the air, delivered by the turbochargers, to clear out the remaining products of combustion and refill the cylinders.

OUTLINE DESCRIPTION

The engine is started by means of compressed air stored at 450 lb/in^2 (31 bar) in storage tanks of about 5·0 m^3 capacity; two tanks are usually carried, either of which can be used.

Fuel is injected in an atomised state at a pressure of between 6000 and 8000 lb/in^2 (say 400 to 550 bar). This pressure is maintained by an engine-driven fuel pump having, normally, one pump ram for each cylinder.

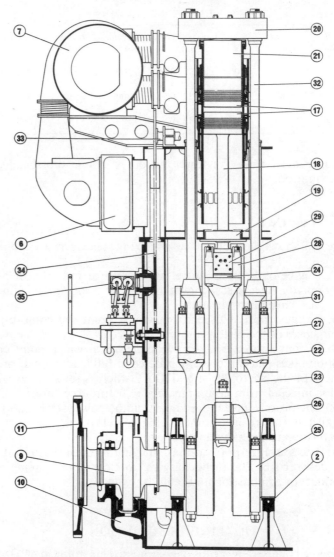

Figure 10.1(a) Longitudinal section of J-type engine

All engines have the cylinders and upper pistons cooled by distilled water circulated in a closed system, the heat being dissipated in tubular heat exchangers cooled by sea-water. The cooling water enters the engine at approximately 65°C, and comes out at approxi-

359

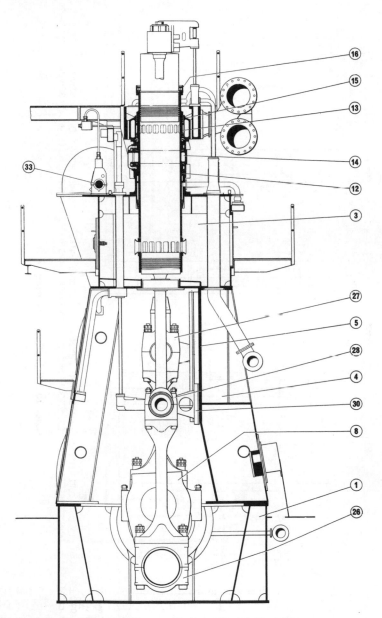

Figure 10.1(b) Cross-section of J-type engine

360

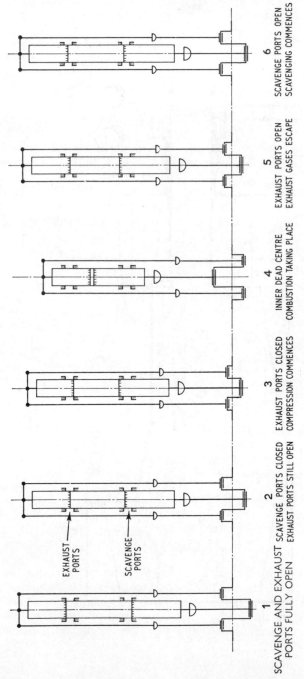

Figure 10.2 Exhaust and scavenging events

mately 75°C. It is pre-heated before starting. The lower pistons of both the P and the J engines are cooled through telescopic pipes by oil.

All crankshaft connecting-rod and crosshead bearings are lubricated by forced lubrication pumps from a common pressure system, which also supplies oil to the thrust block. The oil is filtered after leaving the forced-lubrication pump and is cooled in a tubular cooler by sea-water.

Doxford J-type engines are built with from four to nine cylinders and, in general, the four-cylinder engines have one turbocharger and the six- and nine-cylinder engines have two or three turbochargers respectively connected to three cylinders, as shown in Figure 10.3.

The range of engines covered by the P-type engine of 670 mm bore is shown in Table 10.1, and the range of powers for the J-type engine in three sizes of cylinder is shown in Table 10.2. In all engines the

Table 10.2 POWER OF J-ENGINES (MAXIMUM CONTINUOUS RATING)

Type	bhp	kW	No. of cyls.	rev/min	Length mm	Width mm	Height mm	Weight tonne
10·35 bar, mip								
	5 500	4 000	4	128		3 350	8 640	173
580 ×	6 000	4 500	4	140	7 400	3 350	8 640	173
1850	6 700	5 000	4	155		3 350	8 640	173
10·20 bar, mip								
670 ×	8 000	6 000	4	124	8 380	3 860	10 100	270
2 140	12 000	9 000	6	124	11 500	3 860	10 100	371
10·20 bar, mip								
	10 000	7 500	4	119	9 200	3 960	10 300	336
	15 000	11 200	6	119	13 300	3 960	10 300	472
760 ×	17 500	13 000	7	119	14 700	3 960	10 300	538
2 180	20 000	15 000	8	119	16 500	3 960	10 300	605
	22 500	17 000	9	119	18 200	3 960	10 300	665

thrust housing is arranged to be integral with the aft end of the bedplate, but the thrust-shaft is a separate forging which can be taken out separately from the engine for maintenance purposes. The bedplate, columns and entablature are welded of steel plate, but the cylinder liners, exhaust belts, crosshead guides, etc., are iron castings.

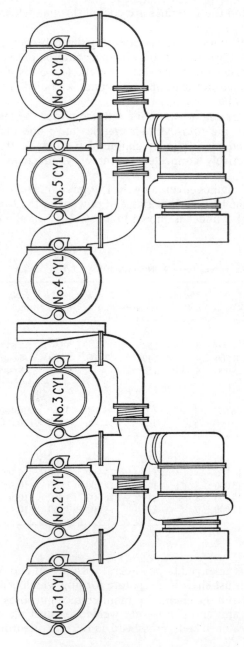

Figure 10.3 Arrangement of turbochargers on a six-cylinder engine

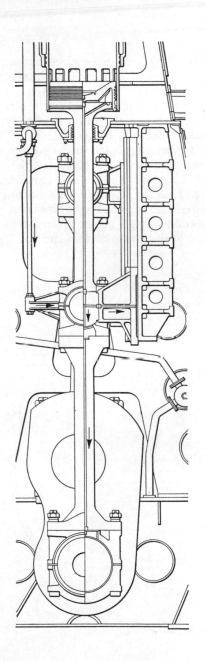

*Figure 10.4 Lubricating
oil and cooling oil circuits*

Crankshafts

In general, crankshafts up to 30 ft in length are in one piece, but those of greater length are in two pieces, with a large-diameter rigid coupling in the centre. For example, on the 76J range of engines the four- and five-cylinder crankshafts are in one piece, but all the others are constructed in two pieces. The thrust block is of the Michell type and is forced lubricated from the forced-lubrication system.

The lubricating oil for the main bearings is fed to the bottom of the housing, which is welded integrally with the bedplate. The oil is fed from the bearing through drilled holes in the side crankpins, thence up the side connecting-rods to the side crosshead bearings. For the centre connecting-rod oil is fed from a telescopic pipe through the centre crosshead to the top-end bearings, thence down a drilled hole in the centre connecting-rod to the centre bottom-end bearing, *see* Figure 10.4.

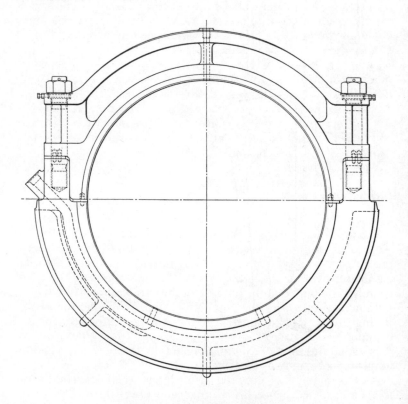

Figure 10.5 Main bearing assembly

Main and Bottom-end Bearings

The main-bearing bottom halves are thin-walled steel-backed bearings lined with thin white metal, and these are fitted into the bedplate, which is of parallel bore. The cast-steel bearing caps are themselves white-metal lined, *see* Figure 10.5. Both centre and side bottom-end bearings are cast steel shells, white-metal lined.

The lower main bearing shells are 50 mm thick, with 6 mm of white metal. They are inserted in the bedplate, which is precision bored, with a slight 'nip'; and the bearing caps are also nipped on to the sides of these bearings, in accordance with normal diesel loco-motive and vehicle engine practice. While not eactly thin-walled bearings, in the sense of automotive bearings, these main bearing bottom halves of 50 mm thick are much thinnerr than the thick white-metalled dove-tailed bearings of earlier days, particularly considering their large diameter, which is about 1200 mm. The connecting-rod bottom-end bearings are all steel castings, white-metalled on to a plain tinned surface without any dovetails, other-wise they are in accordance with normal marine practice. The side connecting-rod bottom-end bearings are similar cast steel bearings. All the connecting-rod top-end bearings, however, are fitted with thin-walled bearings of about 12 mm thick, with 3·0 mm of white metal. They are fitted into precision-bored cast steel shells, with a nip that is now standard practice with such bearings. All these shell bearings are made by specialist firms, although the cast-steel bottom-end bearings may be white-metalled by Doxford or by specialist firms, according to the demand at the time of manufacture.

Columns and Entablatures

The columns of the J-type engine consist of two legs, front and back, which are bolted rigidly to the entablature at the top and to the bed-plate at the bottom, there being a tubular central strut for joining these two legs together and providing rigidity, *see* Figure 10.6. The entablature forms the receiver for the scavenging air, and the cylinders are bolted to the top face of the entablature. The camshaft is mounted on top of the entablature and drives the lubricators, timing valves, starting air distributors and indicator gear for each cylinder.

Entablatures up to 9000 mm long are made in one piece and, for longer engines, in two pieces.

As the engine is of opposed piston type, where the combustion loads are carried between the upper and lower pistons and trans-mitted to the crankshaft through the centre and side running gear,

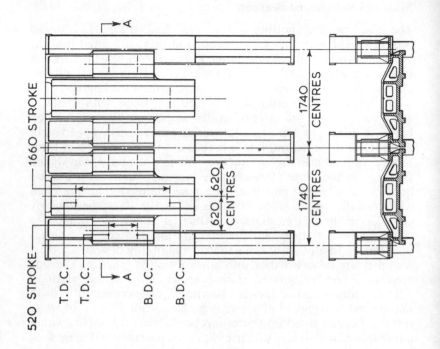

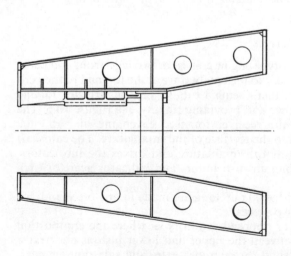

Figure 10.6 Construction of main frames 76J engine

the columns do not have to carry any combustion loads, and, therefore, can be relatively light consistent with adequate stiffness to

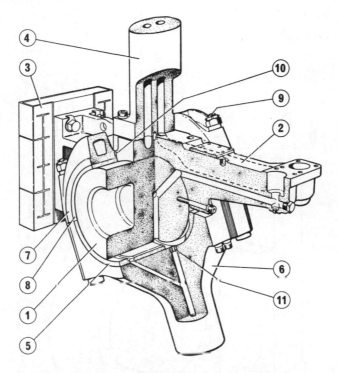

Figure 10.7 Centre connecting rod top end assembly

restrain transverse vibration, and to give sufficient rigidity to the
engine for running in heavy seas. This feature that the columns do
not have to carry any combustion loads, nor do they have to provide
long bolts, or securing features for tie-rods, is one of the reasons
for the inherent lightness of the opposed-piston engine. The back
and front legs of the columns are fabricated from 25-mm thick
plate, with the web plates 19 mm thick.

Crosshead Guides and Transverse Beams (67J and 76J)

The crosshead guide carries the guide faces for the centre crosshead
and for the two side crossheads and is a single heavily ribbed iron
casting. It is bolted against the legs of the back columns, which have
been separated to facilitate the mounting of the crosshead guides.

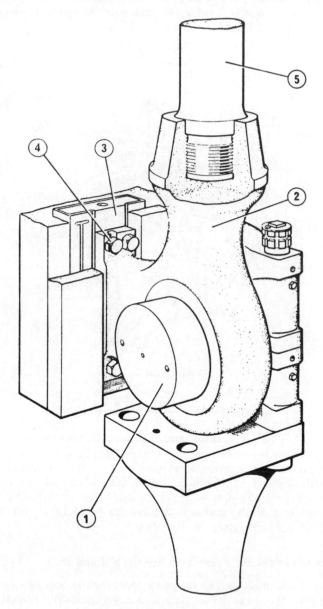

Figure 10.8 Side crosshead assembly

The whole forms a rigid assembly. The guide shoes are of slipper type and are white-metal lined and forced lubricated. The arrangement is shown in Figure 10.7. The side rods are screwed directly into the side crossheads as shown in Figure 10.8. The attachment of the side rods to the transverse beam is shown in Figure 10.9, the side rods passing through the beam and being fixed by large circular nuts. The transverse beam consists of a large steel forging.

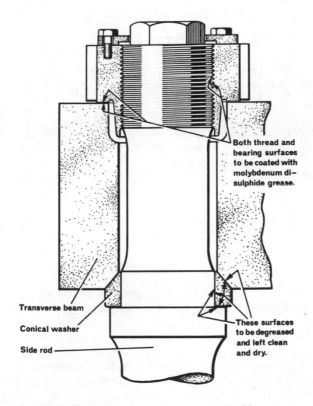

Figure 10.9 Side rod attachment to crosshead beam

In the 58J engine, a different construction is used. The back columns are fabricated in one piece and a heavy steel plate on the inboard side is used as the guide surface for both centre and side crossheads. Cast-iron guide bars are bolted to this plate to take the astern thrust. This construction is very rigid and enables the engine to be mounted on only twelve chocks.

Pistons and Piston Rods

All main piston heads are of forged steel, machined all over. They carry cast-iron spring rings in the ring grooves, which are chrome plated on their lower surface. The lower and upper pistons are identical, and the centre of the piston crown is bolted directly to the piston rod as shown in Figure 10.10. The upper piston is provided

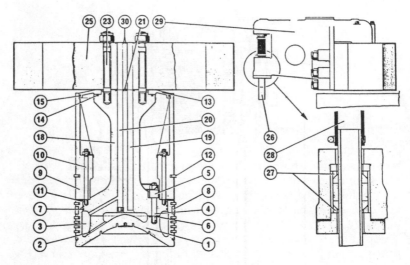

Figure 10.10 Upper piston assembly

with a light cast-iron piston skirt to prevent the exhaust gases from the exhaust ports being blown on to the piston rod and so passing into the engine room. The upper piston head and piston skirt reciprocate in the upper cylinder liner. The lower piston head is attached to the lower piston rod, which reciprocates in a gland box. This gland separates the cylinders from the engine crankcase, Figure 10.11. Sludge and products of combustion from the lower cylinder pass into the well of this gland box, to be drained away. This construction entirely isolates the cylinder from the crankcase and prevents the lubricating oil from being contaminated by the products of combustion.

All piston heads have a broad renewable cast-iron bearing ring which acts as a rubbing band and centralises each piston in its cylinder.

The piston heads are made from a very ductile carbon-manganese steel, which yields readily to the thermal stresses in the piston without cracking. It was customary for many years to weld-in a hardened

crucible steel ring under each piston ring to minimise ring groove
wear, but more recently the ring grooves have been chrome-
hardened, and this process is giving satisfactory service. There are
four compression rings above the cast-iron wearing ring previously

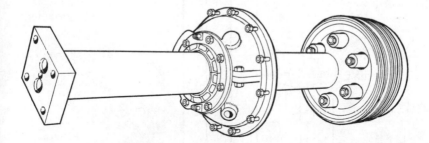

Figure 10.11 Gland box on piston rod

mentioned, and these compression rings are of substantial cross-
section, being 15 mm wide by 21 mm thick. There is also a stepped
oil spreader ring below the cast-iron wearing ring. One or two
grooves are machined in the crown of the piston head to give
flexibility and permit the crown to expand without undue stresses.
These grooves have eliminated the cracking which was prevalent in
pistons, many years ago, before this feature was introduced. A
groove is also machined above the top piston ring, to act as a heat
barrier to minimise the flow of heat into the upper piston rings and
thus reduce their operating temperature.

Piston-cooling Arrangement

Both pistons are cooled through telescopic pipes. The lower
telescopic pipes are attached to a bracket mounted on the centre
crosshead, and they reciprocate in tubes welded integrally with the
entablature. The glands for these telescopic pipes are mounted so
that they can be adjusted. Any leakage of cooling oil drains into the
crankcase. The arrangement is shown in Figure 10.12.

The upper pistons are water-cooled, again through telescopic
pipes, which are mounted on the transverse beams for the supply
of water to and from the upper piston via the upper piston rod; *see*
Figure 10.13. The bracket in which these upper telescopic pipes
reciprocate is attached to the exhaust belt and is provided with
glands to prevent leakage of the water.

The lower pistons are oil-cooled through telescopic pipes, the

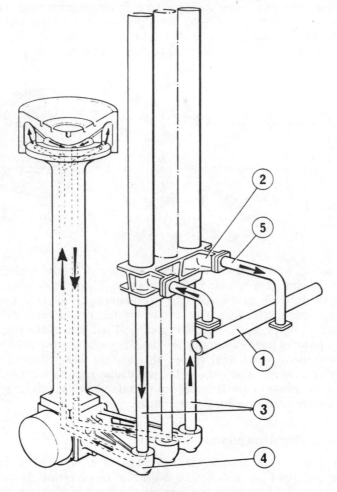

Figure 10.12 Lower piston cooling system

same oil being used as is supplied for the lubrication of the main
bearings and the connecting-rod bearings. The oil inlet temperature
is about 43°C, and the flow is ample to maintain the outlet temperature below 55°C, even at full load under tropical conditions. If the
cooling-oil temperature is maintained below about 63°C there is
no danger of carbonisation in the piston heads; with an operating
temperature at, say, 55°C, there is an ample margin of safety to
prevent carbonisation. The oil is supplied at about 2·0 bar from

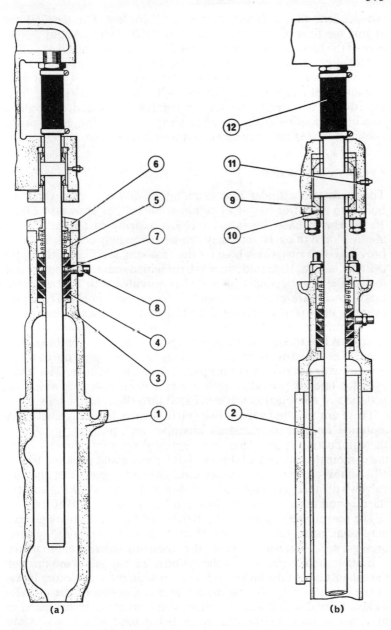

Figure 10.13 Upper piston telescopic pipes

independent motor-driven pumps and coolers. On the 760-mm engine the flow of oil/cylinder h is about 20 tonne. About 2·5 per cent of the fuel heat is taken away by the piston cooling oil.

The upper pistons are water-cooled as previously described, and heat is taken away by water at an inlet temperature of about 63°C and an outlet temperature of about 74°C. With water-cooling there is no danger of the piston surfaces becoming carbonised, as would be so with oil-cooling at these higher temperatures. The upper piston cooling surfaces run very clean, without any deposit.

Cylinder Construction

There are two cylinder liners, an upper and a lower, which are bolted to a central cast-steel combustion belt, as shown in Figure 10.14. The cylinder liners are of hard-wearing cast iron, and are about 25 mm thick, so that they can be adequately cooled. They are provided with ribs which bear on the cast-steel sections of the upper cylinder jackets, to provide strength for withstanding the combustion loads. The lower cylinder liner is also provided with a tubular steel jacket to ensure cooling above the scavenging ports. The upper cylinder liner is also arranged with a cast-steel jacket bearing on ribs to provide strength; and it is surrounded by the exhaust belt, in which it is free to expand. Rubber rings provide a seal for the cooling water. The lower cylinder liner contains the scavenging ports, which are fed with air from the air space of the entablature. The upper cylinder liner is provided with exhaust ports through which the products of combustion are evacuated into the exhaust belts.

There are two fuel valves, one starting valve and one relief valve mounted on each combustion chamber and protruding towards the combustion space. These are mounted on joints directly on to the combustion space and do not require any gland packing. Figure 10.15 shows a fuel valve in section. The arrangement of the fuel valves with their cooling water is shown in Figure 10.16, and the starting and relief valves are shown in Figures 10.17 and 10.18.

The scavenge-air ports at the bottom of the cylinder are given a tangential inclination to cause the air to swirl throughout the compression and combustion cycles, thus assisting efficient combustion.

Longitudinal expansion of the cylinder liner is permitted through the exhaust belt at the upper end, and through the lower water jacket at the lower end by sliding rubber joints. Cooling of the cylinder jackets is by distilled water treated with potassium bichromate, or by a non-toxic inhibitor, the latter being used where any 'Atlas' evaporator supplies drinking-water. The fuel valves are cooled from a separate valve cooling pump.

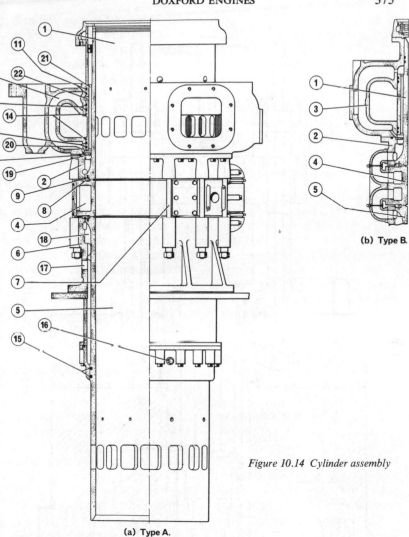

(b) Type B.

Figure 10.14 Cylinder assembly

(a) Type A.

Piston Lubrication

In each size of engine, eight lubrication points are provided for the upper piston, and eight for the lower. Quills at each of these points have inwardly opening non-return valves and are supplied with oil by means of the Doxford distributor lubrication system shown in Figure 10.19. In this system a double pump unit for each cylinder,

376

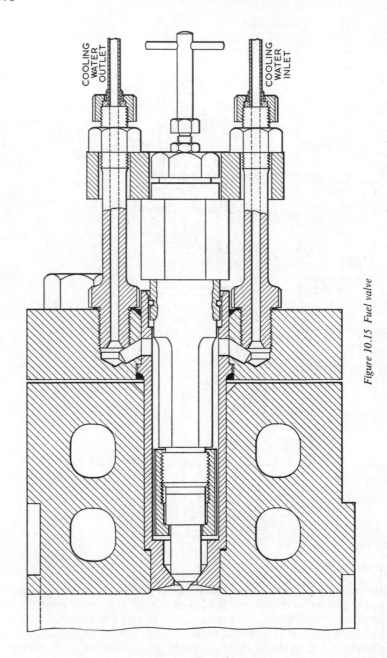

COOLING WATER OUTLET

COOLING WATER INLET

Figure 10.15 Fuel valve

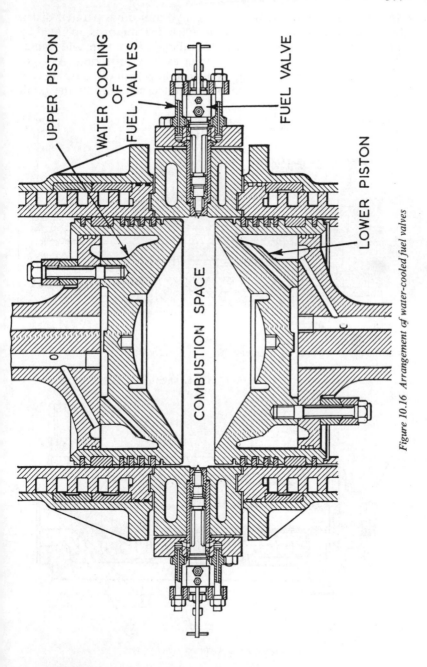

Figure 10.16 Arrangement of water-cooled fuel valves

driven by two cams, supplies oil to hydraulically operated distributors for upper and lower pistons. Each distributor is operated by a plunger on the return stroke of the oil injection pump, and rotates through one-ninth of a turn between each oil injection. At eight distributor positions a passage is opened to permit oil to be injected into one of the quills for the piston concerned, and at the ninth

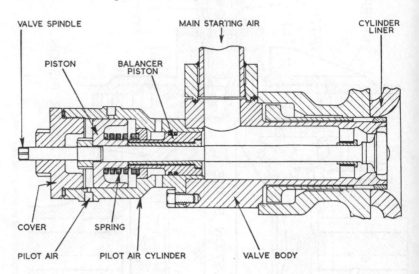

Figure 10.17 Air starting valve

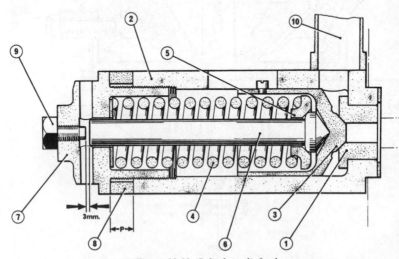

Figure 10.18 Cylinder relief valve

position the oil passes through an indicator to demonstrate that the system is working correctly. Each pump unit also has a measuring device mounted on the top cover by which the amount of oil being delivered to each piston can be checked. The lubricator pump units are supplied with cylinder oil from a main line connected to a common service tank.

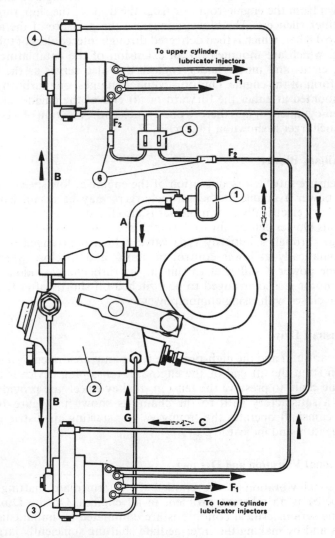

Figure 10.19 Cylinder lubricator arrangement

Turbochargers

In recent years all engines have been turboblown by air delivered by turbochargers driven by the exhaust gases of the engine. The turbochargers are single-stage gas turbines and single-stage blowers, the impeller of the centrifugal blower and turbine rotor being mounted on the same shaft. The air to the centrifugal blowers is drawn from the engine-room or from the deck of the ship, through air filter silencers. The blowers increase the pressure of the air to 0·7 to 0·8 bar, which is then delivered through intercoolers of tubular type, which are mounted on an extension of the entablature. On six-, eight- and nine-cylinder engines this also serves as the back platform of the engine. On four-cylinder engines, one turbocharger is mounted at either the forward or aft end of the engine, and on seven-cylinder engines there is one at each end. A section of a typical turbocharger is shown in Figure 10.27.

Auxiliary Blower

To ensure satisfactory operation of the engine at low speeds, when the power available at the turbochargers may be insufficient, an auxiliary electrically driven blower is also fitted.

This blower delivers air to the entablature at about 400 mm water gauge through a butterfly type valve, which is arranged to open automatically at lower control positions and to close when the engine power is sufficient to run on the turbochargers alone. The fan motor is also arranged to be switched-off shortly after the flap valve closes with rising engine power.

Camshaft Drive

The camshaft and the high-pressure fuel pump are driven by a roller chain from the aft end of the engine; a tensioning device is fitted on the chain to preserve the tension. Jockey wheels are provided to give a satisfactory path to the chain, as shown in Figure 10.20. The camshaft operates the timing valves, starting air distributors, lubricators and indicator gear.

Torsional Vibration and Detuner

Torsional vibration of the crankshaft, intermediate shafting and propeller is an inherent problem in all engines. On the Doxford engine serious critical conditions are eliminated by initial calculations and by making the intermediate shafting sufficiently large to eliminate serious torsional critical speeds. Where necessary, two-

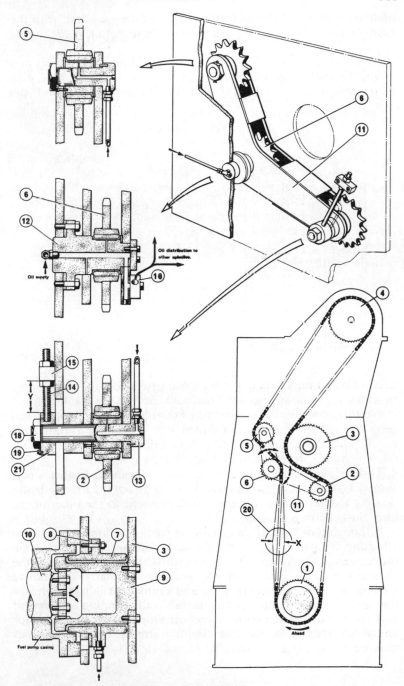

Figure 10.20 Camshaft and fuel pump drive (high level fuel pump)

node criticals are suppressed by a Doxford detuner, but, with the rigid crankshaft of the J-type engine, these detuners are rarely required.

As will be seen from Figure 10.21, the latest detuner consists of a double flywheel mass mounted on either side of a fixed hub, with plate springs between the hub and the floating masses. Both the

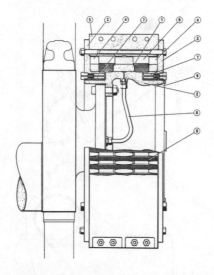

Figure 10.21 Detuner

fixed hub and the floating flywheels are provided with curved slots in which the plate springs are fitted and, should the crankshaft get into a torsional vibration, the springs then bend around the curved teeth and change the natural frequency to detune the vibration. A casing is fitted over the flywheels to retain the springs and to contain oil, which is fed from the forced-lubrication system.

This detuner can also act as an axial vibration damper since, should axial vibration take place, the oil between the fixed hub and floating masses is then squeezed from one side to the other of the hub, thus creating oil damping.

Although a detuner is, in a sense, a particular kind of torsional vibration damper, it has certain notable advantages. Firstly, the movement of the floating flywheel against the springs changes the natural frequency of the engine system, and secondly, the relative movement between floating mass and crankshaft is much greater than on a normal damper. Thus the effect of damping is increased and much more reduction of vibration amplitude is obtained, for any given detuner inertia, than for a normal friction or viscous damper.

MANOEUVRING AND REVERSING GEAR
AND FUEL-INJECTION SYSTEM

On engines built in recent years, with the timing valve injection system, the fuel cams are fixed symmetrically about top-centre so that the injection has identical timing for both ahead and astern directions of rotation of the engine. Similarly, the starting air distributor is arranged to supply air to the cylinders correctly for either direction, so that there is no necessity to change the timing of the camshaft for ahead and astern running. Starting air is supplied through a pilot control valve to the top side of the air distributor for ahead running, and to the bottom side for astern running; and it is arranged for the starting air lever to be pushed forward for ahead or pulled backward for astern operation.

The arrangement of this starting system is shown in Figure 10.22, from which it will be seen that the starting air lever operates the pilot control plunger, which regulates the air supply to the upper side of the air-distributor rotor for starting ahead and to the lower side for starting astern. The rotary air distributor then supplies the starting air to a pilot-air piston on the starting valve of each cylinder in turn, in correct phase, and for the correct duration.

The starting air is supplied to the engine from receivers of about 5·0 m³ capacity at 31 bar, and is admitted through a valve pneumatically operated from the starting lever. There is one air distributor for three- and four-cylinder engines, two on six-, seven- and eight-cylinder engines, and three for nine-cylinder engines.

Fuel-injection System

In the timing-valve injection system a multi-ram fuel pump, with usually a pump for each cylinder, supplies fuel at a high pressure of 6000 to 8000 lb/in², say 400 to 550 bar, through a pipe system and distributor block to accumulator bottles mounted on the entablature of the engine. These bottles are then piped to timing valves actuated by cams and levers. When a timing valve is lifted by its cam and lever, fuel flows from the high-pressure fuel bottle, through the timing valve and piping, to the automatic spring-loaded fuel injectors of Bryce or similar type. The fuel-injector springs are loaded and are set to lift at a pressure of 170 bar. Each timing-valve actuating lever is mounted on a sliding rod, which is operated from the manoeuvring lever at the control station of the engine to give the period of injection required according to the quantity of fuel to be injected (*see* Figure 10.23).

The fuel pressure is controlled by means of an air-loaded spill

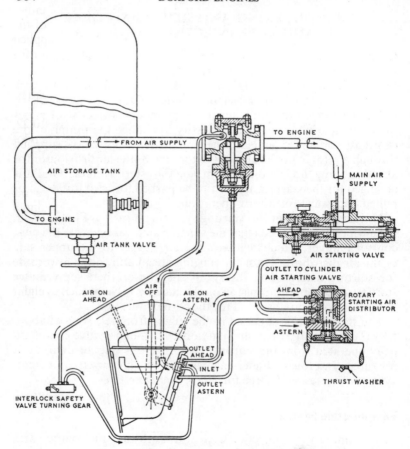

Figure 10.22 Air starting system

valve, Figure 10.24, in which the air loading pressure can be varied
by means of a regulating valve at the control station. The spill valve
has a hardened tool steel seat and a Stellite hemispherical valve lid
held to the seat by air pressure acting on a larger diaphragm. At the
inlet to the spill valve there is a high-pressure filter consisting of a
number of discs with slots only 0·002 in deep. This filter can be
cleaned by blowing compressed air backwards through the element.
The arrangement of the fuel system, using timing valves and spill
valves, is shown in Figure 10.25.

Before initially starting an engine a small air-driven pump is used
to raise the pressure in the fuel system to about 1500 to 2000 lb/in²,

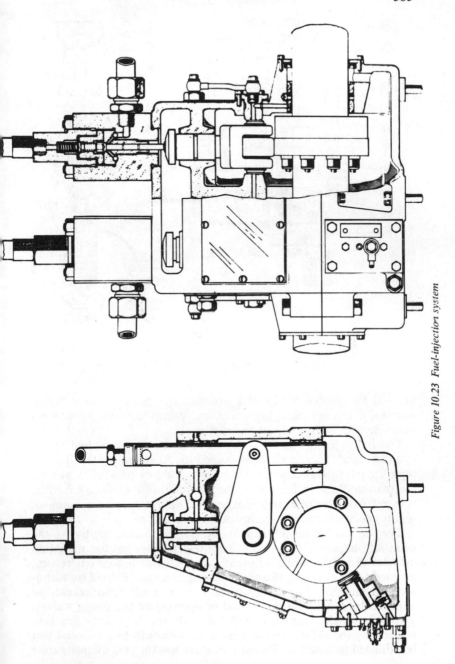

Figure 10.23 Fuel-injection system

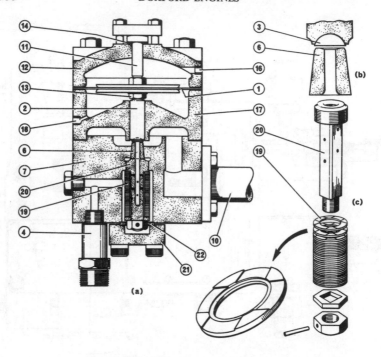

Figure 10.24 Fuel spill valve with built-in filter

i.e. 100 to 140 bar. Once this pressure has been raised it is not necessary to use this high-pressure pump during subsequent manoeuvring or running of the engine.

The fuel injectors sit on a cone-end in a sleeve attached to the cylinder, and they are water-cooled by distilled water from a separate pump and cooling system to avoid any possibility of contamination of the jacket water. Replacement of the injector nozzles is a relatively simple and inexpensive operation, these being of highly specialised and standardised manufacture.

The fuel cam toe is adjustable and can be rotated relative to the camshaft, to permit of earlier or later injection so that the maximum cylinder pressure can be adjusted. This cylinder pressure is recommended to be between 65 and 70 atmospheres at full load on turbocharged engines. The quantity of fuel to each cylinder can be adjusted by regulating the period of opening of the timing valves. Two adjustments are provided for each timing valve. The link connecting the sliding rod to a lever on the control shaft above can be adjusted in length to increase or decrease the fuel quantity over

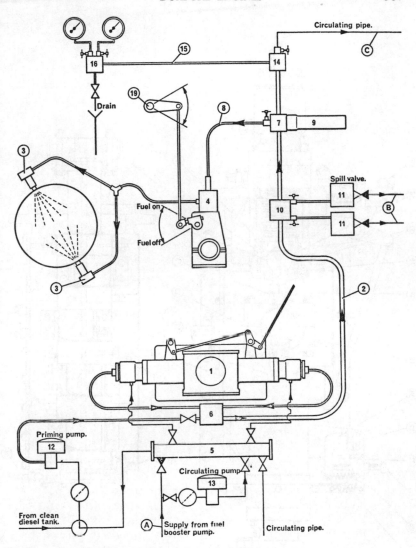

Figure 10.25 Diagrammatic arrangement of engine fuel system

the whole power range, and the lever on the control shaft has an eccentrically mounted pin which alters the effective lever length and enables full-load fuel to be adjusted without affecting the low-load setting.

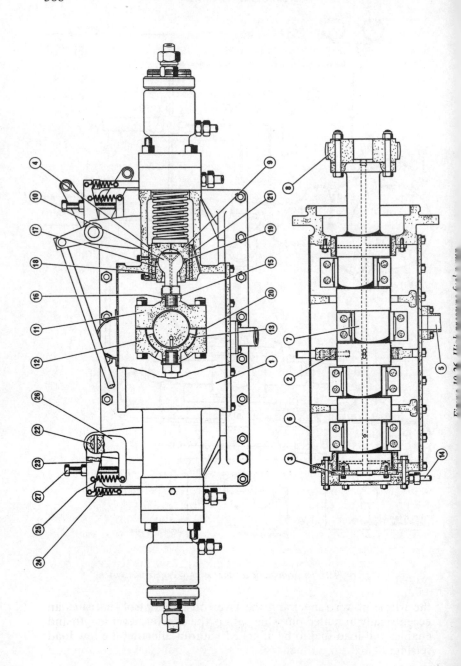

Figure 18.3 Hydrocarrier fuel pump

The high-pressure fuel pump, Figure 10.26, supplying fuel to the timing valves at 400 to 550 bar has four, six or eight plungers, driven by eccentrics and arranged in opposed cylinder form. Although normally the pump is left running at maximum output, and excess fuel is returned to the supply tank through the spill valve, means for controlling the pump output in an emergency is provided by helical lands on the rotatable pump plungers. At full output each plunger delivers over a period of about 130° of drive shaft angle, giving much smoother operation than the normal jerk pump which has to deliver the full load quantity over a period of about 25° of crank angle.

The fuel pump mechanism is forced lubricated from the main engine system and the plungers are spring-loaded towards the cross-heads so that in the event of a plunger seizure the other cylinders can continue to operate. The pump units consisting of plunger, barrel, spring, and delivery valve, can be removed and replaced individually.

The fuel pumps have been standardised with a plunger diameter of 39 mm and a stroke of 50 mm, and the drive-shaft speed in relation to engine crankshaft speed is varied on different engines to give the required fuel quantity.

SUPERCHARGING

The object of turbocharging is to increase the power given by an engine, by increasing the quantity of air in the cylinder at the commencement of the compression stroke. When the exhaust is released from the cylinder, at the end of the power stroke, it still contains a considerable amount of energy which cannot be used by expansion in the engine cylinder but which can be used to drive a turbine wheel which, in turn, can drive a blower impeller to increase the pressure of the air taken into the engine cylinder above the pressure of the atmosphere. Figure 10.27 shows a section through a typical turboblower which has a turbine wheel and a blower impeller mounted on the same shaft.

Turbochargers have been developed to the required stage of efficiency to perform the dual duties of evacuating and charging the cylinders of two-stroke engines. They have been assisted by the employment of intercoolers to cool the air from the temperature at which it is delivered by the blower down to near the sea-water temperature.

Development of Doxford Turbocharged Engine

The first Doxford turbocharged engine was built in 1952. During the

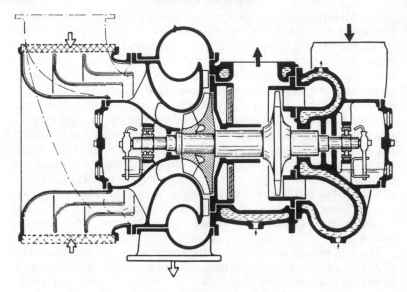

Figure 10.27 Section through typical turboblower

development and experimental period this engine produced a power of 50 per cent more than that of the same size of normally aspirated engine, and thus provided the data for the subsequent development of four- and six-cylinder turbo-charged engines.

The next turbocharged engine to be produced was a six-cylinder engine of 670 mm bore, 2320 mm combined stroke, to give 8000 bhp (6000 kW) service power at a speed of 115 rev/min. To obtain improved performance, an increased lead was given to the side-cranks connected to the upper pistons; and the exhaust ports were opened earlier to give a more powerful impulse of the exhaust gases to the turbocharger. The engine-driven scavenge pumps were retained on this engine to improve the slow-running and astern operation of the engine and to enable the engine to function at reduced power should the turboblowers break down. Many Doxford turbocharged engines have since been built. Later P and J engines have been designed specially as turbocharged engines. In order to obtain more power from the turbochargers, so that they could provide more air, the side-cranks of these engines were given a still greater lead than on previous engines and the exhaust ports were opened earlier to provide a more powerful impulse. Consequently, the overall performance of the engines was improved, so that the engine-driven scavenging pumps could be dispensed with, leading to reduced fuel consumption and more reliable running in both ahead and astern directions.

The blowers of the turbochargers draw their air through filter silencers direct from the atmosphere of the engine room or from the deck of the ship and deliver it through intercoolers into a receiver connected to the entablature of the engine. The exhaust gases rush from the cylinders, when the exhaust ports are opened, into the turbines and, after passing through the turbine nozzles and impulse wheels, they are discharged through a large exhaust pipe to the exhaust silencer and then to atmosphere.

When installed in a ship, an exhaust boiler is fitted in the exhaust pipe, according to normal motor-ship practice, to raise steam for heating and auxiliary purposes. The exhaust turbines are cooled by the normal engine-cooling water service and the intercoolers are cooled by cold sea-water. This lowers the temperature of the air from that at which it is delivered by the turbochargers, thus providing a denser air charge. It is usual practice for the exhaust boiler to be operated, when the engine is not in use, by its own self-contained fuel pump complete with filter.

GOVERNING

All J-engines are now fitted with hydraulic governors for controlling the engine speed and, in addition, there is an overspeed trip to stop the engine if by some mischance the hydraulic governor should fail to operate.

The hydraulic governor arrangement is shown in Figure 10.28 and is of Woodward type, incorporating a variable output control as well as the speed control. Input to the governor is controlled pneumatically by means of an actuator operating the input lever; each position of this lever corresponds not only to an engine speed but also to a maximum rate of fuel delivered. With this arrangement it is impossible for large amounts of excess fuel to be injected into the cylinders in conditions such as those occurring in rough weather, when the propeller re-enters the water after being only partly immersed. In this way possible thermal shock on the engine is avoided.

The overspeed trip is shown in Figure 10.29, and is a simple bob-weight device attached to the camshaft drive wheel which operates by releasing air pressure from the spill valve control system, and thereby preventing fuel reaching the engine cylinders. The bob-weight and spring arrangement is designed deliberately to be unstable, so that once it starts moving it immediately flies to its outermost position to give a quick positive action.

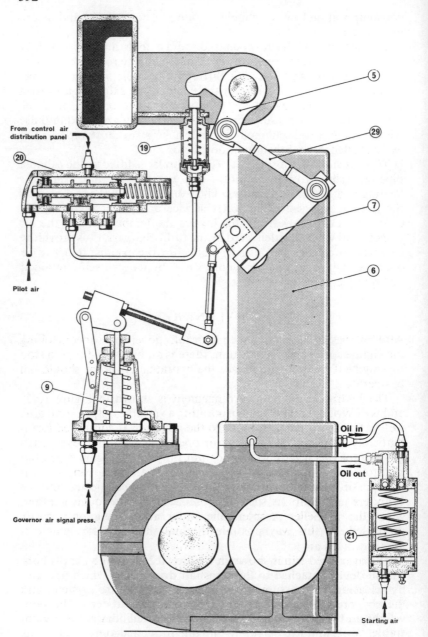

From control air
distribution panel

Pilot air

Governor air signal press.

Oil in

Oil out

Starting air

Figure 10.28 Arrangement of governor

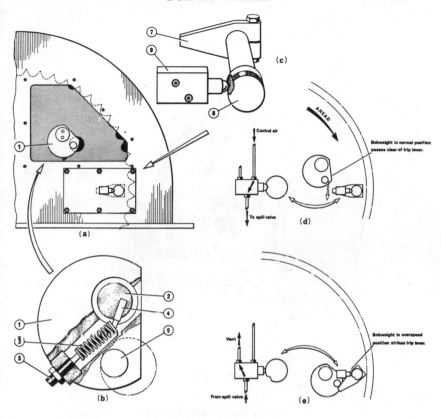

Figure 10.29 Overspeed trip

Controls

The normal control box, shown in Figure 10.30, has two levers and a small handwheel. The main lever controls the speed of the engine by adjusting the air pressure to the governor input lever actuator. This in turn, through the governor, alters the period for which the timing valves are held open. For emergency use, provision is made for connecting the main control lever directly, by mechanical linkage, to the timing valve control shaft.

Fuel pressure is controlled by the small handwheel which adjusts the air pressure on top of the diaphragm of the spill valve.

For starting, the starting air lever is moved forward for going ahead, and backward, towards the operator, for going astern. This lever operates a slide lever which lets pilot air into the correct side

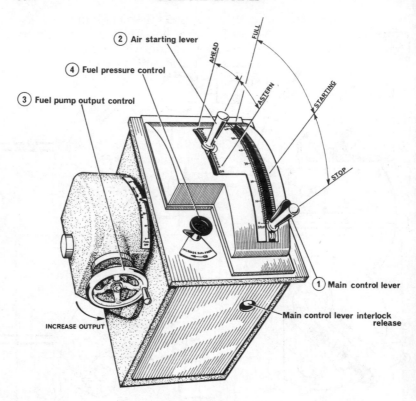

Figure 10.30 Engine controls

of the starting air distributors. As soon as the engine has gathered speed (15–20 rev/min) the main control lever is pushed to the 'gate' position, notch 21, and the engine will fire. When the engine fires, the starting air lever should be allowed to return to the 'off' position, and the main control lever can be adjusted up or down to give the required engine speed. A safety interlock is provided which prevents fuel being admitted to the engine until starting air has been admitted, and prevents the main control lever being moved beyond the 'gate' position until the starting air lever has been returned to the 'off' position.

No action beyond moving the starting air lever in the right direction is required to ensure that the engine will run either ahead or astern. A wrongway alarm is fitted on the camshaft to give audible warning if the engine should inadvertently be started in the opposite direction to that required by the bridge telegraph.

As an extra safety device on J-engines, a fuel pump control is also fitted on the side of the main control box which adjusts the fuel pump output and enables the engine to be run without the spill valve.

Normal fuel pressure is controlled at 4000 to 6000 lb/in^2, say, 275 to 400 bar for manoeuvring, and raised to 7000 lb/in^2, i.e. 500 bar for full ahead running.

Remote Control

The remote control system enables commands from the bridge to be applied at the engine by electro-pneumatic means.

On the bridge there is a telegraph and a four-position switch indicating: BRIDGE CONTROL, ENGINE ROOM CONTROL, FINISHED WITH ENGINES and STAND-BY. (Figure 10.31.)

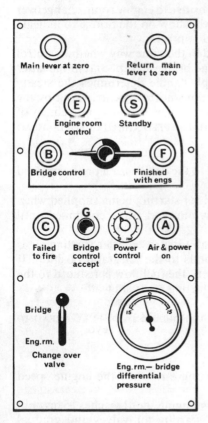

(a)

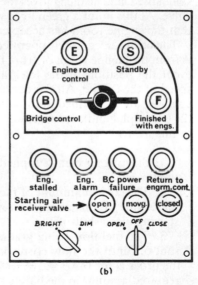

(b)

Figure 10.31 Control panels for remote control gear
(a) Engine room panel
(b) Bridge panel

Movement of this switch sounds a gong in the engine room and shows a warning light at the engine control station. The engineer replies by moving a similar switch to the instructed position. When transferring to bridge control he also moves his main control lever to STOP and moves the changeover valve handle from BRIDGE to ENGINE ROOM. This valve is fitted deliberately to make it necessary to take action so that movement of the changeover switch cannot by itself transfer control.

When transferring from bridge control to engine room control, the officer on the bridge makes his request by turning his switch to ENGINE ROOM, but this does not transfer control until the engineer has accepted. To do this he first moves his main control lever to a position which makes the engine room–bridge differential pressure zero, which ensures that the engine will continue running at the same speed, and he then moves the bridge to engine room changeover valve. At this point a green light will show on the bridge to indicate that the engine room has accepted control.

The bridge telegraph is operated in the same way whether control is from the engine room or from the bridge, except that in the latter event the position of the telegraph handle determines the steady speed of the engine. All the operations normally carried out by the engineer are performed automatically. For instance, movement of the telegraph handle from STOP to HALF-SPEED AHEAD or FULL-AHEAD results in:

1. Starting air being supplied to the engine for a predetermined time;
2. The correct amount of fuel for starting being supplied when the engine attains about 15 rev/min, and being continued until starting air is shut-off;
3. The fuel flow being gradually increased after starting air is shut-off until the flow corresponds to the telegraph position. If the order is for DEAD-SLOW AHEAD, the fuel flow is reduced to the required amount immediately starting air is shut-off.

Again, movement of the telegraph handle from FULL-AHEAD to FULL ASTERN results in:

1. Shutting-off fuel;
2. Application of astern starting air, when the engine speed drops to 25 rev/min.
3. Application of fuel when the engine speed reaches 15 rev/min astern, followed by closure of starting air valves and gradual increase of fuel as required.

If, at any time, the engine fails to start at the first attempt, then the starting process is repeated up to four times. If the engine still fails to start, a warning light appears at the bridge control and normally an order would be given from the bridge to revert to engine room control.

The air reservoirs in the engine room are so arranged that only part of the starting air can be used while the engine is under bridge control. That is, if control reverts to the engine room, a further supply of starting air is immediately available.

An engine tachometer is also provided at the bridge as well as warning lights to indicate excessive temperature of exhaust gas, lubricating oil, or cooling water, and insufficient pressure in oil or water systems.

All connections between the bridge and engine room are electrical, thus avoiding time-lag and making the distance between the two stations unimportant. In the engine room the electrical signals control pneumatic valves and cylinders, as required to operate starting air and engine speed controls. The main electronic and pneumatic units are grouped in protecting cabinets in the engine room for easy maintenance. All electronic units are duplicated and arranged in such a way that should any unit become faulty it can be located by a very simple test procedure and replaced without special tools.

The normal mechanical controls at the engine are retained with the exception of the fuel pump control handwheel. Fuel pressure is maintained automatically at a level preset by the engineer and the priming pump is arranged to come into action to maintain this pressure if necessary during engine stoppage. When engine room control is in use, orders are transmitted from the bridge by the telegraph in the normal way.

The design of the system is such that as well as providing for control from the bridge, any number of other control stations may be provided either remote from, or in, the engine room. At any of these stations the actions required would be similar to those used at the bridge.

A diagrammatic arrangement of the control system is shown in Figure 10.32.

Engine Performance

Figure 10.33 shows typical performance curves of a six-cylinder engine on the test bed. Compared with older engines without turbochargers, modern turbocharged engines save about 6 per cent of fuel, mainly because of improved mechanical efficiency resulting

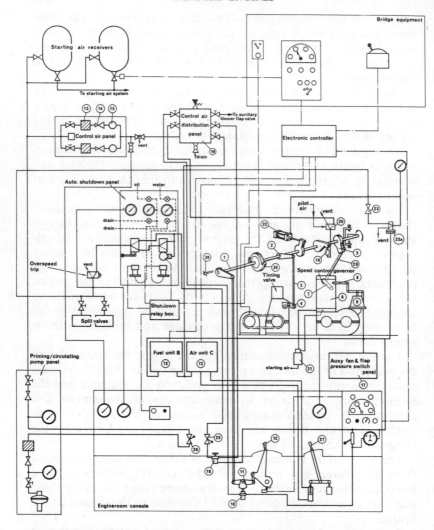

Figure 10.32 Diagrammatic arrangement of speed controls and other pneumatic controls (including remote control)

from there being no engine-driven scavenge blowers. Under sea conditions the exhaust temperature may be 20–40°C higher than the test-bed figures because of engine room temperature and normal slight fouling of the compressor and turbine systems. Increases greater than this indicate some mal-adjustment of the engine.

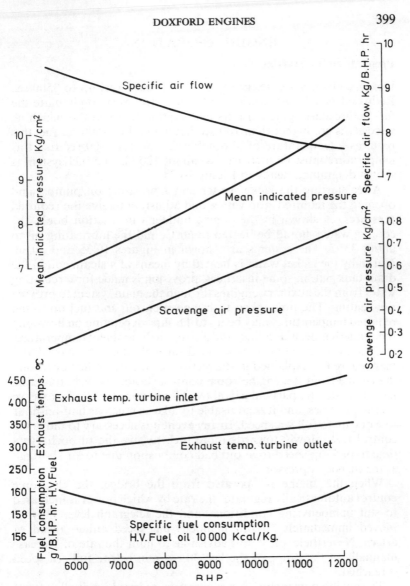

Figure 10.33 Performance curves for six-cylinder engine

The specific fuel consumption at sea normally remains the same as on the test bed, except in that some heavy fuels are of lower quality and, consequently, the consumption will be increased in inverse proportion to the net calorific value.

ENGINE OPERATION

Preparation for Starting

Doxford engines are designed to run on heavy fuel up to 3500 sec Redwood No. 1 and, consequently, it is necessary to circulate the fuel before starting, to raise its temperature to a point at which its viscosity is not higher than 100 sec Redwood. For 1500 sec fuel this requires a temperature of about 104°C, and for 3500 sec fuel this temperature must be increased to about 120°C. The fuel system is shown diagrammatically in Figure 10.34.

After starting the jacket water and lubricating oil pumps, and opening the required stop valves and adjusting to give the required pressures, as shown in the engine builder's instruction book, the cooling water should be heated to 60°C, and the lubricating oil to about 33°C. The systems are shown in Figures 10.35 and 10.36. Normally the jacket water is heated by means of a steam coil in the drain tank but, in some instances, provision is made for circulating water from the auxiliary engines through the main system to provide pre-heating. The time taken to bring water, oil, and fuel up to the required temperatures may be up to 4 hours, depending on how long the engine has been standing, and also upon the ambient temperature.

Once the engine has been warmed-through, it can be started and manoeuvred as explained in the section 'Controls'. When operating the engine from the engine room control station, power should be increased slowly, particularly above 80 rev/min, to avoid excessive thermal stresses, and it is advisable to take as much as half-an-hour to work-up to full sea speed. In any event it is necessary to move the control lever slowly towards more fuel, to give the turbochargers time to pick-up speed to avoid bad combustion due to air shortage at the turbocompressor.

When the engine is operated from the bridge, the electronic control automatically regulates the rate by which power is increased to suit manoeuvring conditions, and the telegraph lever may be moved immediately to full manoeuvring speed either ahead or astern. Nevertheless it is still advisable to limit the rate of increase manually in the range of the last 30 rev/min before full sea speed is reached.

The engine power should preferably be reduced gradually after a full speed run, and, after stopping, the lubricating and piston cooling oil pump and jacket water pump should be kept running for 3–4 hours with the jacket water and lubricating oil coolers by-passed to allow the engine to cool down slowly. During the cooling down period the engine should be turned through one revolution at intervals by means of the turning gear.

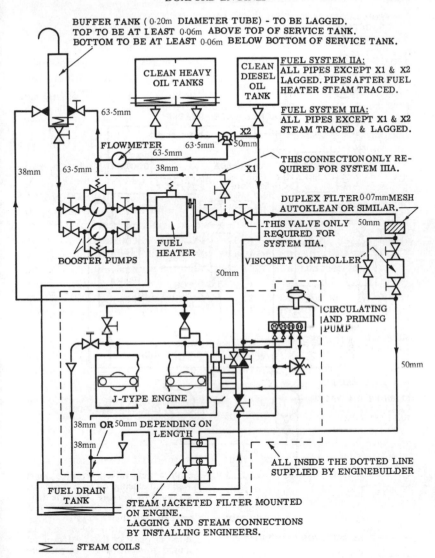

Figure 10.34 Diagrammatic arrangement of fuel system

Maintenance

Present-day engines are designed to run with the minimum of maintenance, but there are still some points which require routine attendance, particularly when using heavy fuel.

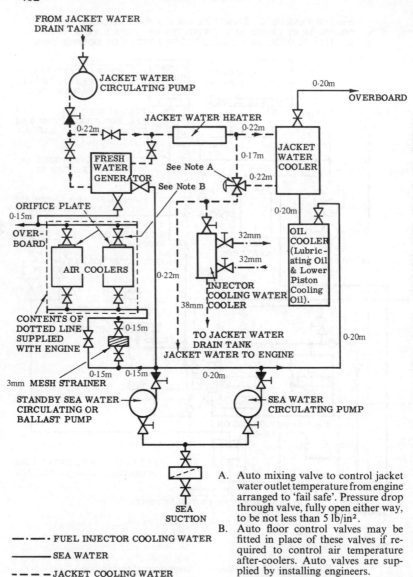

FROM JACKET WATER
DRAIN TANK

JACKET WATER
CIRCULATING PUMP

0·20m
OVERBOARD

JACKET WATER HEATER

0·22m

0·22m

JACKET
WATER
COOLER

0·17m

FRESH
WATER
GENERATOR

See Note A

See Note B

0·22m

ORIFICE PLATE

0·15m

OVER-
BOARD

AIR COOLERS

0·22m

0·20m

OIL
COOLER
(Lubric-
ating Oil
& Lower
Piston
Cooling
Oil).

32mm

32mm

INJECTOR
COOLING WATER
COOLER

38mm

CONTENTS OF
DOTTED LINE
SUPPLIED
WITH ENGINE

0·15m

TO JACKET WATER
DRAIN TANK
JACKET WATER TO ENGINE

0·20m

3mm MESH STRAINER

0·15m   0·15m

0·20m

STANDBY SEA WATER
CIRCULATING OR
BALLAST PUMP

SEA WATER
CIRCULATING PUMP

SEA
SUCTION

—·—·— FUEL INJECTOR COOLING WATER

———— SEA WATER

— — — JACKET COOLING WATER

A. Auto mixing valve to control jacket
    water outlet temperature from engine
    arranged to 'fail safe'. Pressure drop
    through valve, fully open either way,
    to be not less than 5 lb/in².
B. Auto floor control valves may be
    fitted in place of these valves if re-
    quired to control air temperature
    after-coolers. Auto valves are sup-
    plied by installing engineers.

Note that sea-water pipe sizes are based
on maximum velocity for aluminium
brass pipes. Other materials may require
larger pipe sizes.

Figure 10.35 Cooling water system

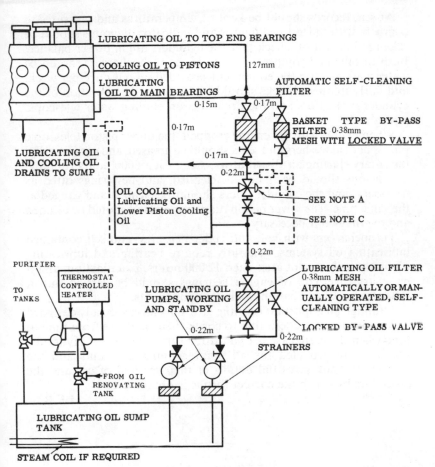

LUBRICATING OIL TO TOP END BEARINGS

COOLING OIL TO PISTONS

LUBRICATING
OIL TO MAIN BEARINGS

127mm

AUTOMATIC SELF-CLEANING
FILTER

0·15m   0·17m

0·17m

BASKET TYPE BY-PASS
FILTER 0·38mm
MESH WITH LOCKED VALVE

0·17m

0·22m

LUBRICATING OIL
AND COOLING OIL
DRAINS TO SUMP

OIL COOLER
Lubricating Oil and
Lower Piston Cooling
Oil

SEE NOTE A

SEE NOTE C

0·22m

PURIFIER

TO
TANKS

THERMOSTAT
CONTROLLED
HEATER

LUBRICATING OIL
PUMPS, WORKING
AND STANDBY

LUBRICATING OIL FILTER
0·38mm MESH
AUTOMATICALLY OR MAN-
UALLY OPERATED, SELF-
CLEANING TYPE

LOCKED BY-PASS VALVE

0·22m   0·22m

STRAINERS

FROM OIL
RENOVATING
TANK

LUBRICATING OIL SUMP
TANK

STEAM COIL IF REQUIRED

If filters of the self-cleaning type are not used, duplex filters are required both before and after the coolers.

A. Automatic mixing valve arranged to control oil inlet temperature to engine. High temperature overrides to operate from lower piston cooling oil outlet. Valve to 'fail safe'; pressure drop through valve, fully open either way, to be between 6 and 12 lb/in².

C. Valve to adjust pressure drop through by-pass. Handwheel to be removed after adjustment.

Figure 10.36 Lubricating and cooling oil system

At sea, records should be kept of temperatures and pressures to compare with the test bed figures and indicator diagrams should be taken at intervals to check that the cylinders are in power balance. Both turbine and compressor ends of the turbochargers should be water washed, with the equipment provided, about once per week, and fairly frequent checks should be made on the operation of the cylinder lubricators and the upper piston cooling water telescopic pipe glands.

When in port with the engine stopped, the upper piston telescopic pipe spherical washers and seats should be greased, and occasionally, the rotary starting air distributors. After each 6000 hours running, the pistons should be removed, cleaned, and new rings fitted as necessary, and the cylinder liners should be cleaned and gauged at the same time. The lower piston diaphragm gland should be cleaned and overhauled if necessary.

Turbochargers with ball and roller bearings, and self-contained lubricating oil systems, generally require bearing and lubricating oil pump replacement after each 12 000 hours. Examination, and if necessary, overhaul of engine bearings should be carried out at times to suit Classification Society requirements.

Although all important running gear nuts have specially designed locking devices, it is desirable to check their tightness from time to time when the crankcase is opened for survey purposes. Hydraulic spanners are provided for all main running gear nuts and the instruction book gives full details of their method of use and the procedure by which the correct torque is obtained.

J.F.B.

Chapter 11

Indirect Drives: Geared Engines

There is more scope for variation with geared diesel engines than there is with direct-coupled engines. Accordingly, for the same horse-power, different men can be expected to choose different engine sizes, different rates of revolution and different gearing ratios.

The geared diesel engine is the most satisfactory form of indirect drive, reckoned as an alternative to the direct-coupled engine and considered in terms of weight, space occupied, first cost and so on.

In general terms, the claims made for the geared drive are:

(i) increased reliability, by having more than one engine per screw;

(ii) one or more of the engines can be shut down when the ship is running light or in partly loaded condition, the others then being operated at their most efficient rating;

(iii) maintenance is easier, because the engines are of more manageable size;

(iv) engines can be overhauled at sea;

(v) by modifying the numbers of engines per ship and cylinders per engine, the propelling machinery of a fleet of vessels of different sizes and powers can be standardised upon a single cylinder size, with advantage to initial cost, delivery time and replacements.

How many of these factors really become operative must depend upon circumstances.

As an alternative to the above, the claims for the diesel-electric drive have much in common with those for the geared diesel drive,

(i) increased reliability, by having several engines instead of one;

(ii) easier maintenance, the engines being relatively of small size and weight, with all parts interchangeable;

(iii) one or more engines can be shut down at sea, for overhaul;

(iv) with the ship running slow, or in ballast, the necessary units can generate power at their most efficient load while the remaining engines are held in reserve;

(v) the total installation weight, in running condition, is less, and the engine-room height is much reduced;

(vi) the propeller and engine revolutions can be made to suit the respective requirements;

(vii) by varying the number of cylinders per engine and engines per ship, one, two, or at the most three, cylinder sizes can cover the complete range of likely powers.

Certain additional claims can be made for the diesel-electric alternating current drive, these are:

(a) flexibility of power distribution, because any desired number of engines per shaft can be installed;

(b) the engines can be located anywhere, the motors being arranged aft, thus eliminating tunnel shafting;

(c) the diesel engines are non-reversible;

(d) complete bridge control can be obtained;

(e) a quicker turn-round in port can be arranged, based upon a system of running overhaul.

Alternating current and high voltages, while they materially assist in bringing down the first cost and the weight of the electrical equipment, are accompanied by certain problems for the diesel engine. Thus, the engines must always run in synchronism. For steady running this is not difficult to achieve, as speed-governing within close limits is possible; and the alternators, being electrically linked, can drag the engines into synchronism. But, when manoeuvring, the revolutions of the engines must rise and fall with the propeller revolutions, and at the same time synchronism must be maintained among all the engines. In reversing, the engine revolutions are reduced to their minimum and then, immediately before reversing the propulsion motor, load is completely taken off the engines. Immediately afterwards, when load is restored to the engines, the back torque transmitted from the propeller to the propulsion motor, caused by the 'way' on the ship, may much exceed what the engines are capable of at the low speed at which they may be running at the moment. Although FULL ASTERN from FULL AHEAD, with way on the ship, is not a common order from the bridge, the machinery must nevertheless be capable of carrying it out in a reasonably short time. In single-screw ships, for maximum safeguard against breakdown, the propulsion motor can have a double armature.

The propulsion motor is usually arranged as far aft as possible and is connected by cable trunk to the engine room. The cable trunk must be large enough, in cross section, for a man to pass along. In addition to housing the cables it must accommodate bilge, fresh-water and oil-fuel pipes as necessary. Ventilating fans, coolers and trunks are self-contained with the alternators and motors. Assuming 96·5 per cent both for alternators and propulsion motor, the combined efficiency of all the electrical equipment, from alternator coupling to propulsion motor coupling, is 92 per cent.

COMPARISON OF DIRECT AND INDIRECT DRIVES

Analysis of Arrangements

Few engineers outside the marine industry have any conception of what a machinery room really contains. Nothing can be more misleading than a superficial comparison of direct and indirect engine drives based upon the main units only, thus tacitly assuming that everything else is the same. In a careful comparison of a direct-drive engine scheme with a geared arrangement of smaller engines, or with a diesel-electric layout, it will be found that many unsuspected items must perforce be different, different in weight or size or cost. A comparison to be worth anything at all must be painstakingly thorough, otherwise it is misleading and disparate.

As every piece of machinery inside a ship is a monetary charge upon the shipowner, a reasonable inception is a hull having a normal design of double bottom but completely devoid of machinery; then, inside that hull, are arranged all such items and things of the necessary quality and standard as are needed for the propulsion of the ship at the specified speed when containing the stipulated amount of cargo deadweight and bunkered with the required weight of fuel for the stated length of voyage or steaming radius.

To summarise: a complete analysis of two machinery installations determines, in the first place, the overall size, tonnage and weight of ship necessary to fulfil the required conditions of deadweight, cubic cargo, speed and propulsion radius. Thereafter the comparison leads to the service weight and space occupied by the machinery. Finally, over and above all, arise the questions of cost of ship and machinery. Fuel and oil costs, engine-room personnel, maintenance and its effect on itinerary are separate matters. For the same machine power, the size of ship may not be the same for the indirect drive as for the direct drive.

Direct Drive

A direct-coupled heavy-oil engine installation must include the following items, namely:

(i) propelling engine complete with turbochargers, exhaust and scavenging air manifolds; incorporated thrust block and shaft; tunnel and propeller shafting, plummer blocks, stern tube, propeller;

(ii) machinery room and ship service pumps;

(iii) auxiliary diesel generators and ancillary equipment;

(iv) settling and daily service fuel-oil tanks complete with mountings; lubricating-oil and sundry tanks for all purposes;

(v) silencers and auxiliary boilers with exhaust and other pipes to atmosphere; starting air reservoirs;

(vi) all piping systems, complete with valves and fittings; ventilation system, with motors and fans; workshop equipment and engineers' stores;

(vii) floorplates, supports, ladders, gratings, lagging;

(viii) spare gear for main and auxiliary engines, pumps, propeller and propeller shaft; bolts and nuts, springs and all sundry details;

(ix) lifting gear and tackle for all purposes;

(x) thick plates on tank top, with intercostals and all stiffening under engines;

(xi) seatings, platforms, brackets, straps, clips, hangers, for all pumps, tanks, reservoirs, auxiliary boilers, silencers; holding-down bolts, chocks and other gear;

(xii) water, fuel and oil, in all systems;

(xiii) main funnel and internal gear;

(xiv) weight of bunker steel.

Indirect Drives

Taking the above schedule as a basis, an indirect-drive arrangement will involve numerous alterations. There will be the deletion of many items and the introduction of many others. Thus in a diesel-electric installation there will be the several high-speed diesel alternator sets complete with all incorporated items, also exhaust pipes, silencers and other gear; there will be the main propulsion motor, shafting; cables, control gear, different seatings, additional hull work as needed, ventilation requirements, and other things.

The pipe arrangements will be different; in some respects they could be more complex, as there will be a number of engines to be served with cooling water, lubricating oil and fuel oil; standby requirements will be different, as will emergency governing and so on.

For certain types of vessel it is a distinct advantage to have a series of engines low down in the hull. Manoeuvring capabilities are in favour of the indirect drive, if this should be diesel-electric. There are then no sudden injections of cold air blasts into hot cylinders, engendering conditions that could lead eventually to liner failures. The bridge control of machinery may or may not be easier with indirect drives than with direct-coupled engines. It is not the engines themselves that constitute the essential problem but the auxiliaries that must operate sympathetically with the propulsion units.

It is always assumed, but not tacitly granted, that the replacement and maintenance costs of a battery of small high-speed engines are lower than the corresponding costs for a large engine. But the bane of a superintendent's existence is not the main engine; it is the aggregation of all the other things—pumps, pipes, valves and so on. That is where most of the money goes.

Diesel-electric Considerations

It is said, from time to time, that the large direct-coupled diesel engine is inherently heavy for its output, compared with the diesel-electric drive; this is incorrect. It is not accurate to describe the large direct-coupled diesel engine as an anachronism; on the contrary, it is the most profitable form of diesel propulsion at present known. If it became the fashion to install the indirect, in preference to the direct, drive it would be a change of practice, but it would not be progress. Enthusiasts do not always sufficiently appreciate that the weight and cost of such things as engine seatings, pipe systems, pumps and all the ancillary gear which a large number of engine units on shipboard entails, can more than offset any savings which may be made in the diesel units.

Another erroneous notion is that there are difficulties in the making of large direct-coupled diesel engines, and that therefore it would be a good thing if they were superseded. There are no difficulties. On the contrary, if there is one single factor more than another which has been responsible for the tardy adoption of the diesel-electric, or other form of indirect, drive in Britain it is the facility with which large direct-coupled diesel engines can be manufactured and operated.

The chief disadvantage of the high-powered, direct-coupled engine is that, for certain types of vessel, its height can encroach upon valuable ship space. The chief disadvantage of the diesel-electric drive is the power dissipated by the double transformation of energy.

In installations comprising a small number of large units this loss may possibly be as low as 8–9 per cent, but, with a large number of small units, it may rise to as much as 20 per cent, proportionately augmenting the fuel consumption and necessitating larger bunkers for the same operating radius, to the detriment of the deadweight carrying capacity of the ship. That is, the fuel bill is increased and the ship's earning power decreased. If, towards offsetting the greater fuel consumption, the propeller revolutions are reduced, then larger propulsion motors, shafting, propellers and so on become necessary, with correspondingly enhanced first cost. For the best all-round compromise for a diesel-electric drive, the propeller revolutions are not much lower than for a direct-coupled engine. If high-speed engines are applied weight may be reduced, but seldom the over all first cost—notwithstanding the larger number of small standardised units.

Although the foregoing comments may bring the diesel-electric drive for ocean-going ships into correct perspective *vis-à-vis* the direct-coupled engine, it is not to say that there are not numerous instances where a diesel-electric drive is not only justifiable but can be the most desirable type of prime mover to install.

The fact that a particular method of propulsion, geared turbines, turbo-electric, diesel machinery or whatever it may be, is apparently favoured by one community, or in one country, must be viewed against the background of facilities available and the conditions prevailing there. The answer to the same problem is not the same everywhere. In Great Britain and Northern Ireland, where facilities are equally available for every kind of machinery, and there is an incomparable wealth of sound experience and knowledge in the marine engineering industry, shipowners have only to consider one problem, namely, what is likely to be, for them, the most profitable form of machinery.

REQUIREMENTS FOR INDIRECT DRIVES

Three requirements must be met to ensure a wider application of indirect drives, especially the geared diesel engine. These requirements are:

(i) ability of the engine to run continuously and satisfactorily on heavy fuel oil;

(ii) the use of a gear reduction ratio of not less than 4:1 and preferably at least 5:1;

(iii) a level of engine speed not lower than, say, 450 rev/min, or thereabouts, with high mean effective cylinder pressures.

Until recently it had not been practicable to meet these requirements; hence the dominance of the direct-coupled engine.

Heavy Fuel

Before seriously considering the purchasing of a geared installation,
it is prudent and indeed necessary to arrive at a conclusion regarding
the likely fuel bill. In this connection there are the following matters
to be assessed:

(a) the engine builder will doubtless state that his engines will
run continuously on heavy fuel; but what does he mean by heavy
fuel? In direct-coupled engines the term implies a fuel having a
viscosity of, say, 3500 sec, upon which the engines will con-
engines, the higher the viscosity the more smoothly and satisfactorily will the engines perform in service. Can the proposed
medium-speed engines equal this performance?
speed engines equal this performance?

(b) If not, what is the heaviest and cheapest fuel upon which the
engines can be relied to run in service and what will be the annual
fuel bill in comparison with that for direct-driven engines?

(c) Taking the wear and tear of cylinders, pistons, fuel valves,
etc., for the direct-coupled engines as datum, a comparative
assessment for the geared installation should be attempted.

Propeller Revolutions

Compared with direct-driven engines, there are certain factors which
are adverse to the geared installation, namely, the greater fuel
consumption rate, the higher lubricating oil losses and the lower
efficiency of the transmission components. To set against these
factors there is the potential advantage of being able to choose
revolutions at one end that will enable a high-speed engine to be
used and, at the other end, that will ensure a propulsive efficiency
higher than that attainable with direct-coupled engines.

Thus, comparing a direct-driven engine at 110 rev/min with a
geared engine at 90 rev/min, the overall improvement in propulsive
efficiency is 6–7 per cent in favour of the latter. If, for the geared
engine, the propeller speed is reduced to 80 rev/min, the overall
improvement will be of the order of 10–11 per cent.

Propeller speeds of 80–90 rev/min are almost exclusively used in
the large tanker class, where machinery powers are in the region of
20 000–30 000 kW. The deep draught at which they operate presents
no problem as regards the immersion of a large-diameter propeller.

For cargo ships generally, those of the slow type which operate with direct-coupled engines have a propeller speed of 120–130 rev/min. The medium-speed ships operate at 105–110 rev/min and the fast types at 110–115 rev/min. If turbine machinery were installed the propeller speed would probably be lowered to 105 rev/min.

The comparative results are not always as satisfactory as those mentioned above. Thus, in comparisons for a bulk carrier, single-screw and of typical design, for which a propeller of 8 metres diameter could be provided, a geared engine propeller speed of 68 rev/min showed a propulsive efficiency of 74·1 per cent, against 70·2 per cent for a direct-driven unit at 114 rev/min, i.e. a gain of 5·5 per cent for the geared set.

For a cargo liner, with a 6·5 metre diameter propeller, a geared engine installation having a propeller speed of 97 rev/min, when compared with 114 rev/min for a direct drive, showed that the propulsive efficiencies were respectively 69·4 and 67·8 per cent, i.e. only 2·3 per cent in favour of the geared engines.

Overall Assessment

A shipowner who is attracted to the application of geared engines for his ships should request his staff to prepare a closely detailed estimate and technical statement respectively for the actual direc-driven engines that he would normally have bought and for the geared machinery which will have made the most favourable impression on him. He should put aside the many comparisons to which his attention will doubtless be directed. Most of these will be found, upon careful analysis, to be either incomplete or prejudiced. Moreover, there are far too many variables in the problem for a general statement to be applied to a particular instance.

C.C.P.

MEDIUM-SPEED ENGINES

In several of the earlier chapters, i.e. those dealing with direct-coupled engines, descriptions are included of medium-speed engines of in-line and V-types, which are specially suited for indirect drive arrangements. Accordingly there is only a limited amount of additional space available for examples of other proprietary engine types.

STORK-WERKSPOOR ENGINES

The original Werkspoor engine was described in the first edition of this book and in the second edition, a description of the Stork crosshead turbocharged two-stroke engine introduced in 1952 was added.

The amalgamation of Stork and Werkspoor in 1954 resulted in the introduction of a Stork-Werkspoor crosshead engine, by incorporating the successful constructional features of the Werkspoor-Lugt engine into the Stork direct-coupled design. This engine has since been presented in the successive editions of this book.

In view of the rapidly growing market for high-powered medium-speed engines for the propulsion of ocean-going ships, Stork-Werkspoor introduced their new medium-speed engine type. This engine became the successor of the crosshead engine. The production of the latter engine has been discontinued.

Arising from this sequence of events, the following description deals with the Stork-Werkspoor four-stroke trunk piston, heavy-fuel, medium-speed engine, with type designation TM410. This engine has been specially designed for geared marine propulsion, but it is also very suitable for land-based power stations, pump drives on board dredgers, etc. (*see* Figure 11.1).

Stork-Werkspoor Diesel also supplies auxiliary engines for electric power on board ship from their range of small four-stroke engines—comprising the basic models F240, R210 and R150, with cylinder bores from 240 to 150 mm and the power range from 1500 to 180 bhp (1100 to 135 kW) at 720–1500 rev/min. Logically these smaller engines are also widely used as geared propulsion units for inland craft and small sea-going ships, e.g. tugs, coasters, fishing vessels.

The TM410 engine is a 'first generation size—second generation power' design with potential up to 850–900 bhp/cyl. With turbocharging and aircooling, the engine is available in unidirectional as well as direct reversible form to suit the application.

The main data for the in-line engines with six, eight and nine cylinders and V-type engines with ten, twelve, sixteen, eighteen and twenty cylinders are set out in Tables 11.1, 11.2, 11.3 and 11.4.

Figure 11.2 shows a cross-section of the in-line engines and Figure 11.3 illustrates a cross-section of the V-type engine.

Bedplate and Main Bearings

Figure 11.4 shows the bedplate to be a U-shaped strong iron casting, in which the main-bearing caps are fitted with a serrated joint to form, with the bearing saddles, a rigid housing for the thin-wall steel main-bearing shells.

These bearing shells have copper-lead lining and lead-tin plating. Both upper and lower shells can easily be removed by lifting the

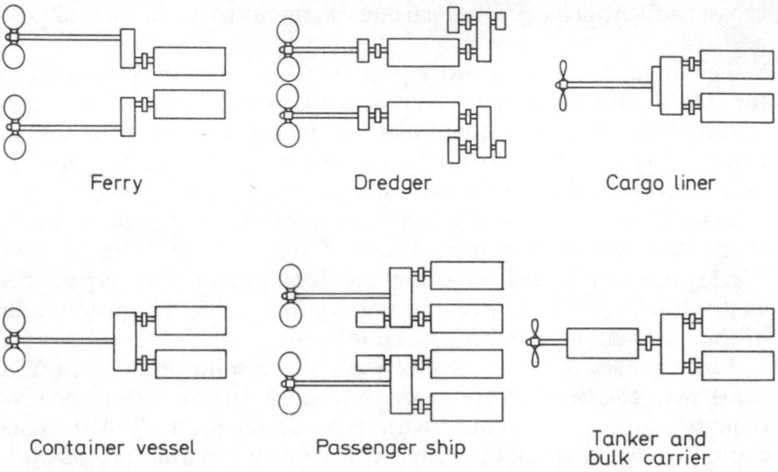

Ferry   Dredger   Cargo liner

Container vessel   Passenger ship   Tanker and
                                             bulk carrier

Ferry. Two engines each driving a variable pitch or fixed blade propeller. Very low engine room to create roll-on/roll-off deck for cars.

Dredger. Two engines each driving a variable pitch propeller. On front power take-off for sand pump and shaft generator. Engine can run at max. torque down to 80 per cent. of max. rev/min.

Cargo liner. Two direct reversible engines, through clutch couplings on one twin-input gearbox, driving one fixed blade propeller. Manoeuvring with one engine running ahead and one astern.

Container vessel. Two engines, one gearbox, driving a variable-pitch propeller. Low and small engine-room, large cargo space for containers.

Passenger ship. Four V-form engines, driving two variable-pitch propellers through clutch couplings and two gearboxes. Board electricity supply from shaft generator, jacket water can be used for desalination plant. Well balanced engines.

Tanker and bulk carrier. Three engines on one gearbox driving a fixed blade or variable-pitch propeller. Drive of cargo pumps from engine power take-off. High output in small engine room, saving weight and installation costs.

Figure 11.1 Typical applications for TM410 engines

bearing cap, *see* Figure 11.5. Large inspection openings in the bedplate enable easy access to the crankcase. The inspection covers are fitted with relief valves.

Integrally cast columns in the bedplate accommodate alloy-steel tie-rods, to connect bedplate and cylinder block tightly together in a rigid construction and to prevent high tensile stresses from the cylinder pressures being transmitted to these cast-iron components. In the V-type engine also, two rows of tie-rods are applied. As these rods are in an oblique position, a number of short bolts are fitted in addition in order to prevent relative movement of cylinder block and bedplate.

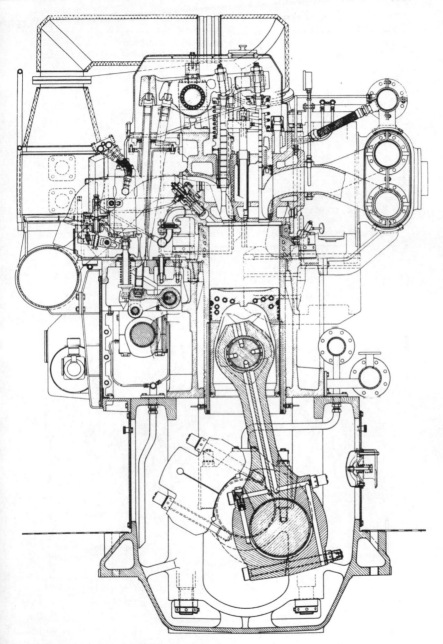

Figure 11.2 Cross-section of 'in-line' engine

Table 11.1 TECHNICAL DATA FOR IN-LINE AND V ENGINES

Type:	Four-stroke, direct reversible.
Configuration:	6, 8, 9 cyl. in-line, left handed and right handed; 10, 12, 16, 18, 20 cyl. 40° V form.
Aspiration:	Pressure charged and intercooled.
Bore and stroke:	410 × 470 mm.
Swept volume per cylinder:	62 litre.
Fuel specification:	Heavy fuel, diesel oil and gasoil.
Lub. oil specification for heavy fuel:	Crankcase and cylinder: viscosity: SAE 30 quality: detergency/dispergency and oxidation stability at Series 3 level. alkalinity: 20–30 TBN
Lub. oil specification for diesel oil and gas oil:	SAE 30. MIL–L2104A TBN 5–7.
Cooling water specification:	Water treated to prevent hard scale and corrosion.

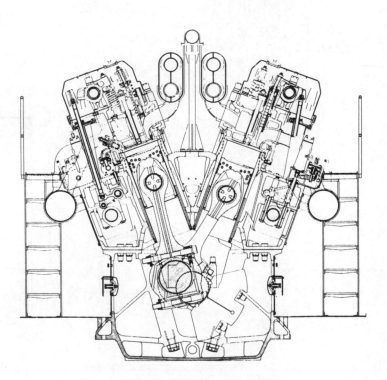

Figure 11.3 Cross-section of V-type engine

Table 11.2 ENGINE POWERS AND SPEEDS

| Outputs* | Engine speed (rev/min) | Metric shaft horsepower Number of cylinders | | | | | | | | Mean effective pressure (kg/cm²) |
		6	8	9	10	12	16	18	20	
MAX. CONTINUOUS RATING										
Ship propulsion	550	4 000	5 100	6 000	6 500	8 000	10 500	12 000	13 000	17·6
One hr per 12 hrs 10 % overload according to BS.649 and DIN 6270 A	500	3 800	4 850	5 700	6 200	7 600	10 000	11 400	12 400	18·4
RECOMMENDED HEAVY CONTINUOUS SERVICE RATING	550	3 600	4 600	5 400	5 850	7 200	9 450	10 800	11 700	15.8
	500	3 400	4 400	5 150	5 600	6 800	9 000	10 200	11 200	16.4

Ambient conditions: Intake air   30°C   Derating for tropical climate roughly 5%
                      Water for charge-air cooler   25°C
                      Atmospheric pressure   750 mm Hg
                      Exhaust back pressure   300 mm

Table 11.3 ENGINE WEIGHTS AND LENGTHS

	Number of cylinders							
	6	8	9	10	12	16	18	20
Engine with standard flywheel, kg	52 000	68 000	76 000	85 000	95 000	125 000	140 000	155 000
Heaviest part for erection, kg	11 000	13 500	15 000	15 000	18 000	24 000	27 000	30 000
Heaviest part for maintenance, kg	800	800	800	800	800	800	800	800
Engine length from front to coupling flange, mm	6 020	7 920	8 620	5 075	5 550	8 230	8 430	9 475

Table 11.4 CONSUMPTIONS AND CAPACITIES

	Number of cylinders								Mean piston speed m/sec
	6	8	9	10	12	16	18	20	
Fuel g/bhp.h at lower calorific value	155	157	157	157	155	156	155	157	8·6
10 000 kcal/kg	155	157	157	157	155	156	155	157	7·8
Lubricating oil, litre/h	3·5	4·5	5·3	5·8	7·1	9·3	10·6	11·6	

									Head m
PUMP CAPACITIES									
Fresh water (jacket cooling) m³/h	70	90	100	115	140	180	200	230	20
Raw water m³/h*	110	140	165	155	160	220	240	280	20
Lubricating oil m³/h	55	75	80	90	110	145	160	180	80
Lubricating oil circulating pump m³/h	70	90	100	115	140	180	200	225	15
Fuel m³/h	2	2·7	3	3·5	4	5·4	6	7	50
Fresh water (injector cooling) m³/h	1·2	1·6	1·8	2·0	2·4	3·2	3·6	4·0	20

*For C.S.R. and 32°C seawater, for main engine cooling only.

Figure 11.4 Bedplate and crankshaft

Crankshaft

The crankshaft is a fully machined one-piece forging. The large diameter journals and crankpins are provided with obliquely drilled holes for the transmission of lubricating and piston cooling oil. *See* Figure 11.4 for general construction of the crankshaft.

Counterweights are fitted on all crankwebs, being secured by means of two hydraulically stressed studs and two keys.

Cylinder Block with Camshaft

The cylinder block is a rigid iron casting and includes the cooling water jackets and the camshaft space.

For the inspection of cams and rollers, the cylinder block is provided with covers on the camshaft side. Three roller levers are fitted per cylinder, one each for the inlet and exhaust cams and one for the fuel pump drive.

The pushrod passages are fitted with seals to prevent oil leakage from entering the camshaft space. The camshaft is ground to a single diameter over its entire length. The cams are of hardened steel, hydraulically shrunk-on with the aid of tapered bushes.

When necessary, the complete camshaft can be removed sideways. The camshaft is driven from the crankshaft by Werkspoor nodular cast-iron 'Sferolite' gearwheels and runs in white-metal lined steel bearings. The direct-reversible engine is provided with double cams and a hydraulic reversing gear, to move the camshaft in an axial direction.

Connecting Rod and Piston

As will be seen from Figure 11.6 the connecting rod has an extremely

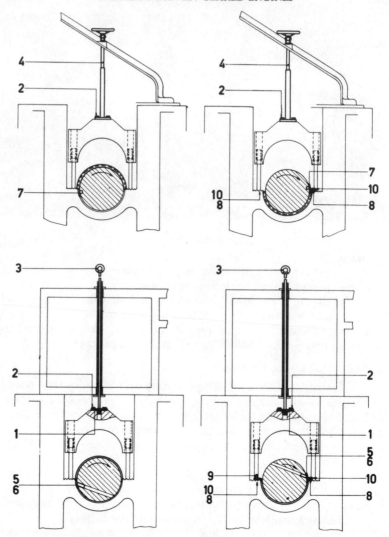

Figure 11.5 Main bearing removal

heavy big-end, to form a rigid housing for the copper-lead lined
lead-tin plated thin-wall steel bearing shells.

To allow the rod to be removed through the cylinder liner, the
big-end is split by serrated joints in two planes. The advantage of the
design is the low headroom required, together with easy dismantling.
The big-end bolts are stressed hydraulically.

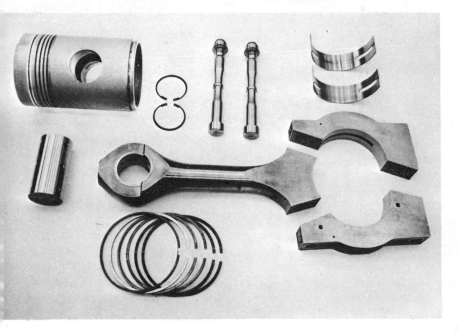

Figure 11.6 Connecting rod and piston components

The light-alloy piston has a cast-in top-ring carrier and a cast-in cooling-oil tube. The piston gudgeon pin is fully floating. The piston pin, connecting rod and big-end are provided with two sets of drilled passages, one for the cooling oil flow from the crankshaft to the piston, the other for the return from the piston to the underside of the big-end. This reduces the amount of splash oil.

Cylinder Liner

The cylinder liner is made of special cast-iron and is provided with cooling-water passages drilled to a hyperboloid pattern in its thick upper rim. This special feature ensures an intense cooling of the upper liner part and also ensures, by equalising the temperatures of the connected liner rim and the cylinder block, a perfectly circular liner when the engine is in operation, *see* Figures 11.7 and 11.8.

Two holes for cylinder lubrication are drilled in each liner from the bottom, thus avoiding oil pipes through the cooling-water spaces. Each hole feeds one lubricating-oil quill arranged half-way along the liner length. A normal 'Assa' cylinder lubricator is provided.

Figure 11.7 Cylinder liner

Cylinder Head and Valves

There are two designs of cast-iron cylinder head. These are respectively the three-valve and the four-valve head types shown in Figures 11.9 and 11.10.

The original three-valve head has two exhaust valves in separate valve cages and one large inlet valve; the four-valve head has the same exhaust valve cages but two smaller inlet valves.

The four-valve head has been developed for larger air inlet and exhaust gas areas and for a fully enclosed valve gear. The first feature ensures an impressive uprating potential—beyond the 585 bhp/cyl limit of the three-valve head—up to 850–900 bhp/cyl. This increase has been realised in a first-stage already, by an uprating to 670 bhp/cyl. The second feature is particularly useful for land applications in dusty surroundings.

The cylinder head also accommodates the injector and the starting air valve. Much attention has been given to efficient cooling, to avoid dangerous heat stresses. The cooling water, entering the

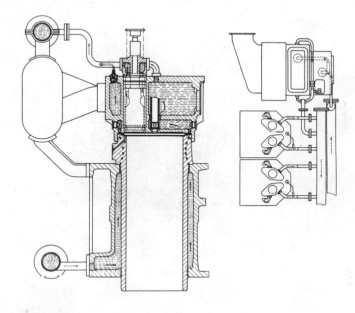

Figure 11.8 Cooling water system

head by drilled passages in the bottom periphery, is therefore guided over the bottom and along the injector by a horizontal partition wall.

The exhaust valves have Stellited seating faces; they are fitted in separate water-cooled valve cages, *see* Figure 11.11. The total water flow per cylinder is forced in parallel streams through the cooling spaces, extending close to the seat surfaces of the two exhaust valves. This results in very low exhaust valve temperatures, which are a prime requisite for long periods of service between overhauls when using residual fuels.

Hardened cast-iron inlet-valve seat inserts are mounted directly in the cylinder head.

Valve Gear

The cam profiles have been designed to avoid rapid acceleration changes and thus to minimise noise and dynamic stresses. The valve rockers are fitted with needle bearings which require no oil supply;

Figure 11.9 Three-valve cylinder head

all other contact faces within the cylinder head covers are lubricated by separate impulse oiling equipment. The lubricator for this is driven, in parallel with the cylinder lubricator, from the camshaft gear. This system is applied to the valve gear of the three-valve head as well as to the four-valve head, *see* Figure 11.12. The oil used for these purposes is drained separately, to prevent contamination of the crankcase oil by leaking fuel.

Fuel-injection System

One separate E-size injection pump is fitted per cylinder. The system is designed for high injection pressures to obtain good combustion at the high brake mean effective pressures used. The injector is equipped with an easily replaceable nozzle, which is water-cooled to prevent carbon deposits when using residual fuel.

Figure 11.10 Four-valve cylinder head

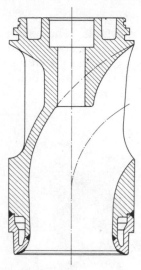

Figure 11.11 Lower part of exhaust valve cage

Safety Devices

The mechanism for the starting-air pilot valves is also used to stop the engine at overspeed. In that event the mechanical overspeed trip actuates a pneumatic valve, to allow air pressure into an auxiliary cylinder which then keeps every fuel injection pump lifted after one last injection stroke. Figure 11.13 shows the fuel injection-pump drive gear with the starting-air pilot valve and the pump lifting piston.

Safety devices for low lubricating-oil pressure and for low cooling-water flow are integrated in the engine systems and are thus independent of the external electrical alarm system. Standard electric alarm equipment, or alarm equipment and other safety functions to the specifications of clients and classification societies, can be installed in separate panels.

Controls

The engine has no handwheel or mechanical control levers, but one or more pneumatic single-handle controls. One of these is built into a manoeuvring desk which can be situated on or near the engine, *see* Figure 11.16. This desk contains most of the pneumatic equipment and also accommodates the necessary gauges for operation of the engine.

In addition a remote control column or columns can be installed anywhere in the engine room, or outside at any distance, *see* Figure

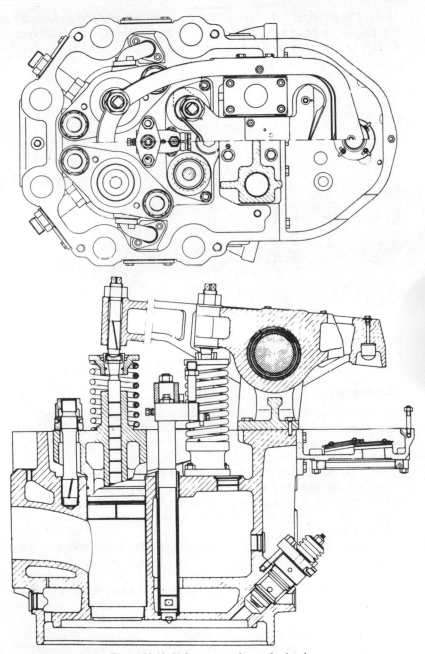

Figure 11.12 Valve gear on four-valve head

11.17. The pneumatic governor control has been specially developed for parallel service in geared installations. Unidirectional engines can also be electrically remote-controlled as an alternative.

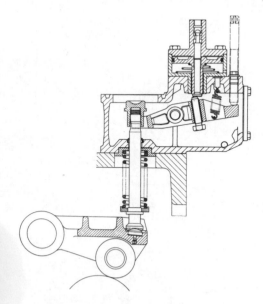

Figure 11.13 Fuel pump drive

Maintenance

Special attention has been paid in the design stage, to the requirements for quick and easy maintenance. Some of the matters dealt with are mentioned below.

    (i) Hydraulic tightening for all important bolts and studs;

    (ii) Easy removal of the big-end bearing parts, to facilitate the withdrawal of a piston, by the dismantling of both bearing caps along a horizontal slide through crankcase openings, *see* Figure 11.14.

    (iii) A gasket-free joint between cylinder head and exhaust pipe.

Some results of these and other measures for quick maintenance are illustrated by the following review of removal times:

Cylinder head and piston, with connecting rod, $1\frac{1}{2}$ hours;

Set of main-bearing shells, 1 hour;

Valve cage (complete with valve), 20 minutes;

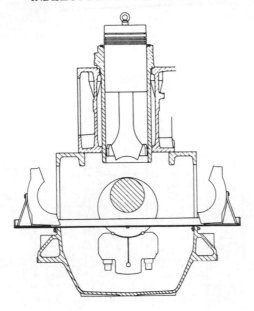

Figure 11.14 Removal of piston and connecting rod

Fuel injector, 10 minutes.

The periods between maintenance operations, based on actual service results, are as follows:

After every 1500 operating hours:
  Inspection of valve gear and crankcase;
  Check of valve clearance.
After 3000 hours:
  Inspection of fuel injectors;
  Sampling, for check, of crankcase oil.
After 6000 hours:
  Inspection and, when necessary, lapping of exhaust valves;
  Renewal of fuel atomizers;
  Inspection of inlet valves in one cylinder;
  Inspection of piston, piston rings and big-end bearing in same cylinder;
  Inspection of one main bearing;
  Inspection of all starting-air valves;
  Check of fuel pump timings.
After 12 000 hours:
  Measurement of cylinder liner bores.

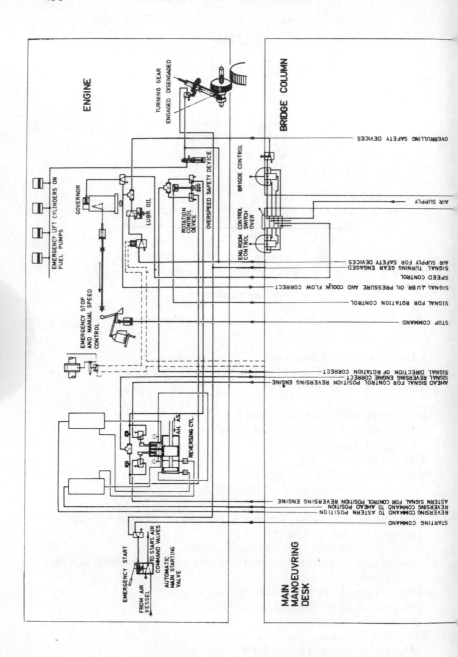

The above periods set for preventive maintenance have been estimated on the safe side. When more operating experience with these engines has been accumulated, the above maintenance intervals may be increased if possible.

Remote Control

The direct-reversible TM410 engines are equipped with a pneumatic control system without any use of mechanical controls.

This control system is a fully automatic one-lever system, which means that the lever can be put from any position (direction of rotation and engine speed) into any other position, without waiting or checking. All functions of decreasing speed, stopping, reversing, air starting, fuel admission and speed setting are performed in the right sequence and at the right moment. The system even repeats starting efforts, after a predetermined time, should the engine not fire at the first start.

The components of the system are fitted at three places: the engine; the main manoeuvring desk in the engine room; and as many

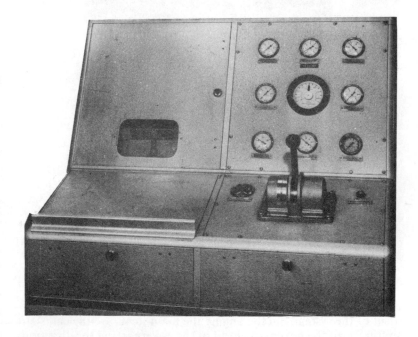

Figure 11.16 Main manoeuvring desk

Figure 11.17 Bridge control column

remote control columns as required. Figure 11.15 shows the arrangement of the system. On the engine the main items are the camshaft
shifting gear, the pneumatic head of the governor and the direction-
of-rotation indicator. A number of essential safety functions, which

do not depend on any electrical alarm or automation system, are integrated in the pneumatic system. These are: turning-gear-out check, overspeed trip which acts on the fuel pumps, *see* Figure 11.13, lubricating-oil pressure check and cooling-water flow check.

At the main manoeuvring desk, Figure 11.16, the air cleaning system, also all valves, tanks and nozzles of the system are located with, of course, one control lever and a change-over valve to connect either the engine room or the bridge control to the system.

The standard bridge column is very simple and comprises, in addition to the operation lever, a few indicators for engine alarms, a tachometer and two air pressure gauges, Figure 11.17.

Engine Room Installation

Figure 11.18 shows, by way of example, the engine room installation of a 600 passenger ferry, with its particular requirements, which are: high manoeuvrability; low engine room height for an uninterrupted car deck; short engine room length; unmanned engine room; unrestricted operation on heavy fuel oil.

These requirements have been met by the following arrangements. Twin-screw installation with one engine per shaft, controllable pitch propellers and bow thruster; gearboxes with horizontally offset in and output shafts for minimum engine-shaft height; auxiliaries for principal systems, e.g. pumps, filters, etc., combined to form clearly arranged and easily accessible vertical pump modules; bridge control for main engines and couplings; essential systems are automatically started and thermostatically controlled for automatic take-over by standby units, when triggered by the appropriate alarm and datalogging installation; steam heating of fuel lines and pre-heating of injectors at main engines; simple fuel system with special self-cleaning fuel oil filters instead of centrifuges.

A separate auxiliary engine room is provided for the three a.c. 650 kVA self-supporting flexibly-mounted Stork-Werkspoor diesel generator sets. The sets are automatically controlled to suit the requirements of the unmanned engine room. A small emergency power set, with compressor, is installed well above the waterline.

The principal auxiliary systems are: Fuel oil system for 3500 sec heavy fuel oil and for diesel oil comprising settling and day tanks, transfer pumps, fuel oil filtering and heating having automatic viscosity control, and booster pumps for adequate main engine supply pressure; lubricating oil system, separate one for each engine, comprising pumps, filters, cooler, centrifuge and drain tank; fresh water jacket cooling system, with pumps, cooler, deaerator and

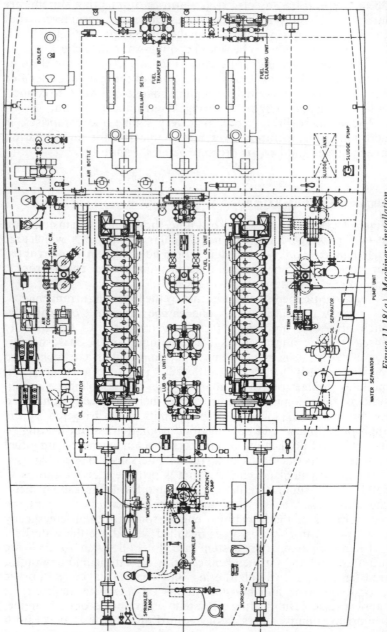

Figure 11.18(a) Machinery installation

435

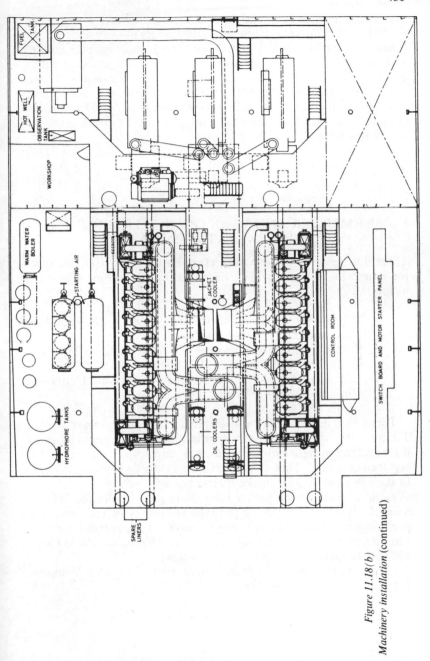

Figure 11.18(b)
Machinery installation (continued)

expansion tank; with special heating arrangement for warming-up —the hot-cooling water from the main engines in normal operation being used for fresh water generation; fresh water injector cooling systems, with pumps, cooler and observation tank provided with a heating coil for cold starts on heavy fuel oil; sea-water cooling system, with pumps and coolers, the latter in series for charging air, lubricating oil and jacket cooling water, and in parallel for injector cooling water, gearbox lubricating oil, shaftline lubricating oil and air compressors.

J.H.W.
A.H.

BURMEISTER AND WAIN GEARED PROPULSION AND GENERATOR ENGINES

Three Burmeister and Wain non-reversible four-stroke engine types for geared installations will be described in this section. These are as follows:

(i) 225 mm bore, 300 mm stroke, designated T and V 23H for the 'in-line' and the 'V'-types respectively;

(ii) 280 mm bore, 320 mm stroke, termed S and U 28H, also respectively for the 'in-line' and the 'V'-types.

(iii) 500 mm bore, 540 stroke, designated S50H and U50H also for the 'in-line' and the 'V' types respectively.

Table 11.5 indicates the power particulars per cylinder for the T and V 23H engine. This engine type is built as in-line engines having three and five to eight cylinders and, as V-engines, with from eight to eighteen cylinders. Thus the power range extends from 265 to 1920 brake kW (360 to 2600 brake metric horsepower).

Table 11.6 shows the power particulars per cylinder for 280/320 S and U 28H engine. The engine type is built as in-line units with five to eight cylinders and as V-engines with ten to eighteen cylinders. Thus a power range extending from 810 to 3500 brake kW (1100 to 4800 brake metric horse-power) is available.

Figure 11.19 shows performance curves for a 12 cylinder, V-engine, 225 mm bore, 300 mm stroke.

Table 11.5 POWER PER CYLINDER—225 MM BORE, 300 MM STROKE ENGINES
(T & V 23H)

Purpose	Conditions	rev/min	Power (brake)		Mean effective pressure	
			bkW	Metric bhp	bar	kgf/cm²
Propulsion engines	Continuous service	800	92	125	11·60	11·80
	Maximum continuous	825	100	135	12·20	12·80
	Overload	845	107	145	12·70	13·00
Generator engines	Maximum continuous	720	88	120	12·30	12·60
	Overload	720	96	130	13·40	13·60
	Maximum continuous	750	92	125	12·30	12·60
	Overload	750	100	136	13·40	13·70

Table 11.6 POWER PER CYLINDER—280 MM BORE, 320 MM STROKE ENGINES
(S & U 28H)

Purpose	Conditions	rev/min	Power (brake)		Mean effective pressure	
			bkW	Metric bhp	bar	kgf/cm³
Propulsion engines	Continuous service	750	162	220	13·20	13·40
	Maximum continuous	775	176	240	13·80	14·00
	Overload	800	195	265	14·80	15·10
Generator engines	Maximum continuous	720	162	220	13·80	14·00
	Overload	720	176	240	14·80	15·20
	Maximum continuous	750	170	230	13·80	14·00
	Overload	750	184	250	14·80	15·20

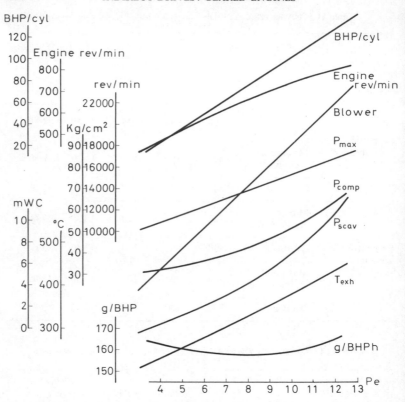

Figure 11.19 Performance curves, twelve-cylinder V-type engine, 225/300 size

General Description, 225/300 and 280/320 Engines

The cross-sections in Figures 11.20 and 11.21 are so nearly alike for the respective engine types T and V 23H and S and U 28H that the same description will serve for both.

The frames are sturdy, one-piece castings of a high-grade cast-iron. The crankshafts are carried in underslung bearings with precision shells. The cooling water space walls are also integral with the frame, and the cylinder liners have upper collars by which they are clamped to the machined upper faces of the frame by the cylinder covers.

Charging air is led from the air cooler to the charge-air space that is also integral with the frame. The air space for the V-type engine is arranged between the banks; and for the 'in-line' engine at the aft side. From there the air is taken through elbows to the intake duct in the cylinder cover. The exhaust pipes are also supported on the frame.

Figure 11.22 shows the layout of turbocharger, air cooler, and connection to the exhaust pipes for an 'in-line' engine.

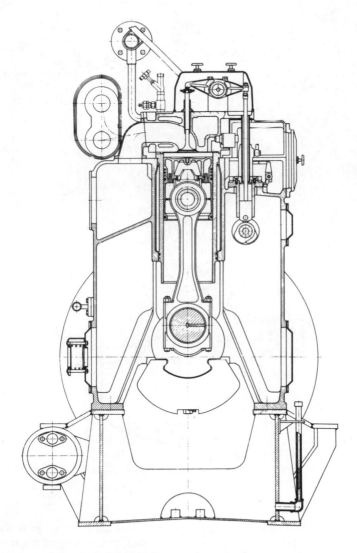

Figure 11.20 Four-stroke 'in line' engine

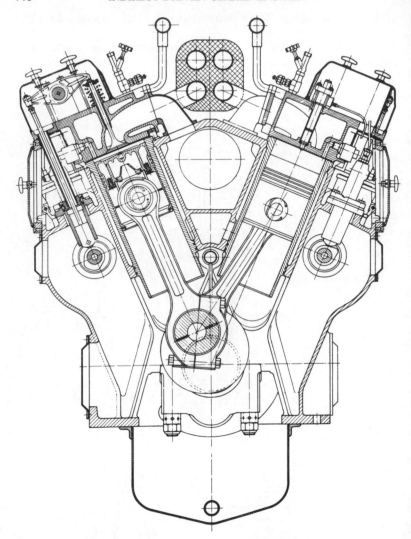

Figure 11.21 Four-stroke V-type engine

The camshafts are carried in bearings that are inserted in bosses in the frame. The valve motion and the fuel injection equipment are oiltight-enclosed in such a way that leakages from the fuel oil system cannot mix with the lubricating oil system.

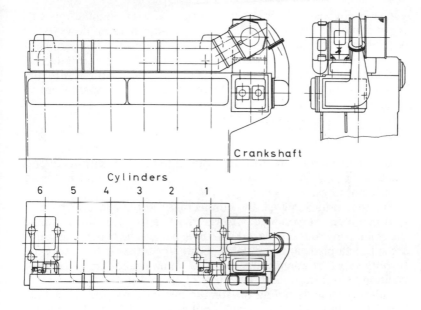

Figure 11.22 Arrangement of turbocharger

Pistons

The pistons, Figure 11.23, are oil cooled by a jet from the connecting rod. Each piston is a casting of special grey iron, having relatively thin walls and a rigid rib structure to transmit the gas forces to the

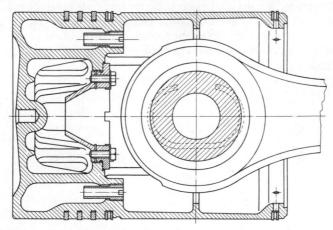

Figure 11.23 Cross-section of piston

gudgeon-pin bosses. Lubricating oil enters as a jet from the connecting rod into the central conical bushing from whence it flows to the cooling space in the piston. The oil outlets are near the periphery of the cooling space and placed at such a height that an effective cocktail-shaker effect is obtained. This, in combination with the thin walls, ensures low piston temperatures, thus enabling intermediate viscosity fuel oils to be used.

Connecting Rods

The connecting rods are drop forgings, fitted with precision big-end bearing shells as for the main bearings. The top-end bearings have bronze bushings.

For the 'in-line' engine, the connecting rod big-end bearings are split in a plane perpendicular to the shaft centre. For the V-engine the connecting rods are placed side-by-side and the big-end bearings are split in a plane at an angle of about 30° to the shaft centre-line. In both types of connecting rod, the joining faces are secured in position by serrations and by screws of alloyed steel.

Lubricating and cooling oil for the piston flows through a hole bored longitudinally along each connecting rod from the big-end bearing to the top-end and from there to the piston.

Crankshaft

Figure 11.24 shows the crankshaft design. The crankshaft is of forged, alloy steel, with ground journals. Lubricating oil is supplied to the main bearings, whence it flows through holes bored in the crankshaft to the connecting rods. The outlet holes into the connecting rods are perpendicular to the centre-line plane of the crank throw. That is, they are horizontal when the crank throw is standing in the vertical plane.

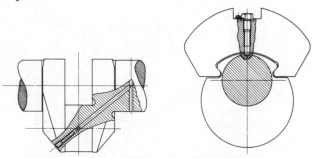

Figure 11.24 Section of crankshaft

Where balance weights are necessary they are fitted to dovetailed recesses as shown in Figure 11.24, being located by tap-bolt.

Main Bearings

The main bearing shells are of the precision type, steel-backed, lead-bronze lined, with a soft running-in coating, for the V-engines. For in-line engines, where the load is less, the steel shells are white-metal lined. The bearing keeps have a tight, sidewise fit to the frame. They are fastened by two heavy studs to the frame. The nuts are tightened by means of hydraulic jacks. Lubricating oil is supplied from a pipe that is inserted above the bearing.

Cylinders

The cylinder liners are made of perlitic cast-iron of high wear resistance. Tightening from the cooling water space is obtained by two lower rings of synthetic water- and oil-resistant rubber and above by the pressure between the collar and the frame. In the V-engine, cooling water enters from the lowest trapezoidal canal between the cylinder banks.

The cylinder covers are made of special cast-iron and each is clamped to the top of the cylinder liner by four studs in the frame, the nuts of which are tightened simultaneously by hydraulic jacks. In the covers are arranged an air inlet valve, an exhaust valve, a fuel valve and a safety valve.

The air inlet valve and the exhaust valves are seated directly in the covers, but for running on intermediate viscosity fuel oils, the exhaust valves may be provided with interchangeable seats of heat-and wear-resistant alloy cast-iron. In event of wear, both inlet and exhaust valves may afterwards be provided with such seats.

Valve Motion

The camshaft, Figure 11.25, is driven from the end of the engine by a spur gear train. The camshaft proper is assembled by flanging together drop-forged and machined sections for each cylinder. The thick flanges function as journals for the bearings and these, and the cams, are hardened and ground. The roller guides move in housings that are bolted to a face that is parallel to the top face on the frame. The pushrods are surrounded by pipes that, by synthetic rubber rings at their ends, tighten to the top flange of the roller guide housing and to the upper wall of the cylinder cover.

The oil-tight cover over the valves and valve gear is partitioned

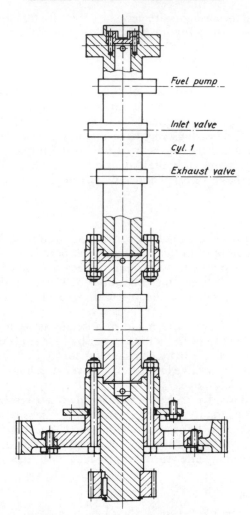

Figure 11.25 Camshaft

into two oil-tight separated spaces, the inner one containing the fuel valve and the fuel pipes, from which any possible fuel leaks drain down into the fuel pump space in the frame above the cam-shaft, and from thence to a drain box, float-controlled or with sight glasses, and so to the fuel oil drainage tank, *see* Figure 11.26.

The valve rocker arms, Figure 11.27, move on bronze bushes on hardened journals that are fixed in supports bolted to the cylinder

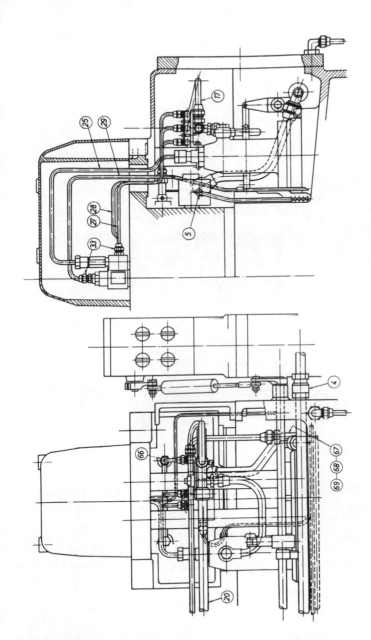

Figure 11.26 Arrangement of oiltight covers

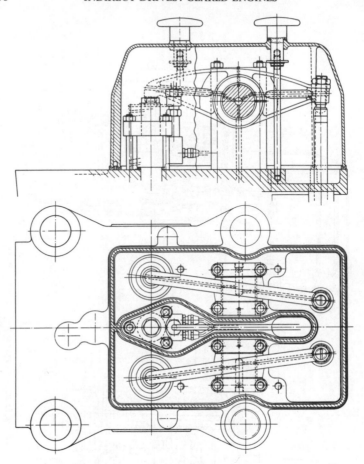

Figure 11.27 Valve rocker arms

cover. The rocker arms are forced-lubricated. The oil drains to the crankcase through the previously mentioned two pipes and past the roller guides to the crankcase.

The fuel injection system is of Bosch design and manufacture. In the path of the fuel pump movement, Figure 11.28, is inserted a seal, 3, to prevent fuel oil from leaking past the plunger to seep down into the crankcase.

Governor

A speed governor is located at the generator end of the engine and is

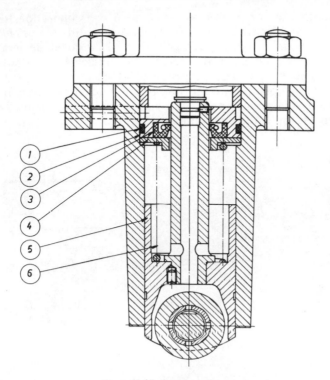

Figue 11.28 Fuel injection movement

driven off the camshaft gear train. The governor which is used, is one of the several types of Woodward manufacture, the prccise form depending upon the requirements as regards regulation. For a constant-speed generator drive, the governor is usually of the UG8-type. For ship propulsion, with remote engine control and variable speed, one of the PG types of governor is applied. The capabilities for manoeuvring are as described later for the 50H engine types.

At the forward end of the engine there are two gear-pumps for lubricating oil, driven from the crankshaft direct or by spur gearing. In the drive cover a space is provided for a Holset torsional vibration damper, should this be necessary.

Also at the forward end, camshaft-driven, are a fuel oil booster pump and an overspeed trip, *see* Figure 11.29. When the speed exceeds the overspeed limit, the centrifugal force on flyweight 3 overcomes spring force 12 and the weight rapidly moves to its outer position, pressing arm 15 down, to be held by pawl 16. Valve 8 is connected to compressed air at A; at B is a connection to the actuating cylinder at C. In the position shown, ball 14 closes and the actuating cylinder is de-aerated. When arm 15 is down, de-aeration ceases, the ball is pressed from its seat by spindle 14 and admits air to the actuating cylinder, the piston of which moves forward and brings the fuel pumps into the stop position against a spring in the linkage from the governor. The engine is stopped manually by pressing button 1, thereby bringing down arm 15.

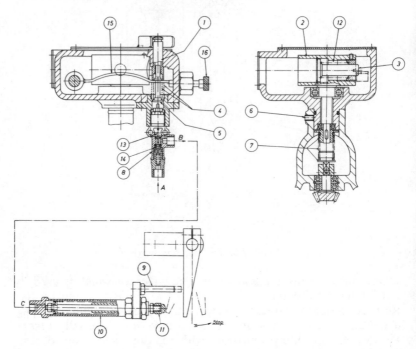

Figure 11.29 Overspeed trip

General Description, 500/540 Engine

The designation S50H and U50H refer to the line-in-line and the V-type versions of the four-stroke cycle, high-pressure, turbocharged engines having cylinders 500 mm bore and 540 mm stroke. The engines are built as geared propulsion engines and are also used as generator engines. Table 11.7 gives the power particulars per cylinder.

The engines are built with five to nine cylinders in-line per unit, and eight to eighteen cylinders in V-form. Thus, maximum continuous shaft powers ranging from 2750 to 9900 brake kW (3750 to 13 500 metric brake horse-power) are available, per engine. Figure 11.30 shows the outline of a twelve-cylinder V-type propulsion engine U50H.

Table 11.7 POWER PER CYLINDER—500 MM BORE, 540 MM STROKE ENGINES (S50H & U50H)

Purpose	Conditions	rev/min	Power (brake) bkW	Metric bhp	Mean effective pressure bar	kgf/cm²
Propulsion engines	Maximum continuous service	465	550	750	13·4	13·6
Generator engines	Maximum continuous service	428	520	710	13·8	14·1
	Maximum continuous service	450	550	750	13·8	14·1

There is one turbocharger and one charging air cooler at either end of the engine. They are carried on rigid-welded structures bolted to the engine frame. The induction pipes traverse either side of the engine and the cylinder exhaust pipes from the turbochargers are arranged between the cylinder banks. Depending upon the arrangement of the engines in the ship, the exhaust pipes from the turbochargers may be led away individually or connected to a common outlet.

A section of the V-type propulsion engine is shown in Figure 11.31.

Entablature

The main structure consists of a cast iron frame that carries the underslung main bearings and has two integral cylinder cooling jackets that are clamped on spigots between the frame and the cylinder covers. On either side of the frame there are two camshafts; and on top of the frame are provided roller guides for the actuation of the inlet and exhaust valves and also the fuel pump.

The valve motion gear is completely separated from the piston motion system; it has its own lubricating arrangement for preventing fuel leakage to the main system.

The camshafts are inserted through slots in the frame sides and may thus be removed for inspection without requiring space in the longitudinal direction.

450

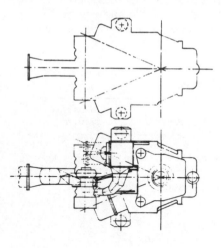

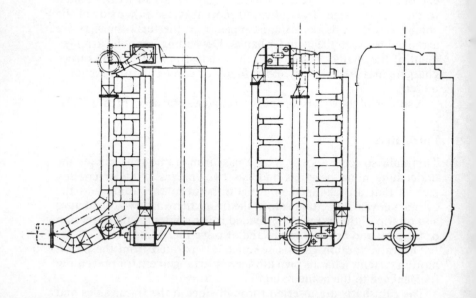

Figure 11.30 Twelve-cylinder V-engine, 500 mm bore, 540 mm stroke

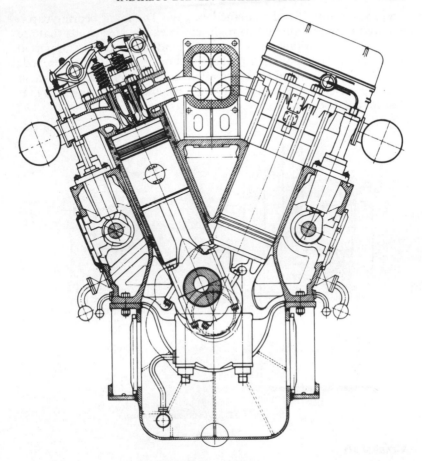

Figure 11.31 Cross-section of V-type engine

Bedplate and Main Bearings

The bedplate is a fabricated structure, the lower part of which forms the oil pan. Large doors on the vertical side girders provide easy access for the inspection and overhauling of the main bearings and connecting rod bottom-end bearings.

The main bearing shells are of the precision type with steel-backed lead-bronze, coated with a thin layer of a relatively soft alloy. The method of main bearing overhaul is unique and is particularly easy of manipulation. As shown in Figure 11.32, transverse girders are placed immediately underneath the crank webs and are dimensioned to provide room for the balance weights. The main bearing cap is secured to the frame by two high-tensile elastic steel studs that are tightened by hydraulic jacks. When dismantling, the cap is supported on the central telescopic hydraulic jack shown; the nuts are loosened; and the cap is lowered to the position shown, from which the main bearing shells can be withdrawn sideways under the crank web that has no balance weight.

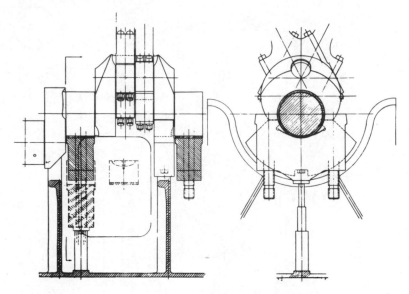

Figure 11.32 Main bearing removal

Crankshaft

The crankshaft is made of forged, high-tensile steel, dimensioned to provide ample bearing areas, together with strength and torsional rigidity. In design and manufacture it fulfils the requirements of the classification societies, *see* Figure 11.33.

The balance weights are dovetailed to the crankwebs and secured by thrust screws. By loosening the crews the balance weights may be withdrawn sideways without dismantling anything else.

The connecting rods are arranged side-by-side on the crankshaft journals. Lubricating oil for the crankshaft bearings and cooling oil for the pistons is led to the main bearings from whence it flows through drilled passages in the crankshaft and enters the connecting rod bottom-end. To reduce the magnitude of the centrifugal forces, the passages in the crankshaft journals are large in diameter and are

453

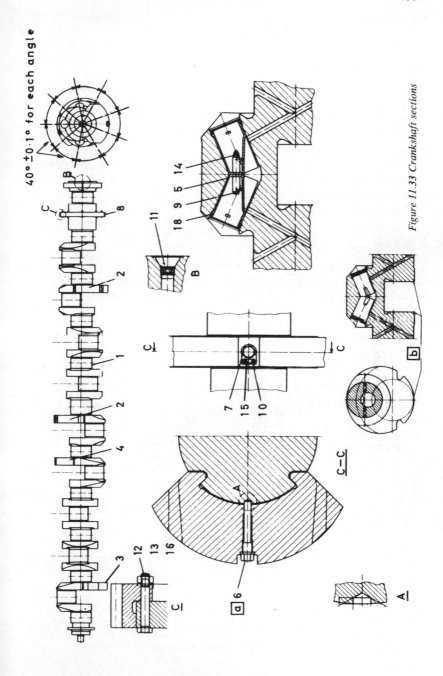

40° ±0·1° for each angle

Figure 11.33 Crankshaft sections

fitted with aluminium inserts in such a way that accumulation of oil sludge by centrifugal action is prevented.

Connecting Rods

The connecting rods are made from drop-forged, plain carbon steel. Each bottom-end is secured to the rod by a serrated joint and four elastic high-tensile steel bolts. The bottom-end of the connecting rod is so dimensioned that it permits withdrawal through the cylinder liner, together with the piston.

The bottom-end bearings have bearing shells and the closed small-ends have bushings of the same type as the main bearings. Drilled passages in the connecting rod convey the oil to the small-end bushing and the piston cooling.

Pistons

As shown in Figure 11.34, the piston is a two-piece design having a cast-steel top and a cast-iron skirt that sustains the guide pressure. The piston top is secured to the body on a rim about 0·10 of the diameter by means of four relatively long elastic studs of high-tensile steel. In this design the walls of the piston top can be made relatively thin, particularly in the ring zone that is not required to transmit gas pressures.

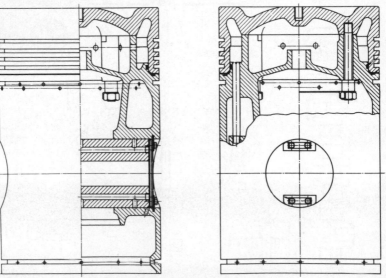

Figure 11.34 Sectional view of piston

The piston body is a ribbed structure that, with a minimum of distortion, transmits the gas forces to the gudgeon-pin eyes. The gudgeon-pins are of the floating type, made of alloyed carborising steel. The cooling and lubricating oil is led from the connecting-rod bushings to the ends of the gudgeon-pins, through drilled passages from which the cooling oil enters the annular outer chamber of the piston. From there the oil flows through holes in the supporting rim to the central chamber; and so through the central hole in the cooling-chamber bottom. The passages in the annular and central chambers are placed at such a height that an effective splash cooling of the piston crown is obtained.

Figure 11.35 shows piston temperatures plotted against mean effective pressures, as measured on a S45 engine. It will be seen that very favourable low temperatures are obtained all over the piston. This is important for the successful running of the engine on low-grade fuels. There are four piston rings located in flame-hardened lands in the crown and two oil scraper rings in the skirt.

Cylinder Liners

The cylinder liners are made of perlitic cast-iron of a composition that gives high wear resistance. There are four lubricating quills to each liner to ensure that there is a sufficient amount of high alkaline oil in the piston ring zone for running on low-grade fuels having a relatively high sulphur content.

Each liner is machined all over and has a high top collar that is clamped between the frame and the cylinder cover. Cooling water enters at the annular space between frame and liner, where a rotational motion is imparted. From there it passes through the oblique-tangential drilled passages in the collar to an annular space at the top of the liner, and then to the cylinder cover. The rotating motion of the coolant and the form of the passages in the collar ensure an efficient cooling of the liners, particularly in the zone corresponding to the piston rings in top position. Figure 11.35 shows temperatures measured on a U45H engine. With the modified cooling of U50H, the temperature at E will be even lower and the difference between temperatures at D and E will also be reduced, with equivalent reduction to the thermal stresses.

Cylinder Covers and Valves

The cylinder covers are made of high-strength cast-iron, and each cover accommodates two air inlet valves, two exhaust valves, one fuel valve, one starting air valve and one safety valve. The air intake

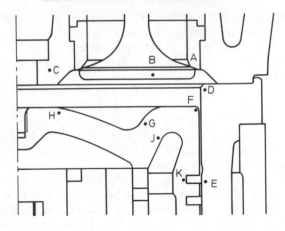

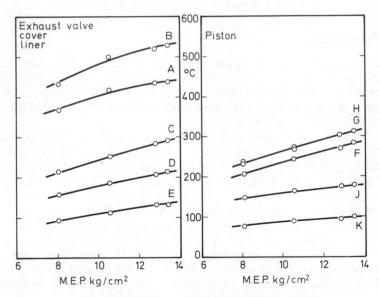

Figure 11.35 Piston temperature curves

is led from the outboard side of the cover, through ducts that are integral with it.

The seats for the air inlet valves are provided with shrunk-in and replaceable inserts of wear-resisting molybdenum cast-iron. The exhaust valves are located in separate water-cooled housings and the exhaust gases escape through ducts in the cylinder cover towards the centre of the engine.

There are two types of exhaust valve, namely, one for running on gas or diesel oil and one for running on lower grade fuels having a higher sulphur content. The plain exhaust valve, Figure 11.36, comprises a cast-iron housing with inserted spindle guides having replaceable bushes and a valve seat of special cast iron. The seat on the valve head is stellite faced.

The valve with water-cooled seat, Figure 11.37, has a shorter cast-iron housing, with inserted spindle guides as described above, but

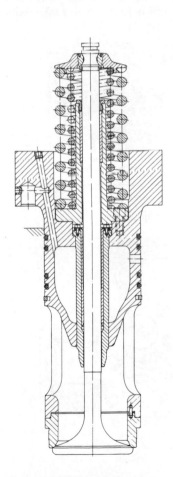

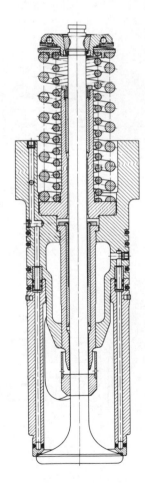

Figure 11.36 Exhaust valve, plain   *Figure 11.37 Exhaust valve, water-cooled*

the valve seat-piece is elongated so as to contain windows for the exhaust gases. The seat-piece is made of steel and to its lower end is welded another steel ring so that an annular cooling groove is formed close to the valve seat. The water is led to this cooling space by a separate pipe from the water inlet manifold, and through bored holes in the valve housing and seat-pieces; it escapes into the valve cooling chamber. The valve seats are also stellite faced. For heavy oil operation the exhaust valves are provided with Rotacap valve rotators.

The arrangement of the valves and rockers is shown in Figure 11.38. The rocker arms are oiltight, enclosed under an easily detachable and light cover of reinforced polyester. The air inlet valve

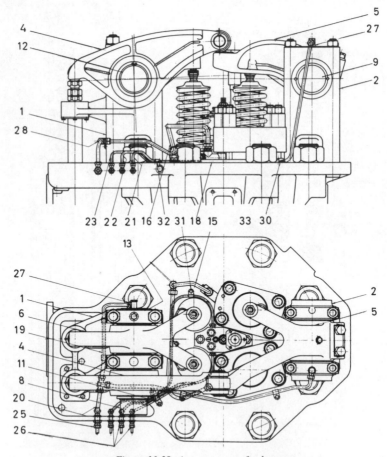

Figure 11.38 Arrangement of valve gear

rocker is of symmetrical *Y* shape and oscillates on a fixed hardened steel shaft, that is extended beyond the right fixpoint to accommodate the master rocker for the exhaust valve movement. Both of the rockers have bronze bushings. The exhaust valve rocker forms a symmetrical *V* shape for the exhaust valve contact points, but has one extended arm for contact with the master rocker. The rocker arm is fixed to the hardened shafts that oscillate in the two symmetrical outer bearings having bronze bushings.

The method of removing the exhaust valve housing for valve overhaul is unique and unexcelled. By removing a circlip ring and a washer, the master rocker may be moved sufficiently to the right, on the shaft extension, to become disengaged from the pushrod and the exhaust valve *V* arm. Both arms may be swung away and thus provide very easy access for removing the exhaust valves without dismantling anything else, *see* Figure 11.39.

Figure 11.39 Overhauling exhaust valve

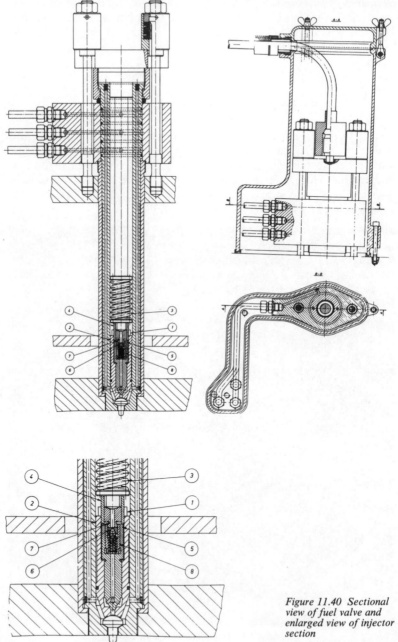

Figure 11.40 Sectional view of fuel valve and enlarged view of injector section

Fuel Injection System

The fuel injection valve, Figure 11.40, placed centrally in the cylinder cover, is of a new design that permits hot boiler oil to be circulated down to the injector. The valve is clamped to the cylinder cover; and the injector is secured to the valve housing by the top flange, via the central injection pipe and the thrust collar 1 which rests on top of the spindle guide 2. The spring 3 that is located around the injection pipe presses the spindle 5 against its seat via the four forks of the thrust piece 4.

Between injections, the check valve 6 rests against its seat 1 with a pressure that is slightly higher than the boost pressure. By this means, leakage of fuel to the cylinders through a leaky or hanging valve spindle is prevented, and a small amount of fuel oil escapes to the fuel oil system whereby the injection pipe is kept warm in standby periods. At the beginning of injection, the valve 6 opens and makes connection to the hollow of the slide 7 and the valve spindle. Next the slide 7 lifts to tighten against 1, whereby the spill 7 is closed and the full injection pressure reaches down to the bottom of the spindle that lifts by the difference of pressure on the area 5 of the spindle and the area of slide 7.

On top of the cylinder cover there is an aluminium housing. This tightens against the cover and contains the fuel valve, high-pressure pipe connections, also the cooling oil and drain pipes, from which

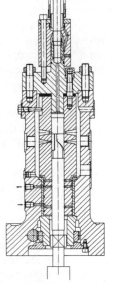

Figure 11.41 Fuel pump section

any possible oil leakage is drained. The high-pressure pipe is surrounded by an oil-tight flexible hose, from which any possible leakage is drained away at the fuel pump. By removing the small cover on the top of the housing, also the high-pressure pipe and the valve retainer nuts, the fuel valve can be withdrawn through the cooling oil connection piece without having to loosen these connections.

The fuel pump, Figure 11.41, is of the usual type, with regulation by helices at the upper end of the plunger. By rotating the latter, the position of the helices in relation to the bores in the cylinder is changed. The connection to the governor is obtained by a rack and pinion arrangement at the base of the housing. Fuel enters the annular space between the housing and the cylinder, whereby the cylinder and the plunger are maintained at an even temperature, thus ensuring a constant clearance. The cylinder is secured to the top flange of the housing by studs and is located by a spigot. Shims between the cylinder and the flange permit adjustment of the beginning of injection and the magnitude of the firing pressure.

The rounded ends of the high-pressure pipe tighten directly on the top flange, to which it is clamped by means of the conical topped bush. This bush is so dimensioned that the tightening produces a firm but not too hard a grip on the fuel pipe, which is thereby supported against vibration. Figure 11.41 shows the mode of drainage from the protecting hose around the high-pressure pipe.

The tightening arrangement provided against fuel oil seepage to the lubricating oil has no seal and, therefore requires no maintenance. The fuel oil that leaks between plunger and cylinder is led back to the annular fuel space from the upper groove. Below, there are two other grooves; the lower is connected to the lubricating oil system and the other to the fuel oil drainage system. As the distance between the two grooves is slightly greater than the stroke of the plunger, and as there is a higher pressure in the lower groove, it follows that no fuel oil can seep through this seal. As the clearance between plunger and cylinder is very small the loss of lubricating oil is negligible.

The fuel cams and the inlet and exhaust cams are fastened to the camshaft on conical bushings by the SKF hydraulic method.

Turbochargers

Figure 11.42 shows a section through the turbocharger designed by the Elsinore Shipbuilding and Engineering Co. specially for this engine. It has a single-stage radial flow blower driven by a single-stage axial flow turbine.

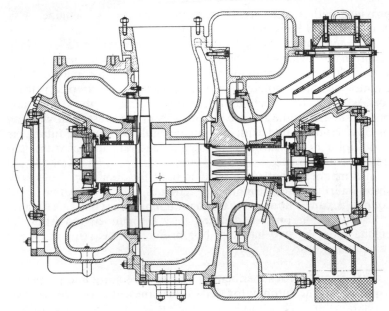

Figure 11.42 Section through turbocharger

The turbine disc is forged in one piece with the shaft, and the turbine blades are secured to the rotor by fir tree feet. The blower wheel is made of a high-strength aluminium alloy and is in two parts, namely, the radial wheel proper and pre-rotor, both of which are fastened to the shaft by splines. The shaft is carried in sleeve bearings at both ends and, at the blower end bearing, the axial forces are sustained by thrust bearings.

The leakage from spaces having pressure differences at the rotating parts is reduced by labyrinth packings. Those around the shaft take sealing air from the blower involute. The housings surrounding the exhaust gas spaces are water-cooled.

Manoeuvring

The medium-speed engines are not directly reversible, but are connected to a reversible reduction gear that drives a fixed-blade propeller or, alternatively, to a non-reversible reduction gear that drives a variable-pitch reversible propeller. With the latter arrangement an electric generator, large enough to provide all the necessary current at sea, may also be connected to the gear. For installations with more than one engine per propeller, the reduction gear is provided with a disengaging friction clutch for each engine. Also it usually has a built-in thrust bearing.

The requirements for governing and manoeuvring differ widely according to owners' specifications for ship and machinery services. For multi-engine installations, remote control for manoeuvring engines, flexible couplings, gearing, propellers and coupled generators is necessary. Such manoeuvring arrangements are usually pneumatic-hydraulic and are obtained from specialist firms working in close co-operation with the engine builder, gear manufacturer and shipbuilder, to meet the particular requirements for vessel and trading conditions.

In a manoeuvring system that is used for some types of cargo ships, starting and stopping of engines, also manoeuvring of couplings, can be done in the engine room by three control handles.

The propeller pitch and speed may be manoeuvred from the engine room by two handles. For bridge manoeuvring there are two possibilities:

(i) Simultaneous manoeuvring of speed-setting and propeller-pitch over the combinator that adjusts these in a pre-determined relationship. This mode of operation is used only during manoeuvres in port or in restricted waters where manoeuvres can be expected. The generator is electrically disconnected during the operation.

(ii) Manoeuvring of propeller pitch only. This mode is used when sailing in free waters, with constant engine speed set in the engine room, the generator being disconnected.

The speed governors are of the Woodward PG type with pneumatic speed setting that, when both engines are working, is adjusted over a common pressure regulating valve. The speed setting membrane and the speed droop of the governor are accurately adjusted so that an even load sharing is obtained.

At constant engine speed the load on the engines may vary considerably, due to sea and wind. Accordingly, warning lamps are lighted on the bridge when the load exceeds a predetermined fuel regulating setting. If the warnings continue for too long or are too frequent, the propeller pitch should be reduced. There is also a fuel stop to prevent excessive loading.

In some installations the Woodward PG-L types of governor have been used for the simultaneous regulation of engine speed and propeller pitch, to maintain constant power irrespective of the instantaneous torque-speed characteristic of the propeller.

465

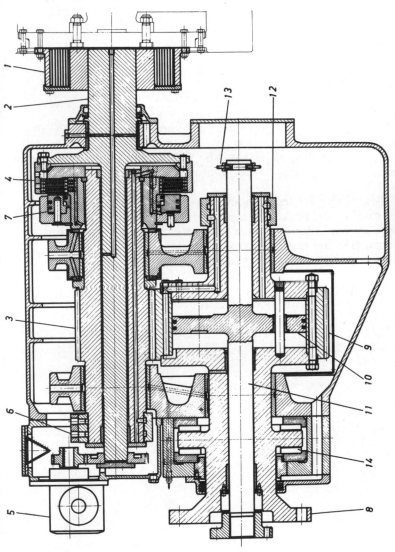

Figure 11.43 Reduction and Manoeuvring gear, variable pitch propellers

Reduction Gear for Variable Pitch Propellers

The gear that is shown in Figure 11.43 is used with the Burmeister and Wain Alpha T and U23HU engines, through an elastic coupling (1) it is connected to the drive shaft (2) that runs through the pinion quill shaft (3) and connects to the wet multiple disc clutch (4).

On its left end the quill shaft drives, through a stepping-up gear, an oil pump (5) that draws from the gear sump and provides oil pressure for lubrication and manoeuvring of the gear. The pinion shaft that is integral with the pinion is supported in two bearings and carries the clutch on its right end.

The clutch is, by a slide valve, manoeuvred by pressure oil that flows through the distribution ring (6) and the bores in the pinion shaft, to be brought to bear on the appropriate side of the clutch piston (7). The pinion drives the output shaft (8) through the gear rim (9).

The cylinder for the manoeuvring piston for the propeller (10) is formed by the flanges on the output shaft and the gear rim. The manoeuvring piston is connected to the propeller blades through the rod (11) and is manoeuvred by pressure oil through the distributor ring (12) and the bores in the left shaft part and the gear rim. The manoeuvring piston is kept in the desired position by a feedback connection (13) to the manoeuvring slide valve, not shown. Manoeuvring of both slide valves is done remotely from the wheel house.

The thrust bearing (14) is of the Glacier pivoted path type and has its collar integral with the shaft. The oil system has its own cooler, filter and spare pump.

S.H.

PIELSTICK ENGINES

When marine engineers refer to the Pielstick engine, they have in mind the PC2 type, which is built under licence in France, Germany, Sweden, Finland, Japan, U.S.A. and the U.K. The licensors, Société d'Etudes de Machines Thermiques (S.E.M.T.), include in their design range the PA type, which is a high-speed series of engines used for rail traction, power generation and, to a lesser extent, for marine propulsion.

This Chapter covers the PC type, including the PC2 and the later design of larger bore and stroke, the PC3. The latter extends the PC power range up to 12 600 kW immediately and higher powers will become available from continuing development. The engines are turbocharged, intercooled, four-stroke; their characteristics are given in Table 11.8

Table 11.8 GENERAL CHARACTERISTICS

		PC2	PC2.5	PC3
Bore		400 mm	400 mm	480 mm
Stroke		460 mm	460 mm	520 mm
Maximum continuous power		368 kW/cyl	480 kW/cyl	626 kW/cyl
Corresponding	rev/min	520	520	460
	Mean piston speed	8 m/s	8 m/s	8 m/s
	Brake mean pressure	14·7 bar	19·1 bar	17·3 bar
Number of cylinders, in-line engines		6, 8, 9	6, 8, 9	—
Number of cylinders, V-engines		8, 10, 12, 14, 16, 18	8, 10, 12, 14, 16, 18	12, 14, 16, 18

The design gives a high power-to-weight ratio and a high power-to-space ratio as illustrated by Table 11.9.

The power ratings are developed under CIMAC reference conditions as follows:

Ambient temperature	20°C
Ambient pressure	736 mm Hg
Relative ambient humidity	60 per cent
The air cooler inlet water temperature to be	20°C

For conditions other than these, power ratings are fixed by reference to the engine manufacturer.

Table 11.9 POWER TO WEIGHT/SPACE RATIOS

Engine types	A	B	C	D	E	Approx. weight of bare engine*
	m	m	m	m	m	Tonne
6PC2L	6·565	3·30	1·776	2·10	2·910	34·4
8PC2L	8·347	3·063	1·794	2·10	2·910	44·0
9PC2L	9·087	3·063	1·794	2·10	2·910	49·2
8PC2V	4·905	2·775	3·28	3·75	2·765	38·0
10PC2V	5·841	3·018	3·52	3·75	2·765	46·2
12PC2V	6·581	3·018	3·52	3·75	2·765	54·4
14PC2V	7·31	3·018	3·52	3·75	2·765	61·5
16PC2V	8·061	3·85	3·52	3·75	2·765	68·5
18PC2V	8·80	3·85	3·52	3·75	2·765	76·0
12PC3V	8·288	4·26	3·66	3·90	3·67	110·0
14PC3V	9·148	4·26	3·66	3·90	3·67	125·0
16PC3V	10·00	4·26	3·66	3·90	3·67	140·0
18PC3V	10·868	4·26	3·66	3·90	3·67	160·0

*Standard engine without flywheel and driven pumps. Gearbox excluded.
Note. All engines are now normally fitted with two turbochargers with the exception of the 6PC2L engine which has one.

PC2L engines

Minimum height for withdrawing pistons

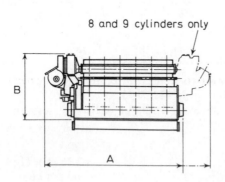

8 and 9 cylinders only

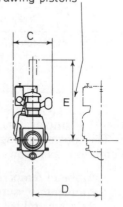

PC2V and PC3V engines

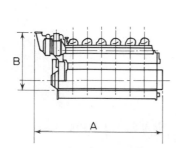

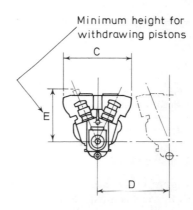

Minimum height for
withdrawing pistons

All ratings in Tables 9, 10(a) and 10(b) are available, using light
or marine diesel fuel and heavy fuel up to 860 centistokes (3500 sec
Redwood No. 1).

Table 11.10(a) RATING OF IN-LINE ENGINES — PC2 RANGE

		Engine type:	6PC2L	8PC2L	9PC2L
	Number of cylinders:		6	8	9
		rev/min	kW	kW	kW
Maximum continuous rating and engine speed		350	1 600	2 150	2 410
		400	1 900	2 530	2 840
		450	2 010	2 680	3 010
		465	2 050	2 730	3 180
		520	2 200	2 940	3 310

Table 11.10(b) RATING OF V-ENGINES — PC2 RANGE

	Engine type:	8PC2V	10PC2V	12PC2V	14PC2V	16PC2V	18PC2V
Number of cylinders:		8	10	12	14	16	18
	rev/min	kW	kW	kW	kW	kW	kW
Maximum	350	2 150	2 680	3 220	3 760	4 280	4 840
continuous	400	2 530	3 160	3 800	4 430	5 060	5 680
rating and	450	2 680	3 350	4 030	4 690	5 350	6 020
engine	465	2 740	3 420	4 100	4 800	5 460	6 150
speed	520	2 940	3 680	4 410	5 150	5 880	6 600
PC2·5	520	3 820	3 780	5 750	6 750	7 650	8 600

Table 11.11 RATING OF V-ENGINES—PC3 RANGE*

Engine type:		12PC3V	14PC3V	16PC3V	18PC3V
Number of cylinders:		12	14	16	18
	rev/min	kW	kW	kW	kW
Maximum continuous	400	7 380	8 610	9 840	11 070
rating and engine speed	460	8 400	9 800	11 200	12 060

*There is no 'in-line' version of the PC3 range.

Construction

Figure 11.44 shows a cross-section of the 'V' engine and a longitudinal view is illustrated in Figure 11.45.

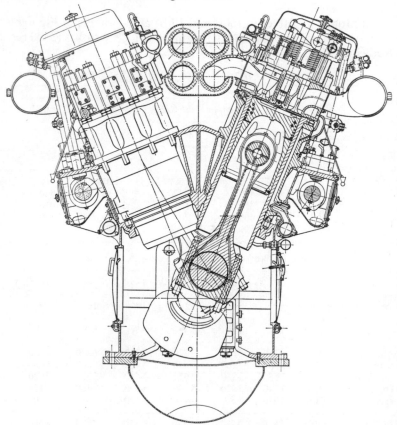

Figure 11.44 Section of V-type engine—PC2V400

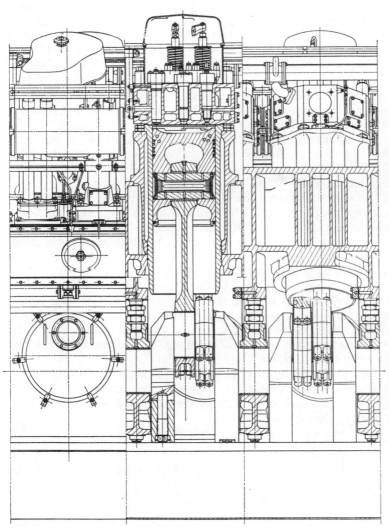

Figure 11.45 Longitudinal section of V-type engine—PC2V400

The main frame is of all-welded construction, built up from steel plate, steel castings and steel forgings, *see* Figure 11.46. All welded joints have prepared edges and are located in regions of low stress. This remark applies particularly to the welds which carry direct loads which are carefully designed to be easily executed and inspected. The main bearings are carried in the frame by bearing housings secured by long through-studs, forming an underslung design which contains all stresses within the frame itself, *see* Figure 11.47. The design is such that conventional main bearing caps are provided on top of the crankshaft. They are readily removable upwards so that, once the engine has been assembled, inspection of bearings is dealt with in a normal manner. The bearings themselves are steel-backed thin-wall copper-lead, with a lead-tin overlay.

The crankshaft is a single-piece forging. Each balance weight is held by means of notches in the crank webs and by a jack screw. The latter is actually relieved of some of its load when the engine runs up to speed.

The connecting rods are H-section steel stampings in manganese–molybdenum steel. The bottom-end bearings are steel shells lined with copper-lead, with lead-tin oyerlay. The top-end bearings are phosphor-bronze bushes and the piston pins are fully floating.

The cylinder liners are of special cast-iron, giving exceptionally good wearing properties. Each cylinder has its own separate cast-iron water jacket, making for effective heat transfer in the cooling system and for easy replacement. Cooling water at no time comes into contact with the steel frame. The design is such that leakage of cooling water, should it occur, cannot result in water entering the crankcase: nor can any possible leakage of oil from the crankcase enter the cooling water.

The cylinder heads are of cast-iron. Each head has four valves, i.e. two inlet and two exhaust. The exhaust valves are housed in water-cooled cages which can be easily removed and replaced, without disturbing the cylinder heads.

Three types of exhaust valve may be fitted.

1. Orthodox narrow-seat valve.
2. 'Rotocap' wide-seat valve which is automatically turned through about 15° each time the valve lifts.
3. Water-cooled wide-seat valve.

Type 1 is intended for use with light fuels, including marine diesel.

Type 2 is intended for use with heavy fuel in which the vanadium content does not exceed 150 parts per million.

Type 3 is designed for fuel having more than 150 parts per million of vanadium.

Figure 11.46 Main frame
of V-type engine

All three have seats with hard facings of Stellite type, which can be remachined with a diamond tool in a lathe and eventually can be recoated.

The pistons, Figure 11.48, are of aluminium alloy and are cooled

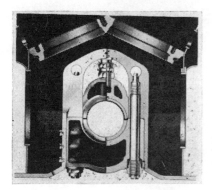

Figure 11.47 Main bearing arch—V-type engine

Figure 11.48 Piston

by the circulation of oil under pressure from the lubricating oil system of the engine. Figure 11.49 shows the route taken by this cooling oil. It is conducted from the connecting rod bottom-end up a passage into the rod and so into the piston pin through passages in the piston pin, thence to the cooling coil in the piston. Starting at one piston boss and circulating around the ring belt, the oil returns to the other piston boss. Having again passed through passages in the piston pin, it is returned down the rod by a passage similar to the one by which it ascended, and is thus discharged at the bottom

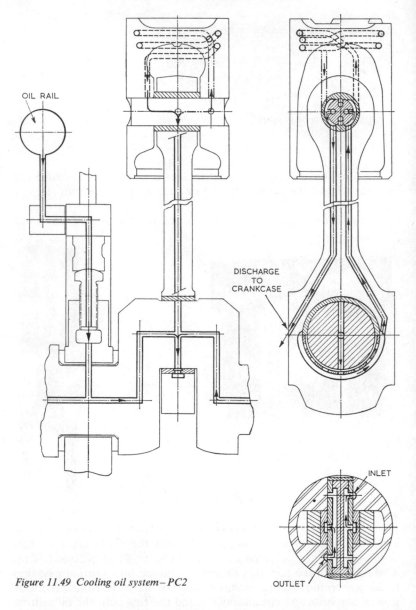

OIL RAIL

DISCHARGE
TO
CRANKCASE

INLET

Figure 11.49 Cooling oil system– PC2

OUTLET

end. By these means, an excessive amount of oil in the bottom of
the cylinder liner is avoided and the inertia effects of the columns of
oil in the rod cancel each other out. This method of cooling gives an

exceptionally low piston-ring temperature, maintaining conditions under which the rings can be easily lubricated. The top compression-ring groove is armoured with a cast-iron insert. There are four compression rings and two scraper rings.

Fuel-injection System

The pumps are of conventional jerk type, with metering helix. Each fuel pump is located close to the cylinder, so that a short fuel pipe connects it to the injector. This pipe is of double-wall construction, so that any leakage takes place outside of the cylinder-head covers. The injectors are of conventional differential spindle form and are water-cooled down to the tip of the nozzle.

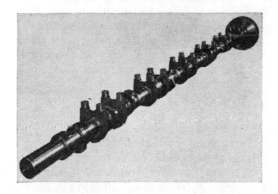

Figure 11.50 Camshaft of V-type engine

The fuel pumps and cylinder-head valves for each bank of cylinders are operated by a camshaft. This is located about the mid-height of the cylinders, at the top of the frame. This camshaft, Figure 11.50, is carried in bearings bolted directly to the fuel pumps, thus relieving the camshaft chamber of all pumping loads. The camshaft can be removed sideways from the engine, without disturbing either the valve gear or the fuel pumps.

Starting and Reversing

The engines are either unidirectional or direct-reversing. Reversing is accomplished by moving the camshaft axially, using hydraulic power controlled by compressed-air signals from the engine control panel, or direct from the bridge. Starting is by means of compressed air, which is operated by the same lever that controls the reversing mechanism.

A speed-setting lever is pneumatically connected to the governor which controls the speed of the engine throughout the speed range. There is, in addition, an overspeed trip which would limit the maximum speed of the engine in an emergency. A fuel-setting control is also provided, by means of which the fuel delivered to the engine can be limited to any desired amount, from full-load to no-load.

Lubricating Oil System

Lubricating oil can be circulated around the engine, either by a gear-pump driven directly from the engine or by a separate motor-driven pump.

The lubricating oil supply for the system is normally contained in a separate tank. The oil is drawn from this tank by an oil delivery pump, which delivers it through a filter and cooler to the main lubricating oil distribution manifolds on the frame. A pipe supplies lubricating oil to each bearing through the main-bearing cap jacking screw. This oil finds its way through bored holes in the crankshaft to the main bearings and the connecting-rod bottom-end bearings, up the connecting rod to the top-end bushes and finally to the piston-cooling arrangement: as previously described. The oil returns via the top-end bushes and the drilled passages in the connecting rod, eventually to find its way to the engine sump.

A branch system for lubricating oil is situated at the coupling end of the engine. This subsidiary system feeds oil to the outer thrust-bearing, and to all bearings of the gear train and pump drives.

Another branch system supplies oil to the camshaft at low pressure, which is obtained by the introduction into the pipe-line of a reducing valve or an orifice protected by a fine filter.

On many engines the valves and valve rockers are lubricated from a system which is independent of and sealed from the main system. Oil is pumped around this circuit from an engine mounted tank by a pump which is either engine or electric motor driven. A stand-by motor/pump set is normally supplied with the engine.

The tank is maintained at a minimum level by a float-controlled valve which takes filtered oil from the main system. An alarm is actuated by a high-level switch in the tank to indicate water leakage contaminating the oil.

A lubricating oil pressure-control valve, which can be adjusted by hand, enables the operator to set the oil pressure in the main system distribution manifold to the required figure of about 5·5 bar. A thermostatic diversion valve is also fitted to the oil system, to ensure quick warming up of the oil on starting. The valve also controls the oil temperature under varying load conditions.

The bearings of the turbocharger have their own self-contained lubricating oil system. There are some points on the engine, in particular the control linkage and the injection pump racks, which are lubricated by means of grease supplied through grease cups or nipples.

The engine is provided, in the lubricating oil system, with a low-pressure alarm which is connected to a shut-down device. This comes into operation if the lubricating oil pressure drops to a figure which may lead to bearing damage.

Cooling Water System

The engine can be provided with both circulating and raw-water pumps driven direct from the engine; as an alternative, motor-driven pumps can be used.

The engine is cooled by a closed fresh-water system. The fresh-water circulating pump supplies water to the engine after the water has passed through a heat exhanger. A vent and make-up tank is incorporated in the system. There is a water inlet connection for each cylinder, the water circulating between the jacket casting and the liner. From there, the water passes through an external pipe into the cylinder head; thence it flows to the outlet manifold. The exhaust-valve cages are cooled by a branch system; each valve cage is provided with a connection which receives water from the cylinder head and returns it to the cylinder head. A thermostatic diversion valve is provided in the cooling water system to ensure quick warming up during starting. The valve also has the purpose of controlling the cooling water temperature under varying load conditions.

Small pipes are led from the high points of the cylinder jacket and the cylinder head to connect with the high-level water manifold. This arrangement ensures good venting of the water spaces.

A fresh-water branch system is provided for the turbochargers. The air coolers associated with the turbochargers are sea-water cooled. If the water outlet temperature from the engine rises above the normal limit, an automatic alarm gives warning, with eventual shut-down.

Oil Fuel System

The oil fuel system is so arranged that the engine is able to operate on either distillate fuel or heavy fuel. When the engine operates on distillate fuel, the fuel is usually supplied by gravity or by a motor-driven booster pump.

When heavy fuel is burned, distillate fuel is also made available;

this is primarily intended for use during the starting and warming-up periods, after which the engine is changed over to heavy fuel for normal continuous operation. It is also usual for distillate fuel to be used for a short time immediately before shutting down the engine, thus ensuring that all pipe-lines and working parts in the fuel pumps and injectors are cleared of residues.

When the engine is operated on distillate fuel, the fuel is supplied through a three-way change-over valve to a mixing vessel. From the mixing vessel there is a gravity feed to an electric motor-driven booster pump which delivers the fuel through duplex filters to the main fuel rail. From the rail, the individual injection pumps are supplied. At the end of the main fuel rails there are pre-set orifice plates which determine that the main rails are completely full of fuel, thereby ensuring that the injection pumps are completely filled before each pump stroke. Excess fuel from the main rails is led by a return pipe to the mixing vessel.

After the engine has been started on distillate fuel it is desirable to change over to heavy fuel as soon as possible. To facilitate this, the engine cooling water and lubricating oil systems are fitted with thermostatically-controlled diversion valves which prevent any cooling until the systems have reached the correct operating temperature. This ensures the rapid warming up of the engine to a temperature which is consistent with running satisfactorily on heavy fuel.

The heavy-fuel service tank is usually fitted with a steam-heating coil inside the tank, and also a heater in the delivery pipe. Both heaters may be supplied with steam during the initial period when running on distillate fuel and before the engine is actually started. The engine can be started and run on heavy fuel, provided the fuel is kept at the correct operating temperature before the fuel-injection pumps.

When steam is being used for heating the fuel, and the engine has reached normal operating temperature, the steam is supplied to the final fuel line heater, to the jackets of the fuel filter, and to the engine main fuel rails. When this has been done, the change-over valves can be turned to heavy-fuel operation. In this condition heavy fuel is supplied by gravity from a service tank to the mixing vessel. From the mixing vessel the fuel flows by gravity to the electric-motor-driven booster pump; from there it proceeds, under pressure, through the line heater and filter and so to the engine. Excess fuel is returned to the mixing vessel.

When heavy fuel is used the necessary treatment plant for ensuring cleanliness of the fuel before it enters the engine system must be provided.

Injector Cooling System

The fuel injectors are cooled with fresh water taken from the main cooling water system. The water is cooled before use by passing it through an auxiliary heat exchanger. The cooling water outlets from the injectors are led away individually to a tank so that a visible return-flow can be observed. If operation is intended to include starting from cold on heavy fuel, this system includes thermostatically controlled heaters.

Supercharging

A turbocharger or turbochargers, according to the size of the engine, supplies the cylinders with fresh air at a pressure exceeding atmospheric pressure.

The intake air is first compressed by a centrifugal blower operated by a turbine which is driven by part of the energy of the exhaust gases expanding in the turbine. The centrifugal blower and the gas turbine are keyed on the same shaft, so as to constitute an independent machine. The turbocharger is therefore not mechanically connected to the drive shaft of the engine. The supercharging system is self-controlling, the speed of the turbocharger adjusting itself in accordance with the power required from the engine.

The turbocharger is mounted at the end of the engine on a special fabricated steel bracket bolted to the engine frame. One turbocharger is used per bank of cylinders. In early versions of the sixteen- and eighteen-cylinder engines in V form, four turbochargers were employed.

The turbocharger has its own lubricating system and is cooled by water which is by-passed from a feeder connected to the engine cooling water system. The air delivered to the engine by the turbocharger is cooled before reaching the intake manifold. The air cooler is therefore connected between the blower outlet and the intake manifold. Sea water is used for the turbocharger air cooler, because this water should be as cold as possible to ensure a steady supply of freshly cooled air to the engine cylinders.

It is not uncommon for the turbochargers to be fitted with water-washing equipment on either the turbine or compressor, or both. It is usually necessary to use this equipment frequently (at intervals of between 40 and 400 hours, depending upon the load-cycle and the environment) as it is ineffective if deposits in the turbocharger are allowed to become heavy. If water-washing of the compressor is used, the effect on fouling of the air side of the intercooler needs to be watched.

Specific Fuel Consumption and Range of Operation

The specific fuel consumption of PC2 engines in relation to the power per cylinder and the revolutions is shown in Figure 11.51. The nett calorific value of the fuel is 42 900 kJ/kg.

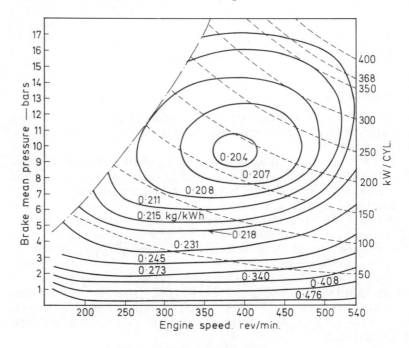

Figure 11.51 Iso-consumption lines

The fuel consumption at full-load is about 0·214 kg/kW h. The minimum consumption is in the neighbourhood of 0·204 kg/kW h (0·330 lb/bhp h), and the speed range that can be covered in full-fuel notch position extends from full-speed down to about 70 per cent of full-speed. This can be an advantage in ships propelled by two engines coupled to one shaft, as it is possible, by running on one engine, to keep the specific consumption down to about the same amount as that under full-load while slowing the speed of the ship to less than half-speed. This is shown in Figure 11.52.

Figure 11.52 also shows the operating range over which one engine can be allowed to run, the ship speed being reduced to only 70–75 per cent of full-speed. With a variable-pitch propeller, the regular service speed when running on one engine alone is about 80 per cent of the speed obtained on two engines.

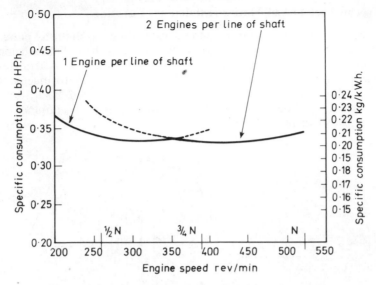

Figure 11.52 Specific fuel consumption, two engines per shaft

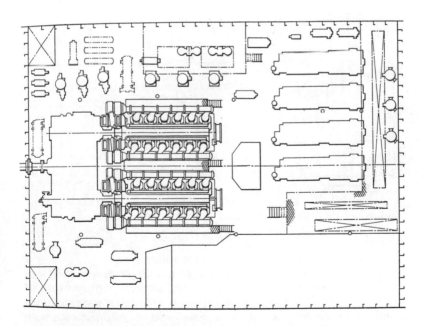

Figure 11.53 Geared arrangement of V-type engines—plan view

Typical Examples of Marine Installations

The PC engine has been used in many propelling installations, either as a single-engine unit or as a multi-engined gear drive. One scheme of particular interest and merit is the two-engined geared arrangement shown typically at Figures 11.53 and 11.54. This arrangement is the one most often favoured with medium-speed heavy-duty engines. Couplings of all kinds are now used, often in conjunction with disc or drum clutches.

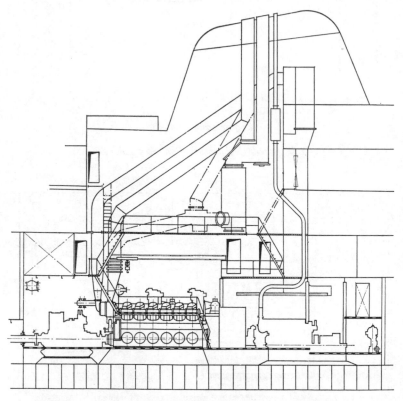

Figure 11.54 Geared arrangement of V-type engines—cross-section

The scheme with two engines on one shaft increases safety in operation because, with only one engine running, a proportion of power is still available and the vessel can proceed at a speed reduced to only 70 or 75 per cent of full-speed, or to only 80 per cent with variable-pitch propellers.

The use of clutch couplings, with the two engines turning in contrary direction, gives an excellent means of manoeuvring in and out of port. The propeller can be coupled, at will, to one or other of the engines, one of which has been started ahead and the other astern. There is thus no need for compressed-air starts or for repeated moving of the camshafts.

The PC engine has been successfully used for twin-screw installations having two engines geared to each shaft as in Figure 11.55. With such an installation, sets of engines developing an aggregate power of more than 50 000 kW can be offered.

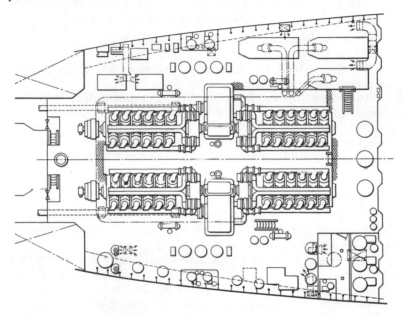

Figure 11.55 Twin-screw arrangement, 20 000 shp total

Auxiliary Generating Equipment

In many installations it is sound policy to fit generators of considerable power to the free ends of the main engines, or to the high-speed shafts of the reduction gears. These generators can be switched into the ship's circuit when 'full away'. If the engines have clutch couplings the generators can be used to provide current for pumps or other machinery, thus reducing significantly the installed power of the ship's generating sets and obtaining the savings consequent upon the reduction of installation, maintenance and running costs.

Maintenance

The maintenance of the PC engine is greatly facilitated by the light weight of most moving parts, and the ease with which they can be removed.

In recent years, much attention has been given to improving ease of handling and maintenance. PC engines can now be fitted with hydraulic tightening of large-end and main bearing nuts, cylinder heads and PC2 main bearing jack-screws. The PC3 main bearing saddle is raised and lowered hydraulically for bearing inspection. The exhaust valves, which may be removed without taking down the cylinder head, can be taken out by hand by one man.

Typical maintenance periods are indicated below:

(a) Every 1000 to 1250 hours, replace fuel injectors, the injectors removed being reconditioned afterwards.

(b) Every 5000 or 6000 hours, replace exhaust valves, the valves removed being reconditioned afterwards.

(c) Every 10 000 or 12 000 hours, remove pistons and renew the top piston ring.

(d) Every 20 000 hours examine large-end and main bearings, and renew all piston rings.

In propulsion installations which comprise several engines it is possible to carry out maintenance without stopping the working of the ship, assuming that it can be done during a period when full power does not have to be used.

Some owners work on a progressive maintenance system of two cylinders at a time, while others carry out an annual survey of one cylinder bank of one engine. Others, again, simply overhaul two complete engines after a fixed number of running hours.

The scheme adopted depends largely on the type of duty and the consequent working schedule of the ship. Where operation is with unmanned engine-room, maintenance becomes a shore-based and carefully planned function.

D.C.

RUSTON AND HORNSBY ENGINES

The present state of development of the turbocharged medium-speed engine allows powers in the region of 375 kW per cylinder to be obtained. From single units having up to eighteen cylinders in V-form, powers up to 6000 kW are available. Single-shaft powers up to 15 000 kW can be provided by coupling two or more engines through appropriate reduction gearing. Design techniques have been evolved which ensure successful operation on residual fuels up to 0·85 mm²/s (3500 sec) viscosity without excessive maintenance requirements.

In the near future powers up to 15 000 kW will be available from a single unit. Both two-stroke cycle and four-stroke cycle engines are currently available to operate at speeds in the range 400–600 rev/min, and at brake mean effective pressures up to 1·03 bar for two-stroke engines, and up to 1·73 bar for four-stroke engines.

The application of medium-speed geared propulsion systems offers a number of advantages in comparison with direct-coupled engines of powers up to 15 000 kW. These advantages receive attention in the succeeding paragraphs. The machinery room spaces are necessarily arranged to suit the engine requirements.

Capital Cost

The medium-speed geared propulsion machinery, comprising engine and gearbox, at present available, can show a saving in first-cost of 4–5 pounds sterling per horse-power over an equivalent slow-speed engine. There is also a reduction in the weight and space requirements of the geared system allowing a slightly smaller ship to be built for the same cargo-carrying capacity and service speed, with a corresponding reduction in the propulsive power and in the capital cost for the complete vessel.

Fuel Consumption

A specific fuel consumption of 0·212 kg/kW h is available with present-day medium-speed engines, compared with a consumption of 0·200 kg/kW h in the slow-speed engine.

The losses associated with gearing are approximately 2 per cent. The various forms of slip-coupling which can, but need not, be employed, account for a further loss of 2–3 per cent.

The consumption of lubricating oil in the medium-speed machinery is in the order of twice that for the slow-speed engine.

The medium-speed system has a distinct advantage in that the propeller speed can be arranged to suit ship operating conditions regardless of engine revolutions. The propeller revolutions for the slow-speed engine are essentially a compromise, to suit the engine revolutions. For the geared system, by a suitable design of propeller, a higher propulsive efficiency can be achieved, which more than compensates for the transmission losses, and the higher fuel and lubricating oil consumptions.

Maintenance

The length of life of the components in the slow- and medium-speed engines is about the same. Detailed comparisons of routine maintenance schedules for equivalent direct-coupled and geared installations indicate that maintenance man-hour requirements are approximately equal. That is, the overhauling of the larger number of components comprising the geared units is offset by their smaller size and the ease of handling them.

The cost per unit for spares replacements, resulting from quantity production, ensures for the medium-speed engine an overall lower spares cost. The medium-speed engine also lends itself more favourably to partial repair by replacement of complete component sub-assemblies. This feature is likely to show increasing economies in the future, due to the reluctance of ship-board personnel to undertake maintenance work.

Available statistical information suggests that the reliability of medium-speed machinery does not suffer in the ratio of the increased number of parts. In fact, the number of failures per component is reduced by comparison with the slow-speed engine, and this offsets the increased number of components at risk. Reliability of the geared system is further improved where two or more engines are coupled to a single propeller shaft, as with this arrangement maximum flexibility in operation can be achieved under all conditions of ship loading.

THE RUSTON AO TYPE ENGINE

Characteristics

An example of an engine, of most recent design, which is eminently suitable for large vessel propulsion, is the Ruston Type AO engine.

This two-stroke cycle engine is a trunk-piston, valve-in-head, through-scavenge, pressure-charged and intercooled design. As an in-line engine it is available in six, eight and nine cylinders. In the V form it is built with twelve and sixteen cylinders.

The engine is directly reversible and has been designed and developed for operation on residual fuels.

All the engines have a common bore and stroke, namely 362 mm by 470 mm. The continuous rating of the engine, when running on residual fuel oils with viscosities up to 0.85 mm^2/s (3500 sec Redwood No. 1 at 100°F) is 375 kW per cylinder at a brake mean effective pressure of 1.03 bar and 450 rev/min, thus giving a power range of 2250–6000 kW from single units.

Overall Dimensions

The overall dimensions of the various cylinder combinations are stated in Table 11.12. In Figures 11.56(a) and (b) typical performance data are shown. The range is 100–450 rev/min, and the basis is a propeller law. A cross-sectional arrangement of the sixteen-cylinder engine is illustrated in Figure 11.57.

Table 11.12 DIMENSIONS OF RUSTON AO ENGINES

Engine size	Continuous hp output 450 rev/min kW brake	Overall length bare engine mm	Height above crank c/l mm	Overall height mm	Max. width over engine mountings mm	Approx. dry weight bare engine tonne
6AO	2 240	4 750	2 580	4 000	1 870	34·5
8AO	2 980	5 512	2 835	4 460	1 870	45·7
9AO	3 360	6 050	2 580	4 250	1 870	50·8
12AO	4 480	5 210	2 824	4 380	1 793	53·9
16AO	5 960	6 290	2 824	4 380	1 793	68·1

Design Structure

The main structure is formed by cast-steel members extending axially one cylinder pitch and joined together by welding on transverse planes through each cylinder centre-line. The structure is closed by a separate bracing member in a plane parallel to the crankshaft axis and bolted between the lower extremities of the main structure. This member forms an integral part of the engine sump and is extended to form mounting point attachments, a feature which removes the disadvantage of poor accessibility normally associated with an underslung crankshaft arrangement. Crankshaft removal in service is accomplished by lowering the shaft on to the bracing member, which remains on the engine seating and takes the place of a bedplate in the alternative design.

The design allows an air chest of ample proportions to be incorporated readily and, because of the disposition of the structural members, allows close proximity of engine cylinders without air-port masking, a factor which has contributed to the short overall length of the engine.

The crankshaft is supported in detachable bearing caps bolted to the main structure at the lower extremities of members, which also carry cylinder-head attachment loads. These members react firing loads directly. In addition, the structure incorporates a system of interconnected diagonal members in planes parallel and perpendicular to the crankshaft axis. These members impart a high degree

488

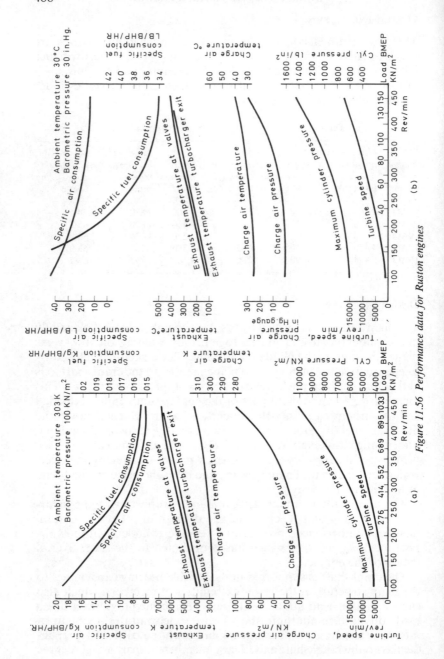

Figure 11.56 Performance data for Ruston engines

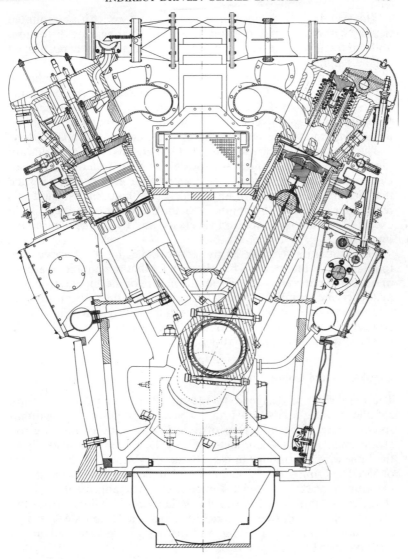

Figure 11.57 Cross-section of AO engine

of torsional rigidity. This rigidity reacts torque-loading applied normally to the crankshaft axis and produces load-sharing between members associated with several cylinders when a particular cylinder is acted on by firing loads.

The AO engine, because of its rigid structure, can be mounted flexibly without the risk of producing abnormal bearing distortion, and this feature relaxes the requirement for an accurately positioned engine seating.

Because of the discrete nature of each load-carrying member in the frame, loads are introduced and transferred to reaction points without having to diffuse into, or concentrate out of, plate sections. Maximum-to-mean stress approaches unity, giving high material utilisation; and the design eliminates stress concentrations entirely.

The method of fabrication adopted has ensured that all welds are ideal butt welds occurring at sections of constant area where stresses can be accurately predicted. The design of the engine frame is such that the maximum stress in any weld is less than 300 bar, and this feature ensures that the engine will have a definite fatigue life in excess of ten thousand million reversals, or 25 years of continuous operation.

The structure is completed by removable skins which serve only to retain fluids and noise. This allows a further advantage to accrue in respect of noise emission. From the nature of the engine structure, load-carrying members are disconnected from the outside surface, and the response of the latter to internal exciting forces is low. In addition, because the surface skin fulfils only a limited requirement, its efficiency as a sound radiator is closely controlled.

Crankshaft and Connecting Rods

The crankshaft is designed to Lloyds' Rules, and the maximum specific bearing-loads conform to present practice for medium-speed engines. The adoption of a fork-and-blade connecting-rod arrangement allows a compact engine to be achieved. It also allows the same air-port timings in each bank of cylinders, with a V angle of 55°. The firing order for each engine in the range has been chosen to ensure a satisfactory pulse sequence to the arrangement of turbochargers, without impairing engine balance and torsional vibration stability. The crankshaft is machined from a 55-ton steel; it is a continuous grain-flow forging, and the design represents advanced medium-speed engine practice.

For the fork connecting rod, a three-piece 55-ton steel forging, with horizontal split and inclined bolts, is employed. The blade rod is an automotive type, with a diagonal serrated joint between rod and cap. Both rods can be withdrawn through the respective cylinders. They are articulated to large-diameter hardened steel gudgeon-pins, fixed to the piston body.

Lead-bronze, steel-backed, bearings are utilised for the small ends and for the large-end of the blade connecting rod, the latter operating on hard chrome journals formed on the fork rod block. Overlay plated, steel-backed, copper-lead bearings are employed for other large-end and main bearings.

Pistons

The pistons are composite structures, each comprising a domed profile steel crown attached to a cast-iron skirt from the underside through the gudgeon-pin attachment. Three compression rings are housed at the upper extremity of the piston body. The crown is positively cooled by oil supplied and returned by a system of telescopic tubes. A positive oil-flow path within the piston crown, together with a geometrical heat carrier above the ring belt, ensures excellent cooling and contributes to the engine's ability to withstand high thermal loading.

One compression ring and two oil-control rings are fitted to the piston skirt and form a seal between the crankcase and the air chest.

Cylinder Liners

The liners are of single-piece design, cooled above the port belt. Separate cast-iron water jackets are located on the upper plate of the engine frame; they support the liners, which are additionally located in the upper and middle longitudinal plates of the frame.

Coolant is admitted to the water jackets and is deflected around the periphery at entry. Scalloped ports transfer the coolant from the liner to the cylinder head and ensure efficient cooling of the portion of the liner exposed to combustion.

Inlet ports are machined in each liner and provide all directional stability for the scavenge air. Chrome plating is applied to the running surface of the liners.

Cylinder Heads

Each main head structure, of cast iron, houses a steel flame plate, four exhaust valves and a central injector. Hard-faced valve seats are formed in the flame plate; these have separate cooling passages of closely controlled section, accurately positioned in close proximity to the seating surface. Each passage is connected by single radial port to a manifold formed between the periphery of the flame plate and the liner water jacket. After passing around the valve seats, coolant is first directed to a collecting duct formed around the injector boss and subsequently directed to the main body of the head.

The sectional area of the coolant passages around the valve seats is chosen to provide the optimum compromise between heat transfer and the absence of scale formation on the passage surface. There are no abnormal coolant requirements. The design construction does not employ high-pressure seals between flame plate and the main head structure; the parts are readily dismantled and assembled.

Four masked exhaust valves are incorporated in each head; they operate in dry valve guides.

In service the complete flame plate can be replaced more quickly than can conventional seat inserts. Due to the superior valve-seat cooling achieved, the requirement for seat reconditioning is considerably extended beyond that with conventional designs.

Under operating conditions the flame plate is sandwiched between the cylinder liner and the main head casting. The cylinder-head assembly is attached by four studs passing directly into the engine frame.

The valve-rocker housing, the cylinder head and the water jacket are designed to produce an even distribution of load at the seal face between the liner and the head. The design of the retaining studs ensures that the joint force is adequately maintained throughout combustion.

Valve Gear

Two exhaust valve cams per cylinder each operate a pair of valves through a conventional rocker and pushrod system. The camshaft is driven directly from the flywheel end of the engine, through a system of spur gears; it is supported along its length in discrete bearing blocks attached to the engine frame. These blocks house separate fuel pumps, and support the cam followers which operate the pushrods.

The valve cams are bolted together in pairs, one cam in each pair being for ahead running and the other for astern running. The fuel pump is actuated by the same cam for both directions of rotation.

Reversing is achieved by a lost-motion device which retards the camshaft and fuel cam relative to the crankshaft and moves the valve cam followers to cooperate with the separate cams which correspond to the respective directions of rotation.

Starting the engine is achieved by compressed air and starter valves in the cylinder heads. These are connected to a common manifold and are actuated by pressurised servo-air fed in the correct sequence to the valves by a distributor which is phased with the engine crankshaft. Starting air can be applied to the engine during reversing, to facilitate engine braking.

The complete engine system is designed to ensure that events in the starting, stopping and reversing cycles occur in definite sequence. Fuel cannot be admitted to the engine unless both crankshaft and camshaft are rotating in the selected direction, and the exhaust valve cam-shift actuator has moved to the position corresponding to the selected direction of engine rotation; also, unless the engine-oil pressure exceeds the predetermined limit.

Fuel Injection and Control Equipment

To accommodate inertia loadings at maximum operating speed, individual spring systems are incorporated in the tappets and in the fuel pumps.

Each fuel pump contains a double helix plunger and is actuated through a pushrod, by a barrel tappet, from the engine camshaft. An effective seal between the fuel pump and the camshaft chamber is provided on the pushrod to prevent contamination of the lubricating oil by fuel leakage. A constant-pressure delivery valve is incorporated at the outlet of the pump and a special design of conical seal is used at this point to contain high-pressure fuel. A through-flow of fuel is arranged in the pump supply circuit, to facilitate operation on residual fuels.

Fuel is discharged from the fuel pump to a cooled low-inertia fuel injector which delivers fuel directly into the combustion chamber. The injector is housed in a machined passage through the centre of the cylinder head and valve-rocker supports, and a seal is incorporated between these two components. Separate valve covers for each pair of valves and the arrangement of the fuel connections to the injectors ensures the isolation of fuel from lubricant in the cylinder-head assembly.

Pump-rack position, and hence fuel delivery, is controlled by a series of rotating links attached to a layshaft along the engine length. This layshaft, in turn, is actuated by a hydraulic governor located on the upper plate of the engine frame. The governor is shaft-driven from a spur and bevel-gear system engaging with a spur gear at the flywheel end of the engine crankshaft. The system allows for incorporation of shut-down safety devices and can be readily adapted to provide a series of alternative governing and control characteristics.

Turbocharger System

The engine is fitted with a simple turbocharger system and dispenses with any external air supply.

Four turbochargers operating on a pulse system are used on the

494

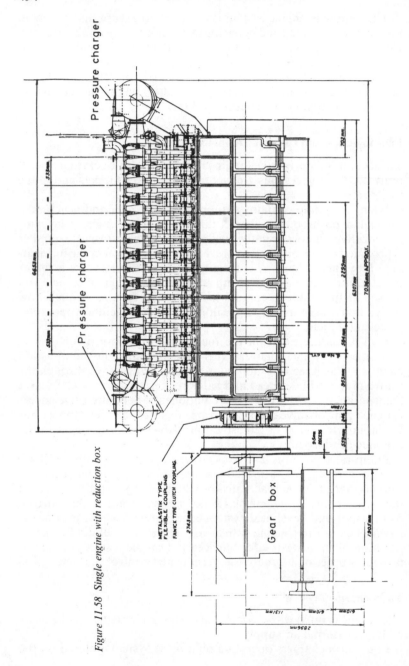

Figure 11.58 Single engine with reduction box

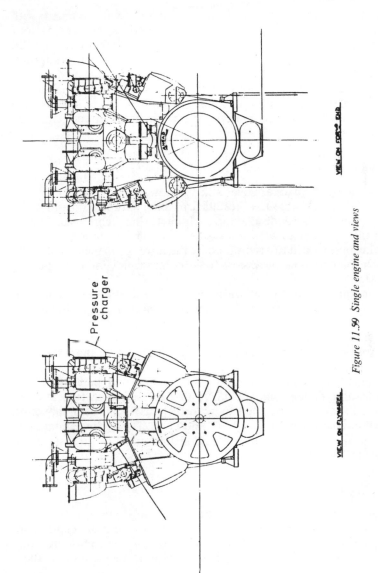

Pressure charger

VIEW ON FLYWHEEL

VIEW ON DRIVE END

Figure 11.59 Single engine and views

sixteen-cylinder engine, each turbocharger being supplied with exhaust gas by short pipes from four cylinders. Groups of four cylinders are also used on the eight-cylinder 'in-line' engine. All other engines in the range, however, have three-cylinder groupings.

Charge-air is fed to a common air chest, incorporated in the engine frame, through coolers mounted directly on the frame. The coolers are formed from standard stacks. Modified headers allow the arrangement to be accommodated within the cylinder banks on V-form engines.

Reduction Gearing

Reduction gearboxes are available for powers up to 15 000 kW per shaft input. Trouble-free results can be guaranteed from units employing the latest design and manufacturing techniques. Reduction ratios of 3:1 to 5:1 are in general use. These ratios can beneficially be extended to accommodate the lower propeller revolutions which may become necessary for obtaining maximum propulsive efficiency.

For single-engine installations, epicyclic and spur-gear reduction units are available, the former showing advantages to an increasing extent in cost, weight and space requirements, as powers and reduction ratios increase. Co-axial input and output shafts are a feature of the epicyclic gearbox and can also be achieved with more complex spur-gear units.

Figures 11.58 and 11.59 show a typical single-engine installation. The leading dimensions are shown in Table 11.13. A typical twin-engine installation, coupled to a parallel-shaft spur-gear reduction gearbox, is shown in Figures 11.60 and 11.61. The leading dimensions for various combinations of engine and gearbox are stated in Table 11.14.

Coupling Engine to Transmission

Where a single engine is utilised, direct coupling to the gearbox offers the simplest and cheapest solution. Where two or more engines are coupled to a single output shaft, a means of connecting and disconnecting the engine from the gearing is necessary to allow maximum flexibility in operation.

In both cases, to provide torsional stability in the overall driving and driven system throughout the operating speed range of the engine, adequate torsional flexibility is necessary. This is normally obtained by introducing a suitable coupling between the engine and the gearbox input.

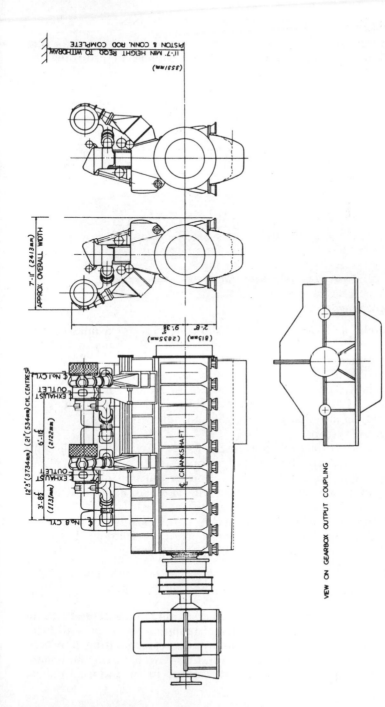

Figure 11.60 Twin engine with spur-gear reduction gearbox

Several forms of coupling are available which, when used either singly or in complementary pairs, are capable of providing the required operating characteristics.

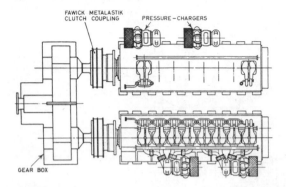

Figure 11.61 Twin engine with spur-gear reduction gearbox

Slip-couplings

Hydraulic and electromagnetic slip-couplings are available from fully proved designs. These combine torsional flexibility with ability to disconnect the engine from the transmission system. Both types are capable of allowing full-power engagement and disengagement indefinitely. They completely eliminate torsional resonance between driving and driven system, but they suffer from the disadvantage of relatively high initial cost, weight and bulk when compared with alternative systems.

There is a further inherent disadvantage associated with the slip-couplings, namely that, at full torque, slip between driving and driven components is necessary for power transmission and, under these conditions, energy is absorbed. Thus, an additional power transmission loss of about 3 per cent is incurred.

Variations are available which incorporate positive locking of the two components under continuous operating conditions, but additional penalties associated with first cost, weight and bulk are thereby incurred.

Elastic Couplings

Simple elastic couplings are available which can be adjusted to remove any undesirable torsional instability from single- and twin-engine geared systems. For a geared system incorporating more than two engines, a wide range of operating characteristics can occur, dependent upon the number of engines in operation. In these

Table 11.13 SINGLE RUSTON AO ENGINES AND GEARBOXES

Engine size	Power kW brake	kW shaft	Engine weight tonne	Gearbox weight tonne	Total weight tonne	Overall length mm	Overall width mm	Overall height mm	Height above crank c/l mm
6AO	2 240	2 130	34·5	9·1	43·7	7 080	2 410	4 000	2 580
8AO	2 980	2 830	45·7	10·2	55·9	8 150	2 410	4 460	2 835
9AO	3 360	3 190	50·8	10·2	61·0	8 750	2 410	4 250	2 580
12AO	4 480	4 270	53·9	12·2	66·1	8 060	3 050	4 380	2 824
16AO	5 960	5 660	68·1	13·2	81·3	9 150	3 050	4 380	2 824

Table 11.14 TWIN RUSTON AO ENGINES AND GEARBOXES

Engine arrangement two off	Power kW Brake	kW Shaft	Engine weight tonne	Gear-box weight tonne	Total weight tonne	Overall length mm	Overall width mm	Overall height mm	Height above crank c/l mm
2× 6AO	4 480	4 260	69·1	25·4	94·5	7 380	6 100	4 000	2 580
2× 8AO	5 960	5 660	91·4	28·4	119·8	8 450	6 100	4 460	2 835
2× 9AO	6 720	6 380	101·6	28·4	130·0	9 050	6 100	4 250	2 580
2×12AO	8 960	8 540	107·7	32·5	140 2	9 030	7 080	4 380	2 824
2×16AO	11 920	11 320	136·0	35·6	171·6	10 190	7 080	4 380	2 824

conditions the elastic coupling can have severe limitations. Where it is possible to use an elastic coupling, simplicity, compactness and low initial cost are achieved.

Friction Clutches

Where a disconnecting device is necessary this has to be provided in addition to torsional flexibility, and when a separate device has to be added to an elastic coupling the additional cost advantage is reduced although not eliminated. Disconnecting devices are available in the form of friction clutches variously actuated by hydraulic or pneumatic means.

When compared with slip-couplings, friction clutches in general are limited in respect of continuous full-power manoeuvring. Transmission of a continuous steady torque presents no problem. Designs exist where torsional flexibility is combined as a separate function, but in the same unit as a friction clutch. Because the friction clutch operates without slip, there is no associated transmission loss under continuous power transmission.

Manoeuvring Requirements

The selection of suitable coupling combinations is dependent largely on the method of manoeuvring and reversal adopted in any particular application. In single-engine installations, reversing is most economically achieved by reversing the engine in the case of a fixed-pitch propeller or with a variable-pitch propeller operated in astern pitch. In multi-engine systems a variable-pitch propeller can be used to achieve reversing.

With a fixed-pitch propeller, reversing can be achieved with direct reversing engines by operating one engine in the appropriate direction without using any form of disconnecting clutch, or by operating one engine ahead and one engine astern and engaging as necessary the appropriate disconnecting device.

Slip-couplings are ideally suited to manoeuvring operations, and no limitation need therefore be placed on powers and speeds used during manoeuvring. Friction clutches are limited in their power absorption capacity, but can accommodate in a twin-engine system unlimited manoeuvring at vessel speeds below one-half.

H.W.

DOXFORD ENGINE

The Doxford Seahorse geared engine has been developed jointly by Doxford and Sunderland Limited and Hawthorn Leslie (Engineers) Limited, who have formed for this purpose a new Company called Doxford Hawthorn Research Services Limited.

The engine is a two-stroke opposed piston design, with crosshead and diaphragm construction, suitable for burning heavy fuel and developing 2500 bhp (1840 kW)/cylinder at 300 rev/min. Engines can be built with from four to seven cylinders per unit; and up to four units can be geared to a single propeller shaft. Power outputs available are given in Table 11.15.

As indicated in Table 11.15, all powers from 10 000 to 70 000 bhp/shaft (i.e. 7350 to 50 000 kW) are covered in steps not greater than 25 per cent. Intermediate powers can be obtained by using three engines or, alternatively, by installing two 6-cylinder and two 7-cylinder engines.

The Seahorse engine is designed for ocean-going ships and, accordingly, no attempt has been made to reduce either the height or the specific weight to a level comparable with that of V four-stroke medium-speed engines specially intended for ferries, where low height is essential. But, against this, emphasis has been laid on robust reliability and on ability to burn heavy fuel in the relatively large

Table 11.15 POWER OUTPUTS

I. Single engine per propeller shaft

No. cylinders per engine	4	5	6	7
bhp, metric	10 000	12 500	15 000	17 500
kW equivalent	7 350	9 200	11 000	12 850

II. Two engines per propeller shaft

No. cylinders per engine	4	5	6	7
bhp, metric	20 000	25 000	30 000	35 000
kW equivalent	14 700	18 400	22 000	25 700

III. Four engines per propeller shaft

No. cylinders per engine	4	5	6	7
bhp, metric	40 000	50 000	60 000	70 000
kW equivalent	29 400	36 800	44 000	51 400

cylinder having a diaphragm construction which separates the combustion from the mechanical parts. Ease of maintenance is an important feature, resulting from the small number of cylinders.

Resulting from the vertical in-line arrangement of the engines, the gear centre distance between pairs of engines is only 3·6 metres. This is less than can be attained with V engines of comparable power.

The overall weights and dimensions of the Seahorse engine are given in Figure 11.62, which also shows the general arrangement of the engine. The principal characteristics of the engine will be clear from Table 11.16.

Construction

Propulsion engines often rely on the ship's structure for maintaining the alignment of the crankshaft. In heavy seas, this can result in distortion of the engine structure and crankshaft. Changes in ship loading can have a similar adverse effect. Moreover, because of its being attached to the cold double-bottom of the ship, the engine can be distorted as it warms-up to the running temperature.

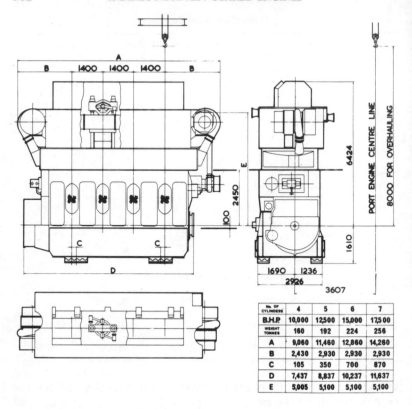

No. OF CYLINDERS	4	5	6	7
B.H.P.	10,000	12,500	15,000	17,500
WEIGHT TONNES	160	192	224	256
A	9,060	11,460	12,860	14,260
B	2,430	2,930	2,930	2,930
C	105	350	700	870
D	7,437	8,837	10,237	11,637
E	5,005	5,100	5,100	5,100

Figure 11.62 Overall dimensions of Doxford Seahorse engine

To avoid the difficulties arising from the causes named, the Seahorse engine has been designed to have an extremely rigid structure; also it is mounted on only four points, thus ensuring that bending of the ship does not affect the engine alignment.

The general construction of the engine can be seen from Figure 11.63, which shows a longitudinal section and also a cross-section. The bedplate is deep and its upper face on the camshaft side is raised above the crankshaft centre-line to ensure stiffness and to allow sufficient height in the bedplate for a man to stand for maintenance purposes. At the other side of the engine the top face of the bedplate is below the crankshaft centre-line, to permit easy access to the running gear. The main bearing keeps are very stiff steel castings. They are bolted to the bedplate, both vertically and horizontally, at back and front, to enable them to serve as substantial strength members, thus stiffening the crankcase structure.

Table 11.16 GENERAL DATA

Cylinder bore	580 mm
Piston stroke, lower piston	880 mm
upper piston	420 mm
total	1 300 mm
Bhp metric, (max. cont. rating) per cyl.	2 500
kW (max. cont. rating) per cyl.	1 840
Rev/min	300
Bmep	10·9 kg/cm^2 (10·7 bar)
Mip	12·0 kg/cm^2 (11·8 bar)
Max. cylinder pressure	106 kg/cm^2 (10·4 bar)
No. of cylinders per unit	4 to 7
Cylinder centres	1 400 mm
Crankpin dia. centre and side	520 mm
Crankshaft type	Semi-built with forged main webs and pins
Main journal diameter	840 mm
Centre connecting rod length, between centres	1 520 mm
Side connecting rod length, between centres	1 300 mm

On the top of the bedplate, at the back, there is bolted a box girder the heavy steel plate inner face of which forms the guide surface for the crosshead shoes. The girder also contains a balance shaft extending the length of the engine and driving the camshaft and the auxiliary blower. In addition there is located a large oil main from which lubricating oil is supplied for all necessary places and cooling oil for the lower pistons.

The front of the engine is closed-in by a girder structure to produce great stiffness, but at the same time to permit easy access through hinged doors to the running gear. Bolted to the top of the box girder at the back of the engine, and to this front column structure, there is a strong scavenge-air entablature which carries the cylinders and camshaft, and which serves, structurally, to complete the girder effect produced by bedplate and columns.

The entablature is fitted with a double bottom plate to form a cofferdam so that, in the event of a scavenge fire, heat is not transmitted to the crankcase. As seen in Figure 11.63, the inner plate slopes from both back and front of the engine, down to a gully above the inboard side of the guide structure, to provide good drainage and to simplify cleaning.

The four mounting feet for each engine are positioned to give minimum bending of the engine structure. They are of a patented design, with rubber inserts which permit expansion of the bedplate radially from a central point to maintain correct alignment in all

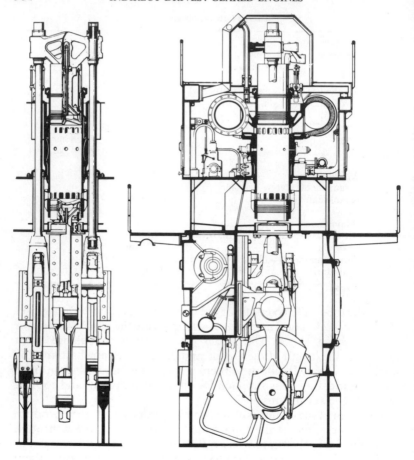

Figure 11.63 Sectional views of Doxford Seahorse engine

directions. They are not resilient mountings in the ordinary sense of the word because the stiffness of the mountings is very high in all directions except that in which expansion is allowed.

Running Gear

The crankshaft is semi-built and is made up of forged steel horseshoe pieces, comprising main crankwebs and centre crankpin, and 'dog legs' formed of side crankpins and main journals. The main journals are slightly smaller in radius than the outer part of the side crankpins. This results from the side crankpin being considerably greater in

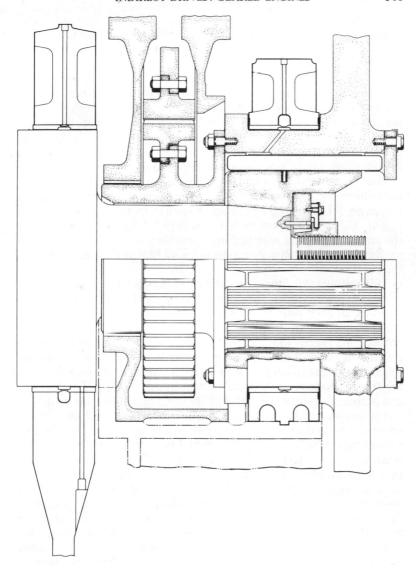

Figure 11.64 Detuner coupling

diameter than is needed for strength, in order to give greater stiffness and larger bearing surfaces. The design also provides a forging shape in which good grain flow can be obtained. There are no bolted couplings in the crankshaft; engines up to seven cylinders have crankshafts shrunk together in one piece. No integral thrust block is fitted, as on the J-engine, because with geared propulsion the thrust has to be taken on the propeller shaft. The aft main journal has flanges which cooperate with white metal rings on the corresponding bearing keep and housing, to provide location.

At the forward end of the crankshaft is fitted the flexible coupling shown in Figure 11.64, which is used to provide a smooth drive for the gears to the balance shaft, auxiliary blower, and camshaft. The turning wheel is also fitted on the floating part of this coupling at the forward end of the engine and provides a flywheel effect so that the coupling is used as a torsional vibration damper.

The centre connecting rod is conventional in design, except that the bottom-end has thin shell bearings, as have all major bearings on the engine. The top-end bearing is similar to that used on the J-engine, but it is expected to have an even longer life because, with the geared engine, the inertia forces provide a reversal of load during each cycle, which helps to maintain an oil film at the loaded part of the bearing.

Lubricating oil for the connecting rod top-end and piston cooling oil for the lower piston is supplied through the crosshead shoe. This is slotted at each side, receiving oil from an opening in one side of the crosshead guide and discharging it at the other side. The top-end bearing receives lubricating oil from drillings in the crosshead pin and has longitudinal grooves arranged to mate with a drilling in the connecting rod in such a way that there is always a flow through the grooves, to ensure adequate lubrication and cooling. The bottom-end bearing receives its oil through the drilling in the connecting rod.

The piston rod has a large central bore, which is fitted with an internal tube so that piston cooling oil passes up the central tube and returns down the annular space around it. In the forged steel piston head, cooling is effected by cocktail-shaker effect and by convection in a large number of radial holes passing between the inner and outer cooling chambers. For guidance purposes in the cylinder, a short cast-iron skirt is bolted to the underside of the top flange of the piston rod. The piston head itself is supported on a ring at about 0·7 of the outside diameter, the ring belt being free to expand. This construction enables a relatively thin crown to be used without excessive bending stress due to pressure, thus keeping thermal stresses to a minimum.

The side connecting rods are steel castings with through-bolts taking the load from top-end to bottom-end keeps. The top-end bearings are the same size as the bottom-end bearings and run on bobbins held in place in cast steel crossheads by shrunk-in steel pins. The side rods carrying the load from the upper pistons are screwed directly into the crossheads and hold the transverse beam by means of collars on the underside and nuts on the top face.

The transverse beams are steel castings in the form of 'A' frames, designed to give maximum strength with minimum weight.

The upper piston heads are similar to those of the lower pistons, and the load is transferred to the transverse beams by means of short piston rods. Again, a cast iron skirt is attached to the piston rod, but here it is relatively long because it has to cover the exhaust ports at inner dead-centre and to provide a surface for the scraper rings attached to the top of the cylinder liners. In addition the skirts carry two sealing rings, to prevent hot exhaust gas from reaching the scraper boxes.

The upper pistons are water cooled through a tube and annular space in the piston rod, similar to the arrangement in the lower piston. Cooling water is supplied and discharged by means of swinging links pivoted on the transverse beam and on specially designed flexible standpipes. The construction is such that the joints in the swinging links are lubricated by the cooling water. The glands can be quickly replaced when required. The small movement needed at the top of the standpipes is accommodated by means of a synthetic rubber hose inside a system of links and trunions which carry the inertia loads of the link system, but permit slight malalignment of the transverse beam to accommodate normal piston movement within the bore clearance.

The diaphragm gland separating the entablature from the crank chamber has a pack of inward-springing rings similar to those on the J-engine, but strengthened to suit the higher speed. It is attached to the entablature by means of a bolted plate underneath, in such a way that it can either be withdrawn with the piston and rod during piston overhaul, or dropped down towards the crosshead with the piston still in place, for examination and ring replacement.

Cylinder Construction

The cylinder liner shown in Figure 11.65 is a one-piece iron casting with the cooling surface around the combustion area formed by a large number of holes drilled at an angle to the vertical axis of the cylinder. By this means, the water cooling surface is fully machined and is much closer to the gas side of the liner than is attainable by any other means. The part of the liner casting outside of the cooling holes functions as a strong-back to take the pressure stresses, while thermal stresses are kept low because of the small distance between the gas and the water faces. Four fuel injector valves, one air starting

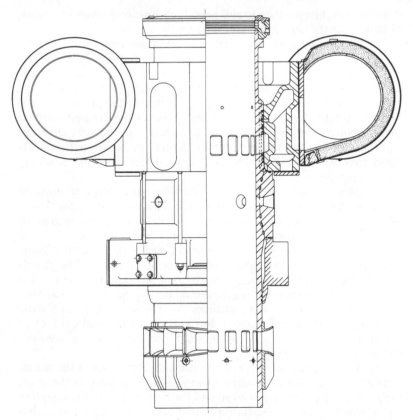

Figure 11.65 Cylinder assembly

valve and one combined relief and indicator valve are fitted in the
heavy central part of the liner at the middle of the combustion zone.
The liner is clamped between the exhaust belt and a lower cast iron
jacket which rests on and is bolted to the top face of the entablature.
Cooling water enters the lower jacket and passes through the drillings
in the central part of the liner into an annular space at the bottom
of the exhaust belt. Here the stream divides, part of it passing up
through drillings in the liner through the exhaust port bars, and the
remainder cooling the exhaust belt. Attached to each exhaust belt
are two sections of exhaust manifold, at the front and the back of
the engine respectively, which are connected to corresponding
sections on the adjacent cylinders by means of flexible pipes.

The liner, jacket, and exhaust belt construction is such that a liner
assembly complete with all valves, cylinder lubricators, inlet port

vanes, exhaust belts and exhaust pipes can be lifted from the engine
without dismantling.

Starting

The Seahorse engine is fully reversible. Starting is effected by
injecting air at up to 450 lb/in² (31 bar) into the cylinders during
the expansion stroke, either ahead or astern as required. To give
precise timing, the starting air control mechanism shown in Figure
11.66 operates the cylinder air inlet valve mechanically. For each
cylinder the camshaft carries two starting air cams. There are two
levers, each of which can operate the cylinder starting air valve.
These levers are mounted on eccentric fulcra arranged to be brought
into operating position by means of low pressure air cylinders.

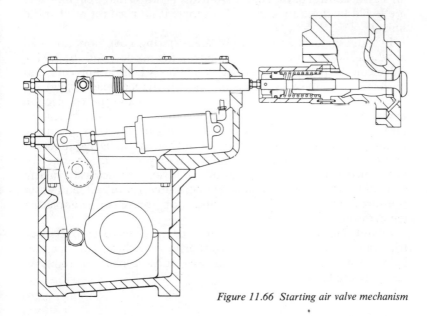

Figure 11.66 Starting air valve mechanism

When ahead starting is required, the ahead air cylinders for each
engine cylinder bring the required cam into operation; air is injected
into whichever cylinder has pistons in the suitable position; and
the engine turns. Similarly for astern starting, the astern air cylinders
bring the correct cams into operation. Because of the precise timing,
astern air can be used for engine braking when manoeuvring from
ahead to astern.

Control and Governing

The engine is arranged for remote control, either pneumatically from a position in the engine room, or electrically from the bridge. On the engine structure itself, simple mechanical controls are fitted for emergency use if the electrical and pneumatic systems should fail. The engine is fitted with a hydraulic governor driven from the camshaft, with a hydraulic amplifier, to control the timing valves, supplied with oil from the engine system at 70 lb/in^2 (4·85 bar). The governor is of the torque-limit type, and both governor output position and speed setting are controlled by an air pressure signal, between 3 and 15 lb/in^2 gauge (say 0·2 to 1·0 bar). Fuel pressure is controlled by air pressure on the diaphragm of the spill valve, as in the J-engine, and, because starting is also performed by means of an air signal, control of the engine from any position in the engine room is effected by three air signals. Thus there is no need for mechanical linkage.

In multi-engined installations, load-sharing governors are used in which the governor on one engine is the master, and the timing valve control position on the other engine is held in line with that of the master engine by means of a pneumatic feed-back signal.

When bridge control is fitted for the engines, the connection between the bridge telegraph and the engine room is electrical, as on J-engines, to avoid the use of long pneumatic lines. As the engine is completely enclosed and no routine attention is required for lubricating small parts, it is comparatively easy to arrange for unmanned engine room operation by fitting the necessary alarm systems for bearing and exhaust temperatures, for oil, air, and water pressures and temperatures, and for scavenge entablature temperature.

In addition to the hydraulic governor, an emergency overspeed trip is also fitted on the balance shaft drive gearwheel. This operates by releasing the air from the spill valve control line, thus reducing fuel pressure to zero.

Fuel Injection

The timing valve common-rail fuel injection system, as fitted to earlier Doxford engines, is used; but to ensure the quick injection necessary for this higher speed engine, a number of modifications have been made. The whole system is designed to withstand line pressures up to 10 000 lb/in^2 (say 700 bar), and for this purpose all high-pressure pipes have flanged fittings and are made of extra heavy tube arranged so that any pipe can be dismantled without bending.

The fuel pump is of the opposed cylinder type, as previously, but has plain plungers without scrolls and without means of adjusting output. Instead, pressure is controlled by one of two air-operated spill valves and, for safety, there is a third spill valve operated by lubricating oil pressure set at a higher pressure than that for the controllable valves, to serve as a safety relief valve.

The timing valves use the mechanism shown in the chapter on J-engines, but have modified valve blocks to give approximately 50 per cent more flow area; four fuel valves are fitted to each cylinder instead of two, to give ample nozzle area and good fuel distribution in the combustion space without excessive air swirl. Instead of fitting normal edge-type filters in the timing valves and fuel injectors, fuel from the timing valves is taken to distribution blocks for each cylinder fitted with disc pack-type high-pressure filters, which are easily removable for cleaning without disturbing the pipe system. Fuel has to pass through these filters before going to the four pipes which lead to the cylinder injectors. Arrangements for heating and filtering heavy fuel, and for circulating before starting-up, are similar to those on the J-engine.

Lubrication

For crankcase lubrication, oil is supplied at 70–75 lb/in² gauge, (say 4·8–5·2 bar), from an external electrically driven pump to a large main fitted in the guide structure. From this main, pipes and drillings carry the oil to the main bearings, the crosshead guides for lubricating the centre connecting rods, the lower piston oil cooling, and the balance shaft, auxiliary blower gearbox, balance shaft gear drive, and fuel pump. Oil is supplied from this main to the governor hydraulic amplifier and to the servo-valve which controls the scavenge air supply from the auxiliary blower.

The main bearing journals are drilled to supply oil to two drillings in each side crankpin. From here the oil flows up a tube in each side connecting rod to lubricate the side top-end bearing and side crosshead. The detuner coupling at the forward end of the engine is supplied with oil from the bearing surrounding the floating member.

Cylinder lubrication is provided by the Doxford timed distributor system, with eight lubricator quills for each piston. These are fitted in the liners above the exhaust ports and below the scavenge ports, to inject oil on to the respective ring packs at approximately outer dead-centre. The cylinder lubricator pump units are similar to those used on direct-drive engines, but with modified cams to suit the higher engine speed. The cam and follower mechanism is enclosed and lubricated.

Scavenge and Exhaust

Because of the high cylinder output of this engine in relation to its size, the provision of adequate air throughput is more difficult to achieve than on the normal slow-speed direct-drive engine. To overcome this problem, the boost pressure is increased to 2·4 atmospheres absolute from the normal 1·75; and an engine-driven auxiliary blower is fitted to supplement the exhaust-driven turbochargers.

The engine-driven blower is of centrifugal type and is driven through speed-increasing gears from the balance shaft, with an arrangement of two SSS clutches which ensures that the blower impeller always runs in the same direction, regardless of the direction of engine rotation. In the speed-up gear there is a fluid coupling to absorb shock and vibration, and to avoid excessive gear loading during acceleration. The complete speed-up gear is made as a unit with the auxiliary blower. It is flange-mounted on the aft end face of the guide structure, and the drive from the balance shaft is made through a gear tooth coupling to provide for easy removal and to overcome alignment problems.

To ensure minimum pressure-drop through the engine, the scavenge ports at the lower end of the cylinder are fitted with streamlined aluminium inlet guide vanes. The exhaust ports, which are all around the upper cylinder, are sloped in the direction of gas flow. The exhaust belt shown in Figure 11.67 is designed for the freest possible gas flow, and the passages at back and front are streamlined to lead the gas smoothly into the two exhaust manifolds.

The engine is provided with two single-entry turbochargers, one at each end of the engine. The forward turbocharger receives exhaust

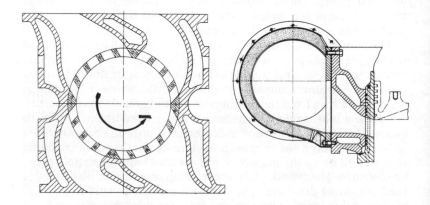

Figure 11.67 Exhaust belt arrangement

gas from the front manifold and the aft turbocharger is fed from the back manifold. The turbochargers deliver air through trunking into coolers incorporated in the ends of the scavenge entablature fabrication. The auxiliary blower delivers air into the aft trunking through a special flow divider, which prevents surging of either turbochargers or auxiliary blower.

Each engine is fitted with four cooler stacks which can be withdrawn transversely from their mounting in the entablature ends. By using two stacks at each end of the engine, the length of each stack is reduced sufficiently to enable the inboard stacks to be withdrawn in the space available between a pair of engines. If required the stack can then be cleaned without further removal, by the use of a portable cleaning tank. At the boost pressure ratio of 2·4:1, as used in the engine, there is no gain by employing pulse turbocharging. Accordingly the engine is designed for constant pressure turbocharging, which simplifies the exhaust manifold and enables the same power per cylinder to be obtained for all cylinder numbers.

Balance Shaft

Each cylinder line has near-perfect balance, resulting from the opposed piston arrangement; but, as the exhaust cranks are at 172° to the main cranks to give the exhaust piston an 8° lead, there is a small residual imbalance. This, on a relatively small high-powered engine, becomes of some importance. To overcome it, the balance shaft arranged in the guide structure rotates in the opposite direction to the crankshaft, and it is fitted with opposed balance weights to counteract the residual primary couples of the engine.

Because of the perfect primary balance, the firing order for each cylinder number configuration can be so chosen that the secondary couples are either non-existent or are of extremely small magnitude. The internal couples are insignificant, because of the small number of cylinders and the very stiff structure.

The power absorbed by the auxiliary blower is about three per cent of the engine power and has to be carried by the drive to the balance shaft. Because of this, gears are used instead of a chain drive. There are four wheels in the gear train and the fuel pump is driven from the third of these at a speed slightly above engine speed. The intermediate gears have different numbers of teeth to the crankshaft and balance shaft gears. To ensure silence all gears are mounted in a rigid cast-iron casing having accurately positioned centres. The final gear, which is mounted in its own bearings in the cast-iron casing, drives the balance shaft through a toothed flexible coupling. The drive wheel is attached to the floating mass of the detuner coupling and has its own bearings. Hence it is not affected by crankshaft movement either transversely, axially, or torsionally.

Camshaft

To drive the timing valves, lubricators, air starting valves and governor, a light camshaft is arranged on the top of the entablature, and is driven at the centre by roller chain from the balance shaft. The camshaft is divided into separate modules, one for each cylinder, and these modules comprise a timing valve, upper and lower piston lubricators, and the air starting valve mechanism for the particular cylinder. The separate shafts are coupled by means of split cone couplings, so that the timing of the units for each cylinder is a matter of simple adjustment. Although the individual units can be over-hauled in place, it is also possible to remove and replace a complete module quickly. The hydraulic governor is driven from one end of the camshaft through a flexible coupling and speed-up gearbox.

Main Drive Gear

For twin-engine installations, the standard gear arrangement consists of a horizontally split gear casing aft of the engines, with a simple gear train comprising a helical toothed pinion for each engine shaft driving the main helical toothed wheel which is attached to the propeller shaft. All of the spindle centres are in the horizontal plane of the casing split. A thrust block integral with the gear casing is arranged on the propeller shaft, either forward or aft of the main gear wheel, as may suit the engine room arrangement. To provide the required torsional flexibility, each pinion is driven from the corresponding engine through a quill shaft, the quill-shaft coupling being movable for disconnecting either engine if required. The gearbox is mounted on three or four feet, with the main mounting point at the thrust block and the other points designed to permit expansion relative to the tank top. The arrangement of mountings and quill shafts permits malalignment and movement between engines and gears without causing gearwheel distortion.

The gear arrangement described above is a simple form, treating the two engines as a single power unit, but more elaborate designs can be arranged, with power take-offs for generators or pumps, and with provision for disconnecting either of the engines or the propeller by means of clutches while the engines are running. Such an arrangement is suitable for tankers, in which it may be advantageous to use one or both engines for pumping purposes in harbour. A simple twin-engine arrangement is shown in Figure 11.68.

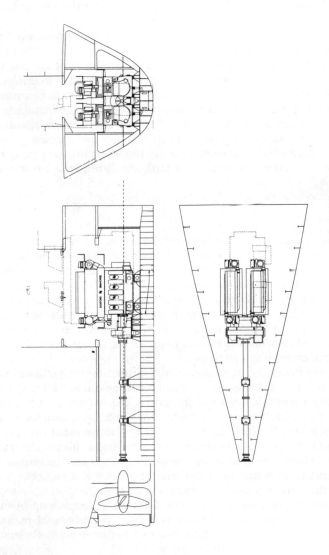

Figure 11.68 Arrangement of two geared engines

The normal arrangement for a quadruple engine installation comprises two main gear wheels, with port and starboard engine pairs respectively in fore-and-aft line. The two engines forward of the main gears drive the forward main wheel, and the two engines aft of the main gears drive the aft main wheel.

To enable the most convenient multiple engine arrangement to be attained, the Seahorse engine is designed in such a way that the drive can be taken from either end; also the direction of crankshaft rotation can either be clockwise or anti-clockwise, when looking on the drive end. There are thus four types of engine available, using the same components. Therefore in a quadruple engine installation the camshafts can all be outboard and all running gear overhauling can be carried out in the central space between the engines.

The main gearbox is designed to use the same oil as the engine crankcase, so that a common drain tank and lubricating oil system can be used.

Performance

For two reasons a geared engine inevitably has greater mechanical losses than a direct-drive slow-speed engine. Firstly, for the higher speed engine there is more frictional loss in the bearings; secondly, the auxiliary blower absorbs about three per cent of the engine output.

The design of the Doxford Seahorse engine incorporates two features to offset the losses mentioned and to provide sufficient improvement in specific indicated fuel consumption to ensure that the brake fuel consumption is as good as, or better than, that of competitive direct-drive engines.

Firstly the higher boost pressure, in conjunction with efficient air cooling after the turbochargers, results in the fuel/air ratio, at full load, being slightly lower than in, say, a 76J engine at full load. Secondly provision for a much higher maximum pressure, and for quick injection of the fuel, permits a higher effective expansion ratio after combustion to be obtained, and therefore a higher thermal efficiency. These two factors are more than sufficient to ensure a specific brake consumption at the level of direct-drive engines.

In addition to frictional losses in the engine, there is a loss of 2–3 per cent at the main drive gears. However, the running of the propeller at the best speed to suit the ship, regardless of engine revolutions, will almost invariably ensure a higher overall efficiency than is attainable with the direct drive.

As with most medium-speed engines, the high maximum cylinder pressure and the high rate of pressure rise tend to induce noise. However, the very stiff structure and the complete enclosure of all running parts, together with the solid one-piece liner construction, combine to lower the overall noise to an acceptable level.

J.F.B.

ELASTIC COUPLINGS

Geared engines have occasionally been made with a heavy flywheel as the only damping agent between engine and gearing, but it is the consensus of well-informed opinion that, in the present state of knowledge, an elastic coupling of some kind should be interposed between engine and gearing. The functions of a flexible coupling are:

(a) to serve as a cushion, preventing the transmission of detrimental torque pulsations from engine to gearing;
(b) to function as a quick-disconnecting clutch—for use when manoeuvring;
(c) to limit the transmissible torque to, say, 1·5–2·5 times its normal value and thus obtain a measure of protection if there should be a seizure in one of the engines.

The forms which such a coupling can take are: (i) mechanical; (ii) electric; (iii) hydraulic, and (iv) pneumatic. The first-named cannot easily be made to serve as a clutch. Cost, weight, space and reliability are the factors to be considered when comparing the other couplings. Because of the exigencies of space, outline description is herein restricted to the electric and hydraulic coupling forms.

Figure 11.69(a) shows two forms of geared units.

Electromagnetic Coupling

The mechanical power supplied by a prime mover to an electrical generator is converted through the air gap between stator and rotor into electrical power. If the stator, as well as the rotor, is arranged to rotate about its own centre, mechanical instead of electrical power is given out. This is the basic principle of the electric coupling.

The coupling consists of two electromagnets. One, the primary element, is excited from the ship's direct-current supply; the other, the secondary, is excited inductively. Figure 11.69(b) shows, diagrammatically, the elements of the coupling.

The primary element is a multi-polar magnet ring. It has the greater moment of inertia and is attached to the pinion. The secondary element, which is provided with squirrel-cage windings having short-circuiting end rings, is electro-mechanically more

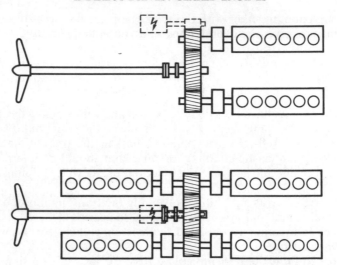

Figure 11.69(a) Geared sets, with two and four engines

robust and can better endure variable torque than can the salient pole windings; it is therefore connected to the diesel engine. In one form of magnetic coupling the primary element is on the inside and the secondary member on the outside; in another design the primary part is on the outside and the secondary part on the inside. Both forms are indicated in Figure 11.69(b). These variations do not affect the coupling characteristics.

The two members, which may be cast steel or fabricated steel, are overhung on their respective shafts and are separated by a radial air gap which may be anything from 5 mm to 10 mm. The shafts, also

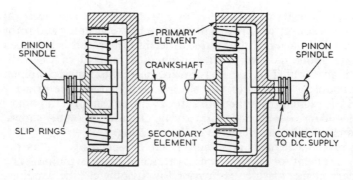

Figure 11.69(b) Principle of electromagnetic coupling

the slip-coupling flanges and the mating flanges, are of ample dimensions; the coupling bolts are numerous and sturdy; the flanges are spigoted. British designers, especially, always strive to avoid constructions in which there are heavy, overhanging masses. With the electric coupling it is difficult to avoid overhang, the alternative being very cumbersome indeed.

The working of the coupling depends upon the principle that, when the primary element is excited, a magnetic field is created; the lines of force pass from the poles across the air-gap, cutting the conductors of the secondary element and inducing in them an electromotive force, or voltage, sufficient to drive through the conductor bars and end-rings a current of the amount needed. The interaction of this current and the magnetic field produces a torque, causing rotation of the secondary element. Under the influence of this torque the speed

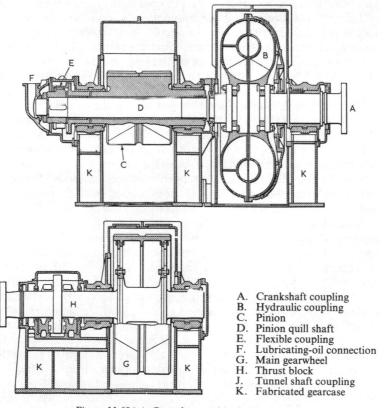

A. Crankshaft coupling
B. Hydraulic coupling
C. Pinion
D. Pinion quill shaft
E. Flexible coupling
F. Lubricating-oil connection
G. Main gearwheel
H. Thrust block
J. Tunnel shaft coupling
K. Fabricated gearcase

Figure 11.69(c) Gear-drive and hydraulic coupling

of revolution of the secondary element increases until it reaches a value just sufficiently below the speed of revolution of the primary member to circulate the secondary current required to transmit the torque. The small difference in rotational speed between the two elements is termed the *slip*.

During the transmission of the torque a small fraction of the power is lost, as is always so in power transmission. Excitation and induction power losses appear as heat in both elements; there are also iron and windage losses, as well as resistance losses in the conductors.

As the torque across the air-gap must of necessity be the same as the engine torque the power losses do not appear as a difference in torque; they become apparent as a difference in rotational speed between the primary and secondary elements. The excitation current, which is necessary for creating and maintaining the magnetic field, can be expected to be about 1 or 2 per cent of the transmitted power.

There is no doubt that the magnetic slip-coupling, sometimes called the electric air-gap coupling, while transmitting the mean torque, reduces to negligible proportions the shocks which have their origin in torsional irregularities of the engine; the oscillations on the pinion side correspond in frequency with those on the engine side but have greatly reduced amplitude. Resonance cannot occur at the coupling. Under sudden changes of load the coupling tends to change relatively slowly to the new conditions, thus smoothing out the acceleration forces engendered. Pitching in a seaway is an example. As the propeller leaves the water the engines accelerate, as in a direct-coupled arrangement, until the governors cut off the fuel. When the propeller descends again the suddenly imposed loads, as the blades meet the water, are not transmitted in their intensity to the crankshafts, thus relieving the shafting system.

When the engine is stopped the coupling is still capable of transmitting torque. The transmissible torque increases with increased speed difference between the elements, i.e. with the slip, up to the maximum allowed by the design. This may be 1·5–2·5 times the full-load at, say 6 or 7 per cent slip. At greater slip the transmitted torque begins to fall. With one engine out of service the excitation current may be reduced and the slip increased, reducing the ship speed until the propeller torque lies within the capacity of the remaining engine or engines. Full torque at low speeds, especially with a coupling member which has a small wr^2 value, may cause the firing impulses to accentuate the turning moment irregularities.

The lowest revolutions per minute at full excitation are 50 per cent of the normal revolutions. The approximate maximum static torque at full excitation is 1·7 times the full-load torque, thus enabling the engine to be reversed, when running at full speed, with fully excited couplings, without the coupling halves being stalled. Torque at 100 per cent slip, i.e. when one element is rotating at full speed while the other is at rest, is 50 per cent approximately; the slip at normal torque is approximately 1 per cent. The excitation current at 220 volts is about 1 per cent of the main-engine output—which must be allowed for when computing the electrical load on the diesel generators. The runaway speed is 25 per cent above the normal designed revolutions.

By reason of wear and slight inaccuracies in initial setting, the two elements may not be exactly concentric and thus the air-gap will not be uniform. A radial magnetic attractive pull between the elements at the place of minimum air-gap is thus created. The maximum value of this force is reached when the excitation current is much below normal and falls well below maximum at full excitation. Normally the stiffness of the shafts, the adequacy of the bolting and the insignificant amount of wear which occurs at the bearings render negligible the effect of the magnetic pull. The width of the air-gap is checked periodically by the insertion of gauges.

Teeth, for the diesel engine turning gear, can be cut on the circumference of inner-pole type slip-couplings if so desired. The circuit breakers, resistance, switches, fuses, and other devices are mounted in a suitable cubicle.

The couplings are air-cooled by a self-acting fan arrangement incorporated in the design. Ducts from the engine-room ventilation system are led to the neighbourhood of the couplings to minimise the drawing-in of oil mist. A wire-mesh guard surrounds the couplings. As about one-half of each coupling is normally below the flooring, splash guards are desirable, although the couplings are designed to expel entrained water. Toe-plates and portable floor plates are provided as required.

The couplings are designed and constructed in accordance with Lloyd's rules for electrical machinery and for service in the tropics, where dampness and condensation can be expected.

In the ordinary magnetic coupling the slip serves no purpose other than to generate the low-frequency current which excites the secondary element.

The torque transmitted by the coupling is not dependent upon the engine speed but, apart from the excitation, is determined only by the actual amount of the slip. The engine speed changes, but the relationship between torque and actual value of the slip remains the same. Reduction of excitation current is followed by a relative increase in slip and enables the propeller torque and revolutions to be reduced, the engine speed remaining constant.

In Figure 11.69(b) the secondary element is driven by the diesel engine; the primary element therefore has a rotational speed less than the secondary by the amount of the slip. Excitation current is continuously applied to the couplings when the engines are in use, and the latter are started, stopped, reversed and controlled exactly as for direct-coupled engines.

Hydraulic Coupling

The hydraulic coupling will transmit a torque equal to the input torque, a result which is obtained by the use of two elements; a primary section, or impeller, and a secondary section, or runner. *See* Figure 11.69(c). The impeller is driven by the engine and imparts kinetic energy to the working fluid which is contained in the pockets formed in its face. The runner is provided with pockets opposed to those in the impeller and receives energy from the fluid flowing back towards the axis of the coupling, preparatory to a further cycle through the impeller. Thus the torque is transmitted by means of energy changes in a rotating vortex of liquid.

For the cycle to operate, i.e. for the vortices to form, there must be slip between impeller and runner. Hence, for any required torque, there will be a corresponding slip. At full-power rating the relative velocity between impeller and runner is low, hence the rotational velocity of the oil in the vortices is low. The slip is then usually 2–4 per cent. The rotational velocity will only rise to a high value if excessive slip occurs, e.g. when manoeuvring the engines or if there is 'stalling'. The output torque being always equal to the input torque, and no external power being applied, efficiency = 100 per cent — slip per cent.

The coupling can tolerate an appreciable amount of misalignment, as there is a facial clearance of about 5–10 mm between the impeller and the runner.

There is always an axial thrust, tending to separate the two rotating members. Attempts have been made to reduce this thrust, e.g. by cutting relieving holes in the back of the runner; but this causes increased slip and reduces the efficiency. A Michell thrust bearing, arranged on the pinion shaft, can take the thrust on the driven side, i.e. at the runner; on the engine side the thrust is taken by the engine thrust bearing. Because of this end thrust, single helical gearing, only, should be used in geared installations. The axial thrust from the pinion shaft, resulting from the single helical gearing, may be utilised to balance, in part, the thrust from the runner component. Double-unit couplings, comprising two impellers and twin runners, back to back, are sometimes used. In them the thrust is balanced.

The hydraulic coupling will not transmit torsional vibrations to any appreciable extent; for vibration calculations the engine may be assumed to be independent of gearing and shafting. Momentary changes of torque, such as may arise in an engine having few cylinders, are effectively smoothed away, as a rule.

Two methods of coupling control are used, namely *scoop* control and gravity, or pump fed, *ring slide-valve* control. The scoop-control method is in general use for the lower ranges of power and higher engine speeds, also where it is desired to use the hydraulic coupling for speed reduction, e.g. when manoeuvring at speeds below the idling speed.

So far as machinery operation is concerned, a simple lever is all that is required for either method of control.

Several different methods of construction are used for the impellers and runners. The smallest types of coupling, operating at moderately high speeds, may have the two elements made in die-cast or sand-cast light alloy. Fabricated steel constructions have been used for high-speed engines. Low-speed and medium-speed marine couplings are normally cast either in iron or steel. In large low-speed couplings the increase of slip, arising from higher frictional resistance to flow in the chambers, is so small as to be negligible. If desired, however, a slight increase in the coupling diameter will compensate for this.

Various liquids have been tried in the hydraulic coupling, and, as a result, oil is most generally used. The oil reservoir and header tank, if fitted, can conveniently be combined either with the gearing or with the engine lubrication system.

REDUCTION GEARING

The gearing which is interposed between the diesel engines and the tunnel shafting is always single-reduction and, most usually, double-helical.

In steam-turbine machinery the ratio of reduction may be from 12:1 to 20:1 for single-reduction gearing, and up to 40:1 for double-reduction gearing—if the best overall results are to be obtained, i.e. from an efficient slow-moving propeller at one end and an economical, and therefore fast-moving, turbine at the other end. Generally speaking, the ratio of reduction with geared diesel engines has hitherto seldom been as high as 4:1; it has frequently been 2·5:1 and 2:1; and occasionally it has been as low as 1·5:1. As it becomes possible to use higher rates of revolution, with the confidence necessary for marine work, the ratio will be increased.

Table 11.17 is typical of installations which have entered service in past years.

Table 11.17 PARTICULARS OF REDUCTION GEARS

kW propeller	3 100	3 300	3 600	4 500	5 200	5 700	6 000	6 400	6 700	12 000	13 000
kW pinion	1 550	1 650	1 800	1 125	1 300	2 850	3 000	1 600	3 350	3 000	3 250
Rev/min engine	218	225	250	210	215	210	217	237	223	212	215
Rev/min propeller	90	94	110	75	77	86	100	85	100	140	94
Dia. gear wheel, mm	2 690	1 950	1 983	2 300	2 295	2 440	2 489	3 040	2 533	2 293	2 230
Dia. pinion, mm	1 110	810	912	820	818	1 000	1 156	1 090	1 134	1 506	970
Teeth on wheel	213	120	276		348		196	299	361	245	160
Teeth on pinion	88	50	127		124		91	107	162	161	69
Gear ratio	2·42	2·4	2·18	2·8	2·79	2·44	2·15	2·79	2·23	1·51	2·30
Pinion length, mm	1 120	810	457	1 290	1 200	1 150	1 016	970	915	1 580	1 050
Pinion length/diameter	1·0	1·0	0·50	1·57	1·47	1·15	0·88	0·89	0·81	1·05	1·08
Tooth pitch, normal, mm				15			35	29	19	25	
Tooth pitch, circular, mm	40	51	23		21		40	32	22	30	44
Engine centres, mm	3 800	2 760	2 895	3 120	3 113	3 440	3 645	4 120	3 670	3 800	3 200
÷ No. of engines per propeller	2	2	2	4	4	2	2	4	2	4	4

The standard propulsion reduction gear units for marine trans-
missions as made by David Brown Gear Industries Ltd. are designed
for association with most of the leading makes of medium-speed
diesel engines, with output ratings starting at about 3000 shp for the
smallest single-input units and rising to 42 000 shp for the largest
twin-output units. They cover a propeller speed range of 90 to 180
rev/min. The gearing is designed for use with controllable-pitch
propeller installations or for direct reversing engines. The units are
suitable for use with all leading makes of clutch and coupling combinations.

The gearing is of the single-helical type, using low helix angles
with adequate overlap. Maximum use is made of surface-hardened
steels for gear elements. Figure 11.70 shows a twin-input, single-
output David Brown gearbox.

Figure 11.70 David Brown gearbox

The pinions are made in case-carburising steel or in nitriding steel,
the choice depending on the loading and other requirements. In the
former material, the pinion teeth are hobbed, gas carburise-

hardened and profile ground. Nitriding steel pinions are finish hobbed before being nitride-hardened by the ammonia gas process. Wheel rims are made from nitriding steel or through-hardened steel of appropriate strength. Small wheels may be made from solid forgings and keyed to their shafts, but large wheels are of fabricated construction with mild steel centres fabricated and welded to steel hubs pressed and keyed on to carbon steel shafts. Rims are welded or shrunk and pegged-on to the centres.

The combination of surface-hardened pinions meshing with surface-hardened or through-hardened wheels ensures maintenance of ideal tooth meshing contact throughout the life of the gears. Gear loadings are chosen to conform with the regulations of classification and safety authorities. To give economies in space and weight, maximum advantage is taken of the loading limits allowed by these bodies, for various combinations of gears.

The main load-carrying sections of gearcases are of stress-relieved welded steel construction, with substantial internal ribbing and stiffening to give a rigid structure. In the twin-input, single-output range the wheel and pinion bearing housings are in the form of cast pedestals, heavily dowelled and bolted to the surface of the main structure. Inspection covers are located at appropriate positions.

Journal bearings are of the white-metal-lined, plain type, secured in their housings with substantial covers. One bearing in each gear line is provided with means of adjustment. This is to simplify any re-alignment which may be necessary through possible damage in service. There are no loose shims. All bearing covers can be removed without disturbing the main gearcase covers.

Main thrust bearings are of the tilting-pad type. They are supplied as separate units for twin-input, single-output gearboxes, and as integral units for single-input, single-output gearboxes. Access for periodic inspection or maintenance is a simple matter. Pinions are located axially by means of small tilting-pad type thrust bearings, or thrust locating rings placed adjacent to the forward journal bearing. Each gear mesh is spray lubricated and each journal and thrust bearing is pressure lubricated. Spray manifolds are arranged for easy removal through openings in the gearcase wall.

Single-reduction series gear units have gears whose pitches range from $3\frac{1}{2}$ to 2 diametral pitch, whereas the twin-input range has pitches ranging from $3\frac{1}{2}$ to $2\frac{1}{4}$ diametral pitch. All pitches stated are normal and are not measured in the circular section as they vary according to the degree of helix angle.

Helix angles for the single helical gears are arranged so as to control the end thrusts which ensue and, overall, are in general of the order of 10°. Auxiliary or power take-off units to drive alternators, cargo pumps etc. can be accommodated on the gear case structure using either direct drive from the high speed shaft or, when the facility is required, by a flexible coupling and quill shaft passing through the high speed shaft. Gear units are fitted with integral lubrication systems.

Figures 11.71(a) and (b) show a five-wheel design of a Lohmann and Stolterfoht twin-input, single-output reduction gear, incorporating two elastic clutches of Pneumaflex design. The input power is developed by two medium-speed engines, the rating of which is 6000 metric brake horse-power per unit, i.e. 12 000 metric brake horse-power total. If the engines are of Pielstick 12PC2V size, as described earlier in this chapter, the rotational speed will be 515 rev/min. If the prime mover is of Ruston 12AO type, also described in this chapter, the rev/min will be 450. The propeller rotates at 120 rev/min and is of controllable-pitch design.

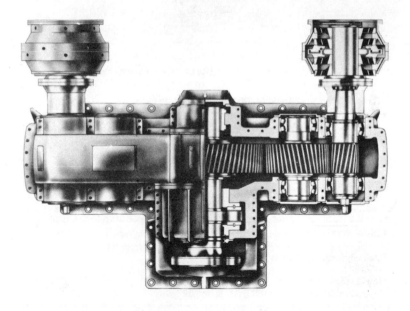

Figure 11.71(a) Lohmann and Stolterfoht reduction gearing

The distance between the engine centres is 3750 mm, being the aggregate of 660 mm between pinions and intermediate wheels and 1215 mm between intermediate wheels and main wheel. The gearing particulars are indicated in Table 11.18.

The Pneumaflex type friction clutches transmit the engine torque

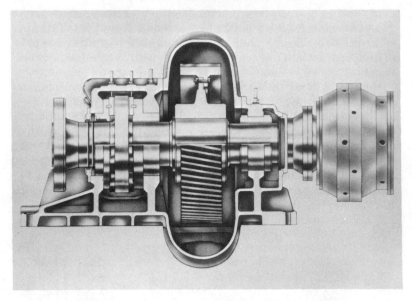

Figure 11.71(b) Lohmann and Stolterfoht reducing gear

Table 11.18 PARTICULARS OF GEARING

	Distance between centres = 660 mm		Distance between centres = 1 215 mm
	Pinion	*Intermediate wheel*	*Main wheel*
Number of teeth	22	48	83
Module	18	18	18
Helical angle, degrees	10	10	10
Pitch circle diameter, mm	402·109	877·329	1 517·047
Outside diameter of gear wheel, mm	459·9	927·7	1 569·9

to the reduction gear unit. The high degree of torsional elasticity, characteristic of the embodied rubber ring elements, allows of the balancing of the natural frequency of the complete main propulsion drive against the frequency of the vibration exciter. The dangerous torsional vibrations are suppressed to below idling speed and thus the total operating speed range can be used without restriction. The

Pneumaflex clutch can withstand unexpected alternating loads, e.g. those caused by cylinder misfiring, or damage to the propeller. This type of clutch has no spline connection and therefore it works chatter-free. The friction cones, carried by the rubber ring elements, are dimensioned to allow a momentary engaging or disengaging of the main engines to be made at full torque.

The friction linings have a high isolating efficiency. The generated heat is transmitted mainly to the clutch housings and from there is dissipated to the ambient air.

The five-wheel unit, by its flat construction, better suits the foundation arrangements at the aft end of vessels than does the normal three-wheel system. The proper distribution of stiffness and elasticity is decisive for the successful installation of high powers.

The tooth flanks of the single helical spur gearing are case-hardened and ground. All gear rims are connected to their hubs by fitted bolts. The input and intermediate shafts are mounted in anti-friction bearings. The output shaft is carried in slide bearings. The propeller thrust of 140 000 kgf is absorbed by a Michell type thrust block, with tiltable thrust pads.

The A.G. 'Weser' gearing comprises four components; the re-duction gear; the coupling, whether hydraulic or high-elastic type; the step-up gear for driving auxiliaries, e.g. generators, if required, and the auxiliary equipment such as turning gear, shaft brake, cooler, filter and valves.

The range of powers that can be provided extends from a single engine of 4000 hp to two engines of 18 000 hp each, three engines of 10 000 hp each and four engines of 10 000 hp each, i.e. 40 000 hp total. The reduction ratio varies from 2:1, or even less, to 5:1 and more, according to the requirements of the clients.

Figure 11.72 shows an A.G. Weser twin-input, single-output gearbox. The two engines deliver 6000 hp each at 510 rev/min, i.e. 12 000 hp aggregate. The propeller speed is 100 rev/min. The gearbox is welded, being torsionally rigid. The main wheel is welded; the thrust bearing is built-in. The gearing teeth are shaved, the teeth being cut in an air-conditioned room. The bearing brasses are so arranged that disassembly does not require the removal of the gearbox cover.

In Figure 11.72 the engine centres are 3750 mm; the distance from base to engine centres is 900 mm; the overall breadth 6100 mm; overall length 3200 mm; height from base to top of box 2500 mm. The weight of gearbox complete is 42·0 metric tons.

The Vulcan hydraulic coupling consists of a driving primary wheel which is bolted to the engine crankshaft flange, a driven secondary wheel which is attached to the pinion of the gearing, and an enclosing

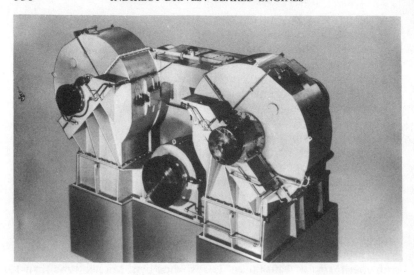

Figure 11.72 A-G 'Weser' gearbox

cover which is fitted to the driving wheel. The two wheels are positioned close together, but without mechanical contact. The hollow space formed between the two wheels, which have radial vanes, is filled with oil. When the primary wheel is set in motion, the generated centrifugal force causes the oil to flow, thus bringing about movement of the secondary wheel. The transmission of torque from the primary wheel to the secondary wheel is effected by means of a turbulence ring which has been incorporated in this design.

By reason of the weight of the contained oil and the weight of the half-coupling and cover, it is possible to utilise the driving section of the coupling as flywheel. The hydraulic coupling provides compensation for irregular torque and surging; it smoothly engages and disengages under working conditions; its efficiency is 98 per cent.

One of the advantages of the hydraulic coupling is that any desired low propeller speed, to suit reduced ship speed, can be obtained, even with high-speed engines of high power output, simply by increasing the slip. The coupling requires no maintenance. The carrying away of the power loss, by means of heated oil, is especially simple. The oil used in the coupling is exactly the same as that used for lubricating the gears and the bearings.

In event of a sudden propeller stoppage, say when passing through ice, the coupling can temporarily withstand 100 per cent slip without suffering any damage. This means that there is no danger of the gearing being damaged.

The emptying of the coupling is effected by special emptying valves, the pistons of which open when the lubricating oil pressure falls off. The valves are shut by the pressure of the lubricating oil. The number of emptying valves depends on the desired time of discharging.

On the engine side, the primary section runs in slide bearings. After removing the cover of the pinion bearing, without taking-off the coupling cover, the labyrinth sealing of the cover on the primary side can be checked and maintained from the gear side.

As it is often desired to utilise the primary side for driving auxiliary units such as generators, and so on, irrespective of the operation of the gearing, a transmission gear is provided, being connected to the driving shaft of the coupling. In generators with a single end bearing it is possible to utilise a bearing of the transmission gearing for the rotor of the generator.

The auxiliary ancillary equipment comprises the oil pumps which, depending on the circumstances, either pump the oil up into a gravity tank, supplying the coupling and its bearings with oil, or directly into the coupling and its bearings.

Generally, electrically-driven geared pumps are provided, but directly-driven oil pumps can also be used. The oil coolers are double or single pipe radiators, designed for the power loss at the hydraulic coupling. A turning gear as well as a shaft brake can be built-in upon request.

The Vulcan hydraulic coupling appropriate to the reduction gearing shown at Figure 11.72 is 2200 mm diameter outside, 2000

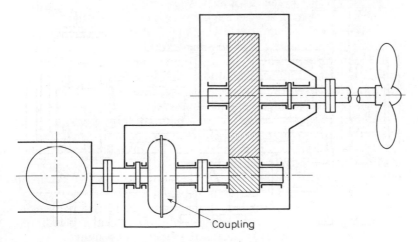

Figure 11.73 Arrangement of A-G 'Weser' Vulcan coupling

mm inside, 670 mm outside width, and weighs 4030 kg. The location of the coupling for a single-engine geared installation is illustrated at Figure 11.73.

A gearbox for four 9000 hp engines running at 465 rev/min, reduced to 90 rev/min propeller speed, weighs 113 metric tons, the overall dimensions being 6900 mm breadth, 4500 mm length, with engine centres 4400 mm.

When a geared installation comprises three engines, one engine is arranged above and abaft the main wheel; the other two engines are located forward of the main wheel at normal level. Thus, for 30 000 hp total, the crankshaft centre of one engine is arranged 1950 mm vertically above the main wheel centre, and the other two units on the same horizontal plane as the main wheel centre, being 1950 mm on each side athwartships, i.e. 3900 mm between crankshaft centres.

With engines running at 430 rev/min and the propeller at 110 rev/min, the overall breadth of gearbox is 6900 mm, with overall length 5300 mm. The gearbox complete weighs 105 metric tons.

Figur 11.74 shows a reduction gear arrangement, of special registered design, made by F. Tacke, KG.

The diagram shows a double gearbox with electromagnetic slipping clutches. The torque from the diesel engines is transmitted

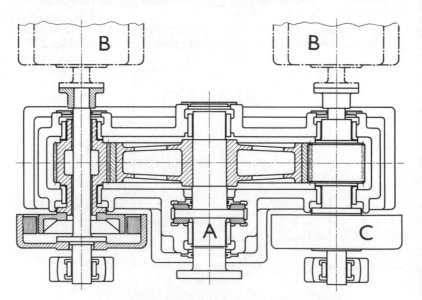

Figure 11.74 Tacke reduction gear with slipping clutches

through the rigid flange connection, and the clutch shaft, to the primary component of the electromagnetic slipping clutch. The latter is flanged on to the clutch shaft. The primary component transmits the torque to the secondary component which is rigidly connected to the hollow bored pinion shaft through a flange.

This arrangement relieves the diesel engine bearings from the forces of the electro-magnetic slipping clutch, while the pillow block bearing is relieved of the weight of the primary unit and the pinion shaft bearing from the weight of the secondary unit. The secondary unit of the clutch has a lever arm which is so short that the loading on the pinion shaft bearings is much more favourable than in previous designs. This reduces the influence of the electro-magnetic slipping clutch on the bearing characteristics of the tooth system.

It must also be noted that the concentric running of the primary and secondary units in relation to each other has been considerably improved by comparison with previous models. The displacements which occur between the engine and gearbox foundations are practically cancelled out by the long lever arm of the clutch shaft.

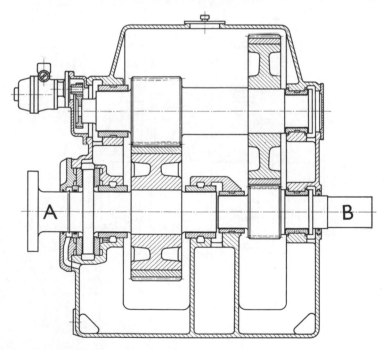

Figure 11.75(a) Tacke single-engine gearbox; coaxial shafts

In the design the slipping clutches are arranged on the side of the gearbox remote from the diesel engines. This arrangement can be used both for electro-magnetic and for hydraulic slipping clutches. The main advantages of the design are: the load on the diesel engine bearings, on the driven side, is reduced considerably; and there is considerable reduction in the effective installed length of the gearbox and slipping clutches.

The standard range of Tacke gearboxes has been developed to meet the special requirements of marine engine builders. These considerations are reflected in the compact construction of the single-type marine gearboxes and in the possibility of selecting double gearboxes with varying axial distances for given powers.

The gearbox housing, made of high quality grey cast-iron or, if requested, in welded design, is normally split horizontally. It is torsionally rigid and has a vibration damping effect. The upper section of the housing has a significant curvature and is provided with strong fins.

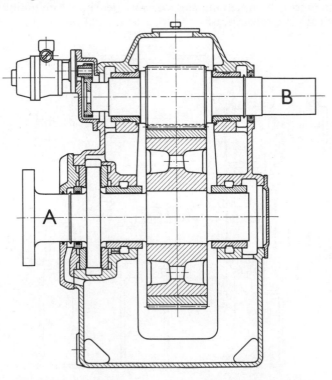

Figure 11.75(b) Tacke single-engine gearbox; superimposed shafts

Depending on the size of the gearbox, single-type gearboxes have single- or double-helical teeth. The teeth are case-hardened and ground. The shafts run in antifriction metal slide bearings with basic elements in steel. The thrust bearing is built to a Michell design. Oil is supplied to the bearings and tooth system by a gear pump which is fitted as standard. An oil filter and an oil cooler are provided. The operating pump and the stand-by pump are interlocked by check valves in the pressure oil line. A relief valve is provided.

Figures 11.75(a) and (b) illustrate single-engine gearboxes, of Tacke make. The design at (a) shows co-axial shafts; that at (b) shows superimposed shafts. The engines are either reversible or have variable pitched propellers.

Lubricating oil is supplied to the thrust bearing at the lower end, while oil is drained out of the highest point, so that the entire thrust bearing chamber is permanently filled with oil. The bearings and teeth are lubricated and cooled directly with fresh oil.

In Figures 11.74 and 11.75, A is the output shaft, to propeller; B is the input shaft, from diesel engine and coupling; and C is the electro-magnetic coupling.

C.C.P.

Chapter 12

Machinery Maintenance

Marine diesel engines, if operated with proper care and attention, provide a high level of reliability under arduous conditions of service. Proneness to fatigue from mechanical and heat stresses, however, necessitates continual watchfulness on the part of all engine designers and operators. Wear is the direct and unavoidable result of running the machinery, and occasional failures are therefore to be expected. These failures, depending upon their location, generally result in the cutting-out of the cylinder line affected. If suitable arrangements have been made for the provision of spare parts there should be little or no difficulty in effecting the necessary renewals at the terminal port. The cost is confined to that of renewal and repair. Normally, no delay to the ship should be incurred.

Wear and tear in internal-combustion engines, although controllable and widely variable, is inevitable. Each start made with cold air causes rapid change in heat gradient, with consequent change in thermal stress and eventual tear. Every revolution of the engine makes its contribution to wear. The effect of inexpert operation and overhaul may not be obvious in the early stages, but an increase in the rate of deterioration duly shows itself. There is diminishment in the maximum output.

In the engine-builder's organisation conceptions of design and directions regarding manufacture originate in and radiate from its technical centre. In the shipowner's organisation, perception of faults and their immediate correction are activities to be found at the periphery of the operating department. The correction of discovered faults tends to be confined to restoration to the original conditions. That is, the underlying cause is not always sought, and therefore remains undiscovered. Where faults recur, there is often a facile tendency to regard them as part of the accepted pattern. Many instances could be cited to illustrate the unwisdom of correcting a visible fault without attempting to identify and eliminate the original cause.

It should be the practice of operating staffs to ensure that information regarding faults, especially recurring incidents, should reach the responsible technical officials of the engine-builder. It is then the duty of the latter to weigh and interpret the observed facts, in terms of improvement for embodiment in succeeding designs of engine.

It is standard practice for engine-builders to supply a fully detailed book of instructions on operation and maintenance to the chief engineer of every ship propelled by their proprietary types of machinery. This book of instructions normally remains in the care of the chief engineer and, regrettably, its contents are not always available to the ordinary members of the engine-room staff.

In this chapter some guidance notes of a necessarily general nature on operation, overhaul and maintenance are given.

SOME OPERATIONAL NOTES

Preparations for Starting Engine

The recommended sequence of preliminary steps is summarised below. These steps should be taken methodically and unhurriedly.

1. The jacket cooling water should be heated slowly, by circulating fresh water from the auxiliary generator discharge through the main engine system. Where such a connection is not provided, steam may be arranged to percolate into the cooling water while it is being circulated by the fresh-water pump. The fresh-water cooler should be by-passed during this operation. The pipe system and cylinder jackets should be examined for leaks.

2. The amount of oil in the fuel service tank should be checked.

3. The low-pressure fuel-oil filters should be examined and cleaned—if necessary; all connections to the fuel-service pump should be opened.

4. The lubricating oil filters should be inspected and cleaned— if necessary.

5. The lubricating oil pump should be started, after ensuring that all the appropriate valves are open; the oil coolers should be by-passed; the oil system should be examined for leaks and the piston cooling oil-flow returns checked.

6. If there is a crankcase vapour extraction fan, this should be started.

7. The turboblower lubricating oil pump should be started, checking the bearing-oil temperature.

8. The cylinder lubricators should be filled and primed by hand pumping. A check should be made for leaks at pipe-joints and plunger stuffing boxes.

9. All hand lubrication points—e.g. those on the manoeuvring gear, reversing gear links, etc.—should be oiled.

10. The automatic valve should be moved by the handle provided; the air-distributor operating piston should be tried, by moving the test lever, to ensure that it operates freely; the components should be lubricated.

11. After opening the indicator cocks, the engine should be moved through at least one complete revolution by means of the turning gear. This is important, especially if the engine has been stopped for an appreciable length of time, because if water—for one reason or another—has accumulated in the cylinders, damage is thereby obviated. (Cylinders have been known to be wholly or partially flooded, by way of the silencer and piping, when in a tropical port during the wet season.)

12. The fuel-oil system should be primed, as may be described in the builders' operating instructions.

13. The manoeuvring air compressor should be started and the air reservoirs charged to the required pressure.

14. The turning gear should be disengaged.

15. The auxiliary—or emergency—scavenge air blower should be started, if such a unit is part of the installation.

16. The air-reservoir stop valve, the air-distributor stop valve and the main-engine stop valve should be opened. All air drains should be shut-off.

17. If conditions external to the ship are safe, and if permission is given by the bridge, the engine should be tried, ahead and astern, on starting air.

18. The engine is now ready for manoeuvring. When STAND-BY is rung on the telegraph from the bridge, the indicator cocks should be closed.

Starting the Engine

Immediately the first order has been given by the bridge telegraph, the engine-reversing handle should be moved into the appropriate position, be it ahead or astern.

The manoeuvring handle is then pushed over to START. This movement will cause the air pilot valve to be lifted, admitting air—by way of the automatic valve—to the air distributor and the cylinder starting valves.

Immediately the engine gathers speed, the manoeuvring handle should be pushed over to FUEL. When firing begins at the cylinders the handle is positionally adjusted, as may be appropriate to the required engine speed.

If the engine fails to pick up on fuel, a second or even a third application of starting air will be essential. After a third unsuccessful attempt it can be assumed that the fuel system is airlocked. Re-priming will therefore be necessary before any further attempt to start the engine is made.

While the engine is running slowly, the pressure-gauge readings should be observed; especially should the exhaust pyrometers be carefully watched, for assurance that all cylinders are firing properly. The air-inlet pipe on each starting valve should be felt; heat is an indication that a valve is sticking in the open position. If a leaking starting valve cannot be made gas-tight by turning the spindle on its seat the engine should be stopped and the valve be changed. If the engine is allowed to run with a leaky starting valve the oil on the spindle—and on the other starting-valve spindles also—will become dry and ineffective. All the valves will therefore be liable to stick when the engine is started on the next occasion.

In no circumstances must the starting-air valves be eased or freed by the application of petrol, paraffin or any kind of inflammable liquid when in position on the engine.

When the order FULL-AWAY is received the auxiliary scavenge air blower should be stopped. The starting air stop valve should be closed and all air drains opened.

Keeping Watch

On the way to the engine room the colour of the funnel exhaust gases should be observed.

The cylinder exhaust-gas temperatures should be noted and con-firmation made that the power of the engine is well distributed among the cylinders. The cylinder-jacket outlet-water temperatures should be observed and, by manipulation of the test cocks on the outlet pipes, it should be seen that there are no air-locks. The water level in the fresh-water heater tank should be checked. If the air-inlet pipe of a starting valve is hotter than the others the valve should be changed at the earliest opportunity. Observation should be made of the turboblower lubricating oil temperatures and pressures, also the exhaust-gas temperatures before and after the turbines. It should be confirmed that the amount of fuel oil in the service tank is ample for the duration of the watch.

The cylinder lubricators should be examined for satisfactory operation. The telescopic piston-cooling pipes and the scraper glands for the piston rods should be examined for leakage. All pressures and temperatures, as registered by the various gauges and thermometers, should be regularly observed for abnormalities. The amount of lubricating oil in the drain tank should be checked by sounding. If lubricating oil filters of the edgewise cleaning type are fitted the handles should be given a few turns. The sea temperature should be noted and the temperatures at lubricating oil and fresh-water coolers observed.

A keen sense of hearing is desirable. It is by his ears that the engineer becomes aware of abnormal happenings in the running gear.

Before a fuel service tank is brought into use it should be drained of water and sediment. If two tanks are installed the empty tank should be pumped up immediately.

Fuel-oil filters should normally be cleaned once every week; but in bad weather, when the sediment is liable to be disturbed, they may have to be cleaned several times a day.

During manoeuvres, the fresh-water temperature should be regulated by throttling the salt-water supply to the fresh-water cooler.

In shallow water the high sea-water suction—commonly termed the high injection valve—should be used, for minimising the inflow of sand.

Special attention should be given to the rectification of leaks of all descriptions, immediately they become apparent. Vital parts of the engine should be examined as frequently as practicable. If the crankcase is opened for investigation, naked lights must not be used until the inside of the crankcase has been fully ventilated.

All tools and spanners should be maintained in good order and systematically stored.

Stopping the Engine

At the end of a voyage, before STAND-BY is rung by the bridge on the telegraph, the air automatic valve and the air distributor should be lubricated and tested. On receiving the order to stand-by, the main air stop valve should be opened, all air drains should be closed and the auxiliary scavenge air blower should be started.

It is desirable that there should be a *modus vivendi* between engine room and bridge whereby, before the beginning of engine man-oeuvres, the engine revolutions will be gradually reduced. During this time care should be taken that the cylinder-jacket outlet temperatures are maintained.

During the period of manoeuvring an engineer should be stationed on the top platform for observing the working of the fuel valves and for noting those which are faulty in operation or sluggish in firing.

Careful attention must continue to be given to the jacket-water temperatures, the salt-water supply to the fresh-water cooler being severely throttled or, if necessary, completely shut-off, for ensuring a satisfactory temperature level.

On receiving the order FINISHED WITH ENGINES the main air stop valve should be closed; all the air drains should be opened; the auxiliary scavenge air blower should be stopped; the turboblower lubricating oil pumps should be stopped; the main fuel-oil inlet valve should be closed. The starting air in the air reservoirs should be raised to full pressure; a full flow of lubricating oil should be maintained in circulation for at least fifteen minutes before there is any thought of by-passing the cooler, reducing the pump speed or shutting down. By this means the deposition of carbon will be minimised, especially inside the pistons if these are oil cooled. Similarly, the flow of cooling water should be maintained for about fifteen minutes, for minimising the rate of change of cylinder-liner temperature. By observing the water-jacket outlet temperatures, a correct decision can be made regarding the moment to begin by-passing the cooler and reducing the pump speed.

If, when in harbour or at anchor, the engine-room temperature cannot be maintained above, say, 2°C, all cooling water should be drained from the engine jackets and piping system, also from the fresh-water cooler and pump.

Reversing from Ahead to Astern

If an order to reverse the engines is received from the bridge while the ship is manoeuvring in and out of harbour the ship will usually be moving slowly, and reversal can speedily be made without difficulty.

If, however, the vessel is proceeding at full speed the prolonged application of a powerful astern torque will be necessary. The starting air is only capable of turning the engine at reduced revolutions. It is obvious, therefore, that it will have to be applied over some specific period of time during which the force of the water acting on the propeller has to be overcome.

Only when the speed of the ship is broken sufficiently will the starting air power be able to overcome the above force completely and bring the engine to a stop. When the engine has actually been stopped its internal friction is generally sufficient to prevent it from beginning to run ahead again.

It should be realised that immediately the starting air is applied in the opposite direction to that in which the engine is running it has full effect on one cylinder at a time and for only one revolution or perhaps slightly more. After that the effect will diminish because the pressure of the trapped starting air, after the main pistons have passed their top dead-centres, will counteract the original braking effect. It is therefore advisable in such conditions that the reversing procedure should be as follows:

1. The manoeuvring handle is brought to the stop position. The auxiliary scavenge air blower is started.

2. The reversing handle is moved, *unhurriedly*, from the ahead to the astern position.

3. The manoeuvring handle is pushed to the starting position, thereby applying the starting air.

4. After not more than about two revolutions the handle is pulled back to the stop position.

5. Movements 3 and 4 are repeated, the starting air being applied and then cut-off.

6. On a third application of starting air the engine can usually be expected to stop and to begin moving slowly in the astern direction. (It is necessary to be absolutely sure that this is so before applying fuel.)

7. If, after the fourth air impulse, the engine is only creeping astern a fifth application of starting air, as described previously, is advisable. By then, sufficient engine speed astern will have been obtained for it to be safe to push the handle as quickly as possible from the starting to the full-fuel position without any risk that the engine will again move ahead.

8. Sufficient fuel must now be admitted for the engine to be able quickly to gather speed in the astern direction. If there seems to be a tendency to lag and slow down, the manoeuvring handle is pushed somewhat further on to fuel. One or two cylinder-relief valves may lift slightly while the engine is moving slowly. If all the cylinder-relief valves lift heavily it is a sign that the engine is running in the wrong direction, as will be observed from the direction indicator.

For a reversal from astern to ahead, with full way on the ship, the same procedure as above described will be followed. It is then likely that fewer starting-air impulse applications will be needed.

The time required for the complete operation of reversal need not be more than 30–35 seconds, at the most. Attempts to shorten the procedure can be dangerous and, indeed, will usually increase the time required. Despite what has just been mentioned, it is by no means unusual for a longer time for reversal to be required, depending upon ship and propeller conditions.

SOME WORKING DIFFICULTIES

Some difficulties which may be experienced in service are itemised below. The probable causes are stated.

When an Engine Will not Start

Should an engine start on air but move in the wrong direction, one or more starting valves must be leaking or sticking.

If an engine will not start on air the reason may be one of the following: the starting pressure is too low; stop valves between air reservoirs and engine are shut; starting or distributor valves are sticking; the pilot valve may be sticking; a starting valve is leaking on one of the cylinders as the piston moves upwards under compression; or the engine is being braked, either by the main or bottom-end bearings being too tight, or because of entanglement at the propeller or by reason of the turning gear being engaged.

When an Engine Turns Slowly at Starting

If an engine starts very slowly on air and there is no ignition, the cause may be one of the following: the starting-air pressure is too low; the automatic starting valve does not lift sufficiently, or is leaking; the starting valves are leaking; the pistons on top of the starting valves are leaking; the pilot distributor valves are sticking; the air-distributor chain is either slack or stretched; or the starting stop valve may not have been opened sufficiently.

When an Engine Will not Fire

If an engine starts on air, but there is no ignition subsequent to the starting handle being thrown over to oil, one of the following causes may be responsible: valves between settling tanks and surcharging pump are closed; the fuel pump is air-locked; fuel valves are leaking; unsatisfactory fuel oil, which may be too heavy or contain too much water; fuel-valve by-pass is open; air is in fuel-oil system; fuel-oil filters are choked; no fuel oil in service tank; no fuel-oil pressure because of service-pump fault; air-compression pressure too low because of faulty piston rings or loss of scavenge air pressure.

Should a cylinder refuse to fire when the engine is running, there may be air in the fuel pump, pipe-line or fuel valves; the remedy is to open the priming valve on the fuel valve and the air valve on the fuel pump until there is a steady flow of oil. Alternatively, there may be a choked fuel valve, necessitating a change of valves.

Engine Exhaust not Smokeless

Should the exhaust gases become visible and contain either grey or black smoke, the cause may be: overloading of engine; unsuitable fuel oil; nozzle holes not suitable for fuel used; holes in nozzles partly choked; broken fuel-valve spring; injection pressure too low; fuel valves leaking; air in fuel system; fuel-valve lift incorrect; ignition too late; dirty inlet strainers; one or more of the fuel pumps may have ceased to function properly, or have become mis-timed, because a fuel-cam timing gear has slackened back, thus overloading the other cylinders; the air-compression pressure is too low, because of leaking piston rings or scavenge air blower fault; the exhaust back-pressure is too great; or the fuel-oil temperature may be too high for its viscosity.

An admixture of blue smoke in the exhaust gases usually signifies that lubricating oil is being burned in the combustion space. The cause may be a leak in an oil-cooled piston. A white exhaust is usually an indication of misfiring in one of the cylinders.

Engine Knocking

If a knock is heard while the engine is running at slow speed, or on starting from cold, it may be only the characteristic knock which is liable to occur in most compression-ignition engines in these circumstances; it will probably disappear on the attainment of normal running speeds and temperatures. If, however, the knocking is persistent, or if it occurs while the engine is running at normal revolutions, an investigation should immediately be made and the cause be uncovered.

If the knocking is traceable to one cylinder the fuel supply can be by-passed, thus revealing whether the knock is due to faulty combustion or to a mechanical defect in a working part.

Apart from overloading, knocking may be caused by: too much 'play' in oscillating parts; ignition too early; injection pressure too high; leaking or sticking valves; unsatisfactory fuel atomisation; ignition too late; uneven distribution of fuel to different cylinders.

Slowing-down of Engine

Should the revolutions fall, with the manoeuvring handle in its normal position, the cause may be: a seized or leaky fuel-pump plunger; a component of the regulating gear having slackened back; a leaking joint, causing air-lock; a leaking priming valve or sticking fuel-valve spindle, causing air-locks; a burst fuel-delivery pipe;

choked atomising holes; fuel-valve lift too small; choked fuel filters; water in the fuel oil; leak in service-pump by-pass valve; empty service tank; air leak on suction side of fuel system; choked air-inlet strainers or filters; air-compression pressure too low, because of faulty piston rings or deficiency in scavenging air pressure; seizure of an engine component; overloading of engine; fouling of propeller by extraneous object; increased propeller slip because of heavy weather, especially head winds; or increase of helm to turn ship.

Irregularity of Running

If the engine runs with irregularity the cause may be: faulty governor or governor gear; air or gases in the fuel lines; water in the fuel; fuel too viscous; choking of fuel-oil filters; faulty fuel valve or valves.

Scavenge-belt Fires

To obviate the combustion of lubricating oil in the scavenge spaces, the undermentioned precautions should be taken.

The piston rings must be maintained in good order, to prevent blow-past. In this connection, the correct timing of the cylinder lubricators can be an important factor.

Although the cylinder lubrication may clearly be normal and adequate, nevertheless, if the surfaces of the cylinders and the pistons are dry it is a sign that the piston rings need attention. Broken and worn rings must be changed.

Scavenge belts and spaces should be cleared of all carbonised oil as often as practicable. The exhaust ports should be cleared of carbon deposit. Care should be taken that no cylinder is overloaded relative to the other cylinders.

So long as liquid can be drained from a scavenge belt there is little likelihood of fire. If, however, a fire should occur, the fuel pump on the cylinder concerned should be lifted off its cam and the suction valve of the pump should be closed. The scavenge-space drain cocks should be shut-off. The supply of lubricating oil to the main piston, only, should be increased.

Indicator Diagrams

Before attaching the indicator, the indicator cocks should be blown-through thoroughly to remove carbon and other matter. The indicator piston should be taken out frequently, for cleaning and oiling.

After an overhaul, during which the driving gear has been disconnected, it is desirable to check the indicator-cam positions. Compression cards are therefore taken, with fuel cut-off, by opening the fuel-valve priming valves.

In a true compression diagram the compression and expansion lines exactly coincide. Slackness or tightness in the indicator or in the driving gear may cause the lines to cross and the compression card to show an enclosed area. This may wrongly indicate that positive or negative work is being done in the cylinder. The working card, obtained while firing is taking place, will therefore be either fuller or narrower by this amount. A positive indicator compression card can usually be corrected by retarding the cam slightly; a negative card requires the cam to be advanced in the direction of rotation. On a positive card the expansion line will remain in front of, or above, the compression line, until nearly the toe of the card is reached; a negative card is recognisable by the expansion line joining the compression line near, or before, the centre of the card. That is: on a positive compression card the two lines tend to remain a longer time apart than when the card is negative. If the two lines coincide during the up and down stroke, until near the centre of the card, and then part slightly towards the toe, the card may be accepted as satisfactory. Any further retardation of the indicator cam will cause a definite loop on the down stroke, and the card will become negative. The tendency of the lines to remain apart, when running horizontally, is explained by the friction of the pencil against the paper, and by the slight clearance in the pencil lever rods.

The approximate amount the indicator cam should be moved on the circumference of the shaft is the measurement of the widest part of the loop, negative or positive, multiplied by two.

If an engine runs too fast the taking of a true compression card may be impracticable; the open by-pass valves may not prevent fuel from entering and firing in the cylinder. If a fuel valve leaks, fuel may enter the cylinder during the stroke and fire at the end of compression. A small working card, instead of a compression card, will thus be obtained. When in doubt, the fuel-pump stop valve should be closed and the fuel-valve priming valve opened fully. Should a compression card show that firing is still occurring, there may be leakage from the piston-cooling oil system. Examination should be made for vapour rising from the piston-cooling outlet pockets or smoke from the exhaust cocks.

All cards from the same engine, except those from the top and bottom cylinders of double-acting engines, should be to the same hand, but there is no significance in this.

Indicator-card heights vary with cylinder load and engine revolutions. Approximate figures to be maintained will be stated on the adjustment and instruction sheets for the engine. Firing heights and mean pressures should be checked by taking indicator cards regularly. If a card exceeds the maximum height permitted—the engine being normal—the fuel-pump plunger should be lowered by about one-half of the amount that the card is too high. Alternatively, the fuel valve may have been wrongly adjusted, to open at too low an injection pressure; or the fuel-valve spring may be broken. If a card is too high, and its mean pressure is higher than the average for the cards taken, then the fuel supply should be reduced on the fuel pump.

If, in a twin-screw ship, one engine is shut down for a time, cards should be taken from the other engine to ensure that initial pressures do not rise too far above those which are permissible.

Low indicator cards are usually caused by: fuel-valve lift too small; choked fuel valves; leaking or sluggishly operated fuel valves; leaky pipe or filter joint; fuel pump sticking, or roller not running on its cam continuously; or fuel-pump plunger working loose. If the fuel-pump setting is normal an improvement in height and mean pressure can be effected by increasing the fuel supply height—by adjusting the fuel-pump regulating rod. If no fault can be found from the foregoing suggestions the cause of the low card may be a leaky plunger, for a plunger can leak excessively from the pressure to the suction side without oil reaching the plunger bottom. A spare pump must then be fitted and precautions taken—as directed on the adjustment sheet—for obtaining correct plunger height.

Light spring cards are taken for determining the pressures in the cylinders during the exhaust and the air-intake periods. It is sometimes useful to keep records of the exhaust-pressure heights from the atmospheric line, and the intake-air pressure at the beginning of the compression stroke. From these records it can be seen, for example, when the exhaust ports in a two-cycle engine should be cleaned, or if the exhaust turboblower or air valves in a four-cycle pressure-induction engine need attention.

Compression Cards

The ideal compression card is shown in Figure 12.1, diagram 1, wherein, for the length of the card, the compression and expansion lines coincide. In 2 the cam is probably correctly placed, but the loops signify that there is a time lag in the drive, caused by tight gear or/and a loose indicator pencil lever. Diagram 3—which is positive in area—shows the expansion line in front and above the compression line for the length of the card; the cure is to retard the indicator cam 5–6 mm. In 4—which is a negative diagram—the expansion line lies behind and below the compression line for half the length

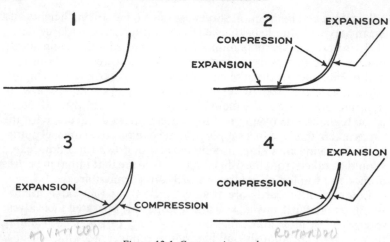

Figure 12.1 Compression cards

of the card; for rectification the indicator cam should be advanced 3–4 mm.

Two-stroke Engine Indicator Cards

In Figure 12.2, diagrams 5 and 6 are normal cards for single-acting two-stroke engines. In 5 the mean indicated pressure is about

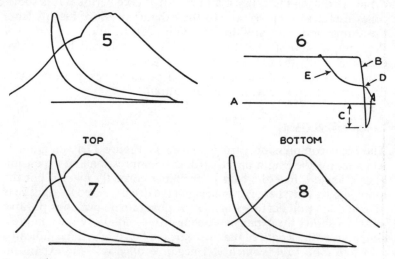

Figure 12.2 Two-stroke engine indicator cards

7·60 kgf/cm², the compression height about 38 mm, the firing height about 56 mm. The scale of all normal indicator diagrams is 1 mm = 1 kgf/cm². A light spring diagram is reproduced at 6; the scale of such a card is: 45 mm = 1 kgf/cm². The atmospheric line is lettered A; B is the line of falling exhaust pressure; C the lowest pressure in the cylinder during scavenging; D the pressure at the beginning of compression; E the compression line.

Diagrams 7 and 8, Figure 12.2, are normal diagrams for two-stroke double-acting engines. In diagram 7—for the top of the cylinder— the mean indicated pressure is about 7·1 kgf/cm², the compression height about 34 mm, the firing height about 47·5 mm; for the cylinder bottom the mean indicated pressure is about 6·7 kgf/cm², the compression height about 35 mm, the firing height about 48 mm. In the full-load diagram 9, Figure 12.3, the effect of a leaking fuel-pump plunger is shown. The full lines are the actual, the dotted lines the normal, shape of the indicator card. The compression height is normal; the firing height is too low. The fuel-pump regulating arm has been adjusted to provide an increased fuel charge to make up leakage losses. If the fuel-valve filter or nozzle holes are choked, the fuel-injection pipe or the fuel-valve leaking, the diagram will also lose height, and the appearance of the card will be similar to 9.

The light spring diagram 10, which may be from the top or bottom of a double-acting two-stroke engine, shows the normal card in dotted lines, the actual card in full lines. Either the exhaust ports

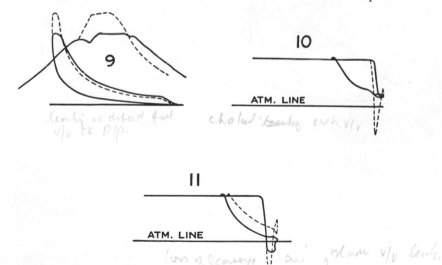

Figure 12.3 Two-stroke engine indicator cards

are partly choked by carbon or there is too much resistance in the exhaust system. Card 11 indicates loss of scavenge air; probably the blower change valves are leaking or are not properly closed.

Four-stroke Engine Indicator Cards

Figure 12.4 shows normal cards at 12 and 13 for a four-stroke, single-acting engine. On the full-load working card 12, Point Y shows where the exhaust valve begins to open. On the drawcard, taken by pulling the indicator cord by hand, X shows where fuel injection begins at the top of the compression stroke. Cards 13 are light-load diagrams.

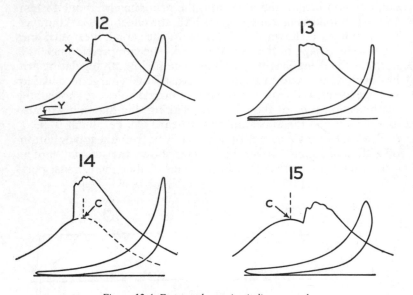

Figure 12.4 Four-stroke engine indicator cards

Diagram 14 indicates the effect of too early ignition, probably caused by the fuel-pump timing being too early, the fuel-valve spring being set to lift at too low a pressure or the fuel-valve spring being broken. The maximum pressure is too high; the extended dotted compression curve shows firing taking place before top dead-centre C.

Card 15 shows the effect of too late ignition. The maximum pressure is too low; the draw-card shows that firing has taken place after the crank has passed the top dead-centre C. The fuel-pump timing may be too late, or the fuel valve and its filter can be at fault.

Figure 12.5 illustrates light spring diagrams at 16, 17, 18 and 19. At 16, which is a power diagram taken with a weak indicator spring, 12 mm = 1 kgf/cm², A is the air-inlet suction line, B the compression line, C the expansion line, D the exhaust line. The exhaust valve opens at E. The atmospheric line is dotted. In 17 the exhaust valve opens too late and closes too soon; the cam clearance is too great. In 18 the exhaust resistance is too great, perhaps caused by an obstructed exhaust outlet. In 19 the resistance in the air intake is too great, perhaps the result of an obstructed air-inlet strainer or too small an opening at the air-inlet valve. Alternatively, the cam clearance may be too great. The cylinder-air volume V is reduced by the amount S which the piston traverses before reaching atmospheric pressure. The dotted vertical line shows where the compression line C intersects the dotted atmospheric line.

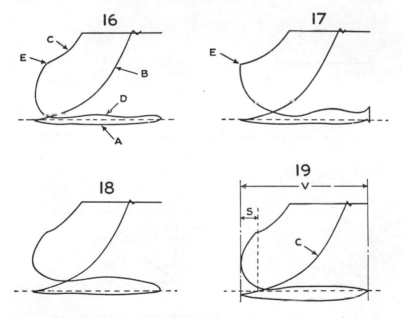

Figure 12.5 Four-stroke engine light spring cards

In Figure 12.6, diagrams 20 and 21 respectively show normal working diagrams and light-load diagrams for single-acting four-stroke engines, pressure-charged on the Büchi system. In 20 the mean indicated pressure is about 9·1 kgf/cm², the firing height about 46 mm, the compression height about 35 mm. In 21 the mean indicated pressure is about 4·5 kgf/cm², the firing height about 39 mm, the compression height about 30 mm. Light spring diagrams, 45 mm = 1 kgf/cm², are illustrated at 22 and 23, where *A* is the air inlet, *B* the compression and *C* the exhaust. Line *C* differs in the two diagrams—it depends upon the number of cylinders and the exhaust-pipe length—but both are normal.

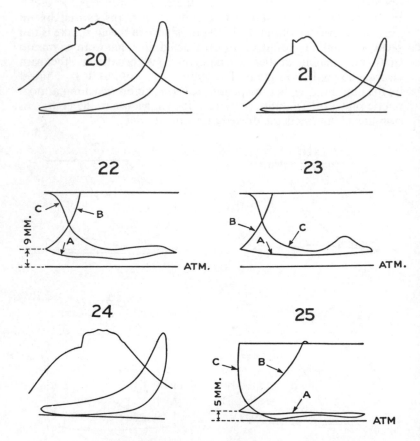

Figure 12.6 Four-stroke engine indicator cards

Cards 24 and 25 are typical for single-acting, four-stroke, under-piston, pressure-charged engines. Diagram 24 is for overload work-ing, with mean indicated pressure about 10·5 kgf/cm², compression height about 35·5 mm, firing height about 45 mm. Normal and light indicator cards for such engines are the same as for exhaust turbo-blown engines. Diagram 25 is a light spring card, 20 mm = 1 kgf/cm² for an under-piston charged engine. *A* is the air-induction, *B* the compression and C the exhaust line. The line C, in this type of pressure-charged engine falls below line A (compare with diagram 22). The pressure at the beginning of compression is 0·25 kgf/cm² above atmosphere.

Mean Indicated Pressures

If there is any doubt about an indicator card showing the correct mean pressure—assuming that the indicator drive is in a state of proper adjustment—it is advisable, in the first instance, to rely upon the indicator card rather than upon deductions from the exhaust temperature as shown by pyrometer.

To assist in removing or confirming the doubt, the exhaust temperature of each cylinder should be checked against that of the other cylinders. The same mercury thermometer should be used for all the cylinders. By checking all the cylinders in this way, the reliability of the pyrometers can be determined, and a useful comparison made with the indicator card.

If, for any cylinder, the mean pressure appears to be low and the exhaust temperature high, the explanation is, usually, shortage of combustion air. This may arise from carbon-choked ports or broken piston rings.

OVERHAULING AND MAINTENANCE

Overhauling Gear

Engine-room cranes and overhauling gear are matters of real importance. Expeditious overhauling of machinery requires, as a concomitant, a high degree of labour saving. It is not the size of an engine which makes overhauling difficult; it is lack of appropriate facilities. A large and powerful engine, well planned for easy overhaul and well provided with lifting and transporting gear, can be much easier to handle than a small engine having no equivalent gear.

Wherever possible, main pistons and piston rods should have a straight vertical lift. Ship considerations can, and do, override this desideratum, but, nevertheless, every effort should be made, in planning the engine room, to attain this result.

Pistons

The rings of the main pistons should be examined monthly, if possible, during the first half-year of service. If the condition of the rings is satisfactory, then an examination every six months is all that is necessary.

Pistons should be taken out for inspection once a year and all cooling spaces opened up and cleaned.

Leaky pistons cause low efficiency in an engine. Lubricating oil is blown away from the piston rings; friction increases, wear and tear become greater. When new rings are fitted care must be taken to ensure that there is sufficient clearance in the laps to allow for the expansion of the rings. In trunk engines the scraper rings are often placed away from the piston rings; their lower edges are made sharp for preventing crankcase oil, which has splashed on to the cylinder walls, from passing the rings and being burned in the cylinder. If combustion gases are blowing past the pistons and the piston rings are not sticking, the cause may be wear of the rings and the gaps having opened so much that the combustion gases have forced their way through the entire group of rings. The cure is to fit new piston rings, as it is of the utmost importance that the pistons should be tight.

Where there is a common system for bearing lubrication and piston-oil cooling, it is important that all bearings and bearing liners are maintained in good condition, thereby preventing oil from escaping too freely, with consequent loss of oil pressure. The piston-cooling-oil outlet temperature must not be allowed to exceed 70°C. For controlling the temperature a regulating valve is usually fitted to the bearing-oil system. By throttling the oil supply here, more oil will flow to the pistons. The control valve for the bearing-oil supply is so designed that it can never cut off the supply completely.

Oil holes in the cylinder liners, for piston lubrication, should be cleaned periodically. In crosshead engines a scraper-ring device for the piston rod is fitted on the crankcase top. Occasionally it should be confirmed that the segments of the ring are not butting, thus preventing the ring from functioning efficiently.

To prevent fires occurring in the scavenge spaces, the precautions to be taken are:

(a) piston rings to be maintained in good order to prevent blow-past;

(b) when cylinders and piston surfaces are dry—although the cylinder lubrication appears to be normal—the piston rings should be attended to;

(c) scavenge belts and spaces should be cleared of carbonised and oxidised oil as frequently as practicable;

(d) care to be taken to keep the exhaust ports clear of carbon;

(e) one cylinder unit must not become appreciably overloaded, in comparison with the others;

(f) if, despite all precautions, combustion occurs in a scavenge space, the fuel-valve by-passes for the cylinder should be opened, the drain cocks closed and the lubricating oil to the main piston increased until combustion has ceased.

As long as lubricating oil in the liquid state can be drained from scavenge spaces there is little likelihood of fires starting.

Cylinder Liners and Jackets

When the pistons are withdrawn, the condition of the cylinder liners should be noted and carbon deposits removed from the ports. If the exhaust temperature steadily increases over a period of time, and if this rise is accompanied by an increase in air pressure, carbon deposits in the ports can be expected.

The cylinder jackets are provided with inspection doors through which the water spaces can be examined. This should be done every six months.

It is important that rubber rings should not be volume-bound nor wedged in the grooves. That is, the rings should not project more than 1 mm above the metal surface. If a jacket rubber ring is oversize in diameter and the desired size is not available a piece should be cut out of the length and a scarfed joint made with rubber solution. If the diameter is 10 per cent oversize, then 20 per cent of the length should be cut out; and so on, *pro rata*. The increased stretch will reduce the diameters to the size required.

After fitting a new cylinder liner, or new rubber rings, or a new piston in an existing liner, the engine should be 'run-in' slowly, as if new.

Fuel Valves

Fuel valve designs necessarily differ according to the proprietary engine types. A characteristic design is described below.

Two fuel valves per combustion space are usual in two-stroke engines. Normal practice is for the spindles and nozzles to have flat seats except in small engines, when they are conical. In some engines the valves are oil-cooled by a separate circulating system. Fuel valves are always fitted with air vents and air-release ball valves, which are used for priming. Normally each ball valve is screwed down tight, but, when priming or forcing the air out of the fuel system, the plug on top is released; the oil and air then pass out through a drain pipe.

There is no special delivery valve, or other non-return valve, between fuel pump and fuel valves. It is therefore essential that fuel valves do not leak, otherwise the fuel injection will fail. The upper face of the valve-spindle sleeve forms a seat against the lower end of the valve box, and is carefully ground in. The top face of the nozzle, or pulveriser, is also ground and forms a seat against the bottom face of the valve-spindle sleeve. Both are firmly secured to the valve body by the bottom coupling-nut and are prevented, by steady-pins, from turning.

The nozzle, except in small engines, is made in two parts which are pressed together. The outer part has a diagonal hole for the fuel-oil inlet, and the inner part is provided with grooves which form passages for the oil to circulate around the nozzle-piece, flowing out through the outlet groove into the fuel-valve-spindle chamber. This arrangement helps to keep the nozzle cool when no separate cooling system is provided. When the fuel valve is being assembled it is important to guard against the steady-pins being damaged or sheared, thus resulting in the oil flow through the head of the spindle-case being blanked.

The fuel-valve spring is arranged in a space above the spindle. A guide washer at the bottom of the spring transmits the spring-pressure to the fuel-valve-spindle top. The spring is adjusted as mentioned when dealing with pressure-testing. An indicator rod is arranged in the hollow adjusting screw and, passing through the spring, rests on the fuel-valve-spindle rod. By pressing a finger on the end of the rod it can be ascertained if the valve is working properly.

Fuel-valve Examination

When examining fuel valves, all parts must be washed clean with solar oil, or paraffin, and dried in a warm place—without using cleaning rags. The reason for this is that minute particles of fluff will adhere to the cleaned parts, eventually to find their way into the injection holes, to impede the spray and to cause the injection pressure to rise, thus reducing the quantity of fuel oil injected. Increasing the fuel delivery, by adjustment of the length of the pump-regulating rod, will only assist slightly. If rags and cotton waste have been used for cleaning fuel-valve parts during overhauling the consequences may be burst pipes, leaky joints and the necessity for the frequent changing of fuel valves.

After being washed in clean paraffin, all parts should be placed on warm dust-free plates, to dry before reassembling. During the first voyage of a new ship all fuel filters should be frequently removed for cleaning, even if the valves seem to be working perfectly. Later, with the continued use of properly purified fuel oil, the filters can remain undisturbed until the fuel valves themselves require over-hauling; this may be from, say, six to eight weeks. When a filter is taken out to be cleaned the housing must be washed out also. Clean paraffin should be used, with a small brush, to remove the dirt. The use of cotton waste or rags is to be avoided, as previously stressed.

When changing a nozzle-piece great care should be taken not to damage the valve spindle or its sleeve. While the nozzle-piece is out of the fuel valve, the centre-hole should be cleaned with a spiral drill and the pulveriser-holes with a special cleaning needle. Should the nozzle face be pitted or scratched, the defects can be ground away against a surface plate or against the face of another nozzle. A nozzle with a damaged face should never be re-used.

Each fuel-valve spindle and sleeve are matched. Should the spindle be damaged, the sleeve should be returned to the makers for matching with the new spindle. Hard spots on valve spindles can be polished away by the use of a fine hone, after which the spindle may be lapped into its sleeve with jeweller's rouge. Traces of scoring on new valves can be treated in the same way.

If, during normal running, a cylinder should stop firing by reason of a defective fuel valve, priming valves of both fuel valves should be opened and the outflow of fuel oil into the drain funnel observed. The fuel valve which discharges oil vapour, or aerated fuel, will be the faulty one. A steady stream of darker-coloured oil will be discharged from the tight fuel valve. If the faulty fuel valve is leaking but slightly it may be possible at full load—by shutting the priming valve of the satisfactory valve and leaving slightly open the priming valve of the faulty fuel valve—for the satisfactory fuel valve to continue to operate; the gases entering during cylinder compression and firing can then find an easy outlet between the strokes of the fuel pump.

It should be superfluous to state that each fuel valve should be perfect, in all respects, before being used. The spindle should be a tight fit in its housing, but, at the same time—when perfectly clean and held at an angle of about 45° to the horizontal—it should be able to slide out of the housing by its own weight. Before trying a fuel valve in this manner all oil must be washed off with clean paraffin. If the spindle surface is not absolutely smooth and free from all tool marks and blemishes the fuel valve will operate satisfactorily for only a very short time; fine, solid matter in the fuel will lodge in the surface undulations and blemishes, and cause the spindle to operate sluggishly. If the valve does not close snappily after injection is completed the combustion products will flash through the fuel valve. This may cause overheating and distortion of the spindle, so that leakage begins and the fuel-injection pump becomes inefficient in its working. The pump must then be replaced at the earliest opportunity.

Fuel-valve Lift

The springs of fuel valves are adjustable; the opening pressure is stated on the adjustment sheet supplied with the engine. The valve lift should never exceed the lift stated on the adjustment sheet, otherwise the springs may be overstressed and break. If the lift is below 75 per cent the fuel may be wire-drawn at full load and the combustion be impaired, because of reduced injection pressure at the nozzle. In these circumstances the indicator cards will show a reduction in height.

Before replacing a fuel valve in an engine it should always be tried on the test pump. The lift height should be checked, by ascertaining how much the lift stop-screw can be tightened up. After the priming valve has been opened it is possible—while running—to check and readjust a fuel valve having incorrect lift. Maintenance of correct lift will reduce spring breakages and also ensure minimum load being carried on pumps and pressure pipes.

As previously mentioned, when assembling a fuel valve great care must be taken not to shear the dowel-pin in the nozzle end, because the result may be either to blind the oil supply to the nozzle entirely or wrongly to direct the fuel spray, whereby an important part—such as a piston-rod sleeve or a cylinder-cover wall—may become burned and cracked.

Fuel-valve Testing

To pressure-test a fuel valve: the valve is connected to a test pump and then, after fuel oil has been pumped through the line and all air forced out through the valve air-vent, the pressure at which the valve actually opens is observed on the pressure gauge. The correct lifting pressure is stated on the adjustment sheet for the engine. The adjusting screw for the spring is now set so that the spindle lifts at this pressure. The screw is then locked in position and the lift pressure rechecked. Next, the nozzle is wiped thoroughly clean and pressure re-applied, this time to 10 kgf/cm^2 below the injection working pressure. If the pressure remains steady for a few minutes the valve is tight. A trace of oil at the nozzle-holes is of no importance, as the valve will normally be worked-in completely after a few minutes of running. Should, however, the nozzle become wet, or should drops appear, then replacement or regrinding of the valve is necessary.

If the injection pipe to a fuel valve becomes hot, and the valve is not leaking, there may be choking of nozzle holes, a dirty filter or too small a valve-lift. While running slowly, it is possible to determine if the two fuel valves in a cylinder are set to open at the same pressure. A pressure difference will cause uneven fuel distribution and inferior combustion at full load. The valve which is set to the higher pressure will cease to operate, or will react feebly, when the engine is running light. If a pair of fuel valves on the same cylinder stop functioning it is usual to find only one valve leaking. As already mentioned, if the leak is small it is possible to ascertain which valve is at fault, from the gases which blow out from the open priming valve or by-pass drain pipes. If the leak is heavy both drain pipes may be blowing out air; it will then be necessary to feel the valve bodies, for temperature, to determine which one is at fault. When a leaky fuel valve has been withdrawn for overhauling the lower part may show heat discoloration. This discoloration should be removed by emery cloth.

A record should be made showing the behaviour of each fuel valve; working and spare valves must be maintained in perfect condition— there is no alternative. A valve which repeatedly fails after only short periods of service is useless.

See also earlier reference in this chapter to fuel-valve pressure-testing.

Fuel-valve Priming

When preparing an engine for starting it is most important to have the air cleared from the fuel lines and every fuel valve properly primed with fuel oil. For this purpose, the engine-manoeuvring gear handle must remain in its stop position, so that the cylinder fuel-pump plungers do not block the free passage for the fuel oil. All intermediate shut-off valves between the fuel service tank and the fuel valves are then opened. The priming, or air release, valves on the fuel valves are opened up, and fuel oil passed through by hand-pumping until the oil is completely air-free. As soon as a steady stream of oil is issuing from a fuel valve its priming valve may be shut.

When changing a number of fuel valves it is desirable to prime only one cylinder at a time, because, if many priming valves are open together, the force of the oil through air-locked fuel pumps and fuel valves may not be strong enough to dislodge the air in all the pockets. While priming with the hand-pump, a pressure of at least one bar should be maintained and a careful search should be made, prefer-ably with a torch-light, to discover any leaking high-pressure fuel-oil joints. Defects should be rectified immediately. In no circumstances can even a very small leak be tolerated anywhere in the fuel-injection system.

If fuel oil should refuse to flow through any particular pair of priming valves the cause may be that either the stop valve of the corresponding fuel pump has not been opened or that the regulating lever of the pump has not been brought back to the no-fuel position by its spring, with the result that the pump plunger has been lifted by the fuel cam and the free passage of oil through the pump has been blocked.

If, during manoeuvring, an engine is running dead-slow for some time it is strongly recommended that the priming valves be opened slightly on any pair of fuel valves which, for one reason or another, may not have been operating satisfactorily at light load, and thus release all air and aerated fuel which could accumulate in valves and pipelines. On closing the priming valves, when the next order from the bridge is received, all cylinders will then fire. For this and similar reasons, at least one engineer should be stationed on the upper platform until all manoeuvres in and out of port have been completed. Before entering a port, when the engine is at STAND-BY, the engineer should open the priming valves on both fuel valves of all cylinders and carefully inspect the fuel-oil outflow. He will then be able to pick out any valve which it may be advisable to change when reaching port. He will also be forewarned of the valves which may be likely to be unsatisfactory during manoeuvres.

Fuel-injection Pumps

The fuel valve is the only delivery valve in the fuel-injection line of a normal two-stroke engine. There is therefore a relatively large volume between the top of the fuel-pump plunger and the fuel valve. Moreover, the suction efficiency is entirely dependent upon the vacuum created during the downward stroke of the plunger. When the plunger top edge begins to open to the fuel-pump suction holes the fuel must rush in and fill the space thus created. If any air— either from a leaky fuel-valve seat or from a leaky joint—enters the system during this period the vacuum will be proportionately vitiated and a reduced charge of oil will enter the pump delivery chamber. During the delivery stroke the entrained air must necessarily be compressed before the pump plunger can force any oil through the fuel valves into the engine cylinder. If the air leakage becomes great enough the pump will not be able to cope with it, and fuel injection will stop. Only one fuel-valve seat need leak for both valves to cease operating. If a pump is unable to deliver fuel the air or gas from a leaky fuel valve or valves will accumulate. As the system cannot then rid itself of the air, it may be necessary to shut the stop valve on the pump concerned—to prevent its neighbours from becoming air-locked.

If a fuel-pump stop valve is shut-off the pump should be hung up, to prevent the plunger from running dry and seizing. If, however, it seems undesirable to hang up the pump the stop valve should be left slightly open to ensure lubrication of the plunger. The priming valve of the leaky fuel valve should also remain open for the escape of the accumulated air and gas. If a fuel-pump plunger suddenly shows signs of sticking in its sleeve it will frequently be found that a leaky fuel valve is the cause; i.e. the pump has ceased to deliver fuel normally, over-heating by hot gases has occurred and the plunger has seized. As soon as the fuel valve has been located and changed, the pump will immediately begin to function properly again, unless the abnormal conditions have persisted so long that the plunger, when seizing, has scored the sleeve.

After a fuel pump has been overhauled its plunger height should be rechecked by means of the fuel-pump mandrel, as directed on the engine-adjustment sheet. If the plunger height has not been disturbed when taking the pump adrift it is not always necessary to use the mandrel. Then, all that is required when linking-up the pump lever, is to adjust the length of the regulating rod so that, with the starting handle in the stop position, the pointer indicates the normal number of degrees on the scale. When running the engine it will be observed, by comparing indicator cards and exhaust temperatures, if the fuel delivery of the pump is correct, or if adjustments are needed. Fuel-pump settings are also mentioned elsewhere in the chapter, when referring to indicator diagrams.

Shock Absorbers

The shock absorbers are intended to prevent the fuel oil—which during the delivery stroke of the plunger is spilled back into the suction line—from causing excessive surging in the line. The shock-absorber pistons are displaced by the fuel-oil pressure and returned by their spring load; by reducing pipe-surge, they assist in maintaining a steady charging pressure for the fuel pumps. Drain pipes are usually fitted to the shock absorbers, and it can be observed from them if the shock absorbers are functioning properly. Normally, only drops of oil should leak from the drain pipes.

If difficulties arise through broken shock-absorber springs, the lift of the pistons may be reduced, within reasonable limits; but their free movement must be ensured, to obviate hammering in the suction line.

The spill-line carries away the air which is entrained with the fuel or which is blown back through a pump. If a fuel valve leaks badly, so that it cannot operate, the non-return valve in the spill-pipe must be unable to release the air or gas through the line. The fuel should then be cut-off as described earlier.

Fuel-surcharging Pump

The fuel pumps are usually charged by a service or surcharging pump, located between the fuel-oil service tanks and the fuel pumps, and driven direct from the engine. It is fitted with a by-pass valve which lifts at about 2·5 kgf/cm² service pressure. A hand-gear is incorporated, whereby the surcharging pump can be operated and the pipe-lines primed and freed from air before starting the engine. An independent, motor-driven, rotary pump is sometimes fitted instead of the hand-pump. A spring-loaded hand-regulated by-pass valve is then usually arranged on the manoeuvring platform. During stand-by periods and prolonged stops the fuel should be by-passed to the service tank. In trunk engines a cog-wheel type of surcharging pump is often arranged on the end of the camshaft or on one of the blower-rotor shafts.

A fuel-oil filter is arranged between the settling tank and the fuel service or surcharging pump. This filter consists of two or more compartments, each fitted with a cartridge. By means of a change-cock these cartridges can be isolated, one by one, and taken out for cleaning. Indicator plates show which filter is in service. The service pump discharge pressure should be maintained at about 2 kgf/cm² ; it can be regulated by the by-pass valve. If the filter should become choked with dirt it may cause the engine fuel pipes to become air-locked from minor leaks in the surcharging-pump suction line.

Fuel Cam

The fuel cam usually consists of two main components, one being used for ahead running and the other for astern running. The components are mounted on a taper, on the camshaft, and are held in place by fitted bolts through slots in the cam. During the shop test of the engine the position of the cam for optimum combustion conditions is determined. When the test is ended, wedge-pieces are fitted to prevent the cam from shifting. To provide a continuous surface for the cam roller to work upon, the joint between the ahead and astern cams is tongued and grooved. When the wedge-pieces are fitted and the retaining nuts tightened-up, locking-washers prevent the nuts from slackening back. A tapped hole for a starting screw is provided in each half-cam, for easing same off the camshaft taper, should any alteration in timing be required.

To adjust a fuel cam: the nuts are removed from the fitted bolts;

the locking plates are removed; the wedge-pieces are removed from the ahead or the astern side of the cam—or both sides—depending upon which cam requires adjusting; the cam is moved until the fuel-pump lift at the corresponding main-piston top dead-centre is equal to the required figure; then new wedge-pieces are fitted and the cam reassembled.

Starting Gear

The starting gear normally comprises: (i) an automatic valve; (ii) a pilot valve; (iii) a distributor; and (iv) starting valves. The automatic valve, operated by the pilot valve, is worked by the starting handle. The starting valves are also automatic and are operated by air-pressure from the distributors. These, in turn, are operated by circular cams in phase with the engine cranks.

Before starting the engine, the main stop valve for the automatic valve is opened; air passes through a small pipe across the pilot-valve top and then through another pipe to the top of the automatic valve. The air, pressing upon the large area of a differential piston, keeps the automatic valve shut. When the starting handle is moved from the stop to the starting position, the pilot valve is lifted so that its air inlet is blocked; the pipe connection to the top of the valve piston is vented to atmosphere; the air pressure on the valve differential piston is relieved; the air pressure below the piston opens the automatic valve and air flows simultaneously to all starting valves and to the distributor.

The starting valves and their pilot valves in the distributor are held off the cams by springs under the spindle heads. When starting air reaches the distributor it tends to open its pilot valves; but the cams prevent this for all except that pilot valve whose spindle end can enter into the cam depression. This pilot valve opens and air passes through the connecting pipe into the appropriate starting valve, entering above the piston on the valve spindle. The starting valve lifts and air enters the engine cylinder. As soon as the engine has turned through the appropriate angle, the distributor cam shuts the pilot valve, and the air trapped on top of the starting-valve piston is vented to atmosphere through an outlet pipe on the distributor pilot valve. The starting valve is immediately closed by the spring at the top. The next cylinder unit then receives its quantum of starting air in similar manner.

As soon as the engine has attained the necessary speed, the starting handle is pushed further over, from the starting to the fuel position. This causes the pilot valve for the automatic valve to be tripped and the air pressure to be transmitted to the top of the differential piston again, immediately to close the valve. The air trapped in the starting-air lines, between the automatic valve and the starting valves, is vented through a special outlet in the valve, leading through a pipe into an air silencer. The air between the valve and the distributor is released to atmosphere through the same outlet. All air used for starting the engine is thus cut-off and released, rendering the starting valves inoperative.

The automatic valve should be lubricated occasionally with a few drops of oil, but never more than once a day. Over-lubrication of the starting service is most undesirable, because of explosion risks. At no time, nor in any circumstances, can solar oil or paraffin be allowed.

The automatic valve and the pilot valve should be examined twice a year, and seats ground if required. The distributor valves should be tried by hand, before manoeuvring. Their springs should be able to return them snappily, when released from contact with the cams. The valves should be cleaned and lubricated every three months. The starting valves should be turned on their seats daily, to ensure that they always work freely. After turning, each valve spindle should be left in the same position relative to its body as before; otherwise the valves may be likely to leak. They should be lubricated and overhauled just as is the starting air automatic valve.

All starting valves can be tested simultaneously thus: (i) the shut-off valve to the distributors is closed; (ii) all indicator cocks are opened; (iii) the main stop valve to the starting service is opened; (iv) compressed air is admitted to all starting valves, by placing the manoeuvring handle in the starting position.

Care must be taken to ensure that the turning gear is not in mesh during this test.

A leaky starting valve will become apparent from the air which will blow through the indicator cock of the corresponding cylinder. Such a valve should be exchanged for a spare valve, and immediately reconditioned, to be ready again for use.

When working on starting valves, the main stop valve on the manoeuvring platform—as well as the pipe lead to the distributors—should be kept closed; all drain cocks on the pipe-lines should be opened.

Manoeuvring Gear

Usually, a pilot starting air distributor is operated from gear driven from the camshaft, a lost-motion coupling being provided in the drive. If the engine turns freely over the dead-centre in either direction on starting air, but does not pick-up on fuel, then the fault will be in the lost-motion coupling movement. If the engine turns sluggishly on starting air and all starting valves are in order, then either the timing or the condition of the pilot valves in the air distributor is at fault. The distributor valves are operated by negative cams. The ahead and astern cams are arranged alongside each other so that, in the astern position of the reversing gear, the astern cams take up their positions below the distributor valves.

If any of the gear has been disconnected, a check on the distributor timing should be made as follows:

(i) turn any crank, preferably the crank of No. 1 cylinder, if its distributor valve is easily accessible, to its top dead-centre;

(ii) measure the distance, on the corresponding air-distributor valve, from the spring collar to the distributor block face;

(iii) push the valve as far down as it will go, by pressing a finger against the spindle end and measure the compressed length between the spring collar and the distributor block face;

(iv) without turning the engine, put the reversing gear into the astern position and measure the compressed length between the spring collar and the distributor block face. If the difference in the ahead direction between the compressed and uncompressed lengths is only a few millimetres, and if the corresponding difference in the astern direction is, say, 12 mm or more the deduction is that the intermediate wheel of the distributor driving gear is not in correct mesh.

Care of Scavenge Belts

Cleanliness in scavenge belts is a paramount requirement. This implies frequent and thorough attention to all places where oily carbon can accumulate. So long as lubricating oil can be drained from the scavenge belt there will be no fires, but if, due to blow-past, the lubricating oil becomes carbonised, then the walls around the scavenge ports will gradually become dry, and danger of fire will arise.

The carbonising of exhaust ports, with consequent reduction of area and increase of exhaust pressure, can result in hot blasts penetrating into the scavenge belt and causing fires.

Camshaft Drive

When connecting-up the camshaft chain, the points to be observed are:

(i) the camshaft is turned so that the line marked on the end of the shaft is horizontal and from the fuel-cam position it will be noted which crank is required to be on top dead-centre;

(ii) the crank is placed on top dead-centre, according to the flywheel mark or gauge supplied;

(iii) the chain is put on in such a way that the camshaft setting mark remains horizontal when the chain is tightened up;

(iv) the fuel-pump lifts are checked with the respective cranks on dead-centre and should correspond to the adjustment-sheet records.

Periodically it is necessary to tighten the chains. The procedure is:

(i) the locknuts underneath the tightening-bolt boss are slackened back; the limit-movement studs are screwed back; the nut on the top of the bolt is tightened until the first pressure mentioned on the engine builder's adjustment sheet is reached;

(ii) the locknuts, with their ball washers, are screwed up against their faces and locked;

(iii) the spring is tightened further, until the second and higher pressure stated on the sheet is reached;

(iv) the top nut is secured by its locknut;

(v) the limit movement studs are adjusted to the clearance stated on the engine builder's drawing.

After the chain has been retightened it is necessary to check the position of the camshaft relative to the crankshaft. With the crank on top dead-centre the corresponding fuel-pump cam should have raised the plunger the amount stated on the engine adjustment sheet.

The driving chains should be inspected at the end of each long voyage. Particular attention should be paid to wear of rollers and also chain tightness. The chain-lubrication sprayers should be examined carefully and the flow of oil from each sprayer checked.

The chain-wheels should be examined for wear of teeth, as frequently as possible. Any variation in alignment will become evident by wear on one side of the teeth. The flow of oil to all jockey-wheel bearings should be checked.

The amount of chain wear which takes place is directly proportional to the percentage elongation. In general, an elongation of 2 per cent is regarded as marking the end of the useful life of a chain.

Bearing Clearances

The clearances of connecting-rod top- and bottom-ends should be checked every six months. At the end of each long voyage the nuts should be tested for tightness. Once a year the main-bearing clearances should be checked. Wear-down readings should be compared with the crankshaft-deflection readings.

The thrust block, with its bearings and thrust pads, should be examined annually and the clearances checked. All oil passages should be thoroughly cleaned and tested for a full and free flow of oil.

Tightening of Piston-rod Nuts

The correct tightening of piston-rod nuts, especially in double-acting engines, is a matter of the utmost importance. The instructions which are issued by the engine builder for each engine, should be carefully followed.

During crankcase examinations the locking devices should be inspected and all nuts tested with feelers for slackness. During the overhaul of cylinder units, or when time permits, the locking plates on the piston-rod nuts should be removed and the nuts hammer-tested.

Double tightening-up of nuts is necessary, to guard against possible defects on the pressure surfaces. The first tightening of the nuts will smooth out such faults, and thereby provide a reliable datum line for the final securing of the piston rod during the second tightening-up operation.

Connecting-rod Bolts

If a piston seizure, or something equally drastic, occurs, an engine may be pulled-up suddenly. Shock-loading of the connecting-rod bolts, with permanent injury to them, may be a consequence of such a mishap. The bolts should then be scrapped forthwith.

If an engine has been running with connecting-rod bolts insufficiently tightened, examination of the shanks of the bolts will show bright belts of rubbing; the undersides of bolt heads and nuts will also show bright hammering marks. Bolts should be rejected if they show: thread stretch; excessively bright marking under head or nut, indicating prolonged and severe hammering; or excessively bright marks on the shank, caused by long and heavy 'working'.

Very seldom is there any difficulty with main-engine connecting-rod bolts. The author has only experienced two or three failures, out of thousands of connecting rods examined.

Cylinder Pressures

Compression and firing pressures vary according to engine type. The correct average figures, for full-load, are usually recorded on the adjustment sheet provided by the builders of the engine. It is important that the engineer should try to maintain the pressures as closely as possible to the figures on the adjustment sheet. Therefore, for continuous satisfactory running, indicator draw-cards, from all cylinders, should be taken fairly frequently. The compression and firing pressure heights are measured from the atmospheric line. The compression pressure is measured to the top of the compression curve, and the firing pressure should start rising from there. The maximum firing pressure can, of course, also be measured on the ordinary indicator diagram.

Piston Rings

Cylinder-liner surface should be considered in conjunction with piston-ring problems. It is often believed, quite wrongly, that the best finish for a cylinder liner is imparted by honing or grinding. Experience shows, however, that if a liner is turned to a reasonably good finish the innumerable tiny hollows in the surface may serve as lubricating oil receptacles, and thus may tend to reinforce the oil film which is so important. An initially smooth surface is not conducive to long liner life. The limit of permissible wear on liners, before replacement, is about 1 mm per 100 mm of diameter.

To state that the materials, design and manufacture of piston rings should be such that there is neither blow-past nor sticking, that the friction and wear are the least possible, and so on, is easy; to satisfy these desiderata is much less easy. Non-marine men tend to criticise the number of piston rings which are fitted to propelling engines. They frequently suggest that the number could, with advantage, be halved. Experience, however, has repeatedly demonstrated that the customary numbers of rings yield the most satisfactory results.

The first ring groove should be located as far away as practicable from the piston crown, because it is important that the maximum amount of heat from the combustion space should be conveyed away before the top piston ring is reached; otherwise this ring is likely to stick from heat expansion. The first and second rings should always be made to float more easily in their grooves than those further down. The edges of piston-ring working faces should be bevelled, or rounded, to assist in retaining the lubricating oil film on the cylinder wall until the rings and liners are worn smooth. Thus, for a 620 mm diameter piston, a 2 mm radius would be suitable.

The end-butting of rings can be troublesome, especially in two-stroke engines, if the ring gap is too small. It is possible for end-butting measurably to lower the mechanical efficiency; the effect can sometimes be felt at the engine turning gear, if used when the engine is warm. For the two top rings of main pistons, an adequate amount of axial clearance is necessary. Adequacy may imply twice normal clearance.

The incidence of scavenge fires is often determined by the type and the state of the piston rings. With the proper fitting of piston rings in their grooves, with minimum end-gaps and with a suitable amount of lubricating oil applied to liners at the right moment, scavenge fires are unlikely. In this connection the piston-ring joint design is important. Figure 12.7 shows an overlapping end-joint, sufficiently robust to avoid fracture, which prevents the passage of gas. A generous amount of end-clearance, without blow-past, is obtainable with this design. For main pistons, such rings should certainly be fitted to the third and fourth ring grooves.

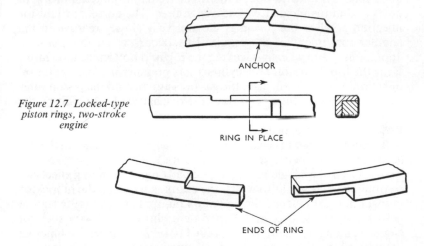

Figure 12.7 Locked-type piston rings, two-stroke engine

The use of positioning pins for piston rings is unsatisfactory. A much more robust alternative, obtainable at slight additional cost, is the anchor piece which is shown in Figure 12.7. Vertical wear is minimised by its use, and the rings are enabled to mate perfectly with the liner. No cylinder completely retains the same form when cold and when hot. Experience shows that an unanchored ring can tend to move circumferentially somewhat. The ring ends are arranged to coincide with the broad bar at the scavenge ports. A correctly made ring, when closed-in the predetermined amount, should present a truly circular working surface. Rings which are not truly circular should be avoided.

The surface finish of piston-ring grooves is important. It avails little if excellently finished rings are fitted into roughly finished grooves; blow-through with new rings is often attributable to this cause. The piston-ring grooves should be dimensioned radially inward from the outside of the piston; that is, they should not be machined to a diametrical dimension. To reduce likelihood of seizures during the running-in period of a new engine, lead-bronze rings fitted into machined grooves in the piston circumference are very useful, the face of the rings being about 0·1 mm above the piston surface.

Timing of Cylinder Lubricators

The difference between the genuine timing of cylinder lubricators —where this is achievable—and the indefinite injection of lubricating oil is reflected in rates of cylinder-liner wear, in the carbonising of ports and in the incidence of scavenge fires. The correct instant for injection is when the piston is moving very slowly relative to the angular movement of the crank. This occurs when the piston is approaching and when it is leaving the top and bottom dead-centres. Near the top dead-point the cylinder gas pressure is too great for oil injection. Lower down, also, the gas pressure behind the piston rings can be sufficiently high to prevent the discharge of lubricant by the lubricator plunger. There remains the lower end of the stroke, and this is the most practicable region for the purpose.

Because of the uncertainties, some engine builders make no attempt to time their cylinder lubricators.

In four-stroke, single-acting, crosshead engines a timing effect can be obtained. The point to which the crank is set when the lubricator plunger has just reached the end of its pumping stroke is 30 degrees before bottom dead-centre. Experiment shows that, with such an engine running normally at, say, 100–110 rev/min, there is a time-lag between plunger movement and oil injection of approximately 20 degrees of crank angle; i.e. injection has been completed by the time the piston is about 10 degrees of crank angle from the bottom dead-point. But in experiments on lubricating oil injection settings at 30 degrees after bottom dead-centre, under conditions closely simulating those in a four-stroke trunk engine running at 135 rev/min, there was at best a continuous dribble, with a minor periodic pulse superimposed upon it.

As ordinarily made, the cylinder lubricator has a very short effective stroke and, in ships which travel from cold to hot and from hot to cold climates, it is in continuous need of adjustment, because of the oil-viscosity variations which are inseparable from the changing ambient temperatures. The incorporation of a small, thermostatically controlled, heating element into the lubricator overcomes the need for viscosity adjustment. A speed-reducing gear of say 1/3, by which the effective plunger stroke is increased and the number of strokes per minute reduced, can be helpful. The injection lag is, however, thereby increased.

The non-return valve, which is always provided on the lubricator discharge pipe, should be placed as near the cylinder as practicable, to assist the timed impulse of oil. If the non-return valve is mounted on the cylinder there may be carbonisation difficulties.

Lubricating Oil Filters

If the lubricating oil filters contain wire-gauze elements, these should be changed and cleaned regularly. After a crankcase overhaul, or the cleaning of lubricating oil drain tanks, the filter elements may have to be washed several times at short intervals. Where other types of filter are used, the precautions specified by the makers as necessary for continuous service must be carefully followed. The pressure-differences on the gauges before and after the filters will normally be sufficient indication of when the filters are dirty and require changing.

Where cloth is used as the strainer material, it is important that the oil pressure before the filter should be watched. Excessive pressures will cause by-passing of the oil, or bursting of the cloth and its cages. Dirty lubricating oil will then enter the bearings, to the detriment of the engine. Filters of the fabric type accordingly need frequent cleaning. Normally their use should be avoided.

In no circumstances must gasoline, petrol or low-flash spirit of any kind be used for cleaning oil filters.

Lubricating Oil Coolers

For propelling engines the oil cooler is usually arranged with a by-pass on both the water and oil sides; these should be judiciously used during manoeuvring, especially in cold climates.

For small engines, in which the lubricating oil pump is engine-driven and there is no independent stand-by pump, and in which the cooler is arranged with a by-pass pipe for the oil: the regulating valve should be fully opened during starting operations. It is important that the lubricant should reach the crankshaft bearings with the least possible delay, after the engine has started to turn. When the oil is cold and viscous the resistance in an effective cooler can be very great, and the resulting increase in pressure can therefore cause the lubricating oil to be discharged back into the sump, through the spring-loaded by-pass regulating valve, instead of being delivered to the bearings.

Lubricating oil coolers should be cleaned, on the oil side, at reasonable intervals; the decreasing temperature-difference between oil inlet and oil outlet will be a sufficient guide.

There are many proprietary cleansing fluids on the market. An effective cleansing medium is coal-tar naphtha, but trichlorethylene may be preferred. The cooler to be cleaned should first be drained of oil, through the drain cocks or bottom plug. The drains are then closed and the oil side of the cooler is filled with the cleaning medium, which is admitted through the air-cock or thermometer boss at the top, by means of a funnel. In large coolers the filling is more conveniently done by a hand-pump, which draws from a drum and discharges through a flexible steel hose to the funnel. The fluid should remain in the cooler for at least three or four hours; then the dirty fluid is drained away to an empty drum.

The fluid may be used again, after being cleaned in the oil purifier, but care must be taken that it is not mixed with the lubricating oil in the system. All pipes between purifier and lubricating oil tank should therefore be disconnected. Expensive cleansing fluids should be sent ashore and purified by partial distillation.

Should a cooler be very dirty, it may be necessary to repeat the cleaning process.

Lubricating Oil Pressure

If the lubricating oil pressure is too low the cause may be: an insufficient amount of oil in the tank; leaky pipe unions or joints inside the crankcase; dirty filters; a defect in the lubricating oil pump; excessive clearance at bearings.

Cooling Water System

Although fresh water is used for cooling the cylinders and turbo-blowers, nevertheless all accessible spaces should be periodically inspected for deposition of scale.

To maintain the cylinder-liner wall temperature above the dew point, the cooling water inlet temperature should be about 50°C when running at full speed, rising to about 55°C during slow running. Observance of this temperature level is important if cylinder-liner wear is to be minimised. These figures are for general guidance and reference should be made to the engine builder's instruction book.

A liberal flow of water through the engine is desirable. The cylinder and turboblower cooling water outlet temperature should not normally exceed 70°C and should preferably be kept about 65°C or as may be indicated in the instruction books. The general outlet temperature should be regulated by adjusting the salt-water supply. The valve on each inlet pipe should always be full-open. The outlet temperature for each cylinder is regulated by manipulation of the outlet valve, which should not normally be opened more than one or two turns. A thermometer is provided on each cylinder and turbo-blower for indicating outlet temperatures.

If a cylinder jacket becomes so hot that steam issues from the test cock, then the fuel supply to the cylinder should be cut-off and the engine revolutions reduced to allow the cylinder to cool. Only after the cause has been discovered and eradicated should an attempt be made to put the cylinder on load again. If neither water nor steam issues from the test cock the cooling water pipe must be choked somewhere. The engine is then stopped and the obstruction dealt with. The unit must be allowed to cool slowly before any attempt is made again to circulate cooling water through the cylinder.

The normal cooling water pressure, as shown by the starting-platform gauge, may be anything from 0.5 to 1.5 kgf/cm^2, according to the engine size. If the water pressure should suddenly fall, the cooling water pumps should be changed-over and a search be made for the cause of the difficulty. If the pumps are main-engine driven the independent stand-by pump should be started; and if the pressure cannot be restored and maintained by one pump, then both pumps should be used. If it is not possible to keep the outlet temperature below 70°C the engine speed must be reduced until the system has been cleared.

If, after a shut-down, the engine-room temperature cannot be raised above 2°C, the cooling water should be drained from the cylinder jackets and piping system, to avoid fracture by freezing. An engine is, naturally, more difficult to start when cold. Normally, arrangements are provided for warming-through the main engine from the auxiliary engine circulating water discharge line, or by equivalent means. The salt-water regulating valve on the fresh-water cooler should be throttled and, during manoeuvring, this valve may be closed completely for a time.

Air Reservoirs

Manoeuvring air reservoirs are constructed of welded steel plates and strong dished ends. They are fitted with stop, safety and drain valves; a manhole and door are arranged at one end. Reservoirs are inspected regularly; precautions must be taken against internal corrosion and pitting, especially at the top and the bottom. It is of great importance that reservoirs should always be well drained, and that a protective coating should be applied as necessary.

A spare bottle is often supplied, so that if all the air is lost from the manoeuvring reservoirs an auxiliary engine may be started by the bottle and the reservoirs filled by the manoeuvring air compressor. The spare bottle should always be fully charged to the maximum pressure. Should the air be lost from this bottle also, the emergency compressor can be started up for recharging. Double drain valves are fitted on the bottom of the bottles, for draining away condensed water and oil. To manipulate a double drain valve, the inner valve should first be opened fully, and then the outer one should be opened slightly, for blowing-off. At least once in two years air bottles should be emptied, the bottle-heads taken off, the inside cleaned with boiling caustic soda solution, then well washed with fresh water.

Fuel Oil

Particulars of recommended fuels are given by the engine builders to the shipowner. The specification should indicate gross calorific value, viscosity, flash point, ash content, hard asphalt, water and sediment, coke value, pour point, cetane number and diesel index.

If a fuel analysis is not available, a sample of the fuel oil should be tried in one of the auxiliary engines. With a poor-quality fuel, combustion at light loads is irregular and there is usually smoke at full load. Sulphur, as sulphur dioxide, is identifiable by smelling the exhaust gas. Water content can be traced by shaking an oil sample with benzol in a bottle. If the mixture emulsifies and becomes lighter in colour the water content is probably too high. The fuel should then be accepted only on an analysis.

Engines which have been started on lighter oil may work satisfactorily for some time on inferior quality fuel, but the water and ash percentages will soon be detrimental to the valves. If the oil is more viscous than specified, fuel-valve adjustment should be made to suit, i.e. the spray holes may have to be enlarged. When lighter oil is again purchased readjustment may be necessary.

There are usually two settling tanks. One is used for unpurified and the other for purified oil. The former should be pumped full, twelve hours before use. Drain-cocks should be opened, and all water and sediment drained off, before using a tank.

All fuel oil should be passed through the purifiers on its way to the service tanks. If a new supply of fuel is being used, before transference the fuel-oil filters should be inspected and cleaned within twenty-four hours. Settling tanks should be cleaned every year.

For the successful use of heavy or furnace oils, sufficient time should be allowed, before starting the engine, for heating the fuel in the service tank and for circulating it through the engine-fuel system. When the oil is circulating through the engine freely, and when it has reached the temperature appropriate to its viscosity, the engine will be ready for starting (Table 12.1).

Table 12.1 HEATING REQUIRED FOR HEAVY FUELS

Viscosity, sec (Redwood No. 1 at 38°C)	Approximate temperature in °C at fuel pumps to reduce viscosity to 250 sec	Temperature of fuel in tank before circulation begins, °C
3 700	80	85
3 000	75	80
2 000	70	75
1 500	65	70
1 000	60	65
750	55	65
600	50	60
400	45	55
200	—	50

If the viscosity is below 1000 scc at 38°C, it is not necessary for the fuel entering the injection pump to be heated above 60°C.

The burning of heavy fuels receives attention in another chapter. The fuel-injection system is fully capable of dealing satisfactorily with oil of 260 sec. For purification, it is desirable to heat the fuel to about 85°C, irrespective of its viscosity.

Lubricating Oil

Lubricating oils should be pure mineral oils, free from water. Those that are produced from stocks having a naturally detergent base are suitable.

It is necessary to distinguish between: inhibited oils—often of naturally detergent stock or base—which have been rendered resistant to oxidation by the addition of an anti-oxidant inhibitor; and the oils which have been rendered highly detergent by special additives having the property of holding in suspension carbonaceous matter which would otherwise be deposited on the hotter parts of an engine, e.g. in way of the piston rings.

Inhibited oils can be used in the crankcase of all engines; they can also be used as dual-purpose oils for crankcases and cylinders if so desired. Highly detergent oils are not recommended for crankcase lubrication, but they can be used as cylinder lubricants in crosshead engines, i.e. where the cylinder oil cannot become mixed with crankcase oil.

For air compressors, special non-carbonising oil must be used.

The circulating oil should be purified as often as possible. Every half-year lubricating-oil sumps and tanks should be cleansed of sediment. From time to time the lubricating oil gauges should be checked.

The correct amount of lubricating oil should be distributed to each cylinder; the mechanical lubricators should be adjusted to provide the minimum amounts needed. When an engine is new the lubricating oil allowed for the cylinders is generally more than twice the amount required later, when piston rings and cylinder liners have been run-in. After the sea trials a beginning should be made to reduce the amount of oil; after two or three weeks in service the amount should be not more than normal. The drops of oil which pass up the glasses of each cylinder lubricator should be counted; each mechanical lubricator should supply the same amount in a stated period.

A special Instruction Sheet is issued with each engine by the builders. This provides detailed information regarding amounts of cylinder oil per day.

Inspection of Engine Details

The undermentioned particulars are included for general guidance purposes only. For each proprietary engine type, the engine builders provide specialised information.

AT INTERVALS OF SIX WEEKS

Fuel valves: to be taken out; atomisers and filters cleaned; seats tested. If condition of valves is good inspection intervals can be extended.

AT INTERVALS OF ONE MONTH

Upper piston rings: to be examined monthly, if possible, for the first six months. If condition continues to be satisfactory inspections can be extended to six-monthly periods.

AT INTERVALS OF SIX MONTHS

Upper pistons: if cooled, to be examined for carbon deposits in cooling spaces and cooling pipes.

Exhaust belts and manifold: to be examined for carbon deposits.

Cylinder ports: to be examined for carbon deposits; also when indicator diagrams show that exhaust back-pressure is increasing.

Cylinder liners: to be examined externally for scale deposits. If the deposits are too difficult to remove by flushing with water, then liner should be withdrawn for cleaning. Wear to be measured. Allowable wear on liners and/or pistons is a total taper of 0·75 per cent of bore; then liners should be renewed.

Piston-cooling gear: to be thoroughly examined.

Fresh-water coolers: the salt- and fresh-water spaces should be examined.

Connecting rods: top-end and bottom-end clearances to be examined.

Starting valves: to be overhauled and tested. (Spindles should be moved twice weekly.)

AT INTERVALS OF ONE YEAR

Manoeuvring gear: to be examined for wear at the joints of levers and rods.

Governor gear: to be examined; to move without undue play and without sticking.

Crankshaft: clock-gauge readings to be taken; shaft alignment adjusted, if necessary; lubricating-oil channels to be cleared of deposits.

Main bearings: to be examined; wear-down readings taken.

Thrust block: to be examined and clearances checked.

Starting-air piping and air bottles: to be cleaned and steamed out.

Lubricating oil system: to be thoroughly examined and cleared of deposits.

AT FREQUENT, CONVENIENT, INTERVALS

Fuel pumps: examine and adjust when necessary.

Automatic starting valve: move occasionally.

Pistons: examine for cracks.

Chapter 13

Recurrent Problems

In engine design the primary criterion is not strength but stiffness. Only in machinery components under dead load can strength alone be a satisfactory criterion. In heavy oil engines the components, almost without exception, are either under fluctuating stresses or alternating stresses. Where the stresses are bending, or compounds of bending and direct stresses, or a combination of torsional and other stresses, it is the stiffness that is the yardstick. Stiffness is ensured, in the design office, by utilising simple bending stress or combined-stress formulae—which, incidentally, do not by any means comply with the fundamental assumptions of the theory—and accepting an appropriately low figure for the skin stress, a figure which experience shows will provide the correct degree of stiffness. It is the only practicable way. If bedplates and frames, for example, were calculated on a basis of strength only the deflections and variations of deflection which would occur under running conditions would lead to trouble at bearings, guides and other places. That is: although there are in general two ways of designing a thing, namely, to make it sufficiently rigid or to make it sufficiently flexible, it is in rigidity rather than in flexibility that the normal solution lies.

Some Comments on Design

For his computative work the designer obtains assistance from three main sources, namely: fundamental formulae (seldom); trial-and-error results (most frequently); and small-scale tests (occasionally).

Thus, a simple bending test to destruction on, say, a small, true-to-scale, cast-iron bedplate, can yield many helpful data, notwithstanding that the bedplate behaves very differently in service from the model under simple bending. Against this, small specimens of

578

different kinds of alloy steel, tested to destruction for fatigue, can yield misleading results when applied to engine components of substantial size. The respective results of these two examples are different from what might normally be expected.

Occasionally the stress values yielded by conventional routine formulae are very close to observed results. But this is not usual; often the differences are appreciably large. In general terms, a designer is more interested in comparative than in absolute figures, because every design is either an interpolation or an extrapolation of some earlier work.

It is necessary to discriminate between general weakness of design and local failure. General weakness implies a lack of understanding of the problem. Local failure is something quite different; with correct prognosis and persistence it can usually be overcome.

Experienced marine-engine designers strive to avoid the use of costly materials, especially alloy steels. Heavy marine-engine practice thus differs from that of small highly rated engines, where alloy steels find an important place. The marine practice is sound, not only on commercial but also on technical grounds. Large engine components which are subjected to heavy impact forces must be capable of absorbing energy; therefore a reserve of ductility is needed in the material used. Mild steel has a wonderful self-restoring propensity which is absent from the higher-grade materials. The fatigue limit under fluctuating loads is higher than the limit of proportionality. Consequently, plastic flow can occur at loads below the fatigue limit, and this is likely to facilitate 'bedding down' and thus eliminate some of the stray stresses which are not always suspected, and therefore difficult to assess. There are, in short, many things to be considered before a departure is made from mild steel for important components. For example, in, say, a mild-steel rod of 10 in. diameter there are no locked-up stresses; but in a similar rod of alloy steel—say forged manganese–molybdenum steel—the internal stresses may be twice the working stresses, according to some metallurgists. Phenomena experienced in service are only explicable on this basis. To realise the benefits of high-tensile alloy steels in fatigue, particular care must be paid to surface finish, and this is not always practicable in large engine parts. In the author's experience, manganese–molybdenum steel piston rods have fractured after only twelve or fifteen weeks of service. Indeed, if they did not fail within six to twelve months they continued without any deterioration for the whole life of the ship. It is an accepted fact that, although a plain test-piece under fatigue will in general show a fatigue limit bearing a definite relation to ultimate stress, the effect of a stress-raiser is to lower the fatigue strength of alloy steel in greater proportion than is so with low-carbon steel. Small-scale laboratory tests have shown an absolute notched fatigue superiority of about 10 per cent in alloy steel in conjunction with the lower fatigue-stress/ultimate-stress ratio of the alloy steel. Although each laboratory test has established superiority of the alloy steel, full-scale experience has shown otherwise.

Further comment is made on alloy steels versus mild steel in another section.

The identification of stresses in an engine member can be difficult. It is so easy to focus attention on the wrong thing, e.g. upon the

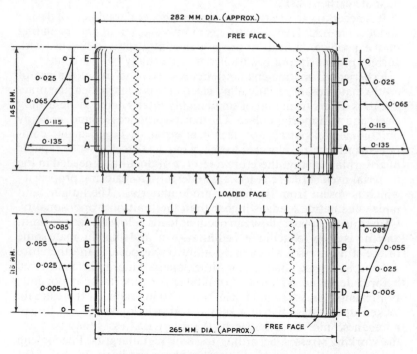

Figure 13.1 Dilation of nuts

workmanship of the screwed ends of a member under alternating stress, instead of upon the adequacy of the body against buckling.

Figure 13.1 shows how a nut, under steady loading, dilates at the face, by reason of the couple on the face of the nut—caused by the longitudinal load along the thread and the reaction across the nut face—and the radial component of the thread loading. The distension releases the load on the lower threads and concentrates it on the upper threads, which is where thread stripping is almost invariably found. The mathematical theory that the stress in a screwed rod is greatest at the loaded face of the nut is therefore not in accordance with observed facts. If the threads and the nut faces had been coated with, say, molybdenum disulphide there is no doubt that the dilation would have been even greater for the applied loading.

Similitude and Proportion

It is seldom that the principle of similitude can be effectively applied in engine design; moreover, the short cut to success which it might seem to offer is too often a snare. On one occasion, in the midst of a complex combustion problem, a well-known professor suggested to the author that, taking as the basis an engine with a satisfactory system, the principle of similitude should be applied to the problem under consideration and extended to the full range of cylinder sizes. When one thinks of the many variables and sub-variables involved—the fuel pressure, the bore and length of piping, the number and size of nozzle holes, the fuel-particle size, the direction of the jets, the size and shape of the combustion chamber and so on—he would indeed be a credulous man who would seek a sheet anchor in the principle of similitude. In combustion problems repeated experience shows that the only sound procedure is to treat each engine size and type as a separate entity. The data might not appear to be consistent: that does not matter; the important thing is to obtain the best possible result for each engine, apparent inconsistencies notwithstanding.

It is surprising how slight departures from customary engine proportions can sometimes bring about unexpected difficulties for no apparent reason. An example of this kind of perversity, with which the author had at one period to deal, was a double-acting, two-stroke engine 450 mm bore, 1200 mm stroke, the stroke/bore ratio being 2·67. For established engines of the same generic type, of 530, 620 and 660 mm cylinder bore, the stroke/bore ratio had been 2·26. The author's firm engined, to designs which were prepared elsewhere, two twin-screw ships with nine-cylinder units of the 450 mm size. Although each component of the design had normal characteristics, the engines as a whole required substantially more attention in service than any other engine of the range. The adverse results were so abundantly clear that the engine size was never repeated.

Fillets and Radii

Fillets and fastenings must surely cause more failures than everything else added together in the design, construction and running of engines. The drawing-office worker omits to dimension the fillets and radii; or, if the dimensions are indeed stated, the turner ignores the drawing instructions and produces sharp corners. Stress-raisers are thus engendered and the way is made easy for creeping cracks to begin.

The function of a shoulder on a shaft is often two-fold: (i) to serve as a stop, probably for a driven-on boss; (ii) to serve as the borderline between two different assemblies. Condition (i) makes it highly desirable that part of the shoulder should be straight, and equally desirable that there should be a well-defined fillet. Disregard of (ii) can have unsatisfactory consequences; e.g. if a shaft is made of constant diameter, with a driven-on coupling flange at the end, and a bearing in juxtaposition. With this arrangement, the hole in the coupling boss must be made a special diameter to ensure a driving fit for the coupling; also a stress raiser is set up at the boundary of coupling and bearing.

For keys and feathers the distance from the end of a key seat to the shoulder should not be less than, say, three times the fillet radius.

Recurrent Failures and Their Causes

When an engine component, or assembly of components fails repeatedly the underlying cause may be starkly clear. The remedy then will doubtless be equally obvious, even if proportionately costly. But it is not always thus. One of the most perplexing of the many experiences which have befallen the author extended over a period of more than ten years and centred around the piston-rod/crosshead attachment of certain types of double-acting, two-stroke engine. There were nearly one thousand piston rods in service at the time.

A predominant number of the rods had completely trouble-free lives. The distance separating complete success from the adventitious results actually obtained must have been small. But the precise reasons why one rod was a success and an adjacent rod was not a success were undiscoverable; there was never any discernible common factor.

Although, reckoned on a basis of percentages, the yearly failures may not have been high, the perpetual feeling of anxiety engendered by uncertainty was very wearing to those concerned. The cost of a piston rod, *per se*, was not great; the anxiety was that if a piston rod should break in a certain position and with a force sufficient to bend the connecting rod—as had happened in a number of instances—then one or more crank webs could be shifted and much incidental damage be caused. Immobilisation of the ship for many weeks, for partial crankshaft replacement, inevitably followed.

Many theories were formulated to explain the failures. But no single theory embraced all the occurrences; there always remained one or more types of failure which were unexplained. Where complex and obscure problems of this kind are encountered, it is reasonable to conclude that the design is not fully adequate for its purpose— everything is too near the safety line; therefore, certain rods fail for one apparent reason, other rods fail for another apparent reason and so on. But the real underlying common cause is a slight general weakness. If an all-round strengthening could be made—it need, perhaps, only be slight—the distance separating indifferent success from complete success would be bridged, and all such difficulties would evaporate. Figure 13.2, which concentrates in one rod all the types of failure, supports this conclusion. To focus attention on them, the characteristic failures are marked 1 to 6.

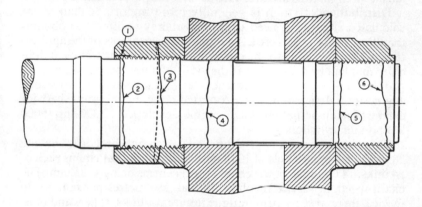

Figure 13.2 Piston-rod failures

Resulting from an analysis of the different ways in which piston rods and threads failed, the final conclusion was that if the rods were made 10 per cent larger in diameter the position would be transformed. Unfortunately, in an existing engine, this 10 per cent was beyond attainment. In new installations, however, by modifying the design, it was possible to obtain a 15 per cent increase, and the problem was solved.

Chain Drives

Difficulties with chain drives in service are remarkably few. The safety factor of chains should never be less than 25, and the loading upon which this factor is based is the maximum which is realisable under the most irregular conditions of working. Figures 13.3 and 13.4 show a typical arrangement of a camshaft chain drive. There is a 0·45 carbon cast-steel sprocket wheel constructed in halves and keyed to the crankshaft, a forged-steel intermediate wheel—where the chain lead requires such a wheel—and an adjustable spring-loaded wheel for chain-tightening. The chain is of duplex design. In large engines, where there may be a double duplex drive, the pairs of chain are matched by the chain maker to ensure that the load is equally shared.

It will be observed that the chain-tightening sprocket wheel is located on the slack side of the chain. This is the preferred arrangement.

The tensile strength of a chain varies as the square of the link pitch, or of the angle between adjacent sprocket teeth. Increase of tensile strength thus involves greater increase of accelerating forces.

Distribution of strain is generally more important than a low calculated stress. The need to absorb energy is often less obvious than the need to resist force. An outstanding example of the application of this reasoning to the overcoming of a serious technical difficulty that had been gnawing at the vitals of a number of engineering people for a long time concerned four double-acting two-stroke engines of a design which incorporated a secondary crankshaft for exhaust piston actuation. Each engine developed 12 000 shp (9000 kW) on ten cylinders.

The original arrangement comprised two chain wheels, each having 28 teeth on a pitch-circle of 1313 mm, and two duplex chains each of 54 links, 147 mm pitch, the chain-wheel centres being 1775 mm. The chain speed, at service revolutions, was 380 metres per minute. In service, there were frequent fatigue failures of links, rollers and pins. The surface of the pins showed abnormal bearing pressure. The chains were examined throughout at every port, and defective sections were replaced. There were many theories formulated to explain the failures, most of them being altogether unsupportable.

Eventually the drive was replaced by one comprising two chain-wheels, each having 38 teeth on a pitch circle of 1230 mm, and two three-strand chains of 78 links, 4-in. (say, 100 mm) pitch. Although the six single chains, compared with the two duplex chains, showed a reduction of 28 per cent, nevertheless the substitution of the lighter chains completely solved the problem.

In the original drive the spring-loaded jockey wheel was located above the slack side of the chain and was arranged to press downwards upon the chain. In the revised scheme the jockey wheel was located under the slack side of the chain and pressed upwards upon it. Any advantage which this change may have made was not at all

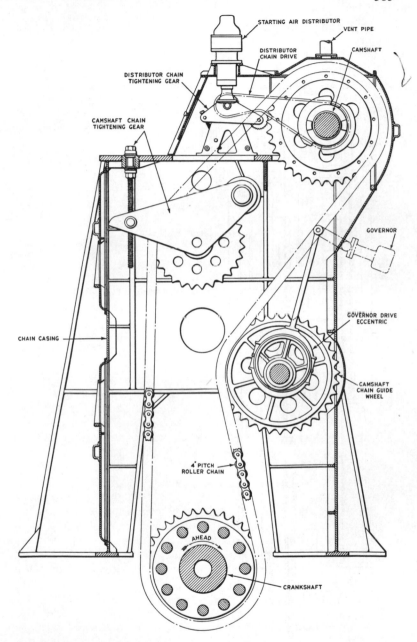

Figure 13.3 A typical chain drive

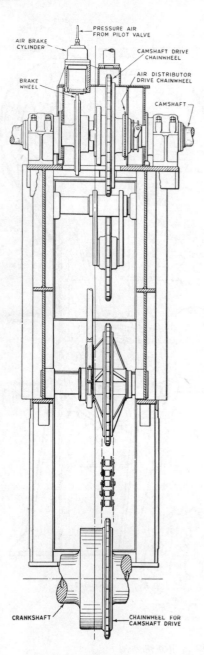

Figure 13.4 Chain drive

significant. It should be stated that the chain drive was approximately 20 degrees to the horizontal.

Polygon Action of Chains

In addition to the normal load which a chain connecting two sprocket wheels has to carry, there is a momentary load due to the alteration in chain length as a link passes over the tangential point. This is the so-called polygon action. It can be shown from first principles that this alteration in length $= 0\cdot62I/n^2$,

where $I =$ length of link in mm;
$n =$ number of teeth in the wheel.

The polygon action of chains in a chain drive is not always negligible. The absolute strain on the chain will depend upon the rate of change of momentum arising from sprocket diameter, chain pitch and chain velocity. The strain ratio, and consequently the stress, will vary inversely as the chain length. In the extreme example of a horizontal chain between two sprockets each having six teeth, the relative angular velocity of the wheels will vary throughout each pitch from R_2/R_1 to R_1/R_2, where $R_1 =$ vertical distance of chain pin, with pins on vertical centre-lines, $R_2 =$ vertical distance of chain pin, with pins on horizontal centre-lines. *See* Figure 13.5. Acceleration at each engagement is a function of the angle between adjacent teeth of the sprocket and of the chain velocity. The resulting forces are the product of this acceleration and the specific weight.

Polygon action makes it desirable—really necessary sometimes—for chain-wheel centres to be made a multiple of the chain pitch.

The matter is sufficiently important to merit attention in greater detail below.

Chain drives are an attractive alternative to the trains of gear-wheels that were commonly used for the camshaft drives of tall four-stroke engines. The form of the gear-wheel tooth provided constant

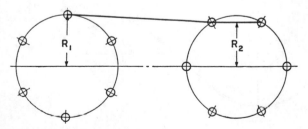

Figure 13.5 Polygon action of chain drive

relative velocity of the driving and the driven members of the gearing train. That is, there was no relative acceleration at engagement and disengagement of the individual tooth.

The chain does not comply with the above-stated characteristic. Acceleration at the engagement of each chain roller is a function of the angle between adjacent teeth of the sprocket wheel and of the chain velocity. The resulting forces are the product of this acceleration and the specific weights involved. A short chain drive will aggravate the effect of the accelerating forces.

The acceleration effect of the angle between adjacent sprocket-wheel teeth is illustrated diagrammatically in Figure 13.6. For simplicity, the smaller wheel shows the extreme example of a sprocket with only six teeth. In the upper diagram (*a*) the link joints are on the vertical centre-line for the large chain-wheel, and in the lower diagram (*b*) the link joints are on the vertical centre-line for the smaller sprocket wheel. Inertia of the driving and the driven shafts, and their gear, prevents them from reacting to the varying ratio of angular velocities required by the chain as the wheels rotate. The

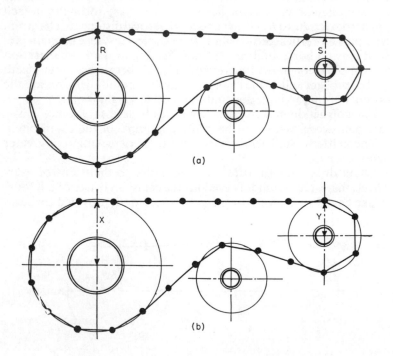

Figure 13.6 Chain drive. Acceleration effects

ratio varies from S/R to Y/X during each period of engagement and disengagement. The accelerating effort of the chain results in abnormal stress in its parts.

Vibration and Noise

Noise and vibration are transmitted from the machinery room to the accommodation spaces mainly by way of the steel structure. The amount of airborne noise is, by comparison, insignificant.

If a structure, or a machine component, is intended to carry heavily fluctuating bending forces there are two general ways of making the component sturdy enough to fulfil its function. One is to embody in the design a sufficient amount of material to ensure adequate stiffness against the bending action of the forces. The other is to introduce a strut, or a tie, directed to the point of maximum flexure, thus obtaining stiffness and rigidity with only a fraction of the weight of material.

Many of the problems which arise on shipboard are problems of resonance, and they can appear in a multitude of guises. There is space for only one example.

In a new passenger liner there was a group of very expensive suites on the bridge deck, and on the first voyage serious complaints about vibration were made. A representative of the builders made a trip to investigate the complaints. His vibrograph as used in the normal manner provided no information. The investigation was made in the small hours of the morning so that passengers should not sense anything unusual. There came a time when the tired and baffled man laid the vibrograph on his bed while he cogitated. Something in the behaviour of the instrument attracted his attention and, lying down beside it, he solved the problem. A very small vibration in the hull was synchronising with the natural period of the loaded mattress. Accordingly, all the mattresses in the suites were removed at the end of the trip and replaced by others with different springs. There were no further complaints.

The vibrations which form the subject of most investigations are those in which force and damping are in such ratio that the problem becomes one of estimating acceptability against comfort and stress. And it is in the stress that the real problem of vibration is encountered. For reasons which have not been really explained, the strength of a material is greatly reduced if the applied load is not steady but cyclical. Its ability to withstand stress decreases, within limits, with every cycle of the applied load. Vibrations of even comparatively low frequencies can soon attain 10 million cycles if the vibration is continuous. Sooner or later failure will result if the fluctuating stresses caused by the vibration are in excess of the fatigue strength of the material. If, however, the maximum stresses induced by the vibration fall below the fatigue strength of the material the body will not fail, no matter how many reversals of stress occur.

A type of vibration which is often difficult of solution is the drumming of flat surfaces and the shaking of component parts which have been excited by impulses from the propeller. Vibrations of this type are at a frequency which is a product of the number of propeller blades and the revolutions of the shafting. The intensity may vary greatly, even in ships of comparable features. The origin of the impulses lies in the passage of the propeller blades through zones of varying wake velocity, the load on a blade being greatest when it is passing through the dead-water zone in line with the stern frame. Difficulty from this source can be experienced in ships of all types and sizes, and is related to the design of the propeller, stern frame and after body of the ship. There are many practical difficulties in measuring the variables associated with this type of vibration.

Synchronising Gear

In high-speed, twin-screw passenger ships problems of vibration are always present, and its elimination, or even its mitigation, can provide some complex puzzles for unravelment. With single-screw ships there is not usually much scope for change after the vessels are in service; against this, it seldom happens that single-screw ships carry many passengers.

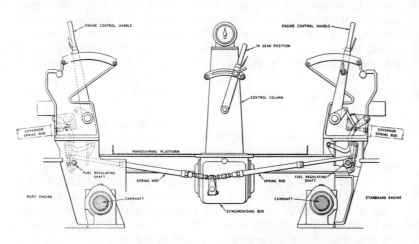

Figure 13.7 Synchronising gear

Hull vibration which originates in the engines and/or the propellers can be successfully eliminated by the application of a suitable type of synchronising gear. Such a synchronising gear, as illustrated in Figure 13.7 may comprise four separate mechanisms, viz.:

   (i) a differential gear;
   (ii) a phase adjuster;
   (iii) a synchronising box;
   (iv) a fuel control gear.

When both engines are running in the ahead direction and at exactly the same speed the differential shaft is stationary. Upon the slightest variation in speed, the differential shaft turns in the same direction as the slower-running engine, this movement being utilised to equalise the revolutions.

The phase-adjuster is an adjustable coupling arranged between the differential shaft and the roller shaft of the synchronising box. It enables the angular displacement of the engine crankshafts to be varied minutely while the engines are running. When the best position is found the coupling can be locked permanently.

The synchronising box contains a mechanism for operating the fuel-regulating gear; also a means whereby the synchronising gear can be rendered inoperative; and a graduated dial with a pointer, which will show the relative phase position of the two engines.

The engine control handles are connected to the fuel-regulating shafts in such a manner that, when the synchronising gear is inoperative, both engines can be manoeuvred as though there were no synchronising gear. When the synchronising gear is operating the fuel is automatically reduced to the faster engine and increased to the slower engine, without causing any movement to the control levers on the sector brackets.

Capacities of Ancillary Pumps

The respective pumps which serve a main engine vary in relative size according to the engine type. The following particulars are for guidance only. It is always advisable that reference should be made to the engine builders for particulars of their practice.

A tolerance of 10 per cent is permissible, to allow a standard size of pump to be used. The divisors are for tropical conditions; for ships trading solely in temperate zones the capacities of the salt-water pumps may be reduced by, say, 25 per cent. The lubricating oil and fresh-water pumps remain unchanged.

$$\text{Pump capacity, tonnes/hour} = \frac{\text{engine kW}}{F}$$

Single-acting, Four-stroke Engines, Crosshead or Trunk, with Oil-cooled Pistons

Salt-water circulating pumps	$F = 16$
Fresh-water circulating pumps	$F = 22$
Lubricating oil pumps	$F = 22$

Single-acting and Double-acting, Two-stroke Engines, Crosshead or Trunk, with Oil-cooled Pistons

Salt-water circulating pumps	$F = 16$
Fresh-water circulating pumps	$F = 19$
Lubricating oil pumps	$F = 12-15$

Pressure-charged, Single-acting, Two-stroke Engines with Oil-cooled Main Pistons and Water-cooled Exhaust Pistons

Salt-water circulating pumps (including oil cooler, water cooler and air cooler circulating)	$F = 17-22$
Fresh-water circulating pumps (including exhaust-piston circulating)	$F = 22-30$
Lubricating oil pumps (including main-piston circulating)	$F = 22-34$

For the salt-water circulating: three-fifths of the total quantity passes to oil and water coolers in series; two-fifths to turboblower air and oil coolers.

If fitted, the fuel-valve cooling water pump, in tonnes/hour

$$= \frac{\text{engine kW}}{1100}$$

The capacities given above are for the working pumps; stand-by pumps, as may be required, are additional. A stand-by pump may often be a dual-service unit.

Surface of Coolers

$$\text{Cooler surface, in square metres} = \frac{\text{engine kW}}{C}$$

Single-acting, Four-stroke Engines, Crosshead or Trunk, with Oil-cooled Pistons

Fresh-water cooler	$C = 48$
Lubricating oil cooler	$C = 28$

Single-acting and Double-acting, Two-stroke Engines, Crosshead or Trunk, with Oil-cooled Pistons

Fresh-water cooler	$C = 40$
Lubricating oil cooler	$C = 16$

Size of Exhaust-gas Boilers

$$\text{Weight of exhaust gas, kg/h} = G = E + W$$

where $E =$ weight of fuel burned in engine, kg/h;
$W =$ weight of air, kg/h.

Four-stroke Engines

$$W = \frac{V + 40 \text{ per cent excess}}{0.875}$$

where $V =$ total swept volume of cylinders, m^3/h;
$0.875 = m^3/kg$ at 40°C.

Two-stroke Engines

$$W = \frac{B}{0.875}$$

where $B =$ scavenge-blower capacity, m^3/h;
$0.875 = m^3/kg$ at 40°C.

Weight of steam raised, kg/h $= S$

$$S = \frac{G \times t \times s \times 0.9}{H}$$

where $G =$ weight of exhaust gas, kg/h;
$t =$ temperature-drop in exhaust gas, °C $= (e - b)$;
$e =$ temperature of exhaust gas entering boiler, °C;
$b =$ steam temperature plus 40°C;
$s =$ specific heat $= 0.25$;
$H =$ total heat of steam, from feed inlet temperature, kcal/kg;
$e = 480°C$, four-stroke engines;
$e = 370°C$, two-stroke engines;
$e = 350°C$, two-stroke, pressure-charged engines.

For pressure-charged, single-acting, two-stroke engines:

Weight of exhaust gas, at full load service rating = 10 kg/kWh.
Approximate quantity of saturated steam obtainable at 7 kgf/cm²
(6·85 bar) (gauge) = 0·45 kg/kWh.

The normal evaporative capacity required from the boiler is
arranged to be obtained from the exhaust-gas weight and temperature
at 80 per cent of the average service power. But the boiler must also
be able to pass the full-power weight of gas, with a boiler back-
pressure not exceeding 150–200 mm of water. At 80 per cent power
the exhaust temperature may be down 20 per cent.

Size of Compressed-air Reservoirs

The Classification Societies stipulate an air-reservoir capacity
sufficient for twelve consecutive starts for each main engine. As a
rule, an engine builder provides a capacity well in excess of minimum
requirements—say 50 per cent. The aggregate reservoir capacity may
vary from 5·5 to 7·0 times the total swept colume of the engine. For
some engines, say double-acting two-stroke, the ratio is as low as 4·5;
for other engines it may be as high as 8·0. This is for an initial starting
air pressure of 25 bar. An engine, so designed, can usually be started
with air down to 10 bar, but for calculation purposes a lower limit
of 15 bar is assumed.

Heat Losses

For pressure-charged, single-acting, two-stroke engines, with oil-
cooled main pistons and fresh-water-cooled exhaust pistons, the
undermentioned guidance figures for heat losses may be useful, in
the absence of other data, viz.:

Fresh water circulating to cylinder jackets = 11 per cent
Fresh water circulating to exhaust pistons = 2·5 per cent
Fresh water circulating to blower casings = 2 per cent
Lubricating oil to engine bearings = 2·5 per cent
Lubricating oil to main pistons = 2 per cent
Sea-water circulating to blower air cooler = 3 per cent
Sea-water circulating to blower oil cooler = dependent upon size
of blower.

The gross calorific value of the fuel is assumed to be 10 750 kg/cal,
the net value 10 150 kg/cal.

Relative Weights and Costs

In weight the main propelling engine, over the crank-ends, may account for 40–50 per cent of the total machinery weight for single-screw tankers and cargo ships, and 50–55 per cent for twin-screw vessels—according to the size and kind of ship. In approximate cost the engine, over the crank-ends, may be from 35 to 50 per cent of the total installation cost. The main propelling engine is less costly than any other component section of the installation reckoned in pounds sterling per ton weight. On the same basis the most costly section is the pipe-arrangement work.

Burning of Low-grade Fuels

The successful burning of low-grade fuel oils depends, fundamentally, upon two things, viz.:

(i) provision for heating the fuel to a high level, say to 120–130°C, to ensure successful atomisation;

(ii) the thorough elimination—by series centrifuging—of water, sludge, solid matter and slow-burning constitutents.

There are various ways of achieving these results. One is to heat the fuel in the unpurified oil-settling tank to 50°C; pass it gravitationally through a coarse filter and through a magnetic filter, in series; then heat the oil to the required temperature level, as it falls to the separator and clarifier, and so to the daily service tank and the engine. Heating grids are provided in the bunker and settling tanks; the pipe from the settling tank is well lagged, with a small steam pipe in contact with the fuel pipe under the lagging. The heating and purifying scheme, and its details, belong to the machinery-room pipe arrangement and not to the propelling engine, which is the essential subject of this book.

It is important that hot-oil circulation should be possible through the system right up to the fuel valves, to ensure that there is no difficulty in moving and atomising the fuel after periods of stoppage.

Granted the embodiment of the foregoing precautions, the burning of low-grade fuels causes no difficulty in the mechanical running of an engine. Combustion, in many instances, has been better with the lower-grade oils than with diesel oil. In watching an engine running it is, often, not possible to detect when it has been changed over from diesel oil to heavy oil.

The burning of lower-grade fuels, naturally, is accompanied by increased maintenance costs. Even so, the net results are profitable.

Low-grade fuels, of viscosity 860 centi-stokes, are very successfully burned in double-acting, two-stroke engines—the most exacting form of prime mover for the purpose.

If, in the burning of heavy fuels, maintenance costs are to be low, then the fuel-oil purifiers and clarifiers must be of ample size. In the author's opinion many purifiers are much too small. It seems to him to be prudent to choose purifiers having listed outputs of at least twice what is required. The additional cost is well worth while.

Record of Engine Behaviour

It not infrequently happens that, when the engine builder is requested to give an opinion on difficulties which have arisen with an engine in service, there are few, if any, data readily available for assessing general behaviour. On each outward and homeward voyage, therefore, one set of normal indicator cards and one set of out-of-phase cards, i.e. draw-cards, should be taken, and a simple table compiled as indicated below. Test-bed and trial-trip records, similarly arranged, should be available for comparison.

GENERAL DATA

Cylinder	1	2	3	4	5	6
Mip						
$P_{max.}$						
$P_{comp.}$						
Fuel-pump index						
Exhaust temperature						

For example, if $P_{max.}$ slowly falls, over a succession of tables, the fuel pumps may be worn and leaky; if suddenly, then fuel valves may be choked; if $P_{comp.}$ goes down, then piston rings may be sticking or broken, or, much more infrequently, the exhaust valve may be leaking, and so on.

Heat-balance Approximation

A superintendent engineer may occasionally make a request to his representative for an analysis of engine heat losses. By way of example, a simple approximation—which will be suitable for most purposes—is detailed below.

Test-bed figures:

Gross calorific value of fuel = 10 840 k cal/kg.

(a) *Fuel burned per hour* = 1089 kg

$$kW - 5000$$

Given the gross calorific value G of the fuel being used, then the net calorific value N may be obtained from the approximate formula:

$$N = 2515 + (G \times 0.707)$$

i.e.
$$N = 2515 + (10\,840 \times 0.707)$$
$$= 10\,177 \text{ kcal/kg.}$$

$$860 \text{ kcal} = 1 \text{ kWh.}$$

(b) *Brake thermal efficiency* $= \dfrac{860 \times 5000}{10\,177 \times 1089} = 39$ per cent

From the test-bed:

E = weight of exhaust gas in kg/h = weight of air plus weight of fuel = 43 680.

T = exhaust gas temperature after turbine minus air inlet temperature = 372°C.

C = weight of cooling water, kg/h = 59 870.

R = water outlet at engine minus water inlet temperature = 28°C.

L = weight of lubricating oil and cooling oil, in kg/h = 104 500.

S = oil outlet from engine minus oil inlet temperature = 22°C.

(c) *Heat lost to exhaust* $= E \times T \times$ specific heat = 43 680 × 372 × 0.2372 = 3 855 000 kcal.

(d) *Heat lost to cooling water for cylinders, turboblowers and air coolers* $= C \times R \times$ specific heat = 59 870 × 28 × 1.0 = 1 660 000 kcal.

(e) *Heat lost to lubricating and cooling oil* $- L \times S \times$ specific heat = 104 500 × 22.2 × 0.50 = 1 160 000 kcal.

The results are summarised in Table 13.1.

The relative figures for oil and water may differ slightly, depending on the quantities passing through the engine; but, added together, they ought not to vary much from 26 per cent.

It is essential that suitable measuring devices should be fitted to the blower-air intakes, also to the water-inlet and oil-inlet connections. The temperature of the air at the engine should be taken close to the blower inlet.

Table 1

Category	kcal/h (approx. test figures)	kcal/h (totals)	Per cent
(a) Fuel consumed	1 089 × 10 177	11,090 000	100
(b) Useful work	5 000 × 860	4 300 000	39
(c) Exhaust losses	43 680 × 372 × 0·2372	3 855 000	35
(d) Cooling-water losses	59 870 × 28 × 1·0	1 676 000	15
(e) Lubricating and cooling system losses	104 500 × 22·2 × 0·5	1 160 000	10·5
(f) Radiation, etc.	—	—	0·5

The heat losses in the cooling water for the turbochargers and the charge-air coolers, as well as the heat loss in their lubricating oil supply, are included in the figures for the items (d) and (e).

Lubricating Oil Flow

It is erroneous to suppose that oil pressure at any point in a forced-lubrication system is, by itself, a satisfactory criterion of oil flow. Oil flow should be interpreted in a way analogous to current flow in an electrical circuit, where pressure, resistance and flow are correlated in terms of Ohm's law. The resistance of the whole circuit affects the flow of oil; the pressure at any one point, by itself, may be entirely misleading; it is the quantity of oil which is flowing that really matters. Lower oil pressure, by reason of, say, greater running clearances, may imply a greater oil flow, and may therefore be fully satisfactory; conversely, a higher pressure, with finer clearances, may be concomitant with a diminished and unsatisfactory oil flow. An oil-flow indicator—especially at the highest point of a lubricating oil circuit—is more likely to impart confidence to an engineer than a pressure gauge will do.

The pressure of lubricating oil at every point throughout a cooler from inlet to outlet, should always be greater than the pressure of the salt water there; otherwise salt water may enter the lubricating oil, to emulsify it or to form sludge.

Running Clearances

An old-time marine rule for running clearances in bearings allows one-thousandth of a millimetre per millimetre of shaft diameter. For diesel propelling engines this amount is normally too great; three-quarters of this amount is more representative; indeed, some engineers successfully reduce their running clearances to one half.

Main bearing clearances can sometimes be influenced by variations in the torsional stiffness of crankpins, as mentioned in another chapter. A slight lack of crankpin rigidity—by throwing the centre-line of one or more journal-pieces out-of-line with the remainder of the crankshaft—may make it necessary to increase the main-bearing clearances to an abnormal amount if 'wiping' is to be avoided.

If one or two main bearings show relatively high loading in the design stage it may be advisable to fit balance weights to the adjacent crank webs of such magnitude and at such angles as may be necessary to reduce the loading, having due regard to the overall dynamic balancing of the engine.

The use of ball bearings and sleeve bearings on the same spindle is always unsatisfactory, by reason of problems of centring, differential wear, lubrication and so on. Ball bearings must work with the closest accuracy; when harnessed with sleeve bearings, therefore, they are liable to break.

Critical Speeds

In every engine there is a series of torsional critical speeds at which in some instances it is not desirable, and in others dangerous, to run. These critical speeds appear whenever the pulsations in the engine torque coincide with the natural frequency of the shafting system, producing conditions of resonance. There are critical speeds other than torsional. For example, there can in certain circumstances be whipping, measurable at the connecting rod foot as very heavy pressure on the crankpin; also there may be critical fore-and-aft vibrations, measurable at the free end of the crankshaft, setting up bending stresses.

Reduction of stress may be obtained by increasing the shaft stiffness; by substituting semi-built for fully built crankshafts; by fitting vibration dampers or de-turners; and sometimes by altering the sequence of cylinder firing. The last-named is bound up with certain constants used in the calculations, by which crankshaft diameters are determined.

More specifically, for certain crank combinations in engines located right aft, the incidence of torsional critical stresses can make necessary the substitution of semi-built cranks—with their less heavy revolving masses—for fully built cranks. Each pair of crank webs and the associated crankpin then constitute one steel casting. An equivalent result can, however, be achieved by introducing unequal crank angles and retaining fully built shafts. The turning moment is then somewhat less regular than with the normal and preferred arrangement of cranks; but it is fully satisfactory.

Figure 13.8 shows, for a six-cylinder, double-acting, two-stroke engine, the stresses caused by the torsional vibration of the crankshaft and tunnel shafting, which are additional to the total stresses otherwise present. They are of negligible magnitude.

The curve shows that the one-node third harmonic produces a vibration stress of approximately 400 kgf/cm² at 60 rev/min. At these revolutions the power torque is very low, but, even so, some

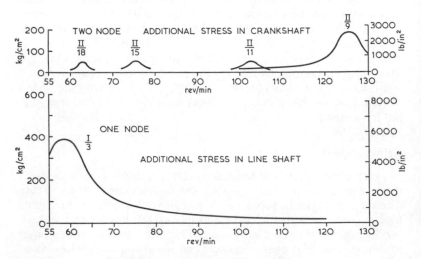

Figure 13.8 Torsional critical stresses

designers would think that a vibration stress of this magnitude is rather on the high side and would prefer a closed period over the range 55–65 rev/min, the vibration stress being thus reduced to about 200 kgf/cm², which is accepted as a satisfactory figure.

Torsion in Crankpins

It is not sufficiently appreciated by marine engineers that crankpins and crank webs, no less than crank journals, are in torsion. It is too commonly assumed that, although journal pieces are under torsion and bending, crankpins are subjected to bending forces only. In certain types of engine it is possible for the crankpins to have insufficient torsional rigidity and, as a result, consecutive journals do not remain truly in line longitudinally, but are transversely displaced, throwing additional loads on to the corresponding main bearings, especially towards the aft end of a multi-cylinder engine. Only if the crank webs are relatively flexible can this additional load be proportionately mitigated. Insufficient torsional rigidity is more likely to occur in engines in which the bending forces are low and where, in consequence, the crankpins do not benefit from the additional diameter otherwise allowed in excess of torsional requirements. Figure 13.9 shows how the crankshaft of a six-cylinder engine, of two-stroke, double-acting, standard type, moves about in its eight main bearings. The bearings are numbered I, at the forward end of the engine, to VIII, at the aft end. The twelve readings per revolution of journal were taken vertically and horizontally, at crank-angle intervals of 30°. When at rest each journal was at position 0; at top dead-centre it was at position 1; at bottom dead-centre it was at

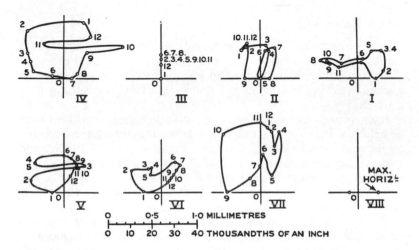

Figure 13.9 Movement of crankshaft in its bearings

position 7. For bearing VIII, due to an inadvertence, the vertical readings were not taken; at bearing III there was not any measurable horizontal movement. The engine was running at full load and full revolutions, i.e. 4500 kW at 104 rev/min.

Movement of Crankshaft in Bearings

It is a matter of some doubt whether a heavy crankshaft really lifts from its main bearings under the impulse of upward inertia forces and gas pressure, or whether the forces expend themselves in slight, local, flexural displacements which mean, in effect, a follow-up by the stressed bedplate girders without separation of shaft and bearings. To establish this point, suitable apparatus was fitted to the main engine mentioned in the last paragraph, when running on the test-bed. The results for the foremost and aftermost main bearings are given in Figure 13.10 from which it will be seen that movement does, in fact, take place to the limit of the running clearance. The respective conventional polar diagrams for the bearing loads are also shown. As the gas pressure is balanced within the running gear, the bearing loads are those caused by the dead-weight, inertia, centrifugal force and torque reaction. Although Figure 13.10 shows diagrams for the end bearings only, there is some degree of movement at every bearing, notwithstanding that, at some bearings, the load—according to conventional calculation—is always downward.

Engine Balancing

Balancing problems are not affected by cylinder pressures and crank-shaft torque; these enter only into questions of turning moment. (Sometimes the levelling-up of ihp among the cylinders is termed by marine engineers 'balancing an engine'—but this is something quite different.)

In engines having more than one crank the weights must perforce be arranged in more than one plane, hence the disturbances created by the moving parts consist both of forces and couples. Forces tend to move the engine as a whole, i.e. to shift or to shake it bodily up and down and sideways; couples to tilt it vertically or horizontally. For an engine to be balanced dynamically, i.e. when running, the respective systems of forces and couples must be in equilibrium.

The moving mechanism consists of revolving masses and recipro-cating masses. For analytical purposes it is convenient to separate the two. The disturbances caused by the reciprocating masses are divisible into primary and secondary forces and couples.

There are thus, within an engine, six separate systems to be balanced, viz.:

(a) forces: revolving; primary reciprocating; secondary recipro-cating;
(b) couples: revolving; primary reciprocating; secondary reciprocating.

Equal and opposite parallel forces, acting on a body, constitute a pure couple; its moment is the product of one of the forces and the perpendicular distance between them. The effect of a couple is independent of its location in a plane. If, in Figure 13.11, the couples X, Y and Z are of equal magnitude each will have the same rotative effect upon the body, about point O. This is important; it means

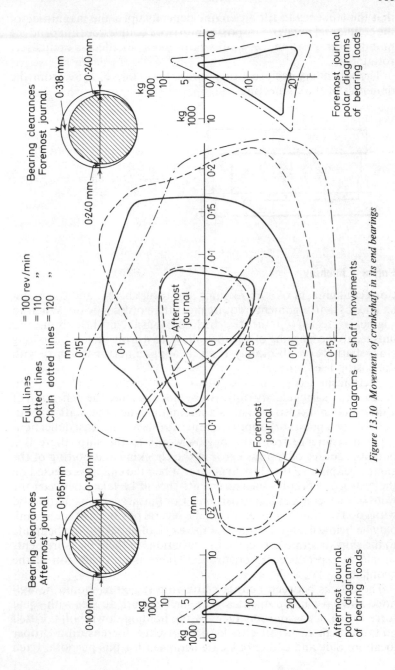

Bearing clearances
Foremost journal

0·318 mm
0·240 mm

Foremost journal
polar diagrams
of bearing loads

kg
1000

kg
1000

Full lines   = 100 rev/min
Dotted lines   = 110   „
Chain dotted lines = 120   „

0·240 mm

mm

Aftermost
journal

Foremost
journal

mm

Diagrams of shaft movements

Bearing clearances
Aftermost journal

0·100 mm
0·165 mm
0·100 mm

Aftermost journal
polar diagrams
of bearing loads

kg
1000

kg
1000

Figure 13.10 Movement of crankshaft in its end bearings

that the tendency to tilt an engine depends upon the magnitude of the couple and not upon its position. Also, a couple does not produce motion of translation, i.e. bodily movement; its effect is exclusively rotational.

The secondary reciprocating forces and couples arise from the finiteness of the connecting rod.

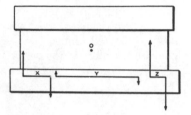

Figure 13.11 Effect of couples

Engine Chocking

Correct alignment of a crankshaft and thrust block, and the maintenance of that alignment, require more than ordinary care. When an engine is erected on the test-bed the journal bushes should be finished to the marking of a thin, hollow, cast-iron mandrel. No long crankshaft is ever absolutely true. Its apparent error will vary with the positions of support.

A crankshaft is unsuitable for use as an alignment gauge; first, because of its irregularity of form; second, because the deflection of a shaft due to its own weight is a maximum when the shaft is solid. Between two points of support, a thin tube shows the least deflection.

On transference from the engine works to the ship, there is a potential source of serious error in the chocking and bolting of the engine bedplate to the ship structure. When the engine is erected on the test-bed deflection measurements should be taken between the webs of each crank in four positions. For the larger crankshafts, and with good workmanship, errors in the several positions of each crank may lie below 0·20–0·25 mm. As the work of chocking the bedplate to the ship structure proceeds, the variations in these measurements should be reproduced to ensure that there is no distortion of the bedplate.

The chocks between bedplate and ship structure should be well fitted and have ample surfaces. The same remark applies with equal force to the heads and nut faces of the holding-down bolts. Fitted bolts through cast-iron chocks do not exist for ensuring proper location. Side and end chocks are arranged for this purpose. Each chock must support the bedplate immediately around the holding-down bolt, as shown in Figure 13.12 at *b*. The chock at *a* is unsatisfactory.

If a bedplate is properly chocked and bolted initially, then, during the whole life of the ship, fretted chocks and broken holding-down bolts may be completely unknown. The effects of bad chocking may be slow in development, but serious in their eventual consequences. The signs are: loose and broken holding-down bolts, followed by fretting abrasion between chocks and tank-top seating, and/or between chocks and bedplate. Once the fault has appeared, correction can become a major undertaking; repeated renewal of fastenings is the only practicable course. The importance of good chocking is usually more apparent to the operating engineer than to the engine builder.

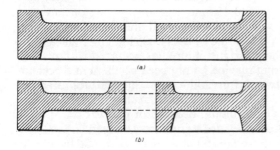

(a)

(b)

Figure 13.12 Bedplate chocks

Holding-down bolts must make a watertight connection if they pass through the inner bottom. The bolt is screwed through the tank-top plating, with nut and grummet underneath. Not infrequently the bolt finds the toe of a floor angle as a seating for the lower nut, making it impossible to obtain a fair surface for the nut face. As a result, the fastening loosens in service.

Practice varies regarding the dead load carried by the fitting strips on the chocks. One engine builder allows 14 kgf/cm² of effective chock area; another allows 17 kgf/cm²; and the practice of a third well-known builder is to allow a loading of 20–35 kgf/cm².

Bolt-tightening

Experiments have shown that there can sometimes be only a narrow margin between a satisfactory degree of bolt-tightening and a state of over-tightening in which the bolt is damaged and given a permanent set. Admittedly there can be difficulties in the way. But the custom of flogging-up important nuts by spanner and tup until they ring solid is barbarous, at the best; at the worst it is highly inimical. It should be borne in mind that the point at which a spanner 'rings solid' is determined by the weight and swing of the tup, the cross-section and length of the spanner and so on. It does not by any means prove that the bolt is tightened the correct amount. Often the bolt is over-tightened, but it may equally well be under-tightened. A successful result depends upon establishing a suitable relationship between the variable factors named. In the end, therefore, success is dependent upon the human equation—the judgment of the man supervising the operation. That is why the tightening-up of important bolts by hydraulic or equivalent means should receive wider application.

For bolts which sustain intermittent loads the contacting surface must be true with the face of the nut. For example, if the nut of a 75 mm diameter spindle is 0·25 mm open at one side, there may be a stress in the spindle of 1500 kgf/cm^2, according to conventional calculation. This assumes static loading. If the out-of-squareness were, say, 0·4 mm the stress would be over 2000 kgf/cm^2. The author can recall instances where fatigue failure has occurred within a few months of a ship entering service simply because there had been an out-of-squareness between nut and contacting surface of from 0·10 mm to 0·40 mm. Calculated stresses, such as the above, are unlikely to be realised in actuality, because of plastic flow and for other reasons, but at least they are a pointer to danger.

Important nuts and bolt-heads on moving parts should have their faces smooth-scraped, also the contacting surfaces. The little ridges on a machined surface are usually able to sustain the tightening-up loads, but they become flattened by the fretting impact loads when running, and are thus a potent cause of slackness. Connecting rod palms and bearing-bush surfaces should similarly be scraped plane; so should the joints of bushes.

This remark applies to a wide category of components and conditions. Thus, Figure 13.13 illustrates the tie rod of an opposed-piston engine. The collar c is provided with flats f for holding the collar when tightening the nut at the lower end of the rod. The arrangement is shown in Figure 13.13(a) after initial tightening of the nut. That is, the load is sustained by the area of collar, diameter d, minus the two segments x.

Under working conditions the collar will tend to rub a slight recess into the surface at the area of contact. If the positioning pin, shown in Figure 13.13(b), is sheared the flats after subsequent tightening can assume a different position, as indicated where the segments have moved to y. This means that the load is then carried by the two small segmental areas x, in Figure 13.13(a). As these areas become fretted away, the attachment will hammer and become slack. The difficulty can be avoided if flats f do not extend the full depth of the collar.

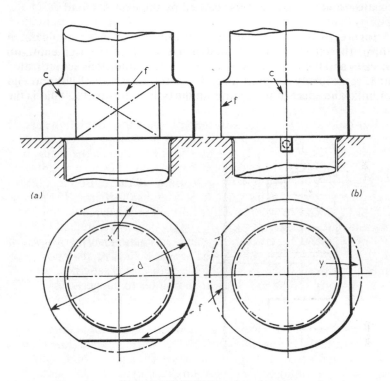

Figure 13.13 High spots from fretting

To take another example of the same principle: the distance between the top edge of the top piston ring and the bottom edge of the bottom ring plus the working stroke of the piston should exceed the length of the cylinder-liner barrel by an amount sufficient to obviate the formation of circumferential ridges on the liner, after making due allowance for wear-down of bearings. A tapered entrance to the barrel working surface is usual.

Stress Effects of Tightening-up and Working Loads

The subject of bolt-tightening seems to hold two misconceptions. These are:

(i) that the total working stress in any tension member under dynamic loading never exceeds the tightening-up stress, if the dynamic load is not greater than the screwing-up load;

(ii) that the total working stress is the sum of the tightening-up stress and the tensile stress caused by the external load.

Figure 13.14 shows diagrammatically, albeit in an exaggerated form,- the effect upon a bolted flange joint of the tightening-up stresses and the working stresses. The initial conditions are indicated at 1, respectively for joint face, flange top face, top of nut and end of bolt. The effect of tightening-up the bolt is shown at 2. That is the

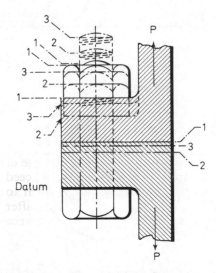

Figure 13.14 Effect of tightening and working loads

bolt is lengthened and the flange is compressed. Upon the application of the working load p there is a partial relaxation of the flange and a further elongation of the bolt, as indicated at 3. It is under the last-named condition that the flange joint must remain pressure-tight. In an actual flange connection the amounts of the compression and relaxation are, of course, very small dimensionally; indeed they are normally minute. But the principle is there.

Figure 13.15 shows, in outline, a simple bearing block.

If a tightening-up force $P_1 = P_2$ is applied at the spanner, the bolt elongation $l_2 = P_2 L_2/a_2 E_2$ and the block compression $l_1 = P_1 L_1/a_1 E_1$. The protrusion of the bolt end beyond the nut $= l_2 + l_1 = x$.

If $l_2/l_1 = K$, where $K = $ constant; $l_2 = l_1 K$; $l_2(1/K + 1) = x$. Given x, derived as above, and knowing the a and E values, and

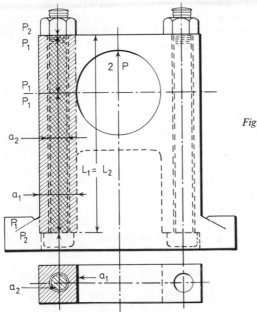

Figure 13.15 Effect of tightening and working loads

therefore K, the magnitude of l_2 can be obtained. Also $l_1(1+K)=x$

Tensile tightening-up
stress in bolt $=f_2=l_2 E_2/L_2$ (13.1)

Compressive stress in block,
due to tightening-up $=f_1=l_1 E_1/L_1$ (13.2)

The area of block under simple compression is empirically chosen.

Application of the external load P causes the block to relax a certain amount and the bolt to stretch a like amount, the block and the bolt being bound together. It can be shown that the additional tensile stress in the bolts caused by the working load $=p_2/a_2=P/(1+K)a_2$. The reduction in the compressive stress in the block $=p_1/a_1=P/(1+1/K)a_1$. $P=p_1+p_2$.

The total tensile stress in the bolts, due to tightening-up plus working load $=l_2 E_2/L_2+P/(1+K)a_2$ (13.3)

The total compressive stress in the block, due to tightening-up plus working load $=l_1 E_1/L_1-P/(1+1/K)a_1$ (13.4)

In the above: $a_1 a_2$ = cross-sectional areas of block and bolt.
      $L_1 L_2$ = initial length of bolt and block. $L_2 = L_1$.
      $E_1 E_2$ = moduli of elasticity of block and bolt material.
      $1_1 1_2$ = alterations in length of block and bolt.
      $f_1 f_2$ = stresses in block and bolt.
      P = working load on block
      $P_1 P_2$ = tightening-up loads on block and bolts; $P_1 = P_2$.
      $p_1 p_2$ = alteration of loads on block and bolt; $P = p_1 + p_2$.

Example. A cast-iron bearing block is held down by steel bolts as in Figure 13.15. Determine the stresses in the bolts, given the following particulars:

Cross-sectional area of one bolt $= a_2 = 13 \times 10^3$ mm^2.
Cross-sectional area of stressed region of block $= a_1 = 39 \times 10^3$ mm^2.
Length $L = 1780$ mm. $E_2 = 20 \times 10^5$; $E_1 = 12 \times 10^5$ bar.
Upward thrust per bolt due to external load $= P = 45\,500$ kg.
Bolt is initially tightened by turning the nut through 80°, the pitch of screw thread being 6·00 mm.

$$1_1/1_2 = a_2 E_2/a_1 E_1 = 13\,000 \times 2\,000\,000/39\,000 \times 1\,200\,000 = 0\cdot556.$$

$1_1 = 0\cdot556\ 1_2$ and $1_1 + 1_2 = $x. i.e. $1\cdot556\ 1_2 = x= 80 \times 6\cdot00/360$
   $= 1\cdot333$ mm.

$1_2 = 1\cdot333/1\cdot556 = 0\cdot86$ mm.

Stress in bolt tightening
$$= 1_2 E_2/L_2 = 0\cdot86 \times 2\,000\,000/1780 = 966 \text{ bar.}$$

Stress in bolt due to tightening plus working load
$$= 966 \text{ bar} + P/(1+K)a_2 = 966 + 122 = 1088 \text{ bar.}$$

Proportions of Flange Joints

Precisely what relationship exists between flange thickness and distribution of pressure along and across the face of the joint illustrated in Figure 13.16 is not clear. The compression is not uniform. Where the load is transmitted along a wall of metal perpendicular to the flange, distortion at each bolt-hole, by the flange bending as if it were a cantilever, tends to reduce the compression between the flanges. If the compression is diminished to zero, the contained fluid leaks under the flange to deflect it.

A suitable criterion for design would be the taking of a definite contact pressure at the flange faces midway between the bolts. The bolt area and tightening-up stress to give this pressure would then be calculated. But that is impracticable. It is therefore necessary to fall back upon a method which experience supports and which has the added virtue of simplicity.

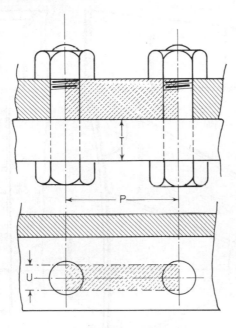

Figure 13.16 Bolted flanges

For Figure 13.16, the design involves the pitch and diameter of the bolts and the flange thickness. A strip between adjacent holes may be regarded as an encastré beam of unit width U.

Let $d =$ deflection of strip.
Then $d = Pp^4/32Et^3 = kPp^4/t^3$
or $Pp^4/t^3 = d/k = K.$

As the numerical value of K is large, it is more convenient to take its fourth root, thus $C^4 = K.$

Formula connecting pitch of bolts and flange thickness:
$$= Pp^4/t^3 = C^4.$$

The bolt sizes are determined in accordance with normal practice. The stress in a 40 mm dia. bolt may be 500 bar, with one-half of this stress for a 20 mm dia. bolt. The bolts must be adequate in size safely to provide a grip on the flanges of sufficient intensity that, when the

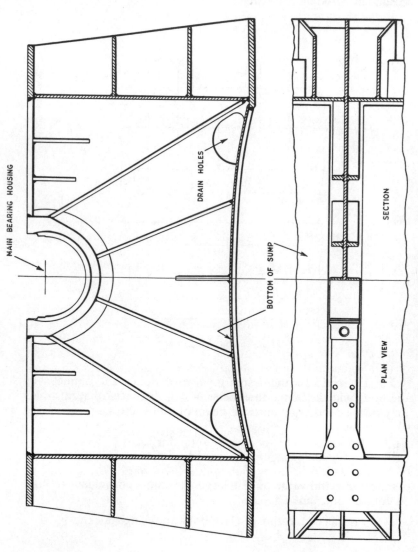

MAIN BEARING HOUSING

DRAIN HOLES

BOTTOM OF SUMP

SECTION

PLAN VIEW

Figure 13.17 Cross-girder of bedplate

bolt pitch and flange thickness are determined from the above rule, the joint is stout enough to obviate leakage. The total load on the bolts is the product of total surface and working pressure.

In the foregoing: P = working pressure;
p = pitch of bolts;
t = flange thickness;
C = constant.

The value of C^4 is proportional to the modulus of elasticity of the material.

In pound inch units, a value of $C = 13$ has been widely used for cast-iron and gunmetal flanges. Alternatively, $C = 11$ for cast-iron and 12·5 to 13·5 for steel and gunmetal have received general acceptance. Usually, comparative figures will be obtainable from current designs of proven value.

The Ribbing of Structures

One of the subjects upon which the author finds himself at variance with many engineers concerns the application of ribbing. While by no means insensitive to the aesthetics of design, the author necessarily places simplicity, robustness and competitive costs in the first line of requirements for any design. Therefore, unlike some engineers, he does not go out of his way to avoid the use of ribs.

Figure 13.17 shows the cross-girder of a bedplate for an opposed piston engine.˙ It is economical in the weight of material used. Rigidity is ensured by the ribbing which holds apart the bearing housing and the heavy base flange. Ribs, if necessary at all, should be of substantial thickness, usually not less than 1·20 to 1·25 times the plate thickness. This remark applies equally to castings and weldings. The welding design of Figure 13.17,is simple and direct. To obtain equivalent results by the thickening of the plating or the substitution of a box-section would increase the first cost.

In general there are two ways of obtaining the structural stiffness needed for dynamic machinery. One is by the use of a heavy weight of material; the other is by the application of ribs or struts directed to the point of movement or deflection, thus to reinforce a somewhat lighter structure and attain the necessary rigidity thereby.

Chapter 14

Creeping Cracks

Creeping cracks are common phenomena in marine machinery. They appear in many guises, and it is therefore desirable to be able to make the appropriate deductions from the appearance of such cracks.

While it is convenient, in conformity with everyday speech, to use the expression 'fatigue cracking', the term is, nevertheless, a complete misnomer. There is no tiredness nor deterioration in the metal after repeated stressing. Test pieces taken closely adjacent to so-called fatigue cracks—more accurately termed 'creeping cracks'—invariably bear testimony to the soundness of the material.

There are many fatigue failures in the diesel engine. Sometimes their origin is obscure. Rarely are they related to functional or design stresses. Often the cause has to be sought in a stress-raiser, such as a badly fitted bolt, or in a design which over-estimates the capacity of the engine fitter. In some difficult problems the cause may be secondary accelerations which were overlooked in design.

In the initial phase of the propagation of a crack, the repetitive loading causes a gradual breakdown in the inter-atomic locking of an individual crystal, leading to the generation of a minute crack. The subsequent alteration in local stress distribution causes an extension of the crack to contiguous crystals. The separation thus initiated slowly extends. The smooth and even surface of the crack at this stage is attributable to friction between the severed crystals. A creeping crack is trans-crystalline and not inter-crystalline. That is, the breakdown under repeated stress first takes place within the crystals, and the crack does not follow the crystal boundaries. Accordingly, there are no changes in the inter-crystalline structure of the metal in so-called fatigue failures.

It is extremely improbable that a creeping crack ever has its origin in a shock load.

According to the author's experience, there is no relationship between a violent blow and fatigue cracks. Catastrophe and fatigue have no association, and if by any chance they concur, it is only by coincidence. It may be that laboratory tests could point towards a different conclusion, but it is to be questioned if fatigue as it is explored in a laboratory, and fatigue as it is known in the running behaviour of piston rods, connecting rods and so on are the same phenomena. In the former a structural change in the material may be induced more or less throughout the test piece. In the latter, structural change is generally confined to dimensions of microscopical order.

Failure from fatigue is the concern of the designer. Shock from accidents is the affair of the superintendent engineer.

Appearance of Creeping Cracks

Creeping cracks have a distinctive appearance, and show three progressive phases. Starting at a point of stress concentration, there is a tiny crack. This is the first phase. The separation of surfaces slowly extends, the appearance of the surfaces at this stage being smooth and even. The place of origin of the creeping crack is usually unmistakable; lines are observable radiating from it, and there are wave-like markings—successive crack boundaries—the axis of which indicates the starting-point. As the crack creeps across the section the separated surfaces tend to become increasingly less and less smooth, terminating in a region which is probably rough and may be angular. This is the second phase. When the crack has penetrated so far that the residual section can withstand the repetitive loads no longer sudden rupture occurs, cleaving the section and showing a characteristic shock fracture, brightly crystalline, in contrast to the darker, smoother surface of earlier regions. It often happens that, after rupture, there is rubbing contact between the two severed sections, and this is liable locally to alter the configuration of the surfaces. A creeping crack in alloy steel is, usually, relatively smooth and plane across the whole section.

Examples of Creeping Cracks

In Figure 14.1, where failure was by bending, an attempt is made to illustrate the above features clearly. Figure 14.2 is a photograph of the section from which Figure 14.1 was prepared. The point of crack origin is deducible from a study of the characteristic conchoidal markings.

Figure 14.3 is another characteristic fatigue failure by bending.

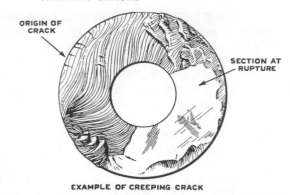

Figure 14.1
Characteristic
creeping crack

Figure 14.4 is an excellent example of fatigue failure. It shows the section of an exhaust-valve spindle 40 mm in diameter. The main crack had its origin at the point marked *X*, and the steps in its creeping penetration, i.e. the successive crack boundaries, are well defined. Additionally, at the places marked *S*, three secondary cracks are seen to have made their appearance.

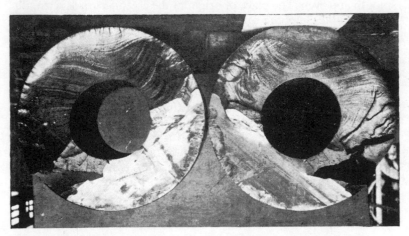

Figure 14.2 Fatigue, or creeping crack failure

With torsional creeping cracks the genesis is similar; a crack tends to follow a more or less helical path, being smooth and even in the early stages, but becoming increasingly less smooth as it pursues its way. This is shown in Figure 14.5. The crack began at the tapped hole which held a key in a keyway at a chainwheel drive. The tapped hole was eliminated in later constructions.

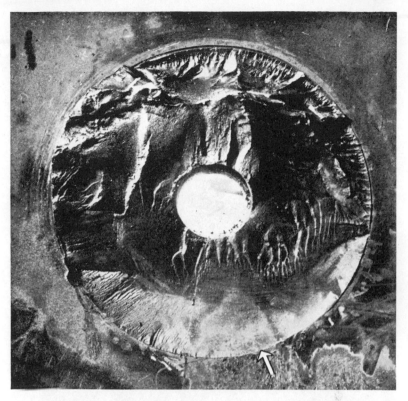

Figure 14.3 Creeping crack by bending

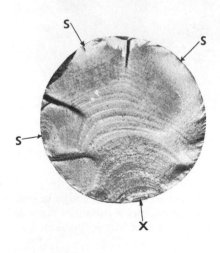

Figure 14.4 Exhaust valve spindle

Figure 14.5 Torsional creeping crack

Figure 14.6 shows the fatigue failure of a hollow gudgeon-pin. The bright ends were unbroken. In Figure 14.7 a fractured tie-bolt is illustrated. The crack has started at a defect below the skin, and has crept across the section until rupture has occurred almost diametrically opposite the point of origin.

Figure 14.8 is an enlarged section of a screw-thread subjected to heavy alternating loads. When such a thread fails, a creeping crack

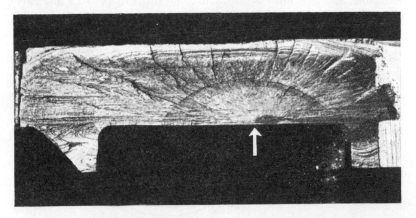

Figure 14.6 Creeping crack in hollow gudgeon pin

begins at X and remains smooth until it reaches Y, when it becomes rougher and finally ruptures in the neighbourhood of Z.

If two or more bolts or bars equally sustain a member which is dynamically loaded and there is failure, a creeping crack will usually

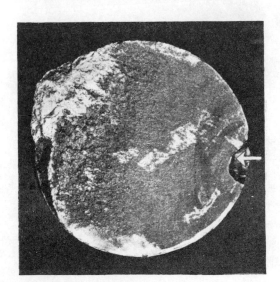

Figure 14.7 Fractured tie-bolt

be found in one bolt only. Subsequent to its failure the other bolt or bolts are ruptured by violence.

It is not uncommon for creeping cracks to be generated in more than one plane simultaneously. This implies that conditions are unstable, and that local dynamic loading shifts its peak of intensity for a time from one locality to an adjacent one.

Figure 14.8 Creeping crack on screw-thread

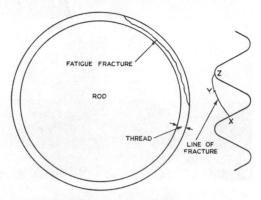

Sometimes a member in simple tension, say the long tie-bolt of a four-stroke engine, fails and the broken section shows rupture by violent overloading without any trace of creeping cracks. The

Figure 14.9 Fractured slave-rod pin

explanation is probably that the engineer has repeatedly flogged-up the bolt when it was cold and has generally treated it as if it were, say, a bottom-end bolt instead of a static member. The whole section may then resemble the upper part of Figure 14.3.

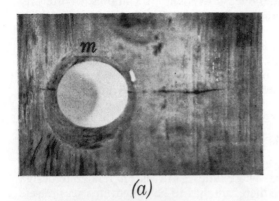

(a)

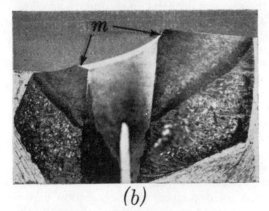

(b)

Figure 14.10 Macrograph of oil holes

Figure 14.9 shows the end portion of a fractured alloy steel slave-rod pin of a V engine. There are two well-defined fatigue cracks running longitudinally. They originate at the outer ends of opposite oil holes, at the countersinking. The fact that the cracks were directly opposite to each other would suggest that the pin had not been floating, as intended, but had tended to remain in one position.

An undesirable feature of the oil holes was the sharp corners at the countersinking, for it was here that the fractures originated. The oil holes penetrated the bore where there was an abrupt change of section, thus intensifying the stress concentration effect. The mouths of the holes in the bore were examined by the penetrant method, and all were found to be cracked on both sides, diametrically opposite, and running in a lengthwise direction.

A macrograph of the oil hole marked m in Figure 14.9 is shown in Figure 14.10(a). Short cracks were found on each side of the hole, in the bore. These cracks were exposed by suitable cutting and exhibited the characteristics of fatigue failure, as shown in Figure 14.10(b).

The results of examination showed that the pins were over-strained at the oil holes. It need scarcely be mentioned that sharp corners at oil holes should always be eliminated; moreover, the holes should be so located that they will not penetrate the bore at a change of section.

Flaws and Stress-raisers

The reasons for the start and the growth of creeping cracks can often be difficult to determine. These failures are seldom related to design stresses, and the cause, therefore, has to be sought in stress-raisers such as sharp corners, the absence of fillets, in secondary accelerations which are liable to be overlooked and so on.

Figure 14.11 is an example of a creeping crack in a component which, according to calculation, strain-gauge analysis and long experience, should have been completely immune from failure. The photograph shows a cast-steel eccentric strap; this, in service, is under a maximum bending stress of not more than 1 tonf/in² (1·57 kgf/mm²). At the tension edge of the casting there is a deep flaw, the characteristics of which suggest a 'hot tear'. At this flaw a creeping crack started, spreading almost completely across the section before final rupture occurred. The grain size of the steel is reasonable for a casting having the mass of an eccentric strap. The microstructure is generally consistent with correct heat treatment. Sulphur printing indicated freedom from the segregation of impurities. Test specimens cut from the casting, closely adjacent to the fracture, showed: yield point 14·6 ton f/in² (23 kgf/mm²); ultimate stress 29·2 ton f/in² (46 kgf/mm²); 31 per cent elongation on 3 in. (75 mm) and 50 per cent reduction in area. A 1·0 in. × 0·75 in. (25 mm × 19 mm) piece bent to 180° on 0·25 in. (6.4 mm) radius remained without fracture, izod impact values were 23, 22, 20 ft lb (3·2, 3·0, 2·8 kg mm). On the evidence failure was attributable to stress concentration at an original defect.

In a number of cast-steel eccentric straps which failed by fatigue, and which presented a perplexing problem, it was finally proved that the cracks started inside the castings, at a point where there was heavy residual internal stress.

Where fractured surfaces display the characteristics of fatigue failure and the creeping crack has extended across, say, 95 per cent of the cross-sectional area before final rupture has occurred, crack propagation has probably progressed relatively slowly after the initial crack took place; also, the operative stress has been well below the endurance limit of the material. Fatigue fractures usually appear brittle because they are unaccompanied by any large-scale plastic flow; this is despite the fact that the material may possess a high measure of ductility.

As a further example of a cast-steel eccentric strap failure: on a high-class passenger-cargo vessel a strap failed after 20 000 hours of service. A crankcase inspection had been made shortly before the failure. There was no indication of distress in the strap until a dull thudding noise was heard. The engine was immediately stopped, the fracture located, and a spare strap fitted by the ship's staff.

At the time of this occurrence, there were in service 660 cast-steel eccentric straps of which eight top-half straps had fractured, all at the same place, as in Figure 14.11. One thousand forged steel straps

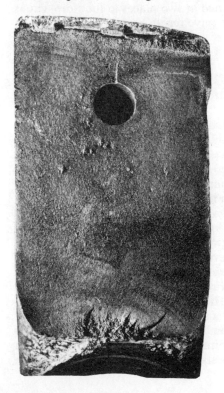

Figure 14.11 Creeping crack in eccentric strap

were at that time also in service of which two had failed, in each instance because of bolt slackness. Strain gauge measurements normally showed a working stress of 0·90 ton f/in² (1·42 kgf/mm²), maximum at the place of fracture. With slack bolts the resisting couple at the strap was vitiated, as a result of which the local stress could rise to 3·25 ton f/in² (5·12 kgf/mm²). This stress was, in itself, very moderate, but, with a surface defect or a sharp edge, a fatigue crack could begin.

The point of origin of the creeping crack in this cast-steel strap was a small casting defect on and immediately below the fillet adjacent to the nut facing for the strap bolt. The defect consisted of a porous area in which small pellets of steel were embedded. This type of defect may arise from slight seepage of metal in casting from an imperfectly fitting plug in the pouring basin before the plug is actually lifted and the small pellets so formed rise to the top of the metal in the casting and do not become completely fused to the remainder. Segregation was found over several areas, notably in way of the crack origin.

Mechanical test results obtained at two places in the strap, cut as near to the fracture as possible, gave results as follows:

	First point	Second point
Yield point, ton f/in²	18·8	19·2
Yield point, kgf/mm²	29·6	30·3
Ultimate stress, ton f/in²	30·6	31·6
Ultimate stress, kgf/mm²	48·2	49·8
Percentage elongation	13	27
Percentage area reduction	21	38
Izod impact, ft lbf	38, 34, 34	40, 35, 35
Izod impact, kgfm	5·3, 4·7, 4·7	5·5, 4·8, 4·8

Bend tests: bent to 180° on 16 mm without fracture.

The ductility at the first point is distinctly poor and not consistent with the bend tests.

In Figure 14.12 a section through the upper portion of an exhaust piston yoke of a double-acting two-stroke engine is shown. The yoke is a steel casting and there is evidence of some internal shrinkage during cooling. Crack origins are indicated at three points, at places where there are casting flaws. From these points the cracks spread outwards through the section. The yoke, in service, was under intermittent bending stress, which placed the upper one-third of the yoke, i.e. the part illustrated, in tension. The creep waves are smooth, thus implying a slow fatigue rate. Final rupture occurred at the rough triangular area between the points of crack origin.

Pulsating Stresses

Figure 14.13 shows the genesis of creeping cracks in a cast-iron bedplate. Beginning at point *A* (full line), the crack crept along to *B*, *C* and *D*; then started at *F* and proceeded to *G* and *E*. On the other side of the girder a crack simultaneously appeared at point 1 (dotted line) and crept to 2, 3 and 4. Corresponding cracks also appeared at *X*, and proceeded through *Y* to *Z*. The family of cracks, as shown, took less than one year to grow.

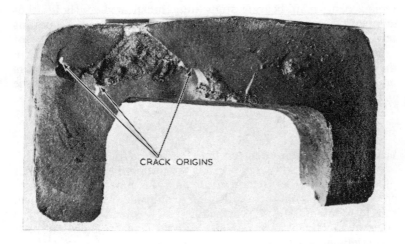

Figure 14.12 Exhaust piston yoke

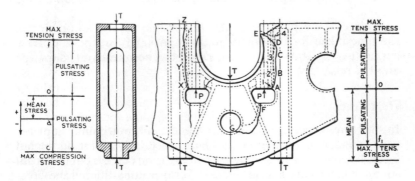

Figure 14.13 Creeping crack in cast-iron bedplate

The construction at A was undoubtedly a 'stress raiser'. Each time the crank approached top dead-centre, on the exhaust-stroke, a heavy tensile pull was transmitted through the main bearing bolts to the casting. On the downward stroke, and on the compression stroke, there was a down thrust T, which tended to buckle the vertical walls, each wall being a strut. These two interactions led to the initiation and growth of the cracks. But, serious though these cracks may seem, the engine was not in jeopardy; the strength region between crankshaft and tie-bolts was but little impaired. In the replacement, main-bearing studs were substituted for bolts, thus eliminating side holes; and a tubular construction of casting obviated buckling.

In calculating the stresses in such a casting, use may be made of the method shown diagrammatically in Figure 14.13. Starting from point a, ac = maximum compressive stress, af = maximum tensile stress. The pulsating stress $= oc = of = \left(\dfrac{ac + af}{2}\right)$, and the mean stress $= ao = \left(\dfrac{af - ac}{2}\right)$. The total stress (mean + pulsating) should be within the appropriate stress limit for such a structure.

It is surprising how widespread is the notion that the whole body of a forging, or other part, is infected by the presence of a creeping crack. Thus, the author recalls a large shipside plate, located near the stern bossing of a ship, which had a creeping crack in it about 400 mm or 500 mm long, near one end of the plate. The whole plate was condemned as being unsound, because of the presence of this crack. Steel specialists of wide experience, also the author, would have been fully satisfied by cutting off the plate a short distance from the crack.

With most creeping cracks it is impossible to form an opinion of the time taken for the cracks to grow. All that can be said, from surface examination, is that one crack has been relatively slow and another relatively rapid.

Heat Cracks

In structures which are heated on one side and cooled on the other— as in cylinder covers and liners—heat cracks may occur on the hot faces. It is often said that they are compression cracks; but this is not so. Such cracks are tension cracks. Temperature differences across the section set up bending, by the hot side trying to expand relatively to the cold side, thus inducing compressive stresses on the hot face. If severe enough, a certain amount of plastic flow on the hot side follows, the metal on the hot face accommodates itself to the slightly different contour, and stress equilibrium is restored. On cooling, relatively greater contraction occurs on the hot face, high tension stresses are induced locally and cracks appear. There must be restraint, somewhere, to cause this phenomenon. It is not found, for example, in a simple cylindrical, unrestrained liner, unless it is very thick. But it can happen if there is a cooled annular belt around the liner, connected by ribs. Fissures in the hot faces of pistons, and internal cracks traceable to temporary failure of the cooling medium, provide other examples. Contiguity of masses of metal and thin walls can cause a kindred phenomenon.

Welding Failures

During the maiden voyage of an important refrigerated cargo-liner which was propelled by supercharged single-acting two-stroke engines there was heavy cracking of the cylinder liners at the cast-steel combustion chamber belt between the upper and lower liners. As events proved, the failures were not by any means confined to this one ship. The four pockets provided respectively for fuel valves, starting and relief valves were separate steel forgings welded to the combustion chamber. The cracks originated at the fuel-valve pockets and quickly extended vertically, to such an extent that the combustion belts had to be condemned at sea and all the spares fitted. The replacements were no better and the ship arrived home with one-third of the cylinders out-of-action.

Figure 14.14 shows a valve pocket and part of the combustion chamber. The crack, which penetrated the chamber casting completely, extended vertically from C to C.

Figure 14.15 shows a fuel-valve pocket in section. The metal was roughly polished and etched in way of the welding. For such a high-pressure–temperature component, fusion welding of the highest order of excellence was essential. Actually the workmanship fell far short of requirements. The external welding showed a lack of fillets. The two welds at C show that there was no fusion at the 'nose' between the welds. Also the nose of ligament was twice as long as that specified, being 6 mm instead of 3 mm. The fatigue crack originated at this unfused zone between the welds. In Figure 14.14 the fatigue crack which resulted in failure started at the unfused zone C on the side of the pocket.

Micro-examination of the specimen cut out at P, Figure 14.15, revealed cracking which ran just inside what should have been the fused zone. Figure 14.16 shows an unetched low-magnification enlargement. The slag inclusion at the extremity of the nose, to the left of the photograph, will be noted. In Figure 14.17, at the upper

Figure 14.14 Combustion chamber failure

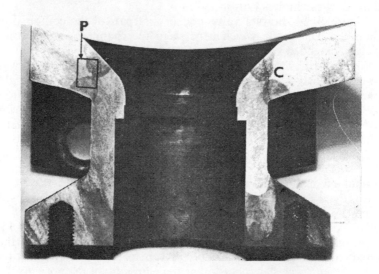

Figure 14.15 Fuel valve pocket

section, the crack runs just inside the fusion zone, and this was considered to be the result of the stress-raising effect of the cavity present, originally due to the lack of fusion. The welding itself was clean and normal in structure, as shown in the lower section of Figure 14.17.

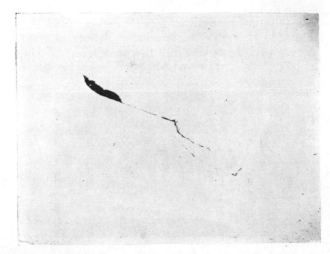

Figure 14.16
Crack at
unfused zone

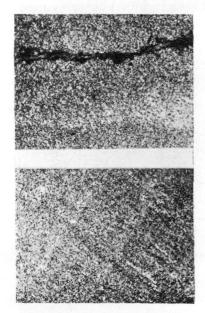

Figure 14.17 Sections etched
in two per cent nital

The sections shown in Figure 14.17 were photographed at high magnification, after etching in 2 per cent nital.

As a result of the long list of failures, the practice was changed and the valve pockets were cast integrally with the combustion chambers.

Casting Strains

Figure 14.18 shows the sawn-through section of an exhaust piston intended for a single-acting two-stroke engine 530 mm bore. This molybdenum steel casting was condemned because of heavy shrink-

Figure 14.18
Casting shrinkage:
exhaust piston

age porosity. It was so porous that it could not withstand more than a few kilogrammes of water pressure before profuse leakage occurred.

The cracked cast-iron piston of Figure 14.19 is characteristic of another kind of failure, brought about, essentially, by unrelieved internal casting strains. It is a customary requirement for piston castings to remain in the sand for at least seventy-two hours. Occasionally, however, such castings are dug out as soon as they are

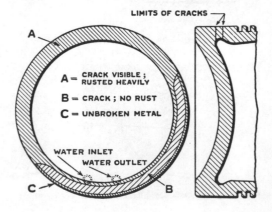

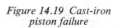

*Figure 14.19 Cast-iron
piston failure*

sufficiently solid to keep their shape. Metallurgical examination may reveal no abnormality, but a short time in service brings about failure.

The vagaries shown by failures of complicated castings under heavy pressures, high temperatures and severe internal strain are very puzzling; and it can be really difficult to decide whether to strengthen a casting against pressure or to make it more flexible for reducing temperature stresses. Sometimes, in service, there may be a self-annealing process at work, and if a casting does not fail within, say, a few months it may not fail at all. Cracks, as already mentioned, are almost invariably caused by tension, however difficult the causation may be to identify; sometimes—but seldom—shear forces are responsible.

Figure 14.20 shows some characteristic failures of double-acting-engine pistons. At *A* a piece of metal has completely broken away

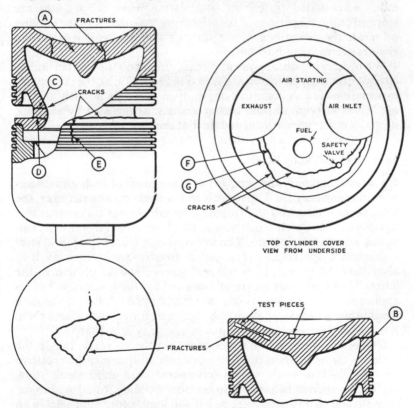

Figure 14.20 Cylinder cover and pistons

in the middle of the crown; the typical creeping crack B has begun on the inside of the piston, under the crown, and made its way across the metal section until, at the final rupture the crown has been completely severed. At C there is a circumferential crack a few inches long and at D a similar creeping crack has encircled the piston waist, breaking the piston in halves. The vertical crack E is unusual.

Fractures of the type A are completely obviated by the fitting of screwed plugs. Creeping cracks B start as 'grooving'. To ensure uniformity of thickness and to identify the grooving before the crown is seriously weakened, the pistons are now machined inside. Porous metal under the crown is undoubtedly a factor in the initiation of creeping cracks B. To correct tendency to porosity, chills are introduced into the core. Test-pieces, taken from the places indicated, have proved the metal to be sound at the crown.

Tendency to fracture circumferentially below the crown is probably accentuated by crown overheating when the engines are stopped or during periods of manoeuvring. At such times the cooling oil inside the piston is not in a state of agitation as it is when the engines are running normally.

When cracking occurs simultaneously in piston tops and cylinder-cover bottoms, as indicated at F and G in Figure 14.20, the customary explanations fail. A common origin, then, can only lie with the fuel oil. While showing normal characteristics, as revealed by analysis, it produces an intense localised heat at the time of firing.

Mild Steel and Alloy Steels

It may be wondered why greater use is not made of high-alloy steels in marine engineering. The reply is: alloy steels may be stronger, the yield point higher and the fatigue strength greater on comparable test-pieces; but notch sensitivity is also higher, and this, alone, can nullify all other desiderata. The self-restoring tendency of mild steel —due to the appreciable yield-point stretch—has no equivalent in alloy steel. Moreover, high internal stresses can be present in the latter. Thorough heat treatment can reduce these stresses, but its application cannot always be depended upon. Alloy steels save weight only where strength is the criterion; for equal stiffness there is no saving, because the modulus of elasticity is unaltered.

One of the things which experience over the years has taught the author is the uselessness of relying upon small specimens for relative tests. High-class steels which, compared with mild steel, show markedly superior behaviour in tension, bending, twisting, fatigue strength and so on as test-pieces, will fail long before mild steel in an actual engine. The fatigue strength of mild steel, as exemplified by failures in the component parts of heavy engines, is much lower than is commonly supposed. It can, sometimes, be only 20 or 30 per cent of ordinarily accepted values.

A structure which is subjected to impact effects must be capable of absorbing energy, hence to produce an economical structure it is essential for the material to have a reserve of ductility. The use of a brittle material, although very strong, is to be avoided. When material with notches or other stress-raising changes of section has to withstand impulsive or fluctuating loads the rate of stress variation becomes a matter of importance. Sudden blows may cause a local rise in the stress rate which is greater than the critical rate and thereby start a brittle type of crack. How far such a crack will spread must depend upon the general stress conditions over the originating area. If the immediate neighbourhood is already highly stressed a crack once started may travel a long way.

Ten million stress-reversals, without failure, is usually taken as implying indefinite life. But there have been many instances where engine moving parts have withstood one hundred million stress-reversals and have then broken. The explanation is probably that there have been some subtle changes in the tightness or loading of the system.

One hundred million, rather than ten million, reversals are necesary before a secure conclusion can be reached. The connecting rods illustrated in Figure 14.21 must have had hundreds of millions of reversals before the fractures appeared.

The author's philosophy regarding failures is simple. One failure: anything may explain it. Two failures: the omens are not so good. Three failures: doubt becomes almost a certainty, and every such part may be reasonably expected to fail.

Pseudo-compressive Cracks

Creeping cracks normally appear in tension members and on the tensile faces of structures in bending. Once in a long while, shear cracks are to be seen. Occasionally, cracks have been reported as occurring on compression faces, but investigation has disposed of this notion.

On one occasion the managing director of a Continental foundry which specialises in propellers came to see the author for guidance. On the forward faces of his stainless-steel propellers, after eighteen months in service, fatigue cracks were found at the root of the blades. Interrogation elicited the fact that his bronze propellers were free from cracks. What perplexed the propeller man was the incidence of the cracks on the compressive face. The author corrected him on this point and said that, despite appearances, the cracks were tensile cracks. Although the ordinary stresses showed this to be a compressive face, obviously there must be other stresses to make the force which caused the fatigue cracks into a tensile force.

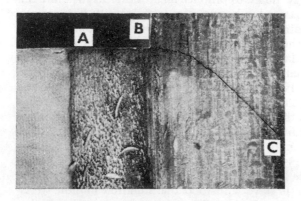

Figure 14.21
Connecting rod
bolt-face crack

The essence of the problem was to explain the difference in behaviour between bronze and steel propellers. On the evidence tendered, the author suspected that the steel propellers were vibrating. The bronze propellers, which did not crack, lacked the resonating characteristics of the steel propellers.

Investigation proved the correctness of the surmise, and changes were made to the thickness, etc. There was no recurrence of the failures.

Effects of Service on Moving Parts

The effects upon fully built and semi-built crankshafts of years of working are liable to misinterpretation. For example, a twin-screw vessel whose diesel engines had just been overhauled after nine years of arduous service was slowly proceeding to sea, under power, when one of the propellers fouled some quayside piling. After a brief trial run the ship was berthed and the crankshaft opened up. At most of the cranks, in the after half, feelers could be inserted for the whole of the circumference, at the main-bearing sides of the webs. The depth of separation of surfaces was almost constant, being about 6 per cent of the web width. The crankshaft, which was of semi-built construction, was condemned by the superintendent engineer as exhibiting the effects of sudden shock. The propeller was undamaged. The author has no doubt whatever that, if as careful an examination had been made before the mishap as after it, the feelers would have

CREEPING CRACKS 635

entered the webs for precisely the same distance. Any crankshaft of the same age and usage would have shown exactly the same characteristics, and there is little doubt that the crankshaft would have lasted the life of the ship.

In a four-stroke single-acting engine, having eight cylinders 740 mm bore, a thorough examination after twenty-two years of service revealed that all the connecting rods in the engine were cracked in way of the landing face for the bolt-heads. Figure 14.21 is a photograph of the sectioned rod. It will be observed that there is a complete absence of fillet at the knifed-out recess where the crack has started. Figure 14.22 shows the separated surfaces in way of the crack. That is, face A is the horizontal machined bolt-head face; the face B is the vertical wall of the knifed-out recess; the two faces C of Figure 14.22 are the separated surfaces of the crack C in Figure 14.21.

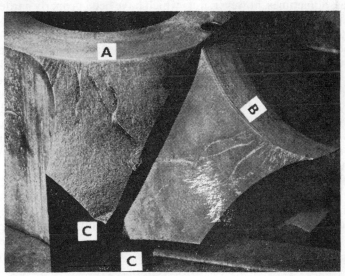

Figure 14.22 Creeping crack at bolt faces

Corrosion Fatigue

A problem which is often bound up with stress fatigue is corrosion fatigue. When minute relative movement occurs between two steel blocks under high surface pressure there is 'fretting', caused by the mechanical tearing of particles from the steel surfaces. These particles rapidly oxidise, under the local heat which is generated, forming a brownish corrosion product; and small corrosion pits are formed on the surfaces. This fretting corrosion action results in reduction of fatigue resistance. Thus, in a screwed member, small corrosion pits can form on the threads, and the notch-effect of the pitting is to increase the tendency to fatigue. Another example is a bolted connection which is insufficiently tightened to ensure a frictional load great enough to counteract the tendency for the nut face alternately to dilate and contract under pulsating load. Then the minute relative movements occur.

Experience shows that fretting may reduce the fatigue limit of steel in reversed bending by as much as 50 per cent, and more. Fretting action can sometimes be minimised by treating with molybdenum disulphide.

Undoubtedly one of the predisposing causes of failure with bolted connections is the under-tightening of nuts and the fretting at nut faces. Sometimes, however, nuts which have been properly hardened up are found to be slack after a term of service, although the locking plates remain unaltered. Stress-raisers may be the result of corrosion in service or may have their origin in the design, or may be caused by the workmanship. The highly localised surface stresses, which the stress-raisers are responsible for setting up, have no necessary relationship with functional stresses; consequently, they require only very small amplitudes of movement to establish the strain which starts the trans-crystalline cracking. The creeping cracks continue across the section, to the point of rupture, without any structural change being made in the metal immediately adjacent to the fracture.

It is sometimes stated that creeping cracks always begin at the surface. This is not so. In the casting described in Figure 14.12 the the fatigue failure originated inside the casting. In the eccentric straps mentioned in connection with Figure 14.11 the cracks began inside the castings at a point of heavy residual internal stress.

Stress-corrosion Cracking

No constituent part of the diesel engine has been more difficult to bring to near-perfection than has the cylinder liner for pressure-charged two-stroke engines. It is not the concern of this paragraph to review the current forms of cylinder-liner joints, but to present a story showing that, from evidence seemingly clear and complete, an entirely erroneous conclusion was reached and a wrong decision made in connection with a far-reaching cylinder-liner problem. It is an illustration of the principle that any theory, to be sound, must embrace every observed fact. Otherwise, as in this example, effect can be mistaken for cause and cause for effect.

Figure 14.23 shows the design of liner joint for a new type of turbocharged two-stroke engine, as stipulated by a leading ship-owning company having vast experience with marine diesel engines. The noteworthy points were:

(a) the joint was located in the cooling water space;
(b) the bolting consisted of a proprietary brand of chrome–molybdenum alloy steel;
(c) the outer annulus, as well as the inner annulus, had to be arranged to take the load.

To the author, for the engine builders, the position was:

(a) they, i.e. the builders, had had over fifteen years of successful experience with ordinary two-stroke liner joints being immersed in the jacket water spaces, and thus no objection could be made to this arrangement;
(b) their normal practice was to use stainless-steel studs, but, as the steel stipulated by the shipowner was a higher-grade alloy and more expensive, it was assumed that for such an important joint it would be superior;
(c) as it is general practice for the total load to be taken by a carefully ground joint on the inner annulus only, the outer annulus having a clearance of one-thousandth of an inch, the clients' requirement that the outer annulus should share the load was a strange one, but, against this, they were engineers of great experiential knowledge, and therefore it was unavoidable that their request should prevail.

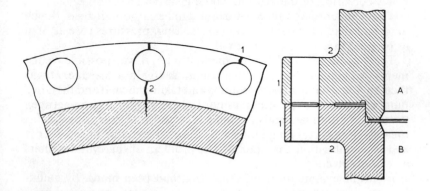

Figure 14.23 Stress corrosion cracking

The design was quickly accepted by other shipowners also, and everything augered well. At a certain point in time, however, when there were many hundreds of cylinders in service, serious troubles developed and soon became widespread. In rapid succession, scores and scores of liners began seriously to leak at the combustion joints. The vital problem was to replace the combustion chambers without delay, regrind the joints and keep the ships moving.

On investigation, many flange bolts were found to be broken, showing fissures and a multiplicity of transverse cracks that tended to wander through the metal, giving a coarse appearance to the fractured surface. Failure had undoubtedly been caused by stress-corrosion cracking, as distinct from corrosion fatigue.

Stress-corrosion cracking is a progressive type of fracture, beginning with a small crack and proceeding across the section perpendicularly to the tensile stress. The resulting fracture is brittle. For stress-corrosion cracking to occur, it is not necessary for the bolts to have been over-strained in tightening-up; on the contrary, many bolts had lost more than one-half of their load-carrying capacity. Strained metal will corrode much more rapidly than unstrained metal in a corrosive environment. Some bolts were not fractured, but showed transverse cracking.

The evidence seemed clear that combustion gas leakage at the joint faces had followed the failure of the bolts.

An early occurrence was the splitting of a number of the ligaments. These are marked 1 in Figure 14.23. This, by itself, was of no significance, until some of the cracks began to penetrate inwards from the bolt-holes towards the liner proper, as indicated at 2. These proved to be stress-corrosion cracks; but, curiously, they had originated on the *inside* of the bolt-holes and not at the ligaments. There was very heavy corrosion of the external cooling surfaces.

The cylinder relief valves were found to be carbon-clogged to such an extent that, at starting and manoeuvring, pressures rose as high as two and three times the normal.

There came a day when, for the first time, it was possible to dismantle a cylinder that was just beginning to show leakage. It was then obvious that the outer annulus had taken the load and that, in a number of places at the inner annulus, there was separation between the faces. This immediately explained the bolt-hole corrosion cracks, the type of bolt cracking and the local rough exterior of the liner A and the combustion chamber B. The problem of the cylinder liners had been solved.

In all the examinations of liners that had been made, by metallurgists, designers, sea-going engineers and others, the wasted bolts were assumed to have been a primary occurrence, leading to leakage at the joints. Now, at last, it was fully clear that the leaking joint was the first cause, and the wasted and broken bolts the sequel.

Thereafter the liner joint was radically redesigned.

Stress Concentration at Fillets

Figures 14.24 and 14.25 illustrate the effect of fillet radius upon the fatigue strength of a bolted flange connection for the centre-section of a 750 mm bore cylinder liner. Provided that the bolts are not too closely pitched, a flanged connection having a large fillet radius and spot-faced recesses for the bolt-heads is superior in fatigue strength to a similar flanged connection having a smaller fillet radius and no spot facings.

In the photo-elastic experiments of Figures 14.24 and 14.25, in which stress patterns are compared, the flanges were bolted together

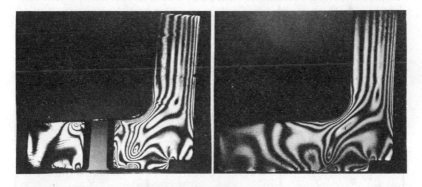

Figure 14.24 Cylinder liner flanges

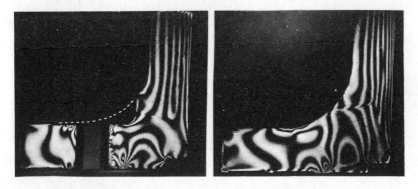

Figure 14.25 Cylinder liner flanges

and the working temperature stresses simulated by applying a uniform bending moment over the bolted section. The model was then stress-frozen and sections cut between and also through the bolt-holes.

In Figure 14.24 the fillet radius is 18 mm and in Figure 14.25 the fillet radius is 45 mm, with recessed spot-facings in way of the bolts. The differences in the stress patterns will be duly noted.

Simple Destructive Tests

When failure in a complex structure has occurred under running conditions and an investigation into causes is pending, realistic simulation by means of scale models and fashioned test-pieces is only possible infrequently. As a last resort, the best that can be attempted may well be the conducting of simple, steady-load tests on pieces having but faint resemblance to the actual component that has failed. Even so, this procedure may be useful, if interpretation and deductions are sensibly made.

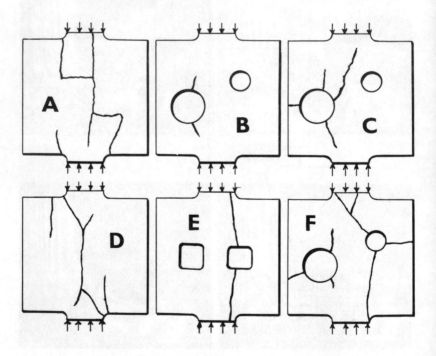

Figure 14.26 Destructive compression tests

Thus, in a series of propelling engines, failure occurred in the main cast-iron structure. Accordingly the author was faced with a problem of deep perplexity. To make a complete model of say, one-tenth full size, would have been very costly; moreover it would have been a futile proceeding, because destructive static tests would not even remotely simulate the dynamic forces at work in the engines. Eventually it was decided to make a series of compression tests on a sequence of small slabs. Figures 14.26 and 14.27 indicate a few random results. Surprisingly, some very valid and apposite deductions were possible, leading to a correct assessment of causes. The forms of failure in the slabs were not those that were expected beforehand.

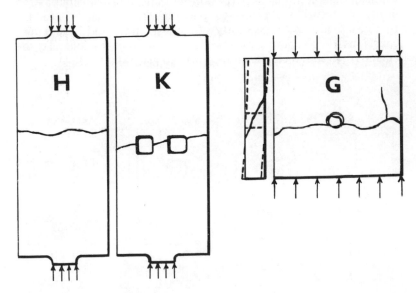

Figure 14.27 Buckling and crushing tests

The slabs shown in Figure 14.26 at *A*, *B* and *C*, were 65 mm long, 60 mm high and 11 mm thick. All surfaces were machined to the dimensions stated. The material was hard homogeneous cast-iron. The slabs were exposed to gradually increasing loads, applied at the areas shown by the arrows. The plain slab *A* broke when the applied load reached 14·73 metric tons—now termed tonne. Slab *B* showed fractures at the large hole when the load reached 9·65 tonne. In specimen *C* cracks appeared at 10·7 tonne and it broke completely at 11·5 tonne.

Test-pieces D, E, and F were 9·5 mm thick, and of fairly soft cast iron. Slab D broke at 13·5 tonne, E at 8·2 tonne and F at 8·3 tonne. The specimens H and K in Figure 14.27 were 150 mm high, 65 mm wide, and 5·7 mm thick. Slab H buckled and cracked at 5·8 tonne; K cracked through the holes at 4·3 tonne. Slab G, which was 65 mm long, 60 mm high and 11 mm thick, was loaded over its full length. The slab cracked at 39 tonne and fractured at 43 tonne.

Importance of a Reasonable Finish

Although it would be unreasonable to expect that time and money should be expended by a builder in making an engine—either as a whole or in its component parts—other than an instrument of strict utility, nevertheless a pleasing appearance can often be attained by the simplest and least costly of means. This could have a subconscious effect upon a prospective non-technical client. To the engine room staff it can be an incentive to general tidiness.

Chapter 15

Crankcase Explosions

It is surprising how prevalent is the notion that a crankcase explosion occurs without prior warning, with instantaneous suddenness and with irresistible force; that it is a hazard to be accepted as part of the engineer's life; in other words, that it is futile to attempt to do anything about the matter. This notion is as erroneous as it is common.

Forced-lubricated, totally enclosed, reciprocating machines, aggregating many millions of horse-power and comprising diesel engines, steam engines, air compressors and so on, function with complete success year after year without any precautions being taken to safeguard the machines against crankcase explosions. Once in a while, however—adventitious in time and place—there occurs a crankcase explosion with dire results, destructive to machine and fatal to man. As in all actuarial problems, the average and the general afford neither refuge nor solace to the individual. In the absence of positive safeguards, an element of uncertainty in the running of enclosed forced-lubricated machines must always be present. But as the necessary precautions for ensuring complete safety are simple to apply, there is no need for the continuance of uncertainty.

A crankcase explosion can originate at any moving element in an enclosed forced-lubricated engine. More explicitly, crankcase explosions are known to have originated, respectively, at pistons, gudgeon-pins, cylinder liners and liner details, fuel valves, piston rods, top-end bearings and crossheads, bottom-end bearings, main bearings, camshaft bearings, jockey-wheel bushes, chain rollers, roller bearings, gear teeth, emergency governors, lubrication systems, engine-driven pumps and so on.

Contrary to popular belief, trunk engines are not more predisposed to crankcase explosions than are crosshead engines. Many

643

of the explosions which have occurred in trunk engines could equally have taken place in crosshead engines. The converse is also true. There are forms of crosshead engine with long piston skirts which dip into the crankcase. Such engines behave as trunk engines. In a true crosshead engine the cylinders are completely separated from the crankcase by a stout horizontal diaphragm which extends the full length of the engine and which forms the crankcase top. Piston-rod scraper boxes are arranged in this diaphragm.

CAUSE AND CHARACTERISTICS OF EXPLOSIONS

The Hot Spot

All recorded occurrences have one factor in common, namely a hot spot. Without a hot spot there can be no explosion. An occasional element in the case histories of crankcase explosions is the incidence of starting and stopping. Sometimes an explosion has occurred as an engine was stopping or had just stopped, sometimes when it was starting or had just started; sometimes an explosion has followed the restarting of a heated engine on compressed air. In no example known to the author has there been any suggestion of spontaneous explosion in the absence of a hot spot.

An alternative to a hot spot can be the passage of flame along the piston of a trunk engine into the crankcase.

The sequence of events leading to an explosion seems to be explicable on the basis that a mixture of lubricating oil particles and air can become converted, by a hot spot, into a combination which can explode. The hot spot is thus both the cause of the crankcase contents becoming explodable and the source of the igniting agent. Precisely what constitutes an explosive medium is a problem outside the province of the mechanical engineer.

It is impossible to guarantee that any engine will operate for the whole of its life without, somewhere, at some time, a hot spot appearing. Therefore it is essential that such precautions should be taken that if a hot spot does occur and if it does remain undetected an explosion will not result.

Wherever the overheating may begin, it seems ultimately to be well down in the crankcase that the main explosion has its seat. In some of the reports of explosions this point is clearly brought out, e.g. in references to the throwing-up of splash guards in examples where the overheating began at the highest point of a tall crankcase.

Conditions Favourable to Explosion

If a hot spot makes its appearance, somewhere, oil particles in the neighbourhood can be expected to evaporate. This local volatilisation may cause the formation and concentration of quantities of condensed oil mist in cooler regions, distant from the hot spot, the quantities being dependent upon temperature variations throughout the crankcase. The oil mist particles may reasonably be expected to be smaller than mechanically atomised globules of oil. Rapid combustion can presumably be expected to take place more readily when the oil is vaporised than when it exists as oil mist, although the latter may be explosive. It seems to be a matter of total heat of vaporisation. With the continued generation of heat at the hot spot, volatilisation and augmented concentrations of condensed oil mist, away from the overheated region, can proceed apace. Increase in size of the cloud or clouds of mist can be expected to occur concurrently with the development of the hot spot. Together with the vaporisation of the oil, some decomposition into inflammable gases can be expected at the same time. Eventually, over a substantial part of the crankcase, the ratio of oil vapour to air falls inside the upper and lower limits of inflammability. Then, if all the circumstances are propitious, and if the hot spot, in itself or by its consequences—e.g. by a falling piece of hot metal—can provide the necessary heat energy for the ignition of vapour, an explosion may occur. This explosion may be mild or it may be severe, depending upon all the circumstances.

Granted that the oil–air ratio is within the inflammability range, the speed of burning may vary from a few inches per second—with negligible heat release and no sensible pressure rise—to many times that speed, accompanied by a great release of heat and an instantaneous pressure rise of several atmospheres, depending upon whether the oil–air ratio is just inside the edge of the inflammability range or is near the middle of the range.

As stated, an explosion of the oil–air mixture requires the presence of a hot body. The temperature of this hot body may be great enough locally to produce gaseous products such as hydrogen and acetylene, to be accompanied by intermediate substances such as aldehydes and carbon monoxide. The ignition-promoting compounds, e.g. peroxides and aldehydes, may ignite at a lower temperature than would oil mist, and may therefore provide a trigger action.

The propagation of an explosion flame throughout a long chamber, if the facilities for heat dissipation and pressure-relief are inadequate for damping it, might result—by reason of a pressure build-up which causes the explosion effect to be augmented in a ratio greater than that of the increase in volume—in an acceleration of the speed of combustion to 1000 ft/sec, or more, with the possibility of detonation and a vastly increased rate of pressure rise.

If a safety door opens before the peak of an explosion is reached an unburnt mixture of air and oil particles is first expelled, followed instantly by a burning mass. The length of the issuing flame, *inter alia*, will depend upon the linear distance between the point of origin of the explosion and the relief door. Until all the ejected inflammable material has been consumed—or until it has fallen in temperature to below ignition point—active flame will persist.

Development of Explosion Pressures

When an explosive mixture has been ignited the flame at first travels slowly—the term is relative. Except in lean mixtures, i.e. those near the lower and upper limits, the flame may proceed with vibratory motion, causing a general overall increase in flame velocity. Under these conditions, compression waves are initiated, and, in a closed vessel, these waves may accelerate the flame speed and the pressure development. If the containing vessel has adequate length, and if the mixture is of suitable composition within the inflammability range, the extreme state of detonation may finally be set up.

In the main, pressure development depends upon the temperature attained by the flame. If the explosive mixture is in a state of agitation, or turbulence, pressure development may be more rapid. With explosions developing slowly, energy may be dissipated by heat transference to cooler parts, and pressure development may be retarded accordingly. The maximum overall pressure generated in the explosion of a hydrocarbon–air mixture can normally be up to about eight times the initial pressure, depending upon mixture composition and rate of flame travel. An explosion implies a flame associated with a high pressure, which is developed by the flame as it ignites the gas. Without the high pressure, the flame is no more than a fire.

Shock Waves and Detonation

Detonation requires the formation of a sufficiently intense shock wave. In a shock wave, or blast, the pressure is great and the initial velocity is very high. A shock wave may be formed on the rapid disruption of a body; but, as it travels, the pressure in the wave is dissipated and its velocity is reduced until, ultimately, the pressure wave degenerates into a sound wave.

In true detonation the pressure in the wave is not dissipated but is maintained by the adiabatic combustion of the explosive mixture. The velocity of detonation through an explosive mixture is normally of the order of 2·5–3·5 km/sec, and the pressure in the wave about

30 bar. In general, it may be assumed that the pressure developed by the explosion of an explosive mixture in a confined space is evenly applied, unless detonation is set up.

Detonation produces a hammer-blow effect which can be expected to shatter any normally constructed containing vessel.

It is possible to transmit a shock wave through a standing plate, from the outside atmosphere to a crankcase interior; its magnitude depends upon the characteristics of the plate. This possibility might explain—when other theories fail—the transmission of an explosion from one engine to another engine near by.

Effects of Pressure Wave

A pressure wave has no tendency to turn around corners. If, in its path, it meets an elastic surface the pressure will tend to push forward that surface until the impulse dies away. During the reflex suction phase, which immediately succeeds the forward pressure phase, the surface will be brought back again as far as its original position, or even farther. If, say, the flat surface is brittle, e.g. a glass window, the initial pressure wave will push in the window and shatter it. Then, before the broken pieces can travel more than an extremely short distance, the succeeding suction wave will draw out the broken pieces. As the suction phase is of much longer duration than the pressure phase, the pieces may be drawn back not only to the original plane, but to a plane beyond the original, thus creating the erroneous impression that the glass window was blown outwards by an internal explosion.

A slight difference in resistance, in an upward direction, between one part of an engine room and another will determine precisely at which place an uprush of hot gases will occur.

Maximum Realisable Pressures

The author has had reason to assume that the maximum realisable live pressure in a crankcase may be of the order of 7 or 8 bar, unless there is detonation. With detonation the pressures are far higher. In experiments made in the U.S.A. with propane–air mixtures a maximum pressure of 7·0 bar was obtained, when the air–propane ratio was 11·76. The highest explosion pressures were produced when the spark was most distant from the relief valve, i.e. when the flame travel distance was longest. The maximum pressure which is realisable in an actual engine crankcase containing air and lubricating oil/vapour mist may be different from this figure; possibly it may be lower.

Actual Explosion Pressures

In many explosions the actual crankcase pressures have not been high, notwithstanding the disruption caused. Almost all of the bulged and disrupted doors, castings and so on that have come to the author's notice could be duplicated, on a static water-pressure basis, by pressures ranging from about 0·3 bar to 6 bar. Thus, it is common to find chequered floor-plates standing on end after an explosion. But it only needs a pressure of one-tenth bar, applied for 0·10 sec, to lift such an unbolted floor-plate to a height of 600 mm. Floor-plates are seldom rebolted to their bearers once they have been taken up.

Figure 15.1 shows the form of graph for an explosion without any attempt at time-pressure scales.

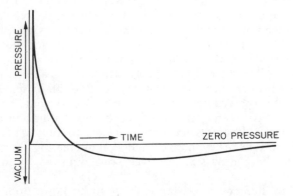

Figure 15.1 Diagrammatic representation of explosion curve

Explosion Wave Effects

Where a crankcase door has been blown off near one end of a long engine the explosion wave, if not thus dissipated, can pass along the inside of the engine, blowing off other doors in sequence, either at one or both sides of the engine. During the time that the explosion wave has travelled along the inside of the engine, or probably more rapidly, the heat wave issuing from the first-opened door has caused a sub-atmospheric pressure outside the same side of the engine; hence, other things being the same, there may be a greater tendency for doors to continue to blow off on that side.

The heat energy released by a heavy explosion can produce a tremendous up-draught—sometimes, on board ship, with flame rising through open sky-lights and extending half-way up the funnel

—and in its train a vacuum depression of much longer duration than the explosion wave, in the course of which one or more doors can be brought off an adjacent engine. The general temperature level may well be sufficiently high to start the explosion process all over again in the crankcase of the second engine, by exploding the droplets and by creating the requisite oil–air ratio inside the second crank-chamber.

The author has not seen a crankcase door knocked in by the instantaneous pressure wave, nor has he seen a casting broken from the outside. Possibly what happens is that the duration of the pressure wave is so extremely short, to be reckoned perhaps in milliseconds, that the impulse tending to cause deformation of the elastic plate is immediately reversed by the lower negative pressure of the suction wave—which persists for a much longer time and thus produces a substantially greater impulse—always supposing that the suction pressure is intense enough to cause bulging of the crankcase doors.

The degree of violence which accompanies an explosion may bear some relation, or some inverse relation, to the size of the engine room. As in mining explosions, the pressure wave seems to seek the nearest outlet. If the cross-section of the space is small and the outlet passages are restricted there can be outbursts of great violence; if the engine-room volume is great the effect may be reduced.

The negligible amount of damage done to engines by crankcase explosions is noteworthy. An engine room may be the embodiment of chaos, but as soon as the crumpled doors are cleared away and the disarranged gear is straightened out, there may be little or no remaining evidence of anything untoward having occurred. The engine surfaces may not only be free from all marks of fire but may also even be oily.

Crankcase Doors

In many engine designs the crankcase doors are lightly held at their edges by widely spaced and readily operated handles, clamps or clips, as in Figure 15.2. Removal is the work of a moment.

The equilibrium of such a plate is unstable. Under a live pressure of about 0·2 bar the dishing which results from plate instability can pull out the plate boundary from under the clamped points. Under a live, internal pressure of substantially less than one bar a door of the type of Figure 15.2 can be dislodged from its fastenings and blown clear of the engine. Such a door, therefore, is not robust enough to withstand explosion pressure, should a safety door fail to open. It may not even be stout enough to prevent its being 'sucked' off during the negative pressure period which follows the pressure wave.

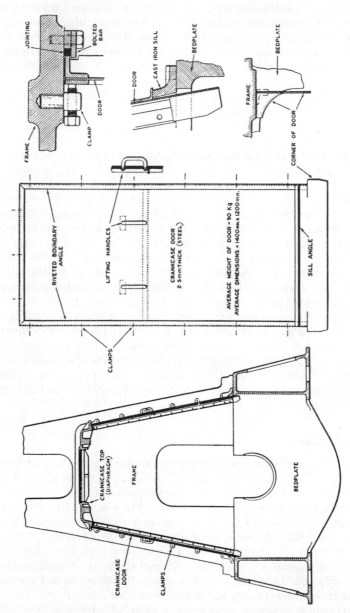

Figure 15.2 Crankcase doors

A bolted-on door can be made stiff enough to withstand a very substantial crankcase pressure, for only an insignificant increase in weight. Thus the door of Figure 15.3, which is 1960 mm high, 1012 mm wide, 3 mm thick, curved in one direction, can sustain a water pressure of 8 bar before there is any sign of distress, although the plate is distorted and the centre deflection is 100 mm. Leakage is then observed at the encastrément. A plate of the same dimensions, but dished vertically and horizontally to 100 mm, will withstand about 12 bar without distress, apart from permanent deflection.

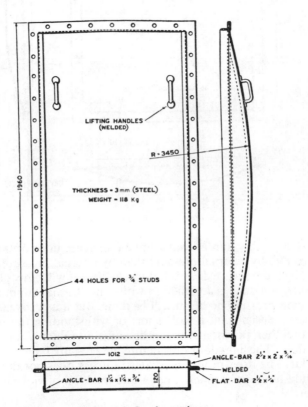

Figure 15.3 Crankcase door

The rectangular dished door of Figure 15.4, 1460 mm high, 1170 mm wide, 3 mm thick, can sustain a steady water pressure of 12 bar before any leakage at the flange joint begins.

The reader can transmute water pressures into dynamic pressures for himself.

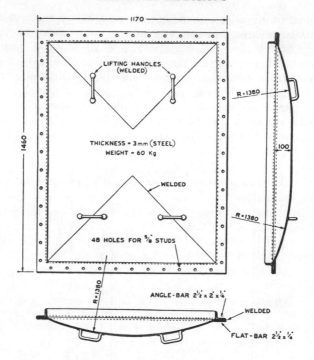

Figure 15.4 Crankcase door

It is negligibly harder to disrupt a crankcase door of the form of Figure 15.2 by external pressure than by internal pressure.

If a light crankcase door is lightly clamped it will blow off at a low pressure. If a door is designed to withstand the maximum realisable explosion pressure no harm will be done. But if a crankcase door is of such a design that it falls short of withstanding the maximum pressure, then potentially it can be much more dangerous than the light door. The light door fails before the pressure build-up has gone very far. The door of intermediate stoutness does not fail until the pressure build-up is much greater and the level of violence is much higher.

Crankcase Contents

It is commonly said that the normal crankcase contains a mixture of air and oil vapour too rich to be inflammable. This, however, is not so. The normal content of a crankcase is air. In this air there are oil globules innumerable; the number and size of the particles per cubic unit of space vary widely throughout the crankcase. The globules are presumably formed by the mechanical atomisation of the oil as it is sprayed from the edges of bearings and other places; as it falls upon internal ledges and surfaces; and as it is thrown about and churned by the quickly moving parts. Temperature differences inside the crankcase are not usually great enough to cause substantial concentrations of oil mist.

When an engine is started up normally or is working normally the lubricating oil return temperatures are moderate and the running temperatures of the moving parts are also moderate. Lubricating oil is not a volatile liquid—its flash point is above 200°C—and the temperature level inside the crankcase is insufficiently high to cause concentration of vapour.

The highest figure known to the author for oil concentration was less than one-third of that needed to reach the lower limit of inflammability for oil mists produced by mechanical atomisation or vapour condensation. In trunk-type auxiliary engines the greatest concentration was at 150 mm below the splash-guards; at 225 mm above the splash-guards the concentration was only one-quarter of this.

In a crankcase atmosphere it is not the temperature that is important *per se*; it is rather the dispersal and size of the oil particles. The reader will no doubt, be familiar with the part played by coal-dust particles in mining explosions, and with particles of flour in flour-mill fires. During the war, for example, many a large flour-mill was destroyed by a single small bomb, weighing only 25 kg. This small bomb was the 'hot spot'; the mill atmosphere was normal; the myriads of highly explosive flour particles, with which the atmosphere was charged and which lay about floors and beams, constituted the destructive agent.

A condensed-oil mist closely resembles a white fog, and is quite different in appearance from the black smoke associated with incomplete combustion. Before they can be ignited, condensed-oil mists must possess considerable optical density. This implies that, under normal running, the comparatively clear crankcase atmosphere is unlikely to be readily ignitable by a hot spot.

PRECAUTIONS AGAINST EXPLOSIONS

Practicable Safeguards

In general terms, there are three problems to consider, namely:

(1) to prevent the genesis and growth of explosion conditions;
(2) to provide relief and safety if explosive gases should form;
(3) to ensure that gases are not ejected from the engine as flame.

Two safeguards which can be applied to all new engines are:

   (i) an ample number of self-closing relief doors of appropriate size;

   (ii) a strong form of crankcase door.

These, together, will ensure complete safety for an engine, as distinct from the personnel.

The cost of relief doors is a small premium to pay for the effective safe-guarding of an engine, therefore an ample number should be provided, always taking care that, where the doors are not well above man-height, they are properly shielded. At frequent intervals the relief doors should be tried by hand to ensure that they will open easily.

If it is correct that explosion pressures cannot much exceed 7 bar, crankcase doors economical in design and weight can be produced for the required conditions. The structural parts of engines, e.g. bedplates, frames and entablatures, are normally capable of withstanding such pressures.

For fully safeguarding the operating staff, additional precautions are necessary, e.g. the fitting of effective flame-traps to the relief doors—or equivalent means of preventing flames, hot oil and scorching gases from reaching the engineers and greasers; the provision of a carbon dioxide drenching arrangement; the application of a photo-cell system to each crankcase and chain casing; or the fitting of explosion suppressors.

Automatic Relief Doors

Automatic self-closing relief doors should be provided on all enclosed engines, except small ones.

In marine propelling engines each cylinder crankcase should have its own relief door. The author would extend this requirement downwards to all moderate-speed engines of about 75 kW per cylinder. Below this size a door at each end of the engine should suffice.

Safety doors should be as lightly constructed as it is practicable to make them, because reduction of inertia is most important. The door should permit a straight and direct outflow for the gas; changes of direction are to be avoided. Equally important is it for the door to be self-closing, thus preventing a return-flow of atmospheric air into the crankcase. According to the evidence, secondary outbursts can far exceed in violence the primary explosion.

Only three elements are needed for an ideally constructed relief door: a hinge, a lid and a self-closing sneck. Elaboration in design is not only out of place; it is a snare.

Figure 15.5 shows a widely applied and very successful type of safety door. The diagram is self-explanatory. The circular lid or flap, also the circular frame, are made of aluminium. The lid is held in position by a spring-loaded, double-mitred sneck. When correctly set, the door can be pulled open by one's finger acting on the knob. After opening to discharge flame and smoke it instantly closes again with a snap. The double-mitre sneck construction permits this. A coil spring is fitted to the hinge of the lid. As a safe-guard against the non-functioning of the sneck spring, a counterweight is sometimes provided, i.e. when requested by a client. The safety door is made in standard sizes, from 200 mm to 400 mm bore.

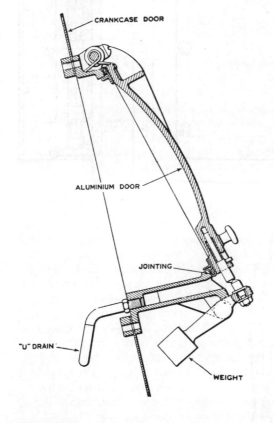

CRANKCASE DOOR

ALUMINIUM DOOR

JOINTING

"U" DRAIN

WEIGHT

Figure 15.5 Automatic self-closing safety door

It is more satisfactory for relief to be provided at several small safety doors than at a single large door. With a number of small doors, relief is given before the combustion-wave has travelled very far, and therefore before the pressure has reached a high level. The farther the relief door is from the place where burning begins, the greater is the flame speed and the steeper is the pressure-rise by the time the relief door is reached.

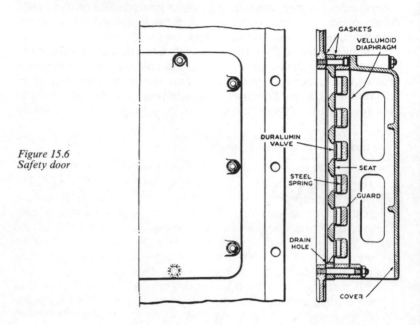

Figure 15.6
Safety door

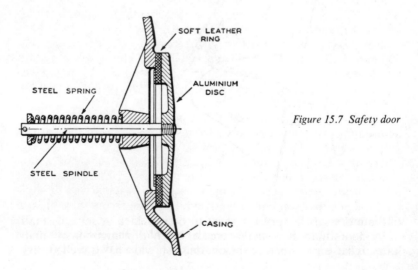

Figure 15.7 Safety door

Figures 15.6 and 15.7 show other forms of safety door. These, however, do not provide the straight-line exit which is so essential for safety; the momentum of the swiftly moving gases must be arrested and their path redirected at right angles before they can freely escape to atmosphere. In heavy explosions this characteristic could easily cause the destruction of the safety device, with corresponding danger from secondary explosions.

For heavy oil engines in power stations the author has many records of the safety doors having lifted and having emitted flame and/or dense black smoke. When the engines have been stopped and examined, seizures incipient and otherwise have been discovered. But for the safety doors there would have been active explosions.

Size and Number of Relief Doors

The relation between the aggregate free escape area of safety doors and the crankcase volume is important.

In large crosshead engines, of different types, known to the author, where the lifting of the safety door, or doors, relieved the crankcase pressure and prevented an active explosion, the free area of the safety door orifice was 20–23 cm² per cubic metre of crankcase volume, gross, per cylinder. As none of the crankcase doors on the engines mentioned could withstand a live pressure of more than 0·5–1·0 bar above the normal ambient atmospheric pressure, without complete dislodgement, it follows that the internal pressures in the crankcases must have been only a small fraction of the pressures named when the safety doors lifted. In many explosions the lifting of only one or two safety doors has been sufficient completely to relieve the crankcase internal pressure.

Lloyd's Rules require that in engines having cylinders exceeding 300 mm bore, at least one valve is to be fitted in way of each main crank throw. The combined free area of the crankcase relief valves fitted on an engine is not to be less than 115 cm²/m³ based on the volume of the crankcase.

The free area of each relief valve is not to be less than 45 cm². In determining the volume of the crankcase, the volume of the stationary parts within the crankcase may be deducted.

Crankcase relief valves are to be designed to open at a low pressure, of about 0·10 kgf/cm². The discharge from the valves is to be shielded where necessary by flame guard or flame trap to minimise the possibility of danger and damage arising from the emission of flame.

In the author's opinion, where the height of the crankcase much exceeds the transverse dimension, there should be two safety doors.

Figure 15.8 is an example of current marine practice. Where they are not well above man-height, safety doors should be shielded. The lower safety doors of Figure 15.8 would normally be arranged at the

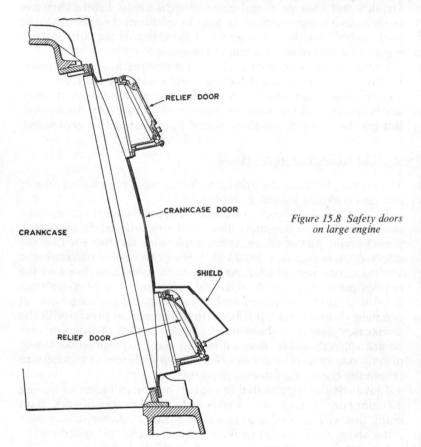

Figure 15.8 Safety doors on large engine

back of the engine, the protecting shields being larger and more effectively directed downward. Complete protection by shielding is very difficult to attain.

Some Alternative Relief Devices

There are other devices in use; most of these are to be avoided.

Paper discs, gripped around their circumference, have been used. As such discs are liable to pulsate and fail in normal service, when unsupported, they are sometimes backed by a perforated grid.

Alternatively, instead of paper, millboard is often used. A variant of this device is a thin metal disc, backed by a perforated plate, with a fixed steel cutter or pointer directed towards the centre of the disc. The theory is that the metal disc deflects under a slight crankcase pressure and is punctured by the metal instrument.

All such devices have one serious defect: even if they burst at the proper time and relieve the crankcase pressure—which is more than doubtful—there is nothing to prevent a flow-back of atmospheric air into the crankcase, to set off a secondary explosion.

Despite what has just been written, the author has records of cardboard discs which functioned effectively. Thus, to quote but one example, in a certain auxiliary engine a fuel valve nipple end broke and a hole through the piston was a consequence. The cardboard disc on the crankcase blew off, and the engineer stopped the engine. There was no secondary explosion and there was no damage.

Stiffness of Metallic Discs

The pressure that a thin metallic disc will withstand before bursting is much greater than might be expected. Thus: a flat steel disc 395 mm external diameter, 320 mm dia. of hole, 30 l.s.g. (0·315 mm) thick, gripped circumferentially by a bolted steel ring 45 mm wide and 13 mm thick, will withstand a steady water pressure of 5·5 bar before showing the least sign of distress at the circumferential fixing. By that time it has become a dished plate having a permanent deflection of 35 mm at the centre. Except at the encastré edge, the sheet will be perfect. A similar flat steel plate 18 l.s.g. (1·219 mm) thick will withstand a water pressure of 17 bar without so much as a leak. An aluminium plate 18 l.s.g. (1·219 mm) thick will carry 6 bar before tearing at the circumferential fixing.

Spring-loaded Crankcase Doors

Sometimes it is suggested that the crankcase doors should be arranged to function as pressure-relief valves, by being held in place on the engine framing by spring-loaded studs. The reasoning is that such a plate would move bodily under pressure and that the gas would quickly escape through the openings formed at the plate boundary.

The objections are: first, the imprisoned gas has to overcome the inertia of the door and springs; second, the gas has to change direction before being able to escape.

With a crankcase door of any reasonable size, weight and construction, it could be expected that the arrestation of the momentum of the gas by the door would cause the door to be blown off before the gas escaped. The author has among his records an account of an engine which suffered a crankcase explosion, in which the crankcase doors were spring-loaded. Two were blown off.

Safeguarding of Engine Operators

With relief doors of a simple, self-acting type of reasonable size, the engines themselves can be completely safeguarded against damage in event of explosion. Until, however, an equally positive dictum is possible regarding the operating staff, the position will not be fully satisfactory.

There are two ways of obtaining safety:

(a) by the prevention of explosions;
(b) by nullifying the effects of explosion.

Preventive measures fall into two groups, namely:

(i) those under the control of the operator for use when conditions become ominous;
(ii) those which are self-acting when an explosion mixture is being built up.

The effects of explosion can be nullified in various ways. One is to provide simple ducts of large cross-section to carry away the flames and hot black smoke. Such a scheme for a multi-cylinder engine, although not perhaps too costly, is unsightly and interferes with the rapid taking-off of crankcase doors. An alternative is the provision of effective flame-traps on the relief doors. The simplest form of flame-trap comprises a system of copper gauze, arranged on the principle of the miner's lamp.

Flame-traps

If across the path of hot, swiftly moving explosion gases there is interposed something that can quickly absorb large quantities of combustion heat, then the burning comes to an end. This is the principle of the flame-trap. The requirements of an effective design are: a large surface offering as much area of contact as possible to the moving gases; a low frictional resistance; a robust mechanical construction. The material used in flame-traps may normally be metal gauze of high heat conductivity.

Flame-traps said to have been effective have been made by stretching across the safety-door openings five layers of gauze in close contact, the two layers nearest to the relief door being 20 mesh, 0·50 mm dia. wire, 36 per cent clear area, and the other three layers being 40-mesh, 0·25 mm wire, 36 per cent clear area. The clear area through the flame-trap should not be less than 30 per cent in excess of the free valve area. It is necessary for the gauze to be in close contact with the metal supporting frame.

An alternative construction is a shallow conical structure, also composed of sheets of gauze, attached at the rim to the circumference of the relief-valve orifice, the apex of the cone pointing into the crankcase. The cone ensures stiffness and provides an enhanced free area. There are six sheets of gauze, namely, two coarse, two medium and two fine.

Experiments have shown that oil-wetted gauze is a much better flame-retarding agent than is dry gauze. Gauze attached to the inside of a flame door can be expected to remain oil-wetted.

When a safety door opens and gases are expelled most of the visible flame is caused by ignition of the oil particles ejected from the crankcase ahead of the burning gases. The flame produced inside the crankcase, or the amount of heat to be absorbed by the gauze, is only a small part of the flame observed when no flame-trap is provided.

Likelihood of flame passing from one engine to another by way of the oil-suction pipes can be obviated by making the lines discontinuous, by arranging suitable pump connections and by ensuring that a convenient length of piping is always 'drowned'. If flame-traps are required here they may be cylinders of metal gauze or perforated plate.

Care should be taken to avoid direct interconnections between adjacent engines. Oil-sump vapour pipes should be led separately to atmosphere.

Lloyds require that, where crankcase vent pipes are fitted, they are to be made as small as practicable and are to be led to a safe position on deck. Lubricating oil drain pipes from the engine sump to the drain tank are to be submerged at their outlet ends. Where there are two or more engines, vent pipes and lubricating oil drain pipes are to be independent.

Smoke Detection Apparatus

Oil mists can readily be detected at concentrations far below that required for explosions, hence the automatic detection of the growth of oil mists is a very effective method of obviating crankcase explosions.

The apparatus used is a modification of the photo-cell equipment used in steam boiler plant for the detection of smoke in flue gases or that used in the cargo spaces of ships.

The detector can be made completely automatic by providing a trigger in the bell circuit, which releases carbon dioxide from bottles and floods the crankcase as soon as the oil mist reaches a prearranged density. Alternatively, the trigger can be hand-operated by the watch-engineer as soon as he hears the bell and satisfies himself that it is not a false alarm. The time interval between the ringing of the alarm bell and the incidence of an explosion is ample to enable suitable action to be taken.

B.S.R.A. System. The apparatus developed by the Graviner Co. and the British Ship Research Association is shown in Figure 15.9. It has received wide and successful application.

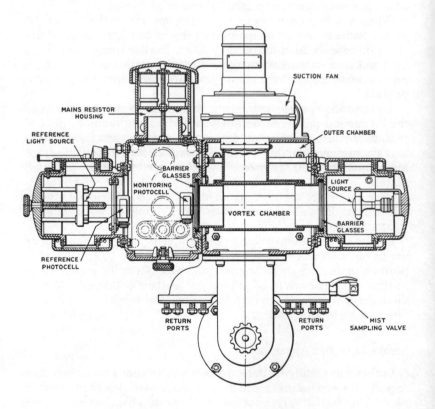

Figure 15.9 Graviner oil-mist detector

The mist detector operates on the principle of measuring the degree of mist density by photo-electric cells which are normally in electrical balance. The value of the out-of-balance current is indicated either on an instrument or on a chart recorder. The instruments provide a continuous indication of the condition of the crankcase atmosphere. A warning gong rings at the appropriate setting for which the instruments have been calibrated, namely, 2·5 per cent of the lower explosive limit. Depending upon the free volume of the crankcase, there will be ample time between the warning and the occurrence of dangerous conditions, for slowing down or stopping an engine.

The detector consists of an outer chamber, which is provided with a short, large-diameter suction pipe in direct communication with the crankcase. Within the outer chamber is a second, or vortex chamber, in direct connection with a suction fan, having apertures at each end in communication with the outer chamber. Two circular sleeves, with protective sealing glasses at each end, protrude into the vortex chamber. The design effectively prevents the obscuration of the protective glasses by oil droplets or mist condensation. A light source is arranged to throw a beam across the vortex chamber, through gas-sealed windows, on to a photo-electric measuring cell. A further light source, located in an isolated compartment, energises a second or reference cell. Continuous sampling of the crankcase atmosphere is thus obtained by the suction fan drawing a large volume of slow-moving oil vapour/air mixture through the chamber and the vortex chamber.

The connection between the detector mist chamber and the crankcase is controlled by a valve operated by a central knob. The control panel on the detecting apparatus incorporates the main on/off switch, the sensitivity control and warning reset push button, a checkmeter, a green (normal) signal lamp, a red (warning) signal lamp and a sensitivity check. A remotely positioned mist-density indicating meter is provided, with a graduated scale divided into green, amber and red sections.

As the crankcase atmosphere is continuously passing through the detector, the slight haze associated with normal engine running will be detected by the apparatus and will cause the mist-density indicating needle to rise above zero; but it will still be within the green sector of the scale. Should the indicator needle move within the red sector of the scale, the green indicator lamp will be extinguished and be replaced by the red lamp; the suction fan will cease to operate, and the engine-room warning gong will ring until the equipment is switched off. The engine-room staff will be warned in sufficient time to prevent the generation of explosive oil-mist in the crankcase from becoming dangerous before action is taken.

B.I.C.E.R.A. Explosion Relief Valve

As already mentioned, the provision of pressure-relief valves on the crankcase of enclosed engines does not, *ipso facto*, ensure the safety of the engine-room staff. Indeed, unless such valves are provided with effective flame-traps, they may actually increase the danger to the personnel, because explosions too weak to damage a crankcase can be responsible for the ejection of large masses of flame from unprotected relief valves.

Figure 15.10 illustrates a most effective oil-wetted wire-gauze flame trap. It was devised by the British Internal Combustion Engine Research Institute after a most thorough investigation. Compared with designs in which the wire-gauze is placed on the outside of the relief valve, the internal arrangement flame-trap, shown in Figure 15.10, can absorb about three times as much heat before allowing the passage of flame. Further, the capacity of the gauze is again approximately doubled by coating it with lubricating oil. This is achieved by arranging the gauze assembly in the path of the lubricating oil which is sprayed about the interior of the crankcase by the moving parts of the engine. The combination of the two factors named makes the internal oil-wetted flame-trap about six times more effective than an external gauze flame-trap.

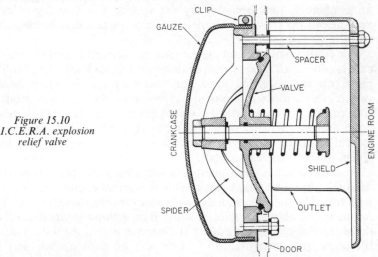

Figure 15.10
B.I.C.E.R.A. explosion
relief valve

In the B.I.C.E.R.A. explosion relief valve the flame-trap is arranged to form a single unit with an incorporated relief valve. In Figure 15.11 the crankcase door to which the valve is fitted is sandwiched at X between the two components of the valve. The internal element comprises the frame for the mild-steel woven-wire gauze layers and the spider which supports the spindle on which the relief valve rides. The external element is a combined valve cover and deflector made of aluminium. The deflector exit opening, 120 degrees in extent, is turned in the direction which may be safest for the issuing hot gases. The relief valve proper is an aluminium alloy casting having synthetic rubber oil- and heat-resisting seals. It is retained in the closed position by a compression spring which presses against a stop in the spider.

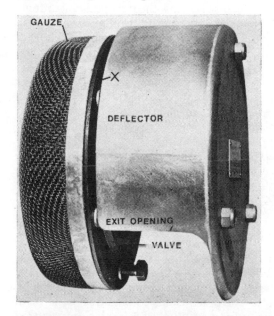

Figure 15.11
B.I.C.E.R.A explosion
relief valve

B.I.C.E.R.A. valves are available in four standard sizes, the nominal diameters of valves being 100 mm, 150 mm, 250 mm, and 350 mm. The valves have been approved by Lloyds, Bureau Veritas, American Bureau of Shipping and other classification societies, as well as by the safety authorities, including the Board of Trade.

The licensee for the manufacture of B.I.C.E.R.A. valves is The Pyropress Engineering Co. Ltd, of Bedford.

Crankcase Exhauster Fans

Normally, the crankcase of a diesel engine is provided with an open vent pipe, or other form of breather, to allow for the expansion of the warm air inside the crankcase.

To reduce the explosion risk on shipboard, systems of exhauster fans have been applied fairly widely. With this arrangement, pipe connections from the top of the crankcase are led to a motor-driven exhauster fan. This fan may, or may not, be fitted with an oil trap. The discharge from the fan is led to atmosphere. There is no free access of air to the crankcase. The action of the suction fan, therefore, is to induce a slightly sub-atmospheric pressure in the crankcase, experiments having shown that, with such an arrangement, the risk of explosion is reduced.

If the atmosphere in a crankcase is below the inflammability range, and normally it is well below the lower limit, the admission of fresh air is an advantage and not a danger. Danger arises only when fresh air is admitted to a crankcase which is already filled with a heated over-rich mixture.

For engines with lightly attached crankcase doors, the exhauster system reduces seepage from the joints of doors, frames, bedplates and so on. In a normal engine the leakage of air into the crankcase— as at, say, the sump tank air pipes, or the small annular space which may be found in some types of trunk engine where the cylinder liner passes through the crankcase top—can be beneficial; it can help to keep fresh the crankcase atmosphere. If the atmosphere grows dangerous by the creation of oil vapour the fan should assist in staving off trouble.

Experiments on Vapour Extraction

According to the author's experience, vapour extraction fans increase the margin of safety against crankcase fires. Years ago, in Belfast, a long series of experiments on explosive mixtures of lubricating oil vapour and air was made. The conclusions to be drawn from them were that the most favourable conditions for explosion occurred when the oxygen content was high, i.e. around 19 per cent. At this concentration a spark could start a violent explosion at a temperature as low as 95°C; also a mild explosion could readily occur when the gas mixture was in contact with a hot body having a temperature of approximately 175°C. If the oxygen content of the vaporous mixture were reduced the temperature necessary for explosion increased. The presence of 7 per cent carbon dioxide in the vaporous mixture prevented explosion of the mixture, when sparked. A vapour extraction fan was shown to ensure freedom from explosion if there was no ingress of air into the experimental chamber. If oil vapour is being created in substantial quantities by, say, a hot bearing, under conditions where there is a decided air ingress, there is a risk of explosion if the air supply is cut off.

In the experiments mentioned above, which were of necessity restricted to laboratory scale, painstaking effort was made to obtain the very worst conditions. This explains the violent explosion at 95°C. Reckoned in terms of oxygen content, the atmosphere was practically normal, but it was carefully charged, artificially, with oil particles of such sizes and quantity that the peak of explosibility was reached. Under rather different conditions explosion required a higher temperature, namely 175°C, and a hot body instead of a spark.

A bearing temperature of 95°C is not uncommon in an engine, but the crankcase atmosphere is approximately a normal fresh-air atmosphere; it is not then artificially charged with oil particles in the careful manner of the experiments mentioned. That is an important difference. The same remarks apply to the explosions at 175°C. A temperature of 500°C is more likely to be needed to fire an oil mist in an actual engine than the lower figures quoted from the carefully manipulated laboratory experiments.

Air Circulation of Crankcases

As an alternative to closed crankcases and exhauster fans, it is occasionally suggested that a free current of air should be drawn through the engine crankcase, thereby ensuring that there cannot, in any circumstances, be a pressure build-up. This proposal implies the arranging of large openings in the crankcase at suitable places and the provision of capacious fans and ducts, with oil traps and other appurtenances. The expense of such an arrangement would be high; moreover, the engine-room ventilation system would doubtless need revision, with aditional capacity provided for fans and air trunks.

Use of Exhaust Gas in Crankcases

Another type of scheme, which receives periodical reference, is the passing of engine exhaust gas through the crankcase on its way to the atmosphere. For such a scheme to be satisfactory, gas-washing arrangements and effective coolers are necessary, in addition to fans and trunking. Apart from the cost, the weight and space requirements of these and similar schemes have hitherto made them uncommercial.

Subdivision of Engines

It may be prudent to subdivide a long engine by one or more cross-partitions, so that if an internal explosion should occur near one end it will not sweep right through the engine, greatly to increase in violence and destructiveness as it proceeds. It is impracticable to isolate each cylinder unit crankcase; there must be openings in the frames for the lifting of main bearing keeps, openings at the bottom of the bedplate for the passage of return oil and so on.

When an engine room is so constructed that the space around the engines is cramped, especially if the engines are long relative to their height, platforms of the open-spill design should be provided in preference to chequer plating. The underlying idea is that the explosion wave should be encouraged to rise, rather than be allowed to tear its way around inter-engine passageways and spaces, to wreak destruction upon the machinery as it passes.

Bearing Materials

Opinions differ regarding the materials to be used for lining the bearings which are located inside crankcases. In marine crosshead engines the main bearings, top- and bottom-end bushes and guide shoes are white-metal lined. Intermediate chain-wheels and similar components, also gudgeon-pin bearings in trunk engines, are, more often than not, lined with bronze-type alloy. Sometimes, by reason of design requirements, the specific loading is too great for white-metal to withstand. Sometimes, also, the use of white-metal does not increase the safety, i.e. immunity, factor. Of thirteen explosions known to the author, which originated at gear drives inside crankcases, seven of the seized or melted bushes involved were of bronze, six of white-metal. In one of the examples a white-metal-lined connecting rod top-end bush, of increased size, was substituted for the bronze bush, but overheating was not thereby prevented.

The author would prefer white-metal as a lining for all bearings inside the crankcase; otherwise he would use leaded gunmetal. The alloy constituents are: 80 per cent copper, 10·50 per cent tin, 7·50 per cent lead, 1·00 per cent nickel, 0·75 per cent antimony, 0·20 per cent zinc; when melted and cast within the appropriate temperature limits about 7 per cent of the tin forms a soft solid solution in the copper, the remaining 3·5 per cent becoming the harder tin–copper compound, i.e. the delta constituent. The lead, in the form of small segregated particles, mixes with the tin–copper solution. Thus, not being dissolved in the tin–copper compound, the lead retains its anti-friction characteristics. The zinc is a deoxidiser. A leaded gunmetal, such as that described, differs from lead-bronze, which is a mixture of about 30 per cent lead and 70 per cent copper, with up to 1 per cent nickel to assist 'freezing'.

The fitting of lead-bronze rings to trunk-engine pistons will materially assist the safe running-in of the pistons and liners. These rings are turned 'proud' by 0·10 mm. By the time the rings have worn flush with the piston surface any rough-running tendency which might have been present initially should have completely disappeared.

Piston Blow-past

The effect of piston 'blow-past' is the injection into the crankcase of quantities of hot combustion gases, of approximate composition 5–6 per cent carbon dioxide, 14 per cent oxygen, variable but small amounts of sulphur gases and the remainder nitrogen. These gases, by themselves, reduce the explosion risk, but their high temperature tends in the opposite direction. The carbon dioxide percentage is not sufficiently high to inhibit explosion in otherwise favourable circumstances. The author understands that 500°C is regarded as the minimum temperature needed to 'set-off' a lubricating oil mist, as mentioned earlier.

Lubricating Oil Dilution

It is improbable that the dilution of lubricating oil by fuel oil has any significance in the causation of crankcase explosions. In the author's experience, fuel oil dilutions of 8 per cent and 10 per cent have been consistently carried for years with impunity. For propelling engines 10 per cent may be accepted as an allowable maximum. The author knows diesel locomotives which run with 15 per cent dilution without the slightest difficulty, the viscosity being lowered 50 per cent thereby. The permissible limit of dilution is determined by other factors. Lubricating oil analysis figures taken after explosions have shown the dilution percentages to vary from 2·7 to zero. Apart from dilution, the age of the oil is not a recognisable factor.

Hydrogen in Crankcases

The presence of hydrogen in a crankcase can only arise from dissociation caused by iron at a red heat, say, at a minimum of 700°C. This dissociation is a balanced action; that is, it proceeds in one direction or the other, as determined by the excess of vapour or of hydrogen. The amount of water-vapour present in a crankcase is very small relative to the other gases, and the temperature conditions are unfavourable to the initiation of the reaction. Concentration of hydrogen in the upper parts of a crankcase arising from, say, a hot piston is, at best, a remote possibility. It is still more remote if an exhaust fan is coupled to the crankcase.

Introduction of Air into Hot Crankcases

The introduction of air into a heated crankcase can only be potentially dangerous if the crankcase atmosphere is over-rich in oil mist, and if the aerial dilution brings the mixture inside the limits of inflammability. Restoration of temperature equilibrium, disturbed by the increase of cold air, takes from 15 to 30 sec under experimental conditions.

Experiments to determine the rate of disappearance of oxygen from crankcase air, when the air is shaken up with lubricating oil, have shown no change.

Inspection of Overheated Engines

When there is reason to suspect overheating it is important that crankcase doors should not be taken off until an ample amount of time has elapsed, for in such circumstances it is impossible to be sure that the crankcase contents are safe. The principle should be applied to all crankcase openings, irrespective of size. A distinction must be drawn, however, between the taking off and the leaving off of a door when a running engine is cool, and when it is overheated. One day, during sea trials, the skew-gear drive of a propelling engine became overheated. An engineer unclasped the lid of a small inspection opening and, seeing smoke issuing therefrom, blew upon it with his breath. The smoke changed to flame, to his physical hurt.

Time Notions

The terminology, units employed, background of thought and approach which are habitual to the mechanical engineer are necessarily very different from those which an explosion expert brings to his problems. When an engineer speaks of a failure being rapid he is thinking in terms of a bursting boiler tube, the failure of a bottom-end bolt, the fracturing of a steam-engine cylinder-end, or the breaking of a steel bar under tensile test. In explosions, however, time notions take on a totally different sense. Thus, an engine room may be disrupted in an interval of time which is measurable in hundredths of a second.

Proneness to Explosion

The assumption current in ill-formed quarters that the larger the diesel engine, the more is it liable to crankcase explosions is utterly devoid of foundation. The author has been responsible for many diesel engines of 5000–15 000 kW per screw, and in none of them has there ever been the slightest suggestion of proneness to crankcase fire or explosion. On the contrary, the larger the engine, the safer is it likely to be from such hazards. One reason for this is that the more powerful and the more costly the engine, the less is the designer likely to take liberties with loads, running speeds and materials, if only because of the financial risk involved to the engine builder.

There is, at the best of times, only a narrow market for really powerful engines, and the building of a prototype is not therefore practicable. Of the largest engines, probably not more than half-a-dozen installations are ever made from the same plans. If designers could be as venturesome with large and powerful engines as they can afford to be with small engines, then all engines, irrespective of size, would probably have a common denominator of explosion risk.

SOME TYPICAL CRANKCASE EXPLOSIONS

Outline particulars of some characteristic crankcase explosions are given in the following pages. In number they are sufficient to establish reasonable, consistent conclusions. One inescapable deduction from the descriptions is that, when two pieces of metal rub together in the oily atmosphere of an enclosed, forced-lubricated engine crankcase a potential focal point of danger from explosion is thereby created. Another deduction is that, more often than not, there are premonitory warnings of danger. And a third deduction is that suitable precautions, simple in their essence, can ensure safety.

Of the explosions described below, twenty five per cent had fatal consequences for one or more men on duty in the machinery spaces.

Piston-rod Crosshead. A five-cylinder 650 kW unit, of four-stroke, single-acting, crosshead design, running at 215 rev/min, was behaving normally when the cast-steel bottom half-bush of No. 4 top-end bearing broke in halves. The crosshead pin at that place dropped, causing the guide shoe to run 'cape-and-corner' in the guides, thus to produce an overheated region.

The first intimation of something amiss was the issuing of smoke from the crankcase. The engineers immediately started up another engine to take the load and, while the smoking engine was slowing down, an explosion of considerable intensity occurred. But for the large dimensions of the engine room, the results might have been disastrous. A cast-iron cover about 300 mm dia. and 19 mm thick, was projected from the oil-sump end; a hole was blown through the sheet-steel casing which enclosed the crankshaft damper; blazing oil was extruded through all apertures; crankcase doors were blown off; oil was ejected in every direction; there was a roaring flame from the sump and from the crankcase openings; and a sheet of fire enveloped one part of the engine room.

The engine was not fitted with an anti-explosion device.

Piston Rod. A new double-acting, four-stroke, crosshead type, six-cylinder engine, developing 3000 kW at 95 rev/min, had entered service.

Shortly before the explosion No. 3 piston rod became very hot, throwing out sparks. The excessive heating was thought to have had its origin in a defective bottom fuel valve, which, giving rise to after-burning, permitted combustion to continue while the piston rod was exposed. Normally, combustion would terminate while the rod was being shielded by the moulding provided on the piston for that purpose. The overheated piston rod, entering the crankcase, caused the explosion. In this make of engine the piston rods were not provided with cooled cast-iron sleeves.

Actually there were two explosions. The first occurred in the forward part of the crank chamber and was of some violence; among other things it ignited the lubricating oil. Some seconds later there was a second explosion, which was thought to have occurred in the after part of the crank-chamber. The damage was considerable. Apart from the crankcase doors, the engine-room doors, of teak 50 mm thick, were blown out into the alleyways in a badly splintered condition; the skylight operating gear was broken, and the substantial operating rods were badly strained; handrails and gratings were twisted and deformed.

The cardboard safety discs in the crank-chamber ends remained intact.

Jockey-wheel Bush in Crankcase. This example also concerned a double-acting, four-stroke, crosshead engine. It was an eight-cylinder unit developing 5600 kW at 100 rev/min. The mishap occurred on the sea trials.

The anchor was raised at midnight, and two hours later the engines were running at full power. Full-power trials ended at noon next day. Between 12 noon and 1 p.m. a series of manoeuvring trials were made at full power, ahead and astern. An anchoring test followed, the main engines working at varying revolutions. Then the engine was stopped for a short time to allow a vibrograph to be arranged. At 1.23 p.m., shortly after restarting, when the engine was running at about 90 rev/min, a slight explosion inside the crankcase occurred, followed immediately by a violent explosion in the engine room. The damage to the machinery was small.

The cause of the explosion was the overheating of a jockey-wheel bush in the camshaft chain drive. The cast-steel jockey wheel was fitted with two bronze bushes, driven hard into the wheel; each bush was further secured by a tap-bolt. The wheel rotated on a steel shaft, which was secured to a triangular-shaped casting pivoted on a fixed pin, the appropriate tightening being obtained by an adjusting screw. The bronze bushes in the jockey wheel had heated and seized on the steel shaft, the securing pins had sheared and the wheel had rotated on the outside surface of the bushes. The heat generated had been intense.

The paper safety discs, on the ends of the engine, were intact after the explosion.

Chain-drive. A two-stroke, single-acting, crosshead engine, designed for 6000 kW at 110 rev/min, had had eight months' sea service when a crankcase explosion occurred. The explosion was of such severity that all the crankcase relief valves lifted—there were two on each crankcase unit but none on the chain casing—emitting blazing oil, flame and smoke, which, rushing up the engine casing and out through the open skylight, almost reached the top of the funnel. The first explosion was followed by at least one further explosion. The engine was immediately slowed down to 40 rev/min and was so run for three-quarters of an hour, to allow the engine to cool.

Although the free area through the safety valves was greater than classification society requirements, every valve opened. The force was such that three of the valves had their attachments broken.

Three hundred gallons of lubricating oil were lost.

A post-explosion examination showed that the oilway supplying one of the chain-wheel bearings was blocked by metal shavings and chips of wood. This and other occurrences of like category point to the desirability of having more than one oil supply to such hidden, sensitive places as chain-drive bearings. The cost of doing this is relatively insignificant.

The chain-wheel bearing, which was the seat of overheating, was white-metal lined.

Chain-wheel. A double-acting, two-stroke, crosshead engine, fifteen years old, developing 7500 kW on ten cylinders, had an explosion of such severity that eight out of ten relief doors lifted. From the permanent deflection of the crankcase doors, the explosion pressure had been less than 0·10 bar. The cause was a fractured copper oil pipe, 13 mm bore, which supplied a chain jockey wheel.

Camshaft Bearing. This example concerns a six-cylinder engine, developing 4500 kW at 98 rev/min. The engine was of two-stroke, double-acting, crosshead type and was eighteen months old.

When on a long voyage the ship called at an intermediate port to take in bunker fuel. The ship arrived at 9.54 p.m. one day and left at 1.14 a.m. the next day. The forced-lubrication pumps were not stopped while the ship was in port and no adjustments of any kind were made. At 4.00 a.m., when the watch was changed, everything was running normally. At about 4.20 a.m. the engineer of the watch noticed smoke issuing from the top of the chain casing. He telephoned the bridge and slowed down the engine. At 4.30 a.m. he stopped the engine, because the camshaft bearing was apparently on fire. The tell-tale was showing a continuous flow of lubricating oil through the bearing. The engineers then went aloft to attend to the hot bearing. There is reason to think that they cut off the oil supply to the bearing and also took off a small inspection cover near the bearing.

At about 4.35 a.m. there was a heavy explosion. Crankcase doors were buckled and blown off; evidence of damage was widespread in the engine room; there was a fire zone extending from the middle of the engine room to the ship's skin.

The ship, which was twin-screw, had been running for twenty-seven days in the open sea when the mishap occurred.

Examination of the bearing after the explosion showed the journal surface to be normal; the oil supply hole was clear. The bearing was adjacent to a chain-wheel; *see* Figure 15.12. The location of the bearing in the crankcase is shown in Figure 15.13.

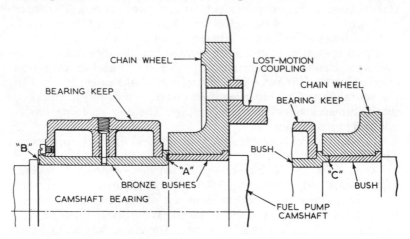

Figure 15.12 Camshaft bearing

The lip of the bush remote from the sprocket wheel, i.e. that which abuts the collar on the camshaft, *B* (Figure 15.12), had a recess approximately 0·50 mm deep for the width of the collar. At the end of the bearing adjacent to the sprocket wheel a recess 15 mm wide,

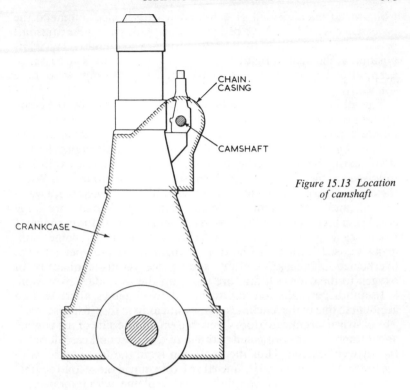

Figure 15.13 *Location of camshaft*

at 15 mm from the inside of the bush, was observed; this recess extended around the half-circumference of the bush, and was 0·40 mm deep. The groove coincided with the sprocket-wheel bushing, *A*. The lower half-bush, which was in place, but on top of the camshaft, had been rotated 180°. The lower half of the bush took the thrust, and it was fused to the sprocket-wheel bushing, *C*.

The sprocket-wheel bushing end was broken away in places and was partly melted. Pieces of bronze were found at various places in the chain casing and crankcase. In size they varied from about 50 mm square down to pieces the size of chippings. Some of the larger pieces had melted and had dropped the full height of the chain casing, into the sump. About 150 mm of the lower bush lip, adjacent to the sprocket wheel, was broken off. The sprocket-wheel bushing had projected beyond the face of the boss and had pressed against the lip of the bearing bush, at *A*, with such intensity that great heat had been created. This pressure had also brought the other lip of the bush, at *B*, into heavy frictional contact with the journal collar.

If the camshaft bearing or the sprocket-wheel bush had been

white-metal lined instead of being lined with leaded gunmetal the occurrence would not have been obviated. This particular camshaft bearing had not much to do; its normal vulnerability lay in its position at the highest point of the lubrication circuit. The cast-iron keep, also the cast-steel base of the camshaft bearing, were quite sound.

The rapid descent of pieces of semi-molten metal down the chain casing probably achieved what many sparks would fail to do. The uninterrupted flow of lubricating oil no doubt added fuel to the fire.

Camshaft Bearing. In a 2250 kW two-stroke trunk engine, a camshaft bearing became overheated and caused a slight, dull explosion, followed by the issuing of black smoke from the crankcase. While the engineers were trying to find out what had happened there was a second, and very violent, explosion. The engines had very large crankcase breathers and there were connections from the crankcases to the scavenging pump suctions. The rotating of the engine, non-firing, caused fresh air to be drawn through the breather into the overheated crankcase, thereby adding the requisite quantity of oxygen to the over-rich mixture to set off the secondary explosion.

In another installation, consisting of two engines, there was an accident to one of the machines, somewhat akin to that just described. The cast-iron crankcase doors were blown off one side of the engine, and a fragment was projected through one of the crankcase doors of the adjacent engine. Thus the explosion from the first engine, with the fire that accompanied it, caused an explosion in the second engine. The system of crankcase ventilation was to blame, with its crankcase breathers and connections to the scavenging pumps.

Lubricating Oil Pump Drive. In a four-cylinder, 400 kW two-stroke trunk auxiliary engine there was a gear-wheel type oil pump at one end of the engine driven by a bell-crank from a pin arranged eccentrically on the crankshaft end. The pin worked loose, its end striking the pump casing as it revolved, creating heat which was transmitted to the crankcase contents, ultimately causing an explosion.

Cylinder-liner Gland Ring. A four-stroke trunk engine of standard eight-cylinder design, rated at 900 kW was running on the test-bed.

At the client's request an explosion door was required on each cylinder crankcase. As the proper explosion doors, for the back of the engine, were not available for the test, two explosion doors were fitted temporarily on the front of the engine.

After running, at different powers, for a total period of 5 h 40 min, an explosion occurred without warning.

The two safety doors lifted; flame and smoke shot out to a considerable distance; the explosion doors snapped closed; and the attendants stopped the engine.

The cause of the explosion was the distortion of the gland ring which retained in place the synthetic rubber ring which sealed the water-jacket from the crankcase. The gland ring was made of fabricated steel, in halves. It had been bearing on the liner in four places, and the liner had been distorted, causing heavy overheating of the piston and scoring of the liner. A revised design of ring was a complete cure.

Perforated Piston Crown. In a four-stroke trunk engine of 1100 kW output, a hole was burned through a piston crown. This gave fuel oil combustion pressure access to the crankcase, resulting in explosion and fires.

A number of mishaps of this category have been recorded.

Foreign Body between Piston and Liner. In this example the engine was a four-stroke trunk unit, developing 750 kW on four cylinders at 175 rev/min. It was about seven years old and had been running continuously for over two weeks when an explosion occurred.

Smoke, noticed at the breather pipe, was assumed to be caused by piston blow-by. While it was being investigated, No. 1 crankcase door blew out. The engine continued to run and was stopped by hand.

The explosion had occurred in the lower part of No. 1 crankcase, as the splash-guard over the crank had been partly torn and forced upward. The crankcase door had been buckled outwards and torn; it was blown clear of the attachments. The cardboard explosion disc, adjacent to No. 1 crankcase, was intact. The oil in the crankcase was burning.

The first cause was a fired-up piston. Both piston and liner were scored and torn on the thrust side—the piston from the bottom of the skirt to a point above the rings, and the liner for about two-thirds of its length, the worst damage having occurred at a point near the bottom. All piston rings were free and in good order; there was no evidence of blow-past. There were signs of previous firing at several points on piston and liner. The bolted-on piston head had slackened off six times during the previous three years, the securing studs having either broken or slackened. On some occasions fragments of locking plates had been found on the splash-guards.

It was concluded that the accident had been caused by one or more fragments of steel locking-washer becoming wedged between piston and liner, causing heavy overheating. Probably incandescent pieces of metal had fallen into the crankcase.

Gudgeon-pin Bearing. A ten-cylinder four-stroke trunk propelling engine, 4000 kW output at 160 rev/min, was on full-power trials on the makers' testbed. There was an explosion. The chain-case inspection door was temporarily secured by two clips only, and the explosion blew off this door and scattered burning oil.

A sudden and severe piston seizure, occurring when the engine was running at full speed, was one explanation offered. Another was an insufficiency of working clearance between the fitting strip at the cylinder-liner bottom and the bored hole in the crankcase diaphragm; alternatively, the rubber ring near the bottom of the liner had become volume-bound. More probable than either of these explanations, as the engine's subsequent history showed, was a hot gudgeon-pin bearing. Accordingly, the gudgeon-pin and top-end bearing were altered; a white-metal-lined bush was substituted for the bronze bush. Self-acting safety doors were provided on the crankcase doors; previously there had been no safety doors.

The changes in design and material were not effective in preventing overheating, because, subsequently, there were fifteen crankcase explosions in service, all caused by hot pistons. The explosions were without consequential damage, because the safety doors effectually relieved the crankcase pressure, opening momentarily to discharge flame and smoke. Some years later new pistons were supplied throughout. These were fitted with lead-bronze rubbing rings and taper-tightened gudgeon-pins. The alterations in construction went to the core of the problem, and all troubles disappeared. The original piston design was, perhaps, too light.

Seized Piston and Gudgeon-pin. This example is from a quadruple-screw installation of twelve cylinders per engine, developing 13 500 kW aggregate at 135 rev/min. The engines were turbo-pressure-charged four-stroke trunk units. The ship was sixteen years old and the engines had had an unusually successful life. Following a re-conditioning of the vessel, sea trials were held. These had been completed when a violent explosion occurred. All the engines were involved. On each engine many crankcase doors were violently blown off; many splash-guards were displaced upwards; floor plates were overturned; ventilating trunks in the engine casing were locally crumpled; skylight panels were blown off; ducts inside the funnel were compressed; the diaphragm plate across the funnel top was bent open. The engines were brought to a standstill through shortage of fuel oil, consequent upon a main fuel-supply connection being fractured by a flying fragment of metal. From the port outer forward corner of the engine room, diagonally across to the starboard outer after corner, the mechanical damage progessively increased from a relatively quiet minimum to a most violent maximum.

According to the evidence, No. 2 port outer cylinder had been warming up for some time prior to the mishap and, eventually, the heat became so great that the engine was stopped. After a very short interval starting air was admitted to the engine and, within a few seconds, the explosion occurred. Examination showed that No. 2

port outer piston had seized badly, and the gudgeon-pin bush had been severely overheated. Otherwise the engines were completely unharmed. All engine internal surfaces retained their oiliness.

There were no relief doors on the crankcases, but simply a cardboard disc at each end of each engine. There was an exhauster fan system. Figure 15.14 shows a fractured cast-iron end door and Figure 15.15 two typical damaged crankcase doors.

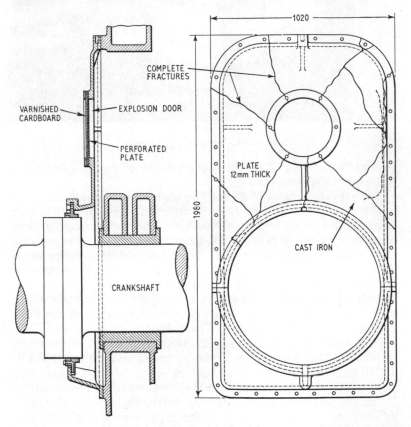

Figure 15.14 Fractured end door

Volume-bound Rubber Ring. A six-cylinder four-stroke trunk engine, 95 mm bore, 600 mm stroke, was in service. About five minutes after starting the engine one day, a crankcase explosion occurred. The cause was a partial seizure of No. 6 piston. The engine had been overhauled, and the seizure was brought about by distortion of the cylinder liner, caused by the rubber rings becoming

Figure 15.15 Crumpled crankcase doors

volume-bound. No. 3 piston showed signs of considerable over-heating for the same reason.

The explosion doors lifted and the engine was undamaged.

Broken Gear-tooth, etc. This example refers to more than one engine of two-stroke semi-crosshead type. The engines were 1300 kW units running at 180 rev/min. On each occasion there was warning of overheating. In one engine the explosion was said to have occurred immediately after the control gear had been brought to the stop position. In another engine the explosion instantly followed the removal of an inspection door. In one engine a broken gear-tooth was to blame; in another the cause was an overheated camshaft bearing. The engines were new. There were no safety doors.

Fuel Valve, etc. This example also refers to more than one installation. The engines were twin-screw, of total power 3000 kW at 220 rev/min. Two ships had been in service about a year; other engines were new. In each instance there was warning of overheating. In one engine the explosion followed restarting. In different engines different causes were assigned to the explosions, e.g. pistons, fuel valves and lubrication system. No anti-explosion devices had been provided.

The lubricating oil returns from the engines to the sump tanks were not submerged, hence oil vapour could be drawn from the sumps into the crankcases. The fuel oil and lubricating oil centrifugal machines were interconnected and, by improper handling, fuel oil could be introduced into the lubricating oil system. Also, some of the ship's engineers dumped badly contaminated lubricating oil from the high-speed diesel generating sets into the main engine sump tanks.

Roller Bearing. In a six-cylinder, double-acting, two-stroke cross-head type engine of 5000 kW output, a roller bearing in the scavenge blower became overheated, causing the bearing bush to become welded to the blower spindle. There were relief doors on the engine; these lifted, emitted flame and closed again. The engine was stopped by hand.

Engine-driven Pump Bearings. This example was a 4500 kW six-cylinder engine, three years old. It was fitted with a crankcase exhauster fan and a safety door on each cylinder crankcase.

The vessel raised anchor one day at 4.35 p.m.; it proceeded slow-ahead; at 4.48 p.m. the full-away order was given; at 5.15 p.m. there was an explosion and the engine was stopped by the engineers. The ship re-anchored. Flames issued from Nos. 4, 5 and 6 crankcase safety doors, which functioned effectively, opening for the emission of flame and then immediately closing again. The occurrence was so sudden and so unexpected that it was impossible for the engineers to seize upon a clue immediately. They shut-off the lubricating oil supply to the engine; the extraction fan continued to run, clearing the crankcase atmosphere. An external examination of the engine showed that, at the chain casing for the engine-driven pumps, the paint had been scorched. In this ship there was a set of rotary pumps, mounted on the back of the engine, for lubricating oil, circulating water, fuel-pump surcharging and so on. The pumps were chain-driven from the engine crankshaft, a sprocket wheel—enclosed in a casing—being arranged at the middle of the line of pumps.

Inspection showed that the pump bearing adjacent to the forward side of the casing had fired; the pump shaft, chain-wheel and after bearing were also very hot. After a suitable amount of dismantling it was discovered that no oil was issuing from the pipes leading to the heated bearings. All the pipes were taken down and steamed-out. A stoppage was detected in the piping leading to the bearings. The pump gear was reassembled, anchor was raised and there was no further difficulty.

The chief engineer expressed the opinion that the crankcase extractor fan had been a sound feature. The three aft relief doors were sufficient to clear the pressure.

Thin Main-bearing Bush. A six-cylinder, 900 kW engine of two-stroke trunk type, was running prolonged trials on the test-bed. One day it was started at 8.12 a.m., to run a preliminary duration trial under full load. Full load was obtained at 8.30 a.m.; at 11.33 a.m. there was a crankcase explosion and the engine had to be stopped.

The crankcase doors, for test-bed purposes, had been secured by only a few nuts, spaced at wide intervals. When the explosion occurred the crankcase doors opened up, emitting flame and smoke; but they did not leave their fastenings. The cardboard safety disc was blown away. There was no secondary explosion. The white-metal in the bottom halves of Nos. 2, 3, 4, 5 and 6 main bearings had run out and the crankshaft had become badly scored, especially at the wide centre-journal of No. 4 bearing. In No. 1 bearing the crankshaft had rubbed hard on the top-half bush.

Under full-load conditions, the steel bearing housing—which was in halves—had closed-in upon the crankshaft creating heat. After the explosion the design was revised. The lower bush was substantially increased in thickness; the upper bush was dispensed with and the keep itself was white-metal lined; also a 'check' was provided at the horizontal centre-line of the bush, to prevent distortion. There was no further difficulty.

Emergency Governor. Figures 15.16 and 15.17 show the governor gear of a two-stroke, double-acting engine of 6000 kW. The lever bearing was served by a hand siphon lubricator. One day, at 7.50 a.m.,

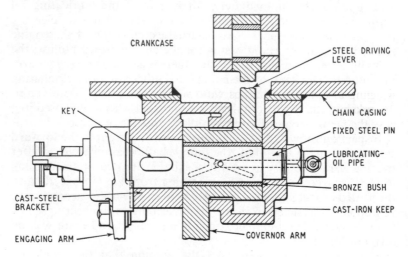

Figure 15.16 Governor gear

the bearing block became red hot and the engine speed was reduced from 104 to 90 rev/min. Oil, poured on to the block, cracked the cover. At 9.20 a.m. there was a heavy explosion, lifting five relief doors. The pressure must have been insignificant, as the large light crankcase doors remained flat.

The oil supply to the lever bush had failed; the gear components had become so hot that the pin had partly melted, as had the bush

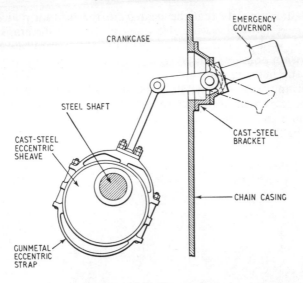

Figure 15.17 Governor gear

and the block. Pieces of metal, which had run out molten, were found.

This is an example of an insignificant component being the cause of a serious explosion which killed a man.

OTHER FORMS OF EXPLOSION

Explosions in diesel engines are normally associated with the crankcase and its adjuncts, including the chain-drive casings of engine-driven pumps and the casings of thrust blocks. But explosions are by no means unknown in scavenge belts and in high-pressure starting-air lines.

In these places, as in the crankcase, there are two prerequisites for the generation of an explosion, namely, an inflammable mixture and a hot spot. In the starting-air line the accumulation of lubricating oil from the cylinders over years of running provides the inflammable mixture; the flash-past of hot cylinder gases through a leaking or sticking valve in the air line provides the hot spot. Explosions in starting-air lines can be particularly violent. Periodical stripping, examination and cleaning of the pipes and fittings is the only certain method of obviating them.

Scavenging air belts, sometimes called entablatures, are more prone to fires than they are to explosions. These fires are most frequently of a mild nature, but sometimes they are serious and prove most difficult to overcome. There are on record instances of fires of such severity that the heat from the bottom plates of the scavenge belts—which were also the top plates of the crankcases—was responsible for raising the temperature of the crankcase contents to explosion point, with fatal results. There will be no scavenge-belt fires if the main pistons are maintained gas-tight, if there are no points in the cycle at which the exhaust-gas back pressure is greater than the scavenging air pressure, and if the scavenging belt is maintained in a clean condition. It is necessary that each scavenge belt should be fitted with a relief door.

Chapter 16

Anti-friction Metals

BEARING PROPERTIES

Anti-friction metals are used as sliding members in journal bearings, usually with a steel shaft as the other member. With proper lubrication and sufficient speed, the journal is lifted free of the bearing liner and floats in the bearing. The load is then transmitted via the lubricant, and the sliding properties of the bearing surface become of minor importance. However, to obtain a proper hydrodynamic lubrication, and to maintain it under heavy alternating loads, an interaction is required between the bearing surface, the lubricant and the surrounding atmosphere, to form adhesive lubrication films. Anti-frictional properties is the vague term applied to this requirement.

Depending upon the size and type of load, very different bearing materials are used, including wood, plastics and metals. Among the metals there is again a wide selection, mostly of alloys, based on tin, lead, copper, cadmium, silver, aluminium, zinc and iron. Tin and lead-based white metals, and copper alloys, are commonly used for bearings in ships' engines, the other metals having fewer marine applications.

Unfortunately, no testing method for bearing properties has been standardised, and the results obtained by different investigations are often not comparable. There is general agreement, however, that a good bearing metal should possess anti-frictional and *running-in* properties, being able to build up adhesive oil films under boundary lubrication conditions; also that it should not be liable to cause scoring of the steel journal, nor itself be corroded by lubricants and the deterioration products of lubricants. A certain fatigue strength is required, as well as a good capacity for carrying static loads. These

685

requirements are to a certain extent contradictory, but they can be met by combining soft and rigid metals in composite or lined bearings, the white-metal lined bearing being a good example of this.

Physical Requirements

The stress on a bearing is commonly expressed as the specific load or bearing pressure, i.e. the load per unit of projected bearing area in bar. The bearing area is simply taken as length × diameter irrespective of oil pockets, actual load distribution, etc. While the specific load thus is an imaginary figure it is used as a relative measure for comparison and for design considerations; and the maximum specific load is often used as a criterion of load capacity for bearing metals.

Another criterion is the product $P \times V$, which is assumed to be a materials constant. In this formula P is the specific load and V is the surface velocity of the journal.

Although it is general experience that high specific loads are permissible only with comparatively low speeds, and vice versa, nevertheless the product is not a true constant; its numerical value depends upon the bearing design.

For bearings with cyclic loads, fatigue life is the limiting factor. Fatigue strength can be measured as the maximum amplitude of stress sustained over a large number of cycles, usually 10 or 100 millions.

The remaining bearing properties cannot easily be measured and expressed in figures; even for those that can, the results depend much on the details of the design and the method of manufacture of the

COMPARISON OF BEARING METALS

Alloy type	Anti-frictional properties	Non-scoring quality	Fatigue strength	Corrosion resistance	Load capacity
Tin-base white-metal linings	Excellent	Excellent	Fair	Excellent	Low
Tin-base white-metal, very thin linings	Good	Excellent	Good	Excellent	Medium
Lead-base white-metal linings	Excellent	Excellent	Fair	Good	Low
Leaded tin bronze	Fair	Fair	Excellent	Good	High
Lead-bronze lined on steel	Good	Fair	Very good	Fair	Medium
Cadmium alloy linings	Excellent	Good	Good	Good	Low
Aluminium-tin alloy linings	Good	Excellent	Very good	Very good	Medium

investigated bearing. Strictly speaking, numerical values apply only to the specific bearing on which they have been measured. In the present state of knowledge, general experience must also be relied upon, and a rough comparison of anti-friction metals can be made as in the accompanying table. Variations within each group of alloys are not taken into account, except with regard to the lining thickness of tin-base white-metals.

WHITE-METALS

General Characteristics

The suitability of certain tin alloys as bearing materials was noted by Sir Isaac Babbitt, who, in 1839, patented a bearing lined with an alloy of approximately 89 per cent tin, 9 per cent antimony and 2 per cent copper. The terms *babbitt metal* and *white-metal* have later been extended to cover all the tin and lead alloys used for bearing linings A multitude of alloys have been marketed, mostly under trade names, to meet the requirements of various types of machinery. Thus, eight white-metal alloys are standardised in BS 3332:1961; similarly a range of tin and lead alloys are specified in American ASTM B23–66, German DIN 1703:1952 and several other national standards. In addition, almost all important engine manufacturers maintain their own standards for white metals. Accordingly, in spite of national standardisations, the alloy selection has remained very wide, often with only slight differences between related alloys.

White-metals are either tin alloys containing antimony, copper and sometimes lead, or lead alloys containing tin, antimony and usually some copper. Other elements, notably nickel, silver, cadmium and arsenic, are added in minor quantities to several of the alloys to impart improved mechanical strength or to be stabilisers against ageing.

Generally speaking, all these alloys have good anti-frictional properties, although not entirely independent of composition. Thus it has been found that lead contributes more than does tin to the ability of white metals to react with lubricants to form the base for hydrodynamic lubrication.

The white-metals as such are mechanically weak, particularly at elevated temperatures, but when thin layers are bonded to steel or bronze shells bearings are obtained with a much increased fatigue strength and load capacity. White-metals are able to accommodate a slight misalignment and to allow the embedding of small foreign particles carried in the oil, without scoring the shaft. In fact, the white-metal lined bearing is one of the best compromises regarding bearing properties, without turning to exotic and costly alternatives.

As with most alloys, white-metals melt and solidify over a temperature interval, called the melting or solidification range. At temperatures within the range the metal is in a pasty state, with some constituents molten and others solid; and this may lead to segregation of the alloying elements during the solidification of a casting. The lead-base white-metals are the most prone, and the high-tin alloys the least prone, to segregation. Hence the latter are easier to cast.

Alloy Groups

For convenience, the range of white-metals can be described according to their tin content. This will also usually determine their price.

One group of alloys contain about 90 per cent tin, alloyed with antimony and about half as much copper, but no lead. Some alloys contain nickel, silver and/or cadmium. With their low alloy content, they are comparatively soft and tough metals with a high fatigue strength. They represent developments of Babbitt's original alloy and they have a very wide field of application in America and England. In other countries their use has primarily been in small, quick-running engines, more particularly in automobile engines, small diesels and semi-diesels. This type of alloy is now being increasingly used also in the crosshead and top-end bearings of large diesels, thus making use of their high fatigue resistance.

Alloys with about 85 per cent tin, the remainder again being antimony and copper, are harder and have a higher capacity for static loads; but their fatigue strength is somewhat lower than that of the alloys mentioned above. They have been used widely for main propulsion diesel engine bearings, although they seem to be losing ground to the high-tin alloys with better fatigue properties and to the group of alloys with better wear resistance, as mentioned below

Notable for their load-carrying capacity and wear resistance is a group of alloys containing about 80 per cent tin and 20 per cent alloying constituents, namely antimony, copper and lead—in this order of decreasing content. Against this, they have a lower fatigue strength than any of the two first groups. In Continental practice their properties are utilised in almost all types of heavy machinery, including the largest diesel engines. Main bearings, bottom-end bearings, stern tubes and propeller shaft bearings are typical examples of application.

The presence of lead in tin alloys gives rise to the formation of a low-melting constituent, a so-called eutectic, in the metal. The tin–lead eutectic melts at 180°C, while the other constituents in white-metals do not begin to melt until about 225°C. This is sometimes considered a harmful effect of lead, making the metal more prone to *wiping*. But if a condition prevails that causes a serious increase in bearing temperature the metal must just begin to melt; therefore it is of little more than academic interest whether melting begins at 180°C or at 225°C. In fact, micro-melting will occur at surface points of contact whenever a bearing begins to move under load and without full lubrication. The low-melting eutectic phase then helps towards an easier polishing of the bearing surface and a better build-up of lubricant films.

White-metals in the range between 75 and 12 per cent tin have inferior mechanical properties and are therefore no longer used to any appreciable extent.

Lead alloys with 5–10 per cent tin are excellent anti-friction metals. They usually contain 10–15 per cent antimony and small amounts of copper, plus additions of arsenic, cadmium or other metals. The high-density lead forms the alloy matrix; the tin, antimony and copper constituents all tend to float upwards in melting and casting operations, when passing through the melting range. This tendency to segregate renders these alloys more difficult to cast; hence, in spite of their much lower price, the use of lead-base white-metals in propulsion machinery is largely restricted to bearings of secondary importance, such as camshaft bearings and the *unloaded* halves of primary bearings. When thoroughly cast in well-designed bearings the lead alloys do, however, compare favourably with high-tin alloys, and many small engines and auxiliary engines run entirely on lead base bearings.

Lead-base bearing metals without any tin are used in large numbers and include alkali-hardened lead alloys, but their role in marine diesel engines is unimportant.

The Design of Bearings

Depending on the type of load a bearing is intended to sustain, its design can vary greatly regarding thickness of layers, choice of materials, lubrication system, etc. The following remarks, however, apply to practically all designs.

A length/diameter ratio of 0·5–0·8 is preferred, to obtain an effective distribution of load without undue risk of edge overloading.

Thin-walled bearing shells require great accuracy in their fitting into the machine frame or bearing housing; but, from the point of view of casting, inspection, control and replacement, they are better than heavy shells or housings with direct linings.

Bearings with thin layers of white-metal have better mechanical properties than those having thick layers. The shell under thin linings, so to say, takes over more of the stresses, provided that the lining is perfectly bonded. There is a marked improvement in fatigue life, and also in static load-carrying capacity, with decreasing white-metal thickness. The proper thickness of the lining is related to journal diameter d, and, in all primary bearings of internal-combustion engines, should be held below $t_{max.} = 0.25 + 0.005d$, measured in mm. In secondary bearings without sudden load variations the lining may be twice the above thickness, or even thicker, for ease of alignment or other reasons. Many existing bearings have thicker white-metal linings than indicated here. This does not mean that they are all faulty, but only that they do not have full load-carrying capacity and fatigue strength.

A clearance is required between the journal and the bearing, to allow the lubricant to be carried around the bearing by hydro-dynamic action. A large clearance will increase the oil flow through the bearing and thus improve cooling by the lubricant. However, a large clearance can allow the shaft to move in an uncontrolled way in the bearing, to cause hammering and subsequent fatigue cracking of the white-metal. With tin-base white-metals the oil clearance is usually held at, or below, 0·1 per cent of the diameter. Lead-base bearings are made with a slightly higher clearance, to allow for their greater thermal expansion at working temperatures.

There is no absolute maximum for the specific load on a white-metal bearing, but for bearings with cyclic stresses—which means most bearings in diesel engines—70 bar is a reasonable limit. Maximum pressures up to 100 bar are sometimes seen, but this can reduce the fatigue life of the bearing. Bearings with constant loads, for instance turbine bearings, can carry much higher loads, say up to 175 bar, because fatigue strength is not a limiting factor. White-metalled bearings, with extremely thin linings, have been successfully operated under much higher loads, in special instances.

Choice of Alloy

The choice of a white-metal alloy for any given bearing is restricted by several design factors, e.g. engine speed and thickness of lining. Referring to the groups of alloys described previously, the mention of, say, 90 per cent metal as being suitable for a type of bearing does not mean that the metal has to contain 90 per cent of tin, but that the group of alloys with about 90 per cent of tin are recommendable, although other types of white metal may be applied in certain circumstances.

High- and medium-speed engines running at more than about

400 rev/min are most often designed with 90 per cent metal in all bearings, for maximum fatigue strength. White-metal thicknesses should be made low, certainly less than 2 mm, to avoid squeezing of the soft metal. Using very thin linings, and with careful manufacture, lead-base metal can also be used throughout. Reduction gears for high-speed engines need more wear resistance than fatigue strength, and can thus run on bearings with 80 per cent metal. The linings can be made thicker.

Most low-speed main propulsion engines run on 80 or 85 per cent metals in all primary, or load-carrying, bearings. Thin linings should again be preferred, but not below 1·5 mm or 2 mm, to retain some plasticity of the bearings. In high-rated, supercharged engines the crosshead bearings tend to become overloaded because of their limited size and show reduced fatigue life. Accordingly, 90 per cent metal is then used, normally with a reduced thickness of lining. The same may be the procedure with bottom-end bearings and with eccentric straps in opposed-piston engines. The harder 80 per cent metal is usually retained for main bearings and guide shoes because of its excellent wearing properties. Secondary bearings such as those for camshafts are regularly designed with lead-base metal; and this may also be used for the unloaded halves of primary bearings. For such applications, there are no strict limitations on lining thickness.

Bonding Principles

Mechanical anchoring, or dovetailing, is still used to some extent in diesel-engine bearings. One of its purposes is to hold the pieces of white-metal in position in event of cracking. However, dovetails cause local variations in white-metal thickness, and this can give rise to fatigue cracking. The white-metal is compressed slightly under load, and the deeper metal in the dovetails is compressed more than the shallow layer between them. In early stages of fatigue failure cracks are often seen to follow the edges of the dovetails.

When dovetails are used they should be kept·away from the pressure-centre and their depth should be held below 50 per cent of the lining thickness. The latter requirement practically rules out dovetails from bearings with thin layers of white-metal. The edges of dovetails should be rounded to avoid notch effects on the white-metal, this being a rule that is often overlooked.

Bonding by tinning makes the bearing a bimetallic composition and ensures much better load distribution between the white-metal and the shell; it also makes for better heat dissipation through the bearing. The overall result is improvement both in mechanical strength and fatigue life.

Mild, i.e. unalloyed, steel whether cast or wrought provides the strongest tinning. It is followed by tin bronzes, gunmetals and phosphor-bronzes. Cast-iron, unless specially treated, also brass and aluminium bronze, are less suitable for tinning. Steel shells must be fitted exactly into rigid housings, to avoid deflections in unsupported areas; bronze shells, however, are able to adapt themselves to minor irregularities.

Some impurities and alloying elements in bearing-shell materials are known to reduce tinning strength, or solderability. Thus, high lead and zinc, and even small amounts of aluminium in copper alloys, give rise to poor tinning; and the same is true with silicon and manganese in steel and cast iron. The graphite flakes, or nodules, in cast iron tend to break the tinning layer; hence the graphite must be wholly or largely removed from the surface, either electrolytically or in a molten salt bath, before a proper tinning can be made. Sometimes steel castings and forgings contain hydrogen that causes *de-wetting* when a tinning layer is applied. In such instances a heat treatment is required to de-gas the surface to be tinned.

Tinning

The tinning of bearing shells involves a number of steps, as is schematically indicated in Figure 16.1.

This is a flow diagram showing the manufacture of white-metalled bearings, including tinning with a tinning compound. If hot-dip tinning is used the operations marked with an asterisk are replaced by fluxing and tin-bath dipping. Across the diagram, operations should be carried out at the same time. It is important that the white-metal is molten and the casting apparatus pre-heated at the moment the bearing shell is ready for tinning.

The final boring of the bearing shell is preferably done without cutting oil. The surface can be rather rough, but without sharp ridges between cuts. Even after dry machining, it is good practice to de-grease bearing shells just prior to tinning, especially if the machined shells have been stored for some time.

Bronze shells can be tinned without further preparation. The same is true of steel and cast iron, but pickling in acid solutions or the use of strong soldering fluxes will increase the bond strength, particularly on cast iron, by removing a thin surface layer with its possible contamination. Pickling must be followed by a thorough rinsing, using plenty of water to remove all acid. Cast iron requires further treatment, if the graphite flakes are to be removed for perfect tinning. Certain electrolytic processes can transform the surface layer to pure iron, and molten chloride and nitride mixtures can attack and dis-

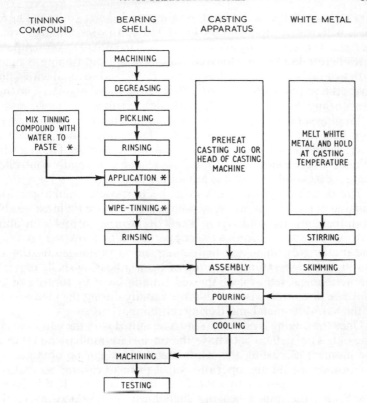

TINNING
COMPOUND

BEARING
SHELL

CASTING
APPARATUS

WHITE METAL

MACHINING

DEGREASING

PICKLING

MIX TINNING
COMPOUND WITH
WATER TO
PASTE ✳

RINSING

APPLICATION ✳

WIPE-TINNING ✳

RINSING

PREHEAT
CASTING JIG OR
HEAD OF CASTING
MACHINE

MELT WHITE
METAL AND HOLD
AT CASTING
TEMPERATURE

STIRRING

ASSEMBLY

SKIMMING

POURING

COOLING

MACHINING

TESTING

Figure 16.1 Flow diagram for white-metalling bearings

solve the graphite. Copper plating is less useful, because thin layers
tend to be discontinuous over graphite flakes, while thick layers have
low internal strength.

The tinning is always carried out with molten tin, either by dipping
in a flux bath followed by a tin bath, or by *wipe tinning* with ready-
made mixtures of tin powder and flux. The tinning compound is
applied on all surfaces to be tinned, and the shell is heated in an oven
or with burners, until the flux and the tin melt and can be worked
into the surface with a steel brush (wiping). The tinning is controlled
as it is being made and more tinning powder can be added as required.
Finally, all flux residues are removed with clean water, without
cooling the shell so much that the tinning solidifies.

Tinning temperatures depend on the shell materials. Bronze
bearings should be tinned at a maximum of 270°C, avoiding
extended dipping or heating time. Mild steel can be tinned at about

300°C, while 350°C is required for alloy steels and cast iron. The tin layer will oxidise rapidly in the air at 350°C. In wipe-tinning, oxidation can be prevented by allowing the shell to cool to lower temperatures before the flux is removed. The best hot-dip tinning is made with two tin baths. One bath is held at 350°C and covered with a flux layer; the second bath, at about 280°C, is skimmed regularly, so that the bearings emerge with a clean, fluxless tinning.

Tinning with pure tin prevents any contamination of white-metals with lead from the tinning layer. Tin–lead alloys (solders) melt at lower temperatures and have less tendency to oxidise. Tinning with solder is thus easier to control, but it must be so carefully controlled that no excess solder metal is left on the bearing.

The described procedure serves the purpose of making a true metallic bond. That is, at every point of the surface tin must be able to diffuse into the underlying steel, or bronze, to make an alloy transition layer. On bronzes the copper–tin alloy forms very readily, and it may grow thick and brittle in event of prolonged heating or too high a temperature. Relining of bronze bearing shells requires the mechanical removal of the old tinning layer by turning or by shot-blasting; otherwise it will grow rapidly during the melting-out of the old white-metal and during retinning.

Once the tinning is perfect, it must be united with the white-metal. The only safe method is to have the tin surface molten and clean at the moment of casting the white-metal. This can be obtained by performing the tinning operations just prior to casting, so that the tinning is not allowed to solidify in the meantime. If this is not practicable the tinned bearing shell must be reheated above the melting point of the tin, and it will usually be necessary to refresh the tinning by means of tinning powder, or flux, to remove oxides and other contamination. It is valuable to check the quality of the bond, but this can only be done after lining.

Casting White-metal

The white-metal linings of diesel-engine bearings are almost always cast. The low temperatures involved, below 500°C, allow the casting of white-metals to be carried out by several different methods. A few basic rules apply in all instances, as indicated below.

1. The shell must be preheated, and its tinning layer must be clean, non-oxidised and molten.
2. The white-metal is held at casting temperature, or near 400°C for most alloys. It is stirred, skimmed and then poured in one operation for each bearing or shell.

3. The metal is brought to solidify *directionally*, from the tinning towards the opposite surface.

4. The metal is brought to solidify *quickly*.

Most of these rules require no further explanation, but the importance of correct solidification should be stressed. Directional solidification prevents the metal from shrinking away from the tinning layer as it cools. Rapid solidification gives a stronger bond and fine-grained metal with better mechanical properties, including fatigue strength, and with improved lubrication ability. It also counteracts segregation. The low solidification rate obtained in sand moulds, or with sand cores, is not permissible for bearing linings. Only metallic (steel) moulds, cores and fixtures are allowable, and if at all possible water cooling should be applied during solidification. This forced cooling is discontinued as soon as the metal has solidified completely, to obviate undue stresses from the differential contraction of white metal and backing.

Casting moulds consist of the bearing shell(s), one or two end plates and a core (except in centrifugal casting). The parts must be easy to assemble and tighten, and they must all be preheated to prevent chilling of the tinning. Machined surfaces of contact require little or no tightening when assembled with spanners or by hydraulic means; otherwise asbestos sheets are useful as gaskets, or various tightening pastes based on asbestos can be applied.

Gravity die-casting requires little equipment; it is used for small-scale production and for off-size bearings. It is recommendable to cast only one half-shell at a time, preferably with its axis in a vertical position, for proper control of the solidification. The other parts of the mould are a base-plate, a core plate and an extra ring to form a feeding head on top of the bearing shell. An additional thickness of 2–3 mm, or more, is allowed for machining the bearing surface.

In gravity die-casting solidification must be directional in two ways: i.e. inwards from the tinning and upwards from the bottom. If the metal is allowed to solidify first in the upper regions its solidification shrinkage will leave cavities or porosity in the lower parts; accordingly, the water cooling should be directed towards the back of the shell, beginning at the bottom and moving upwards as the metal solidifies. This is shown in Figure 16.2, a sectional view of a gravity die-casting rig. Cooling is applied on the back of the bearing shell, but if it is not properly directed as in Figure 16.2(a) the upper part of the white-metal may solidify first, leaving shrinkage porosity in the lower regions. In Figure 16.2(b), forced cooling starts at the bottom, moving upwards with solidification, and shrinkage occurs only in the feeding head. The course of solidification can be followed with a *puddling rod* moved slowly up and down through the still molten metal. Puddling also aids the escape of air bubbles from the mould. The feeding head serves as a reservoir for replenishment of shrinkages, and it may be necessary to heat it gently or to add more hot metal.

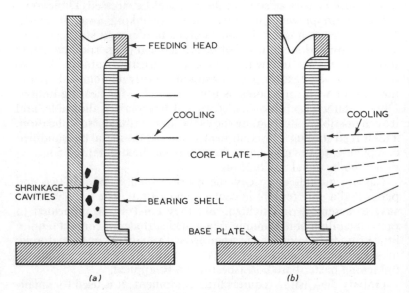

Figure 16.2 Gravity die-casting

Pressure die-casting is similar to gravity die-casting in principle, but instead of being poured through a feeding head, the metal is injected into the mould under pressure and is held under pressure during solidification. The machining allowance can be as low as 1–2 mm. A pressure die-casting machine for bearings is rather complex, and the method is not much used.

In centrifugal casting the bearing, or two half-shells, is rotated about its axis during the pouring and solidification of the white-metal. No core is needed, and the bearing is fixed between two end-plates, one of them being provided with an opening through which the metal can be poured. There is no feeding head, but some shrink-age porosity will appear on the inner surface, which will have to be machined away to a depth of at least 3 mm. A water jet directed towards the outside of the rotating bearing will ensure the desirable rapid and directional solidification. A disadvantage of the process is that the centrifugal force increases the tendency of white-metals to segregate, but this is easily overcome by forced cooling as described. Centrifugal casting is being used increasingly, not least because it is relatively independent of the operator, and because it is well suited for the present-day thin-walled type of bearing shells.

Bearings can also be lined by a welding or soldering technique, using white-metal in sticks or bars. The shell is held horizontally between two end-plates, and a section is filled with white-metal to the requisite depth by means of a torch or a hot soldering iron. When the first section has solidified the shell is turned 30–40° about its axis, and an adjoining section is filled, the two sections being carefully welded together. This method requires special skill to avoid oxide inclusions and to ensure a uniform structure throughout the lining; but it can be used for emergency repairs.

The soldering technique is also used to repair minor surface defects in cast white-metal layers prior to final machining. With large or widespread defects the metal must be metled out, and the bearing must be relined.

Finishing and Fitting

White-metal bearings are finished by dry machining, the last cut being thin to avoid deformation of the soft metal. Grinding or polishing of the surface is not desirable, as it will passivate the metal. The edges of the bearing and of oil grooves must be rounded carefully, so that they cannot break the oil film.

Oil grooves, mostly in the shape of pockets at the horns, supply the bearing surface with lubricant. As a rule, they do not extend to the edges, and they are kept away from the pressure-centre, where they would reduce the effective bearing surface, and where they would act as drainage channels. Notable exceptions are crosshead and other bearings which have an oscillating movement. In these the hydrodynamic action cannot build up a full oil wedge, and it is therefore necessary to have oil supplies at short intervals over the active surface. Accordingly, oil grooves are usually placed lengthwise and spaced at intervals corresponding to the amplitude of the movement, or a little closer. The longitudinal grooves are fed through circumferential, preferably helical, oil grooves. Here also, the grooves do not extend to the edge of the bearing.

Thin-walled bearing shells require careful fitting into housings, particularly with shells of steel. These must be well supported in all areas, otherwise elastic deformation under load can lead to fatigue cracking of the white-metal over unsupported areas. After the assembly of a bearing the white-metal surface may show minor deviations from the true cylindrical shape. Adjustment is then made by hand scraping.

Testing Methods

The best non-destructive test is made ultrasonically, scanning the white-metal surface in the finished bearing. Use is made of the fact that the ultrasonic waves will be reflected from the white-metal/shell interface in areas with defect bonding, while they will pass through a good bond, being then reflected from the back of the shell.

With many engine builders the introduction of ultrasonic testing has practically eliminated bonding failures from their bearings. *Ringing* a bearing with light hammer strokes to observe the different *ring* from bonded and non-bonded areas is somewhat similar to ultrasonic testing, but is far less sensitive. Other test methods are destructive, such as measuring the tensile strength or shear strength of cut-out samples, and chiselling the white metal out of a shell. Such methods are primarily used when inspecting bearings which have failed.

Lubrication

Engine lubricants are invariably based on mineral oils; but all pro-prietary lubricants contain additives, such as anti-oxidants or neutralisers. The former type would delay the unavoidable oxidation of the base oil in closed systems, while the latter would neutralise the acids formed when the hydrocarbons are oxidised. Some lubricants contain emulsifiers, for holding contaminants like water emulsified in the body of the oil.

The selection of lubricants may need a consultation with the oil suppliers. It should be noted that a lubricant should not be more heavily *doped* than is required for the specific machine and operation. Too much anti-oxidation can increase bearing wear, because the chemical interaction between white-metal and oil is withheld, delay-ing the generation of protective oil films.

If water is present in the oil, neutralisers can react to form water-soluble salts that may cause corrosion in bearings. On shipboard salt water is a natural oil contaminant; but, with modern oil centrifuges and sometimes by washing the oil with fresh water to dilute the salt water and thus reduce the danger of corrosion, much can be done to keep it away from the engine bearings.

Some solid lubricants are available that can be applied to bearing surfaces, or carried in the oil, to prevent serious bearing failure in event of momentary breaks in the oil supply. Examples are graphite, molybdenum disulphide and polytetrafluoroethylene (Teflon). Solid lubricants are very seldom used in marine engines, except as self-lubricating bushings with Teflon impregnated surfaces.

Bearing Failures

If not found by routine inspection, the first sign of a bearing failure is either a temperature rise or an emitted noise. Typical failures are described below.

Faulty Casting. Inspection will cause it to be noted that faulty casting is a possible cause of many failures. However, after prolonged running it can be very difficult to determine the original defect, because of subsequent cracking or melting of the white-metal surface.

Wiping. If, for some reason, the white-metal surface is heated abnormally the metal will begin to soften or melt, and it can then be moved over the surface by the rotating journal. This is called wiping. It is usually not a primary cause of failure, but appears as a result of other defects, such as squeezing, or fatigue cracking, or bonding failure. Wiping may also indicate inadequate lubrication. External overheating of a bearing can lead to wiping.

Squeezing. This shows that the white-metal has been loaded beyond its compression strength. There is no cracking of the surface, but the metal is pressed out over the edges and into the oil grooves. Squeezing is caused by too soft metal, or faulty alloy selection, or coarse-grained casting. With the same metal, thick linings are softer than thin linings.

Fatigue Cracking. Beginning as tiny cracks in the bearing surface, the cracks eventually extend in all directions—preferably along the edges of dovetails—finally dividing large areas of the metal into small islands. The cracks also extend downwards into the metal, but usually they bend just over the tinning layer and proceed along the bond. After some time most of the white-metal may bear the appearance of a jigsaw puzzle. If all parts are retained in position the bearing can continue to function for a considerable time, although not at full load.

Fatigue can arise only in bearings with alternating stresses, either as repeated loading/unloading or as cyclic fluctuations between high and low loads. Failure by fatigue will usually take a long time to develop. Most of the possible causes have been referred to earlier, but are here mentioned again. An oval shaft can give load variations for each revolution; careless fitting of the shell can cause undue deflections under load; dovetailing in the pressure-centre reduces the fatigue strength of a bearing, as does excessive lining thickness. The white-metal will have low fatigue strength if coarse-grained or segregated, or contaminated with lead or oxide inclusions. Some alloys have a reduced fatigue strength, particularly tin-base metals with high antimony content and with lead present.

Bonding Failures. Examination shows that the white-metal is loose from the shell in large areas, as distinct from fatigue cracking, wherein the metal is broken up into small fractions, usually with the tinning intact underneath. Once the bonding has failed the lining will be unsupported; local heating and wiping, or fatigue cracking, may then develop. Typical causes of bonding failure are: brittle tinning on bronze shells; pickling acid left on the shell, where it may later attack the tinning; oxidised or chilled tinning that has not united properly with the white-metal; unsuitable shell material that cannot be tinned perfectly; too rapid cooling of the bearing after solidification of the white-metal, which can cause the metal to break the bond at the horns by its contraction.

White-metal Corrosion. This is a rare occurrence, because of the high corrosion resistance of tin and lead alloys. The metal surface first turns grey, or brownish, instead of being gradually polished in service. Eventually a very hard black, or brown, scale may form on the surface, or the attack may penetrate into the metal, thus forming corrosion pitting. The scale may become hard enough to damage the steel journal; but most often it develops so slowly that no harm is done before the bearing is inspected. Bearing corrosion is not yet fully understood but, apparently, several adverse conditions have to prevail simultaneously to cause the phenomenon. Such conditions are: salt water and/or air bubbles in the lubricant; high acidity of the oil; increase of temperature under defective lubrication; electric tension over the bearing, caused by static electricity being generated in high-speed components (superchargers) and *earthed* via the bearings, or due to the potential difference between dissimilar metals in contact with each other.

COPPER-BASE BEARING METALS

General Characteristics

When bearing loads exceed the limits for white-metals copper alloys (bronzes) can be used as bearing materials. Bronze bearings do not possess the anti-frictional properties of white-metals, but their fatigue strength and their load capacity are high. Owing to their hardness, they cannot adjust themselves to any misalignment; nor can they accept embedded foreign particles as can the white-metals; moreover, hardened journals are usually required to prevent scoring.

Solid bronze bearings are manufactured by casting or by sintering from powder. In either case a number of alloys are available, as covered by the British Standard BS 1400:1969, the American ASTN B30–59, the German DIN 17656:1963 and several others. There is a special American standard for sintered bearings, ASTM

B438–66T. Sintered bearings can be made porous, and the pores impregnated with lubricant, to make self-lubricating bearings. Because of their porosity, they have less active bearing surface, but they need no external lubrication nor maintenance, until the oil supply is exhausted.

On shipboard, bronze bushes and bearings are used with low speeds and high static loads, where friction and wear are of minor importance. Also, some high-speed diesel engines run on bronze-lined bearings, consisting of steel shells with a thin layer of lead bronze on top.

Most copper alloys used for bearings contain considerable amounts of tin or lead, or both, because these metals impart excellent anti-frictional properties to the alloy. Other common constituents are nickel in leaded alloys, and phosphorus in tin bronzes. Some tin- and lead-free alloys are used in bearings for special purposes. Reference will only be made here to aluminium bronze, which is used in bearings and other machine parts where very high wear resistance and excellent corrosion resistance are required.

Bronzes

Tin bronzes, with 10–16 per cent tin, are long established as bearing metals. With increasing tin content they become harder and more wear resistant, and the addition of 0·5–2·0 per cent of phosphorus increases their durability and hardness. The 14 and 16 per cent bronzes are rather expensive and tend to be brittle, and the 10 and 12 per cent bronzes are usually preferred.

It has been found that lead adds extra anti-frictional properties to bronzes, as in white-metals. Roughly half the tin, but all the lead, goes to form a good bearing surface. This is because lead does not dissolve in copper but forms small globules in the structure, while tin is partly soluble and hardens the copper base. A range of leaded tin bronzes are cast into bearings, extending from 80 per cent copper alloy with 10 per cent each of tin and lead and similar alloys to high-lead bronzes with up to 30 per cent lead and only about 5 per cent tin. The undissolved lead tends to segregate out of the metal during casting, and the high-lead bronzes are difficult to cast. Nickel is a useful addition, bringing about a more fine-grained solidification with improved dispersion of the lead particles. Specific loads up to about 700 bar can be carried by leaded tin bronze bearings.

True lead bronzes, i.e. alloys of only copper and lead (again with nickel additions) are rarely sand cast, for the reasons already mentioned. Under the names of copper–lead and metal rosé they are used as sintered or continuously cast linings on steel bearing shells.

Excellent anti-friction properties are derived from 30 per cent or 40 per cent lead in the alloy, while the body of the bronze has the toughness and heat conductivity of copper. It is very important that the lead is finely distributed in the alloy, both for its bearing qualities and for corrosion resistance. Copper-lead bearings can fail by rapid corrosion attack, because of galvanic action between copper and lead particles, combined with some acidity of the lubricant. The maximum load is usually held below 300 bar.

Gunmetals

Gunmetals are alloys of copper, tin and zinc, formerly used for casting cannon. With lead additions they become suitable as bearing materials and are called leaded gunmetals (the U.S. term is leaded red brass); they are quite often misnamed bronzes. As with bronzes, high tin and lead improve bearing properties, while zinc is held at or below 5 per cent. Leaded gunmetals are cheaper than bronzes, and are much easier to cast, owing to the presence of zinc. Besides being used in bronze shells for lining with white-metal, they constitute the major part of all bronze bushings used, either cast to the desired shape or manufactured from centrifugally cast or continuously cast material.

Continuous casting has made gunmetals available with a very uniform and dense structure, and with properties comparable to those of some of the more costly tin bronzes. A leaded gun metal with 85 per cent copper and 5 per cent of each of the three metals tin, lead and zinc is in common use practically all over the world; it is designated '85–5–5–5', 'three fives' or 'ounce metal'. For improved wear resistance and bearing properties, other gunmetals contain 7–10 per cent tin, up to 7 per cent lead and down to 2 or 3 per cent zinc. Nickel alloyed gunmetals are also available with improved grain-structure.

OTHER ANTI-FRICTION METALS

Innumerable metals and alloys have been tried as bearing metals. Many have been patented and marketed, and most of them have again disappeared. A few types have remained of importance and should be mentioned, although they have little marine usage.

Cadmium alloys have better fatigue strength than tin and lead-base white-metals, but they are slightly inferior in other respects. Their load capacity is nearly the same.

Silver bearings with thin platings of lead and/or indium are used for high-speed bearings where heat removal is a primary requirement.

Aluminium-tin alloys with 6–7 per cent tin have high load capacity, but their anti-frictional behaviour is inferior to white-metals. The introduction of alloys with about 20 per cent tin, rolled and heat-treated to obtain a so-called reticular tin structure, is a recent development. Supported on steel shells, reticular aluminium–tin shows good anti-frictional and mechanical properties.

Aluminium–zinc alloys of various compositions are sometimes called *white bronze* and are occasionally used for bushes in replacement of gunmetal.

Cast iron can also be used as an anti-friction metal in bearings with low speeds and low specific loads. Pearlitic iron is preferred, and the bearings must be well lubricated.

N.G.

Chapter 17

Chemistry of Combustion

Table 17.1 provides a list of the symbols designating the atoms and molecules of the elements and compounds composing liquid fuels; the atomic weights are given, and the suffix denotes the number of atoms accepted as constituting one molecule of the substance.

Table 17.1 ELEMENTS AND COMPOUNDS IN LIQUID FUELS AND PRODUCTS OF COMBUSTION

Name	Nature	Atomic symbol	Atomic weight	Molecular symbol	Molecular weight
Carbon	Element	C	12·00	C	12·00
Hydrogen	Element	H	1·008	H_2	2·016
Oxygen	Element	O	16·00	O_2	32·00
Nitrogen	Element	N	14·01	N_2	28·02
Sulphur	Element	S	32·07	S_2	64·14
Carbon monoxide	Compound	—	—	CO	28
Carbon dioxide	Compound	—	—	CO_2	44
Sulphur dioxide	Compound	—	—	SO_2	64·07
Sulphur trioxide	Compound	—	—	SO_3	80·07
Sulphurous acid	Compound	—	—	H_2SO_3	82·086
Sulphuric acid	Compound	—	—	H_2SO_4	98·086
Water	Compound	—	—	H_2O	18·016

Tables 17.2, 17.3 and 17.4 summarise chemical changes during combustion. Nitrogen compounds are ignored. Quantitatively, sulphur is negligible in its heating effects.

The weight of oxygen needed is evaluated, from the appropriate equation, for every element in the fuel, and the results are added together. The atmosphere may be assumed to contain 23·15 per cent of oxygen by weight and 20·96 per cent by volume. At standard atmospheric pressure 1 kg of air occupies a volume of 0·83 m³ at 20°C and 0·77 m³ at 0°C.

704

To convert the kcal/kg values of the metric technical system, as stated on Table 17.4, to the SI code:

$$1 \text{ kcal/kg} = 4{\cdot}187 \text{ kilojoules/kg.}$$

Example: Express a fuel calorific value of 10 500 kcal/kg in SI units

$$10\,500 \text{ kcal/kg} = 10\,500 \times 4{\cdot}187 \text{ kJ/kg} = 44\,000 \text{ kJ/kg}$$
$$= 44 \text{ MJ/kg.}$$

Calorific Value of Fuel

If the calorific value of a fuel cannot be determined by calorimeter, but the proximate analysis is available, then the theoretical value can

Table 17.2 COMBUSTION EQUATIONS

Nature of reaction	Equation	Gravimetric meaning
Carbon burned to carbon dioxide	$C + O_2 = CO_2$	12 kg C + 32 kg O = 44 kg CO_2
Carbon burned to carbon monoxide	$2C + O_2 = 2(CO)$	24 kg C + 32 kg O = 56 kg CO
Carbon monoxide burned to carbon dioxide	$2(CO) + O_2 = 2(CO_2)$	56 kg CO + 32 kg O = 88 kg CO_2
Hydrogen oxidised to steam	$2H_2 + O_2 = 2(H_2O)$	4 kg H + 32 kg O = 36 kg steam (or water)
Sulphur burned to sulphur dioxide	$S_2 + 2O_2 = 2(SO_2)$	64 kg S + 64 kg O = 128 kg SO_2
Sulphur dioxide burned to sulphurous acid	$SO_2 + H_2O = H_2SO_3$	64 kg SO_2 + 18 kg H_2O = 82 kg H_2SO_3
Sulphur dioxide burned to sulphur trioxide	$O_2 + 2(SO_2) = 2(SO_3)$	32 kg O + 128 kg SO_2 = 160 kg SO_3
Sulphur trioxide and water to form sulphuric acid	$SO_3 + H_2O = H_2SO_4$	80 kg SO_3 = 18 kg H_2O = 98 kg H_2SO_4

Table 17.3 VOLUMETRIC MEANING OF EQUATIONS

Nature of reaction	Volumetric result
Carbon burned to carbon dioxide	1 vol C + 1 vol O = 1 vol CO_2
Carbon burned to carbon monoxide	2 vols C + 1 vol O = 2 vols CO
Carbon monoxide burned to carbon dioxide	2 vols CO + 1 vol O = 2 vols CO_2
Hydrogen oxidised to steam	2 vols H + 1 vol O = 2 vols H_2O (steam not water)
Sulphur burned to sulphur dioxide	1 vol S + 2 vols O = 2 vols SO_2
Sulphur dioxide burned to sulphurous acid	—
Sulphur dioxide burned to sulphur trioxide	—
Sulphur trioxide and water to form sulphuric acid	—

Table 17.4 HEAT EVOLVED BY COMBUSTION

Nature of reaction	Thermo-chemical equation	Heat evolved per kg of element burned kcal/kg
Carbon burned to carbon dioxide	$C + O_2 = CO_2 + 96\,900$	8 080
Carbon burned to carbon monoxide	$2C + O_2 = 2(CO) + 58\,900$	2 450
Carbon monoxide burned to carbon dioxide	$2(CO) + O_2 = 2(CO_2) + 315\,000$	5 630 (per kg CO burned)
Hydrogen oxidised to steam	$2H_2 + O_2 = 2(H_2O) + 136\,000$	33 900 (a) 29 000 (b)
Sulphur burned to sulphur dioxide	$S_2 + 2O_2 = 2(SO_2) + 144\,000$	2 260
Sulphur dioxide burned to sulphurous acid	—	—
Sulphur dioxide burned to sulphur trioxide	—	—
Sulphur trioxide and water to form sulphuric acid	—	—

Note. (a) Value if the latent heat of the steam formed is to be *included*.
(b) Value if the latent heat of the steam formed is to be *excluded*.

be calculated. The value thus obtained always differs from the actual experimental value, but the discrepancy may not be high. The reasons for the difference need not be pursued here.

Calorific value in k cal/kg of fuel

$$= \frac{8100C + 34\,000\left(H - \frac{O}{8}\right)}{100}$$

where C, H, O are *percentages* of these elements in one kilogram of fuel. Carbon yields 8080 k cal/kg when completely burned, hydrogen 34 000; the oxygen is assumed to be already attached to its proportion of hydrogen—i.e. an amount of hydrogen equal to one-eighth the weight of the oxygen is nullified. The sulphur compounds are assumed to have their combustion heat nullified by the oxy-nitrogen ones.

Numerous variations of this formula are extant, thus:

Calorific value in k cal/kg of fuel

$$= 7500C + 33\,800\left(H - \frac{O}{8}\right)$$

C, H, O being fractions of a kilogram per kilogram of fuel.

The calorific value, as determined by bomb calorimeter, is the *gross* value—i.e. it includes the latent heat of the water vapour

The viscosity of fuel oil decreases rapidly with increase of temperature. Accordingly, it is customary to record viscosities at 20°, 40° and 80°C. The viscosity at 40°C (Redwood No. 1 viscometer) is commonly accepted as a standard of comparison and indicative of general viscidity.

The variation of viscosity with temperature for boiler-quality oil is as follows:

Temp., °C	=95	80	65	50	40
Viscosity	=80	160	300	650	1350

A similar comparison, for typical diesel fuels, shows:

Temp., °C	=65	50	40	25	10
Viscosity	=33–37	37–45	45–60	55–90	70–140

As a guide to the viscosity limit for fuels without pre-heating, the following comparison is given:

. . Temp., °C	=95	80	65	50	40	25
Viscosity	=45	60	100	175	300	550

For medium-sized engines running at, say, 500 rev/min, viscosities up to 100 sec may not cause any difficulties. In large, slow-running engines fuels having viscosities up to 1250 sec at 40°C may be dealt with by heating to, say, 80°C, thereby reducing the viscosity to about 150 sec at the filters, purifiers and pumps. A substantial change in fuel viscosity may necessitate a modification to fuel-valve nozzles, for ensuring satisfactory combustion.

An engine, when run on fuels of different calorific values, but all suitable for the revolutions, may show either constant consumption or consumptions which vary less than the proportionate differences in calorific values. The explanation lies probably in the differences in viscosity. A higher viscosity tends to advance the ignition by reducing the fuel-pump leakage; but fuels of rather high viscosity are, not infrequently, rather low in calorific value. Other things being equal, the fuel consumption can be expected to be inversely proportional to the calorific value, but much depends upon ignition quality; sometimes the result may be contrary to expectations and the apparent evidence.

Coke Value

The Conradson method of measuring coke values requires a special apparatus for determining the percentage of carbon residue remaining after evaporation of the fuel in a closed space under control. The coke value is a measure of carbon-forming propensity and an indication of tendency to deposit carbon on fuel-injection nozzles.

The Conradson method has recently been replaced, to a large extent, by the Ramsbottom method of carbon residue determination. This method gives roughly the same results as the Conradson, but has the advantage that the conditions in which the evaporation takes place can be more readily standardised.

Sulphur Content

Sulphur content has no influence on combustion; but, on burning, sulphur forms sulphur dioxide, with perhaps a proportion of trioxide. If the temperature falls below dew-point sulphur acids are formed by the oxides dissolving in the water which becomes available from the combustion of the hydrogen in the fuel. Corrosion is therefore liable to occur in exhaust pipes, exhaust blowers, silencers and similar places, when cold. Corrosion is also possible in combustion spaces, under low jacket temperatures. To what extent sulphur is responsible for liner wear is a matter on which opinions differ.

Ash

The ash content, which is a measure of the inorganic impurities present in the fuel, usually consists of sand and sundry metallic oxides, of which vanadium is the most important. On ignition of the fuel, the vanadium pentoxide in the ash is deposited on surrounding surfaces; here it has a profound effect, as a corrosive agent, at temperatures above 690°C. When sodium is also present in the ash, as is not uncommon in fuels of boiler quality, it combines with the vanadium pentoxide and forms a compound, the melting point of which is about 630°C. This compound, when molten, penetrates into and destroys the natural protective film of the metals in contact with same, and thereby leaves them prone to high-temperature oxidisation and wastage.

One well-known diesel-engine manufacturer limits the vanadium content in residual fuel oil to a maximum of 125 parts per million of vanadium pentoxide.

Chapter 18

Conversion Factors

SECTION I. IMPERIAL/METRIC UNITS

Because of its continued general usefulness, the following section has been retained for reference, exactly as printed in earlier editions of the book. A further section has been added to serve as an introduction to the SI system.

Marine diesel engines are sometimes built and operated on the basis of British measures, sometimes in accordance with the metric system, sometimes on the basis of a mixture of both systems. Conversion factors are therefore in frequent demand. Accordingly, the more commonly used factors are codified below.

Power

horse-power (metric) $\times$ 0·9863 = horse-power (British)
horse-power (British) $\times$ 1·0139 = horse-power (metric)

Fuel Consumption

grams per horse-power (metric) $\times$ 0·00224 = lb per horse-power hour (British)
lb per horse-power hour (British) $\times$ 447·3 = grams per horse-power hour (metric)

Calorific Value

kilogram calories per kilogram $\times$ 1·8 = Btu per lb (Btu/lb)
Btu per lb $\times$ 0·5556 = kilogram calories per kilogram (k cal/kg)

711

Piston Speeds

metres per second $\times$ 196·85 = feet per minute (ft/min)
feet per minute $\times$ 0·0051   = metres per second (m/sec)

Weights

kilograms $\times$ 2·205   = lb
pounds $\times$ 0·4536   = kilograms (kg)
grams $\times$ 0·0022   = lb
pounds $\times$ 453·6   = grams (g)
tons (metric) $\times$ 0·9842 = tons (British)
tons (British) $\times$ 1·0161 = tons (metric)

Loads

kilograms per sq cm (kg/cm²) $\times$ 14·223 = lb per sq in (lb/in²)
lb/in² $\times$ 0·0703   = kilograms per sq cm
                                                (kg/cm²)

atmospheres $\times$ 14·223   = lb/in²
lb/in² $\times$ 0·0703   = atmospheres

Stresses

kilograms per sq mm (kg/mm²) $\times$ 1422·33 = lb/in²
kilograms per sq mm (kg/mm²) $\times$ 0·635   = tons/in²
lb/in² $\times$ 0·0007   = kg/mm²
tons/in² $\times$ 1·5749   = kg/mm²

Work (and Moments)

kilogram-metres $\times$ 7·233 = foot-pounds
foot-pounds $\times$ 0·1383   = kilogram-metres
tonne-metres $\times$ 3·229   = foot-tons
foot-tons $\times$ 0·3097   = tonne-metres

Capacities

litres $\times$ 0·22   = gallons
gallons $\times$ 4·546   = litres
litres $\times$ 1·7598   = pints
pints $\times$ 0·5683   = litres
litres $\times$ 0·0353   = cubic feet
cubic feet $\times$ 28·3161 = litres

Linear

millimetres $\times$ 0·03937 = inches
inches $\times$ 25·4 = millimetres
metres $\times$ 3·2808 = feet
feet $\times$ 0·3048 = metres

Square Measure

square metres $\times$ 10·764 = square feet
square feet $\times$ 0·093 = square metres
square centimetres $\times$ 0·155 = square inches
square inches $\times$ 6·452 = square centimetres

Cubic Measure

cubic centimetres $\times$ 0·061 = cubic inches
cubic inches $\times$ 16·387 = cubic centimetres
cubic metres $\times$ 1·308 = cubic yards
cubic yards $\times$ 0·765 = cubic metres

Temperatures

To obtain Centigrade (or Celsius) equivalent of a given temperature $t°$Fahrenheit:

$$\text{temp in } °C = \tfrac{5}{9}(t - 32).$$

To obtain Fahrenheit equivalent of a given temperature $t°$ Centigrade (or Celsius):

$$\text{temp. in } °F = (1·8t + 32).$$

Examples

Examples of the application of these conversion factors are given below, viz.:

1. To convert 0·375 lb of fuel per bhp h (British) into the metric equivalent:

$$0·375 \times 447·3 = 167·7 \text{ g/bhp/h}$$

2. To convert a calorific value of 10 070 kilogram calories (k cal) per kilogram to Btu/lb:

$$10\,070 \times 1·8 = 19\,260 \text{ Btu/lb}$$

3. To convert an engine piston speed of 980 ft/min into metres .per second:

$$980 + 0.0051 = 5.0 \text{ m/sec}$$

4. To convert 56 metric tons into British tons:

$$56 \times 0.9842 = 55.12 \text{ British tons}$$

5. To convert a pressure of 894 lb/in² into atmospheres:

$$894 \times 0.0703 = 62.86 \text{ atmospheres}$$

6. To convert a tensile stress of 17 350 lb/in² into kg/mm² :

$$17\,350 \times 0.0007 = 12.15 \text{ kg/mm}^2$$

Additional Notes

In dealing with *alterations* in temperature: the 32 does not enter into the calculation. Thus, a rise in temperature of $100°\text{F} = 100 \times \frac{5}{9} = 55.6°\text{C}$. Similarly, a fall in temperature of $40°\text{C} = \frac{9}{5} \times 40 = 72°\text{F}$.

In the list of conversions reference is made to metric tons and metric horse-power:

$$1 \text{ metric ton} = 1000 \text{ kg} = 2205 \text{ lb}$$
$$1 \text{ metric horse-power} = 75 \text{ kg m/sec} = 4500 \text{ kg m/min}$$

For ordinary calculations, 1 metric atmosphere = 1 kg/cm² = 14.223 lb/in².

The natural atmosphere = 760 mm of mercury = 1.033 kg/cm² = 14.696 lb/in².

The following measures are used for very small quantities, e.g. certain clearances and tolerances, viz.:

1. A micron (μ); this is one-thousandth of a millimetre, and one-millionth of a metre (10^{-6} metres).
2. A mil; this is one-thousandth of an inch (10^{-3} in.).
3. A micro-inch; this is one-millionth of an inch (10^{-6} in.).

The prefix milli- implies a one-thousandth part; thus, a milli-second is the one-thousandth part of a second.

To convert cylinder constants (metric) to British units: the factor is $0.986/14.223 = 0.0693$. Thus, for a 620 mm bore, 1400 mm stroke, double-acting, two-stroke engine, $C = 1.892$ (metric). For engine dimensions in British units the equivalent constant $= 1.892 \times 0.0693 = 0.1312$. Similarly, for a 660/1500 engine, $C = 2.296$ (metric); in British units the equivalent is 0.1591.

In expressing British units of work the sequence is: distance/ weight, e.g. foot-lb. In expressing the moment of a force the sequence is reversed thus: weight/distance, e.g. tons-feet.

SECTION II. THE INTERNATIONAL SYSTEM OF METRIC UNITS (SI)

As many marine engineers are now being confronted with the SI system for the first time, it seems desirable that, in this edition, a brief statement on the evolution of the system should be given, before proceeding with the technical details.

Origins

International standardisation began in 1870 with a meeting of fifteen nations in Paris. This led to the establishment in 1875 of a permanent International Bureau of Weights and Measures near Paris under the control of a General Conference which meets at intervals of six years.

Thus, all international matters concerning the metric system have, since 1875, been the responsibility of the Conférence Générale des Poids et Mesures—usually referred to by its initials CGPM

The metric system first adopted in the United Kingdom was the centimetre-gramme-second system (i.e. the c.g.s. system). These units were very well suited to the needs of chemists and physicists, whose work lies with small quantities. But about the beginning of the present century, metric codes began to be based on the metre-kilogram-second measurements (i.e. the MKS system). The later addition of the ampère produced the MKSA code.

At a meeting of the CGPM in 1954, a rationalised coherent system of metric units based on the four MKSA items, together with the degree kelvin as the unit of temperature and the candela as the unit of luminous intensity, received acceptance. In 1960, with the participation of thirty-six countries, the CGPM formally gave their code the title *Système International d'Unités*. For designation, the symbol SI is now used in all languages.

Coherency

The basis of the SI code is its coherency. A system of units is said to be coherent (Latin *cohaereo*, to cling together; to be connected) when the product, or quotient, of any two basic quantity units in the system becomes the new quantity unit. Thus, in a coherent system, a unit length multiplied by a unit length gives rise to a unit area. For example: a foot multiplied by a foot gives a square foot, which is a unit of area in a coherent system, whereas a square yard is not. A unit of force is obtained when unit mass is multiplied by unit acceleration and a unit of velocity is obtained when a unit of length is divided by a unit of time. That is, a foot divided by a second gives a velocity of one foot per second, which is coherent; one mile per hour is not.

Adoption of SI Units

The change to the SI system for the United Kingdom has been planned for completion by the end of 1975.

The substitution of SI units for the familiar metric technical units should have little or no effect on the everyday life of the marine engineering community. But there are a few necessary rearrangements. The chief of these centres upon the introduction of the term newton as a practical unit of force. This matter will be referred to later.

There will be several incidental problems to be faced. Thus, spare parts will probably provide the greatest anomaly in practice, because inch-dimensional spares for many engine room components must be available for a period of perhaps twenty years.

SUMMARY OF THE SI SYSTEM

The SI system comprises the six basic units enumerated below.

Quantity	Unit	Symbol
length	metre	m
mass	kilogramme	kg
time	second	s
electric current	ampère	A
luminous intensity	candela	cd
temperature	kelvin	K

Two supplementary SI units are: radian (plane angle) and steradian (solid angle). It will be observed that capital letters are used for certain symbols. These are the units which have been named after eminent men.

From the six basic units of SI and with the aid of the two supplementary units of radian and steradian, other units are derived, all of which are coherent. Some of the derived units are named and many have been in use for some time, e.g. volt, joule, and lux. The unit of force is the newton and this is the one unit the acceptance of which has caused the most resistance to the adoption of SI. Some derived units are listed below.

Quantity	Unit	Symbol	Formula
plane angle	radian	rad	
solid angle	steradian	sr	
frequency	hertz	Hz	s^{-1}
force	newton	N	kgm/s^2
work, energy, heat	joule	J	Nm
power	watt	W	J/s

Regarding units of time: internationally recognised multiples of the second, namely, minute, hour, day, week, month, and year will continue to be used; that is, they are not being decimalised.

Similarly, the division of the circle into 360 degrees, with 60 seconds to the minute and 60 minutes to the degree, is also being continued. The radian, which is a supplementary SI unit, will continue to figure in dynamic problems.

The litre is not a basic unit. It is accepted as a special name for the cubic decimetre and, as such, is used as a unit of volume.

Multiples and Sub-multiples

The original intention was that only multiples and sub-multiples separated by the factor 1000, i.e. 10^3, should be used. The complete range is from 10^{12} (tera-) to 10^{-18} (atto-). For marine engineering purposes the following short list covers the usual requirements.

Factor by which basic unit is multiplied	Prefix	Symbol
10^6 (1 000 000)	mega-	M
10^3 (1000)	kilo-	k
10^{-1} (0·1)	deci-	d
10^{-2} (0·01)	centi-	c
10^{-3} (0·001)	milli-	m
10^{-6} (0·000 001)	micro-	μ

There is sometimes a choice between two or more multiples or sub-multiples of a unit. The practice of the major metric-using countries should then be taken as a guide. For example: kilogramme force per square millimetre (kgf/mm^2) replaces tons force per square inch ($tons f/in^2$) and is used for stresses in materials. But kilogramme force per square centimetre (kgf/cm^2) replaces pounds force per square inch (lbf/in^2) as used, say, for steam pressures. This nomenclature violates the original intention that only multiples or sub-multiples separated by 1000 should be used. Nevertheless the convenience and usefulness are overriding.

Energy and Power

The horse-power is the engineer's unit of power. The British horse-power is 33 000 ft lb of work per minute, or 550 ft lb per second. The metric horse-power is 75 kilogramme-metres per second, which is 32 550 ft lb per minute, or 542·48 ft lb per second. That is, the metric horse-power is about 1·4 per cent less than the British horse-power.

In the SI system, energy—whether its type or kind is thermal, electrical, or mechanical—is always basically the product of force and distance. The unit of energy, therefore, is the newton-metre (Nm), which has been named the Joule (J). Whatever form is taken by power, it is a rate of generation or dissipation of energy, and the unit of power is one newton-metre per second, which is one joule per second, which is one watt (W).

Newton

The most notable departure of the SI code from the original form of the metric system lies in the introduction of the term newton as the practical unit of force, instead of the kilogramme (kg) or the kilogramme force (kgf).

The unit of mass, i.e. the amount of matter, in the foot-pound-second (f.p.s.) system is the pound. In the c.g.s. system the unit of mass is the gramme. In the SI scheme it is the kilogramme.

The unit of force, as distinct from the unit of mass, is the poundal in the f.p.s. system. In the c.g.s. system it is the dyne. In the SI system it is the newton.

A newton (N) is defined as the force needed to impart to one unit of mass (i.e. one kg) one unit of acceleration (i.e. one metre per second per second). That is: one newton = one kilogramme-metre per second per second; or, $N = kgm/s^2$.

Mass and Weight

It has been common practice not to distinguish between mass and weight, and this has been observed in Acts of Parliament, in that the units for mass may be used also for weight. In general, engineers have used as their unit that force which, when applied to a unit of mass, produces an acceleration of g rather than unit acceleration.

As the gravitational acceleration g is 9·806 metres per second per second, i.e. 9·806 m/s^2, the force exerted by a stationary mass of one kilogramme will be 9·806 newtons.

1 newton = 0·2248 pound force; and one pound force = 4·448 newtons.

Expressed differently, in engineering work it has been the practice to use weight units as force units; accordingly, the unit of force has been that which, when applied to unit mass, induces an acceleration *g*. That is, the force of a body having a mass of one kilogramme is 9·806 newtons, as previously stated.

The distinction between mass and weight can be clarified by appropriate wording, thus:

a mass of 500 kg is placed on a beam; a force of 5 kN is applied to the beam.

Because acceleration due to gravity varies slightly over the earth's surface, a constant mass has not a constant weight. The concept of a technical force unit has therefore been introduced. This unit is the product of a standard acceleration of 9·806 metres per second per second and a unit of mass. Thus the kilogramme force (kgf) is to be distinguished from the varying local weight of a body of one kilogramme mass. The pound force (lbf) and the ton force (tonf) have similar connotations. The use of the newton, which is a coherent force unit, is to be preferred to the non-coherent but much more widely used unit, kilogramme force.

Derived Units

The units derived from force, e.g. pressure, work, energy, power, etc., now comprise the existing metric units combined with newtons instead of kilogramme force. For energy the symbol is Nm or joule, J; for power the symbol is newton-metres per second, i.e. Nm/s, or J/s, which is the watt. One horse-power = 745·70 W.

Dissatisfaction has been expressed with the term kilogramme for the unit of mass, because the prefix kilo- is not consistent with the designation of a basic unit. A different name, suitable for all languages, has not yet been accepted and it is thought that the present name will never be changed unless unanimous demand for a particular title is forthcoming.

The newton and its derived unit of pressure, i.e. newtons per square metre (N/m^2), have a low value in relation to the expressions normally used by engineers. The difficulty would seem to have been overcome by the introduction of the bar, a term agreed upon at Moscow in 1967 by France, Germany, and the United Kingdom.

The Bar

The bar is 100 000 newtons per square metre, i.e. $10^5 \ N/m^2$.

The bar agrees approximately with a standard atmosphere.

Actually a bar is 14·5 lbf/in², a barometric atmosphere being 14·7 lbf/in², i.e. 1·013 bar. This is also not much different from the metric atmosphere of one kilogramme per square centimetre (1 kg/cm²) or 14·223 lbf/in².

The use of the bar (10^5 N/m²) as the unit of pressure, and the hectobar (10^7 N/m²) as the unit of stress, has become widespread for the reason that, as already stated, the bar approximates to atmospheric pressure and to the kilogramme-force per square centimetre, while the hectobar approximates to the kilogramme force per square millimetre.

SOME CONVERSION FACTORS

Until the SI code is so firmly established that all former records, designs, calculations, etc., in metric technical or in Imperial units have ceased to have reference value, a system of conversion factors will be needed. In this connection the undermentioned particulars may be useful.

Power Units

1 watt (W)	= 1 joule per second (J/s)
	= 1 newton-metre per second (Nm/s)
1 foot-pound force per second	= 1·356 kW
1 kilowatt (kW)	= 1000 W = kJ/s
1 British horse-power	= 0·7457 kW
1 metric horse-power	= 0·7355 kW
1 kilowatt hour (kWh)	= 3600 kJ = 3·6 MJ
1 British horse-power hour	= 0·7457 kWh
1 metric horse-power hour	= 0·7355 kWh

Power Conversion

watts × 0·7374	= foot-pounds force per second
foot-pounds force per second × 1·356	= watts
kilowatts × 1·341	= horse-power (British)
horse-power (British) × 0·7457	= kilowatts
kilowatt hours × 1·341	= horse-power hours (British)
horse-power hours (British) × 0·7457	= kilowatt hours

Fuel Rate Conversion

kilogrammes per kilowatt hour (kg/kWh) $\times$ 1·644 = pounds per horse-power hour

pounds per horse-power hour $\times$ 0·6083 = kilogrammes per kilowatt hour (kg/kWh)

Force

1 kilogramme force (kgf)	= 9·8067 N
1 newton (N)	= 0·10197 kilogramme force (kgf)
1 pound force	= 4·448 N
1 newton (N)	= 0·2248 pound force
1 ton force (British)	= 9·964 kN
1 pound-force-foot	= 1·356 Nm
1 ton-force-foot	= 3·037 kNm

Bar

1 bar $= 10^5$ N/m² = 100 000 newtons per square metre

1 hectobar $= 10^7$ N/m² $= 10$ MN/m² = 10 000 000 newtons per square metre

1 millibar $= 10^2$ N/m² = 100 newtons per square metre

Pressure

1 bar = 100 000 newtons per square metre (10^5 N/m²)
— 1·0197 kgf per square centimetre — 14·5 pounds force per square inch
= 1 atmosphere

1 hectobar = 1 kilogramme force per square millimetre = kgf/mm²

1 millibar $= 10^2$ N/m² = 0·0145 pounds per square inch

1 pound force per square inch = 0·06895 bar

Stress

1 hectobar (h bar) = 100 bar $= 10^7$ N/m²
= 10 meganewtons per square metre (10 MN/m²)
= 0·647 tons force per square inch
= 1450 pounds force per square inch

1 hectobar = 1 kilogramme force per square millimetre (kgf/mm²)

hectobars $\times$ 0·647 = tons force per square inch

tons force per square inch $\times$ 1·544 = hectobar

bar × 14·5 = pounds force per square inch

pounds force per square inch × 0·06895 = bar

Temperature

temperature in degrees Celsius (°C) $= \frac{5}{9}$(°F − 32)
where F = Fahrenheit scale
temperature interval: 1°C $= \frac{9}{5}$°F; 1°F $= \frac{5}{9}$°C
absolute temperature: unit = 1 kelvin (K)
K $= \frac{5}{9}$(°F + 459·7)

Thermal Units

thermal unit	= 1 joule. J = Nm
1 kilojoule (kJ)	= 1000 Nm
	= 1000 × 0·2248 × 3·2808
	= 737 foot pounds
1 BThU	= 778 foot pounds = 1·055 kJ
1 BThU per second	= 1·055 kW
1 BThU per hour	= 0·2931 W
1 BThU per pound	= 2·326 kJ/kg
1 BThU per pound per degree F	= 4·187 kJ/kg °C
1 kilogramme calorie per kilogramme	= 4·187 kJ/kg
1 calorie	= 4·187 J
kilojoules × 0·948	= BThu
BThU × 1·055	= kJ
kW	= BThU per second × 1·055
W	= BThU per hour × 0·2931
kJ/kg = kilojoule per kilogramme	= BThU per pound × 2·326

Noise and Vibration

Noise: 1 cycle per second   = 1 hertz (Hz)
Vibration: kilocycles per second = kilohertz (kHz)

Kinematic Viscosity

There is no conversion factor for centistokes and Redwood visco-meter seconds. Tables of approximate conversion values are available.

Examples: 1500 seconds Redwood No. 1 at 100 deg. F = 370 centistokes (cSt); 3500 seconds = 860 centistokes.

Nautical Terms

1 U.K. nautical mile	$= 1{\cdot}8532$ km
1 International nautical mile	$= 1{\cdot}8520$ km
1 U.K. knot	$= 1{\cdot}8532$ km per hour
1 International knot	$= 1{\cdot}8520$ km per hour

Explanatory Note

In SI nomenclature, the feminine gender is used, thus, kilogramme instead of kilogram; tonne instead of metric ton. Also, the singular and not the plural number is expected to be preferred, thus, 15 bar and not 15 bars; 20 tonne and not 20 tonnes.

Some engineers seem to experience difficulty in interpreting the printed symbols. The explanation lies in the need for compactness in printing; hence the frequent use of the solidus. To take the most familiar of examples: whereas in normal technical literature the term pounds per square inch, or lb. per sq. in., is used, in SI symbolage this becomes lb/in^2. Similarly, one pound per horse-power hour is expressed 1 lb/hph and one kilogramme per kilowatt hour as 1 kg/kWh. The formula 10^7 N/m² $= 10$ MN/m² = ten million newtons per square metre, or 10 meganewtons per square metre—a meganewton being one million newtons; and so on.

Examples of Conversion

In the following examples, typical conversions from Imperial, i.e. United Kingdom, units to SI equivalents are indicated.

(i) Convert a ship resistance of 3203 ehp, i.e. effective horse-power, into effective kilowatt power.

$$3203 \times 0{\cdot}7457 = 2389 \text{ kW}$$

(ii) Convert a fuel consumption rate of $0{\cdot}34$ pounds per bhp hour into kilogrammes per kilowatt hour.

$$0{\cdot}34 \times 0{\cdot}6083 = 0{\cdot}207 \text{ kg/kWh}$$

(iii) Express a brake mean effective pressure of $181{\cdot}3$ pounds per square inch into bar units.

$$181{\cdot}3 \times 0{\cdot}06895 = 12{\cdot}50 \text{ bar}$$

(iv) If the ultimate tensile strength of a mild steel bar is 26 tons per square inch, what is the SI hectobar equivalent?

$$26 \times 1{\cdot}544 = 40{\cdot}2 \text{ h bar}$$

(v) The modulus of elasticity of steel is 30×10^6 lb/in. What is the modulus in SI units?

(a) meganewtons per square metre (MN/m^2) $\times 145 = $ lb/in^2
(b) pounds per square inch $\times 0.00689 = MN/m^2$

$$30 \times 10^6 \text{ lb/in} = 30 \times 10^6 \times 0.00689 \text{ MN/m}^2$$
$$= 206.7 \times 10^3 \text{ MN/m}^2$$
$$= 206.7 \times 10^3 \text{ N/mm}^2$$

(vi) Express a refrigerator temperature of minus 20°F in SI units.

$$\text{temperature } °C = \tfrac{5}{9}(-20 - 32) = \tfrac{5}{9} \times -52 = -29° \text{ Celsius}$$

(vii) Express a calorific value of 18 920 British thermal units per pound in joules.

$$18\,920 \times 2.326 = 44\,000 \text{ kJ/kg} = 44 \text{ MJ/kg}$$

(viii) What, in SI units, is a service speed of 21 U.K. knots?
$$21 \times 1.8532 = 38.9172 \text{ km/hr}$$
$$\text{International knots} = 38.9172/1.8520 = 21.014$$

RECAPITULATORY

The newton (N) unit of force $1 \text{ N} = 1 \text{ kg m/s}^2$

The joule (J)   unit of energy $1 \text{ J} = 1 \text{ Nm}$

The watt (W)   unit of power $1 \text{ W} = 1 \text{ J/s} = 1 \text{ kg m}^2/\text{s}^3$

Length	International nautical mile (1 n mile = 1852 m)
Area	are (a) hectare (ha) (1 ha = 10^4 m^2)
Volume or capacity	litre (l) millilitre (ml) (1 litre = 10^{-3} m^3 = 1 dm^3)
Velocity	kilometre per hour (km/h) knot (kn) (1 kn = 1 n mile/h)
Rotational frequency	revolution per minute (rev/min) revolution per second (rev/s)

Mass	tonne (t) (1 tonne $= 10^3$ kg $= 1$ Mg)
Mass density	tonne per metre cubed (t/m³) (1 tonne/m³ $= 1$ kg/l $= 1$ g/ml $= 1$ g/cm³)
Pressure and Stress	bar hectobar (hbar) millibar (mbar) (1 bar $= 10^5$ Pa $= 10^5$ N/m²)
Viscosity (dynamic)	centipoise (cP) (1 cP $= 10^{-3}$ Ns/m²)
Kinematic Viscosity	centistokes (cSt) (1 cSt $= 10^{-6}$ m²/s)
Work, Energy	watt hour (Wh) kilowatt hour (kWh) megawatt hour (MWh) (1 kWh $= 3 \cdot 6$ MJ)
Temperature	degree Celsius (°C)
Thermal conductivity	watt per metre degree Celsius (W/m °C)
Coefficient of heat transfer	watt per metre squared degree Celsius (W/m²°C)
Heat capacity	joule per degree Celsius (J/°C) kilojoule per degree Celsius (kJ/°C)
Specific heat capacity	joule per kilogramme degree Celsius (J/kg °C) kilojoule per kilogramme degree Celsius (kJ/kg °C)

The following approximations are commonly used:

Standard gravitational acceleration	$9 \cdot 81$ m/s²
Standard atmospheric pressure	$0 \cdot 1$ MPa or 100 kPa or 1 bar
Density of water	1 Mg/m³ or 1 tonne/m³ or 1 kg/litre
Specific heat capacity of water	4200 J/kg °C or $4 \cdot 2$ kJ/kg °C
Specific latent heat of vaporisation of steam (s.a.p.)	2250 kJ/kg or $2 \cdot 25$ MJ/kg

Index